'Deepak Nayyar is the model of a clear-headed, systematic, non-obscurantist thinker in development economics. This collection of essays in Deepak Nayyar's honour, by distinguished economists from around the world, is true to his admirable approach to understanding social change.'

**Will Milberg**, *Dean and Professor of Economics,*
*The New School for Social Research, USA*

'This impressive volume of essays by many eminent economists builds on Deepak Nayyar's work, illustrating that work's range and depth, while itself making a significant contribution to the arguments of which Nayyar is such a formidable exponent.'

**Sir Julian Le Grand**, *Professor, Marshall Institute,*
*London School of Economics, UK*

'This very important book, written in honour of one of India's most distinguished economists, is a must-read and thought provoking critique of current economic theory and policy, which also proposes valuable alternative thinking. It will be of great interest both to heterodox economists, as well as mainstream ones.'

**Stephany Griffith-Jones**, *Professor and*
*Financial Markets Director, Initiative for*
*Policy Dialogue, Columbia University, USA*

'This volume is a fitting tribute to Deepak Nayyar, unquestionably one of India's leading economists. The essays are all of the highest quality, covering a breathtakingly wide sweep of issues and the contributors themselves are a stellar lot. The volume should be of great value to researchers, university students, and the concerned citizen alike.'

**Pulin B. Nayak**, *Professor and formerly Director*
*of the Delhi School of Economics, India*

'The essays in this volume engage in-depth with theoretical constructs and empirical questions for the formation of economic policies with the right social concerns. The volume will undoubtedly become one of the valuable sources of inspiration for the next generation of economists who have to tackle the formidable challenges of securing a sustainable, inclusive development path in a fast-changing world order.'

**Machiko Nissanke**, *Emeritus Professor of*
*Economics, Faculty of Law and Social Sciences,*
*SOAS, University of London, UK*

# Economic Theory and Policy amidst Global Discontent

This book rethinks economic theory and calls for a creative and pragmatic approach to policymaking. It examines what development and sustenance of economic progress mean, and how these may be facilitated. The relevance of this issue has received fresh impetus from the significant changes in the degree and pattern of international economic relations that are unfolding across the world, posing both opportunities and challenges. While globalisation of goods and financial markets may have delivered high growth for some nations, the distribution of the benefits has often been highly unequal, with gains to owners of capital and skills being disproportionately higher compared to that of labour, especially the unskilled.

Widening and persistent inequalities have been at the heart of rising polarisation and spread of conflicts that threaten the social fabric. This work emphasises the relevance of a broad policy framework based on building individual capabilities and in line with a human-centric perspective. At the same time, it points out the crucial need to create policy space for macroeconomic stability and to accommodate heterodox influences, especially when conventional wisdom proves inadequate, as starkly demonstrated *inter alia* during the recent global financial crisis.

This festschrift, dedicated to Deepak Nayyar, presents chapters on diverse themes that address the persisting global problems of poverty, inequality and sustaining development. The book will be of great interest to scholars and researchers of economics, development studies, public policy and governance, and also to policymakers, government officials and those in media.

**Ananya Ghosh Dastidar** is Associate Professor in the Department of Business Economics, University of Delhi, South Campus, India.

**Rajeev Malhotra** is Professor at the School of Government and Public Policy and Executive Director, Centre for Development and Finance at O. P. Jindal Global University, Sonipat, Delhi NCR, India.

**Vivek Suneja** is Professor in the Faculty of Management Studies, University of Delhi, India.

# Economic Theory and Policy amidst Global Discontent

Essays in Honour of Deepak Nayyar

Edited by Ananya Ghosh Dastidar, Rajeev Malhotra and Vivek Suneja

LONDON AND NEW YORK

First edition published 2018
by Routledge
2 Park Square, Milton Park, Abingdon, Oxon, OX14 4RN

and by Routledge
711 Third Avenue, New York, NY 10017

*Routledge is an imprint of the Taylor & Francis Group,
an informa business*

© 2018 selection and editorial matter, Ananya Ghosh Dastidar,
Rajeev Malhotra and Vivek Suneja; individual chapters, the
contributors

The right of Ananya Ghosh Dastidar, Rajeev Malhotra and Vivek
Suneja to be identified as the authors of the editorial material, and
of the authors for their individual chapters, has been asserted in
accordance with sections 77 and 78 of the Copyright, Designs and
Patents Act 1988.

All rights reserved. No part of this book may be reprinted or
reproduced or utilised in any form or by any electronic, mechanical,
or other means, now known or hereafter invented, including
photocopying and recording, or in any information storage or
retrieval system, without permission in writing from the publishers.

*Trademark notice*: Product or corporate names may be trademarks
or registered trademarks, and are used only for identification and
explanation without intent to infringe.

*British Library Cataloguing-in-Publication Data*
A catalogue record for this book is available from the British Library

*Library of Congress Cataloging-in-Publication Data*
A catalog record for this book has been requested

ISBN: 978-1-138-68921-3 (hbk)
ISBN: 978-1-351-13758-4 (ebk)

Typeset in Sabon
by Apex CoVantage, LLC

# Contents

| | |
|---|---|
| *List of figures* | x |
| *List of tables* | xi |
| *Notes on contributors* | xii |
| *Preface* | xvi |

**PART I**
**Introduction** 1

1 Deepak Nayyar: A diverse oeuvre 3
ANANYA GHOSH DASTIDAR, RAJEEV MALHOTRA
AND VIVEK SUNEJA

2 Development complexities: Looking afresh 24
ANANYA GHOSH DASTIDAR, RAJEEV MALHOTRA
AND VIVEK SUNEJA

**PART II**
**Evolving dimensions of globalisation** 39

3 Capitalism, consciousness and development 41
AKMAL HUSSAIN

4 The rise and fall(?) of the ABP (Anything But Policy)
discourse in development economics 61
HA-JOON CHANG

5 Inequality and conflict: Global drivers and interventions 78
FRANCES STEWART

viii *Contents*

6 Economic policy and human rights: Is globalisation
a meeting ground?     98
RAJEEV MALHOTRA

## PART III
## Economic theory and public policy     125

7 The theory of credit and macroeconomic stability     127
JOSEPH STIGLITZ

8 Money and market failures: A theoretical perspective     184
ANJAN MUKHERJI

9 Persuasion and coercion: A transaction costs perspective
on income distribution     198
VIVEK SUNEJA

10 Dual economy models with fixed terms-of-trade     211
AMITAVA BOSE

11 Comprehending the 'in-formal': Formal-informal
conundrum in labour under capitalism     221
SAUMYAJIT BHATTACHARYA

12 Multiple efficient rules and inefficient outcomes     243
SATISH K. JAIN

13 Auctions with an inferior outside option     254
KRISHNENDU GHOSH DASTIDAR

## PART IV
## Lessons from development experiences     273

## Emerging economies     274

14 Beyond *Catch Up*: Some speculations about the next
twenty-five emerging economies     275
SUDIPTO MUNDLE

Contents  ix

15 Latin America's development record and challenges in
   historical perspective                                      305
   JOSÉ ANTONIO OCAMPO

16 The global financial crisis and policy challenges in EMEs   324
   ANANYA GHOSH DASTIDAR

17 Land deals in Africa: Host country effects in the presence
   of skill formation                                          340
   GOURANGA G. DAS

Indian Economy                                                 374

18 Major policy debates in the Indian economy:
   Some reflections                                            375
   Y. V. REDDY

19 Reversing premature deindustrialisation for job
   creation: Lessons for *Make-in-India* from industrialised
   and East Asian countries                                    389
   NAGESH KUMAR

20 Globalisation and the slowdown of the Indian economy:
   A demand-side view                                          416
   MRITIUNJOY MOHANTY

21 Is land a bottleneck for economic development in India?     435
   RAM SINGH

   *Index*                                                     449

# Figures

| | | |
|---|---|---:|
| 5.1 | No. of muslim majority countries as percent of total countries in category | 90 |
| 5.2 | A depiction of global connections among Muslims | 92 |
| 6.1 | Framework for identifying human rights indicators | 109 |
| 7.1 | Central bank assets-to-GDP ratio | 128 |
| 7.2 | M2 to GDP ratio | 129 |
| 7.3 | The relationship between T-bill rate and money market rate | 133 |
| 8.1 | An efficient state | 186 |
| 10.1 | The two equilibria in the Keynesian case | 217 |
| 14.1 | GDP growth 2007 to 2014 and per capita GDP 2014 | 293 |
| 15.1 | Latin America: Moving average of decade-long growth rates | 309 |
| 15.2 | Latin America: Share of manufacturing in GDP, 1950–2015 | 310 |
| 15.3 | Latin America: Human development indices vs. developed countries | 315 |
| 19.1 | GDP and employment growth and elasticity in India, 1992–2013 | 391 |
| 19.2 | Shares of agriculture, industry and services in GDP, 1951–2014 | 392 |
| 19.3 | Backward and forward linkages generated by productive sectors in India based on input-output tables | 392 |
| 19.4 | Share of manufacturing in GDP of select Asian countries | 393 |
| 19.5 | Growth rates of GDP and major productive sectors, 1990–2014 | 393 |
| 19.6 | Movements in nominal and real effective exchange rate of Indian rupee | 397 |

# Tables

| | | |
|---|---|---:|
| 3.1 | International banking, economic activity and international trade | 43 |
| 14.1 | Selected indicators of the next twenty-five emerging economies | 283 |
| 14.2 | Structure of production in the next twenty-five emerging economies, 2014 | 290 |
| 15.1 | Relative position of Latin America in the world economy | 307 |
| 15.2 | GDP growth in Latin America: Dynamics and volatility | 312 |
| 17.1 | Top-10 investor and target countries for pure and mixed deals | 344 |
| 19.1 | Share of imports used in final consumption expenditure in major industry groups, 2001–11 | 395 |
| 20.1 | GDP and expenditure aggregates – growth rates (percent p.a. and at constant 2004/5 prices) | 417 |
| 20.2 | Supply-side contributions to GDP growth (percent) | 418 |
| 20.3 | Macroeconomic balances (percent at current prices-old series) | 419 |
| 20.4a | Average trade ratios (percent of GDP) | 421 |
| 20.4b | Average oil and non-oil goods trade ratios (percent of GDP) | 422 |
| 20.5 | Average trade and current account balances (as percent of GDP) | 424 |
| 20.6 | Manufacturing sector trade ratios (percent of manufacturing GDP) | 425 |
| 20.7 | Export and import growth rates (percent p.a. in current rupees) | 427 |

# Contributors

**Saumyajit Bhattacharya** is Associate Professor in Economics at Kirori Mal College, University of Delhi, India. He completed his education from St Xavier's College, Kolkata and Jawaharlal Nehru University, New Delhi, India.

**Amitava Bose** was former Professor of Economics and Director of Indian Institute of Management Calcutta, Kolkata, India.

**Ha-Joon Chang** teaches Economics at the University of Cambridge, UK. His books include *Kicking Away the Ladder* (2002), *23 Things They Don't Tell You About Capitalism* (2010), and *Economics: The User's Guide* (2014).

**Gouranga G. Das** is Professor of Economics at Hanyang University, South Korea. He completed his doctorate from Monash University, Australia and post-doctoral fellowship from University of Florida, USA. He has published extensively in the areas of international economics, development economics and computational economics.

**Ananya Ghosh Dastidar** is Associate Professor in the Department of Business Economics, University of Delhi South Campus, New Delhi, India. She has a doctorate in Economics from the Centre for Economic Studies and Planning, Jawaharlal Nehru University, New Delhi, India, and started her teaching career at the Department of Economics, Delhi School of Economics. Her research interests are in the area of international economics and development economics, and she has worked on globalisation and inequality. She has published on macroeconomic issues in development, development strategies, income distribution and structural transformation and international trade.

**Krishnendu Ghosh Dastidar** is Professor at the Centre for Economic Studies and Planning, Jawaharlal Nehru University, India. He has

*Contributors*  xiii

published extensively in the areas of oligopoly theory and auction theory.

**Akmal Hussain** is Distinguished Professor and Dean, School of Social Sciences at the Information Technology University, Lahore, Pakistan. He has published on issues of development and served on the Prime Minister's Economic Policy Committee.

**Satish K. Jain** retired as Professor, Centre for Economic Studies and Planning, Jawaharlal Nehru University, New Delhi, India, where he was member of the faculty from 1978 to 2013, and held the Reserve Bank of India Chair during 2011–13. He is currently ICSSR National Fellow affiliated to Management Development Insititute, Gurgaon. He has published on issues related to social choice theory and law and economics.

**Nagesh Kumar** is Director and Head of South and South-West Asia Office of the United Nations Economic and Social Commission for Asia and the Pacific (UNESCAP-SSWA). His earlier positions include Chief-Economist at UNESCAP headquarters, and Director-General, RIS, New Delhi, India.

**Rajeev Malhotra** is currently Professor at the School of Government and Public Policy and Executive Director Centre for Development and Finance at O. P. Jindal Global University, Sonipat, India. A development economist and a civil servant with nearly three decades of experience, he has worked with the Government of India where until August 2012 he was Economic Adviser to the Union Finance Minister. He also worked at the UN Office of the High Commissioner for Human Rights in Geneva and prior to that at the Planning Commission, New Delhi, India. Over the years, he has been a consultant to several international organizations. He has published extensively, including on poverty estimation, human development, fiscal and other issues of Indian economy and on human rights indicators and monitoring. His research interests include macro-economic issues in development policy, human development and human rights in development.

**Mritiunjoy Mohanty** is Professor of Economics at the Indian Institute of Management Calcutta, Kolkata, India. He is also affiliated with the New Trade Union Initiative (NTUI), New Delhi, a federation of independent trades unions in India working in both the organized and unorganized sectors.

**Anjan Mukherji** is Professor Emeritus, Jawaharlal Nehru University and Honorary Visiting Professor, National Institute of Public

xiv *Contributors*

Finance and Policy, New Delhi, India. At the time of his retirement from JNU in 2010, he was the RBI Professor of Economic Theory. He has published on general equilibrium theory, mathematical economics and economic dynamics.

**Sudipto Mundle** is Emeritus Professor at the National Institute of Public Finance and Policy (NIPFP), New Delhi, India, and is on its governing body. He was a member of the Fourteenth Finance Commission, the Reserve Bank of India Monetary Policy Advisory Committee and member and acting Chairman of the National Statistical Commission. Earlier he was with the Asian Development Bank, Philippines.

**José Antonio Ocampo** is Professor at Columbia University, USA. He is a Member on the Board of Central Bank of Colombia (Banco de la República) and Chair of ECOSOC's Committee for Development Policy. He was formerly United Nations Under-Secretary-General for Economic and Social Affairs, Executive Secretary of the Economic Commission for Latin America and the Caribbean, and Minister of Finance, Minister of Agriculture and Director of National Planning of Colombia.

**Y. V. Reddy** is currently with the Centre for Economic and Social Studies, Hyderabad, India. He was Chairman, Fourteenth Finance Commission, Governor Reserve Bank of India, and Executive Director, International Monetary Fund (IMF).

**Ram Singh** is Professor at the Delhi School of Economics, University of Delhi, India. His areas of research interests are contract theory, public economics, public–private partnerships and law and economics. He is recipient of the Ronald Coase Fellowship in Institutional Economics, and Fulbright Senior Research Fellowship in Economics.

**Frances Stewart** is Emeritus Professor of Development Economics, University of Oxford, UK. She has published extensively and her many publications include *Horizontal Inequalities and Conflict: Understanding Group Violence in Multiethnic Societies* (2008).

**Joseph Stiglitz** is University Professor at Columbia University, USA. He is the winner of the 2001 Nobel Prize in Economics and Chief Economist of the Roosevelt Institute.

**Vivek Suneja** is Professor, Faculty of Management Studies, University of Delhi, India. He completed his doctorate from the University of Reading, UK. He taught at the University of Salford (1995–97) and at the Open University Business School, UK (1997–2005), before joining as Professor at the University of Delhi. He has been Dean, Planning, University of Delhi (2005–13) and Pro-Vice-Chancellor, University of Delhi (2010–13). His research interests lie in the areas of strategy, public policy, culture and development economics. His books include *Markets: A Multi-Dimensional Approach to the Market Economy* (2008), *Policy Issues for Business* (2002) and *The Economics of Marketing* (1998).

# Preface

The desire to acknowledge the role of Deepak Nayyar, our teacher, in encouraging us to explore the fascinating discipline of economics, his contribution in shaping our thinking as we pursued our professional interests, and for being a mentor and a constant source of inspiration over the many years of our association led us to conceive this volume in his honour.

The task of identifying potential authors and getting them to commit their contribution to this volume turned out to be a pleasant experience because of the enthusiastic and encouraging response that we received to our proposal. We sought contributions for this volume from some of his students, whom he taught in UK and in India, and some of his colleagues, with whom he engaged and collaborated over a career spanning nearly five decades. They all agreed, without exception. The fact that we ended up with a very eminent list of contributors, each one of whom scripted an original essay for inclusion in this volume, is indicative of the regard that Deepak Nayyar enjoys among his peers and students, alike.

The range of issues, related to economic theory and development policy, covered in this volume reflect nothing less than the breadth and diversity of Deepak Nayyar's engagement with the discipline of economics. The book covers many of the evolving dimensions and challenges of globalisation. Importantly, it seeks to rethink economic theory and practice in that context and draws lessons for policy correctives by re-examining development experiences from different parts of the world. We cannot claim that all relevant economic policy issues at the current global conjuncture have been covered, yet the larger picture that emerges from this book provides a story that must be read as policymakers across the world gear up to confront the challenges that they face.

Globalisation of goods and financial markets has delivered significant growth, yet distribution of the fruits of growth has been highly

*Preface* xvii

unequal, with gains to owners of capital and skills being disproportionately higher compared to that of labour, especially the unskilled. The widening and persistent inequalities across the world have been at the heart of rising polarisation and spread of conflicts that threaten to tear apart the social fabric in many countries. This calls for a rethink of development theory and a creative and pragmatic approach to policymaking to sustain progress. The relevance of a policy framework that builds on individual capabilities and promotes a human-centric approach in resolving the challenges that nations face cannot be over-emphasized. Equally important is the need to create policy space for macroeconomic stability and to accommodate heterodox influences, especially when conventional wisdom proves inadequate, as starkly demonstrated *inter alia* during the recent global financial crisis. Indeed, the world requires creative and imaginative approaches and solutions to the pressing global problems of persistent poverty, inequality and environmental sustainability. This compilation of essays attempts to respond to that call and, in the process, resonates with the large body of Deepak Nayyar's research and applied work as a policymaker.

We owe an immense debt of gratitude to each one of the contributors to this volume. The spectrum of their research interests and economic persuasions has enriched this publication. In particular, we are thankful to Amitava Bose who, we deeply regret to say, passed away in January 2017 and could not see this volume in its published form. We are also thankful to Ajit Singh, who had agreed to write an essay, but unfortunately passed away before this volume took shape.

On the personal front, the editors would like to thank their families for their encouragement and understanding in the course of undertaking this project. In particular, Ananya would like to thank her brother Anindya, brother-in-law Anirban and especially her husband Krishnendu, daughter Kheya and mother Srilata Sen. She also fondly remembers her father Amar Sen and mother-in-law Kalpana Ghosh Dastidar, both of whom passed away before this volume could be published. Likewise, Rajeev would like to thank his wife Meenakshi, daughter Sukriti and son Madhav for their support in all his endeavours. Vivek would like to thank all his family, particularly his wife Sonjuhi, his father Dr R.K. Suneja and his dear brother-in-law Dr Sanjeev Chibber.

This book would not have been possible without the support of the editorial team of our publishers. We would like to thank them all and especially Shoma Choudhury, for her patience and cooperation throughout the publication process and Nitasha Devasar for encouraging and facilitating this work.

# Part I
# Introduction

# 1 Deepak Nayyar
## A diverse oeuvre

*Ananya Ghosh Dastidar,*
*Rajeev Malhotra and*
*Vivek Suneja**

Deepak Nayyar – a great teacher, an eminent academic, a distinguished policymaker and a leading thinker of our times – is a man of many parts. He has donned several hats and shouldered diverse responsibilities with great distinction. In a life that presented him with interesting and varied professional opportunities and challenges in both academia and the policymaking world, he epitomises the saying 'the whole is greater than the sum of its parts'. At heart, he remains a teacher who regards interaction with students as an invaluable learning experience. This has shaped his thinking, research and evolution as an economist. Time and again, he has chosen to return to the classroom from the exalted positions he has held and from opportunities that have beckoned him. At the same time, perhaps guided by a sense of a larger purpose in life, he has not hesitated in taking up several responsibilities outside of academia, which to a typical academic would have appeared to be daunting and off the beaten track. He left each of those engagements richer for the experience, which is, perhaps, a major reason for his professional success.

We reflect here briefly on his achievements and the person that he is, the body of his work and how that situates within the discipline of economics. His academic work is especially relevant at the current historical conjuncture, when economics and its practice face challenges emanating from governance and policy failures within countries situated in a wider global context that is in flux.

---

\* In writing this chapter, the authors have drawn on the website www.deepaknayyar. com and on several interviews of Deepak Nayyar published in leading newspapers (including 'The Tuesday Interview/Deepak Nayyar', *The Economic Times*, February 18, 1992 and February 25, 1992; and his interviews marking 25 years of economic reforms in India, *The Indian Express*, July 6, 2016 and *The Hindu*, July 26, 2016). They have also benefitted from conversations they have had over their long association with him.

# 4  *Ananya Ghosh Dastidar et al.*

## Professional milestones and the person

Deepak Nayyar was born on September 26, 1946. He began his schooling in Shimla, followed by eight years in Hindi-medium schools at different places in provincial India. He completed it at St Xavier's School, Jaipur, where Father Extross was his mentor for the next stage of his journey in life. He studied at St. Stephen's College and the Delhi School of Economics, University of Delhi, for his BA and MA in Economics, respectively, before moving on as a Rhodes Scholar to study at Balliol College, University of Oxford. He obtained his BPhil (1969) and DPhil in Economics (1973) at Oxford. From 1969 to 1973, he was in the Indian Administrative Service (IAS), posted in the state of Uttar Pradesh. But it was not long before he resigned from the service and chose the life of an academic.

In his formative years at the University of Delhi, while learning Economics, he was influenced by Pankaj Ganguli and N.C. Ray as an undergraduate in St Stephen's, and by Amartya Sen, Sukhamoy Chakravarty and K.N. Raj at the Delhi School of Economics. At the University of Oxford, he especially remembers Max Corden, John Hicks and Robert Solow as teachers. The closest association at Oxford was with Paul Streeten, his DPhil supervisor, who brought home to him the significance of the heterodox and the unorthodox in economics. It was, however, the brief exposure to the realpolitik of the civil administration, and the hard reality of feudal India in Uttar Pradesh, that, as a young IAS officer, Deepak Nayyar began to form his moral and ethical premises that were in the future to define his ideological approach to the discipline of economics and his work.

At the centre of his approach has been the concern for the human and for all things humane. It recognises the failings of the unhindered functioning of markets and the unfettered intervention of the State alike, and perceives the role of markets and the State as being complementary to each other. Having learnt to resist the authority of the printed word early on in his student days at Oxford, he was led to persistently question the dominant thinking of the time. This allowed him to escape the confines of a dogmatic approach to thinking and an exclusive reliance on orthodox analytical constructs. It also prevented him from turning into a 'pragmatic' – swimming with the tide of the time. Although he chose to be eclectic in his classroom teaching of economic theory – exposing his students to the different schools of economic thought, from the left to the right – he has remained remarkably consistent to the ideological framework that he adopted early on to the study and practice of economics. It is, therefore, no surprise that

## Deepak Nayyar: A diverse oeuvre  5

his peers on the ideological right often find him too left in his thinking and those on the left do not see him on their side of the fence.

Deepak Nayyar has taught economics at the University of Oxford (1972–73), the University of Sussex (1973–80) and the Indian Institute of Management, Calcutta (1980–83). He was Professor of Economics at Jawaharlal Nehru University (JNU), New Delhi (1986–2011) and Distinguished University Professor of Economics at New School for Social Research, New York (2008–12). At present Deepak Nayyar is Emeritus Professor of Economics at JNU, New Delhi. For most of the period since the early 1970s, the academic world has been his home and he has mostly engaged in teaching and research. However, he had a somewhat different incarnation as an academic from 2000 to 2005, when he was appointed as the Vice Chancellor of University of Delhi. He has often described the University as a miniature Republic of India that was almost as difficult to govern.

The job of a Vice Chancellor was indeed a challenging one, requiring enormous commitment. He had to address the widespread decay, intellectual and institutional, that had set into a premier institution of higher learning in the country. His approach was to persuade all stakeholders to come together, overcome inertia and reinvigorate institutional practices to pursue reforms. His priorities were restructuring courses and curricula that had not changed for decades, searching for excellence in academic appointments that had been progressively eroded and creating physical infrastructure, since what existed was poor or on the verge of collapse. Of course, the essential objectives were an academic renaissance in teaching and research, the restoration of academic morale and the creation of a milieu that was conducive to learning. These were amongst the numerous complex challenges he addressed with remarkable success. It was a time-consuming and arduous job demanding enormous patience, with results showing up gradually, but ultimately few doubted the very significant transformation of the University during his tenure. In this role, Deepak Nayyar took inspiration from the record of a most distinguished predecessor, C.D. Deshmukh, who was Vice Chancellor of Delhi University, for the five years that he was a student at the same university. Despite his gruelling schedule at the University of Delhi, Deepak Nayyar managed to keep up with his academic writings and responsibility to his research students.

Besides his current position at JNU, he continues his academic engagement as an Honorary Fellow of Balliol College (Oxford), a Distinguished Fellow of the Centre for the Study of Developing Societies (Delhi) and a Distinguished Professor at the Council for Social

## 6 Ananya Ghosh Dastidar et al.

Development (New Delhi). He is Chairman of the Sameeksha Trust, which publishes the *Economic and Political Weekly*. He has received the VKRV Rao award for his contribution to research in economics and has been a President of the Indian Economic Association.

Deepak Nayyar's distinguished career in academia has been interspersed with appointments in the government in the world of public policy. Besides his brief tenure in the IAS from 1969 to 1973, he worked as Economic Adviser in the Ministry of Commerce from 1983 to 1985. This was the time for him to rethink India's trade policies and redraft its operative regulations and guidelines in order to begin the process of reform and change. He was also closely associated with multilateral trade negotiations in the General Agreement on Tariffs and Trade (GATT). In this period, he learnt the art of policymaking as an exercise in persuasion, and he developed an understanding of the politics of decision-making.

He served as Chief Economic Adviser to the Government of India and Secretary in the Ministry of Finance from 1989 to 1991, and was perhaps the youngest to serve in that position. It was a politically turbulent era as governments at the centre changed thrice and, in fact, the most testing time for the Indian economy and its policymakers in its post-independence history. During this period, India was on the verge of default in its international payment obligations, with foreign exchange reserves running perilously low. The crisis had come about as a result of fiscal profligacy and piecemeal attempts at trade policy reforms in the second half of the 1980s. In the absence of a stable government at the centre, Deepak Nayyar found himself handling the acute crisis on a day-to-day basis. Several desperate measures had to be taken, such as rescheduling international payment obligations on an almost ongoing basis, borrowing overnight in international capital markets, imposing hefty cash margins to stifle imports, shipping gold confiscated from smugglers and negotiating loans with the IMF and later with the World Bank. He led these negotiations, and managed to secure the loans on conditions that were much less demanding than for other countries, which went to the IMF and the World Bank in similar crisis situations. A sharp devaluation of the rupee and measures to drastically reduce the fiscal deficit were put into effect. It was touch and go, but India managed to avert default and gradually stabilise the balance of payments situation.

Subsequently, the focus changed from managing the acute balance of payments crisis to macroeconomic management that would stabilise the economy and return it to a path of sustained growth. He was closely involved in preparations for the landmark Union Budget that was presented in July 1991. It heralded the macroeconomic reforms spanning the fiscal policy, monetary policy, financial and banking sector, trade policy, industrial policy and economic liberalisation that India embarked upon. This was the time for him to learn and understand the nature of the Indian State and the limitations of politics in a parliamentary democracy from a unique vantage point. It had a significant bearing on his thinking and later work. The tenure at the Ministry of Finance, at a difficult time, also brought to the fore the professional conviction and the courage with which he has approached his responsibilities. This courage of conviction also meant that, when differences arose on policy matters, he resigned from the government at the end of 1991, and returned to the classroom in his academic home at JNU.

Deepak Nayyar has worked in diverse organisational contexts, where his innate ability to lend his expertise and leadership to strengthen institutional foundations, streamline extant practices and build capacities to sustain change and develop future visions has come to the fore. This is especially true of his tenure as Vice Chancellor of the University of Delhi, where he is credited with many firsts. It is also true of Sameeksha Trust where he has been instrumental in raising much needed resources for the organisation, which transformed the financial situation of the *Economic and Political Weekly*, in his long association as a Trustee and now as the Chairman of the Trust. Over the years, this talent has been tapped by several organisations, in India and abroad.

He has, for instance, been Chairman of the Board of the World Institute for Development Economics Research (UNU-WIDER), Helsinki (2001–08). He was on the Board of Directors of the Social Science Research Council in the United States (2001–07) and was Chairman of the Advisory Council for the Department of International Development, Queen Elizabeth House, University of Oxford (2004–07). He was Vice President of the International Association of Universities, Paris (2004–08). In the other context of international agenda setting on research and policy, he was a Member of the World Commission on the Social Dimension of Globalization (2002–04). More recently, he has been a Member (2005–11) and then the Vice Chairman (2011–14) of the Board of the South Centre, Geneva. In India, he has served as a member of the National Knowledge Commission (2005–09).

He has chaired and convened several committees that reviewed the working of national and international institutions of higher learning engaged in teaching or research. These include the following: the Review Committee, Ambedkar University, Delhi, (2012, he also Chaired the Committee that led to its establishment); the Evaluation Committee, Institute of Social Studies, The Hague (2012); the Review

## 8 *Ananya Ghosh Dastidar et al.*

Committee, Indian Council for Social Science Research, New Delhi (2011); and the Evaluation Committee, United Nations Research Institute for Social Development (UNRISD), Geneva (2006). During 1997–98 he chaired the Review Committees for four premier research institutions and centres of higher learning in India, namely, Centre for Development Studies, Trivandrum; Institute for Social and Economic Change, Bangalore; Madras Institute of Development Studies, Madras; and Centre for Economic and Social Studies, Hyderabad, contributing significantly to their revitalisation.

Deepak Nayyar's professional success and considerable achievements across the diverse spectrum of his activities, over the past five decades, can be attributed to at least three qualities that he possesses in ample measure: a sincerity of purpose, integrity of the highest level and an ability to approach the task at hand in a dispassionate and knowledgeable manner, without any axes to grind. This allowed him to fully immerse himself in the work that came his way, sometimes out of the blue, and perform commendably in the pursuit of excellence. Ideologically, he remained consistent in the way in which he approached all his work. This enabled him to speak out his mind and retain his professional autonomy, both within and outside academia. He worked with dignity and could walk away when he felt the time had come for him to move on.

It was Aristotle who said: 'Excellence is never an accident. It is always a result of higher intention, sincere effort, and intelligent execution; it represents the wise choice of many alternatives – choice, not chance, determines your destiny'. When confronted with accidents of history and when opportunities came knocking on his door, Deepak Nayyar exercised his choices with care and executed them with intelligence and diligence. No wonder, when asked to identify the one aspect of his life that he would have liked to have lived differently, if given a choice, he responded in the negative and said that he enjoyed, and also learned, from everything he did. He is committed to his work and enjoys the thrill of confronting new challenges. Yet, he is a contented and a grounded person.

To his students, owing to his intellectual stature, Deepak Nayyar sometimes – at first sight – presented a formidable persona. This impression invariably changed once they got to know him, and learnt of the deep respect with which he regards all his students, and his capacity for supportive, friendly and wise guidance and mentoring. For his colleagues, he has been a well-reasoned, dependable and a straightforward person, always generous in lending a helping hand. Many of his students and colleagues would happily and gratefully attest to that fact.

Deepak Nayyar is married to Rohini, whom he met as a young student in 1965. Rohini Nayyar, an eminent economist and person in her own right, has been a critical anchor throughout his professional and personal life. Like him, she resigned from the IAS and moved with him to Oxford. She has not only been immensely supportive in all his endeavours, but has read and provided comments on everything that he wrote. They have two sons, Dhiraj and Gaurav, who are both economists. In fact, there is more to Deepak Nayyar than just Economics. Photography has been a hobby and a passion for more than 50 years ever since he got his first primitive box camera when he was not quite 12 years old. He recently published a book that brings together a collection of his photographs that have been taken over the past four decades. Apart from the camera, he loves travel and enjoys cooking.

## The body of his work

Deepak Nayyar's research interests are diverse and wide ranging, impressive in both their depth and breadth. They lie primarily in the areas of international economics, macroeconomics and development economics. While he has written extensively on economic development in India, he has also worked on development experiences of some Asian, African and Latin American countries, often placing those in the context of broader developments in the world economy. Given the range of his research interests, mirrored in his publications, it is not easy to organise Deepak Nayyar's academic writings into a few themes in order to understand his body of work, or to locate his predominant expertise in the discipline of economics. He has worked on several themes, often overlapping, with each theme addressing a cluster of issues. Furthermore, his work on these themes, or related issues, does not necessarily follow a distinct chronological sequence. He has returned to, or revisited, several issues at different points in time. Such is the case, for instance, with his writings on or related to macroeconomics, or India's economic development. Even so, it is possible to discern clusters and themes in his work.

Like most other economists, Deepak Nayyar started his journey in the discipline of economics with a focus on the relatively narrow, international trade – theory and policy – and much of his early research was on India's trade policies. Yet, soon enough, his field of study expanded in several directions, towards an engagement seeking a larger perspective, for instance on the theme of industrialisation, macroeconomics of development, trade theory, economic liberalisation, globalisation

## 10  *Ananya Ghosh Dastidar et al.*

and, more recently, on the long-term analysis of growth trajectories of nations and on inequality. His own instinctive preference, as he has written, is to sketch the big picture with bold strokes on a wide canvas instead of attempting to join the little dots (Nayyar 2013a, p. ix). However, unlike many of his peers, he consciously approached the subject of his study by exploring intersections of often competing but relevant domains, sometimes even spanning different disciplines in the social sciences. Thus, he has chosen to work on the overlapping and interdependent aspects of macroeconomics and development economics, theory and policy, national economies and the global context, and international economics and economic development. In analysing themes that he has taken up, he has not hesitated in stretching interdisciplinary boundaries, for instance, between economics and history; economics and politics; economics, law and philosophy; or economics and sociology. This preferred method of enquiry, along with his ideological disposition to the study of economics, as outlined, has been a key guiding factor in the advancement of his brand of heterodoxy, involving an unconventional analysis of problems and policy imperatives. Indeed, it has often resulted in a distinct perspective on issues that he has reflected upon.

In the early part of his academic career, following his DPhil thesis on 'India's Exports and Export Policies in the 1960s', he worked in the area of International Economics during the 1970s and the first half of the 1980s, covering issues on world trade, multilateral institutions, foreign direct investment, transnational corporations, international financial markets and cross-border movements of people. This overlapped with work on India's external sector followed by writings on industrialisation, analysing policies and strategies for growth and development. The intersections that he explored in this work relate, in part, to theory and policy or practice and, in part, to international engagement and economic development. His writings in this period include his seminal work on India's exports that provides deep insights into key areas needing policy attention and remains relevant even today for improving export performance (Nayyar 1976; 1988b). His work on industrial stagnation (Nayyar 1978) has been an important contribution to the literature on industrial development in India that soon became the point of departure for a large body of research on the topic, including several PhD dissertations.[1]

In the period from mid-1980s to the mid-1990s, his research engaged with several issues related to international trade not only in goods but also in services, as well as the international factor mobility of capital and labour. In each case he provided both theoretical constructs for explaining emerging trends and policy insights relevant in the contemporary context. He explored the implications of multilateral trade negotiations (Uruguay Round) and plurilateral trade agreements (like NAFTA) for developing countries (Nayyar 1988c; 1989; 1992; 1995c) to emphasise the multidimensional nature of the issues involved, which warranted a cautious and nuanced approach for policymakers. His work on international migration flows broke fresh ground as it provided an analytical framework for understanding how industrialisation strategies and development processes can explain or shape migration transitions in economies. In doing so, he explored the connection between turning points in rural-urban migration within countries and international migration from countries (Nayyar 1994c). In that context, Nayyar (1994a) was another original contribution in terms of its empirical research and its theoretical analysis of the macroeconomic implications and consequences of labour flows and financial flows attributable to migrants for their home countries. He also worked on the cusp of theory and policy in analysing international trade in services and providing insights on policy implications, especially in the context of the multilateral trading system (Nayyar 1988a; 1988c; 1989).

Although he continued his writings on issues related to world trade, he shifted his attention to Development Economics and Macroeconomics around this time. He approached the study of economic development using a macroeconomic framework of analysis and not through a conventional application of a micro-theoretic tool kit. He has worked on open economy macroeconomics and, in the context of developing countries, argued for fiscal and monetary policies to address the objectives of stabilisation (management of inflation and balance of payments) and growth, with an explicit focus on employment generation. It is employment that links macroeconomic objectives with human development and structural transformation of an economy. He has emphasised the need to seek alternative analytical frameworks that straddle time horizons to guide the restructuring of developing countries in their transition to become industrialised. This has led to his thinking on macroeconomics of development. He has hands-on experience in redesigning trade policies and in rethinking industrial and macroeconomic policies, including macro-stabilisation and structural-adjustment policies, where he has always argued that it is essential to pursue stabilisation *with* growth because stabilisation and growth are not *either/or* choices as orthodoxy sometimes suggests. His tenure at the Ministry of Finance complemented his theoretical understanding of these areas of economics acquired as a student,

## 12   Ananya Ghosh Dastidar et al.

teacher and researcher. It is this enriched perspective, founded on the examination of the interdependence of theory, experience and institutions that is evident in his writings on development in the context of economic liberalisation.

The outlines of a holistic macroeconomic framework for analysing the role of international trade, balance of payments constraints and its implications for industrialisation and growth strategies for countries like India and China emerged from Nayyar's research in this period (Nayyar 1988d; 1993). It provided an analytical framework, grounded in heterodox theory, for understanding the country's experience with stabilisation policies and structural reforms as it made a transition from an era of planned development towards a more market-based, open economic regime (Nayyar 1995a; 1995b). The monograph (Nayyar 1995a) based on his R.C. Dutt Lectures underlined the macroeconomic issues that acquired importance in the context of India's economic reforms initiated in 1991. It presented an early assessment of the reform process, for which he did much of the groundwork and laid the foundation for others to build on, during his tenure as the Chief Economic Adviser in the Ministry of Finance. This was entirely academic in its approach and contents. In contrast, his book, co-authored with his colleague and friend Amit Bhaduri (Bhaduri and Nayyar 1996), helped in creating a popular understanding of the reform process. It turned out to be a bestseller, translated into many languages – including Hindi – that reached out to citizens. It presented the then ongoing debate on economic issues in a language that was freely accessible, free of jargon and dogma. In the wake of the far-reaching policy reforms undertaken in the early 1990s, the authors argued for a system that could adapt to the impending changes in society and polity, and reflected on areas where the market and the State had roles to play.

In the period since mid-1990s, Deepak Nayyar worked on globalisation and the world economy, and continues to do so even now. He was, perhaps, the first among his generation of economists in India, indeed even elsewhere in the world, to analyse globalisation. His writings have played a major role in emphasising the importance of incorporating external sector issues (such as role of remittances, outward foreign direct investment from developing countries and balance of payments constraints) in standard macroeconomic analysis for India and other developing countries in the era of globalisation. His work on globalisation has explored many intersections: globalisation and history (Nayyar 1996a; 2006a), globalisation and development (Nayyar 2002a; 2004a), governing globalisation (Nayyar 1997; 1998a), globalisation and education (Nayyar 2008a), globalisation and democracy

(Nayyar 2015a) and globalisation and employment (Nayyar 2016a; 2015d). It is worth mentioning two of his books on the subject. Nayyar (2002b) brought together invited papers from distinguished scholars on the theme of governing globalisation. It was among the earliest texts on the subject and became a standard reference. A volume of his collected essays (Nayyar 2012a paperback edition, earlier printed in 2008) coherently presented in one place some of his writings on the subject of globalisation.

In respect of the world economy, he has analysed economic growth and development experiences, and the role that international institutions and global governance have played in that process (Bhaduri and Nayyar 1997). He has examined the structural transformation of the world economy and its constituents in Asia, Africa and Latin America – the parts and the whole (Nayyar 2008b; 2009; 2012b). He has written on the impact of the financial crisis and Great Recession (Nayyar 2011a) on the developing world, pointing out that large domestic markets can provide much-needed fallback options for countries like Brazil, China and India and indeed that these may even emerge as engines of growth for their respective regions, if not the world economy. He has also analysed other issues related to growth, technological capabilities and governance for emerging market economies (Nayyar 2011b; 2017) including the BRICS (Nayyar 2010a; 2016b) as well as other country groups (Nayyar 2010b). His analyses underscore the importance of external constraints on domestic growth, on the one hand, and highlight the relevance and contribution of the developing world in international context, on the other. In his work on the world economy, he has explored the consequences of political hegemony in a world of unequal partners, increasing macroeconomic interdependence in a world of capital mobility, and global public goods or global public bads in a world where positive or negative externalities spillover across national boundaries.

Much of Deepak Nayyar's work on growth and development of the world economy in the long-term historical perspective, spanning nearly two centuries, is reflected in his recent book that examines whether developing countries (that were once world leaders when viewed in a historical context) will catch up with the developed countries (Nayyar 2013a). He notes that in the six decades since 1950 there is a catch up underway, although it is concentrated in a few countries, and there is a discernible beginning of a shift in the balance of power in the world economy. There is, however, exclusion of many people and many countries from the process of catch-up. He has argued that rapid economic growth has not always been transformed

14   *Ananya Ghosh Dastidar et al.*

into meaningful development for improved well-being of all. He suggests that the developing countries can sustain their rise only if they ensure inclusive development, where economic growth, human development and social progress move hand-in-hand. The book highlights that there is no one uniform, or unique, path to development, as has often been assumed in orthodox economic thinking. Indeed, States and markets are complements rather than substitutes and countries that have succeeded have done so by minimising both market failure and government failure.

This brings us to his work on the theme of people and human well-being, spanning both developing countries and industrialised economies. Much of this work has been undertaken by him during the last 15 years or so. In his writings, he has highlighted that development outcomes have often failed to conform to the predictions stemming from dominant theories of development, wherein free markets and political democracy are expected to ensure efficiency and equity in the process of social transformation. Markets respond more to the demands of the rich than to the needs of the poor. They tend to exclude people without entitlements – those lacking assets or market relevant capabilities. Yet, markets seek to expand themselves by including more and more people. He has argued that the challenge is to focus on the creation of livelihood opportunities that can support gainful participation of the excluded in markets, improve entitlements and help raise their well-being. This is an issue that orthodox economic theory largely glosses over due to its preoccupation with growth and the aggregate level of national income. Similarly, he notes that although democracy includes people constitutionally and electorally, it often excludes or marginalises (the interests of) those without a voice, or numbers in their support, from the development mainstream. In the absence of purchasing power or economic bargaining power in the market, and voice or supportive interest groups in the political arena, the poor and the marginalised remain excluded. The beginnings of this thinking are discernible in some of his earlier work (Nayyar 1996b; 2001). Since then, he has written on issues of work, livelihood and rights (Nayyar 2003a); inclusion and exclusion in democracy and markets (Nayyar 2003b); macroeconomics of human development (Nayyar 2012c; 2013b); discrimination and justice (Nayyar 2011c); poverty, inequality, employment (Nayyar 2014); and the relationship between social development and economic progress (Nayyar 2015b). These writings have explored the interdependence between economy, polity and society to examine the relevant issues. More specifically, he has examined the relationship between employment, growth and development;

## Deepak Nayyar: A diverse oeuvre   15

poverty, inequality and growth; and economic growth, human development and social progress.

At various points in his professional career, Deepak Nayyar has engaged with and written on economic theory. It started with welfare economics, particularly social choice, and orthodox trade theory, but soon he moved away to engage with other issues. Subsequently, beginning in the early 1990s, he returned to economic theory in international economics and macroeconomics. Many of his publications reflect that engagement, as for instance, his works on trade theory (Nayyar 1988a; 1996; 1998b; 2007a), macroeconomic theory and policy (Stiglitz et al. 2006; Nayyar 2007a; 2007b; 2008c; 2011d; 2014) and international migration (Nayyar 1994c; 1998a; 2002b; 2008e). His analyses have served to emphasise the need to develop a nuanced approach towards stabilisation policies and policies of external sector liberalisation. In particular, he has argued that policy choices should be grounded in theories about trade and macroeconomics, so as to take into account market failures and structural rigidities that have critical impact in shaping outcomes in developing countries.

His writings on India's development experience are interspersed throughout his work on other issues. Indeed, his engagement with India's developmental journey and its experience has often provided the backdrop for his writings on other themes. He has written on myriad aspects of the Indian economy, polity and society and their institutions in the last decade and a half (Nayyar 2006b; 2006c; 2015c). From his unique vantage point of both ivory tower academic and policy practitioner, he has provided rare insights into the politics of policymaking (Nayyar 1998a) as well as incisive analyses of various facets of India's reform process (Nayyar 2000; 2002c; 2004b). As with his book on remittance flows and their implications in the 1990s, he was first among Indian academics to analyse the implications of the emerging trend of internationalisation of Indian firms (Nayyar 2008d). Nayyar (2012a; 2012d), bringing together some of these writings on India.

## Contribution to the discipline of economics

The considerable body of his work, across a range of themes and issues, places Deepak Nayyar among the foremost development thinkers of our time. The fact that his work has been guided as much by the pursuit of academic rigour as by the hands-on experience in the real world of policymaking, often at times of crisis and reforms, also makes him a leading practitioner of the subject. The intellectual integrity and the deep sense of scholarship with which he has approached

## 16  Ananya Ghosh Dastidar et al.

the subjects of his study have enabled him to look beyond the obvious and the orthodox. It has empowered him to recognise the relevance of alternative perspectives, pursue unconventional thinking using distinct analytical constructs and offer workable responses to address the realities of a changing developmental context. It is a context that is characterised by a shrinking presence of the State and an ever-expanding role for markets, against the backdrop of a sweeping buildup towards the globalisation of economies, people and cultures across the world. The reality of this rapidly changing context at the national level requires taking cognizance of the interplay and interdependence of markets and the institutions of political democracy, and their respective limitations, and to understand the nature of economic problems, related challenges and the policy response for the remedies.

In the methodological approach followed in his enquiry of the subject, Deepak Nayyar has taken on board the concerns, emerging out of the realities of the context that confront the contemporary world in which we live, not only in poor developing countries but also in rich, industrialised countries. He has also championed the need for research and economic policy analysis to be directed at goals that go well beyond the preoccupations of orthodox economics. The result has been the shaping and enriching of a heterodox approach to economics, which is not only relevant for its scope of study, but also encouraging in its results, especially for application in developing countries. With his distinct perspective, a flair for writing and lucidity of expression, he has contributed handsomely to the success of heterodox thinking in economic analysis and to its access and acceptance among the students and the practitioners of the subject in India and abroad.

Apart from the impact of his work on heterodox thinking in economics, Deepak Nayyar has contributed to the literature on globalisation in its different facets, both from the perspective of the world at large and that of developing countries, as well as India. He has been among the few who have examined and written on macroeconomic theory for developing countries and on the macroeconomics of development. This work spans a wide range of issues: stabilisation programmes, structural adjustment, public finance, economic reforms, industrialisation, trade liberalisation or financial deregulation and capital account liberalisation. In the process, he has enriched the relevant literature immensely. Moreover, he has put all this knowledge from his diverse thinking and writings to good use in examining the evolution of the world economy in a long-term perspective, to focus on what are now described as developing countries. In doing so, he sketches the big picture across continents in space and centuries in time. This constitutes a departure from much of the literature on the subject and contributes to an understanding of economic development in its much wider historical context. Indeed, liberating such work from the confines of economic history and extending it to the macroeconomics of development, imparting it with an appeal that is meaningful and universal in its reach and application across disciplines, has been a major achievement.

The phenomenon of globalisation witnessed in the 20th century is not new in human history. While it has provided significant opportunities to the developing countries to catch up with the industrialised world, there are various aspects of it that pose serious challenges to the growth of the world economy and the ability of people, especially those excluded, to benefit from it. The challenges emanate from the pace of globalisation – in the increased openness, interdependence and integration – and the inadequacy in global governance. Globalisation is being driven by markets, and open markets are not easy to govern, more so when they transcend national boundaries. There is a problem of regulating externalities in production and investment risks, when the economic space (of markets) and the political space (of governments and regulators) do not overlap. There is also the issue of shrinking national policy space due to unequal and, sometimes, hegemonic enforcement of global policy regimes, an unfortunate and undesirable accompaniment of the globalisation process. It undermines the State's capacity to promote equity and inclusion in the economies of latecomers to development. Indeed, globalisation, in its current era, has made it more difficult for governments to intervene and address exclusion. There is, hence, a need for improved global governance to address asymmetries in rules governing economic activities that are getting globalised (tradeable) and those that remain relatively insulated (non-tradeable). For example, trade and capital flows are relatively free, but technology and labour flows remain restricted to the disadvantage of the excluded and the poor residing in developing countries.

Deepak Nayyar has written extensively on these issues, often ahead of others. Importantly, he has been at the forefront of efforts at the international level to set the agenda for global governance reforms, and to promote global public goods and regulate global public bads through the reform of the existing international development, finance and trade institutions.[2] He has sought to address the emerging issues and the missing institutions in the areas of global macroeconomic management, international financial architecture, transnational corporations and cross-border movements of people through his research on, and engagement with, multilateral organisations and international institutions.

18  *Ananya Ghosh Dastidar et al.*

In his work on macroeconomic theory, Deepak Nayyar has consistently highlighted the differences between the economies of industrialised countries and those of the developing countries. It has necessitated an approach that relates economic theory to institutional context and exploring heterodox perspectives for analysis, diagnosis and prescription. He has argued that macroeconomic constraints on growth operate across time horizons and short-term policies have inevitable long-term consequences. That makes the distinction between short-term macroeconomic models and long-term growth models quite redundant in their application to developing countries. It also allows him to make a case for the use of macro-theoretic frameworks, suitably modified to reflect the needs of the local context, in understanding and guiding the process of structural transformation in developing countries.

In rethinking development, Deepak Nayyar has emphasised the importance of initial conditions, the significance of institutions, the relevance of politics in economics and the critical role of good governance, all of which collectively define the eventual outcomes of a development process. He has argued that the conventional approach to trade and industrialisation is narrow in its focus and selective in the use of theory and experience. There is more to trade policies than the choice between outward and inward orientation and there is more to industrialisation than trade policies. While the causation between trade and industrialisation runs both ways, the macroeconomic determinants of, and constrains on, industrial growth and trade are significant and, therefore, cannot be ignored in developing countries. He has highlighted the importance of the demand side, the implications of demand-supply linkages and the pitfalls of overlooking the role of technology. He has argued that the degree of openness and the nature of State intervention in the process of industrialisation are strategic choices that cannot be exercised once and for all. Those choices are dependent on the context and the stage of development and therefore must be allowed to be changed over time.[3] In his work, Deepak Nayyar has not only exposed the limitations of economic orthodoxy, but has successfully advanced the analytical and policy guidance frontiers of the discipline pertaining to the industrialisation of developing countries.

## Conclusions

In conclusion, Deepak Nayyar's contribution to bridging the gap between the world of academia and research on the one hand, and the art of policymaking on the other, cannot be overemphasised. His contribution to revitalising several institutions of higher learning – universities, research institutions, and research-for-policy initiatives – is equally significant. There is also an engagement with the public sphere. He has played the role of the public intellectual in society, whose task is to be independent and unbiased in judgement on issues that are economic, societal or political. Neither dogmatic nor doctrinaire, he has never accepted simple propositions as articles of faith that leave no room for nuances. His ability to question every assumption, the capacity to criticise both orthodox and unorthodox thinking, the readiness to not just attempt different answers but pose different questions, always with rigour and incisiveness, while steadfastly keeping in mind the well-being of the common man, has been refreshing and remarkable. This century requires creative and imaginative approaches and solutions to pressing global problems such as persistent poverty, inequality and natural environment sustainability – some of which are attempted in this book by his colleagues and students. Indeed, Deepak Nayyar's work points out the direction in which we may need to proceed.

## Notes

1 His work on India's Industrialisation and some related contributions were subsequently brought together in a well-received edited book, Nayyar (1994b).
2 See, for instance, Nayyar (2002b) and the review of the body of his work on globalisation in the earlier part of the chapter.
3 See, for a brief elaboration, the introduction to Nayyar (2012d) or its 2008 hardbound print.

## Bibliography

Bhaduri, Amit and Deepak Nayyar (1997), 'The Washington Consensus and the Liberalization of Economies', *Revue Tiers Monde*, April–June.
––––––– (1996), *The Intelligent Person's Guide to Liberalization*, Penguin Books, London.
Nayyar, Deepak (2017), 'BRICS, Emerging Markets and the World Economy', in P. Anand, F. Comin, S. Fennell and R. Weiss eds. *Oxford Handbook on BRICS*, Oxford University Press, Oxford, (forthcoming).
––––––– (2016a), *Employment, Growth and Development*, Routledge, New Delhi (forthcoming).
––––––– (2016b), 'BRICS, Developing Countries and Global Governance', *Third World Quarterly*, Volume 37, Number 4, pp. 575–591.
––––––– (2015a), 'Globalisation and Democracy', *Brazilian Journal of Political Economy*, Volume 35, Number 3, July–September 2015, pp. 388–402, and *Economic and Political Weekly*, Volume 1, Number 19, 9 May 2015, pp. 47–54.

20   *Ananya Ghosh Dastidar et al.*

——— (2015b), 'Social Development and Economic Progress: Some Reflections on the Relationship', in Imrana Qadeer ed. *India Social Development Report 2014*, Oxford University Press, New Delhi.

——— (2015c), 'Birth, Life and Death of Development Finance Institutions in India', *Economic and Political Weekly*, Volume 1, Number 33, 15 August 2015, pp. 51–60.

——— (2015d), 'Globalisation and Employment', *Indian Journal of Labour Economics*, Volume 58, Number 1, 2015, pp. 87–97.

——— (2014), 'Why Employment Matters: Reviving Growth and Reducing Inequality', *International Labour Review*, September.

——— (2013a), *Catch Up: Developing Countries in the World Economy*, Oxford University Press, Oxford and New York.

———, ed. (2013b), *Macroeconomics and Human Development*, Taylor and Francis, London.

——— (2012a), *Trade and Globalization*, Oxford University Press, Delhi (paperback edition), earlier printed in 2008.

——— (2012b), 'The Emerging Asian Giants and Economic Development in Africa', in Akbar Noman, Kwesi Botchwey, Howard Stein and Joseph Stiglitz eds. *Good Growth and Governance in Africa: Rethinking Development Strategies*, Oxford University Press, Oxford.

——— (2012c), 'Macroeconomics and Human Development', *Journal of Human Development and Capabilities*, February.

——— (2012d), *Liberalization and Development*, Oxford University Press, Delhi (paperback edition), earlier reprinted in 2008.

——— (2011a), 'The Financial Crisis, the Great Recession and the Developing World', *Global Policy*, January.

——— (2011b), 'Economic Growth and Technological Capabilities in Emerging Economies: National Specificities and International Context', *Innovation and Development*, October.

——— (2011c), 'Discrimination and Justice: Beyond Affirmative Action', *Economic and Political Weekly*, 15 October.

——— (2011d), 'Rethinking Macroeconomic Policies for Development', *Brazilian Journal of Political Economy*, July–September.

——— (2010a), 'Economic Growth and Technological Capabilities in BRICs: Implications for Latecomers to Industrialization', in Xialon Fu and Luc Soete eds. *The Rise of Technological Power in the South*, Palgrave Macmillan, London.

——— (2010b), 'China, India, Brazil and South Africa in the World Economy: Engines of Growth?', in Amelia Santos-Paulino and Guanghua Wan eds. *Southern Engines of Global Growth*, Oxford University Press, Oxford.

——— (2009), 'Developing Countries in the World Economy: The Future in the Past?', *WIDER Annual Lecture 12*, UNU-WIDER, Helsinki.

——— (2008a), 'Globalization: What Does It Mean for Higher Education?', in Luc E. Weber and James D. Duderstadt eds. *The Globalization of Higher Education*, Economica, Paris and London, reprinted in *Economic and Political Weekly*, 15 December 2007.

—— (2008b), 'The Rise of China and India: Implications for Developing Countries', in Philip Artesis and John Eatwell eds. *Issues in Economic Development and Globalization*, Palgrave, London.

—— (2008c), 'Macroeconomics of Structural Adjustment and Public Finance in Developing Countries: A Heterodox Perspective', *International Journal of Development Issues*, June.

—— (2008d), 'The Internationalization of Firms from India: Investment, Mergers and Acquisitions', *Oxford Development Studies*, March.

—— (2008e), 'International Migration and Economic Development', in Narcis Serra and Joseph Stiglitz eds. *The Washington Consensus Reconsidered: Towards a New Global Governance*, Oxford University Press, Oxford.

—— (2007a), 'Globalization and Free Trade: Theory, History and Reality', in Anwar Shaikh ed. *Globalization and Myths of Free Trade*, Palgrave, London, 2007.

—— (2007b), 'Macroeconomics in Developing Countries', *Banca Nazionale del Lavoro Quarterly Review*, September.

—— (2006a), 'Globalization, History and Development: A Tale of Two Centuries', *Cambridge Journal of Economics*, January.

—— (2006b), 'India 2025: Illusions, Realities and Dreams', in B.G. Verghese ed. *Tomorrow's India: Another Tryst with Destiny*, Penguin Books, New Delhi.

—— (2006c), 'India's Unfinished Journey: Transforming Growth into Development', *Modern Asian Studies*, July.

—— (2004a), 'Globalization and Development', in Ha-Joon Chang ed. *Rethinking Development Economics*, Anthem Press, London, 2004.

—— (2004b), 'Economic Reforms in India: Understanding the Process and Learning from Experience', *International Journal of Development Issues*, December.

—— (2003a), 'Work, Livelihoods and Rights', *Indian Journal of Labour Economics*, January–March.

—— (2003b), 'On Exclusion and Inclusion: Democracy, Markets and People', in A.K. Dutt and J. Ros eds. *Development Economics and Structuralist Macroeconomics*, Edward Elgar, Cheltenham.

—— (2002a), 'Globalization and Development Strategies', in J. Toye ed. *Trade and Development: New Directions for the Twenty-First Century*, Edward Elgar, Cheltenham.

——, ed. (2002b), *Governing Globalization: Issues and Institutions*, Oxford University Press, Oxford.

—— (2002c), 'Capital Controls and the World Financial Authority: What Can We Learn from the Indian Experience?', in J. Eatwell and L. Taylor eds. *International Capital Markets: Systems in Transition*, Oxford University Press, New York.

—— (2001), 'Economic Development and Political Democracy: The Interaction of Economics and Politics in Independent India', in N.G. Jayal ed. *Democracy in India*, Oxford University Press, Delhi, earlier printed in *Economic and Political Weekly*, December 1998.

## 22 Ananya Ghosh Dastidar et al.

———— (2000), 'Macroeconomic Reforms in India: Short-Term Effects and Long-Run Implications', in W. Mahmud ed. *Adjustment and Beyond: The Reform Experience in South Asia*, Palgrave, London.

———— (1998a), 'Democracy, Markets and People in the Context of Globalization', *Public Policy*, January–March.

———— (1998b), 'International Trade and Factor Mobility: Economic Theory and Political Reality', in Deepak Nayyar ed. *Economics as Ideology and Experience*, Frank Cass, London.

———— (1997), 'Globalization: The Game, the Players and the Rules', in S.D. Gupta ed. *The Political Economy of Globalization*, Kluwer Academic Publishers, Dordrecht.

———— (1996a), 'Globalization: The Past in Our Present', *Indian Economic Journal*, January–March.

———— (1996b), 'Free Trade: Why, When and for Whom?', *Banca Nazionale del Lavoro Quarterly Review*, September.

———— (1995a), *Economic Liberalization in India: Analytics, Experience and Lessons*, Orient Longman, Calcutta.

———— (1995b), 'Macro-Economics of Stabilisation and Adjustment: The Indian: Experience', *Economie Appliquee*, Number 3.

———— (1995c), 'Implications of NAFTA for South Asia', in ESCAP *Implications of the North American Free Trade Agreement for the Asian and Pacific Region*, United Nations, New York.

———— (1994a), *Migration, Remittances and Capital Flows: The Indian Experience*, Oxford University Press, Delhi.

————, ed. (1994b), *Industrial Growth and Stagnation: The Debate in India*, Oxford University Press, Bombay.

———— (1994c), 'International Labour Movements, Trade Flows and Migration Transitions', *Asia and Pacific Migration Journal*, Number 1.

———— (1993), 'The Foreign Trade Sector, Planning and Industrialization in India', in T.J. Byres ed. *The State and Development Planning in India*, Oxford University Press, Delhi.

———— (1992), 'The Dunkel Text: An Assessment', *Social Scientist*, January–February.

———— (1989), 'Towards a Possible Multilateral Framework for Trade in Services: Issues and Concepts', in UNCTAD *Technology, Trade Policy and the Uruguay Round*, United Nations, New York.

———— (1988a), 'Political Economy of International Trade in Services', *Cambridge Journal of Economics*, June.

———— (1988b), 'India's Export Performance: 1970–1985: Underlying Factors and Constraints', in Robert Lucas and Gustav Papanek eds. *The Indian Economy: Recent Development and Future Prospects*, Westview Press, London and Oxford University Press, Delhi.

———— (1988c), 'Some Reflections on the Uruguay Round and Trade in Services', *Journal of World Trade*, October.

## Deepak Nayyar: A diverse oeuvre    23

——— (1988d), 'The External Sector in Chinese Economic Development', *Social Scientist*, November–December 1987, reprinted in Ashok Mitra, ed., *China: Issues in Development*, Tulika, New Delhi.

——— (1978), 'Industrial Development in India: Growth or Stagnation?', *Economic and Political Weekly*, Special Number, August. Reprinted in A.K. Bagchi and N. Banerji, eds., *Change and Choice in Indian Industry*, Calcutta, 1980.

——— (1976), *India's Exports and Export Policies in the 1960s*, Cambridge University Press, Cambridge, reprinted as paperback 2008.

Stiglitz, Joseph, Jose Antonio Ocampo, Shari Spiegel, Ricardo French Davis and Deepak Nayyar (2006), *Stability with Growth: Macroeconomics, Liberalization and Development*, Oxford University Press, Oxford.

# 2 Development complexities
## Looking afresh

*Ananya Ghosh Dastidar,*
*Rajeev Malhotra and Vivek Suneja*

It was perhaps Albert Einstein who said that "Everything should be made as simple as possible, but no simpler". The quote succinctly sums up a major dilemma that faces any serious researcher or a policy analyst who has to grapple with a complex problem. Making sense of complexity necessarily requires an exercise in abstraction so that the essential can be separated from the insignificant, the substance from the detail, the grain from the chaff. However, there is a double risk involved here: the wrong variables may be chosen as being critical, while certain critical variables may remain completely ignored. Consequently, the learning curve associated with research and analysis of a difficult subject inevitably leaves room for errors, so that learning proceeds as much by benefitting from correction of errors as by building on successes. Such is the case, for instance, in sustaining progress in a socially desired manner in any country, developing or developed.

Development is a multidimensional phenomenon that defies easy characterization. There are very many paths to development and the optimum path for one nation at a particular historical juncture may differ significantly from that of another. Indeed, as the research of Deepak Nayyar and many others has convincingly demonstrated, there is simply no uniform recipe for all nations at all times. A large range of variables influence the feasibility and desirability of development trajectories including the size of nations, resource endowments, institutional capabilities, persistence of colonial and Neo-colonial relationships, role of the State, nature of the political system, cultural factors and so on. It then turns out that the pursuit of development and sustaining progress is a complex affair. While some nations achieve spectacular success, others fail abysmally; a nation that excels on some dimensions of development may fare very poorly on others. History is witness to the fact that initiating economic development is one aspect

## Development complexities 25

of human endeavour and sustaining it over time for meaningfully advancing human wellbeing is another.

In this book, we take a look at both what development means, and how it may possibly be facilitated. The relevance of this issue has received fresh impetus from the significant changes in the degree and pattern of international economic relations that are unfolding across the world today, posing both opportunities and challenges for development. While globalisation of goods and financial markets has delivered high growth, yet distribution of the fruits of growth has been highly unequal, with gains to owners of capital and skills being disproportionately higher compared to that of labour, especially the unskilled. Indeed, the gap between the winners and losers created by globalisation was sharply accentuated during the recent global financial crisis. No doubt, widening and persistent inequalities have been at the heart of rising polarization, spread of conflicts and manifested in totally unexpected and unprecedented outcomes like Brexit and recent political and economic developments in the United States.

Balancing the soaring aspirations fuelled by success stories crafted in the global economy, with the sheer anger and frustration of all those sidelined or left out is possibly the biggest social challenge of our times. Indeed, failure to accommodate these opposing forces threatens to tear apart the very fabric of societies in different parts of the world. The global discontent, more palpable than ever before, must be addressed. As such, there is urgent need to rethink development theory and policy at the current conjuncture when globalisation seems to be in retreat.

Although not by design, the invited contributions for this festschrift fall in three broad categories, which sets the structure for this volume. The authors, who have all engaged or worked with Deepak Nayyar at different points in his professional life, or have been his students, provide fresh thinking on issues that they have written on, or revisited in the current global context. There is something of a common thread that runs through these contributions. We cannot claim that all relevant issues in development have been covered, yet the picture that emerges from this book provides a story that must be read as policymakers across the world gear up to confront the challenges that they face. The first section of the book includes chapters that try to identify some key evolving dimensions of globalisation. In the second section, authors endeavour to rethink some important theoretical and public policy issues in development; and in the final section, an attempt is made to discern some of the key lessons suggested by recent development experiences from India and various other emerging economies.

## 26  *Ananya Ghosh Dastidar et al.*

## Evolving dimensions of globalisation

A critical task in comprehending a dynamic and complex phenomenon like globalisation is discerning its key dimensions. In turn, any analysis of the implications of globalisation calls for a broad-based exploration of numerous dimensions of economic and social progress as development is a holistic concept comprising manifold attributes of human wellbeing. These include inequalities in the distribution of income, expenditure and access to critical services such as health and education among various groups; impact of economic activity on the natural environment; social, cultural and political freedoms; and many other aspects that interact with and influence each other in diverse ways. These relationships may be symmetric or asymmetric and the various factors may not be on the same footing: some may be more fundamental than others in their influence and power over the other dimensions. For example, the systemic forces at work in market capitalism such as the drive for ever increasing profits and capital accumulation may powerfully influence and constrain other elements, such as the ability of a well-meaning capitalist employer to pay more than the market wage to his workers, in cash or in kind. Similarly, while many economic agents may wish to adopt 'clean' technologies, the nature of externalities involved may well make it impossible for individual agents to act in a responsible fashion in the face of market competition.

Market capitalism has been the dominant ideology embraced by the developing world since the 1980s, with country after country dismantling barriers to trade and state controls to usher in the discipline of competition and unleash the efficiencies of private enterprise. Events such as the collapse of the Soviet Union, the adoption of market-oriented policies by communist China and the export-led growth in East Asia no doubt acted as catalysts in this process. However, historical and deep-rooted inequalities across class, caste, race or region often create an unequal playing field, putting some actors in a far more advantageous position to benefit from the opportunities presented by globalisation. Indeed, global integration can trap economic players in vicious cycles of dependence and immiseration just as it can provide opportunities to participate in virtuous cycles of growth and development. As such, the very outcomes precipitated by market-oriented, open-door policies often unleash forces that threaten to subvert the process of globalisation itself, by creating tensions and conflicts, undermining basic human rights and triggering systemic crises.

Clearly this calls for a creative and pragmatic approach to policymaking. After all, history bears testimony to the vital contribution

*Development complexities* 27

made by developmental states, even after allowing for the influence of other factors like climate, geography and culture on developmental outcomes. In this context, the relevance of a broad policy framework based on individual capabilities and a human-centric approach cannot be overemphasized. Equally important is the need to create policy space to accommodate heterodox influences, especially when conventional wisdom proves inadequate, as starkly demonstrated *inter alia* during the recent global financial crisis.

The chapters in this section deal with various aspects of globalisation and its implications for development policy. In the first chapter 'Capitalism, consciousness and development', Akmal Hussain analyzes the current world economic crisis and the longer-term global environmental crisis in terms of the systemic tendencies of capitalism. At one level, the inherent limitations of the market are identified as the underlying cause of economic instability. At a structural level, the analysis suggests that the particular relationship between humans, commodities and nature engendered by the market-based system has led to an environmental crisis that threatens life on Earth. The limitations of government policy to effectively induce the adoption of green technology and green technological change within a free enterprise system are analyzed in the context of the Paris summit. Finally, an alternative relationship between humans, commodities and nature based on recovering our humanity is presented. This is based on the 'unanimous tradition' of re-awareness of humaneness in which caring for others and for nature can become a vital element in the development of our 'human capabilities'. Such a consciousness could constitute the normative basis for sustainable development and effective cooperation for saving the life support systems of the planet and building a humane society.

The importance of policy in shaping developmental outcomes is underscored in 'The rise and fall(?) of the ABP (Anything But Policy) discourse in development economics', by Ha-Joon Chang. Since the mid-1990s, there has been an explosion in the literature in development economics that tries to explain the poor economic performance in certain developing countries – especially the ones in Sub-Saharan Africa – in terms of non-policy factors, such as geography, climate, history and culture. This chapter contends that these explanations are neither theoretically persuasive nor empirically convincing and thus can only be interpreted as an attempt by mainstream economists to 'explain' why the 'good' policies that were based on their theories failed. The fact that this literature has become less popular with the revival of economic growth in Sub-Saharan Africa in the more

28  *Ananya Ghosh Dastidar et al.*

recent period also confirms the inherently ideological nature of this literature.

The chapter by Frances Stewart, 'Inequality and conflict: Global drivers and interventions' discusses the connections between globalisation, inequality and conflict. It focuses on horizontal inequalities (or between-group inequalities) as contrasted with vertical inequalities (inequalities among individuals). The author argues that it is the horizontal inequalities that raise the risk of conflict. The origin of many of the horizontal inequalities within countries lies in colonialism, but subsequently global forces have contributed to their perpetuation by providing greater resources and markets for the wealthier and better educated groups or regions. Migration flows are also a major source of contemporary horizontal inequalities, including within developed countries. In addition, globally dispersed communities also experience such inequality. Muslims across the globe tend to be relatively deprived in every country where they do not form a majority and on average Muslim countries are less well off than non-Muslim ones. Given the manifold global connections among Muslims, grievances in one country can be transmitted to Muslims in others, with the consequence that these global inequalities become a source of tension and sometimes violence. This is also true of other global groups which have experienced relative privilege or deprivation including Christians, Jews, the Lebanese, overseas Chinese and Roma people. Peaceful development requires inclusive policies with minimal group inequality, nationally and globally.

A case for strengthening heterodox influences and accepting a role for a human rights–based policy approach in development and sustaining progress is made in 'Economic policy and human rights: Is globalisation a meeting ground?' by Rajeev Malhotra. The chapter explores the contours of a meaningful and an effective policy response to the current global economic milieu. It argues that such a response has to be necessarily based on a thinking that consciously departs from the economic mainstream, as the latter has fallen short in delivering desired social outcomes in the developing as well as the industrialised world. It is essential that heterodox economic policy prescription for social problems has its own normative basis, just as it is necessary for that prescription to be evidence based. Furthermore, it is argued that there is a certain inevitability in the human rights normative framework taking centrestage in rethinking economic policy for inclusive development and sustained progress in the current context. The chapter goes on to elaborate how some elements of that desired heterodox economic policy response need to be pursued at the national level.

## Economic theory and public policy

To make sense of the vast amount of data that the working of the economic system generates for policymaking, an appropriate body of theory is indispensable. Indeed, one can go as far as to argue that no meaningful data exists unless there is a theoretical prism through which it can be viewed and measured. This is as true in the social science disciplines as in the physical sciences. In quantum physics, which constitutes the most fundamental level of analysis in the physical sciences, it is universally accepted that it is meaningless to talk of an 'objective' phenomenon that is independent of the manner in which the 'subject' observes and interprets the phenomenon. Physical sciences also recognize the crucial need to explicitly state the assumptions or axioms upon which the deductive superstructure of a particular theory rests. Newtonian, Relativity and Quantum physics hence constitute three separate paradigms, being based upon very different underlying assumptions or views of reality. On the other hand, while social 'sciences', and especially the dismal science, has borrowed its methodological approach in very significant ways from the physical sciences, it has often failed to explicitly examine the appropriateness of its foundational assumptions and the implications of these for explaining real-world phenomena.

The chapters in this section attempt to take a fresh look at theory and policy in development. The urgent need to do so can be appreciated in context of the recent global crisis that brought into stark focus the weaknesses inherent in existing models (which utterly failed to anticipate its onset), as well as in conventional policies (which could not provide solutions to the problems it created). This certainly makes a strong case for re-examining existing macro models and theories and attempting to script unconventional policy measures. The contributions in this section critically examine the mainstream Neo-classical economic theory that dominates economic analysis. Authors explore whether the assumptions of Neo-classical economics turn out to be over-simplified abstractions, which while making the analysis tractable and mathematically elegant, might lead to erroneous conclusions regarding how the real world works. Whether the assumptions that are used in traditional mainstream theory are behaviourally sound, and whether they take account of cultural norms and values that humans as economic agents live by, is also questioned. Behavioural or normative blindness is not a minor aberration – be it in the context of financial markets, labour markets or consumer behaviour. Failure to take account of how people actually make economic decisions can do grave damage to both the quality of our understanding and our policy recommendations.

It needs to be explicitly recognized that many assumptions, often routinely and unquestioningly used in mainstream economic theory, such as, 'men are motivated by their self-interest in making economic decisions'; or 'effort is a source of disutility and hence exerted only if recompensed by income that commands purchase of material products' are essentially cultural assumptions. Since economics cannot do without behavioural assumptions, all economics is necessarily normative – it cannot be otherwise. The distinction often made between positive economics and normative economics is hence misplaced. Given this is so, economists must pay greater attention to the nature of the assumptions that underlie their theoretical models. They also need to recognize that these assumptions can vary from culture to culture – a homogeneous, uniform 'global' science of economics that ignores such cultural variation is an unhelpful and misguided supposition. Whether it is a 'fetish' for the yellow metal, or a more generalized fetish for unbounded personal wealth that overrides all other concerns such as for the natural environment or the welfare of fellow humans is something that needs examination. The discipline of economics has to seriously address how such assumptions are shaped by time and place. In this respect, economics must engage more deeply with the 'social' aspect of the family of social sciences (including the disciplines of sociology, anthropology, history and politics) to which it belongs. Globalisation, by making the exchange of ideas between people belonging to different parts of the world more widespread, needs to be explored in terms of the consequent interaction effects.

In 'The theory of credit and macroeconomic stability', Joseph Stiglitz notes that in the aftermath of the last financial crisis, there is a growing consensus, even among central bank officials, concerning the limitations of monetary policy. The chapter provides an explanation for the ineffectiveness of monetary policy, and in doing so provides a new framework for thinking about monetary policy and macroeconomic activity. It is argued that rather than money supply or the T-bill interest rate, what really matters is the availability of credit, and the terms at which credit is made available. The latter variables may not move in tandem with the former. In particular, the spread between the T-bill rate and the lending rate may increase, so even as the T-bill rate decreases, the lending rate increases. An increase in credit availability may not lead to more spending on produced goods, but increased prices for land or other fixed assets; it can go to increased margins associated with increases in speculative activity; or it may

Development complexities 31

go to spending abroad rather than at home. The chapter explains the inadequacy of theories based on the zero low bound, and argues that the ineffectiveness of monetary policy is more related to the multiple alternative uses – beyond the purchase of domestically produced goods – of additional liquidity and to its adverse distributional consequences. The chapter shows that while monetary policy is less effective than has been widely presumed, it is also more distortionary, identifying several distinct distortions. The second part of the chapter shows how advances in technology may allow for the creation of an electronic monetary system that may permit better macroeconomic management and enable a greater sharing of the rents associated with credit creation to be captured for the national treasury.

The chapter 'Money and market failures: A theoretical perspective', by Anjan Mukherji, considers the problems associated with the introduction of money in the standard general equilibrium model. This discussion is of particular interest given the history of recurrent financial crashes around the globe, and the often serious repercussions of this phenomenon on developing nations. The chapter demonstrates that while the efficiency predictions of the general equilibrium model remain unaltered with the introduction of money as a means of exchange, this no longer holds true when the role of money as a store of value is considered. Under conditions of uncertainty, different economic agents form different expectations about future prices, and this can lead to inefficiency. Hence market failure in financial markets cannot solely be attributed to factors like asymmetric information or government policy; money as a store of value can by itself cause market failure. Moreover, such failure cannot be corrected by imposing taxes (as in the case of externalities) or providing information on quality (as when there is information asymmetry).

In 'Persuasion and coercion: A transaction costs perspective on income distribution', Vivek Suneja argues that transaction cost theories have not adequately addressed the question of income distribution. Team production and transaction asset specificity play a pivotal role in the theory of the firm. However, existing theory has relatively little to say on the nature and degree of bargaining related transaction costs that are likely to be involved in the division of team output or economic rent. The chapter explores how cultural norms and bargaining power can influence the efficiency of transacting and the pattern of income distribution under team production. Transactional efficiency may be enhanced by reducing bargaining costs through 'persuasion' (influencing cultural norms) and 'coercion' (influencing bargaining power). The chapter contrasts the argument presented here against the

## 32  Ananya Ghosh Dastidar et al.

prominent theories of income distribution including the Neo-classical, new institutional economics and Marxian. The author also posits a new explanation for the phenomenon of efficiency wages, under conditions of team production.

The chapter, 'Dual economy models with fixed terms-of-trade', by Amitava Bose,[1] examines the linkages between a traditional (agricultural) sector and a modern non-agricultural sector (manufacturing and services) in a dual economy model with fixed inter-sectoral terms of trade, where output adjustments occur to maintain equilibrium. The author uses two alternate frameworks, the Ricardian framework and a Keynesian framework, and shows that when the terms of trade are given, even though the modern sector may grow faster, it cannot be a 'leading sector' as its growth rate in essence is determined by that of the traditional sector. The relevance of the chapter lies in capturing an important aspect of reality in developing countries, viz., price rigidity (governments often fix the price of food in an attempt to achieve food security). The chapter also has another important implication, namely well-functioning credit markets and interest rate flexibility can play an important role in restoring equilibrium in a market characterized by price rigidity.

In 'Comprehending the "in-formal": Formal-informal conundrum in labour under capitalism', Saumyajit Bhattacharya analyzes the notion of labour 'informality'. The chapter argues that the semantics and framework of structural dualism obfuscates the pivotal role played by 'informal' labour in the capital accumulation process. The Lewisian dual economy model regards the informal sector as a source of cheap 'unlimited' labour supply to the formal industrial sector. A clear separation of the formal and informal and a one-way link from the informal to the formal is a structural feature of this framework. The popularity of the Lewis model in development economics generated a politics of semantics. In-formal, un-organized, un-registered: terms which, apart from being descriptively superficial, signify an 'othering' that obfuscates the nature of the capital accumulation process. The chapter argues that informality as a 'choice' exercised by capital forms the basis of the regime of capitalist accumulation. Moreover, informality as a political choice has been exercised by the regulatory state to facilitate capitalist accumulation in the current phase of globalisation.

Satish K. Jain is concerned with the implications of using more than one liability rule by the courts in 'Multiple efficient rules and inefficient outcomes'. The chapter demonstrates that when a court uses more than one liability rule for apportioning liability between parties and there is uncertainty regarding which rule will be used, then

*Development complexities* 33

inefficiency is possible even if all the liability rules are efficient. A general theorem is established which says that if the court uses more than one efficient liability rule in any particular instance and the two parties do not know in advance which of the efficient liability rules will be used by the court, then outcomes may not always be efficient. The main policy implication is that in any jurisdiction, the use of a single efficient liability rule is generally preferable to the use of more than one efficient rule.

In 'Auctions with an inferior outside option', Krishnendu Ghosh Dastidar explores and models an interesting aspect of consumer behaviour that is especially relevant to developing countries. In societies with shared socio-cultural values and low average incomes, individuals may be willing to spend the bulk of their income on a commodity like gold or liquor. The chapter provides an explanation for such behaviour using an auction theoretic framework. The chapter shows that when bidders consider their outside options to be inferior (e.g. the poor may derive higher utility from consumption of gold or liquor than from food or education), they may be willing to bid their entire income in an auction to obtain objects they value highly. The author considers three different types of auctions and shows that the expected revenue of the seller depends on the type of auction (i.e. revenue equivalence fails to hold), with all-pay auctions yielding the highest and second-price auctions the lowest expected revenues.

## Lessons from development experiences

The developing world has now witnessed over three decades of globalisation and market-based reforms. Yet certain age-old problems and concerns remain. For instance, industrial growth that can create large scale-employment and ensure decent wages and viable livelihoods for the masses still remains elusive in most countries. Also, problems of poverty and deprivation persist on a significant scale, while inequalities of income, wealth and access to opportunities continue to widen across the globe. In this context, lessons from actual country experiences can provide rich insights into policies that work as well as pitfalls best avoided. The chapters in this section cover various country experiences, including India, and draw relevant policy lessons even as the established order, based on global integration and free markets, is under threat.

In particular, at least three key issues are worth highlighting at the current conjuncture. The first relates to the critical importance of industrialisation, especially for generating large-scale employment, vital for reaping the benefits of the so-called demographic dividend.

## 34 Ananya Ghosh Dastidar et al.

Experience shows that while import substitution policies bred inefficiencies, encouraged rent seeking and failed to deliver high growth, they were successful in creating manufacturing capacity. Market-oriented globalisation policies did not necessarily usher in industrialisation on a large scale and, in many cases, were even associated with de-industrialisation owing to import competition. In this context, the success of export-led industrialisation in East Asia (including China) must be understood as much as an example of successful state intervention as of outward orientation.

The second key point relates to the role of the State in the development process. This is now an age-old issue and the importance of strategic state intervention for successful industrialisation is amply demonstrated by experiences of developed and developing nations alike. The recent global financial crisis, which saw a revival of Keynesian policies, also brought into sharp focus the State's role in overall macro management and for crafting sectoral regulations, especially those governing asset markets and the financial sector. Newer regulatory challenges are posed by financial globalisation and the increasingly complex nature of real and financial sector interactions, with speculation-fueled asset price booms often leading to outcomes de-linked from economic fundamentals. This has brought to the fore the use of unconventional economic policy, monetary as well as fiscal.

The third issue relates to the market for an important asset, namely land, that has drawn considerable attention in the recent discourse on development. For instance, economic prosperity, especially among 'the middle class' (the educated class that has been the main beneficiary of market-based reforms and globalisation across developing countries) has enhanced demand for land for housing and urbanization projects. Diversion of land from food production to alternate uses (e.g. production of agro-fuels etc.) is yet another factor behind the growing demand for land and the land acquisition drive in developing countries. In this context, the role of the State becomes critical, both for protecting entitlements to land for the poor and marginalized sections and for creating an adequate regulatory structure that would ensure efficient and optimal use of this scarce and vital resource.

Overall, the diverse historical patterns of development experiences can be broadly understood as outcomes shaped by myriad forces including countries' resource endowments and pace of technological change, with institutional evolution, led by socio-economic and political factors, playing a critical role. Ultimately actual developmental outcomes may be viewed as probabilistic, with the role of policy being just as important as that of the politics behind policymaking.

*Development complexities* 35

*Emerging economies*

The set of chapters in this subsection explores lessons emerging from development experiences from different parts of the world. A broad framework for analyzing development experiences is presented in the chapter by Sudipto Mundle, 'Beyond *catch up*: Some speculations about the next twenty-five emerging economies'. The chapter is inspired by Deepak Nayyar's book *Catch Up: Developing Countries in the World Economy*, wherein he identifies twenty-five developing countries as having the most potential for catching up with the developed nations. This chapter speculates about the likely status of these countries, around the middle of the 21st century. The author first presents the elements of a theory of economic history as the dynamics of interactions between resource endowments, technology and institutions, mediated by the cumulative impact of incremental change as well as transformative shocks at critical junctures. The prospects of the 'next twenty-five' are then assessed through the lens of this theoretical framework, recognizng that outcomes are probabilistic in a Bayesian sense and not deterministic. Since very large and very small countries have their own specific dynamic, the cases of two very large countries (China and India) and two very small countries (Tunisia and Honduras) are separately analyzed. In assessing the prospects of the other twenty-one countries, the chapter attempts to explain why the catch up process has a distinct geographic pattern, working more powerfully in Asia as compared to Africa or Latin America.

The chapter by José Antonio Ocampo, 'Latin America's development record and challenges in historical perspective' focuses specifically on that region's development experience, underscoring the major processes that have shaped economic growth and development over the past two centuries. The processes of convergence, divergence and social and institutional evolution are viewed in context of these countries' integration with the world economy as the author assesses how Latin America fits into the broad trends identified by Deepak Nayyar in his book *Catch Up: Developing Countries in the World Economy*. The author acknowledges the role of State-led industrialisation for putting in place critical capacities, and the failure of market-based reforms to foster adequate manufacturing capability for reducing reliance on natural resource–based exports. It underscores the importance of social policies, especially education, and the need to tie this with a production oriented development strategy aimed at reviving industrialisation for employment creation.

## 36 *Ananya Ghosh Dastidar et al.*

Aspects of economic policy, especially macroeconomic policies, in emerging market economies (EMEs) are discussed in the chapter 'The global financial crisis and policy challenges in EMEs' by Ananya Ghosh Dastidar. The chapter focuses on the problems of growth and macro-management facing emerging market economies in the aftermath of the recent global financial crisis and assesses the challenges for policy in that context. The author questions the relevance of development strategies based on export markets and emphasizes the importance of fostering growth in and strategizing access to domestic markets. The chapter contends that, going forward, a key challenge for EMEs would be to create adequate policy space for accommodating the increasingly complex interactions between asset prices, exchange rates and capital flows and their implications for the real economy. This calls for a creative yet pragmatic approach to policy making that strikes the right balance, especially between the opposing forces of state intervention and market orientation.

One of the most important asset markets across the developing countries today is the market for land. As the chapter by Gouranga G. Das, 'Land deals in Africa: Host country effects in the presence of skill formation' notes, the rush for land acquisition, primarily driven by food price volatility and run for agro-fuel, represents an off-shoring of farm production to relatively land-abundant nations. This chapter reviews the academic literature and debate on the desirability of this phenomenon. While possible benefits include investments in technology, enhancement of physical and human capital and hence productivity in the agricultural sector of host countries, potential adverse effects include large-scale displacement of peasants with poor legal rights to their holdings or weak bargaining power, leading to loss of livelihoods and immiseration. The chapter demonstrates that state intervention in inducing technological efforts via skill, capacity building and infrastructure developments will have favourable effects. Also state efforts to foster governance, especially with regard to owner's legal rights to land, would deter ill-designed land deals with their pernicious effects; a point that is echoed in a later chapter by Ram Singh that focuses on issues related to the land market in India.

### Indian economy

The set of chapters in this subsection draw specifically on the development experience of India with a view to discerning significant lessons for policy. A broad overview of various policy regimes and significant policy transitions in India can be found in the chapter by Y.V. Reddy,

*Development complexities* 37

'Major policy debates in the Indian economy: Some reflections'. It traces the major debates that have shaped the evolution of policies and developmental outcomes in post-independence India. In doing so, it provides an understanding of the contextual backdrop for key policy choices ranging from the adoption of a Soviet-style developmental model based on heavy industries over the Gandhian path of self-sufficient village economies in the 1950s; to the sharp break-away from socialist policies led by the public sector, and emergence of market-oriented reforms based on privatization and liberalisation of domestic and the external sector in the 1990s. Overall, the intricacies of the politics behind policymaking can be hard to assess in the Indian context. The author concludes that strategies with long-term implications have received relatively less attention in mainstream policy debates.

Designing an effective strategy for industrialisation is perhaps the single most important policy priority for India, given its long-term implication for large-scale employment generation. The chapter by Nagesh Kumar, 'Reversing premature deindustrialisation for job creation: Lessons for *make-in-India* from industrialised and East Asian countries', makes the case for building a strong manufacturing sector in India. This is especially important as service sector-led growth has failed to create sufficient employment opportunities. While import intensity has gone up sharply in several industries, overall the manufacturing sector's share in national income has actually declined. Lessons from experiences of present-day developed countries and that of newly industrialising economies in East Asia, clearly demonstrate the importance of state intervention for successful industrialisation. As such, a compelling case for strategic interventions is presented in this chapter for reversing the premature de-industrialisation that the Indian economy has faced and, especially, for meeting the challenge of job creation.

The chapter 'Globalisation and the slowdown of the Indian economy: A demand-side view' by Mritiunjoy Mohanty also finds that India's integration with the world economy had detrimental implications for the development of its manufacturing sector. In fact, the causes underlying the investment slowdown in India, evident since about 2011–12 onwards, can also be explained by India's pattern of integration into the global economy. The high-growth phase (from 2003–04 to 2007–08), witnessed a virtuous cycle of cumulative causation where manufacturing trade, private corporate investment and manufacturing growth fed off each other. However, during the slowdown, this process reversed itself, creating a vicious cycle of cumulative causation where manufacturing imports displaced domestic capacity, leading

38  *Ananya Ghosh Dastidar et al.*

to deceleration in private corporate investment through the expected profitability channel. Further, the chapter argues that import integration during the phase of investment-led growth exacerbated an old structural problem, namely the inability to produce new capital goods.

Currently, as India explores various strategies for industrialisation and faster growth, one of the critical constraints that it faces relates to availability of land. The chapter by Ram Singh, 'Is land a bottleneck for economic development in India?' examines how best to facilitate the transfer of agricultural land for supporting industrial, infrastructure and urban projects. The existing regulatory and taxation framework governing usage and transactions in land imposes considerable costs. It ends up hurting rather than protecting owners of agricultural land by impeding efficient market transactions and creating incentives for tax evasion. Therefore, designing an effective regulatory framework that governs land market transactions is a key policy priority for optimizing land use. Along with these issues, the author also examines the potential impact of a new law governing land transfers and makes suggestions for a future course of action.

## Conclusions

It is hoped that the endeavour made in this volume to take a fresh look at development complexities will fuel further research and ignite a small spark, leading to new insights for theory and policymaking in the coming decades. The 21st century must build on the successes of the preceding experience while learning lessons from the failures of the past, thereby strengthening the foundations for sustainable human development.

## Note

1 The editors deeply regret to record that Professor Amitava Bose, who had been former Director, Indian Institute of Management Calcutta, passed away in January 2017. Professor Bose was one of the finest economists in India, widely revered for the clarity and rigour of his work. It's very unfortunate that he could not see the present volume in its printed form.

# Part II
# Evolving dimensions of globalisation

# 3 Capitalism, consciousness and development

*Akmal Hussain*

Capitalism today is in a crisis in terms of three tendencies located in the very structure of the system. First, markets which are central to the functioning of capitalism have failed to maintain economic stability. The world economy is in the grip of the deepest and most protracted recession since the Great Depression of the 1930s. Second, the tendency of the individual production unit to seek a continuous expansion of production and profits as an imperative of its survival has resulted in a global environmental crisis that threatens life itself. Third, the process of capital accumulation has engendered a form of consciousness in which the individual is driven by an insatiable desire for the aggressive acquisition of commodities without concern for others, much less for nature. This reinforces the second systemic tendency by producing not only goods but also the needs which these goods satisfy. Consequently, it becomes more difficult to reorient the production system to serve humans rather than the needs of capital accumulation. In this chapter I will attempt to first briefly examine each of these features of the contemporary historical juncture to show that the crisis of capitalism today is essentially a crisis of human civilization as it has been shaped by the process of capital accumulation over the last three centuries. Then the threat to the life support systems of the planet will be examined. Finally, the potential of an alternative consciousness for sustainable development with special reference to the South Asian tradition will be outlined.

## The world economic crisis

The financial crisis that erupted in the U.S. in 2008 generated a wave of turmoil that first engulfed the global financial system and then the real economy to generate the protracted recession that continues till today. In this section, we will examine the origins and nature of this

## 42   Akmal Hussain

crisis in terms of the dynamics of the world economy since the Second World War.

### Structural changes and economic fragility

Two key structural changes have occurred in the post-war period:

1   The Multinational Corporation emerged as the dominant institutional form of the production unit in an increasingly globalized economy in the period after the Second World War. The internationalization of production achieved within this framework enabled the MNCs to manufacture different components of a good or elements of a service, in facilities located in different countries to take advantage of country-specific resource endowments. This laid the basis of an unprecedented increase in productivity and profits (Baran and Sweezy 1966: 14–51). Given the problem of investing these profits within the sphere of production, due to demand constraints, profits from the sphere of production began to flow into the financial sphere.[1]

2   Within two decades in the second half of the 20th century (1963 to 1985) the relative weight of the financial sphere in the world economy changed dramatically: it became larger than the sphere of production, in contrast to the preceding two centuries when the sphere of production had far outweighed the financial sphere. The dynamics of this process lay in the interlinkage of financial markets along with the 'I.T. revolution' which enabled individuals and organizations to conduct stock transactions across national boundaries within minutes. At the same time the crafting of new financial products, such as derivatives, laid the basis of explosive growth in what had by the late 20th century become a globalized financial system (Hussain 2010). Thus, as Table 3.1 shows, in 1964 international banking was only USD 20 billion compared to the value of international trade in goods and services which stood at USD 1,605 billion. During the next two decades, the financial sphere grew about 12 times faster than the sphere of production so that by 1985, international banking had become relatively greater (at USD 2,598 billion) than the value of international trade in manufactured goods and services (USD 2,190).

In the next 25 years the financial sphere continued to grow very rapidly so that international banking measured in terms of bank assets had reached USD 126,774 billion by 2013 compared to the value of

*Capitalism, consciousness and development* 43

*Table 3.1* International banking, economic activity and international trade

| | Amount (billions of dollars at current prices and exchange rates) | | | | | | | |
|---|---|---|---|---|---|---|---|---|
| | 1964 | 1972 | 1980 | 1983 | 1985 | 2002 | 2008 | 2013 |
| Gross domestic product (World) | 1,605 | 3,336 | 10,172 | 10,140 | 12,825 | 32,197 | 61,218 | 75,470 |
| International trade in goods and services (World) | 188 | 463 | 2,150 | 1,986 | 2,190 | 8,056 | 19,655 | 23,287 |
| International banking | 20 | 208 | 1,559 | 2,253 | 2,598 | 40,063 | 104,712 | 126,744 |

Sources: For the period 1964 to 1985 the data is obtained from Bryant (1987: 22). For the remaining years, the data on Gross Domestic Product and International Banking is obtained from various editions of IMF Global Financial Stability Reports and the data on international trade is obtained from World Bank World Development Indicators database.

international trade in goods and services in the real economy which was only one-fifth as much at USD 23,287 billion in the same year (at current prices and exchange rates). The emergence of finance as the dominant sphere and the weakening of its links with the real economy imparted to the global economy a new vulnerability and an accentuated tendency for crisis.

### Ill-advised deregulation: Why markets do not necessarily produce efficient outcomes

At the same time, the market regulation institutions for mitigating this fragility had, over the years, been displaced under the influence of the belief that markets deliver efficient outcomes and indeed are self-regulating. The deregulation policies by governments were undertaken in spite of the important research work by Joseph Stiglitz[2] who had rigorously established that both financial and real economies – in a situation of asymmetric and imperfect information, which is inherent to actual world markets, even the most developed markets – "on their own are neither efficient nor stable" (Stiglitz 2011: 231).

Markets in the real economies of Third world countries produce even more inefficient outcomes for society as a whole because of the institutional structure of society and economy in which they are located. Deepak Nayyar in his incisive reflections on the nature of

44    *Akmal Hussain*

markets especially in the developing countries suggests that they produce adverse outcomes for the excluded sections of society. He argues that this occurs in the case of people who do not have skills or physical or financial assets. Citizens deprived in this sense are excluded from the "goods and services sold in the market". The geographic location of the poor can also deprive them of "non-market allocations such as the public provision of goods and services if they live in clusters such as urban slums, or rural settlements where drinking water, sanitation facilities, roads, electricity, or even street lights are not provided" (Nayyar 2014: 572).

In my own work I have argued that in developing countries such as Pakistan, markets cannot be seen as freely functioning, autonomous mechanisms of efficient resource allocation, production and distribution. Markets here are configured by state institutions and power structures such that the poor are systematically discriminated against in terms of access to productive assets, financial resources and governance decisions. My research for the UNDP showed that markets in the rural areas were mediated by local power structures making them asymmetric with respect to the large and small farmers. The poor peasants, where they were operating farms, had to pay a higher price for their inputs and got a lower price on their outputs compared to large farmers. Consequently, poor farmers in the sample data lost 20 percent of their potential income from crop production. Furthermore, pressure from the local administration obliged poor farmers to give to local officials, free of charge, a significant proportion of their output of milk and ghee. Our survey data showed that market asymmetries and extortion by the local police and revenue officials together deprived poor farmers of as much one third of their income (Hussain et al. 2003: 65–67).

Our survey data for the UNDP Report also showed that the poorest peasants were locked in a structure of dependence on the landlord. The extra economic power of the landlord resulted in 50.8 percent of the poorest peasants in the sample data, having to work on the landlord's farm without wages. Another 14 percent worked at a wage of Rs 28 per day which was substantially below the market wage (See Table 14 in Hussain et al. 2003: 63). These and earlier contributions to the literature suggest that markets on their own do not necessarily always produce efficient outcomes in the developed, much less in the underdeveloped countries.

Three key deregulation decisions were taken in the U.S. which were to impact both the developed and developing world. As Skidelsky (2010: 7) has argued, these market deregulation decisions set the stage

## Capitalism, consciousness and development   45

for the subsequent eruption of the crisis. First, there was the Glass-Steagall Act of 1933, which forbade retail banks to engage in imprudent investment activities such as underwriting and selling securities was repealed in 1999. Consequently, banks could package individual mortgages into tranches of varying risk (which included sub-prime mortgages) and sell these to investors. Such securitization became the basis of the housing boom and when the bust occurred, it triggered the collapse of financial markets. Second, the ballooning markets for derivatives were pumped up further by the decision of the Clinton administration not to regulate credit-default swaps. Third, the decision by the U.S. Securities and Exchange Commission to allow banks to increase their leverage ratios[3] from 10:1 to 30:1 (Skidelsky 2010: 7). This enabled banks to massively increase their lending.

### Risk, market failure and crisis

#### The nature of systemic risk and the problem of measurement

There is an important dimension to the tendency for crisis in a finance dominated global economy: the weak institutional framework combined with the nature of risk measurement in economic science. The dynamics of the financial sphere produced escalating systemic risk, and yet it was inherently difficult to measure it, let alone the fact of the absence of an efficient market feedback mechanism for self-correction. While the institutional framework and the state of economic science allowed measurement of individual risk it did not enable measurement of systemic risk. As Michael Spence has pointed out, in a situation where individual risks were positively correlated, systemic risk was virtually impossible to estimate (Spence 2009). This is because in the existing state of knowledge in mathematical modelling, estimation of risk at the aggregate level of the system is based on a particular distribution of individual risk. If, as happened in the case of the current crisis, the distribution of individual risk is changing then, it becomes extremely difficult to accurately model systemic risk (ibid.).

#### Financial fragility and economic instability

The basis of fragility in the global financial system lay in two fundamental features of the new financial edifice:

1   The new financial products were priced by financial experts on the basis of risk estimates drawn from mathematical probability

46  *Akmal Hussain*

which were not transparent to the buyers. This asymmetry of information between producers and buyers of financial products created a tendency for individuals and organizations to undertake overly risky investments without being aware of it. This further accentuated the fragility of the global financial edifice.

2  What made the fragility acute was the fact that many of these financial products such as sub-prime mortgage, debt bonds and risk insurance, while appearing individually distinct products, were actually interlinked and hence created escalating risk at the systemic level – a kind of risk which, as discussed previously, was inherently difficult to measure.

It is these two features of imperfect information at both the micro and the macro levels that gave to the global financial system the potential for market failure within an inadequate regulatory framework. Spiralling production and sale of derivatives, with multiplying systemic risks that were unknown to the individual investors, created a time bomb that could threaten the global financial system and thereby the real economy. The evidence shows that every major financial entity was highly levered and at the same time held potentially toxic assets. This fact exposed all the major financial organizations in the world to extreme financial distress. When the time bomb exploded, some of the most important banks and finance companies suffered simultaneous and major damage, which brought the financial and economic system of the world into the most serious crisis in a century (Hussain 2010).

The current crisis is not historically unique since the world economy is subject to recurrent crises though of varying magnitudes. As John Eatwell observes in an important paper, crises occur on average after every seven to ten years. He argues that risky financial investments by individuals impose "costly risks" on society since these externalities are not part of the cost estimates of the individual (Eatwell 2008: 80). In the absence of public policy to prevent the build-up of such externalities, the market system would be subject to an inherent instability.

Mitigating this tendency of instability will require establishing new institutional structures which restrict high-risk investment in financial products, reduce imperfect information in markets[4] and constrain greed that has historically been celebrated by Neo-classical economists as the driving force of market-based growth. If the institutional structure for providing a semblance of stability to the world economy is to be sustained, then the formal rules have to be rooted in what North calls informal norms.[5] Such a normative structure could be based on a consciousness wherein the pursuit of self-interest is informed by empathy and a sense of responsibility towards the vulnerable sections of society who suffer most during periods of economic turmoil. This feature of culture and individual sensibility as elements in the normative structure underpinning sustainable development is elaborated in "Recovering our humanity for sustainable development" later in this chapter.

## The global environmental crisis

### Global warming, climate change and the threat to life on Earth

Over the last three centuries following the industrial revolution, the rapid build-up of greenhouse gas emissions and the resultant temperature increase could reach a critical level by the end of this century. This global warming is due to the emission of gases such as carbon dioxide, methane and nitrous oxide when using fossil fuels in the process of production, consumption and waste disposal. The Inter-Governmental Panel for Climatic Change (IPCC) has provided evidence that there has been a huge build-up of these greenhouse gases, that this is the consequence of human intervention into the ecosystem and that Global Warming has occurred as a result. For example, the IPCC observes that: "The atmospheric concentrations of carbon dioxide, methane, and nitrous oxide have increased to levels unprecedented in at least the last 800,000 years" (IPCC 2013: 9). Greenhouse gases "have increased markedly as a result of human activity since 1750" and "Warming of the climate system is unequivocal, and since the 1950s, many of the observed changes are unprecedented over decades to millennia . . . the atmosphere and oceans have warmed" (IPCC 2007: 2).

Climate change associated with global warming has caused an increase in the intensity and frequency of extreme climatic events such as droughts, floods, hurricanes and extreme cold in some places and extreme heat in others. These phenomena have caused large-scale destruction resulting in loss of life and livelihood.

The current consensus amongst scientists is that if the increase in average global temperatures goes beyond 2 degrees Centigrade we will enter uncharted territory and the consequences for the life support systems of the planet could be catastrophic. Apart from the threat to human life, if temperatures exceed 1.5 degrees Centigrade, over the next four decades, then approximately 20 to 30 percent of plant and animal species are likely to become extinct (IPCC 2007: 11). Currently the species extinction rate is 2,000 species per year which is 1,000 times the natural extinction rate of two species per year.[6] This has led some scientists to suggest that the Earth may have entered the sixth mass extinction period. But unlike the previous five mass extinction periods, this one has been induced by the forms of production and social life of humans within the capitalist mode of production.

At the same time, during the process of production and consumption, forests and freshwater sources are being depleted. The disposal of toxic materials into soils, the hydrologic system and the atmosphere have reached levels which may be approaching the maximum loading capacity of the planet. As the delicate balance in nature that is now called the ecosystem is being disturbed, the ability of the life support system of the planet to sustain life is being threatened.

### Environmental policy, technological change and the problem of market failure

The recent Conference of Parties (COP-21) held in Paris has achieved a broad commitment from the comity of nations of limiting the average global temperature increase by the end of this century to 1.5 to 2 degrees Centigrade above pre-industrial levels. In the pursuit of this aim, they hope to achieve zero net emissions between the years A.D. 2050 and A.D 2100.

The apparent success of the Paris Agreement is that it has won a commitment from 187 countries to do what they can towards the collective goal of zero net emissions and restricting the temperature increase to well below 2 degrees Centigrade. Its weakness is that there are no specific national goals that can be made consistent with the aggregate global goals, much less an enforcement mechanism to ensure that countries honour their commitments. As it stands, the Agreement creates a zero-sum game: there is an incentive for each country to do less while expecting others to do more.[7]

Implicit in the Paris Agreement in particular and the mainstream literature on Sustainable Development in general is the belief that green technologies will become available and get adopted within the required time frame through the market mechanism regulated by environmental and technology policies of government. This it is assumed can be achieved by states creating the appropriate incentive/disincentive structure through a combination of subsidies and taxes for the private sector.

There are four forms of market failure that render these presumptions unrealistic: first, in the case of green technologies that are available, and are relatively cheaper than non-green technologies, adoption by capitalists quickly and across the board means that the investment embodied in the existing stock of machines would have to be written

*Capitalism, consciousness and development* 49

off. So if green technology adoption is to be financially feasible for firms then the gain from the relatively cheaper green technology would have to be at least equal to the loss resulting from premature replacement of the existing machine stock.

In cases where the green technology in terms of the market calculus is economically infeasible, the magnitude of government subsidies required by profit-seeking entrepreneurs to adopt it may involve a prohibitive fiscal burden for governments already operating under tight budgetary constraints.

A second form of market failure that may operate in the adoption and diffusion of green technologies originates in an aspect of the phenomenon of dynamic economies of scale. This occurs when the gains from technology adoption for one user depend on a number of other users. These gains from the scale of technology adoption may be generated through learning by doing by various firms or network externalities. Such externalities occur in the case of technologies which require operability of components made by different firms, hence the need for standardization and collaboration between firms adopting those technologies (Popp, Newell and Jaffe 2010: 878). Since the financial feasibility of adoption of such technologies for any one firm requires adoption by a number of others, the issuance of a patent by the government to any one party as an inducement for the development or adoption of such technologies may be counter-productive. At the same time, the market would be inherently incapable of internalizing for any one firm the feedback of gains in such cases of interdependence between firms. Thus the development and adoption of those green technologies, which are subject to network externalities, would be uncertain.

A third form of market failure results from information asymmetry between an investor in the production of a green technology and its user. Popp, Newell and Jaffe call this a principal-agent problem which arises when for example a builder invests in the construction of an energy-efficient building which enables a prospective user to save on energy bills. If the magnitude of energy saving estimated by the user is lower than that of the builder due to inadequate information, then the builder may not be able to price the product at a high enough level to recover the investment. Hence this asymmetric information problem may lead to underinvestment in such green technologies (ibid.).

There is a fourth problem with the assumption that economic growth can be sustained through green technological change. In the case of knowledge intensive technologies, the problem arises out of the nature of the relationship between the development of science and the pace and pattern of innovative activity. To begin with, a necessary

50   *Akmal Hussain*

condition for science research to translate into new technologies is the establishment of an institutionalized linkage between science research organizations and industry (Hussain 1988: 87–89). Where technological changes require breakthroughs in science, there is uncertainty that they will occur within the required time frame. This is because even where institutionalized links exist between science research and industry, the fact remains, the domain of pure science is to some extent autonomous. Therefore, breakthroughs in science, their immediate relevance for industry and their timing are not necessarily simply a function of the amount of money made available for science research.

Sometimes scientific discoveries are made without any concern for their applicability, but only later technological applications are undertaken. For example, Harvey Brooks has argued that in some cases opportunities for fulfilling previously identified social needs arise when "a scientific discovery is made in the course of an exploration of natural phenomena undertaken with no potential application in mind" (Brooks 1994: 479). As examples he refers to the discovery of laser which happened to have numerous subsequent applications; similarly, the discovery of X-rays was made in pure science but turned out to have many "applications in medicine and industry" (ibid.). These examples illustrate the fact that scientific discoveries are not necessarily subject to the imperatives of market-driven technological change.

The discussion in this section indicates the uncertain prospects of achieving a time-bound development and adoption of green technologies for making economic growth consistent with conserving the environment.

The limitations of the efficacy of policy as well as markets notwithstanding, governments of the world are expected to strive in concert to seek ways to protect the life support systems of the planet. Since nothing less than life on Earth is at stake, alternative approaches to managing the crisis ought to be considered too. In this context it is vital for the people of the world to seek sustainable levels and forms of production and social life through a change in the existing relationship between humans, commodities and nature: a relationship which has emerged over the last three centuries and which lies at the root of the present crisis.

## Recovering our humanity for sustainable development

Preventing an environmental catastrophe essentially involves achieving a profound change in the consciousness that has emerged within the economic and cultural framework and the underlying institutional structures and forms of production in capitalism. Beyond the immediate mitigation measures, the long-term effort by the human community to restore the life support systems of the planet requires recovering

*Capitalism, consciousness and development*  51

our humanity and a shared sense of the sacred in nature and our own nature.[8] Such a consciousness can underpin the effort to change the mode of production, the trajectory of technological change and the structures of political power.

## The relationship between humans, nature and commodities within capitalism

The social and economic life in the industrial era has shaped a particular relationship between humans, commodities and nature. The relationship between individuals is in most cases structured by the market system where most people are engaged in aggressive competition for profits or consumer goods. The "other" is experienced not as a source of enhancing the self but rather as a means or a threat to achieving material ends.

The relationship of the individual with commodities is also shaped by the market-based production system that has a tendency to continuously increase output. Such a production system has inculcated in the individual an insatiable desire to acquire more and more commodities. Here a commodity is perceived not merely in terms of its functional attributes but as the embodiment of the qualities of physical attractiveness, efficacy, power and success.[9] Thus I have argued elsewhere that "qualities which are inherent to human beings are alienated from them and transposed into commodities. We are then invited by the advertisement industry to acquire commodities not simply to fulfill our material needs but essentially to repossess ourselves" (Hussain 2015: 23).

In an atomized society, where the individual is driven by the single-minded desire to consume and acquire commodities, nature is seen as an exploitable resource to fulfil this desire. Within such a consciousness there is a propensity to objectify nature as if it were divorced from the experience of knowing ourselves as human beings connected to all creation and thereby to a transcendent reality (ibid.).

## An alternative relationship between humans, commodities and nature

Building a new relationship between humans, commodities and nature, will involve overcoming a sensibility in which the ego dominates and pits humans against each other in competition and conflict. Such a sensibility is engendered by a culture wherein accumulation of commodities has become an exclusive measure of human worth and welfare, and where alienation from nature and our own nature leads to the mutilation of both. These forms of consciousness are counter-posed to those implied by the wisdom traditions across the world. If this

## 52   *Akmal Hussain*

"unanimous tradition" is to be brought to bear as a vital element in the social and political process of dealing with the contemporary crisis of civilization, then we need to rediscover the sense of "the sacred, the true and the beautiful" (Perry 1999: 5).

In South Asia, as in many other regions, the interplay of diverse cultures and religious beliefs across centuries has developed a tradition of placing the inner development of a person above the pursuit of commodities. I have suggested elsewhere that this dimension of consciousness lies dormant in many strata of South Asian society, but finds expression in Sufi poetry that continues to resonate in the living folk cultures of various regions. The poor peasants of the Punjab inherit this rich philosophical tradition that is reflected in their comprehension of commodities and forms of social action, through which they create their individual and collective history (Hussain 2010: 80). Thus, for example, the 17th-century Punjabi Sufi poet, Shah Hussain, suggests that the path to the inner Self goes beyond material goods:

> *"Those who have accumulated millions that too is mere dust"*.[10]

Shah Hussain suggests the challenge of an exchange relationship which is counter-posed to the market, where loving the other makes possible a kind of "remuneration" that is nutrition for the inner self:

> *"Become a lover if you want to earn love"*.[11]

Earlier the Vedanta Treatise suggests, according to Parthasarathy, that

> *"Your real Self is the abode of eternal peace and happiness. . . .*
> *Only the rare one who has directed his search inward has*
> *reached the state of supreme bliss"*.[12]

As Kapila Vatsyayan argues, "the voices of poets, the mystics, and the Sufis continue to reverberate in South Asia in rural as also urban milieus" (Vatsyayan 2014: 482).

The journey to self-realization in this tradition is a journey of love for the other. Rabindranath Tagore, the iconic 19th-century Bengali poet bathes in the perennial stream of South Asian consciousness as he recalls this transcendent journey to the other:

> *"You and I have floated here on the stream that brings from the*
> *fount*
> *At the heart of time, love for one another"*.[13]

Capitalism, consciousness and development 53

The relationship of oneness with the other is evoked by the great contemporary Punjabi Sufi poet, Najam Hussain Syed:

"*Every pore is suffused with the warmth of the loved one,*
*There is neither nearness nor distance*".[14]

It is when love and compassion define social and economic relations, rather than commodities alone, that human beings can fulfil themselves and give meaning to their existence.

### Recovering a humane consciousness for deepening human development and achieving sustainable development

The contemporary pre-eminence given to commodities can also be counter-posed by the Classical Greek tradition. Aristotle in his Nicomachean Ethics suggests that goods cannot be of value since they are merely useful. What is of value is human functioning according to the principles of virtue. He argues:

> if . . . we state the function of man to be a certain kind of life, and this to be an activity or actions of the soul implying a rational principle, and the function of a good man to be the good and noble performance of these, . . . if this is the case, human good turns out to be activity of soul in accordance with virtue.
>
> (Aristotle 1999: 11)

### Human functioning and the development of human capabilities

Amartya Sen, 2,400 years later, in taking up Aristotle's insight on human functioning achieved a paradigmatic change in the framework of development thinking by positing the concept of human capabilities (Dreze and Sen 1989: 12). This involved a shift away from income (hence goods) as the aim of development to being a means to an end, which is developing the capability to undertake *activity* which a person may value. The concept of human capability thus broadens the idea of development because while including the ability to earn a higher income, it also includes socially useful activity which a person may consider to be of value (ibid.). Mahbub Ul Haq's work on Human Development based on the Human Development index (income and quantitative measures of health and education, respectively), which had a significant, positive impact on public policy worldwide, was anchored in Sen's concept of the development of human capabilities

54  *Akmal Hussain*

(UNDP 1990). Living a life of virtue as a form of human functioning was raised by Aristotle, however it remains to be brought into consideration in this context.

Amartya Sen does allude to ethical behaviour as a possible feature of human rationality in his powerful critique of the Neo-classical theory of rationality. He rejects the Neo-classical idea of rationality being exclusively restricted to self-interested behaviour on grounds that it is not a good approximation of actual human behaviour. The Neo-classical conception, Sen argues, does not for example take account of varying combinations of individual sacrifice out of group loyalty on the one hand and greater fulfillment of individual interests through the group on the other; much less does it account for an individual's effort to fulfill family obligations that may involve a substantial sacrifice of purely personal gains (Sen 1987: 15–20). Indeed, Sen emphasizes that concern with the lives of others is a "basic human motivation" (Dreze and Sen 1989: 13).

## The self and rationality: An alternative perspective

One could suggest that the missing dimension in the contemporary idea of rationality is the conception of individual choice resulting from a consciousness of the Self that finds fulfillment in its relationship with the other. The development of such a *relational* selfhood and thereby the possibility of virtuous behaviour, as a form of *rationality*, could be considered an aspect of human development. Furthermore, it could be argued that a vital aspect of the development of human capabilities is nurturing a consciousness that could enable a re-awareness of empathy, and hence caring for others, as a form of virtue. Thus the choice of sacrificing narrow self-interest to release the other from suffering, for instance, would flow out of a developed Self which at a fundamental level identifies ontologically with the other. The integrated Self in this conception is *apprehended* in society while the Neo-classical concept of the atomized self is *prior* to society.

The idea of Human Development, so extended, can be seen essentially as a form of education that develops a humane sensibility. At the inner level, it is a journey from the narrowed Self, counter-posed to the other, towards a greater Self into which the other is integrated and which is therefore actualized through its relationship of loving care with the other. Nurturing this dimension of our humanness could make a vital contribution to the process of knowing ourselves: a self-awareness that could reconstruct human relationships so as to form the basis of cooperation in facing the challenge of a planet in peril.

In the context of this discussion, it may be helpful to refer to Karen Armstrong's work. She considers the process of becoming aware of our ability for compassion to be essentially educative (the Latin *educere* means "to lead out"). Armstrong links up with the religious and wisdom traditions of the world in suggesting that compassion "exists potentially within every human being so that it can become a healing force in our own lives and in the world" (Armstrong 2011: 21).

## The normative basis of sustainable development

Developing the sensibility of caring for others can be seen not only as an aspect of human development but can become a material force for Sustainable Development. Consider the original definition of Sustainable Development as formulated by the U.N. World Commission on Environment and Development, chaired by Mrs. Harlem Brundtland: Sustainable Development is development that "meets the needs of the present without compromising the ability of the future generations to meet their own needs" (World Commission on Environment and Development 1987: 8). There are two key aspects of this definition. First, there is interdependence of individuals in the human community both in the present and future. This interdependence, and hence a sense of responsibility of humans towards each other, arises out of the fact that the process of fulfilling material needs by present and future generations occurs within a shared ecosystem. Second, the responsibility towards each other implies overcoming poverty and inequality of opportunity today and in the future. Therefore, human development in terms of nurturing the consciousness of care and compassion becomes an essential normative basis of Sustainable Development.

Of course, recent work by economists has shown that contrary to the view of the economics orthodoxy, inequality has adverse economic and social consequences. Indeed greater equality of opportunity by developing the capabilities of individuals in society, broadening the base of investment and creating greater social cohesion enables long-term economic growth.[15] It can also broaden the knowledge base which can induce a more effective response to government incentives for technological change in a green direction.

The physical environment is seen in the South Asian tradition not in terms of a static and fragmented set of exploitable resources but as an integrated and dynamic natural process that enables material existence. At the same time, meditating upon the beauty of nature is a mode of knowing one's own nature and thereby nurturing our aesthetic and ethical sensibility. Thus the mountains, the rivers, the fertile

## 56  Akmal Hussain

plains and the deserts are experienced in the South Asian tradition as part of a sacred unity that sustains both the physical and intellectual life of the human community. The term intellectual is used here in its Medieval sense of *intellectus*, meaning "the faculty which perceives the transcendent" (Lings 1993: 48). In this context Martin Lings suggests that the term *heart* in both the Western and Eastern traditions is taken to give access to the "centre of the soul", and in the ancient world is "often found as a synonym for intellect" (ibid.).

Religion (from the Latin *religio*) means re-establishment of the ligament with God. The Qur'an invites us to re-establish that ligament whereby in prayer or in beholding God's creation we become aware of His presence as loving mercy (*rahma*):

> "withersoever
> Ye turn, there is Allah's countenance".[16]

In this context Seyyed Hossein Nasr argues that the interrelation between God, humanity and nature is specified within a sacramental view of the physical universe. He observes that many Muslim sages saw the phenomena of nature as "signs" of God (Nasr 1992: 88).

Re-experiencing our humanness through a sense of harmony with nature could create a sustainable relationship with the physical environment. Humans have the potential to harness nature for sustaining physical life and at the same time to experience its transcendent beauty. Cultivating such a sense of beauty could be another element in the normative basis for developing forms of production, social life and ways of being that could underpin Sustainable Development.

## Conclusions

In this chapter the current world economic crisis and the longer-term global environmental crisis have been analyzed in terms of the systemic tendencies of capitalism. This analysis indicates the inherent limitations of markets which at one level underlie the instability of the worldwide capitalist economy.

At a deeper level, the analysis suggests that a market based process of economic growth has engendered a particular relationship between humans, commodities and nature which has led to an environmental crisis that threatens life on Earth. The limitations of government policy to effectively induce the adoption of green technology and green technological change within the market-based system have been analyzed in the context of the aims of the December 2015 Paris Summit.

The concluding section of the chapter presents the possibility of an alternative relationship between humans, commodities and nature. This is based on the "unanimous tradition" of re-awareness of humanness in which caring for others is experienced as a vital, fertilizing force in the growth of the self, and harmony with nature enables both the sustenance of physical life as well as the experience of a transcendent beauty that could enrich human civilization.

The analysis here suggests that the missing dimension in the contemporary conception of the self is the idea of a Self that finds fulfillment in its relationship with the other. Thus nurturing the consciousness of compassion for others and a sense of relatedness with nature, as the source of individual choices, could be another form of rationality. This could be a vital aspect of the development of "human capabilities" which would constitute the normative basis for Sustainable Development. Such a consciousness could also enable a shift away from a zero-sum game in national environmental policies towards meaningful cooperation for saving the life support systems of the planet.

## Notes

1 For a more detailed analysis of growth and structural change in the global economy since the industrial revolution, see Hussain (2004).
2 See for example, Salop and Stiglitz (1977); Stiglitz (1982); Stiglitz (1987); and Hellman, Murdoch and Stiglitz (1996).
3 Leverage ratio is the ratio of total liabilities to net worth of a bank.
4 Perhaps the most influential report proposing institutional changes for financial market regulation so as to reduce instability is a recent report of a UN Commission chaired by Joseph E. Stiglitz, *Report of the Commission of Experts of the President of the United Nations General Assembly on Reforms of the International Monetary and Financial System*, United Nations, New York, September 21, 2009.
5 For a discussion of institutions and how informal norms underlie formal rules, see North (1990: 4).
6 Estimated from World Wildlife Fund (2016) and Ceballos et al. (2015) data.
7 For a discussion of this zero-sum game theoretic constraint to country-level implementation of the commitments in Paris, see: Green Light, *The Economist*, December 19th, 2015, page 89.
8 For a more detailed discussion of this issue, see Hussain (2015).
9 For an elaboration of this point, see Hussain (1991).
10 "Lakh, crore jinhaan de jurriya, so bhi jhuri jhuri", Shah Hussain, *Kaafian*, Majlis Shah Hussain, Lahore, second edition, March 1976, page 22.
11 Aashiq hovain, taan ishq kamaanwain, Shah Hussain, *Poem 11 in Kaafian Shah Hussain (Punjabi)*, Majlis Shah Hussain, Lahore, Second edition, page 25.
12 Parthasarathy (2009: 25).

58  *Akmal Hussain*

13  Tagore (1995: 49).
14  Najm Hussain Syed, *Baar di Vaar*, Rutt Lekha Publications, Lahore, 2000, page 37.
15  See for example, Atkinson (2015); Hussain (2014); and Stiglitz (2012).
    For empirical evidence of the negative impact of inequality on economic growth, see Berg, Ostry and Zettelmeyer (2012); Herzer and Vollmer (2012); and Easterly (2007).
    For an analysis of the relationship between social cohesion and economic growth, see Easterly, Ritzen and Woolcock (2006).
16  *The Qur'an, Surah II, Verse 115*, Translation by Mohammed Marmaduke Pickthall, Tahrike Tarsile Qur'an Inc., New York, 2006, page 34.

## Bibliography

Aristotle. (1999). *The Nicomachean Ethics (Translated by W.D. Ross)*. Kitchener: Botoche Books.
Armstrong, Karen. (2011). *Twelve Steps to a Compassionate Life*. Karachi: Oxford University Press.
Atkinson, Anthony B. (2015). *Inequality: What Can Be Done?* Cambridge, MA: Harvard University Press.
Baran, Paul A. and Paul M. Sweezy. (1966). *Monopoly Capital: An Essay on the American Economic and Social Order*. New York: Monthly Review Press.
Berg, Andrew, Jonathan D. Ostry and Jeromin Zettelmeyer. (2012). 'What Makes Growth Sustianed?', *Journal of Development Economics*, 98(2): 149–166.
Brooks, Harvey. (1994). 'The Relationship between Science and Technology', *Research Policy*, 23(5): 477–486.
Bryant, Ralph C. (1987). *International Financial Intermediation*. Washington, DC: The Brookings Institution.
Ceballos, Gerardo, Paul R. Ehrlich, Anthony D. Barnosky, Andres García, Robert M. Pringle and Todd M. Palmer. (2015). 'Accelerated Modern Human: Induced Species Losses: Entering the Sixth Mass Extinction', *Science Advances*, 1(5).
Dreze, Jean and Amartya Sen. (1989). *Hunger and Public Action*. New York: Oxford University Press.
Easterly, William. (2007). 'Inequality Does Cause Underdevelopment: Insights from a New Instrument', *Journal of Development Economics*, 84(2): 755–776.
Easterly, William, Jozef Ritzen and Michael Woolcock. (2006). 'Social Cohesion, Institutions and Growth', *Economics and Politics*, 18(2): 103–120.
Eatwell, John. (2008). 'Is Capitalism in Crisis', *Public Policy Research*: 80–83.
Hellman, Thomas, Kevin Murdoch and Joseph E. Stiglitz. (1996). 'Deposit Mobilization through Financial Restraint', in Neils Hermes and Robert Lensink (eds), *Financial Development and Economic Growth: Theory and Experiences from Developing Countries*. New York: Routledge.
Herzer, Dierk and Sebastian Vollmer. (2012). 'Inequality and Growth: Evidence from Panel Cointegration', *Journal of Economic Inequality*, 10(4): 489–503.

## Capitalism, consciousness and development  59

Hussain, Akmal. (1988). 'Science, Technical Change and Development', in Akmal Hussain, *Strategic Issues in Pakistan's Economic Policy*, pp. 85–100, Lahore: Progressive Publishers. www.akmalhussain.net/Publish%20Work/StrategicIssuesInPakistansEconomy/chapter4.pdf (Accessed on 29 January 2016).

Hussain, Akmal. (1991). 'Semiology of Advertisement and the Displacement of Desire', *Economic Review*: 15, 32.

Hussain, Akmal. (2004). 'Imperialism', in Syed B. Hussain (ed), *Encyclopedia of Capitalism (Vol. 2)*, pp. 397–401. New York: Golson Books Limited.

Hussain, Akmal. (2010). 'The Global Economic Crisis and South Asia', Paper presented at the 'Pre-Summit Conference, Organized by South Asia Centre for Policy Studies (SACEPS)', Kathmandu, 23–25 February.

Hussain, Akmal. (2014). 'Strengthening Democracy through Inclusive Growth', in Akmal Hussain and Muchkund Dubey (eds), *Democracy, Sustainable Development and Peace: Perspectives on South Asia*, pp. 169–196. New Delhi: Oxford University Press.

Hussain, Akmal. (2015). 'A Planet in Peril and a Civilization in Crisis: Reviving a Sense of the Sacred', in Christian W. Troll and Liam O'Callaghan (eds), *The Sacredness of Creation: Proceedings of the Second Loyola Hall Symposium*, pp. 19–30. Lahore: Multimedia Affairs.

Hussain, Akmal, A.R. Kemal, A.I. Hamid, Imran Ali, Khawar Mumtaz and Ayub Qutub. (2003). *UNDP Pakistan National Human Development Report 2003: Poverty, Growth and Governance*. Karachi: Oxford University Press.

Hussain, Shah. (1976). *Kaafian (2nd ed.)*. Lahore: Majlis Shah Hussain.

IPCC. (2007). *Climate Change 2007: Impacts, Adaptation and Vulnerability, Working Group II Contribution to the Fourth Assessment Report of the Intergovernmental Panel on Climate Change*. New York: Cambridge University Press.

IPCC. (2013). *Climate Change 2013: The Physical Science Basis, Contribution of Working Group I to the Fifth Assessment Report of the Intergovernmental Panel on Climate Change*. New York: Cambridge University Press.

Lings, Martin. (1993). *What Is Sufism?* Cambridge, UK: The Islamic Text Society.

Nasr, Seyyed Hossein. (1992). 'Islam and the Environmental Crisis', in Steven C. Rockefeller and John C. Elder (eds), *Spirit and Nature: Why the Environment is a Religious Issue*, pp. 83–108. Boston, MA: Beacon Press.

Nayyar, Deepak. (2014). 'Some Reflections on Development in South Asia: Markets, Democracy, and People', in Akmal Hussain and Muchkund Dubey (eds), *Democracy Sustainable Development and Peace: New Perspectives on South Asia*, pp. 570–582. New Delhi: Oxford University Press.

North, Douglass C. (1990). *Institutions, Institutional Change and Economic Performance*. Cambridge: Cambridge University Press.

Parthasarathy, A. (2009). *The Eternities: Vedanta Treatise (15th ed.)*. Mumbai: Vakil and Sons.

Perry, Whitall H. (1999). 'The Revival of Interest in Tradition', in Ranjit Fernando (ed), *The Unanimous Tradition: Essays on the Essential Unity of All Religions*, pp. 3–20. Colombo: Sri Lanka Institute of Traditional Studies.

Popp, David, Richard G. Newell and Adam B. Jaffe. (2010). 'Energy, the Environment and Technological Change', in Bronwyn H. Hall and Nathan Rosenberg (eds), *Handbook of the Economics of Innovation (Vol. 2)*, pp. 873–937. Amsterdam, North-Holland: Elsevier.

Salop, Steven and Joseph E. Stiglitz. (1977). 'Bargains and Ripoffs: A Model of Monopolistically Competitive Price Dispersions', *Review of Economic Studies*, 44(3), 493–510.

Sen, Amartya. (1987). *Ethics and Economics*. New Delhi: Oxford University Press.

Sen, Amartya. (1999). *Development as Freedom*. New York: Oxford University Press.

Skidelsky, Robert. (2010). *The Return of the Master*. London: Penguin Books.

Spence, Michael. (2009). 'Agenda for the Next Few Months', in B. Eichengreen and R. Baldwin (eds), *What G20 Leaders Must Do to Stabilize Our Economy and Fix the Financial System*. London: Centre for Economic Policy Research (CEPR).

Stiglitz, Joseph E. (1982). 'The Inefficiency of the Stock Market Equilibrium', *Review of Economic Studies*, 49(2), 241–261.

Stiglitz, Joseph E. (1987). 'The Causes and Consequences of the Dependence of Quality on Prices', *Journal of Economic Literature*, 25(1), 1–48.

Stiglitz, Joseph E. (2009). 'The Current Economic Crisis and Lessons for Economic Theory', *Eastern Economic Journal*, 35(3), 281–296.

Stiglitz, Joseph E. (2011). 'Rethinking Development Economics', *The World Bank Research Observer*, 26(2), 230–236.

Stiglitz, Joseph E. (2012). *The Price of Inequality*. London: Allen Lane (Penguin Books).

Tagore, Rabindranath. (1995). *Selected Poems (Translated by William Radice)*. New Delhi: Penguin Books.

UNDP. (1990). *Human Development Report 1990*. New York: Oxford University Press.

United Nations. (2009). *Report of the Commission of Experts of the President of the United Nations General Assembly on Reforms of the International Monetary and Financial System*. New York: United Nations.

Vatsyayan, Kapila. (2014). 'Pluralism and Diversity in South Asia', in Akmal Hussain and Muchkund Dubey (eds), *Democracy, Sustainable and Peace: New Perspectives on South Asia*, pp. 463–491. New Delhi: Oxford University Press.

World Commission on Environment and Development. (1987). *Our Common Future*. New Delhi: Oxford University Press.

World Wildlife Fund. (2016). 'How Many Species Are We Losing?', *World Wildlife Fund Global*, http://wwf.panda.org/about_our_earth/biodiversity/ biodiversity (Accessed on 3 February 2016).

# 4 The rise and fall(?) of the ABP (Anything But Policy) discourse in development economics

*Ha-Joon Chang*

Development economics emerged as a separate branch of economics in the 1940s and the 1950s on the recognition that the differences in economic and non-economic structures make it necessary to apply different economic theories to different countries. It was argued that the prevailing economic theories – not just Neo-classical but also Marxist theories – had been built assuming the economic and the non-economic structures of developed capitalist economies and therefore could not readily be applied to developing countries.[1]

For example, it was emphasised that a lot of economic problems experienced by developing countries were due to their specialisation in the production of primary commodities, whose prices fluctuate more than those of manufactured products and also show a long-term declining trend against those of manufactured products (Spraos 1983, is a classic review of the early debates on this; Ocampo & Erten 2013, provides an up-to-date review of the issue and updated empirical evidence).

For another example, many early development economists – particularly those who followed the tradition of Chayanovian theory of the 'peasant economy' – argued that the agricultural sector in developing countries cannot be analysed with the tools of Neo-classical economics because farmers in developing countries do not maximise their profits, which producers in Neo-classical economics are assumed to do. This is because developing country farmers work not in capitalist farms but in traditional extended family units, which aim to maximise the average consumption of its members, rather than their profits.

This tendency to emphasise the structural factors saw its apogee in the 1960s and the 1970s in the form of the Dependency theory. The theory emphasised the influences of colonial history and international power relations on the economic structures, the institutions, and the political systems of the 'periphery' countries (i.e., the developing

## 62   Ha-Joon Chang

countries), which perpetuate their status as raw-material producers, thereby condemning them to a state of 'under-development'. Some versions of it became so structurally deterministic that they believed that 'genuine' economic development, based on national capital and technologies, is impossible in the periphery. The recommendation was the destruction of the existing economic and political structures through a socialist-nationalist revolution (see Palma 1978, for a classic review of the Dependency theory). However, the tendency to emphasise structural factors in understanding the developing economies started to come under severe attack in the 1970s with the increasing dominance of Neo-classical economics.

From the day when it was born in the late 19th and the early 20th century, Neo-classical economics has been motivated by a desire to make economics a science. It has prided itself with its ability to provide value-free, parsimonious theories that can be applied anywhere and anytime – from the one-person economy of Robinson Crusoe, through subsistence farming in Ghana and feudal manors in mediaeval Europe, to complex modern industrial economies. However, in the 1950s and the 1960s, in the face of new problems thrown up by the Post-colonial developing economies, it softened its position on the timeless nature of its theory at least in relation to developing countries – for example, in 1969, John Fei and Gustav Ranis, two influential Neo-classical economists of the time, published an article in *American Economic Review* that emphasised the importance of history – and by implication structural factors (Fei & Ranis 1969). However, this proved a brief interlude and, by the 1970s, most Neo-classical economists started to argue again that the core Neo-classical theory that emphasises the centrality of price incentives can be – and should be – applied anywhere.

This resurgence of what Hirschman (1981) called 'mono-economics' characteristic of Neo-classical economics could be seen most clearly from its attack on Dependency theory. When South Korea and Taiwan made impressive progress on industrialisation in the 1960s and the 1970s, against their prediction that industrialisation in the 'periphery' is impossible, the Dependency Theorists wheeled out structural factors to 'explain away' this (self-imposed) puzzle. They argued that these countries could achieve whatever shallow industrialisation that they had managed to achieve (this, of course, turned out to be a total misrepresentation of what was happening in those countries) because they were blessed with geo-political factors (e.g. high US aid and special access to the US market owing to their status as 'garrison states' in the Cold War) or very unusual colonial history (e.g. an exceptionally good manufacturing base and a highly educated labour force left

ABP discourse in development economics 63

behind by Japan; for criticisms of these arguments, see Chang 2006, chapter 4).

Neo-classical economists very heavily criticised this argument (e.g. Bhagwati 1977).[2] They argued that Korea and Taiwan succeeded because they had pursued 'good' (i.e. free-market, free-trade) economic policies, and not because they had been blessed with some special structural conditions. They argued that good economic policies work regardless of the particular historical or political conditions of the countries concerned. The implication was that the countries that did not pursue such policies had only themselves to blame. It was argued that there is only one right kind of economics – Neo-classical economics – and that there is no justification for development economics in the traditional sense – that is, a body of economic theories that is built on the recognition that the institutional (as well as technological) characteristics of developing countries differ significantly from those assumed in Neo-classical economics.[3] Development economics, it was argued, should be no more, or no less, than Neo-classical economics applied to the data sets from developing countries. What is good economics (and thus good economic policy derived from it) in the US or Germany is also good economics (and good economic policy) in Mexico or Ghana.

This view of development economics was fully applied to the real world after the Third World Debt Crisis of 1982. Following the crisis, most developing countries were subject to the Structural Adjustment Programs (SAPs), jointly managed by the IMF (International Monetary Fund) and the World Bank, in which such view of development economics had already become dominant.[4] The SAPs imposed a standardised policy package on all countries – strong anti-inflationary macroeconomic policy, trade liberalisation, privatisation of state-owned enterprises (SOEs), deregulation of foreign direct investment, liberalisation of the capital market, and so on. When the critics raised issues with this 'one-size-fits-all' approach, the response from its defenders was that these policies are universally applicable because they have been derived from a universally applicable science called (Neo-classical) economics. Arguments that countries with different history, politics, and institutions may need different policies were dismissed as the result of 'woolly' thinking on the part of those who pick on minor details because they do not have the intellectual wherewithal to deal with rigorous theories.

Unfortunately for the believers in the universal applicability of Neo-classical economics, the SAPs – and other similar policy packages implemented by the regional development banks (Asian Development

## 64   Ha-Joon Chang

Bank, African Development Bank, Inter-American Development Bank being the major ones) – miserably failed to produce the expected results of accelerated growth and macroeconomic stability. By the late 1980s, it became necessary to find explanations as to why all those 'good' policies based on 'correct' theories had failed to work.

Interestingly, it was not just the failures of policies based on their economic theories that Neo-classical economists had to be explain. They also had to explain how some countries succeeded with policies that were *not* based on their theories. Between the 1970s and the mid-1980s, Neo-classical economists had used the East Asian 'miracle' economies as the ultimate proofs of their free-trade, free-market policies. However, by the late 1980s, the weight of emerging evidence that the East Asian 'miracle' economies heavily used interventionist policies became overwhelming (Amsden 1989 and Wade 1990 are the best known sources of such evidence, but there were many works before, which are reviewed in Chang 1993). Once they acknowledged that the East Asian 'miracle' economies were no paragons of free-trade, free-market policies, they had to argue that those countries could succeed with unorthodox policies only because they had exceptionally good institutions – especially capable bureaucracies – bequeathed by history (World Bank 1993,[5] is the best example).

As a result, in the 1990s, a whole series of arguments emerged that try to explain the continued poor performance of orthodox economic policies (in countries subject to SAPs) and the successes based on unorthodox policies (the East Asian miracle economies) with the help of factors that had until then been considered beyond the domain of economics – or even beneath economists – geography, climate, natural resources, history, culture, and institutions. In other words, economic successes and failures were now to be explained by anything but policy – which is why I collectively call these arguments ABP discourse.

## The arguments

Before criticising them, I will present the ABP arguments one by one: starting from the most difficult-to-change factor, geography, and ending with the factor that is most subject to human intervention – institutions.

### Geography

The geography argument is often, understandably, mixed up with climate and natural resources arguments, which we discuss in the following subsections (Bloom & Sachs 1998; Sachs 2003). However, purely geographical arguments have two main components. First, many developing countries, especially the African ones, are landlocked, and are thus disadvantaged in integrating into the global economy through international trade. Second, many of them are also in 'bad neighbourhoods' in the sense that they are surrounded by other poor countries that have small markets (which restrict their trading opportunities) and, frequently, violent conflicts (which often spill over into neighbouring countries).

## Climate

Developing countries close to the equator suffer from tropical diseases, especially malaria (Bloom & Sachs 1998; Sachs 2003). These diseases become burdens on economic development, as they reduce worker productivity and raise health care costs. Animal diseases are more numerous and virulent in the tropics, thereby reducing the productivity of husbandry.

Acemoglu et al. (2001) have proposed an indirect link between climate and economic development by arguing that the prevalence of tropical diseases discouraged colonial settlement by the Europeans in countries close to the equator. Their unwillingness to settle in those countries meant that the colonisers brought with them only low-quality institutions necessary for resource extraction. It is argued that such low-quality institutions have negatively affected subsequent economic development in those countries.

In addition to the disease-related argument, some commentators have emphasised that tropical soil, especially in Africa, is of poor quality, reducing agricultural productivity (Bloom & Sachs 1998).

## Natural resources

The so-called natural resource curse thesis has held that abundant natural resource endowment hampers economic development (Auty 1994; Sachs & Warner 1997). There are many different explanations of resource curse (see Restrepo 2016, for a review), but the most popular has been that resource abundance generates perverse politics in the forms of corruption and violent conflicts. Other important explanations for why resource-rich countries grow more slowly include the overvaluation of the currency that results in the loss of international competitiveness for the manufacturing sector and the weak linkages that natural resource sectors have with other sectors of the economy.

## 66 Ha-Joon Chang

### Ethnic diversity

High ethnic diversity is emphasised as an explanatory variable for poor economic performance (Easterly & Levine 1997), although some commentators point out that this is not the case in democracies (Collier et al. 2001). It is argued that high ethnic diversity makes people distrust each other, raising transaction costs and making markets function less well. It is also said to encourage violent conflicts, especially if there are a few groups of similar strengths, rather than many small groups, which are more difficult to organise.

### Culture

It is interesting to note that cultural arguments are often presented in rather convoluted ways in order to avoid accusations of racism. However, these arguments boil down to the assertion that some cultures – especially the African ones and the Muslim ones – are bad for economic development (Harrison & Huntington eds. 2000). People from some cultures, it is said, do not work hard, do not save much, do not value education, do not plan for the future, lack discipline, and cannot cooperate with each other – all characteristics that are presumed to be dysfunctional for economic development.

In explaining the economic divergence between South Korea and Ghana, two countries that were at similar levels of economic development in the 1960s, Samuel Huntington, of *The Clash of Civilizations* fame, argues: "Undoubtedly, many factors played a role, but . . . culture had to be a large part of the explanation. South Koreans valued thrift, investment, hard work, education, organisation, and discipline. Ghanaians had different values. In short, cultures count" (Huntington 2000, p. xi). Daniel Etounga-Manguelle (2000), a Cameroonian engineer and writer states:

> The African, anchored in his ancestral culture, is so convinced that the past can only repeat itself that he worries only superficially about the future. However, without a dynamic perception of the future, there is no planning, no foresight, no scenario building; in other words, no policy to affect the course of events.
>
> (p. 69)

And then he goes on to say that "African societies are like a football team in which, as a result of personal rivalries and a lack of team spirit, one player will not pass the ball to another out of fear that the latter might score a goal" (p. 75).

## Institutions

In the late 1980s, institutional deficiency (especially poor political governance and the absence of rule of law) was starting to be mentioned by the World Bank as a possible explanation for the failures of the SAPs, especially in Sub-Saharan Africa. By the early 1990s, institutional explanations had become the dominant explanation in the World Bank and the IMF for the failure of their 'good' policies (Stein 2008, pp. 38–42). The emphasis on institutions was strengthened by the 1997 Asian financial crisis, which Neo-classical economists tried to blame on the institutional deficiencies of the crisis-hit economies – for example, political institutions that generated corruption and cronyism, over-regulation of finance and industry, and deficient corporate governance system, rather than on financial deregulation (for a critical review of the literature emphasising the institutional deficiencies of the Asian countries, see Chang 2000).[6]

## The criticisms

It will be silly to deny that the aforementioned non-policy factors do not matter. However, there are serious problems with the ABP arguments. First, the nature of those 'structural' non-policy factors is poorly understood. These supposedly unalterable 'structural' factors are usually things that can be deliberately changed in the medium-to long-run, as it has happened in today's rich countries (for further arguments, see Chang 2009a, 2009b, 2010). Second, the theories linking non-policy factors and economic performance are very simplistically formulated. In particular, there is no recognition that the actual effects of those factors on economic development may depend on the level of economic development itself. Third, there is a lot of misrepresentation of the empirical facts – especially when it comes to things like culture. Fourth, there is much conflicting evidence on the supposed relationship between the structural factors and economic performance. Let us explore these points in relation to each of the non-policy factors that we discussed previously.

### Geography

#### Landlockedness

Having no natural access to sea routes restricts a country's trading opportunities, but it is not such a binding option, as the stellar economic performances of some landlocked countries show. There are

## 68   Ha-Joon Chang

several rich countries that are landlocked or seasonally landlocked. Switzerland and Austria are two of the richest economies in the world, but they are both landlocked. Before the spread of the ice-breaking ships in the early 20th century, the Scandinavian countries were effectively landlocked for half the year when the sea froze.

Even more intriguing are the cases of Ethiopia and Uzbekistan – two landlocked developing countries. In the last decade or so, Ethiopia has grown basically at China's rate – its per capita income growth rate was 8.2 percent between 2003 and 2014. What is notable is that this acceleration in growth has happened after the country *became* landlocked after Eritrea, which had occupied all the coasts of former Ethiopia, seceded in 1993. During the same period, Uzbekistan, which is the only doubly-landlocked country (that is, you have to go through two other countries to get to the sea) of any size,[7] notched up a 6.6 percent per capita income growth – which is not much below what countries like Korea and Taiwan recorded during their 'miracle' years between the 1960s and the 1980s.

The point is that there are many alternatives to sea transport. There are river, rail, and road transports which will link the landlocked country to other countries' seaports; for example, Ethiopia has been using Djibouti as its main access point to the sea. Air transport is becoming increasingly important – and even essential – for certain industries, like floriculture.

All of this shows that the landlockedness argument is based on a confusion between the cause and the symptom – it is the lack of investment in the alternative transport systems, rather than the geography itself, that is the problem.

### Bad neighbourhood effects

It is plausible that a country's location in a 'bad neighbourhood' full of poor and conflict-ridden countries pulls down its growth. However, the evidence suggests that we need to be careful and not stretch this argument too far. India and, to a lesser extent, Bangladesh have grown very fast in the last couple of decades, despite being in the poorest region in the world, that is, South Asia (poorer than Sub-Saharan Africa). The region also has its share of conflicts. The long history of military conflicts between India and Pakistan, Hindu-Muslim violence in India, and the Tamil-Sinhalese ethnic war in Sri Lanka are well known. Less well known are the resurgent Maoist guerilas in India (the Naxalites) and the 10-year civil war in Nepal with the Maoists (1996–2006).

*ABP discourse in development economics* 69

It may be argued that the bad neighbourhood effects in South Asia were not as severe as those in Sub-Saharan Africa on the grounds that the conflicts in the region have never got completely out of control and that the countries in the region had large domestic markets and therefore did not need the markets of neighbours as much as the small African countries did. However, the most powerful counter to this line of argument is that the recent economic performances of India and especially Bangladesh show that a country in a 'bad neighbourhood' can always generate growth by exporting to richer countries outside the region. Indeed, the East Asian economic 'miracle' was largely driven by exports to richer countries far away – the North American and the European countries – rather than exports to neighbours.

### Climate

When discussing climate, it is implicitly assumed that it is only tropical climate that is harmful for economic development. However, frigid and arctic climates (affecting a number of rich countries, such as Finland, Sweden, Norway, Canada, and parts of the US) also impose economic burdens – machines seize up, fuel costs skyrocket, and transportation is blocked by snow and ice. As mentioned previously, the Scandinavian countries used to be effectively landlocked due to cold weather in winter for half of the year until the 19th century. Indeed, there is no obvious *a priori* reason to believe that cold climate is better than hot climate for economic development. Interestingly, in *Politics* (Book VII, chapter 7), Aristotle argued that the European societies are not very developed, compared to the Greek one, because their climate is too cold, which in his view makes their people unintelligent and less skilled.[8]

We don't even think of their cold climate as an inhibiting factor when we discuss the economic developments of countries like Sweden or Canada – in the same way in which no one complains that tropical climate has hampered Singapore's economic development – only because, through economic development, they have acquired the money and the technologies to deal with it.

The same point can be applied to tropical diseases, which play a particularly important role in the climate argument. Many of today's rich countries (not just Singapore which is bang in the middle of the tropics) used to struggle with malaria and other tropical diseases, at least during the summer – Southern Italy, Southern US, South Korea, and Japan. Of course, these diseases have largely (although not completely) disappeared in those countries, but that is not because they have somehow experienced a dramatic change in their climate (if anything these

## 70  Ha-Joon Chang

countries have become hotter) but because their economic development has enabled them to have better sanitation (reducing the incidences of the diseases) and better medical facilities (allowing them to effectively cure those few cases that still occur).

Thus seen, like the advocates of the landlockedness argument, the advocates of the climate argument are confusing the cause of under-development with its symptoms – poor climate is not the main cause behind under-development; a country's inability to overcome the constraints imposed by its poor climate is a symptom of under-development.

### Natural resources

The alleged negative correlation between natural resource abundance and economic development is sensitive to the methods of measuring natural resource endowment (Restrepo 2016). In particular, the tendency to use the share of natural resources in export of GDP wrongly measures natural resource abundance. Using the 'share' measures, poor countries that have few man-made resources, such as machines, infrastructure, and skilled labour, will inevitably look abundantly endowed with natural resources by default.

Indeed, if we look at their absolute per capita endowments, fewer than a dozen countries in Africa – which is supposed to especially suffer from the resource curse – had any significant mineral deposits as of the 1990s (Chang 2006).[9] Only two countries – South Africa and the Democratic Republic of Congo – are exceptionally well endowed with more than one mineral resource. In terms of land, most African countries may have low population density, but only a small number of them are exceptionally well endowed with arable land (Niger, Liberia, DRC, Chad, Senegal, Sierra Leone, and the Central African Republic).

Moreover, many rich countries have successfully used natural resource abundance as springboards for their economic development – not just the exceptionally well-endowed US, Canada, and Australia, but also the Scandinavian countries (see Wright & Czulesta 2004, 2007, on the role of natural resources in economic development). The fact that in the late 19th and early 20th century the fastest growing regions of the world were resource-rich areas like North America, Latin America, and Scandinavia adds further to our scepticism about the natural resource curse thesis.

### Ethnic diversity

Ethnic conflicts and violence, like other social conflicts and forms of violence, can hamper growth. However, this is different from saying

## ABP discourse in development economics 71

that ethnic diversity itself necessarily leads to mistrust, conflicts, violence, and other negative effects.

Many of today's rich countries in Europe have suffered from ethnic and other (linguistic, religious, and ideological) divides, especially of the 'medium-degree' ones (i.e. a few, rather than numerous, groups) that are supposed to be most conducive to violent conflicts. Belgium has two (and a bit, if you count the tiny German-speaking minority) ethnic groups. Switzerland has four languages and two religions, and has experienced a number of mainly religion-based civil wars. Spain has serious minority problems with the Catalans and the Basques, which have even spawned terrorism. Due to its 560-year rule over Finland (1249 to 1809, when it was ceded to Russia), Sweden has a significant Finnish minority (around 5 percent of the population) and Finland a Swedish one of similar proportion. The examples can go on.

The East Asian countries are supposed to have benefited from their ethnic homogeneities, but they in fact have serious internal divisions. In addition to a tiny native population of Polynesian origin (the so-called Kaoshan people), the 'Chinese' in Taiwan are divided into two (or four, if you divide them up more finely) linguistic groups (the 'mainlanders' vs. the Taiwanese) that are hostile to each other. Japan has serious minority problems with the Koreans, the Okinawans, the Ainus, and the Burakumins. Even though it is one of the most ethno-linguistically homogeneous countries in the world, Korea has serious regional divisions – the animosity between Southeast and Southwest is legendary. In the African context, Rwanda is nearly as homogeneous in ethno-linguistic terms as Korea, but such homogeneity did not prevent the ethnic cleansing of the formerly dominant minority Tutsis by the majority Hutus – showing that 'ethnicity' is a political, rather than a natural, construction.

These examples show that rich countries do not suffer from ethnic heterogeneity not because they do not have it but because they have succeeded in building a nation out of a heterogeneous population (which, we should note, was often an unpleasant and even violent process). Indeed, despite being genetically the most heterogeneous country in the world, Tanzania has been very successful in nation-building in that it has not had any serious ethnicity-based conflicts.

### Culture

Against the cultural explanation of development failure, it should be pointed out that many of today's rich countries used to be criticised for having those 'negative' cultural traits that are supposed to characterise poorly performing economies today (Chang 2007, chapter 9).

## 72   Ha-Joon Chang

Before the mid-19th century, when Germany started industrialising, the British described the Germans to be mentally slow, too individualistic, and too emotional for economic development. For example, John Russell, an early 19th-century British traveller in Germany, remarked: "The Germans are a plodding, easily contented people . . . endowed neither with great acuteness of perception nor quickness of feeling. . . . It is long before [a German] can be brought to comprehend the bearings of what is new to him, and it is difficult to rouse him to ardour in its pursuit" (Russell 1828, p. 394). When travelling in Germany, Mary Shelley, the author of *Frankenstein*, complained that "the Germans never hurry" (Shelly 1843, p. 276).

Until the early 20th century, Australians and Americans would go to Japan and say the Japanese are lazy. Having toured lots of factories in Japan, an Australian engineer remarked in 1915:

> My impression as to your cheap labour was soon disillusioned when I saw your people at work. No doubt they are lowly paid, but the return is equally so; to see your men at work made me feel that you are a very satisfied easy-going race who reckon time is no object. When I spoke to some managers they informed me that it was impossible to change the habits of national heritage.
>
> (*Japan Times*, 18 August 1915)

Even Sidney Gulick, an American missionary who lived in Japan for 25 years and later became a champion of Asian-American human rights after going back to the US, had to admit that many Japanese "give an impression . . . of being lazy and utterly indifferent to the passage of time" (Gulick 1903, p. 117).

The Koreans were considered to be even worse. In 1912, they were condemned as "12 millions of dirty, degraded, sullen, lazy and religionless savages who slouch about in dirty white garments of the most inept kind and who live in filthy mud huts". That comment came from a leading female socialist intellectual at the time, that is, Beatrice Webb of the Fabian movement (Webb & Webb 1978, p. 375), so one can imagine what a regular European male conservative would have said about the Koreans had he visited the country.

Of course, the cultures of Germany, Japan, and Korea today are completely different from what are described. Those transformations happened mainly because of economic development, which created societies in which people have to behave in more disciplined, calculating, and cooperative ways than in agrarian societies.

These historical examples show how weak the theoretical foundations of the cultural arguments are. Theoretically, these arguments

ABP discourse in development economics   73

fail to recognise that the relationship between culture and economic development is complex and that, in the long run, the causality runs far more strongly from economic development to culture, rather than the other way around.

## Institutions

The argument that bad institutions are holding back developing countries should be interpreted with caution (Chang 2007, 2011). The currently popular view is that institutions are the ultimate determinants of economic performance, but the causality is not unidirectional: economic development changes institutions. This can happen through a number of channels. First, increased wealth due to growth may create higher demands for higher quality institutions: for example, political institutions with greater transparency and accountability. Second, greater wealth also makes better institutions more affordable; institutions are costly to set up, run, and maintain, so poor countries cannot afford to have good institutions. Third, economic development creates new agents of change, demanding new institutions; capitalists supported the development of banking institutions against landlords in the 18th century, while workers agitated for the welfare state and protective labour laws against capitalists in the late 19th and the early 20th century.

Indeed, there is quite a lot of historical evidence to suggest that the causality may be stronger from economic development to institutions, rather than the other way around. Today's rich countries had much lower quality institutions than what developing countries have today when they were at similar levels of material development (Chang 2002, chapter 3). If the causality runs more strongly in the direction of development to institutions, it is misleading to blame the underdevelopment of developing countries primarily on their institutional deficiencies.

## Conclusions

This chapter has critically examined what I call the ABP arguments, which attribute the poor economic performance in developing countries to non-policy factors, ranging from climate and geography to culture and institutions.

First of all, arguments citing non-policy factors that do not change over time, such as climate and geography (except for rare things like Ethiopia becoming landlocked due to the secession of Eritrea) cannot explain how the economic performances of the countries in question

## 74  Ha-Joon Chang

have fluctuated a lot since the Second World War. Second, the effects of these factors are often characterised in a biased way; for example, only the negative effects of natural resources are discussed, when they can have positive impacts too. Third, in the long run, some of the non-policy factors are subject to change through human intervention, both directly (through nation-building or cultural reform) and indirectly (through economic development, which is subject to policy intervention). Fourth, many of those factors were (and some still are) present in the rich countries – for example, things like a hostile climate or a disadvantageous geography – but do not matter anymore because those countries have acquired the abilities to deal with them, largely thanks to economic development.

These considerations make us conclude that, while containing some valid points, the ABP arguments have largely served as 'excuses' for the failed orthodox economic policies (and the theories that back them) and, in the process, have actually prevented us from understanding the role of those non-policy factors properly. A more balanced and nuanced look at the mechanisms through which these non-policy factors affect economic performance (as well as the reverse causality) is needed if we are to save the valid ideas contained in the ABP arguments and enhance our understanding of the development process.

## Notes

1 Hirschman (1981) called these economic theories 'mono-economics'.
2 It is interesting to note that the orthodox Marxists were also very critical of the Dependency theorists regarding the explanation of the East Asian industrialisation. The orthodox Marxists argued that capitalism has an inherent tendency to penetrate and destroy the pre-capitalist modes of production, however brutal the process may be, and therefore that there is nothing exceptional in the industrialisation of the East Asian NICs (e.g. Warren 1973, 1980).
3 The view that there can be only one economics is still widely accepted – even by Dani Rodrik, an economist reputed for his emphasis on the importance of institutions. He has titled a recent collection of his essays, *One Economics, Many Recipes*, and very much emphasises the uniquely scientific nature of Neo-classical methodology (Rodrik 2009; also see Rodrik 2016).
4 On the intellectual history of the World Bank, especially in relation to its thinking on the role of institutions in economic development, see Stein (2008).
5 See Wade (1996) for a fascinating account of the politics behind the making of the report.
6 Even though there are those who think that the quality of institutions are determined by long-term historical factors, like colonialism (Acemoglu et al. 2001), many think that, unlike the other ABP factors, institutions are subject

## ABP discourse in development economics   75

to changes through human intervention, so there has been active attempts on the part of the international financial organisations (especially the IMF and the World Bank) and of donor governments to measure the quality of institutions (Kaufmann et al., various years, is the best example) and change them through various "governance-related conditionalities" (Kapur & Webber 2000). These conditionalities have required that the borrowing country implement certain institutions that are thought to improve economic performance, such as an independent central bank, democratic elections, and better corporate governance law.

7  The only other doubly-landlocked country, Liechtenstein, has only 160km² of land and 37,000 people.

8  He said: "Those who live in a cold climate and in Europe are full of spirit, but wanting in intelligence and skill; and therefore they retain comparative freedom, but have no political organization, and are incapable of ruling over others. Whereas the natives of Asia are intelligent and inventive, but they are wanting in spirit, and therefore they are always in a state of subjugation and slavery. But the Hellenic race, which is situated between them, is likewise intermediate in character, being high-spirited and also intelligent. Hence it continues free, and is the best governed of any nation, and if it could be formed into one state, would be able to rule the world" (Aristotle 2001, p. 1286).

9  To this list may be added cases where significant mineral resources have been found recently (e.g. Equatorial Guinea, Ghana), but they are very few in number and do not change the basic picture.

## Bibliography

Acemoglu, D., Johnson, S. & Robinson, J. (2001). 'The Colonial Origins of Comparative Development: An Empirical Investigation', *American Economic Review*, vol. 91, no. 5.

Amsden, A. (1989). *Asia's Next Giant*, Oxford University Press, New York.

Aristotle. (2001). *The Basic Works of Aristotle*, edited by R. McKeon, Random House, New York.

Auty, R.M. (1994). 'Industrial Policy Reform in Six Large Newly Industrializing Countries: The Resource Curse Thesis', *World Development*, vol. 22, no. 11.

Bhagwati, J. (1977). 'Introduciton', in J. Bhagwati (ed.), *The New International Economic Order: The North-South Debate*, MIT Press, Cambridge, MA.

Bloom, D. & Sachs, J. (1998). 'Geography, Demography and Economic Growth in Africa', *Brookings Papers on Economic Activity*, vol. 2, no. 2.

Chang, H.-J. (1993). 'The Political Economy of Industrial Policy in Korea', *Cambridge Journal of Economics*, vol. 17, no. 2.

Chang, H.-J. (2000). 'The Hazard of Moral Hazard: Untangling the Asian Crisis', *World Development*, vol. 28, no. 4.

Chang, H.-J. (2002). *Kicking Away the Ladder: Development Strategy in Historical Perspective*, Anthem Press, London.

Chang, H.-J. (2006). *The East Asian Development Experience: The Miracle, the Crisis, and the Future*, Zed Books, London.

## 76 Ha-Joon Chang

Chang, H.-J. (2007). *Bad Samaritans*, Random House, London, and Blooms-bury USA, New York.

Chang, H.-J. (2009a). 'Under-Explored Treasure Troves of Development Lessons: Lessons from the Histories of Small Rich European Countries (SRECs)', in M. Kremer, P. van Lieshoust & R. Went (eds.), *Doing Good or Doing Better: Development Policies in a Globalising World*, Amsterdam University Press, Amsterdam.

Chang, H.-J. (2009b). 'Economic History of the Developed World: Lessons for Africa', in S. Tapsoba & G. Oluremi Archer-Davies (eds.), *Eminent Speakers Series Volume II: Sharing Visions of Africa's Development*, African Development Bank, Tunis (can be downloaded from: www.econ.cam.ac.uk/faculty/chang/pubs/ChangAfDBlecturetext.pdf).

Chang, H.-J. (2010). *23 Things They Don't Tell You about Capitalism*, Allen Lane, London.

Chang, H.-J. (2011). 'Institutions and Economic Development: Theory, Policy, and History', *Journal of Institutional Economics*, vol. 7, no. 4.

Collier, P., Honohan, P. & Moene, K.O. (2001). 'The Implications of Ethnic Diversity', *Economic Policy*, vol. 16, no. 32.

Easterly, W. & Levine, R. (1997). 'Africa's Growth Tragedy: Policies and Ethnic Divisions', *Quarterly Journal of Economics*, vol. 112, no. 4.

Etounga-Manguelle, D. (2000). 'Does Africa Need a Cultural Adjustment Program?', in L. Harrison & S. Huntington (eds.), *Culture Matters: How Values Shape Human Progress*, Basic Books, New York.

Fei, J. & Ranis, G. (1969). 'Economic Development in Historical Perspective', *American Economic Review*, vol. 59, no. 2.

Gulick, S. (1903). *Evolution of the Japanese*, Fleming H. Revell, New York.

Harrison, L. & Huntington, S. (eds.) (2000). *Culture Matters: How Values Shape Human Progress*, Basic Books, New York.

Hirschman, A. (1981). 'The Rise and Decline of Development Economics' (ch. 1), in *Essays in Trespassing: Economics to Politics and Beyond*, Cambridge University Press, Cambridge.

Huntington, S. (2000). 'Foreword: Cultures Count', in L. Harrison & S. Huntington (eds.), *Culture Matters: How Values Shape Human Progress*, Basic Books, New York.

Kapur, D. & Webber, R. (2000). 'Governance-Related Conditionalities of the IFIs', G-24 Discussion Paper Series, no. 6, UNCTAD, Geneva.

Kaufmann, D. et al. (various associates) various years (between 1998 and 2009). 'Governance Matters' I to VIII, Policy Research Working Paper, various, World Bank, Washington, DC.

Ocampo, J.A. & Erten, B. (2013). 'Super-Cycle of Commodity Prices Since the Mid-Nineteenth Century', *World Development*, vol. 44, no. 1.

Palma, G. (1978). 'Dependency: A Formal Theory of Underdevelopment or a Methodology for the Analyisis of Concrete Situations of Underdevelopment?', *World Development*, vol. 6, pp. 881–924.

Restrepo, R. (2016). *The Resource Curse Mirage: Mimeo*, Instituto de Altos Estudios Nacionales, Ecuador.

## ABP discourse in development economics 77

Rodrik, D. (2009). *One Economics, Many Recipes*, Princeton University Press, Princeton.

Rodrik, D. (2016). *Economics Rules*, Oxford University Press, Oxford.

Russell, J. (1828). *A Tour in Germany*, vol. 1, Archibald Constable & Co, Edinburgh.

Sachs, J.D. (2003). Institutions Don't Rule: Direct Effects of Geography on Per Capita Income, NBER Working Paper 9490, National Bureau of Economic Research, Cambridge, MA.

Sachs, J.D. & Warner, A.M. (1997). Natural Resource Abundance and Economic Growth, Mimeo, Center for International Development and Harvard Institute for International Development, Harvard University.

Shelly, M. (1843). *Rambles in Germany and Italy*, vol. 1, Edward Monkton, London.

Spraos, J. (1983). *Inequalising Trade?*, Clarendon Press, Oxford.

Stein, H. (2008). *Beyond the World Bank Agenda: An Institutional Approach to Development*, University of Chicago Press, Chicago.

Wade, R. (1990). *Governing the Market*, Princeton University Press, Princeton and London.

Wade, R. (1996). 'Japan, the World Bank, and the Art of Paradigm Maintenance: The *East Asian Miracle* in Political Perspective', *New Left Review*, no. 217.

Warren, B. (1973). 'Imperialism and Capitalist Industrialisation', *New Left Review*, no. 81, September/October 1973.

Warren, B. (1980). *Imperialism: Pioneer of Capitalism*, Verso, London.

Webb, S. & Webb, B. (1978). *The Letters of Sidney and Beatrice Webb*, edited by N. MacKenzie and J. MacKenzie, Cambridge University Press, Cambridge.

World Bank. (1993). *The East Asian Miracle*, Oxford University Press, New York.

Wright, G. & Czulesta, J. (2004). 'The Myth of the Resource Curse', *Challenge*, vol. 47, no. 2.

Wright, G. & Czelusta, J. (2007). 'Resource-Based Growth, Past and Present', in D. Lederman & F. Maloney (eds.), *Natural Resources: Neither Curse nor Destiny*, Stanford University, Stanford.

# 5 Inequality and conflict
## Global drivers and interventions

*Frances Stewart*

Considerable research has explored the connections between inequality and conflict. But much less attention has been devoted to the global determinants of the inequality that lies behind much conflict. This is the concern of this chapter. It is an appropriate way to recognize Deepak Nayyar's major contribution to our thinking; he has consistently and systematically addressed the connections between globalisation and inequality, adding greatly to our understanding. Here I attempt to take the issue further by exploring how both globalisation and inequality relate to violent conflict.

The majority of conflicts over the past fifty years have been *within* nations (sometimes termed 'civil war') rather than between nations, although there are often international interventions in these conflicts. This was true in the Cold War era, when international conflict was rare, but many internal conflicts involved interventions from both sides of the Cold War. Post–Cold War, civil wars remain predominant, while international interventions continue, as illustrated by the conflicts in the Middle East. Hence the focus of this chapter is on such civil wars.

There has been considerable research into the factors responsible for civil wars and in particular the issue of whether inequality causes conflict. While no clear connection has been found between vertical inequality and conflict, there is substantial evidence that horizontal inequality (HI) within a country increases the likelihood of conflict. Moreover, global horizontal inequalities may also contribute to conflict. Hence the drivers of horizontal inequalities need to be explored in order to identify policies that are likely to reduce inequality. This chapter discusses both whether and why the drivers of national horizontal inequalities are global, and also the role of global horizontal inequalities in raising the risk of conflict. Finally, it considers some implications for policy.

## Inequality and conflict    79

The chapter is organized as follows: the first section summarizes evidence on the connections between inequality and conflict within countries. This is followed by consideration of the causes of the relevant inequalities, with a particular focus on global causes. The third section is devoted to an exploration of a particular type of global HI, and its connection with conflict. The fourth section concludes.

## Does inequality cause conflict?

De Tocqueville put forward a classic formulation of the view that inequality causes conflict: 'Remove the secondary causes that have produced the great convulsions of the world and you will almost always find the principle of inequality at the bottom. Either the poor have attempted to plunder the rich, or the rich to enslave the poor' (de Tocqueville 1835, quote from 1954 edition: 266).

Yet according to Lichbach (1989), 'In sum, two decades of empirical research in conflict studies have challenged the conventionally accepted view that a strong positive relationship exists between economic inequality and political conflict' (440). More recent studies have also questioned the connection between inequality and conflict (Fearon and Laitin 2000; Cramer 2003; Collier and Hoeffler 2004). However, these studies explored the relationship between *vertical* inequality (or inequality among individuals in a society) and the probability of conflict. In contrast, a large amount of research has shown a connection between *horizontal* inequality (or inequality among religious, racial or ethnic groups) and conflict. The research has shown a connection between HIs and conflict probability, both within nations (Murshed and Gates 2005; Mancini 2008) and between them (Barrows 1976; Stewart 2001; Østby 2008a; Cederman et al. 2013; Cederman et al. 2015).

HIs are inequalities between groups which are bound together by a common identity – which may be on the basis of religion, ethnicity, race or region. The common identity makes it much easier to mobilize people against others with different identities. This is not to say that differences in identity as such create conflict. The vast majority of people with different identities live alongside each other in a peaceful way (Fearon and Laitin 1996). As (Cohen 1974) states: 'Men may and do certainly joke about or ridicule the strange and bizarre customs of men from other ethnic groups. . . . But they do not fight over such differences alone.' But where there are apparent injustices across groups, or inequalities in economic, social, political or cultural dimensions, then the potential mobilizing power of a common identity comes into

## 80    *Frances Stewart*

play. Or as Cohen goes on to say, 'When men do . . . fight across ethnic lines it is nearly always the case that they fight over some fundamental issues concerning the distribution and exercise of power, whether economic, political or both' (94).

Group identities are constructed historically through differences in people's experience, customs, language and so on. Most people have multiple identities, and some identities can be fluid, changing over time. However, leaders and the media often sharpen group distinctions, bringing particular identities to the fore and promoting enmities. Historical analysis of both internal and international wars shows that mobilization by emphasizing difference generally occurs before and during conflicts (Gourevitch 1998; Elon 2002; Akindès 2007). Such mobilization draws on grievances, or HIs. In contrast, where there are limited or no inequalities between groups, such mobilization tends to be ineffective (Ukoha 2008).

HIs are particularly likely to cause conflict if there are both political and socio-economic inequalities in the same direction (Stewart 2001; Østby 2008b; Cederman et al. 2011). This is because, if there are political HIs, then group leaders have limited or no power and therefore have a motive to fight to acquire it, while socio-economic HIs are a source of grievance among the people who are mobilized by these leaders. Inequalities in cultural recognition – for example, outlawing a group's religious practices or refusing to recognize a group's language – can also be a powerful source of grievance. Government treatment of the Tamil language, for example, was a major factor behind the Sri Lankan civil war (Perera 2001; Brown et al. 2003).

While there is good reason and evidence to expect horizontal inequalities to increase the likelihood of conflict, high vertical inequality, without a binding and mobilizing identity, does not seem to raise the risk of conflict. Turning to global drivers, therefore, we will focus on the drivers of horizontal inequality.

## Drivers of horizontal inequalities

HIs generally have historic origins, often as a result of colonialism. This can take a variety of forms: (1) Colonial settlers take over the best land, dominate government jobs and have a privileged position in the private sector. Examples are whites in East, Central and South Africa, and Portuguese and Spanish colonists in Latin America; (2) Colonial regimes favour particular groups and/or regions within the country they settle in, giving some privileged access to education and other resources. Examples are the privileged treatment of the Tutsis in

Rwanda and Burundi, the Igbo in Nigeria and the Kikuyu in Kenya. Sometimes the colonials 'divide and rule,' favouring some groups for education and government jobs and others for the armed forces, as was the case in Nigeria and Kenya; (3) The colonials 'import' labour from elsewhere as indentured labour or slaves. Imported labour is generally treated much worse than the colonial settlers themselves, but are sometimes better off than the indigenous population. Examples are Indians imported to build the railways in East Asia and to work on plantations in Sri Lanka and Malaysia; or Africans transferred to the Americas as slaves.

Another source of HIs, historically, is spontaneous or voluntary migration. The immigrants may be better off financially than local populations as they dominate trade, but they usually do not own land. Examples are the settler/indigenes division in central Nigeria, the Chinese in Southeast Asia and the Lebanese in Africa.

These historic HIs are sustained over time to the extent that the immigrant populations remain, which is the typical situation. The HIs are maintained by a set of factors which reinforce group privilege or deprivation. First, groups with higher incomes are able to secure better education and health for their children, which in turn means higher incomes in the next generation; in addition, the children of those with higher incomes may inherit assets. Second, having more of one type of capital tends to enhance the returns to each type: for example, the returns to education would tend to be higher for those with financial assets and conversely. Third, social capital (networking advantages) is asymmetric in such situations, as people have stronger networks within their own group and inter-group networking can be weak; consequently those in more privileged groups have better networks from an economic perspective than those in poor groups. Fourth, there is often overt or implicit discrimination against particular members of groups. As a result of these reinforcing elements, HIs tend to be persistent, lasting generations and even centuries. Consequently, the initial colonial driver of horizontal inequalities has left a legacy which affects people today (see Stewart and Langer 2008).

There are also contemporary sources of HIs. These include geographic advantages and disadvantages; migration and its consequences; government policies, which are often a reflection of political horizontal inequalities; and environmental degradations. Geography affects production possibilities and efficiencies especially in relation to primary production (agriculture and natural resource extraction). The locational advantages or disadvantages depend not just on geography determining climate and natural resource availability, but also

## 82 Frances Stewart

on technology and markets. Thus coltan has become an important natural resource with the development of mobile phones, of which it is an essential component, whereas previously it was worth little. Similarly, oil became a very lucrative resource after the development of the car industry, while high returns from the production of poppies and coca have transformed opportunities in some Asian and Latin American countries. Having a dynamic neighbouring market leads to opportunities for efficient production, in contrast to situations where neighbouring countries have stagnant low-income economies. Geographic advantages and disadvantages have been, and remain, important sources of HIs in many African countries, where northern areas tend to be less fertile, to have less infrastructure and less dynamic neighbouring markets.

Migration flows also lead to HIs in the host country (and may also do so in the countries from which migrants come). HIs have been created in many European countries with flows of migrants from poorer parts of the world. Here immigrants generally start, and often remain, poorer than the indigenous population. This is the case on average for the Turkish population in Germany, North Africans in France and many Afro-Caribbeans in the UK. Migrants moving between developing countries are also a major source of HIs: for example, the large Philippine population in Malaysia suffers multiple deprivations, as do Somalis in Kenya.

A third contemporary source of HIs is government policy which frequently favours some groups over others, especially where one group is dominant in the government. At the extreme, particular groups are deprived of citizenship and all the benefits that this confers, as, for example, in Cote d'Ivoire in the early 2000s (Gibney 2008). Sometimes the preferences are implicit, as the group in power gives better jobs etc. to people of their own identity. Regional biases in policy are very common, and these imply biases in the distribution of resources among different identity groups where identity groups are concentrated geographically.

Environment degradation, and especially climate change, is a further source of HIs. In general, poorer countries suffer more than richer ones, and are less able to protect themselves. Moreover, within poorer countries, poorer people suffer most, living in the most vulnerable areas. For example, in some African countries, it is the already poor Northern areas and peoples that are likely to suffer most from climate change (IPCC 2014).

Globalisation affects these drivers indirectly in a variety of ways. First, demand for a particular type of natural resource inevitably favours

*Inequality and conflict*   83

the group where the resource is to be found: for example, the global oil market has been a huge source of HIs. Second, the global market favours the haves in poor countries – capital flows to the richer areas, the better educated find better jobs domestically and internationally and are given favourable terms for migration and the poorer areas and groups tend to be left behind. Third, global political interventions often favour one group over another – as is apparent in the interventions in the Middle East. Fourth, international migration and the HIs it creates are intrinsic aspects of globalisation. Fifth, globalisation is a factor in the growing adverse developments with respect to the environment.

We can see a connection between the widening HIs and contemporary conflicts: the impoverishment of Northern Nigeria provides fertile soil for Boko Haram, while similar developments are behind Al-Shabaab in Kenya. Niger and Mali, among others, are also affected by environmental and economic developments which widen inequalities, providing an incentive for recurrent conflict. At the other end of the spectrum, the potential riches that the global economy offers political leaders, through syphoning off money from aid and bribes by corporations, generates strong motives to acquire power, and once acquired to keep it. Hence elections often tend to be the occasion of conflict, as illustrated by the Cote d'Ivoire war from 2002–2004 and the Kenyan riots in 2008 (Langer 2005; Stewart 2010b). A number of leaders have tried to perpetuate their rule beyond the constitutional limits, and this too can lead to conflict. An example is that of Yemen.

In brief, the global economy offers riches to some groups and impoverishes others, and this threatens political stability and peace within particular countries. But there is also a wider threat to global security associated with global HIs. This is discussed in the next section.

## Global horizontal inequalities and global dimensions of conflict

The previous sections have discussed global drivers of inequalities within countries and how these may lead to conflict. This section moves from the national to the global level. Following Stewart (2010a), the section argues that the underlying causes of global tensions are similar to those at the national level. Moreover, global HIs in multiple dimensions – between Muslims and others – underlie many contemporary global tensions. The consequent violence includes domestic and international terrorism and civil wars with major international interventions. The twin towers event represents the extreme (to date)

## 84  *Frances Stewart*

of international terrorism, although there have been many other incidents in Europe and elsewhere; terrorist events occur quite regularly in Pakistan (e.g., where over 30,000 people have been killed since 2001); they also affect many other countries including India, Iraq, Lebanon and Afghanistan. The Afghanistan, Iraqi and Syrian civil wars are examples of civil wars involving extensive international action.

The inequalities that partially underpin these violent events occur at two broad levels: they occur within many countries, both developed and developing, and between Islamic countries and others at a global level. Dimensions of inequalities are of all the main categories – political, economic and cultural. These inequalities can be observed within many nations as well as between them.

### National inequalities

#### HIs faced by Muslims in Europe

Throughout Europe Muslims are disadvantaged compared with the rest of the population. The experience of three countries – the Netherlands, France and the UK – illustrates this. The Muslim populations mainly consist of fairly recent immigrants – from North Africa, in the case of France; Turkey, in the case of Germany; Bangladesh and Pakistan in the UK.

In the Netherlands, Muslims of Moroccan, Turkish and Indonesian origin, as well as refugees from Syria and Afghanistan, form about 6 percent of the total population. In France data are scarce because group categorization is not included in data collection. Estimates of numbers vary: according to Gourévitch (2011), Muslims account for more than 10 percent of the population in France (mainly from North Africa, but also including local converts). In the UK the population with Muslim background is largely composed of immigrants and their descendants, from Bangladesh and Pakistan, together accounting for about 4.5 percent of the total population in 2011.

Extensive evidence shows socio-economic HIs strongly disadvantage Muslims across multiple dimensions – including housing, education, employment and incomes – in each country. Muslims mostly live in low-income areas of major cities. In the Netherlands, one survey found that more than half of Turks and more than 60 percent of Moroccans have an unskilled job, compared with less than 30 percent of native Dutch. There is evidence of discrimination in the labour market and the educational system ([SCP] 2005). The incomes of Moroccan men were found to be more than 40 percent below those of the native Dutch. Poverty rates among the elderly were found to be substantially higher than for native Dutch and education levels are significantly lower for the Muslim community – 40 percent of Turks and 45 percent of Moroccans had no more than primary education in 2006 (Demant et al. 2007).

In France, educational attainments are also worse for the Muslim population than the native population, with more repeat years, higher dropout rates, lower attainments in examinations, less attendance at high school and fewer diplomas. According to a report on Muslims in the EU, French Muslims had higher unemployment than native French and more difficulties in finding long-term, fulltime employment (Viprey 2002).

In Britain, deprivations have been extensively documented by the Equality Commission Review (Equalities Commission 2007). As they state:

> The emergence of British Muslims as a group who are widely recognised to be systematically disadvantaged predates any concern about security. Muslims account for a disproportionate number of people living in areas of multiple deprivation: more than two in three Bangladeshis and more than half of all Pakistanis live in areas in the bottom decile for deprivation.
>
> (Equality Commission Review 2007: 35)

In more detail, the Equality Commission Review notes that the net earnings of Bangladeshi males were reported as just half those of white males (p. 25; Interim Report) and deprivation is evident in education at every level of education. For example, Pakistani and Bangladeshi rates of attainments in language and literacy at an early age were 57 percent of those of whites; their achievement of 5-GSEs was three quarters of that of whites for boys and a bit higher for girls; and they were underrepresented in higher education. However, there is evidence of some catch-up in recent years (Sefton and Stewart 2009). Disadvantages are also reported with respect to health (Equality Commission Review 2007: 75).

There is cultural discrimination in each of the countries, with dress being a particular issue. For example, within schools in the Netherlands, there are frequent complaints about dress, especially the wearing of hijabs. In France too, the issue of the headscarf has created periodic controversy with schools expelling children for wearing them. There is less controversy on this in Britain, however. In all three counties,

## 86   *Frances Stewart*

national holidays are Christian or secular, with no Muslim holidays. There have been periodic cultural controversies – notably in the Netherlands with the murder of Theo van Gogh in 2004, who was making a film attacking Muslim practices.

Political inequalities are also in evidence. In the Netherlands, in 2015, there were no members of the cabinet with Muslim backgrounds (though there had been previously). There is underrepresentation in the police, with only 6 percent of the police in major cities having an immigrant background in 2005, although they account for about 30 percent of the population in the big cities (Demant et al. 2007). In France in 2015, there was just one member of the *Assemblée Nationale* with Muslim background and four senators, far less than proportionate to the population. At the cabinet level, the first Muslim minister was appointed in 2005, but the 2015 cabinet was much more representative with seven members from minorities. In the UK, the number of Muslim members of parliament has been growing, but still, in 2015, accounted for below 2 percent of the total. The 2015 cabinet included one person of Muslim background. Muslims are underrepresented in the judiciary and legal system. Similar political underrepresentation is to be seen throughout (Nielsen 2013).

While this evidence is drawn from just three countries in Europe, similar conclusions apply to other European countries, such as Germany, with its large and underprivileged Turkish population, and Denmark where the Muslim population has been subject to attack in a variety of ways, including from the infamous cartoons. In policy terms, however, a noteworthy exception is the Spanish Zapatero government which 'granted amnesty to a swathe of illegal (mainly Moroccan) immigrants in 2004 shortly after his election and the Madrid bombings.'[1]

### *HIs faced by Muslim communities in Asia*

Where Muslims consist of almost the entire population (Bangladesh and Pakistan), the issue of HIs relative to non-Muslims does not arise and these countries are not considered here; where Muslims are in a majority, as in Indonesia and Malaysia, political dominance can be used to advance their socio-economic position. The most problematic situation is where Muslims are in a minority and suffer consistent HIs across political, socio-economic and cultural status dimensions.

1   *Malaysia*. In Malaysia, the majority are Muslim (the Malay community and other indigenous groups) and account for around two-thirds of the population, while the Chinese (24 percent of

*Inequality and conflict* 87

the population) are mainly either Christian or Buddhist, and the Indian population (6.5 percent) are mainly Hindus, with sizeable Muslim and Christian minorities. There were large inequalities between groups when Malaysia became independent, with the Chinese far richer than Malays; these have been greatly reduced by comprehensive policies since the 1970s. Yet economic inequalities favouring non-Muslims still persist. Politically and culturally, however, Muslims dominate.

2   *Indonesia.* In Indonesia, Muslims account for over 85 percent of the population, with most of the remainder Christian. Muslim incomes, on average, are substantially below all other groups, apart from the small Hindu population, with incomes per head of Christians and Buddhists on average more than 50 percent greater according to the 1995 census. Given the political and demographic dominance of Muslims, these differences are normally not provocative – although there were attacks on the Chinese during the economic crisis of the late 1990s. Muslims have been politically dominant at the national level. In some areas of the archipelago where colonial Christianization took hold more strongly, Christian groups were dominant historically. Amid rapid and extensive decentralization in the post-Suharto era, competition for political and economic power at the local level fed into extensive Christian/Muslim violence in Ambon, North Maluku and Central Sulawesi (which also involved ethnic differences) (Diprose 2011).

3   *China.* There are very little data on the socio-economic position of Muslims in China who account for an estimated 1–2 percent of the total population or around 20 million people, in several ethnic groups, including Hui (largely Mandarin speaking), and Dongxiang and Uigur (Turkic speaking). It seems that Muslims are generally disadvantaged. Data on educational performance show relative disadvantage partly because of the increasing use of Mandarin in schools, with the extent varying among ethnic groups. The Uighur secondary attendance is reported to be about two-thirds of that of Chinese as a whole (Fischer 2014). Repression of political protests and cultural practices is often reported (e.g., see Foust 2010; Hayoun 2015).

4   *Philippines and Thailand.* The relative position of Muslims in the Philippines and Thailand is similar. Both form small minorities living in poor regions and facing relative deprivation within their regions as well as in the country as a whole. Muslims in the Philippines account for about 5 percent of the total population, but a much larger proportion in Mindanao region – around 20 percent

## 88 *Frances Stewart*

today (a sharp drop over the last 100 years largely due to immigration from the rest of the Philippines, encouraged by the state). Likewise, in Thailand, the Muslim population forms a small proportion of the total Thai population (4.6 percent), but a much larger proportion in the Southern region (28 percent in 2000) (Data from CIA and Brown 2008). In both cases, there has been violent opposition – stronger in the Philippines, more sporadic in Thailand – in which the rebels seek greater political autonomy.

In both countries, Philippines and Thailand, the Muslim populations are doubly disadvantaged Brown (2008): first, the regions in which they are located have lower per capita incomes (and growth rates) than the rest of the country; and second, within the region of concentration, the Muslim population does less well than the rest of the population. In the Philippines, incomes in Mindanao have been consistently below national average GDP per capita, while, within Mindanao, the five provinces in the autonomous region of Muslim Mindanao (ARRM) show the worst socio-economic performance in the Philippines (Brown 2008). In Thailand, the Southern region where the Muslim population is concentrated also shows worse economic performance than the rest of the country, while within Southern Thailand, Muslims are disadvantaged relative to the majority Buddhists. For example, in 1987 (the only year for which there are data of this kind), Buddhist males had 1.7 times total years' education of Muslim males (Brown 2008: 273).

### Muslim/non-Muslim HIs in West Africa

Like Asian countries, the demographic position of Muslims varies across West African countries. In some countries Muslims form a significant minority (Benin, Cameroon, Côte d'Ivoire and Ghana), in Nigeria they account for about half the population and in Niger and Mali they dominate the population. In general Muslims are concentrated in the north of each country, so that data on regional inequalities give some guide to Muslim/other HIs.

In the case of Côte d'Ivoire, Ghana and Nigeria, all socio-economic indicators are worse in the four regions in the north where Muslims are concentrated. However, in Benin, while education indicators are worse than the national average in all four northern regions than the national average, and income per head is worse in three, life expectancy is as good or better, possibly reflecting lower rates of HIV/ AIDs among Muslim populations. Data on height differences show

*Inequality and conflict* 89

Northern disadvantage in Cameroon, Chad and Côte d'Ivoire (Moradi and Baten 2005).

While there is generally economic and social disadvantage among Muslims, the situation with respect to political and cultural status varies markedly with demography, as well as national attitudes and practices. In the majority states, Muslim cultural and political status is generally good. But there is considerable variation elsewhere. For example, in Ghana there is a culture of inclusion politically and in relation to general status; but in Côte d'Ivoire, northerners were excluded politically and culturally – indeed this is thought to be a major reason for the outbreak of civil war in 2002 (Langer 2005).

## Inequalities between countries

The evidence thus shows systematic HIs in which Muslims are relatively deprived within countries in much of the world. There is also evidence that Muslim countries (those where Muslims form the majority) are less well off at a global level than non-Muslim ones, in socioeconomic, cultural and political terms.

If we take all countries in which Muslims account for more than 50 percent of the population and contrast them with all countries where other religions (or non-religions) dominate, including Christians, Hindus, Buddhists and secularists, there is a clear and large gap favouring non-Muslims. While Muslim countries form around 20 percent of world population, they account for about 8 percent of world net national income. There are, of course, very big differences within each of these categories: for example, many poor countries are in the non-Muslim group (e.g. Malawi, Nepal, Bolivia), and there are some economically successful countries in the Muslim group (such as Malaysia, Kuwait, Saudi Arabia and Turkey). However, the proportion of countries in the low-income and low human development categories in relation to all countries in that category is much higher than the proportion of countries in medium or high categories (see Figure 5.1).

There is also an imbalance in political power. As indicators of this, Muslim countries have no permanent members on the Security Council; in 2016, they had three non-permanent members or one fifth of the total, while just over one quarter of the countries in the world have a Muslim majority. They account for only 12.8 percent of IMF Voting rights. In 2005 Muslim majority countries were estimated to account for about 8 percent of world military expenditure – in line with their share of world income. By these measures, there are evident political inequalities at a global level.

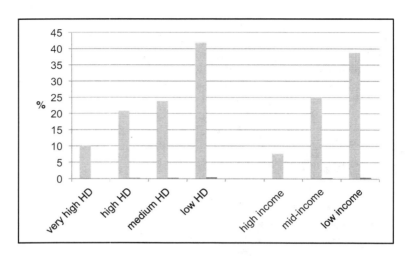

*Figure 5.1* No. of muslim majority countries as percent of total countries in category

Source: World Bank World Development Indicators and UNDO, Human Development Report; and CIA World Fact book for estimates of religious composition of populations

## Some implications of consistent and persistent global inequalities

As indicated previously, there is evidence of consistent deprivation of Muslims relative to others globally, within *and* between countries. Within particular countries, such inequalities can (and often) do underlie group mobilization, sometimes leading to violence, which can take the form of local disputes and violence (as in Indonesia and Nigeria), riots (as in India) or national conflict (as in Côte d'Ivoire).

The question is whether the systematic global nature of the inequalities has implications for global tensions and conflicts. An immediate negative response to this question arises from the many divisions within Islam, often leading to inter-Muslim conflicts as can be observed in Syria and Iraq. Besides sharp divisions between Shiites and Sunnis, there are differences between liberals and radicals, in history, economic activity, education, nationality and language. As (Sivan 2003: 25) notes, 'the movement as a whole . . . is made up of a plethora of groups, more or less structured, loosely coordinated . . . often overlapping.' To argue that there is a common identity would appear to give credence to those who jump from the fact of violence by a minority of

Muslims to the conclusion that all Muslims are potentially violent. Yet to argue the opposite: that there are many disparate groups whose only commonality – that they adhere to Islam – is irrelevant to global mobilization, is, perhaps, equally mistaken, and may lead to neglect of the underlying national and global inequalities that underlie global mobilization and conflict between the West and Islam. An analogy may be drawn from national situations: clearly, the majority of northerners in Nigeria do *not* adhere to the Boko Haram violent movement. Yet the Boko Haram movement is drawn from the northern population, and it is the conditions and inequalities faced by the northern population as a whole which provide a powerful incentive for such mobilization.

The theological basis for global identity among Muslims is the *Ummah*, or the idea of an indivisible community of the faithful. As (Schmidt 2004: 41) states, '[t]he idea of the *Ummah* . . . is not a materialized homeland that one may look up on a map. Rather we are dealing with a mythological homeland that is both nowhere and everywhere offering membership across national boundaries.' The many global connections within this mythical community supports the idea that the pain felt in one area can be reflected in mobilization in others (Stewart 2010a).

The nature of global connections among Muslims across the world is illustrated in Figure 5.2. Connections include family connections, involving a range of communications, marriages and remittances; education and training, in which people travel globally to Asia, the Middle East and to Europe to attend a variety of educational institutions; financial connections (outside the family ones), with finance (and aid) crossing borders, much going from the Middle East, notably Saudi Arabia and Kuwait, to developing countries; the Hajj pilgrimage which takes millions to Mecca; global civil (including religious) and political institutions; and, most recently, media and internet connections.[2] While all these connections enhance a shared Muslim identity, the connections are multi-layered, and the links occur among different groups of people, according to context – including, importantly, differences among religious subsets of Islam – Sunnis, Shia, different *madhabs* within them, Sufism and different Sufi orders, liberals and radicals, and so on;[3] as well as according to differences in economic activities and interests, needs and education. The connections are neither unidirectional nor monolithic. Nonetheless, together, the links are very large in number – some of which touch most Muslims in one way or another.

An example of some of the multiple connections in relation to one person's experience is provided by an article by Tahir Abbas, a British

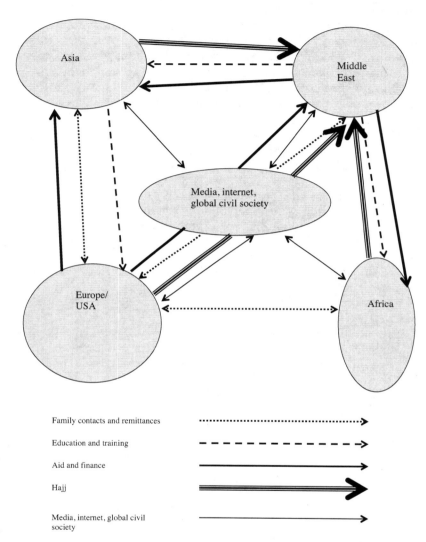

*Figure 5.2* A depiction of global connections among muslims
Source: Derived from Stewart (2010a)

Muslim, reporting on interviews with Moazzam Begg, a second generation British Muslim with a middle-class background, who had been detained in Guantanamo Bay (Abbas 2007, reported on in more detail in Stewart 2010a). Abbas argued that 'exclusion, marginalisation, disempowerment, media bias, political rhetoric, far right hostility,

Inequality and conflict   93

perceptions in relation to British and US foreign policy, a lack of appropriate Muslim leadership in Britain and a regressive interpretation of Islam' accounted for Moazzam's radicalism (Abbas 2007: 430). Moazzam started to look to Islam 'to get rid of the cultural baggage' (Abbas 2007: 432). He 'felt a great affinity towards' Bosnian Muslims (433). In the 1990s he travelled to Bosnia frequently, and gave money to the Bosnian army. After MI5 raided his London bookshop and he married a Pakistani woman, he moved to Afghanistan and financed and built a school just before 9/11. When asked about the London bombings, although he felt 'The targeting of individual is wrong and it shouldn't happen. . . . The overriding factor of the occupation in Iraq and Afghanistan was enough to spur them on to do what they did . . . it was this idea that it is all one and the same: the struggle in Afghanistan and Iraq and even Britain, that it's all connected.' (Abbas 2007: 436, my italics). Moazzam's story is replicated many times (see for example Husain 2007).

The manifold global connections linking Muslims across countries make it likely that grievances in one place will be felt elsewhere – 'it's all connected' as Moazzam stated. Global horizontal inequalities within and between countries among a particular, if loosely defined, identity group can be a cause of both global and national conflict, as seems to be the case today. It is because the inequalities are between a group defined by its culture and religion that such an identity can become a vehicle for mobilization, both of the group itself, and of others who mobilize *against* the group.

While we have illustrated this with the contemporary Muslim example, it is by no means unique. Historically, Christian attacks on Muslims date back to the Crusades and before, while some global groups have been attacked for their relative riches, such as Jews and the Lebanese traders. Some have long been attacked for their poverty, such as the Roma people. These global inequalities and tensions cannot be solved by purely national action as they require a reduction in inequalities at every level where they manifest themselves: in the case of contemporary Islam, inequalities within developed countries, within developing countries and between countries are all needed to reduce potential conflict. Moreover, this action needs to be addressed towards political and cultural inequalities as well as socio-economic inequalities.

## Conclusions

Globalisation has, of course, increased the influence of global factors on national developments. There are many direct ways in which global flows and actions affect conflict: for example, by providing finance

94    *Frances Stewart*

and arms to conflicting parties. However, this chapter is concerned with a more indirect influence – that is the extent to which globalisation affects inequalities which then raise the risks of conflict. The chapter has focused on horizontal inequalities because these, and not vertical inequalities, have been shown to raise the likelihood of violent conflict. While there has been considerable study of whether and how globalisation affects vertical inequality, very little work has been conducted on the influence over horizontal inequality. Here we argue that the origins of many HIs lie in global connections, in particular in colonialism. And modern global forces tend to contribute to the perpetuation and increase in these inequalities by privileging groups and regions that are wealthier and more educated, as against poor groups and regions. Conscious national policy is needed to offset these effects through deliberate targeting of poorer groups for improvements in access to education and health and employment and other economic opportunities. Apart from the global influences over national HIs, globally dispersed groups with a common identity can face global HIs which, in turn, may lead to global tensions and conflicts. This chapter illustrated this with the example of globally dispersed Muslims. While fully accepting that there is no single homogeneous Muslim community, the chapter argues that the identity is sufficiently shared globally such that global inequalities within particular nations and between them are felt not only by those immediately affected by them, but also by the wider community.

We briefly reviewed some empirical evidence showing that Muslims suffer relative deprivation in countries across the world, except where they form the great majority. This includes developed as well as developing countries. Moreover, taking Muslim countries in aggregate they also are less well off than non-Muslim countries, on average, in multiple dimensions. The many connections between people across the world – through families, remittances, pilgrimage and the media – mean that deprivation in one place can motivate people in other places. Hence to reduce global tensions, including terrorism, systematic action is needed globally to reduce these inequalities, as much in developed countries as in developing countries. The story is not unique to Muslims: Christians, Jews, the Lebanese, the Chinese diaspora and Roma people also confront HIs globally, which historically has also led to violent confrontation; in some cases the poorer groups attack the more privileged and in some the reverse obtains. It should be emphasized that these groups do not necessarily self-identify as a group, but are often identified as such by the other. In each of the cases cited, there is a strong element of outside identification, leading to stronger defensive identity by the targeted group.

*Inequality and conflict* 95

At the heart, as with national conflicts and identities, the issue is not one of identity difference as such, but of identity difference combined with inequalities – that is horizontal inequalities. The conclusion – which appears trite but is critical – is that peaceful existence requires inclusive societies with minimal inequalities across groups.

## Notes

1 Personal communication from Mansoob Murshed.
2 For evidence of the magnitude of these connections, see Stewart, F. (2010a). Global aspects and implications of horizontal inequalities: Inequalities experienced by Muslims worldwide. *Global Governance, Poverty and Inequality*. J. Clapp and R. Wilkinson. London, Routledge: 265–294.
3 See e.g. Sivan, E. (2003). "The clash within Islam." *Survival* 45(1): 24–44, who discusses the divisions between radical Islam and liberals.

## Bibliography

Abbas, T. (2007). "Ethno-religious identities and Islamic political radicalism in the UK: A case study." *Journal of Muslim Minority Affairs* 27(3): 429–442.

Akindès, F. (2007). *Mobilisation identitaire, inégalités horizontals et sociohistoire de la violence politique en Côte d'Ivoire*. Oxford, CRISE.

Barrows, W. L. (1976). "Ethnic diversity and political instability in black Africa." *Comparative Political Studies* 9(2): 139–170.

Brown, G. (2008). Horizontal inequalities and separatism in Southeast Asia: A comparative perspective. *Horizontal Inequalities and Conflict: Understanding Group Violence in Multiethnic Societies*. F. Stewart. London, Palgrave: 252–284.

Brown, M. E., S. Ganguly, Belfer Center for Science and International Affairs, Georgetown University, Center for Peace and Security Studies and Pacific Basin Research Center (2003). *Fighting Words: Language Policy and Ethnic Relations in Asia*. Cambridge, MA, London, MIT Press.

Cederman, L.-E., K. S. Gleditsch and H. Buhaug (2013). *Inequality, Grievances, and Civil War*. New York, Cambridge University Press.

Cederman, L.-E., N. B. Weidmann and N.-C. Bormann (2015). "Triangulating horizontal inequalty: Toward omproved conflict analysis." *Journal of Peace Research* 52(6): 806–821.

Cederman, L.-E., N. B. Weidmann and K. S. Gleditsch (2011). "Horizontal inequalities and ethno-nationalist civil war: A global comparison." *American Political Science Review* 105(3): 478–495.

Cohen, A. (1974). *Two-Dimensional Man: An Essay on the Anthropology of Power and Symbolism in Complex Society*. Berkeley, University of California Press.

Collier, P. and A. Hoeffler (2004). "Greed and grievance in civil war." *Oxford Economic Papers* 56(4).

96  *Frances Stewart*

Cramer, C. (2003). "Does inequality cause conflict?" *Journal of International Development* 15(4): 397–412.

Demant, F., M. Maussen and J. Rath (2007). The Netherlands: Preliminary research report and literature survey. O. S. I. Series on Muslims in the EU: Cities Report, EU Monitoring and Advocacy Program.

de Tocqueville, A. (1835). *Democracy in America.* 1954 edition. Vintage Books, New York.

Diprose, R. (2011). A comparison of communal conflict dynamics and sub-national patterns of violence in Indonesia and Nigeria: Central Sulawesi and Kaduna State. D.Phil., Oxford.

Elon, A. (2002). *The Pity of It All: A Portrait of German Jews, 1743–1933.* New York, Metropolitan Books.

Equalities Commission (2007). Fairness and freedom: The final report of the equalities review. London.

Fearon, J. D. and D. D. Laitin (1996). "Explaining interethnic cooperation." *American Political Science Review* 90(4): 75–90.

Fearon, J. D. and D. D. Laitin (2000). *Ethnicity, Insurgency and Civil War.* Stanford, CA, Department of Political Science, Stanford University.

Fischer, A. M. (2014). *The Disempowered Development of Tibet in China: A Study in the Economics of Marginalization.* Lexington, Rowman and Littlefield.

Foust, J. (2010). Terrorism in China. Need to Know on PBS. www.pbs.org/wnet/need-to-know/opinion/terrorism-in-china/3050/ (accessed January 1st 2015).

Gibney, M. (2008). Who should be included? Noncitizens, conflict and the constitution of the citizenry. *Horizontal Inequalities and Conflict: Understanding Group Violence in Multiethnic Societies.* F. Stewart. London, Palgrave.

Gourevitch, J.-P. (1998). *We Wish to Inform You That Tomorrow We Will Be Killed with Our Families: Stories from Rwanda.* New York, Farrar, Straus and Giroux.

Gourévitch, J.-P. (2011). *La croisade islamiste.* Paris, Pascal Galodé.

Hayoun, M. (2015). "China to 'promote its represseion of Uighurs' at Shanghai meeting." *The Independent.* London, www.independent.co.uk/news/world/china-to-promote-its-repression-of-uighurs-at-shanghai-group-meeting-a6773386.htm (accessed January 1st 2016).

Husain, E. (2007). *The Islamist: Why I Joined Radical Islam in Britain, What I Saw Inside and Why I Left.* London, Penguin.

IPCC (2014). Climate Change 2014: Synthesis Report. Geneva.

Langer, A. (2005). "Horizontal inequalities and violent group mobilisation in Cote d'Ivoire." *Oxford Development Studies* 33(1): 25–45.

Lichbach, M. I. (1989). "An evaluation of 'Does economic inequality breed political conflict?' studies." *World Politics* 41(4): 431–470.

Mancini, L. (2008). Horizontal inequality and communal violence: Evidence from Indonesian districts. *Horizontal Inequalities and Conflict: Understanding Group Violence in Multiethnic Societies.* F. Stewart. London, Palgrave: 106–135.

Moradi, A. and J. Baten (2005). "Inequality in Sub-Saharan Africa: New data and new insights from anthropometric estimates." *World Development* 33(8): 1233–1265.

Murshed, S. M. and S. Gates (2005). "Spatial-horizontal inequality and the maoist insurgency in Nepal." *Review of Development Economics* 9(1): 121–134.

Nielsen, J., Ed. (2013). *Muslim Political Participation in Europe.* Edinburgh, Edinburgh University Press.

Østby, G. (2008a). Inequalities, the political environment and civil conflict: Evidence from 55 countries. *Horizontal Inequalities and Conflict: Understanding Group Violence in Multiethnic Societies.* F. Stewart. London, Palgrave.

Østby, G. (2008b). "Polarization, horizontal inequalities and violent civil conflict." *Journal of Peace Research* 45(2): 143–162.

Perera, S. (2001). The ethnic conflict in Sri Lanka: A historical and sociopolitical outline. Background Paper. World Bank.

Schmidt, G. (2004). "Islamic identity formation among young Muslims: The case of Denmark, Sweden and the United States." *Journal of Muslim Minority Affairs* 24(1): 31–45.

[SCP], S. a. C. P. O. o. t. N. (2005). Jaarrapport integratie (integration annual report). The Hague, Sociaal en Cultureel Planbureau.

Sefton, T. and K. Stewart (2009). *Towards a More Equal Society?: Poverty, Inequality and Policy since 1997.* Bristol, Policy Press in association with the Joseph Rowntree Foundation.

Sivan, E. (2003). "The clash within Islam." *Survival* 45(1): 24–44.

Stewart, F. (2001). Horizontal inequalities as a source of conflict. *From Reaction to Prevention.* F. Hampson and D. Malone. London, Lynne Rienner.

Stewart, F. (2010a). Global aspects and implications of horizontal inequalities: Inequalities experienced by Muslims worldwide. *Global Governance, Poverty and Inequality.* J. Clapp and R. Wilkinson. London, Routledge: 265–294.

Stewart, F. (2010b). "Horizontal inequalities in Kenya and the political disturbances of 2008: Some implications for aid policy." *Conflict, Security and Development* 10(1): 133–159.

Stewart, F. and A. Langer (2008). Horizontal Inequalities: Explaining persistence and change. *Horizontal Inequalities and Conflict: Understanding Group Violence in Multiethnic Societies.* F. Stewart. London, Palgrave: 54–78.

Ukoha, U. (2008). Horizontal inequalities and ethnic violence: Evidence from Calabar and Warri, Nigeria. *Horizontal Inequalites and Conflict: Understanding Group Violence in Multiethnic Societies.* F. Stewart. London, Palgrave: 190–204.

Viprey, M. (2002). "L'Insertion des Jeunes d'Origine Étrangère." *Etude du Conseil Economique et Social, Editions des Journaux Officiels.*

# 6 Economic policy and human rights

## Is globalisation a meeting ground?

*Rajeev Malhotra*

The second half of the 20th century has witnessed rapid economic integration and globalisation of nations, along with gradual spread of political democratisation across the world. This process has been facilitated by unprecedented capital mobility, and by information and technology flows that are mutually reinforcing and are advancing in tandem. In recent times, it has also supported a globally widespread, real-time, people-to-people connection. Globalisation, in its economic facet, has resulted in the integration of commodity, capital and (to a lesser extent) labour markets and, in its social and political facet, led to a steady emergence of participatory polity and a momentum towards homogenisation of urban culture across nations. Indeed, these trends feed on each other, supporting and thriving on liberal ethos and appear irreversible in most parts of the world.[1] However, the progress in these trends has neither been linear, nor has the impact on people and communities been uniform. This issue has been extensively analysed for its complexity, using cross-disciplinary perspectives, and is well documented.[2]

Globalisation has created unprecedented opportunities for large populations to improve their material wellbeing. It has supported an extended run of global economic expansion and created conditions for millions in Asia, Latin America and Africa to be lifted out of abject poverty. At the same time, it has also brought economic disruption and hardship to many in different parts of the world, particularly since the 1990s. Indeed, in the post-global financial crisis period, the discontent with economic consequences of globalisation has visibly spilled over to the social and the political arena, resulting in popular backlash extending from Asia to Europe and now even in North America. People are questioning not only the future of globalisation, but that of liberal democracy as well. An anti-market protest has acquired strong nationalist voice against the run of free trade and open borders (see, for instance, Berezin 2015, 2013).[3] There is public clamour for equality, opportunities, entitlements, rights and above all accountability of the state. Importantly, it is posing a challenge for the policymakers to explore fresh grounds and identify sustainable solutions to this predicament and, more generally, to the choice of the desired path to development transformation and sustaining progress, for the development latecomers and the industrialised countries, respectively.

This chapter explores the contours of a meaningful and an effective policy response, at the national level, in the current global economic milieu. It argues that such a response has to be necessarily based on a thinking that consciously departs from economic orthodoxy or the economic mainstream (as commonly understood), as it has fallen short in delivering the desired social outcomes, in the developing as well as the industrialised world. This is despite the considerable leeway and the run it has had in guiding economic policies over the past decades. Furthermore, it is not enough to visualise heterodox economic theory and practice as a mere application of a well-healed orthodoxy, tinkered just sufficiently to address the uniqueness of a context. Rather, it is essential that heterodox economic policy prescription for social problems has its own normative basis, just as it is necessary for that prescription to be strictly evidence-based. The international human rights framework is one such normative basis that could explicitly underpin economic policy heterodoxy in the pursuit of inclusive development and sustained progress. While building on the strengths of market liberalism, the desired policy prescription could benefit from the idea of universalism and individualism,[4] emanating from the constitutive notion and principles of human rights.

Following this introduction, the second section reflects on the inevitability of human rights discourse in taking centre stage in rethinking economic policy for the contemporary globalised world. It discusses the normative and instrumental relevance of human rights in shaping an approach to economic heterodoxy. The third section outlines how human rights norms and standards could be integrated and benchmarked into economic policy options, followed by an attempt to describe the contours of a heterodox economic policy approach to address contemporary challenges in the developing and industrialised world. It describes the implications of that approach for improving country level policy framework, highlighting the macroeconomic policy imperatives for the process to yield acceptable and inclusive outcomes. This is followed by some concluding remarks.

# 100  *Rajeev Malhotra*

## Globalisation and internalisation of human rights values

### *Cross-border networks and social mobilisation*

Human rights embody values that are universal and in fact civilisational in nature, yet it would not be out of place to suggest that globalisation in its modern era, especially in the past two decades, has greatly contributed to the internationalisation and, importantly, to the internalisation of those values by people across the world. There is far greater awareness of human rights and its articulation among people and countries today than ever before in human history. Indeed, human rights have acquired a vital role in the normative guidance of social action across all aspect of human life. The nature of the globalisation process and the outcomes it has generated have both contributed to this improved understanding and application of international human rights standards. This is true of most countries, irrespective of their level of development or attainments on education and social awareness.

The advent of social media and improved access to internet connectivity has multiplied the flow of, and access to, information across national boundaries. It has contributed to an unprecedented people-to-people connect and strengthening of cross-border networks. This has given rise to situations, for instance in the context of the 'Arab spring' and its spillover in some parts of Asia, where people have drawn inspiration and sustenance from each other to come together to give effect to major (previously unthought-of) changes in their societies, although with mixed results. These changes have invariably sought to embrace liberal democratic governance, founded on the ideals of liberty, equality and free enterprise, for improved human wellbeing. Furthermore, the stark images of a war ravaged society, civil strife, hunger and destitution from countries and regions, which are otherwise of little consequence to people and nations in faraway lands (or to the global markets), has invariably evoked a sense of solidarity across the world for preserving human dignity of the affected people. This has encouraged an effective articulation and social mobilisation of the people for the promotion and protection of human rights. Thus, the process of globalisation, as it has unfolded, has led to an overwhelming claim for universal values and norms to anchor and guide policies for social, political and economic change, while meeting the concerns and rising aspirations of people. This is true of people in the developing and the industrialised world and at national and international

*Economic policy and human rights* 101

levels. Alex de Waal's (World Peace Foundation, Tufts University) suggestion that human rights have become the global religion of today is, perhaps, not too far of the mark.

## Rising inequality in economic outcomes and opportunities

The current era of globalisation with its reliance on free markets and characterised by rising average prosperity levels, costless communications, cross-border networks and global footloose capital, has contributed to a shift of power from the state to the people and non-state actors. Yet, it has also resulted in deterioration in inequality of outcomes and opportunity, especially with the economic downturn in the late 1990s (East Asian currency crisis) and, more significantly, post-2008. The growing inequality has fuelled discontent among people and regions that were excluded from the markets and hence were unable to harness the benefits from rapid economic expansion. Indeed, the experience reinforces a belief that market liberalism is not necessarily an inclusive approach to pursue development, particularly so in a globalising world. It is limited by its (largely) market-mediated reach, the accompanying (undesirable) externalities that escape regulatory attention or capacity and affect the poor disproportionately, and increased volatility due to exposure to international contagion risks from multiple channels of cross-border engagement. An excessive reliance on a free-market approach, with its dogmatic focus on efficiency, a non-negotiable requirement of minimal returns for investors in the short term, and an unhealthy appetite for risk-taking, invariably overlooks the importance of addressing structural impediments to trickle-down for the benefit of the marginalised and the vulnerable segments in an economy.[5]

The growing inequality in outcomes and opportunities is a reality of the current times both in the advanced economies and emerging markets and developing countries (EMDCs).[6] Outcome inequality ranges between 0.55 and 0.70, depending on the measure used (reported in Dabla-Norris et al. 2015, based on International Monetary Fund [IMF] Staff estimation). The most common measure of outcome inequality is income inequality tracked through Gini coefficient in gross or net terms (after tax and social transfers), or in terms of income shares accruing to different population segments (by decile/quintile or social/regional groups). Inequality in wealth (assets held by an individual), which complements income inequality is another outcome measure of (monetary) inequality. Inequality of opportunities is generally measured through access of people to basic services (civic amenities, social

102  *Rajeev Malhotra*

services and access to financial services) and opportunities to liveli-hood, or by tracking health, education and human development out-comes by income or social/regional groups.

In the advanced economies, the gap between the rich and the poor in terms of outcome inequality is at its highest level in decades. The top 1 percent now account for around 10 percent of the total income in those economies. This growing share of the top 1 percent in advanced economies reflects both higher inequality in labour incomes as well as a larger share of income (returns) from investments (Alvaredo et al. 2013; Atkinson et al. 2011). Inequality based on Gini coefficients (for gross and net incomes) have increased for most of the advanced econo-mies and, although stable in the EMDCs, they are at a much higher level and exhibit large disparities across EMDCs. The rising income inequality is a result of the top 10 percent now having an income close to nine times that of the bottom 10 percent in the advanced economies, and a shift in the income of the 'upper-middle class' to the 'upper class' in those EMDCs where income inequality has deteriorated (Dabla-Norris et al. 2015). At the same time, while there has been a sharp decline in the poverty incidence (share of population living below a predefined poverty line) in EMDCs (led by China and India), the advanced economies have experienced a rise in poverty incidence since the 1990s (OECD 2011; Dabla-Norris et al. 2015).

Furthermore, inequality is more extreme in wealth (value of finan-cial and real estate assets net of liabilities) than income. On an average, the income Ginis are half of the Ginis for wealth, in both advanced economies and EMDCs. Indeed, almost half of the world's wealth, amounting to $110 trillion, is now owned by just 1 percent of the population and it is sixty-five times the total wealth of the bottom half of the world's population (Fuentes and Galasso 2014). Globally, just eight billionaires have the same wealth as the poorest 50 percent of the world (Oxfam 2017). In most countries where data are avail-able, the share held by the 1 percent wealthiest population is rising at the expense of the bottom 90 percent population (Dabla-Norris et al. 2015; OECD 2011). In the case of India, wealth distribution is more skewed, with the top 1 percent now holding 58 percent of the country's total wealth, and fifty-seven billionaires have a wealth ($216 billion) equivalent to the bottom 70 percent of the population. Stagnancy or slow growth in wages is preventing the middle and lower income earn-ers to improve their savings, and rising wealth concentration at the top end of the income distribution, coupled with a lower propensity to consume by the rich, explains the growing wealth inequality (Piketty 2014). The incomes of the poorest 10 percent of people increased by

*Economic policy and human rights* 103

less than $3 a year between 1988 and 2011, while the incomes of the richest 1 percent increased 182 times as much. In the case of the US, over the last 30 years the growth in the incomes of the bottom 50 percent has been zero, whereas incomes of the top 1 percent have grown 300 percent (reported in Oxfam 2017).

Unlike outcome inequality, which is more or less stable, inequality in opportunities exhibit deteriorating trends and wide variations across EMDCs. This is contrary to advanced economies where, as noted, the outcome inequality is worsening but inequality in opportunities is broadly similar across income groups. For instance, health attainments on infant mortality are twice as high for the poor than the rich households and female mortality rates are disproportionately higher for the lower income group in the EMDCs, while they are broadly similar across income groups in advanced economies. Similarly, use of and access to health care is favourable across income groups in most advanced economies, but there is large disparity across income levels in developing countries and to a lesser extent in emerging economies. This is not to say all is well in the advanced economies. Access to health care is an issue in the US, and the long waiting period to access public health care facilities in the UK is well known. In respect of education inequality, although education Gini (measure of variation in average years of education for different income levels) has declined considerably in EMDCs with improvement in access to schooling for children at lower income end, the education outcomes remain poor for the disadvantaged population groups. The education inequality in advanced economies is significantly lower and has remained unchanged for the decade since 2000 after a decline in the preceding two decades. Disparities in access to financial services exhibit a similar trend across the advanced economies and EMDCs. Not only are there significant differences in the access to financial services across income groups within countries, but the access in advanced economies (80 percent of adults have an account with a formal financial institution) is more than twice that in EMDCs.[7]

This rising inequality in outcomes and opportunity, including for livelihoods, is at the heart of social resentment and discontent. It is a major threat to the sustenance of a liberal economic and political thinking in the medium to long term. The message from recent developments in different parts of the world is that people living in the margins of a market economy, vulnerable to the volatility in economic activity that has accompanied globalisation, are not prepared to wait indefinitely for the trickle down to alleviate their hardship. This is very much true of the developing world, where, in addition, the currently underway demographic transition has resulted in a relatively

## 104  *Rajeev Malhotra*

large pool of the young in the labour force. They are not only restless but also without any ideological baggage of the one or the other kind in demanding the desired social outcomes. They want a quick remedy to their predicament. They want the outcomes of the globalisation process to be sufficiently altered to meet their legitimate aspirations. This makes it necessary to undertake a serious review of the liberal economic underpinnings (the hands-off approach) of the globalisation process and tempering the scope of its influence with the human-centric values, principles and policies.

### *Globalisation and democratisation of governance*

There is another aspect of the current international context that encourages a reliance on human rights discourse in the normative guidance of the globalisation process. This relates to the gradual democratisation of the polity across nations that has accompanied globalisation since World War II. The democratisation of societies has been a human aspiration and an electoral democracy is seen among the best governance options for building the (state) capacity to steer, deliver and sustain human wellbeing.[8] In its 1999 Freedom in the World Survey, Freedom House reported that, in 1900, no country could claim full universal suffrage or regular elections, and only 5 percent of the world's people were able to vote on their leaders. By 1990, this count had grown to 69 countries and 64 percent of the world's people. Since then around 49 new members have been added to the world democratic community to reach a total of 118 in 2013.[9]

Electoral democracies have empowered local stakeholders, including the media and introduced a narrative in the public discourse, which, along with the unifying and aspirational influences of globalisation, make a case for use of human-centric values to guide the process of social transformation and progress. A common ethos that draws upon the human rights normative framework and the human rights obligations of the states (party to international human rights instruments) links the democratic communities across the world. This is notwithstanding the fact that electoral democracies may not necessarily ensure equally the rights and freedoms for all its people or at the same level over time (Freedom House 2016).[10]

The challenge is to translate the human rights narrative for an operational guidance of economic policy. This entails a departure from economic orthodoxy to address the consequences of the globalisation process and, more generally, to provide an approach to social transformation and sustaining progress in the developing and the industrialised world.

## Moving away from orthodox economic policy

Unlike mainstream economics, a move towards economic heterodoxy has to be necessarily anchored in the economic reality of the times. The underlying assumptions of mainstream economic theory are merely a 'blackboard' construct. They reflect, at best, only an outlier situation, applicable to a sector or two, or to limited aspects of a market, where the extant policy framework is able to create the required conditions for competition to thrive (e.g., the aviation or telecom industry currently in an emerging market economy like India or banking and insurance industry in some industrialised countries). To extend the assumption of competitive markets to an economy at large (especially for a developing country) is reckless. It also puts the policy prescription of mainstream economic thinking, howsoever limited in scope (by definition), to a disadvantage even before its application. In the real economy, not only are the economic agents non-atomistic, but they behave strategically and are invariably influenced in their conduct by social norms and beliefs. Indeed, there is a constant moral dilemma that arises from a conflict between individual interest and the interest of society. Therefore, the underlying precept of mainstream economics that the pursuit of self-interest (Adam Smith's 'invisible hand'), with only a minimal state presence, would lead to socially optimal outcome is an oversimplification, far from the reality. This 'godless' and 'stateless' view of the working of an economic system is, perhaps, a major reason for the rising inequality in outcomes and opportunities witnessed in recent decades in a free-market mediated globalisation process (see, for instance, Basu 2011, especially Chapter 3, for a lucid critique of mainstream economics). Furthermore, the attempts to relax the assumptions of a competitive market and model the behaviour of economic agents more realistically are desirable steps in the right direction, but they do not, as yet, provide a macro framework for policy guidance that could arrest the eroding appeal and relevance of economic orthodoxy in the contemporary global context.

There are good reasons to believe that a more equitable and just society than the one we live in at present is feasible (see, for instance, Schumacher 1974). That an appropriate application of norms and institutions can align the individual interests and the resulting behaviour of economic agents with the societal interests and goals.[11] Such an agenda requires policy heterodoxy to respond flexibly to the unique contexts, public concerns and aspirations. Importantly, it demands that the required heterodox economic thinking be anchored in an undisputed normative guidance, which lends a clear direction and predictability to

## 106    *Rajeev Malhotra*

policy action to sustain development and progress (see United Nations 2012a, 2012b). It also requires that the unique methodological tools and goals of heterodox economic policy framework be identified and applied for a normative guidance to support desired outcomes and opportunities at the ground level.

### *Building a normative basis for economic heterodoxy*

In the contemporary context of globalisation, for some of the reasons elaborated in the earlier section, a normative guidance for economic heterodoxy can be effectively derived from the international human rights standards. Human rights are universal legal guarantees protecting individuals and groups against actions and omissions that interfere with fundamental freedoms, entitlements and human dignity.[12] The underlying feature of human rights is the identification of right-holders who, by virtue of being human, have a claim over certain entitlements, and duty-bearers, primarily the state (individually and collectively) which is legally bound to meet the entitlements associated with those claims. Thus, in invoking rights it is not only important to identify the elements that are considered to be entitlements, but also to specify the agents that have the duty to bring about the enjoyment of those entitlements (for a development perspective of human rights see, for instance, Sen 1999, pages 227–248). The human rights duty of the state includes the obligation to respect, protect and fulfil,[13] which could also be categorised as positive and negative obligations, or as the state obligation of conduct and results (see, for instance, United Nations 2012c, pages 10–13, for an elaboration of these concepts). In implementing its human rights obligations, a state is guided by certain principles of conduct, including promotion of non-discrimination and equality, ensuring stakeholder participation, accountability, and transparency and establishing access to remedy and rule of law. The human rights standards and the state obligations contribute to empower the voice of stakeholders in the process of undertaking social change, strengthen the foundations of social contract in the society and improve accountability of public agency in delivering development and good governance to its people (see, for instance, Malhotra 2015).[14]

Furthermore, besides human rights being state-centric, they are characterised as being universal (regardless of political, economic or cultural systems), inalienable (cannot be alienated from the person or group except with due process and in specific situations), interrelated/interdependent (improvement in realisation of any one right is a function of the realisation of some other human rights) and indivisible (all rights civil, cultural, economic, political and social rights are equally important). With these characteristics, human rights standards provide a normative basis for a comprehensive framework of social transformation and sustenance of progress, which is universal in its scope, and a strategy that includes a well-defined redress and accountability mechanisms.

The human rights normative framework, reflected in the provisions of core international human rights instruments and in UN Treaty Bodies elaborations is a narrative, which, as it is, may not be amenable to be incorporated in policy guidance. For human rights discourse to anchor the normative basis and provide instrumental guidance to a heterodox economic policy framework, there is a need for a language of rights that can be accessed and operated upon by policymakers – a language that is less prescriptive and legal, more concrete, accessible and practicable to a broader set of stakeholders, including policymakers and public service providers. Such a language requires a creative use of indicators, qualitative as well as quantitative. The identification of human rights indicators and their application for normative guidance including, for goal-setting, policy articulation, implementation and assessment, offers a potent means to mainstream human rights in economic policy. Importantly, it enables the human rights approach to transcend its absolutist (legal) interpretation, which requires rights to be implemented immediately and fully, to an approach that can work in a real-life context of limited resources and high opportunity costs associated with many social choices. In the latter case, human rights could be seen as aspirational ideals that can be visualised as legitimate objectives of public policy, some of which can be only progressively and partially met through direct state action, but could be realised more comprehensively in the presence of supportive social ethos (see, for instance, Streeten 2003, 1980.) Of course, it could be argued that the state has a role in creating and sustaining the required social ethos for a fuller enjoyment of human rights in a society. Indeed, such a social ethos is the public good that a state must supply, along with other non-state stakeholders in a society.

## Human rights indicators – a normative and strategic anchor for economic policy

A human rights indicator is specific information on the state or condition of an object, event, activity or an outcome that can be related to human rights norms and standards; that addresses and reflects the human rights

## 108  *Rajeev Malhotra*

principles and concerns; and that can be used to assess and monitor the promotion and implementation of human rights.[15]

The framework for identifying and designing human rights indicators (developed by the author of this paper for the UN Office of the High Commissioner for Human Rights and reflected in United Nations 2012c; Malhotra 2013, 2015) builds a common approach to identify indicators for civil and political rights, as well as economic, social and cultural rights. For populating the identified indicators, it focuses on using information and data sets that are commonly available and based on standardised data generating mechanisms (such as official administrative statistics), which most states (party to human rights treaties and other international agreements) would find acceptable and administratively feasible to compile and follow.

The translation of the normative narrative into indicators is based on a two-part approach that includes identifying the attributes of a human right, followed by a cluster of indicators that unpack specific aspects of implementing the standard associated with those attributes. In most instances, the normative narrative of a human right standard can be reduced into a few attributes, such that they are mutually exclusive (to the extent feasible), based on an exhaustive reading of the normative narrative and collectively provide an essence of the content of the right. Attributes are universal in scope as they are derived from universal human rights standards. However, the cluster of indicators for an attribute of a right could be designed appropriately in a context specific manner. In the selection of indicators, the framework focuses on measuring three aspects: (1) the commitments of duty-bearers (mainly the state) to their human rights obligations; (2) the efforts they undertake in implementing those obligations in the form of policies and public programmes; and (3) the results of a duty-bearer's efforts in supporting the enjoyment of human rights by people. Consequently, the framework (see Figure 6.1) uses a cluster of indicators, namely *structural, process and outcome* indicators, or, in other words, *commitment, effort and result* indicators to measure the different facets of a duty-bearer's obligations in implementing the human rights standards.

A structural indicator captures the institutional context of enforcing or implementing a normative (human rights) standard or a policy initiative emanating therefrom. It reflects the state commitment and intent to do the needful once it has accepted a normative standard to guide its policy conduct. Process indicators measure the state's efforts to transform its normative commitments (to human rights) into desired results. A process indicator links state policy measures/instruments

*Economic policy and human rights* 109

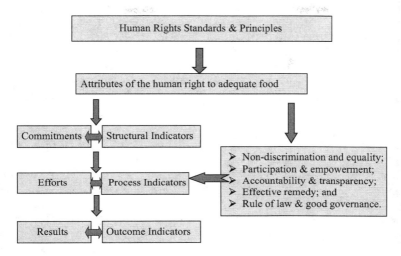

*Figure 6.1* Framework for identifying human rights indicators
Source: Author's work, also reflected in United Nations (2012c)

with milestones that consolidate over time into the desired (human rights) outcomes. By defining the process indicators in terms of an implicit 'cause and effect relationship' and as a 'monitorable intermediate' between commitments and results, the conduct of the process and accountability of a state (for its human rights obligations) can be better assessed. An outcome indicator captures attainment, individual and collective, which captures the enjoyment of accepted normative (human rights) standards in a given context. Indeed, it reflects the consolidation of results from several processes, not all of which may be directly captured by process indicators or be state directed or supported. It is sometimes helpful to view the process and outcome indicators as 'flow' and 'stock' variables, respectively. An outcome indicator being more of a stock variable is often slow moving and less sensitive to capture momentary changes than a process indicator. However, it reflects the sense of wellbeing that an individual enjoys as a result of the underlying (public) action more comprehensively.

The idea of quantifying human rights standards is preposterous for some, especially among the human rights community. Notwithstanding the abstraction of reality, which is inherent in using indicators to quantifying rights (for that matter any event or information set), it is something that has to be accepted with a caveat for human rights to

## 110  *Rajeev Malhotra*

influence policymaking, normatively and instrumentally. The caveat is that human rights assessments cannot be reduced entirely to working with quantitative indicators, there is more to it that requires use of qualitative information and interrogation.

An approach to economic policy design, characterised by the use of structural, process and outcome indicators, embedded in universal human rights normative considerations, not only brings universal social norms and values into play, but also allows for a well-defined institutional context for policy implementation, and its accountability in attaining the desired results. In addition, by responding to the prevailing reality and local priorities for the desired social change, factored through deployment of context appropriate indicators, the said policy approach potentially improves upon the orthodox economic policy prescription. Furthermore, in shaping the contours of a heterodox policy framework, there is also a need for the policymaking process to adhere to human rights principles of non-discrimination and equality, participation, transparency and ensuring an access to remedy in the event of institutional failure in the course of policy design and its implementation. The approach to address some of these concerns through sectoral and macroeconomic policies is discussed in the following sections.

### Contours of heterodox economic policy

A heterodox economic policy that derives its normative basis from human rights standards, and seeks to mitigate inequalities in opportunities and outcomes, needs to necessarily target a context-driven, multiple, sector-specific objectives and follow a flexible macroeconomic policy (unlike a dogmatic orthodox approach), especially so in EMDCs. This could include a major role for fiscal policy in improving social attainments on education, health and environment, social protection, employment generation or on political and financial decentralisation.[16] It could also involve a deliberate use of credit policy as tool for engineering a structural transformation of the economy. In its economic role, the state then evolves from being a minimalist entity to a proactive enabler of social change. In addition, the policymaking and implementation process is characterised by some considerations that distinguish it from mainstream economic policy approach.

First, such a heterodox economic policy explicitly focuses on empowerment of stakeholders (individuals, communities and nations) and accountability of agencies responsible for public goods delivery (the state (individually and collectively), multilateral organisations

*Economic policy and human rights* 111

and civil society) through specific institutional and regulatory arrangements.[17] This may necessitate, for example, the creation of specific legal entitlements for some goods and services deemed necessary to enjoy a human right, and leveraging legal systems to provide redress and accountability in the event of a failure to supply those public goods and services.[18] The basic motivation behind the approach is to remove political, social, economic and bureaucratic barriers for inclusion of the marginalised segments of a society into the mainstream. It seeks to improve the current entitlements of the poor, and also the scope of their future exchange entitlements.[19] In doing so, the policy addresses the vital concerns of equity (fairness in the distribution of benefits from growth and development and access to opportunities), equality (in publicly guided social outcomes and under the rule of law) and non-discrimination (under prohibited grounds by law) in the access of people to the delivery of those goods. Indeed, a policy measure, by virtue of being embedded in a (human rights) legal framework, and, if effectively enforced, could rapidly alter those power relations and structural impediments of a decadent social order and entrenched behavioural dispositions (e.g., the caste system in India or entrenched discrimination on grounds of colour, sex, race or religion elsewhere) that are at the root of persisting inequalities and deprivation across different social groups in a society. This is of particular significance for those electoral democracies, which, due to their context and weakness (such as India with its inherent dependence on vote-bank politics, limitations of the first-past-the-post criterion in multi-cornered electoral contests and a protracted decision-making process) may not always quickly overcome the constraints imposed by its social order through a 'hands-off' orthodox economic policy prescription. A well-defined legal and institutional context for implementation of economic policies, in such cases, could address the structural impediments to social transformation (Malhotra 2015).

It is sometimes argued that implementation of policy measures to address inequality in outcomes and opportunities through creation of legal entitlements is resource intensive. The required public interventions, which besides expanding the bureaucracy, could undermine the fiscal balance and therefore the overall macroeconomic environment of an economy. However, this need not be the case if recourse to establishing legal entitlements is selective, the economic incentives for factor productivity improvement (including enterprise) are not unduly undermined and government's financial liabilities are allowed to expand only with its ability to raise resources in the least distortionary manner for the economy. The creation of new entitlements,

## 112   *Rajeev Malhotra*

particularly in the context of resource-constrained economies, have to be preceded by a revamping of publicly provided services to improve delivery efficiency, and have to be accompanied by a comprehensive rationalisation of extant subsidies and social transfers in the society. Moreover, by leveraging ICT-enabled technologies and an inclusive financial services infrastructure, such an approach need not be inherently statist and, therefore, inefficient.

At the same time, the working of economic policies can be made more effective by creating and enforcing resource-neutral legal entitlements, for instance, the right to information (under the control of public authorities) and formalisation of an identity instrument to improve an individual's access to public service delivery. Such measures go a long way in evolving a level playing field for the poor and marginalised and help in improving governance standards in a society. There is ample evidence to suggest that the poor are disproportionally impacted by corruption and are often denied the benefits of rule of law in practice. Rule of law and administration of justice is the cornerstone in speeding up the social and economic transformation of a society. Overcoming corruption requires transparency in administration, elimination of discretionary powers vested in or deliberately acquired by public officials, improved oversight systems, incisive investigations, time-bound adjudication and effective enforcement of law. All these measures could benefit from a human rights–based approach to economic policies for improving development delivery, governance and market enterprise.

Second, a heterodox economic policy prescription, embedded in human rights standards, seeks to create a coherent, broad-based policy focus on a set of contextually determined and prioritised issues. Indeed, because of interdependence and complementarities among rights (between and across the categories of economic social and cultural rights, and the civil and political rights), the enjoyment of human rights involves a process of co-realisation of all rights. It necessarily implies coordination and coherence across policies at the level of sector-specific interventions and a comprehensive and an inclusive treatment of issues at the level of policy agenda-setting. The issue is how does one prioritise the desired policy mix at the stage of policy articulation as well as in the course of its implementation. Although both these aspects beg a resolution that is essentially context and path dependent and, therefore, evidence based, the rights discourse offers some normative guidance to address these implicit trade-offs.

Two human rights principles, namely the principle of progressive realisation and principle of non-retrogression of a right, together provide a basis for a legitimate prioritisation of policy interventions

*Economic policy and human rights* 113

in the face of competing demands and limited resources. A progressive improvement in people's access to a basket of goods and services associated with (human rights consistent) policy objectives, even when undertaken in a phased manner, is acceptable so long as there is non-retrogression in the enjoyment of any rights, at any point of time. In other words nobody suffers an absolute decline in the enjoyment of a right even as there is improvement in the realisation of some other rights.[20] This is unlike the orthodox economic policy space, where efficiency considerations (related to desirability of having competitive markets, minimal government regulations and private ownership of resources) may invariably allow aggregate normative criteria to assess policy outcome/impact for one group of individuals to trump its consequences for another group of individuals, so long as the former group can benefit to a greater extent than the extent of loss suffered by the latter group.

Third, by virtue of being embedded in human rights standards there are some other considerations imposed on the policymaking process, such as stakeholder participation/consultation in the formulation and implementation of policy, transparency of the process undertaken and establishing a redress mechanism to address the risks and uncertainties associated with the implementation of a policy measure. All this creates an ethical and just basis for prioritising public interventions and, therefore, policy agenda-setting, even when there is a possibility for unequal consequences of policy measures for some people in a society.

Malhotra (2014) revisits the available evidence in India to present a case for a holistic and inclusive economic policy agenda to address social transformational objectives at a provincial (state) level. With development and progress being increasingly viewed as a process to secure broad-based notion of human wellbeing, policy agenda-setting and assessment of policy effectiveness requires consideration of multiple and differentiated human development outcomes. The study focuses on four dimensions of human wellbeing (namely livelihood opportunities, social equality and opportunities, access to civic amenities including connectivity (infrastructure) and law enforcement and administration of justice) to conceptualise and estimate a (public) Policy Effectiveness Index (PEI) for India. Although important, it largely excludes issues related to the quality of policymaking process, such as the efficiency of resource use, political consensus and commitment to reforms, extent of public participation in policymaking and its implementation, from the measurement matrix primarily on account of data limitations. Advancement in indicators (quantitative and, where feasible, quantified qualitative indicators) of different wellbeing

114 *Rajeev Malhotra*

dimensions included in the measure reflects progress in the availability of corresponding (relevant) public goods and, therefore, enables an inference on the effectiveness of underlying policies. A combination of mostly process and some outcome indicators is used to estimate the indices at different points of time between 1981 and 2011.

The analysis throws up some unexpected results. Based on conventional economic measures (e.g., per capita income growth or infrastructure capacities), states that are generally perceived to be doing well are not necessarily in the forefront on the estimated PEI. For instance, states like Kerala and Gujarat known for their success in improving social attainments and infrastructure development, respectively, show relatively weak performance on the PEI. The development trajectories of such states appear to be inadequately balanced to deliver the desired social outcomes and opportunities for their citizens. Glaring and persisting policy gaps and institutional weaknesses suggest a need for a renewed and explicit focus on heterodox economic policy prescription, which is capable of overcoming the ingrained structural rigidities of those societies, to deliver inclusive outcomes and good governance.

## Heterodox macroeconomic policy

A flexibility in the design of macroeconomic policy is a critical element of a heterodox economic policy approach. It is required to underwrite the fiscal consequences of implementing a multisectoral economic/ social policy and to simultaneously sustain a macroeconomic balance in the economy for markets to flourish and contribute to the transformational agenda of a society. The flexibility in macroeconomic policy is necessary to address the current economic problems, including those emanating from rapid globalisation, both in the developing and the industrialised countries, and the growth slowdown since 2008 in the latter.

Macroeconomic policies, irrespective of their impact on macroeconomic aggregates (including income growth, inflation or balance of payments) have significant distributional consequences. In the orthodox tradition, macroeconomic policy is typically meant to ensure economic stability through the pursuit of internal and external balance of an economy. The Keynesian internal balance is defined as full employment and price stability, which supports economic growth. However, with the rise of monetarism in the 1970s, the objective of internal balance reduced to a focus on price stability, with markets on their own expected to ensure full employment. External balance

*Economic policy and human rights* 115

requires an equilibrium in the country's balance of payments. Thus, macroeconomic stability to support economic growth was sought to be achieved through fiscal and external financial sustainability and redistributive objectives of poverty and inequality reduction were left to be met through the trickle-down effect. Unlike this short-term and narrow preoccupation in the industrialised countries, the macroeconomic policy focus in developing countries was broader and supportive of a growth-oriented, long-term development strategy. Here the redistributive objectives were important and sought to be dynamically integrated with the objective of growth, for instance, by specifying the desired rates of income growth for different population groups or sectors in an economy (Chenery et al. 1974).

The 1980s witnessed the macroeconomic policy focus reverting back to economic growth and short-term macro management (without an explicit distributional objective) with international institutions pushing for implementation of the Washington Consensus. Several developing economies in Latin America and elsewhere in Africa and Asia ran into serious macroeconomic imbalances as a consequence of implementing distortionary (import-substitution) policies that resulted, for instance, in overvalued exchange rates, high trade barriers, extensive industrial regulation and inefficient state enterprises. This had significant adverse consequences on both growth and redistribution. There was a collapse of the Soviet Union and the beginning of the rise of China. The East Asian 'miracle' of strong growth with equity also contributed to the thinking that with adequate policies (not necessarily redistributive in nature), there need not be a conflict between economic growth and equitable distribution. It recognised the importance of initial conditions, including attainments on social indicators, for engineering a rapid economic transformation. However, the experience towards the second half of the 1990s suggested that the Washington Consensus had failed to deliver. Although there was evidence of growth convergence across countries, the inequality in outcomes and opportunities for people across and within the developing and the industrialised world were in fact deteriorating. This picture has only got worse since then.

A macroeconomic policy emphasising the pursuit of economic growth has to relate more explicitly to its distributional or micro consequences. Growth, as it has turned out, is at best a blunt instrument against poverty. It works only when that growth is accompanied by a decline in inequality (see, for instance, Ravallion 2004). Therefore, there is a need to be flexible in the design and application of macroeconomic policy, so as to effectively address the evolving reality and sustain

## 116   *Rajeev Malhotra*

desirable social outcomes. This involves a conscious departure from an orthodox thinking on several counts, all of which helps in instituting a heterodox macroeconomic policy perspective and prescription.

First, there are significant differences in the institutions and the context of industrialised and developing countries and also within developing countries, because of which the application of an orthodox (uniform) approach to macroeconomic policy is fraught with challenges. Countries differ in terms of institutional capacity for conducting an evolved and independent fiscal and monetary policy, transmission of policy measures, pace of price adjustments, the depth and the reach of different markets (financial and others), constraints on output expansion, the nature of growth drivers and resilience of an economy to shocks. All this needs to be recognised while designing the policy prescription (see, for instance, Nayyar 2007).

Second, the macroeconomic objective of stability (involving inflation management and sustainability of external balance) with growth depends critically on the policy option exercised about the role of state in the industrialisation of an economy and the adopted degree of its openness. These are strategic choices that depend on the stage of development of an economy and its larger global context and, therefore should not be taken as being sacrosanct and premediated. Indeed, there should be space for considering flexible and unconventional macroeconomic policies, both fiscal and monetary, as well as industrial policy. Budget deficits and quantitative easing are not necessarily a policy taboo, nor should be the case for directed priority sector lending or the use of interest subventions for encouraging a targeted production expansion. The history of the high growth economies of the 20th century and more recent post-financial crisis experience of the industrialised world, especially the economic recovery of the US, attest to the fact that policy flexibility to consider unconventional macroeconomic policies has a place and a definitive role to play in engineering rapid development transformation, economic recovery and sustaining progress. Nations that have succeeded in rapidly transforming themselves from being underdeveloped to developed economics, have invariably done so by adapting and charting their own unique course to development.[21]

Third, a related issue, concerns the case for broadening the goals of macroeconomic policy. The rising inequality and labour dislocation in the context of globalisation reinforces the need for macroeconomic policy to have an explicit focus on employment generation, along with growth. The creation of gainful livelihood opportunities provides a link for macroeconomic objectives with human development and the desired social transformation of a society. It not only supports participation of the excluded in markets, improve their entitlements, capabilities and wellbeing, but also deepen and expand markets – the principle growth driver in mainstream economic policy approach. Besides, the macroeconomic policy would need to factor the necessity of enabling and, where required, providing a social protection floor to ease the likely dislocative consequences of production volatility and economic restructuring on factor productivity in the short term in a globalised world.

Finally, macroeconomic policy, particularly in the context of EMDCs, cannot be an exercise merely in short-term management of the macroeconomic balances. The macroeconomic constraints on growth operate across multiple time horizons. The consequences of short-term policies are invariably felt over longer term. Besides, the transformational agenda, to which all polices including the macroeconomic policy must pay attention to, requires a longer-term engagement. This makes the distinction between short-term macroeconomic models and long-term growth models, perhaps, redundant. Importantly, it makes a case for the macroeconomic policy focus in the EMDCs to be broader and supportive of a long-term development strategy for the desired transformation of the economy.

## Conclusions

Globalisation process and the human rights discourse are both liberal in their underpinnings, yet they are often in conflict when, for instance, in the course of formulating and implementing public policy, the aggregate wellbeing considerations, or the wellbeing of the dominant (those with market power and/or voice) trump the wellbeing considerations of an individual or the marginalised (those without market power or voice or both). The orthodox economic perspective takes precedence over the unorthodox or the heterodox in such instances. The resulting generation of negative externalities and other consequences for the underprivileged are invariably overlooked, or sought to be addressed over time through the improved opportunities that are meant to come their way, but often do not materialise, at least not in a timely manner and in required measures. This outcome is neither desirable nor is it acceptable for sustaining a meaningful process of social change and progress.

Heterodoxy in the space of public policy is often a result of the departure from orthodoxy due to the imperatives of addressing the context. However, for the sake of policy coherence and effectiveness, there is a

## 118  *Rajeev Malhotra*

need for heterodoxy to be normatively anchored and that anchor could well be the human rights standards. In addressing the growing concerns of inequality in outcomes and opportunities, a consequence of the globalisation process in its current phase, this chapter presents a case for applying heterodox economic policy solutions that, while building on the strength of market liberalism, are necessarily tempered by universalism and the inclusionary approach of human rights. An unbridled capitalism may not be the best system to work in, but it need not be the least bad to live in. It is necessary and feasible to move it towards supporting a better context by making a larger space for normative human rights concerns to contest the unfettered liberalism of markets periodically, especially while reviewing the agenda for development and sustaining progress.

## Notes

1 From a historical perspective this may not be so. Over a 100 years ago, the world was as globalised as it is today, if not more. The interwar period witnessed a retreat towards a relatively insular phase, when the proportion of world trade to world GDP dropped by about 20 percent (from over 8 percent in 1913 to around 6 percent in 1950, at 1990 constant USD) followed by a spurt leading to the current phase of globalisation, when the said proportion rose to nearly 14 percent in the early 1990s, see for instance Rodrik (2000).
2 See, for instance, Huntington (1998); Rodrik (2001); Stiglitz (2002); Nayyar (2002); Bhagwati (2004); and Shaikh (2007) for a general discussion on the consequences of globalisation, both the pros and the cons.
3 The backlash against globalisation has taken two forms, ideologically distinct but with a common goal of taming free markets. A left-leaning collective public protest against global capital, driven essentially by non-governmental and civil society actors, which takes the form of organised public demonstrations, disruptions or strife. The other is a right-leaning defence of national sovereignty, which is seen to occur within institutions like nationalist political parties and electoral systems. This is more durable, unlike the sporadic nature of the other, as it is institutionally embedded in the political economy of a society and has gained currency from Asia to the Americas in recent years.
4 In general, universalism is a belief in the existence of a universal, objective or eternal truth that determines everything. It is and must be equally present, or be common to all human beings. It follows that the scope of universalism is far more wide-ranging than the idea of national, cultural or religious constructs. It is, in that sense, a unique approach to look at human life or the world at large. Similarly, individualism is a social outlook or a philosophical approach that emphasises the moral worth of the individual. It seeks to promote the exercise of an individual's goals and desires in her conduct, over that of the state or a social group. It values independence and self-reliance and therefore involves the right of an individual to freedom and self-realisation.

*Economic policy and human rights* 119

5 However, market liberalism with its thrust on efficiency and innovation may well be a means to sustain progress once people have attained certain human wellbeing standards and there are well-functioning markets.

6 The categories of advanced and EMDCs refers to the International Monetary Fund (IMF) categorisation.

7 Various sources, including IMF staff estimates, as reported in (Dabla-Norris et al. 2015, pages 16–18).

8 Freedom House defines an 'electoral democracy' as a country or non-independent territory like Hong Kong with a two- or multiparty political system, regular elections, universal suffrage, and access to media for parties reflecting a representative spectrum of national opinion (see Freedom House 2013).

9 This does not imply that people in these countries are all enjoying rights and freedom unequivocally.

10 Freedom House (2016) while evaluating the state of freedom in 195 countries and fifteen territories during calendar year 2015 notes that 'The world was battered in 2015 by overlapping crises that fuelled xenophobic sentiment in democratic countries, undermined the economies of states dependent on the sale of natural resources, and led authoritarian regimes to crack down harder on dissent. These unsettling developments contributed to the 10th consecutive year of decline in global freedom.' While forty-three countries witnessed an improvement in its score on the freedom measure, seventy-two recorded a decline in 2015.

11 This confidence stems partly from the considerable ethical appeal of an alternative to orthodox economic thinking and partly from the success of heterodox economic policy in the transformation of the high growth economies of the 20th century. Some of those economies succeeded in overcoming the shackles of poverty and underdevelopment and sustained high growth for long periods to significantly improve the living standards of the bottom deciles of their population by adapting and charting their own unique (heterodox) course to development. (See for instance, Commission on Growth and Development 2008; Basu 2000; Acemoglu and Robinson 2012; Lin 2012; Malhotra 2012).

12 Frequently Asked Questions on Human Rights Based Approach to Development Cooperation (United Nations publication, Sales No. E.06. XIV.10), page 1.

13 In the human rights literature, these are referred to as the 'Maastricht principles' that define the scope of state obligations. See "Maastricht Guidelines" on Violations of Economic, Social and Cultural Rights, Maastricht, January 22–26, 1997.

14 The idea of social contract relates to the necessity of having a framework that recognises the rights and obligations of parties and is guided by a sense of justice and equity in the use of available common resources, material or otherwise, in furthering the wellbeing of people. Such a framework has to also evolve in keeping with the needs of the times and the changing context of societies and could, therefore, benefit from being explicitly anchored in a value system that has a universal acceptance and perpetual relevance.

15 See United Nations (2012c, chapter 1, page 16). Defined in this manner, some indicators could be uniquely human rights indicators because they

120 *Rajeev Malhotra*

owe their existence to specific human rights norms or standards and are generally not used in other contexts. This could be the case, for instance, with an indicator like the number of extra-judicial, summary or arbitrary executions, or the number of children who do not have access to primary education because of discrimination. At the same time, there could be a large number of other indicators, such as commonly used socio-economic statistics (e.g., human development indicators used in the UNDP's Human Development Reports) that could meet (at least implicitly) all the definitional requirements of a human rights indicator as laid out here and therefore could be used as human rights indicators.

16 Amartya Sen's emphasis on addressing inequalities in the space of 'capabilities' rather than 'commodities' resonates with objectives of a heterodox economic policy anchored in human rights standards (Sen 1985, 1990).

17 This is relevant for the supply of both local and global public goods at national and international levels, respectively.

18 India, for instance, has established limited legal guarantees for work, education, information with public authorities, food, housing, certain social transfers (pensions) and health (Malhotra 2015).

19 See Sen (1977, 1981) for an elaboration on the notion of entitlements and the importance of improving the exchange entitlements of the poor and the marginalised to lift them out of their chronic deprivation.

20 This is not to say that there is no scope for implementing policy measures with retrogressive consequences on the enjoyment of human rights by people. So long as the affected population group recognises the consequences of the policy measures being undertaken and there is adequate compensation provided to and accepted by them, such measures could be considered by the authorities. This could be the case involving rehabilitation of displaced population from the construction of an irrigation dam.

21 This is apparent in the rise of China and, to a lesser extent, the gradual emergence of Brazil, India, Indonesia, Turkey, Botswana and Chile in recent times. Earlier it was the newly industrialised East Asian economies and Japan. In fact, none of the successfully industrialised countries conformed to the dominant development thinking of the time. They evolved their own policy mix and paths, taking advantage of a favourable global context as they progressed (see also Note 11).

## Bibliography

Acemoglu, Daron and James A. Robinson (2012), *Why Nations Fail: The Origin of Power, Prosperity and Poverty*, New York: Crown Business.

Alvaredo, F., A.B. Atkinson, T. Piketty and E. Saez (2013), 'The Top 1 Percent in International and Historical Perspective', NBER Working Paper 19075, National Bureau of Economic Research, Cambridge, MA.

Atkinson, A.B., T. Piketty and E. Saez (2011), 'Top Incomes in the Long Run of History', *Journal of Economic Literature*, Vol. 49, Issue 1: 3–71.

Basu, Kaushik (2011), *Beyond the Invisible Hand-Groundwork for a New Economics*, New Delhi: Penguin Books.

——— (2000), *Prelude to Political Economy: A Study of Social and Political Foundations of Economics*, Oxford: Oxford University Press.

## Economic policy and human rights 121

Berezin, Mabel (2015), 'Globalization Backlash', Pp. 1–11 in *Emerging Trends in the Social and Behavioral Sciences*, (eds.) Robert A. Scott and Stephen M. Kosslyn, Thousand Oaks, CA: Sage

———— (2013), 'The Normalization of the Right in Post-Security Europe', Pp. 239–261 in *Politics in the Age of Austerity*, (eds.) Armin Schaefer and Wolfgang Streeck, UK: Polity Press.

Bhagwati, Jagdish (2004), *In Defense of Globalization*, New York: Oxford University Press.

Chenery, Hollis, M. Ahluwalia, C. Bell, J. Duloy and R. Jolly (1974), *Redistribution with Growth: Policies to Improve Income Distribution in the Developing Countries in the Context of Economic Growth*, London: Oxford University Press.

Commission on Growth and Development (2008), *The Growth Report: Strategies for Sustained Growth and Inclusive Development*, Washington, DC: World Bank.

Dabla-Norris, Era, Kalpana Kochhar, Nujin Suphaphiphat, Frasntisek Ricka and Evridiki Tsounta (2015), 'Causes and Consequences of Income Inequality: A Global Perspective', IMF Staff Discussion Note: SDN/15/13, June.

Freedom House (2013 and 2016), Freedom in the World 2013, accessed October 15, 2016 at: www.freedomhouse.org/report/freedom-world/freedom-world-2013#.U32y6MKKDmQ

Fuentes Nieva, R. and N. Galasso (2014), 'Working for the Few-Political Capture and Economic Inequality', Oxfam International.

Huntington, Samuel P. (1998), *The Clash of Civilizations and the Remaking of World Order*, New York: Simon and Schuster.

Lin, Justin Yifu (2012), *New Structural Economics: Framework for Rethinking Development and Policy*, Washington, DC: The World Bank.

Malhotra, Rajeev (2015), 'Delivering Development and Good Governance: Making Human Rights Count', in *World Bank Legal Review*, Vol. 6, February, Washington, DC: World Bank.

———— (2014), *India Public Policy Report 2014-Tackling Poverty, Hunger and Malnutrition*, New Delhi: Oxford University Press.

———— (2013), 'Implementing the Right to Development: Towards Operational Criteria and Monitoring Framework', in *Realizing the Right to Development: Essays in Commemoration of 25 Years of the United Nations Declaration on the Right to Development*, Geneva: UN Office of the High Commission for Human Rights.

———— (2012), 'Policy Cauldron: Some Imperatives for Emerging Economies', *Jindal Journal of Public Policy*, Vol. 1, Issue 1, August.

Nayyar, Deepak (2011), 'Rethinking Macroeconomic Policies for Development', *Brazilian Journal of Political Economy*, Vol. 31, Issue 3 (123): 339–351, July–September.

———— (2007), 'Macroeconomic in Developing Countries', *Banca Nazionale del lavoro Quterlt Review*, Vol. 59, Issue 242: 249–269, September.

———— ed. (2002), *Governing Globalisation: Issues and Institutions*, Oxford: Oxford University Press.

## 122   Rajeev Malhotra

Organisation for Economic Cooperation and Development (OECD) (2011), *Divided We Stand: Why Inequality Keeps Rising*, Paris: OECD Publishing.

Oxfam (2017), 'An Economy for the 99%', Oxfam Briefing Paper, accessed January at: www.oxfam.org

Piketty, T. (2014), *Capital in the Twenty-First Century*, Cambridge, MA: Harvard University Press.

Ravallion, Martin (2004), 'Pro-Poor Growth: A Primer', World Bank Policy Research Working Paper No. 3242, World Bank, Washington, DC.

Rodrik, Dani (2001), 'Trading in Illusions', *Foreign Policy*, March–April.

———— (2000), 'How Far Will International Economic Integration Go?', *Journal of Economic Perspectives*, Vol. 14, Issue winter: 177–186.

Schumacher, E.F. (1974), *Small Is Beautiful: A Study of Economics as If People Mattered*, Abacus.

Sen, A.K. (1999), *Development as Freedom*, Oxford: Oxford University Press.

———— (1990), 'Development as Capability Expansion', in *Human Development and the International Strategy for the 1990's*, (eds.) K. Griffin and J. Knight, London: Macmillan.

———— (1985), *Commodities and Capabilities*, North-Holland.

———— (1981), *Poverty and Famines*, Oxford: Oxford University Press.

———— (1977), 'Starvation and Exchange Entitlements: A General Approach and Its Application to the Great Bengal Famine', *Cambridge Journal of Economics*, Vol. 1.

Sengupta, Arjun (2006), 'The Human Right to Development', in *Development as a Human Right-Legal, Political and Economic Dimension*, (eds.) Baard A. Anderson and Stephan P. Marks, Cambridge, MA: Harvard University Press.

Shaikh, Anwar (2007), *Globalization and Myths of Free Trade*, London: Palgrave.

Stiglitz, Joseph E. (2002), *Globalisation and Its Discontents*, New York and London: W.W. Norton.

Stiglitz, Joseph E., Jose Antonio Ocampo, Shari Spiegel, Ricardo French-Davis and Deepak Nayyar (2006), *Stabilty with Growth: Macroeconomics, Liberalisation and Development*, Oxford: Oxford University Press.

Streeten, Paul (2003), 'Human Rights', in *The Right to Development: Reflections on the First Four Reports of the Independent Expert on the Right to Development*, (ed.) Franciscans International, Geneva: Franciscans International.

———— (1980), 'Basic Needs and Human Rights', *World Development*, Vol. 9, Issue 2: 107–111, February.

United Nations (2012a), 'The Future We Want', United Nations Conference on Sustainable Development (Rio+20), accessed at: www.un.org/en/sustainablefuture

———— (2012b), 'Realising the Future We Want for All: Report to the Secretary-General', Especially Towards Freedom from Fear and Want: Human Rights in the Post-2015 Agenda, Thematic Think Piece (May).

###### Economic policy and human rights 123

———— (2012c), *Human Rights Indicators: A Guide to Measurement and Implementation*, New York and Geneva: United Nations Office of the High Commissioner for Human Rights.

———— (2009), 'Report of Commission of Experts on Reforms of the International Monetary and Financial System' (Stiglitz Commission), New York, accessed September at: www.un.org/ga/econcrisissummit/docs/FinalReport_CoE.pdf

# Part III

# Economic theory and public policy

# 7 The theory of credit and macroeconomic stability

*Joseph Stiglitz* *

The post-2008 world has been one dominated by monetary policy, as politics and ideology – and sometimes financial markets – constrain the use of fiscal policy. There have been massive increases in the balance sheets of key central banks – the Federal Reserve's reaching 25 percent (2016) of GDP, Japan, 82 percent (2016), the Bank of England, 21 percent (2016), and the ECB, late to embark on quantitative easing, but as of 2016 already over 31 percent of GDP. But in spite of these increases, the best that can be said is that monetary policy prevented matters from becoming worse; growth in GDP in the advanced countries was an anemic 2 percent.

The growth in base money has become disjointed from the growth in the economies. Figure 7.1 shows the growth in central bank assets and the growth in real GDP for each of the four countries. Rather than GDP growing proportionately to the growth of the central bank balance sheet, the figure shows significant variability in the ratio of central bank assets to GDP, and especially large changes in the money supply being associated with small changes in nominal GDP in recent years in the US.

A simple regression shows a very low correlation between money supply and GDP in recent years, weaker than in the period immediately after World War II. This weak relationship appears robust to a variety of specifications, including variable lags and different measures of money (e.g. the Fed's balance sheet or more standard measures of M2 – see Figure 7.2). These results naturally raise the questions:

---

\* This is a chapter prepared for the volume in honour of Deepak Nayyar, from whom I have benefitted enormously in our many conversations and joint work over many years. The author is indebted to the Institute for New Economic Thinking for financial support, and to Martin Guzman and Andrew Kosenko, for comments and suggestions. This chapter represents a summary of my research in this area and hence the disproportionate number of references to my earlier work.

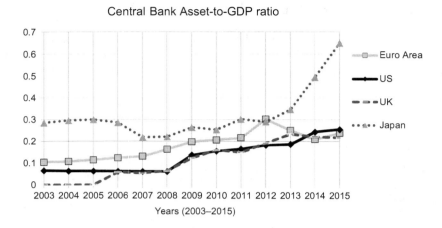

*Figure 7.1* Central bank assets-to-GDP ratio
*Ratio of central bank assets to GDP has varied markedly*[1]
Source: Federal Reserve Economic Database (FRED) (https://research.stlouisfed.org/fred2)

where is the extra liquidity provided by the Fed going? What's happening? Standard theory suggests putting more money into people's pockets should lead to more spending, leading either to higher prices or greater output. If this isn't happening, it suggests a fundamental flaw with standard formulations of monetary theory.

The absence of a clear link between money (however measured) and output (nominal or real) has led naturally to a shift of attention of monetary authorities away from quantitative measures (base money, M2, etc.) to a focus on interest rates. But even here, without further massaging of the data, the relationship is weak. The Appendix discusses the weak relationship between output (nominal and real) and money supply and interest rates (nominal and real). Our empirical investigation suggests, moreover, that the relationship has not been stable over time. In particular, the relationship between money and output has become weaker in the last quarter of a century. As the later analysis makes clear, this should not come as a complete surprise: there have been large changes in institutional arrangements, and one might have expected such institutional changes to be reflected in the relationships discussed in the Appendix.

In the aftermath of the Great Recession, there is a growing consensus, even among central bank officials, concerning the limitations of

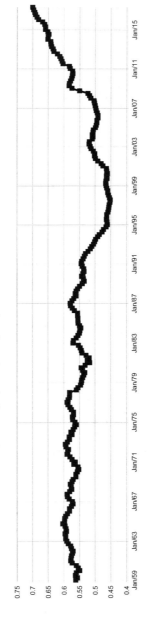

*Figure 7.2* M2 to GDP ratio
*It is obvious that this too has exhibited enormous variability*

Source: Federal Reserve e (FRED) (https://fred.stlouisfed.org)

## 130  *Joseph Stiglitz*

monetary policy. Central banks may have prevented another Great Depression, but they have not restored the economy to robust growth. Our analysis suggests that this experience sheds broader light on the limitations of monetary policy. The first part of the chapter provides an explanation for this extraordinary ineffectiveness of monetary policy, and in doing so provides a new framework for thinking about money and finance.

The second part of the chapter builds on the insights of the first part and shows how advances in technology allow for the creation of an electronic monetary system that enables better macroeconomic management and a greater share of the rents associated with "money", that is, with the payments system, to be captured for the public treasury.

## Towards a new theory of money and credit[2]

Standard modern monetary theory is based on the hypothesis that the T-bill rate is the central variable in controlling the economy, and that the money supply, which the government controls, enables the government to regulate the T-bill rate.

Prevailing economic doctrines earlier argued that there was a simple link between the supply of money (say $M_2$), which the government could control, and the value of nominal GDP. This link is described by the equation:

(1)  $MV \equiv pQ$

where, V is the velocity of circulation, p is the price level and Q is real output. (1) is essentially a definition of the velocity of circulation. Monetarism translated (1) from a definition into an empirical hypothesis, arguing that V was constant. This meant that nominal income and the money supply moved in proportion.

Monetarists like Milton Friedman claimed further that (at least over the long run) Q was fixed at full employment, so that an increase in M would lead to a proportionate increase in p. Shortly after these monetarism doctrines became fashionable, especially in central banks, the links between money supply (in virtually any measure), and the variables describing the economy (income, or even real interest rates) seemed to become tenuous. The velocity of circulation was evidently not a constant. Of course, there never had been a theory explaining why it should be.

Even before this, Keynesians had argued that V was a function of the interest rate. An increase in M is split in three ways – an increase in p,

## Credit and macroeconomic stability 131

an increase in Q, and a decrease in velocity – with the exact division depending on the relevant elasticities (e.g. the interest elasticity of the demand for money, of investment, and of consumption.)

But, beginning in the 1980s, velocity was not only not constant, but it also did not appear to be even a stable function of the interest rate – not a surprise given, as we have noted, the large institutional changes going on in the financial sector (such as the creation of money market funds and the abolition of many regulations). The natural response was a switch from a focus on the quantity of money to the interest rate. But while this experience should have led to a deeper rethinking of the premises of monetary theory, it did not.

Prevailing theories also held that monetary policy provided the best (most effective, least distortionary) regulator of the economy, and that the way it did this was through adjusting the interest rate. A lowering of the interest rate led to more consumption and investment. In an open economy, it led to a lower exchange rate, which led to more exports. The extraordinary ineffectiveness of monetary policy to restore the economy to full economy in the aftermath of the Great Recession has led to a modification of the standard theory: monetary policy is the instrument of choice so long as the economy is above the zero lower bound (ZLB); and to the extent that the ZLB can be breached, it should be.

This chapter questions the primacy given to monetary policy, suggesting that the problem is not the ZLB, but a host of other limitations – effects of monetary policy that were given short shrift. Most fundamentally, we argue that standard theory has given too much attention to the interest rate and too little attention to the primary mechanism through which monetary policy affects the economy, the quantity and terms (including the non-price terms) at which *credit* is available. In normal times, money and credit represent two sides of a bank's balance sheet, so they may be highly correlated. But more generally, and especially in crises, credit may be only weakly related either to the supply of money, or even to the T-bill interest rate. This weak link – and not the ZLB – helps explain the ineffectiveness of monetary policy at certain times, such as the period from 2008 through the present. We further argue that the expansion of credit itself is weakly linked to GDP, with increases in credit going towards multiple uses other than an increase in the demand for produced goods – most notably, towards the acquisition of assets such as land.

The discussion in this section is spread across seven subsections. After setting out the basic argument for the focus on credit in the first, we turn to the determinants of the supply of credit – primarily through

## 132 Joseph Stiglitz

the banking system, observing that changes in monetary policy may be limited in overcoming other changes in the determinants of credit availability, in the second. The third focuses on the demand for credit, noting that there are many other uses to which credit can be put other than an increased demand for produced goods. The fourth then turns to a more expansive explanation of the ineffectiveness of monetary policy. The fifth subsection explains that the distortionary effects of monetary policy may be far greater than earlier analyses have assumed; for instance, the conventional use of an aggregative model hides inter-sectoral distortions. The sixth argues, by the same token, that there may be serious adverse distributional effects which cannot be ignored, and which contribute to the ineffectiveness of monetary policy. The seventh reexamines these issues from the perspective of an open economy, explaining why monetary policy may be more or less effective, and more or less distortionary, with a different set of distributive effects.

The analysis of the relative ineffectiveness of monetary policy provides the background for the second part of the chapter, where we show how a move to an electronic banking system, combined with a direct focus on credit availability, and the use of new monetary instruments described there, can increase the effectiveness of macroeconomic management, even in an open economy.

### The importance of credit – not money

In earlier work, Greenwald and Stiglitz (1991, 2003) argued that what matters for the level of macroeconomic activity was neither the supply of money (the quantity variable upon which monetarism was focused), nor the T-bill rate (the rate of interest that the government had to pay on its short-term bonds, and the focus of recent monetary policy), but rather the *availability* of credit and the *terms* at which credit is available. They thus criticized standard monetary theory in terms of its theory of the determination of the lending rate, the relevance of the T-bill rate, and the assumption that credit markets always clear.

In the standard model, the interest rate is determined by the intersection of the demand and supply for *money*. Government controls the supply of money. In that model, the demand for money is related to income and the interest rate (with the interest rate being the opportunity cost of holding money). But G-S point out that in a modern economy, most money is interest bearing (e.g. money market funds), with the cost of holding money a matter solely of transactions costs, unrelated to either monetary policy or the level of economic activity[3] (see Figure 7.3). Moreover, money is not required for engaging in transactions,

*Credit and macroeconomic stability* 133

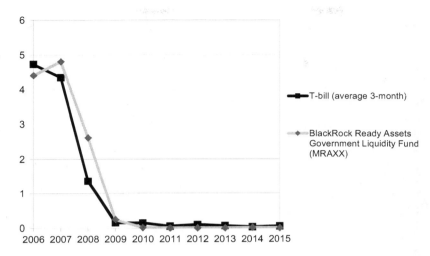

*Figure 7.3* The relationship between T-bill rate and money market rate
*The two track each other almost perfectly, the difference being largely transactions cost, with no significant cyclical component.*

Source: Federal Reserve Economic Database (FRED) (T-bill: https://fred.stlouisfed.org/series/TB3MS;

BlackRock: www.sec.gov/Archives/edgar/data/65109/000119312516426010/d79618d497k.htm)

but rather for credit. Even if money were required for transactions, most transactions are exchanges of assets, and not directly related to the production of goods and services; hence the demand for money is related not just to the level of macroeconomic activity ("Y", GDP), but to other kinds of transactions, and there is no fixed relationship between these and GDP. There is, in short, no theoretical foundation underlying the usual theory of interest determination.

Robertson[4] had earlier proposed an alternative theory of interest determination, based on the demand and supply of savings. Some farmers decide not to consume or plant all their seeds, and some wish to use more than the seeds they have available, and the interest rate equilibrates the supply and demand of "loanable" seeds (see Greenwald and Stiglitz 2003). While such a theory may have made sense in a primitive agriculture economy, it does not describe a modern credit economy, where banks are central and can create credit within constraints imposed by the government. In particular, there is no need for a bank to have seeds on deposit for it to create credit.

## 134   Joseph Stiglitz

While there is thus a lacuna in the theory of interest rate determination, even were we to have a well-developed theory, with a clear link between the interest rate and monetary policy, there is a further problem: it is not clear that the T-bill rate (so determined) plays the critical role assumed in modern macro and monetary theory. First, as G-S show, the T-bill rate is only loosely related to the lending rate.[5] Moreover, the lending rate is not the only variable affecting macroeconomic activity. With credit rationing (Stiglitz and Weiss 1981), the availability of credit matters too, as do other non-price terms of credit contracts (like collateral requirements; Stiglitz and Weiss 1986).[6] These are endogenous, and while they may be affected by the T-bill rate, they are also affected by other policy and environmental variables. In short, modern macroeconomics has focused on certain substitution effects (e.g. the interest elasticity of consumption), and these may be (and we would suggest typically are) overwhelmed by income, wealth, risk, and other non-price effects,[7] or price effects operating in other ways, for instance through their impact on collateral, self-selection, or incentive compatibility constraints.

### The correlation between money and credit

Our analysis emphasizes the role of credit in determining the level of economic activity. For a variety of reasons, data on the money supply (measured somehow) seems more widely available than data on credit, either its "availability" or even the actual level of lending. But these variables are closely related: typically, when a bank lends more, its deposits (or more broadly, the deposits of the banking system) increase (a liability) and so do the bank's assets – the loan. Thus, money (demand deposits) and credit increase in tandem. So too, if a foreigner were to make a deposit in a country's bank, the bank would normally have an incentive and ability to increase lending.

But as we explain later, there are times when this normal relationship breaks down, and policies predicated on the normal relationships may be very misguided. If a bank faces a great deal of uncertainty, it may not lend out as much as it could; it has excess reserves. In the East Asia crisis, the IMF became worried when, say, there were large excess reserves in Indonesia. It meant that, suddenly, the banks could start lending, and that would be inflationary. As a precautionary measure, it thought it was wise to "mop up" the excess reserves or to take other actions to eliminate the excess reserves, for example, tighten reserve requirements. The problem was that with the blunt instruments available, even banks that had no excess reserves were typically affected by

*Credit and macroeconomic stability* 135

the tightening. Their customers lost access to credit – deepening the on-going recession. The cost of tightening was palpable; the risk of inflation that the tightening was supposed to reduce was imaginary – there was virtually no realistic scenario in which the banks with excess reserves would turn around and lend so much that inflation would be excessive.

Economies in deep downturns – recessions and depressions – behave differently than those in more normal times, and policies, including and especially monetary policies, suitable for one situation may not be suitable for the other (see Stiglitz 2016d). Even if the correlation between money and credit were close in normal times, it is not in deep downturns, as banks are willing to hold on to excess reserves. As we explain later, it is this which gives rise to the modern liquidity trap.

## *The supply of credit*

In standard monetary theory, banks play no role. This is true even for the models used by central banks – ironic since if there were no banks, there would be no central banks. In institution-free Neo-classical economics, one sees underneath the institutions to the underlying economic forces. Thus, as we have noted, in standard models, the (real) interest rate is set at the rate that equilibrates the demand and supply of funds (in Robertsonian monetary theory; in Keynesian theory, the demand and supply of money[8]). Though that model may provide a reasonable if incomplete[9] description of the capital markets on which large enterprises raise funds, small and medium-sized enterprises (SMEs) have to rely on banks, and much of the variability in economic activity is related to investment by such enterprises; and much of that variability is related to credit availability.[10] Interest rates are not set at the intersection of demand and supply curves – there may be credit rationing; but even when there is not credit rationing, the supply curve of funds needs to be *derived* from the behavior of banks, and when one does that, one gets a very different picture.

Greenwald and Stiglitz (1991, 1993b, 2003) provide a simple model describing bank behavior, showing how lending is related not just to the T-bill rate, but to banks' net worth, their risk perceptions, their existing portfolio of assets, and the constraints provided by regulators. They describe too how banks adjust not only their lending rate, but the other terms of the contract in response to changes in these variables. Thus, credit (money) supply is determined not just by conventional monetary instruments (open market operations, reserve requirements), but also by macro- and micro-prudential requirements. Indeed, the

## 136 Joseph Stiglitz

two aspects of central bank policy (regulatory and macro-control) cannot and should not be separated.

Their model of banks (combined with their earlier model of the risk-averse firm[11] facing equity rationing; see Greenwald and Stiglitz 1993b; Greenwald, Stiglitz, and Weiss 1984)[12] thus shows how changes in economic circumstances today (such as a shock that affects their net worth or even the value or risk of particular assets[13]) can have large, long-lasting effects. The effects of an economic shock can be persistent. At the same time, they explain why an increase in liquidity – a conventional open market operation, lowering the T-bill or the lending rate – may have little effect on credit availability.[14]

Banks typically respond to a lower cost of funds by lending more, and lending at lower interest rates (whether they choose to ration credit or not). But there are some circumstances in which they do not, or do not do so to any significant extent. In particular, G-S explain why, if risk perceptions have increased and if the risk of the banks' existing portfolio has increased – that is, the risk of both new and past loans has increased – the bank may be at a corner solution, where it will not undertake further loans, even when the interest rate is lowered. And this is especially so if, due to asymmetric information, the bank can only divest itself of the risk associated with past loans by taking large capital losses on its loan portfolio.[15]

This problem is exacerbated by the fact that in severe economic downturns, the value of highly leveraged banks' net worth is severely decreased, so risk-averse banks are even more overly exposed to risk, unless they cut back severely on lending. (The inability to divest oneself of risk generates an important hysteresis effect. There are, in addition, effects on banks' optimal portfolio, e.g. shifting away from more risky lending.)

Changes in government (central bank) policy, as desirable as they may be, typically give rise to new risks, which have their own adverse effects even when the intent of the policy change is to stimulate the economy. Thus, a decrease in the interest rate changes asset values of different firms in different ways, depending on their assets. A firm that has outstanding short-term liabilities and long-term assets (with returns fixed at a higher rate) may be much better off, but a firm with a different maturity structure of assets and liabilities could actually be worse off. Lenders may have to have detailed information about all the assets and liabilities of a firm to know precisely how each firm is affected; and in the absence of that information, uncertainty will have increased. Thus, an increase in the interest rate will have a more adverse effect than anticipated, but a lowering of the interest rate will have a smaller effect – or even an effect that is adverse. This is especially so once one takes into account all the general equilibrium effects. A lowering of the interest rate will lower the exchange rate, thus hurting importers and domestic firms that use imported inputs.

With risk aversion, the benefits of the winners from such changes in relative prices do not offset the losses of the losers. The aggregate effect can be negative (Greenwald and Stiglitz 1993b).

The ability and willingness of banks to lend depends not just on what may be called the environmental variables (risk perceptions[16] and net worth) described in earlier paragraphs, but on all the constraints facing banks today – and the expectations of future constraints. For instance, banks face capital adequacy constraints, specifying, say, net worth relative to outstanding loans. If that constraint is tightened, then the bank must either raise new capital or reduce outstanding loans. But because of capital market imperfections, firms in fact typically face constraints in raising new equity; at the very least, doing so may be very costly to existing shareholders.[17] Hence, an increase in the capital adequacy ratio – or an increase in defaults on loans that reduces capital – reduces lending. But because a quick reduction in lending may be costly, firms need to anticipate that they might face such a situation, and hence well before the constraints bind, banks may curtail lending and firms may curtail borrowing.

This simply emphasizes that all of the constraints facing a bank – whether binding today or possibly binding in the future – can affect lending and borrowing today. And it is not just the standard instruments (e.g. open market operations or the discount rate) by which central banks affect lending activity.

Banks that focus on lending to SMEs face an additional problem: this lending is typically collateral-based, and the collateral is typically real estate. In a crisis such as that of 2008, the value of this collateral decreases enormously, and thus, *given existing rules and constraints*, banks should significantly reduce the amount of their exposure to SME risk. The focus of the bank is thus on reducing SME exposure, not making new loans.[18]

By the same token, severe economic downturns are often associated with increased disparities in *judgments* (probabilities associated with different contingencies). This increased disparity in judgments may give rise to an increase in trading in existing assets, rather than for newly produced assets, and an increase in the demand for credit to support such trades. To see this, consider the 2008 crisis. Some believed that the market had overshot – real estate prices had fallen excessively. The banks argued that that was the case, not wanting to believe that they

## 138 *Joseph Stiglitz*

had made massive misjudgments about the real estate market. The more optimistic market participants believed this contention, and were willing to pay a risk premium to get access to funds to buy these depressed assets. The banks agreed with their judgments (for reasons given in the previous sentence). These *new* borrowers could offer the real estate (at the new low price) as collateral. Thus, from the perspective of the bank, these new real estate loans offered a low-risk (in their calculus), high-return loan – far better than the high-risk loans to *real* firms. From the perspective of the banks as a group, this lending has a further benefit: it raises real estate prices, improving the value of their existing portfolio.[19]

In short, in a deep downturn changes in the balance sheet of the bank and in its risk perceptions typically lead to a significant contraction in the supply of funds and an increase in the interest rate that it charges, and to corresponding changes to its non-price terms; the magnitude of these effects overwhelms any ability of the central bank to stimulate lending by lowering interest rates and other actions designed to ease credit availability.

Of course, when we observe a net contraction in lending in a recession it does not *necessarily* mean that monetary policy has been totally ineffective: it simply means that it was unable to fully counteract the other effects.[20] And even when we see an expansion of credit, it does not mean that monetary policy has been effective: the expansion of credit may not have facilitated the purchase of newly produced goods, and thus may not have contributed to an increase in GDP.

Moreover, a lowering of interest rates on T-bills does not translate into a lowering of the lending rate, and it is that rate that matters for firm and consumer behavior. Further, even that rate may not provide an adequate description of the financial market: there may be credit rationing and collateral and other non-price terms.

We have even identified some circumstances in which lowering T-bill interest rates may be counterproductive (we will identify some further circumstances later), because of the increased risk associated with the *change* in interest rates that increases risk perceptions (in association with the other relative prices effects generated). By the same token, negative interest rates may adversely affect banks' balance sheets, if not carefully designed, and, in doing so, lead to a contraction in lending.[21]

### The demand for and uses of credit

The previous section focused on the determinants of the supply of credit, explaining in particular why an "easing" of monetary policy might not result in a lower lending rate and a greater availability of

*Credit and macroeconomic stability* 139

credit. Here, we explain why the same thing is also true on the demand side: in a severe downturn, risk-averse firms will face an adverse shock to their balance sheets and an adverse increase in their risk perceptions, both of which will lead to a contraction in production and investment. Lowering interest rates *at which they can borrow* (which is not the same as lowering the T-bill rate, as we explained in the previous section) may lead them to borrow more than they otherwise would have borrowed; but this increase may be small compared to the contraction in investment from the increase in risk and worsening of the balance sheet. Moreover, even when interest rates are lowered – for those who can get loans – credit may be rationed.

In addition, for reasons explained earlier, *changes* in interest rates by themselves can give rise to an increase in uncertainty, with adverse effects on the demand for credit. Each firm is embedded in a complex general equilibrium system, in which it has an array of assets and liabilities, some explicit, some implicit, in part related to its economic relations with other entities. A marked lowering of interest rates can increase uncertainty and the perception of risk, and firm risk management may entail a corresponding adjustment in its activities, including decreases in production and investment. Later in this chapter, we shall identify some distributional effects of lowering interest rates that may also result in a reduction in the demand for credit as interest rates fall.

While a change in interest rates thus may not be effective in increasing the demand for and use of credit, even when it does, the increases in credit (money) do not necessarily translate into increases in economic activity – greater consumption or increased investment in newly produced capital goods: there is many a slip between the cup and the lip. Increases in credit (money) can go into several uses:

1  Increased purchases of existing assets, and especially land. Indeed, much of increased wealth is an increase in land values – so much so that the ratio of the value of produced capital to GDP is actually declining.[22] Of course, when more money goes to the purchases of land, it does not lead to more land, but rather, to an increase in the price of land. This wealth effect can lead to more real spending, but this effect is normally likely to be small – far smaller than that which would have been predicted by any model where it is simply assumed that the increase in money leads to more spending on *produced* goods.

2  Increased margin to facilitate taking larger speculative positions, for example, in zero-sum bets, such as futures markets.

140 *Joseph Stiglitz*

3   Increased lending abroad (either for "productive" or non-productive purposes). If the foreign country to which the money goes has an increase in income, it may (slightly) enhance exports, and exports may be further strengthened from the effect on foreign exchange. (Monetary policy in an open economy is discussed briefly further in a later subsection.)

It is, accordingly, not surprising that the link between money and economic activity may be much weaker than standard monetary theory assumed.

### Limitations on the effectiveness of monetary policy

#### Liquidity trap and the Zero Lower Bound (ZLB)

The Greenwald-Stiglitz analysis provides an alternative explanation of the "liquidity trap" to that of Keynes. Keynes' explanation of the inefficacy of monetary policy was that because the demand curve for short-term government bonds becomes horizontal at low interest rates, monetary policy could not push interest rates down below a certain level. Empirically, recent experiences have shown that the interest rate on government bonds can even become negative. Our argument focuses on banks, and their unwillingness to lend more under certain circumstances, no matter how low the T-bill rate is pushed.

So too, our analysis provides a counter to the recent fixation with the constraint on monetary policy imposed by the ZLB. It takes the view that even if the interest rate were lowered below zero, the response would be limited, largely because banks would still not increase their lending, partly because banks would not (fully) pass on the lower cost of funds to their customers, but partly too because the interest elasticity of investment and consumption is low. Of course, if the interest rate became negative enough, to the point where individuals could borrow and effectively never repay, then there would be an increase in economic activity. But that is not what advocates of the ZLB mean.

Elsewhere, I have provided other arguments for why the ZLB argument is questionable: if it were true, there would be other ways of achieving the desired change in intertemporal prices, through investment tax credits and consumption tax rates that change over time. Yet no one is proposing such a scheme. Doing so would provide a test of the hypothesis, and I believe the ZLB theory would be shown to be wanting.

### Credit and macroeconomic stability 141

*Diversion of credit creation and the creation of instability*

Our analysis also provides an additional explanation for the ineffectiveness of monetary policy even short of the ZLB: standard monetary theory *assumes* that any additional liquidity created goes towards the purchase of *produced* goods. But, as we have noted earlier, much of the additional liquidity does not go to the purchase of newly produced assets, but rather into existing fixed assets (such as land), helping create credit bubbles, and into institutionally constrained "gambling" transactions in futures markets in which some form of margin has to be put up. This diversion helps explain the regression findings noted in the beginning of this chapter, showing a low correlation between (the change in) money and the (change in the) value of output.

The observation that increases in credit go into increased speculation and an increased value of fixed assets helps explain why a low interest rate environment is often associated with financial instability. (Other reasons are associated with the distortionary effects of monetary policy discussed in the next subsection.) Guzman and Stiglitz[23] have shown, for instance, that increased gambling in futures markets leads to an increase in what they call pseudo-wealth: all of the market participants believe their wealth goes up as they make more of these bets, simply because they expect to win. But the bets are zero sum: the gains of one person occur at the expense of others. Still, the extent of such gambles can change suddenly, as happened in the lead up to and the aftermath of the Great Recession – and thus the amount of pseudo-wealth can change quickly, and so too the level of aggregate demand. If monetary or regulatory policy tightens, then the extent of such gambles may decrease, and so too the value of the pseudo-wealth. The same thing occurs if there are changes in perceptions and/or the willingness to engage in such bets.

Similarly, if credit is used to finance the purchase of fixed assets, like land (and/or there is borrowing on the basis of land as collateral), an increase in credit can give rise to an increase in the price of land, which, if monetary policy is sufficiently accommodating, can lead to more lending, fueling further increases in prices. This credit-collateral spiral can suddenly break, for example, when market participants no longer believe that the price of land will continue to rise – and in fact, it can be shown that it is impossible for prices to continue to rise *forever* at the rate necessary to satisfy the capital arbitrage equation (giving the same rate of return across all assets). (See Shell and Stiglitz 1967; Hahn 1966; Stiglitz 2015b.)

The problem is not just that additionally provided liquidity goes to these purposes, which do not directly lead to an increase in GDP. It is

## 142 *Joseph Stiglitz*

also that the proportion of any additional money that actually goes to support GDP is highly variable.[24] Hence, without further constraints, monetary authorities cannot be sure about the link between GDP and money (credit).

Of course, if there were a stable relationship between the nominal or real interest rate and GDP, then it could expand or contract the money supply until it reached the targeted interest rate. But the discussions of preceding sections made clear that the relationships were also highly variable between the T-bill rate and either the supply or demand for money/credit on the one hand, and between the T-bill rate and the level of economic activity on the other.[25]

### Distributive effects

In a later section we explain how monetary policy may have adverse distributive effects. There are winners and losers – but if the reduction in spending by the losers is greater than the increase in spending by the winners, then the net effect on aggregate demand may be negative, and these distributive effects may again overwhelm the direct interest rate effect leading each to spend more than they otherwise would have. Moreover, the adverse distributive effects may be compounded by the rationing effects described earlier: the losers may be *forced* to contract their spending, while the gainers may choose to increase their spending only a little; and the lower interest rates may then have no effect on the former.

The argument is parallel to that which has become standard in international economics. There has long been a concern about persistent global imbalances – China's and Germany's surpluses, and the US deficit. The worry is that there will be a "disorderly unwinding" of these imbalances – that if global financial markets suddenly stopped being willing to finance the deficits of the deficit countries (Calvo 1998), the contraction of their spending would not be offset by the expansion of the spending of the surplus countries (see Stiglitz 2010).

### Distortionary effects of monetary policy

Advocates of the use of monetary policy often argue that it is preferable to fiscal policy not only because it can be implemented more quickly, but also because it is less distortionary. That is one of the reasons that so many of those economists supporting the view that monetary policy should bear the brunt of macroeconomic adjustment have been so disturbed by the inefficacy of monetary policy in recent years,

## Credit and macroeconomic stability 143

and why the ZLB argument has become so popular. For it says that their prior view was correct, but that there is a special "regime" under which, when interest rates hit zero, the results are no longer applicable.

But those conclusions are made in the context of highly special models. In this section, we note several reasons why the conclusion that monetary policy should be at the center of macro-stability may be wrong.

### Mispricing of risk

Market participants talk about how the recent low-interest environment leads to a distorted price of risk. They argue that the low-interest environment leads to a distorted price of risk because of the "search for yield", and that, in this low-interest-rate environment, in order to get "yield" there is excessive demand for risky assets yielding a slight risk premium. That drives up the price of these assets, driving down risk premiums to irrational levels, which eventually get corrected.

The consequences of this mispricing have been severe: funds flow into uses where, with more rational pricing, they would not go. And the later readjustment of prices can itself have severe consequences.

But there is a kind of intellectual inconsistency in this perspective. Financial market participants typically believe in the efficiency of markets. That traditionally has been part of their argument against government regulation. But the entire argument for why there is mispricing is based on behavioral finance: market participants fail to take into account the fact that the irrationally low levels of risk premiums will not be sustained.

There are risks associated with such market irrationality – but market irrationality does not just suddenly appear as interest rates get near zero. Market irrationality is pervasive. And because of this, and because of the macroeconomic externalities that are associated with the consequences of both the excessively low risk premiums and of the corrections that follow, there is a need for much greater market regulation than advocates of unregulated markets claim. They cannot have it both ways: to claim that markets are efficient, but that we need to be wary of low interest rates because they create distortions in the price of risk.

They are, however, perhaps correct in their warning against low interest rates, providing a quite different argument for the limitations of monetary policy than provided by Keynes: it is not that interest rates *cannot* be lowered (indeed, some central banks have lowered interest rates below zero); nor is it that lowering interest rates will not

144   *Joseph Stiglitz*

have much effect on real economic activity (true, and even, as we argue later, worse than that); but that the *consequences* of low interest rates mean that central banks should eschew such policies, especially over an extended period of time.

### Inter-sectoral misallocations[26]

The aggregate models so beloved by macroeconomists hide a key problem with the excessive reliance on monetary policy: it gives rise to intersectoral distortions. It makes interest-sensitive sectors bear the brunt of adjustment. It may be desirable to make such sectors bear *more* of the costs of adjustment than others; but there may be (and there typically is) a cost to the reliance on monetary policy.

Optimal macroeconomic policy would distribute the costs of adjustment, which requires both monetary and fiscal policies.[27]

The Ricardo-Barro argument that fiscal policy is ineffective (since it will simply be undone by actions in the private sector) rests on simplistic models. Government spending can be complementary to private spending (either to private consumption or investment) today, and thus affect changes in intertemporal allocations, just as changes in intertemporal prices brought on by monetary authorities can. Even government spending that is complementary to future private spending can elicit more private spending today, for example, because consumers rationally take the future impact on their budget constraints into their current spending (Neary-Stiglitz 1983).[28]

So too, the reliance on using the short-term interest rate for macroeconomic adjustment may lead (even with full rationality) to distortions in intertemporal and risk prices (as we noted), and optimal macroeconomic adjustment may seek to optimize by minimizing the resulting distortions through the use of appropriately designed fiscal policies.[29]

### Choice of technique: Creating a jobless recovery

Here, we discuss one piece of evidence that reliance on changing intertemporal prices for equilibrating the economy may not be optimal. There are many alternative theories attempting to explain why the economy fails to attain full employment, including those related to wage and price rigidities (with those rigidities in fact being endogenous in some variants of these theories). Monetary policy attempts to correct for these distortions by controlling the interest rate (usually the short-term interest rate), setting it at a level different from what it

Credit and macroeconomic stability  145

otherwise would be. But intuitively, if the source of the distortion is in the labor or product market, it might make far more sense to attempt to correct at least some of the distortion more directly.

The standard argument for monetary policy is that it increases investment (and possibly consumption) leading to higher GDP and thus employment today. But there is another effect: lower interest rates induce firms to invest in more capital-intensive technologies, lowering future demand for labor. It affects the choice of technique. Even if real wages go down in a recession, the decline in the cost of capital is even larger. The original distortion is an excessively high price of labor relative to capital because of wage rigidities; the interest rate policy exacerbates that distortion. We see the consequences: firms replacing unskilled checkout clerks and tellers with machines.

Thus, as the economy recovers, there will be a lower demand for labor than there would otherwise have been – it will take a higher level of GDP to achieve a restoration of full employment.

The problem is that we are asking too much from a single instrument, and in principle, there are more instruments in the government's tool kit. The government could, for instance, provide a larger investment tax credit for more labor-intensive technologies. But most governments have eschewed using this broader set of instruments. With a more constrained set of instruments, monetary policy may not only have these adverse distributional effects, but also may be less effective, as we shall explain shortly.

### Distributive effects of monetary policy[30]

The economist's focus on aggregate models with a representative agent has shifted attention away from another important set of effects of monetary policy: their implications for the distribution of income. The presumptions have been the following: (1) The focus of monetary policy should be macroeconomic management, and if there are distributive effects, they are likely to be minor and correctable through fiscal/tax and transfer policies. (2) Ensuring that the economy is at full employment is the most important thing that government can do to ensure the well-being of workers. Higher employment helps workers directly and indirectly: Lower unemployment will lead to higher wages and higher GDP will lead to higher tax revenues and greater benefits for ordinary citizens. Recent failures of monetary policy have highlighted, however, that there can be significant adverse distributional effects, and the politics in the US and Europe have shown that the likelihood of any adverse effects on distribution being offset by government are

## 146   *Joseph Stiglitz*

nil. More generally, research over the past three decades has shown that there are significant costs of such redistributions, and unless the growth benefits are significant, the distributional effects may thus outweigh them.[31]

Among the distributional effects, two stand out: the first, its role in creating a jobless recovery, was discussed in the previous subsection. The second arises from the fact that better-off individuals disproportionately hold equities, while worse-off individuals hold debt, including government bonds. Lowering the interest rate on government bonds to stimulate the economy hurts bondholders, at the expense of those who own equity, thus leading to more wealth inequality.[32] Indeed, elderly retirees who have acted prudently, in a risk-averse manner, holding onto government bonds, have been devastated by quantity easing.

The distributive effects may undermine the effectiveness of monetary policy. Since the marginal propensity to consume (out of income or wealth) of those at the top is much lower than at the bottom, any adverse distributive effect lowers aggregate demand.[33] Moreover, target savers (those saving for retirement, to obtain a down payment on a home, or to finance the education of their children) have to save more to meet their targets.[34] If the distributive effect is large, and the stimulus to investment is small (which has been the case since the 2008 crisis, with investment as a share of GDP actually lower in 2015 than it was in 2007 in spite of QE[35]), then the net effect on the economy of lowering interest rates or more accommodative monetary policies (QE) may have been negative.[36]

### Open economy

The previous discussion focusing on a closed economy emphasized that the government, having delegated the allocation of credit to the private sector, with limited restrictions, had relatively little control over the use to which money/credit would be put, and therefore there was at best a loose connection between monetary policy and macroeconomic activity. Matters are even worse in an open economy for two reasons. Now, there is a further use to which the credit created can be put – purchasing assets abroad. This was evidenced in the aftermath of the 2008 crisis, where much of the liquidity created in the US went to purchase assets and make loans in emerging markets – not a surprise given the boom in these economies and the lackluster performance of the US. In short, the money went where it was not wanted and needed; and didn't go where it was wanted and needed. The stimulus of/to the US economy from this loose monetary policy was thus limited.

*Credit and macroeconomic stability* 147

There is a second effect: now there is an alternative supply of credit from lenders outside the country. Thus, even if monetary authorities tighten credit, there can be an offsetting effect from a flow of money into the country. Indeed, there has been a regular pattern of exactly this happening: when countries tighten credit, raising interest rates, out of concern about overheating, the higher interest rates attract an inflow of capital partially or fully offsetting the domestic contraction.[37] Only by controlling the sources and uses of funds carefully can some semblance of control over the macro-economy be achieved.

### Summing up

Standard monetary theory has sought a neat set of instruments and targets by which the macro-economy could be well-regulated. There was perhaps as much a political drive for such parsimony as an intellectual one: if one could find a simple variable that could lead to macrostability, the nature of government intervention would be very limited; there would be little need for discretion. It was as if, when it was realized that Adam Smith's beautiful economic machine didn't work quite as perfectly as his latter-day descendants believed (though Smith himself was far more aware of these limitations), a slight modification to that machine would ensure its smooth running. Monetarism held that the government should simply expand the money supply at a fixed rate. New theories focused on controlling the interest rate (and indeed, some proposed a simple rule by which that might be done, reflecting inflation, a rule that would work regardless of the source of the disturbance to the economy giving rise to the inflation). Today, these theories are largely discredited (see the various papers in Blanchard et al. 2012; Akerlof et al. 2014). The discussion here has provided the underlying analytics explaining why we should not be surprised at the failures of these simple theories, and of the broader institutional theory attributed to Tinbergen of assigning to the central bank a single target – inflation – and a single instrument – the short-term interest rate.[38]

Government only controls the supply of credit very indirectly through the instruments under its control, and it does even a poorer job at controlling that part of credit that goes to purchase newly produced goods – say machine goods, buildings, or consumption – within the country. As a result, monetary policy is a weak instrument for controlling the economy in the sense that the link between the actions taken and the desired effects are uncertain. In certain circumstances, we have explained why it is an ineffective instrument – it simply may not be able to restore the economy to full employment. Its ineffectiveness goes

## 148  *Joseph Stiglitz*

well beyond the usual "zero lower bound" argument, a generalization of the Keynesian liquidity trap. Indeed, seemingly more accommodative monetary policies may, under certain circumstances, even have perversely contractionary effects, especially when they are not well designed to take into account likely effects on the banking system and broader distributive consequences. Some evidence of this has been seen in recent forays into negative interest rates.

Earlier IS-LM analysis was largely predicated on a stable demand curve for money. What was variable was the "real" economy: the interest rate at which full employment could be attained. Hence, with an unstable IS curve and a stable LM curve, monetary policy sought to increase M, the money supply, to the point where the rate of interest fell, to the level that induced full employment.

It became clear, however, that the LM curve itself was unstable, and this naturally led the government to target the interest rate. In effect, M increased until the desired interest rate was achieved. It was assumed that lowering the (real) interest rate would lead to higher output. Hence, all that needed to be done was to lower the interest rate enough. But then, in the Great Recession, monetary authorities hit the ZLB. Clever economists responded that it was only the nominal interest rate that was constrained. If, somehow, we could raise inflationary expectations, credibly committing to a higher inflation rate, then the real interest rate would fall, and the faith that one could rely on monetary policy to restore the economy to full employment would itself be restored. Putting aside the fact that no one has figured out how to make such a credible commitment,[39] we have argued that this framework is badly flawed.

We have explained that the links between the instruments under the control of monetary authorities and the variables that affect aggregate activity are weak, unstable and uncertain, and even of ambiguous sign. For instance, lowering the T-bill rate may or may not lead to a lowering of the lending rate. Because of distributive effects, we have explained that lowering interest rates may lower aggregate demand. Even when there is a positive elasticity of aggregate demand to changes in interest rates, the interest elasticity may be small, so that the magnitude of the changes in interest rate required will be very large – larger than would be politically acceptable, because such large changes will inevitably have large distributive consequences.[40] We have explained too that changes in interest rates, especially large changes, increase uncertainty; and such increases in uncertainty themselves can have adverse aggregate effects. And this is even more so as monetary authorities stretch themselves, seeing that traditional instruments are failing: there is

## Credit and macroeconomic stability    149

uncertainty associated with these innovative instruments, even if the policymakers were confident about the effects, if market participants are not, there are adverse effects on the real economy of these risk perceptions.

We have also explained why, though monetary policy has long been held out as the instrument of choice, it is an instrument with some adverse side effects, both on efficiency and distribution.

Indeed, it seems peculiar – and inadvisable – to attempt to correct a deficiency of aggregate demand arising from "shocks" to the economy arising, say, from an increase in uncertainty or an adverse change in the distribution of income of wealth (because of a deflationary shock which increases the real indebtedness of firms and households[41]) by changing the interest rate (intertemporal prices). Even if one could do that, it seems preferable to address the underlying problem. If there is an increase in uncertainty, then government can take a more active role in risk mitigation, for example, by issuing income-or state-contingent loans.[42] If there has been a redistribution of wealth as a result of a large deflationary shock, the government might consider a better system of debt restructuring (e.g. through a homeowners' chapter 11; see Stiglitz 2010).

To reflect the central refrain of my criticism of the Washington Consensus,[43] there are broader goals (not just price stability, but employment, growth, financial stability, and even distribution) and more instruments (including a broad set of regulatory tools called macroprudential instruments) than those seeking to employ monetary policy should use. Managing a complex economic system in the face of uncertainty requires as many tools as one can manage; the single-minded focus on short-term interest rates narrowly confined what central banks *could* do, just as the single-minded focus on inflation narrowly confined what central banks *should* do.

We have attempted to dethrone monetary policy from the pedestal on which it has been placed by some economists seeking to put it at the center of macroeconomic management. But at the same time we have shown how we can make monetary policy more effective than those who have focused on the narrow set of instruments that have traditionally been assigned to monetary authorities.

The simple empirical results in the Appendix show that *on average* the link between monetary policy and variables and the real economy is very weak – results that are consistent with the numerous schools of thought (such as real business cycle theory) that have argued that the real economy is affected by real variables, and that monetary variables have, at most, second order effects. The results of the Appendix are

## 150 *Joseph Stiglitz*

especially powerful in discrediting standard formulations, for example, where there is a simple Keynesian demand curve for money that plays a central role in interest rate determination, and this itself is at the center of the transmission mechanism for monetary policy.

But even if monetary policy *on average* has little impact, that is not what monetary authorities care about: they want to know whether, *under the particular circumstances* being confronted at this particular moment, monetary policy can be used to *stabilize* the economy, to *stimulate* the economy when there is excess capacity, and to *constrain* aggregate demand when there are inflationary pressures. It should be clear that there have been particular moments in history when monetary policy has mattered. Hopefully, the analysis of this chapter helps us understand better when monetary policy matters, and when it does not.

In the next section of the chapter, we argue that there are more fundamental reforms to the monetary architecture of the economy – to the system of credit and transactions – making use of 21st-century technology, which will enable monetary authorities in the future to do a far better job of macroeconomic management.

## Creating a new electronic financial system[44]

The 2008 global financial crisis and the subsequent discussion of financial sector reforms highlighted the failures of financial markets and the enormous consequences of these failures for the economic system. These included the following: excessive volatility in credit creation, with a misallocation of capital and a mismanagement of risk; more credit going to the purchase of fixed assets rather than to the creation of productive assets; excessive and volatile cross-border flows of short-term capital, leading to volatility in exchange rates and trade flows; excessive charges for the running of the payments mechanisms; and an array of socially unproductive practices, from market manipulation to insider trading to predatory lending.[45] Around the world, these financial market dysfunctions have had serious macroeconomic consequences. In the case of Europe, misguided credit flows to the periphery countries created the imbalances from which Europe is still suffering. In the case of the US, predatory lending, securitization (often based on fraudulent practices), and derivatives led to the deepest downturn since the Great Depression.

Modern technology provides the basis of a *new* and more efficient financial system, one that would simultaneously lead to better macroeconomic regulation of the economy. The following sections briefly

*Credit and macroeconomic stability*   151

describe the key elements of such a system – a low-cost "medium of exchange" for facilitating transactions and a system of credit creation focused on the *real economy*, managed in a way far more conducive to macroeconomic stability than the current system.

### Creating a 21st-century financial transactions system

The banking and monetary system serves multiple purposes. One of them is as a medium of exchange. The world has several times made a change in the prevailing medium of exchange. Gold was once used as a medium of exchange; then, at least in the United States, there was a move to the bimetallic standard, where gold and silver were used. Finally, we moved to paper (or "fiat") money. For years, it is has been recognized that it would be far more efficient to move to e-money, away from currency. Our payments mechanism has already changed dramatically. We have gone a long way towards an electronic payments mechanism, and in most of the world we could go far further with an even more efficient one, if it were taken out of the hands of the monopolistic financial system. Electronic transfers are extraordinarily cheap, but banks and credit card companies charge exorbitantly for the service, reaping monopoly profits as a result.[46] Electronic money is more convenient for people on both sides of the transaction, which is why it has become the dominant form of payment. It saves the costs of printing money, which has increased as the sophistication of counterfeiters has increased. It has a further advantage, especially in countries where small businesses predominate: it significantly curtails the extent of tax avoidance.[47]

With electronic money, the money *inside* a country's banking system can, in effect, be easily "locked in" simply by not allowing the transfer of money out of the country's banking system. But anybody can transfer the money in his bank account to that of anyone else. Thus, everybody has, in effect, almost full use of his money.[48] Money inside the country's banking system (which for convenience, we will call the G-euro) would be just like any other currency, with a well-defined value relative to any other currency.

Most individuals today have accounts; only the very poor are "unbanked", and in recent years governments and nongovernmental organizations, like the Bill & Melinda Gates Foundation, have been making great efforts to bank the unbanked. In most countries, government pension payments are now transferred through bank accounts, partly to reduce the risk of stolen checks, and partly to reduce the outrageous charges that are sometimes charged by check-cashing services.

## 152   Joseph Stiglitz

Thus, the task of implementing an electronic banking system today is clearly manageable.

### Credit: Creating a banking system that serves society

A big advantage of the use of fiat money was that one could regulate the supply. When gold was used as the medium of exchange, when there was a large discovery of gold – or when the gold supply increased as Spain conquered the New World – there would be inflation, as the price of gold would rise relative to other goods; if there were few gold discoveries, then there would be deflation. Both caused problems. Deflation, for instance, would redistribute income from debtors to creditors, increasing inequality and imposing hardship. America's election of 1896 was fought on the issue of the money supply. The debtors wanted to increase the money supply by moving from gold to a bimetallic standard of gold and silver.

While the modern financial system based on fiat money doesn't suffer from the vagaries of gold discoveries, it has sometimes suffered from something else: volatility in the creation of money and credit by the banking system, giving rise to the booms and busts that have characterized the capitalist system.

Banks effectively increase the supply of money by increasing the supply of credit. In a modern economy, central banks regulate, usually indirectly, banks' creation of money and credit. They are supposed to do it *in just the right amount*, so that there is a "Goldilocks" economy, neither under- nor over-heated but "just right". It is apparent that they have often failed to do so. This is partly the result of the often-noted "long and variable lags" associated with monetary policy – with monetary authorities having to base their actions on predictions concerning the future course of the economy. But more importantly, for our purpose, is "instrument uncertainty", the weak link between what monetary authorities do and the impacts on GDP, since the increased liquidity may go for many uses other than stimulating the economy, as our earlier discussion emphasized.

The traditional view of banking was based on a primitive agriculture economy. Farmers with excess seed – with harvests greater than they wanted to consume or plant the next season – could bring the seed to the bank, which would lend, at interest, the seed to some farmer who wanted more seed than he had, either for consumption (say, because he had a bad harvest that year) or planting. The bank had to have seed deposits in order to lend.[49] Markets on their own equilibrated the demand and supply of seeds, so there was really little need for government intervention.[50]

## Credit and macroeconomic stability    153

But if, for some reason, there was, the interest rate provided the natural mechanism: if for some reason, savings (at full employment) – the supply of seeds – exceeded investment (the demand for seed), then lowering interest rates would cause the supply of seeds to fall and the demand for seeds to increase until the two were equilibrated.

But this reasoning again totally misses the nature of credit in the 21st century. In a modern economy, banks effectively create credit out of thin air, backed by general confidence in government, including its ability and willingness to bail out the banks, which is based in part on its power to tax and borrow.[51]

### Targeted regulation of credit creation

There is a problem in our current system: because the central banks' control mechanisms are typically very indirect, the economy is often over- or under-heated. Sometimes there is too much credit creation, leading to an excess of aggregate demand, and prices rise: there is inflation. Sometimes there is a lack of demand, and prices fall: there is deflation.

The first part of this chapter has explained some of the key reasons for this failure: while central banks can regulate the supply of credit reasonably well, they can't (or more accurately don't) regulate the *use* to which the credit is put. Much of the credit goes to buying preexisting assets, like land. Some of the credit goes to providing margin for bets (e.g. in futures markets). What determines whether the economy is over- or under-heated is the purchase of new goods and services (whether for consumption or investment). Thus, after the 2008 crisis, there was a massive increase in liquidity, as the Fed pumped money into the economy. But relatively little of this went to buy goods and services in the US, so in spite of the huge expansion of the money supply as conventionally measured, the economy remained weak.[52]

In short, even with fiat money, there may still be a deficiency of domestic aggregate demand – a deficiency that could be easily corrected: there are individuals and firms who would like to spend but cannot get access to credit. A near zero interest rate does not mean businesses can get access to credit at such a rate – or at any rate.

### Restoring domestic control over credit creation

The electronic payments mechanism allows a country to assert control over the supply of credit and the uses to which it can be put in a way which is far better than the current system. Think of this most directly

154 *Joseph Stiglitz*

as occurring through a government bank. It can add "money" to the payments mechanism by lending money to a small enterprise with a proven reputation that wants to make an investment. The government simply puts more "money" into the bank account of the enterprise, which the enterprise can then use to pay contractors. Of course, in providing credit there is always a risk of non-repayment, and standards must be established for evaluating the likelihood of repayment.

In recent decades, faith in government's ability to make such evaluations has diminished, and confidence has been placed in the private financial system. The 2008 crisis as well as other frequent crises that have marked the last third of a century have shown that that confidence has been misplaced. Not only didn't the banks make good judgments – as evidenced by the massive, repeated bailouts – but they systematically failed to fulfill what they should have seen as their major responsibility: providing credit to businesses to create new jobs. By some accounts, their "real" lending amounts to just 3 percent of their activities, by others, to some 15 percent. But by any account, bank finance has been absorbed in other directions.[53]

There were always obvious problems in delegating the power of credit creation, backed by government, to private institutions: banks could use their power to benefit their owners, through connected lending. Regulations circumscribed this, motivated by the experience of *bad* lending, perhaps more than by the implicit corruption and inequality to which such lending gives rise.

Circumscribing connected lending didn't address one of the key underlying problems: credit is scarce; giving private banks the right to create credit with government backing gave them enormous "economic rents". Even with connected lending circumscribed, bankers use their economic power to enrich themselves and their friends. Russia provides the quintessential example: those with banking licenses could use that power to buy enormously valuable state assets, especially in natural resources. It was through the banking system that the Russian oligarchs were largely created. In Western countries, matters are done more subtly – but the net result in creating enormous inequality remains (though not of the magnitude of Russia). In many cases, the banks lend money to those whom they "trust" and judge creditworthy, with collateral that they value: in short, the bankers lend money to those who are similar to themselves. Even if banker A can't lend to himself or his relatives, banker A can lend to the relatives of banker B, and banker B can lend to the relatives of banker A. The fallibility of their judgments has been repeatedly demonstrated: overlending to fiber optics at one moment, to fracking at another, to housing in a third.

*Credit and macroeconomic stability* 155

There is a second danger to the delegation of the power of credit creation to private banks. Throughout history, moneylenders have had a bad reputation because of the ruthlessness with which they exploit the poor – especially at moments of extreme need, where without money their family members might die. At such times, there is an enormous asymmetry in bargaining power, which the moneylenders exploit. Virtually every religion has tried to proscribe such exploitation, prohibiting usury, and in some cases, even interest. Somehow, in the magic of Neo-liberalism, this long history was forgotten: bankers not only didn't suffer from the stigma of being called moneylenders, they were elevated to being the paragons of capitalism. In the enthusiasm over their new virtues, as linchpins in the workings of the capitalist system itself, it was simply assumed that such exploitation would not occur, perhaps in the belief that competition would ensure it *couldn't* happen, perhaps in the belief that with the new prosperity of workers, ordinary citizens wouldn't let it happen.

All of this was wishful thinking. Freed of constraints, 21st-century moneylenders have shown themselves every bit as ruthless as the moneylenders of the past; in fact, they are in some ways worse, because they have discovered new ways of exploiting both the poor and investors.[54] The financial sector has enriched itself on the back of the government's credibility, without performing the societal functions that banks were supposed to perform. In doing so, the financial sector has become one of the major sources of the increased inequality around the world.

Even given this history, the government may want to delegate responsibility for making credit decisions to private enterprises, but if so, it should develop strong systems of incentives and accountability, such that the financial system actually focuses on lending for job and enterprise creation and so that it does not make excessive profits as it performs these functions[55] and so the government should be adequately compensated for its backing. In effect, in the current system, all the "value" of the underlying government credit guarantee is captured by the private sector.[56]

### Credit auctions

Here, we consider one possibility for addressing this issue and providing for greater economic stability. First, the central bank (government) auctions off the rights to issue new credit. The amounts would be added to the "money" that is within the financial system. The magnitude of net credit that it allows to be added each month will be

## 156   *Joseph Stiglitz*

determined by the country's central bank on the basis of its assessment of the macroeconomic situation – that is, if the economy is weaker, it will provide more credit to stimulate the economy. The winners of the credit auction then allocate this "money" to borrowers on the basis of *their* judgments about repayment capacity, within the constraints that the central bank may impose (described later).[57]

Note that in this system, banks cannot create credit out of thin air, and the amount of money being created each month is known with considerable precision. The winners of the credit auction can only transfer money from their accounts to the borrowers' accounts.

Conditions would attach to selling the "rights to lend" to the banks. Minimum percentages of the loans would go to small and medium-size enterprises and to new enterprises or to underserved communities; a maximum would go to real estate lending (perhaps apportioned by location, based on local changes in prices), to purchases of other existing assets, or to those engaged in speculative activities, like hedge funds. None would be allocated to socially proscribed activities, like those contributing to global warming or associated with the promotion of death, such as cigarettes. In short, there would be minimum standards for social responsibility. There would be limits on the interest rates charged. Discriminatory lending practices and other abusive practices by credit card companies would be proscribed. So, too, would connected lending. There would be further restrictions to ensure that the loan portfolio of the bank is safe and sound, and there would be strict supervision by government regulators to ensure compliance with the regulations governing any such program.

If it wished, the monetary authority could target credit even more narrowly, to be used to purchase goods which are in excess supply, or which use labor of types which confront high levels of unemployment. There is always a trade-off: such targeted lending may be subject to political pressure in ways that more broad-based measures may not be.

In a 21st-century banking system, a bank's ability to lend is, in a sense, given only temporarily. It is conditional on compliance with the rules and standards established. The government would allow for entry into the banking system; indeed, separating the depository and lending functions and the open auction of rights to issue credit should make entry easier, and thus competition more vigorous than under current arrangements.

Still, since lending is an information-based activity, and the gathering of information is a fixed cost, one would like stability in the new banking system, and this will require that banks not live on the edge – that is, that they be sufficiently well capitalized and sufficiently profitable.

"Sufficiently profitable" should not be taken to mean the 25 percent return on equity that one of the European banks, Deutsche Bank, famously came to expect as normal. Hence, entry of enterprises with sufficient capital and who also satisfy other conditions that enhance the view that they would be responsible lenders, would be encouraged.[58] The system of auctioning of credit would ensure that banks not earn excessive returns; most of the value of the public's backing to the creation of money/credit would be captured by the public, rather than as now by the bankers. At the same time, the new system of credit creation ensures that the social functions of finance are more likely fulfilled, at least better than under current arrangements.

This is an example of how to create a 21st-century banking system, responding to the advantages of electronic technology, doing things that would have been far harder to accomplish in earlier decades – a banking system more likely to ensure responsible lending and macroeconomic stability than the current system, and without the huge rents and exploitation that have contributed so much to the inequality that has stalked advanced countries around the world.

But this reform is about more than curbing bankers' exploitation. It is also about enhancing macroeconomic stability. One of the major contributors to macroeconomic instability is the instability in credit supply, and, in particular, to the supply of credit for the purchase of *produced* goods and services. The 2008 crisis demonstrated that all the advances in markets and our understanding of markets have *not* led to greater stability in this crucial variable – in fact, quite the opposite. The electronic banking system described here not only enhances stability in this critical variable, it also provides the basis of a virtuous circle leading to an increase in overall stability of the economy. One of the most important reasons that small businesses don't repay loans is macroeconomic fluctuation: loans simply can't be repaid when an economy is in depression. Ensuring greater macro-stability (than under the current regime) would do more than anything else to ensure the viability of the banking system and to encourage a more competitive economy.

### Whence bank capital?

The beauty of the modern credit system is that it doesn't really require the same kind of capital as required by banking systems of the past. Recapitalizing a destroyed banking system would not require gold or borrowing to buy seeds as it did in the old days. As we have seen, the government itself can simply create credit.[59]

## 158 *Joseph Stiglitz*

The fact that the money created by the government can be used to pay the taxes that are owed to the government, and that the government has the power to levy taxes, ensures the value of the credit it has created. Indeed, because the credit that has been created is electronic money, the movement of which can easily be monitored, the government does not only have the ability to levy taxes – it also enhances the ability to collect taxes.

The only reason for bank capital in this world is as a partial guarantee that the bank has the capacity to repay the credit – the bank's "purchases" from the government of the right to issue credit are only temporary, and the credit thus created must be repaid to the government. (The fact that the bank will lose its own capital has, in addition, strong incentive effects, incentivizing the bank to make good decisions about whom to give the credit to, and to monitor the loan well.) But if the government is doing an adequate job of bank supervision and has imposed appropriate regulations (e.g., on connected and excessively risky lending), the amount of capital required will be limited. And that fact alone should lead to more competition in the market for the provision of credit – reducing the excessive returns currently received.

### Macro-stability and income-(state-)contingent loans

To achieve full employment may entail an auction of credit at which the price is negative, that is the only terms at which potential lenders are willing to "accept" the temporary use of funds, to be repaid later, entail a negative interest rate. The auction may entail a provision (unlike the current system) where a negative "bank rate" has to be passed on (at least partially) to borrowers, in the form of a negative lending rate. Presumably there is some negative rate at which the desired credit creation – that viewed as necessary to ensure full employment – related to new spending (investment or consumption) is achieved. But it may be a very negative rate, and the distributive and even allocative consequences of that negative rate may be adverse. Accordingly, it makes sense to look for more effective ways of stimulating the economy. One such way – ensuring a trade surplus – is discussed in the next section. Here we consider another way: state-contingent loans, whereby the amount the borrower has to repay depends on the state of the economy.

There is a widespread consensus that one of the reasons that consumption and investment are depressed in a deep economic downturn is "lack of confidence", or, slightly more precisely, uncertainty about the future. Consumers are not sure of their future wages, retirees of the future return on their savings, and producers of the returns on their investment. They worry that if the downturn persists, unemployment may be high, wages low, interest rates low, and sales poor. Traditional monetary policy has tried to compensate for the absence of insurance markets by which individuals might mitigate these risks by changing the intertemporal price. It is, to say the least, a peculiar response: it makes far more sense to try to address the market failure directly, than to increase one distortion in response to another.[60] As we noted in the first part of the chapter, it is not even clear that lowering the interest rate is even an *effective* response, not just because of the distributive and distortionary effects, but because as the interest rate is lowered, risk perceptions may increase, and the adverse risk effects could overwhelm the intertemporal price effects.

### Managing the current account deficit

The analysis so far has been for a closed economy. Extending the analysis to an open economy is at least conceptually easy. When a firm exports some good, say a widget, it receives dollars. The dollars could be kept out of the country, say in a dollar account in New York. But the exporter may want to bring the dollars into the country, depositing them into the country's electronic banking system. The number of, say, G-euros that the exporter would receive in return for the dollars would be market determined; that is, importers may want dollars to buy goods from the US. They thus transfer money in their bank account to the exporter. By the same token, an individual in the country wanting to make an investment abroad, say in the US, might want dollars, and be willing to transfer G-euros in his electronic banking system to someone who is willing to sell him dollars.

These capital flows may, however, be very destabilizing – leading to large fluctuations in exports and imports as the exchange rate changes, leading in turn to macroeconomic instability. The central bank can attempt to offset these effects through the system of credit creation (auctions) described earlier. However, there is another way of regulating trade flows that may be more effective.

### Managing the current account deficit through trade chits

In this proposal, the government would provide to any exporter a chit, a "token" (in this case, electronically recorded – alternatively called trade chits or Buffett chits[61]), the number in proportion to the value of what was exported. To import a G-euro's worth of goods, there would

# 160   *Joseph Stiglitz*

be a requirement to pay, in addition, a G-euro's worth of chits or "trade tokens". There would be a free market in chits, so the demand and supply of chits would be equal; and by equating the demand and supply of chits, one would automatically balance the current account.

In practice, the value of the chit might normally be very small, at least for a country with a small trade deficit.

This system would be a way of managing the high level of volatility in market economies associated with short-term capital flows. With the free flow of capital, the exchange rate is determined by the vagaries of the market. And those capricious changes in exchange rate then drive exports, imports, the trade deficit, and borrowing, and in doing so, give rise to macroeconomic instability. With the system of trading chits, the trade deficit can be controlled, enhancing overall stability.[62]

In the previous analysis, where every import needs a chit, there is neither a trade surplus nor a trade balance. The government could use this system to limit the size of the deficit or surplus as well. For instance, if it wants to limit imports to be no more than 20 percent greater than exports, it can issue 1.2 import chits for every G-euro of exports. When there would be an excessive surplus, every import would be granted an "export" chit. Then every export would require a chit. This would automatically bring exports down to the level of imports. By issuing both import and export chits, the trade balance can be kept within any prespecified bounds.

The fact that the country could thus stabilize the size of the trade deficit or surplus has an enormous macroeconomic advantage: it facilitates macroeconomic stabilization itself. It means, for instance, that a small country doesn't have to suffer from the vagaries of its "external balance", its net export position. These fluctuations impose enormous costs on society, of which the market, in generating them, takes no account.[63]

But ensuring stability in the trade deficit also engenders longer-term stability, for national indebtedness, built up over many years, can suddenly become unsustainable. The market sees the world through very myopic lenses. It is willing to lend year after year – until it suddenly changes its mind.[64] By limiting the trade deficit, a country is in effect limiting national borrowing; this framework thus reduces a key source of instability.[65]

Moreover, we can see how this system would help strengthen the G-euro. In the absence of the chit system, an increase in the demand by Greeks for imports (i.e. for, say, dollars to buy American cars) would lead to a fall in the price of the Greek-euro. But now, with imports discouraged by the necessity of also paying to purchase a chit, the increased demand for imports would be reflected in an increased

*Credit and macroeconomic stability* 161

price of a chit, rather than a decrease in the value of the Greek-euro. The Greek-euro will be stronger than it otherwise would be.

### Economic theory and macro-stability

Some might complain: aren't we interfering with the market? Of course, all monetary policy represents an interference with the market: few believe that interest-rate determination should simply be left to the market.

This proposal entails minimal intervention in the market, and even in doing so, uses market mechanisms. It corrects for a well-recognized externality, the market externality associated with external imbalances. Markets exhibit enormous volatility in both prices and quantities: interest rates demanded of borrowers from different countries have moved violently in different directions, and capital and credit flows have fluctuated in ways that are virtually uncontrollable under current arrangements.

Workers are told that they should simply accept being buffeted by these maelstroms that are not acts of nature but the creations of irrational and inefficient markets. Workers should accept wage cuts and the undercutting of social protections in order for the capital markets to enjoy their "freedom". The electronic payment system, with credit auctions and trade chits, is intended to bring a modicum of order to this chaos, which has not even produced the higher growth in GDP that was promised – let alone the social benefits that were supposed to accompany this higher GDP.

In the Arrow Debreu world with perfect markets, prices play a critical role in ensuring economic efficiency. But in the real world in which we live, as Martin Weitzman (1974) explained long ago, it is often better not to just rely on prices, but to try, as our proposed framework does, to control the *quantity* of credit and net exports, and to regulate the uses to which credit is put. There is a large literature showing that under a variety of conditions, when there is a departure from the first-best world, such quantity controls are a better way of regulating the economy.[66] However, the management of the economy in our proposed framework relies heavily on the use of prices, but not fully so; there is no micromanagement, but more macro-management than exists today.

## Conclusions

Decades ago, we learned that one could not let a market economy manage itself. That is why, for instance, every country has a central bank determining interest rates and regulatory authorities overseeing banking. Some would like to roll back the clock to a world without central banks and with free banking, with no restraints. Anyone who has read his economic history knows what a disaster that would likely be.

But anyone observing macroeconomic performance in recent years will see that things have not gone well in many countries around the world – even in advanced countries, in Europe and the US, with supposedly well-functioning markets and institutions and well-educated individuals to manage the economy. The framework provided here provides a way of improving matters. These are modest reforms that would not upend the system. But they systematically address some of the major weaknesses of current economic arrangements, some of the major instabilities that have proven so costly to our economies and our societies.

There are, of course, many details to be worked out. The system is surely not perfect. It is not intended to eliminate all speculative activity, and it will not do so. But by restraining the uses of newly issued credit it will curb such activities. But almost as surely, it is better than the current system. This framework could lead to greater economic stability and growth.

# Appendix[67]
## On the relationship between money, output, and interest rates

In this appendix, we present some new evidence which supports our reformulation of the theory of money and credit and macroeconomic activity. The evidence is only suggestive, but we believe that, at the same time, it persuasively argues *against* existing formulations, even if it provides only limited support for those advanced here. Each of the models we present here were widely believed among monetary economists, some based on well-articulated theories, others advanced simply as empirical regularities. The data we present for recent years undermines the empirical foundations for these ideas.

### Quantity theory of money

We begin with the (now widely discredited) quantity theory of money, which underlay monetarism:

(A1) $MV = PQ$

where it was postulated that V, the velocity of circulation, was a constant. In the quantity theory of money, government controls the money supply, so (A1) is an equation determining national income, Y, where

(A2) $Y \equiv PQ$,

that is,

(A3) $Y = V M$,

an hypothesis which can be directly tested, in the form of (A3), or in the form of

(A3') $\ln Y = \ln M + \ln V$

164 *Joseph Stiglitz*

or

(A3") $\Delta Y = \Delta M$

or

(A3"') $\Delta \ln Y = \Delta \ln M.$

The quantity theory of money implies that the coefficient in the above regression should be unity. If we run the regression in this form, over the period 1959–2016, using quarterly data, for instance, the coefficient is significantly different from 1.[68]

We can test the model in other ways, for instance, by running the regression

(A4) $\Delta Y = \alpha + \beta \Delta M.$

The hypothesis (A3") predicts that $\beta = 1$ and $\alpha = 0$. We can reject both hypotheses, and the fit of the regression is remarkably poor.[69]

We have run the tests against all the specifications, with flexible lags, using the standard definition of money, M2, and with alternative time periods. We have also run the regressions in logarithmic form, a more natural specification in order to remove scale effects:

(A4') $\Delta \ln Y = \alpha + \beta \Delta \ln M$

The fit worsens, but the conclusion is unaltered.[70]

Often, it makes more sense to express everything in real terms:

(A5) $\Delta Q = \alpha + \beta \Delta M/P$

or

(A5') $\Delta \ln Q = \alpha + \beta \Delta \ln M/P$

Again, if the quantity theory were true, $\alpha$ should be zero and $\beta$ unity. Two striking things stand out from our regressions, done over the period 1959 to 2016[71] (and various subsets of that period) with US data (preliminary work suggests similar results for other countries): (1) $\beta$ is always small, and sometimes even insignificant; and (2) the relationship between a change in Q (or Y) and changes in M/P (or M) has weakened, with a structural break sometime around 1990.[72] That there should be some structural break is hardly a surprise, for there were marked changes in both the financial sector (both in regulations and the creation of new instruments, which serve as effect substitutes to money, the money market funds) and in the conduct of monetary policy (the switch from a focus on the money supply itself to the interest rate, with a greater emphasis on inflation).

It is possible, of course, that our measure of money is "wrong". Moreover, M2 clearly has some element of endogeneity, with banks lending more, creating more money, when income is going up (or is expected to be going up.) Accordingly, we reran our regressions with another notion, base money – the balance sheet of the Fed – which is seemingly a variable more directly under control of monetary authorities than M2. Let B be the size of the Fed's balance sheet (which we take as a crude measure of "base money"). Then the true money supply (here assumed unobservable) is assumed to be a function of B (observable). We again run these regressions, replacing B (or $\Delta B$) for M (or $\Delta M$). The results are similar: either no significant effect, or a small effect.[73,74]

## The demand for money

These are all models suggesting that *somehow* money "drives" the economy. But there is an alternative way of writing all of these equations, more modestly, as simply a demand curve for money. The quantity theory can be thought of as being an equilibrium model based on a special case of the Keynesian demand equation for money

$$\text{(A7) } M^d = k(r)\, PQ,$$

where the demand for money is made proportional to income, with the proportionality factor depending on the interest rate.

### Constant velocity

If $k' = 0$, then $V = 1/k$. If we also assume that we are always (nearly) on the demand curve of money (after all, no one *forces* people to hold money that they don't want to hold), then

$$\text{(A8) } M = kY,$$

with the correlates $\Delta M = k\Delta Y$, etc. As we shall comment further, testing (A8) simply tests whether the economy is "on" a demand function

## 166　*Joseph Stiglitz*

of the given form, a seemingly much weaker hypothesis than that M "drives" the economy. We can test it by running the regression

(A8') $\Delta M = \alpha' + \beta' \Delta Y$,

or, perhaps better (eliminating scale effects)

(A8") $\Delta \ln M = \alpha' + \beta' \Delta \ln Y$,

with the quantity theory hypothesis being $\beta' = 1$ and $\alpha' = 0$.

Our empirical analysis provides convincing evidence rejecting the hypothesis of the quantity theory of money and the related demand theory for money.[75] There are several alternative explanations. The analysis of this chapter has provided one explanation: money is not needed for transactions, and most transactions are not directly related to income (Y) (and there is no reason that they would grow in proportion to Y). There are some difficult econometric problems, which might lead to coefficient bias – but are hardly likely to provide a convincing explanation of the results.[76] The most obvious explanation is that V is not constant.

### Keynesian demand for money

Keynesian monetary theory hypothesized a stable demand function for money, where a linearized version of (A7) gives a corresponding set of equations, such as

(A9) $\Delta \ln M = \alpha' + \beta' \ln \Delta Y + \Upsilon' \Delta r$

or

(A10) $\Delta \ln M/P = \alpha' + \beta' \ln \Delta Q + \Upsilon' \Delta r$

Testing (A9) is testing whether the economy is on a Keynesian demand function. There are, of course, important econometric problems in testing any of these relations, since all of the variables are, in some sense, endogenous. This is true even when government sets M and/or r, because it sets these variables based on expectations of Y, or what Y would be in the absence of intervention, and those expectations may well be correlated with Y or Q itself. We shall return to these problems later.

Here, we simply note that in running the regression, $\alpha'$ should be zero (a value of $\alpha'$ not equal to zero would suggest that there are economies or diseconomies of scale in the use of money. While inventory theories of money might suggest that there are economies of scale, the presumption has been that these are sufficiently small that $\alpha'$ would not deviate significantly from zero), $\beta'$ should be unity, and $\Upsilon'$ should be negative (r here should be the opportunity cost of holding money). The first two hypotheses can clearly be rejected, and the overall fit is sufficiently poor that it suggests we are not on the Keynesian demand function for money. $\Upsilon'$, while of the right sign, is very small.[77,78] These results should create skepticism about the edifice created on the foundations of Keynesian monetary theory.

## Keynesian equilibrium

The standard Keynesian model assumes a stable demand curve for money, while the demand for investment and consumption is somewhat volatile. Investment is a function of the (real) rate of interest. The IS-LM curves give the resulting equilibrium, assuming that inflationary expectations are fixed, so that a change in r translates into a change in R, the real interest rate. The same results hold if, as in more recent models, one assumes consumption is a function of the interest rate.[79] Thus, we write

$$(A11a) \; r = \varphi \, (Y/M),$$

from the LM curve, and insert this into the stochastic IS curve

$$(A11b) \; Y = \phi \, (r) = \phi(\varphi(Y/M)) + \varepsilon,$$

which we rewrite in linearized form[80]

$$(A11b) \; Y = \alpha' + \beta' \, M + \varepsilon$$

or,

$$(A11c) \; \Delta \ln Y = \alpha' + \beta' \, \Delta \ln M + \varepsilon.$$

In the standard Keynesian model, price is fixed (in the short run), so the more interesting variant predicts that an increase in the money supply increases real income.[81]

$$(A11d) \; \Delta \ln Q = \alpha' + \beta' \, \Delta \ln M + \varepsilon$$

(A11c) and (A11d) are, of course, just the "reverse" equation of (A8). and the same as (A4) and (A5), respectively, except now our

## 168   *Joseph Stiglitz*

hypothesis is only that $\beta' > 0$: An increase in the money supply leads to a lowering of the interest rate, and this should increase nominal and real income. But our naïve regressions show that an increase in money lowers real income ($\beta'$ is negative, though not significantly different from zero), though it increases nominal income – with a significant coefficient. It would seem, on the basis of this crude analysis, that if monetary expansion affects national income, it is more by affecting the price level, contradicting the underlying assumption of the Keynesian model that prices are fixed. There are, of course, important simultaneity problems; in particular, monetary policy is conditional on many variables that could themselves be correlated with $\Delta Y$. We will say a little more about this later.

### Government controls r

As the instability of the LM curve became clear, as we noted in the text, it made sense for monetary authorities to switch to a focus on the variable that they (wrongly) believed to be the key determinant of macroeconomic activity, the interest rate. They could control at least the nominal interest rate directly, and if inflationary expectations were fixed, they could thus control the real interest rate. If inflationary expectations were variable and highly unpredictable, of course, controlling the nominal interest rate would leave much of the real interest rate out of the control of monetary authorities. Since different economic actors may respond to *different* interest rates and associated variables affecting the cost of capital, it is not just the T-bill rate that matters. Indeed, the thrust of the first part of the chapter was to argue that the most important variable affecting investment (at least by SMEs) is the lending rate, and that this variable is only loosely connected with the T-bill rate. Tobin argued that it was the price of equity, and this may even be more loosely related to the T-bill rate. Some investments may be more related to the long rate than the short, and the maturity structure itself is an endogenous variable – at least it was before monetary authorities sought to affect it through QE.

We ignore these complexities, postulating that

$$(A11d)\ \Delta Q = \alpha + \Upsilon \Delta r,$$

or in logarithmic form

$$(A11e)\ \Delta \ln Q = \alpha + \Upsilon \Delta r,$$

## Credit and macroeconomic stability    169

where it is assumed that the government controls r (possibly through the control of M). We run reduced form regressions of the form (A11d) and (A11e), obtaining a coefficient on $\Delta r$ of the wrong sign, with again there being a structural break in the late 80s/early 90s, perhaps corresponding to the adoption of the interest rate as the focal point of monetary policy.[82] The logarithmic form does slightly better, but in both, the R2 is very low. There are many things driving the economy. Changes in interest rates do not appear to be among the more important.

In the formulations so far, r enters through the money demand equation, representing the opportunity cost of holding funds. But standard Neo-classical theory suggests that investment and consumption are affected not by the nominal interest rate, but by the real interest rate, R. Changes in nominal interest rates translate into changes in real interest rates if inflationary expectations are constant. But inflationary expectations may well change as r or Q changes. Most simply, assume $\Delta R = f(\Delta Q, \Delta r)$ and $\Delta Q = H(\Delta R)$. We thus obtain in reduced linearized form (A11d) once again. Only the interpretation of the coefficients has changed.

More agnostically, we regress changes in output and the log of output against both changes in nominal and real interest rates, using the interest rate derived from treasury inflation-indexed security, constant maturity, as a proxy for the real interest rate

$$(A12a)\ \Delta Q = \alpha + \Upsilon \Delta r + d\ \Delta R,$$
$$(A12b)\ \Delta \ln Q = \alpha + \Upsilon \Delta r + d\ \Delta R.$$

Several things stand out from these regressions, done over the shorter period 2003–2016 (largely because of data availability) using quarterly data. The R2 is much higher than in any of the other equations. Most significantly, *only the coefficient on the nominal interest rate is significant*. By the same token, if we run the regression on only nominal or real interest rate, nominal does better than real – the real is not significantly different from zero.[83]

We have run regressions with variable lags, and the results remain unchanged.

To be sure, we have not estimated a sophisticated structural model, nor have we massaged the data or engaged in any of the usual data mining. (There are, accordingly, reasons that our estimates may be downward biased.) All that the analysis says – and it may be saying a lot – is that a quick and dirty look at the data doesn't provide the kind of support for many of the maintained hypotheses in conventional

## 170 Joseph Stiglitz

monetary theory and macroeconomics.[84] In particular, most striking are the results on money itself – for the standard hypothesis is that the money demand equation is relatively stable; that the money demand equation is of the general postulated form; and equilibrium analysis requires that the economy be "on" the money demand equation. The data rejects those hypotheses.

### An alternative interpretation?

There are other, more complicated interpretations of the results on (A12) (or the earlier simpler versions). If monetary authorities were perfect in predicting what output would be *in the absence of changes in monetary policy*, and thus changed monetary policy perfectly, to ensure that the economy was always at full employment, there would be no correlation between real output and monetary policy variables. Of course, we know that monetary authorities have been far from perfect in predicting what output would have been in the absence of their intervention, and far from perfect in designing intervention to ensure that output is stable.

Assume that monetary authorities raise interest rates when they expect output to increase next period above trend, and dampen output from *what it would have been* but not relative to the long-run trend. Then periods of high interest rates would be periods of high growth. Monetary policy may have worked – but the regressions don't show it.

Fortunately, we have data that expresses the forecasts of the Fed itself and of the general market consensus. Unfortunately, such forecasts embed both forecasts of the underlying disturbances to the economy and the Fed response, and the fact that such forecasts show systematic deviations from full employment implies that forecasters do not believe that the Fed will fully correct any "shock" to the underlying system. On average, one does not believe that Fed policy deliberately moves the economy away from full employment. Thus, it is reasonable to assume that when forecasters see a larger deviation from full employment, they see an adverse shock that will be partially, but not fully, offset by the Fed (consistent with risk aversion combined with instrument uncertainty; see Greenwald and Stiglitz 1989).

We have data on market forecasts of both interest rates (predictions of Fed policy) and output, and thus can ascertain whether there is any systematic effect on outcomes relatives to forecasts of the Fed's doing something different from what was expected. There does not appear to be. Lest we view what forecasters say about their forecasted interest rate not as reflecting their "true" forecasts, we modeled a forecast of the Fed's policy based on their expectations of output (or other variables), and ascertained whether deviations of policies from these predicted policies had an effect on output. It did not seem to.

The theoretical analysis of this chapter has provided a set of explanations for why none of these results should come as a surprise. They are not "econometric artifacts", likely to disappear if we massage the data enough, but rather should be taken to be stylized facts which economic theories need to take account of.

Nor should the fact that our results show no systematic relationship between money and output be taken to mean that money doesn't matter. Our models explain why it matters, both in normal and abnormal times. In abnormal situations – such as Volker's sudden change in US monetary policy – the credit constraints and soaring interest rates mattered hugely – they threw the US economy into a recession. Our analysis explains why one shouldn't look just to the interest rate – and especially to the T-bill rate – to assess the consequences. In more normal times, our analysis explains why other variables, like changes in expectations and perceptions of risk are likely to be as or more important; and again, the effects of monetary policy may be felt more through credit availability than through small changes in interest rates; and changes in credit availability may be far from perfectly correlated with changes in money supply. Thus, while this chapter takes a somewhat nihilistic stand on some of the monetary econometrics, it is quite positive about the relevance of monetary policy – though it argues that its effects cannot be well-captured in a single variable, like M2 or "r".

## Notes

1  All data in this chapter was obtained from the Federal Reserve Economic Data base (FRED), available at https://fred.stlouisfed.org/.
2  This section represents a development of ideas earlier presented in Greenwald and Stiglitz (2003).
3  In the 2008 financial crisis this relationship broke down temporarily. Apart from that, there appears to be no significant cyclical movement in the difference between the T-bill rate and the money market rate.
4  See Robertson (1934) and Ohlin (1937).
5  That is, the spread between the two is endogenous, and can vary with economic conditions and policy.
6  More broadly, with imperfect information, behavior is constrained by collateral, self-selection and incentive compatibility constraints.
7  Effects which may arise from the change in policy (interest rates) itself – some of which we describe in greater detail later – or which may arise simultaneously from other sources.
8  As we have already noted, as influential as Keynes's work has been, it provides a poor description of a modern credit-based economy. (In the

## 172 *Joseph Stiglitz*

Appendix, for instance, we provide convincing evidence against the hypothesis that individuals are on a stable demand function of the kind hypothesized by Keynes.) But while Robertson's focus on the demand and supply of funds is more convincing, his analysis is flawed, partly because he failed to recognize the central role of asymmetric information in the provision of credit, partly because he failed to take adequately into account the role of banks in the provision of credit (the subject of the discussion here). In the standard loanable funds theory (without banks), the role of government was limited: It was individual farmers who decide how much seed to supply and demand. Our theory, by contrast, says even here there can be a role through the rules government sets for the functioning of the critical intermediary institutions.

9  It leaves out, for instance, the role of rating agencies, investment analysts, etc. That these markets often do not work well is an understatement, evidenced by the problems in the financial crisis of 2008 and the scandals of the early 2000s. See Stiglitz (2003, 2010).

10  Moreover, ultimately, the supply of funds to large enterprises depends on the funds made available to a variety of intermediaries, which in turn depends on the credit creation mechanisms described here.

11  There are other reasons that firms (including banks) may act in a risk-averse manner. Imperfect information means that there is a separation of ownership and control (Berle and Means 1932; Stiglitz 1985) and firms typically construct incentive arrangements that lead managers to act in a risk-averse manner (Greenwald and Stiglitz 1990).

12  Their analysis also assumes that the risks confronting banks (and other firms in the economy) can neither be insured nor distributed across the economy, for example, because of information asymmetries.

13  In their model, bank assets are not fully tradable, because of information asymmetries. Accordingly, if the perceived risk associated with certain assets the bank holds increases, its willingness to undertake more risks may be adversely affected.

14  Their models also explain amplification: Why a seemingly small shock can have large effects.

15  The inability to divest oneself of risk generates an important hysteresis effect. Government regulatory policy may exacerbate these problems: When there are, for instance, capital adequacy requirements and banks' net worth is not evaluated on a mark-to-market basis, then a sale results in the recognition of a loss which is otherwise "hidden". On the other hand, marking to market forces banks to contract lending (or raise new equity) when there is a (what the bankers believe is a) temporary change in market sentiment against the assets which they hold. Of course, the irony is that in other contexts, bankers, as a group, have been the strongest advocates of the "market" and its rationality. But as the 2008 crisis demonstrated, they have shown an impressive level of cognitive dissonance – arguing against subsidies for others (such subsidies would distort markets) but for themselves (without state aid, the whole economy was at risk). See Stiglitz (2010).

16  As we have noted, risk perceptions relate not just to macroeconomic risks, but to risks of particular individuals, firms, and institutions, which in turn have macroeconomic consequences. Thus, it does not suffice to know that

## Credit and macroeconomic stability    173

the value of say equity has decreased *somewhere* in the economic system. A bank contemplating making a loan to a particular firm wants to know the economic situation of that particular firm. Uncertainties surrounding that are affected both by rules governing transparency and the structure of the economy – the nature of the interlinkages among firms.

We need to distinguish too between structural breaks – the move from agriculture to industry or from industry to services – with shocks to the system that, though large, do not fundamentally alter the structure of the economy. Thus, while Greenwald and Stiglitz (1993a, 1993b, 2003; as well as the large number of papers leading up to those studies and cited there) provided the intellectual foundations for what has since come to be called *balance sheet recessions,* they have argued that the current economic downturn is not fully described as a balance sheet recession, but rather is best seen as part of a deep structural transformation. See DelliGatti et al. (2012, 2016).

17  For a review of the arguments, see Greenwald and Stiglitz (2003).

18  I should emphasize that the significant bank contraction in lending to SMEs is not just a response to conventions, rules, and regulations. In 2008 there was a significant increase in risk perceptions, and such changes have a particularly large adverse effect on undercapitalized firms, among which SMEs are heavily represented.

19  This discussion illustrates a more general principle: In markets with asymmetric information, there are marked discrepancies between private and social returns. This can be especially so in the presence of rationing. See Greenwald and Stiglitz (1986).

20  This has been a long standing criticism of Friedman's criticism of monetary policy in the Great Depression. The fall in the money supply does not necessarily mean that the Fed *caused* the depression through its contractionary policy. The fall in money holding could be the result of the reduction in (anticipated) economic activity. And the Fed may have been powerless to overcome the exogenous perturbations giving rise to the decline in GDP. Indeed, while it may not have been able to fully offset the underlying forces, it may still have had an unambiguously positive effect: The decline in GDP could have been smaller than it otherwise would have been. See, for example, Tobin (1970).

21  Not surprisingly, there has been enormous controversy over whether the negative interest rates have had a positive or negative effect. Japan's central bank governor Kuroda tried to design the negative interest rate program in ways which limited the balance sheet effect, while retaining the intertemporal substitution effect. Whether he fully succeeded is part of the debate.

22  See Stiglitz (2015d, 2016b, 2016c) and Turner (2015). Stiglitz (2015b) provides a theoretical model linking monetary policy to land values.

23  See Guzman and Stiglitz (2015, 2016).

24  As the regressions reported in the Appendix amply illustrate.

25  Again, as evidenced in the regressions described in the Appendix.

26  This effect has been stressed by Jonathan Kreamer in his Ph.D. thesis (Kreamer 2015).

27  There may be a loss of intertemporal welfare from the variability in fiscal expenditures. But if the variability takes the form of infrastructure

## 174 *Joseph Stiglitz*

investments, and if the investment authority (say an investment bank, like the EIB) were to keep an inventory of good, high return projects, then the flow of "services" from the aggregate stock of public capital would not be highly variable. If the inputs used in public infrastructure investment were highly substitutable with those used in say private construction, and if one of the main sources of variability in aggregate output is private construction, then the social costs of putting the burden of adjustment on public infrastructure investment may be relatively low.

28 Of course, debt financed government spending may lead to an offsetting effect through the expectation of future taxes, but the conditions under which the adverse consequences of this is fully offsetting are highly restrictive. See Stiglitz (1988)

29 That is, Ramsey showed that optimal taxation entailed distorting all prices a little from their marginal costs, rather than a single price a lot. Modern monetary practice is based on the hypothesis that government intervention should be limited to interventions only in the short-term interest rate. There is, to my knowledge, no general proof that it is optimal to limit interventions in this way.

30 For a more extensive discussion of the issues raised here, see Stiglitz (2015a). Even the Fed has begun to recognize the potential importance of these effects. See Yellen (2014).

31 These are associated with the "repeal" of the second fundamental theorem of welfare economics, implying that issues of distribution and efficiency cannot be separated, as suggested by earlier analyses. See, for example, Stiglitz (1994, 2002a).

32 See Stiglitz (2015a, 2015c). We should expect such differentials in wealth holdings: Life cycle savers have to be more prudent in their wealth management than wealthy "capitalists". Giovannoni (2014, 2015) provides evidence.

33 See Stiglitz (2015d) and the references cited there.

34 This may be especially so if individuals are saving to purchase a home, since the lower interest rate may itself give rise to higher house prices, meaning that the down payment required is also larger.

35 In 2007, gross domestic investment for the US was 22 percent of GDP, and fell to 20 percent by 2015.

36 Of course, these numbers do not answer the relevant hypothetical question: What would investment have been but for the lowering of interest rates? Still, the fact that lowering interest rates from 5 to 0 percent has had such small an effect suggests that lowering the interest rate from 0 to minus 2 percent is unlikely to have a large effect.

37 See Stiglitz (2002b, 2015c) and Guzman and Stiglitz (2013) for a discussion of these issues and the consequent importance of monetary policy coordination.

38 See, for example, Stiglitz (1998b, 2014).

39 Much of the argument for an independent central bank is based on enhancing the ability to make such a commitment. If bankers control the central bank, because they benefit from a low inflation rate, it is more credible that the central bank will act in ways which limit inflation. But the crisis of 2008 showed the flip side risks: A central bank captured by the financial sector will do an inadequate job at financial regulation, exposing the economy to the far greater risks associated with financial instability.

## Credit and macroeconomic stability 175

40 Moreover, such large changes give rise to high levels of uncertainty, with strong adverse effects.

41 The shock does not actually have to be deflationary: All that is required is that the rate of inflation be less than was expected.

42 Australia has provided income contingent loans for a long time. The US has begun doing so in the case of certain student loans. Stiglitz (2014) and Stiglitz and Yun (2013, 2014, 2016) have proposed doing so for unemployment loans, and Chapman et al. (2014) present a range of other examples of such loans.

43 See Stiglitz (1998a, 2016d).

44 This section is adapted from Stiglitz (2016e).

45 Regulators, legislatures, and courts in antitrust actions have finally begun intervening to curtail the high fees and abusive practices, but the fees remain far higher than what they should be.

46 Regulators, legislatures, and courts in antitrust actions have finally begun intervening to curtail the high fees and abusive practices, but the fees remain far higher than what they should be.

47 Cyber security is one of the key problems faced in modern electronic payments mechanisms. The advantages of electronic transactions are, nonetheless, overwhelming, which is why even with monopoly pricing, there has been a shift toward this system.

48 The major exception, for the purchase of goods and services from abroad, is discussed later.

49 The evolution of the banking system from the primitive corn economy toward its modern form is interesting and informative. Early banks were really based more on gold deposits than on corn deposits. Those with more gold than they wanted to spend put it in the bank, and the bank lent it out to others. Soon, banks discovered that they could create pieces of paper, claims on gold, that others would accept, and that they could produce more of such pieces of paper than they had gold, in the knowledge that not all holders of these pieces of paper would ask for their money simultaneously. As it gave gold to some who asked for it, it would receive gold from others.

Occasionally, there would be a panic when holders of these pieces of paper worried whether the bank could fulfill its promises, and, of course, when they panicked and all went to the bank to demand their gold, there was not enough to satisfy their demands. The banks would go bankrupt, and the economy could be thrown into a depression.

Deposit insurance was invented to prevent these panics: The government explicitly stood behind the banks' promises. This gave greater faith that the promises would be honored (so long as there was faith in the government), and this in turn reduced the likelihood of a panic. But if the government was to provide these guarantees, this insurance, it had to make sure that the bank was acting responsibly – for example, lending out money to people who could actually pay it back, and not lending to the owners of the bank and their friends. Gerry Caprio, with whom I worked at the World Bank and who studied government rescues around the world, was fond of saying that there are two kinds of countries – those who have deposit insurance and know it, and those who have deposit insurance and don't know it. Sweden, before its financial crisis in the 1990s, had no

## 176 *Joseph Stiglitz*

deposit insurance, but it rescued its banks nonetheless. In the 2008 crisis, suddenly deposit insurance was extended to accounts that had not been fully insured before.

One can understand government taking on this new role, partially as a result of the magnitude and frequency of the panics and downturns in the market economy in the 19th and early 20th centuries. Moreover, as advanced countries, like the US, transformed themselves from agricultural economies to industrial economies, with an increasing fraction of the population dependent on manufacturing and other nonagricultural jobs, these economic fluctuations took a toll. So long as ordinary citizens had little voice in what government did, so what if so many suffered so much? But with the extension of the franchise and increasing democratic engagement, it became increasingly difficult for government to ignore these mega-failures of the market.

50 The theory of credit rationing based on information asymmetries provided an explanation for why markets on their own might fail.

51 See J. E. Stiglitz (2015c) and Greenwald and Stiglitz (2003).

52 There are several other "slips between the cup and the lips" discussed more fully in Part I of this chapter.

53 See, for example, Kay (2015) and Turner (2015).

54 More broadly, it has been shown that much of the increase in inequality in the advanced countries in recent decades is related to finance. See, in particular, Galbraith (2012) and Stiglitz (2012).

55 See Akerlof and Shiller (2015).

56 This is especially so through the privatization of gains and the socialization of losses that has become a regular feature in economies with too-big-to-fail banks (see Stiglitz 2010).

57 The system is symmetric. The central bank may decide that there is too much money in the economic system – that is, the banks are lending too much, using "money" that they receive in repayment. In that case, the government can buy back rights to issue credit: They buy back the money that they have allowed the banks to effectively manage on their behalf. Again, there can be an open auction for those most willing to give up rights to issue credit. This would literally drain money out of the banking system.

58 Entry would presumably occur to the point where the before-tax return to capital (measured over the business cycle) would be slightly more than the normal return to capital. Some excess return may be necessary to induce more responsible social behavior on the part of bankers.

59 Either through a government bank or through the auction mechanism just described.

60 It should be clear that the generalized Ricardian equivalence theorem (which holds that government financial risk has no effect; Stiglitz 1988) does not hold and that there are real benefits to this socialization of risk. In particular, the firms and consumers who are effectively "buying" this state insurance are engaging in bets which increases their expected wealth, so that there is a pseudo-wealth effect; there is also a "substitution" effect. Both increase investment, consumption, and production.

61 See Buffet (2003).

62 To prevent the buildup of chits – speculators might buy them on the bet that a chit is more valuable some years into the future – the chits should

## Credit and macroeconomic stability  177

be date-stamped; they would have to be used, for example, within a period of one year. (It's possible that some international rules, such as those currently stipulated by the WTO, would need to be changed to accommodate the system of chits, which could be viewed as a system of multiple exchange rates.)

63 These are an example of macroeconomic externalities, such as discussed by Anton Korinek, themselves a generalization of the pervasive pecuniary externalities to which Greenwald and Stiglitz (1986) called attention.

64 See Calvo (1998) for a discussion of sudden stops.

65 The experience of Europe and elsewhere has shown that it is not so much government borrowing that gives rise to crises, but national borrowing. In some cases, the national borrowing was government borrowing (Greece), but in many other cases (Ireland and Spain) it was private borrowing. When a crisis hits, the debt quickly moves from the private balance sheet to the public's.

66 See also Dasgupta and Stiglitz (1977).

67 All the data is from the Federal Reserve Economic Database ("FRED") at the Federal Reserve Bank of St. Louis. Contact the author for information on the exact time series used.

68 The 95 percent confidence interval is [0.7287, 08811]

69 $\alpha = 57.9465$, $95\%CI = [45.7192, 70.1738]$; $\beta = 0.3692$, $95\%CI = [0.2148, 0.5237]$, $R^2 = 0.0895$.

70 $\alpha = 0.0119$, $95\%CI = [0.0091, 0.0146]$; $\beta = 0.2287$, $95\%CI = [0.0796, 0.3777]$, $R^2 = 0.0389$.

71 In the case of (A5): $\alpha = 62.5533$, $95\%CI = [52.1117, 72.9949]$; $\beta = -0.2022$, $95\%CI = [-0.4990, 0.0945]$; $R^2 = 0.081$. In the case of (A5'): $\alpha = 0.0069$, $95\%CI = [0.0056, 0.0082]$; $\beta = 0.0897$, $95\%CI = [-0.0094, 0.1887]$; $R^2 = 0.0141$.

72 To identify the structural break, we used the sup Chow test (Andrews 2003); the tests show that in general there is a lot of parameter instability in the two decades between 1975 and 1995.

73 The only regression in which the coefficient on the assets variable is (barely) significant is a contemporaneous regression of log real output on log real assets – even there it is a meager 0.068. Regressions with lags or leads eliminate significance. Interestingly, there is very strong evidence of a structural break exactly in 2008 in this model.

74 If P is constant, as in Keynesian theories, then the aforementioned equations give a simple relationship between real output (Q) and nominal M, for example,

(A6) $\Delta Q = \alpha + \beta \, \Delta M$ or
(A6') $\Delta \ln Q = \alpha + \beta \, \Delta \ln M$.

75 For (A8'): $\alpha = 34.7090$, $95\%CI = [23.9735, 45.4444]$; $\beta = 0.2423$, $95\%CI = [0.1410, 0.3436]$; $R^2 = 0.0895$. For (A8"): $\alpha = 0.0139$, $95\%CI = [0.0118, 0.0159]$; $\beta = 0.1700$, $95\%CI = [0.0592, 0.2808]$; $R^2 = 0.0389$. The $R^2$ is tiny. It is clear that these do not provide (without further massaging) a good description of money demand holdings.

76 See also the later discussion.

77 (A9): $\alpha' = 0.0127$, $95\%CI = [0.0106, 0.0148]$; $\beta' = 0.2439$, $95\% CI = [0.1294, 0.3584]$; $\Upsilon'' = -0.0023$, $95\%CI = -0.0035, -0.0011]$; $R^2 = 0.0954$.

# 178   *Joseph Stiglitz*

(A10):   $\alpha' = 0.0052$, 95%CI $= [0.0033, 0.0071]$; $\beta' = 0.2768$, 95%CI $= [0.1015, 0.4521]$; $\Upsilon' = -0.0037$, 95%CI $= [-0.0053, -0.0020]$; $R^2 = 0.0924$

78  As we have emphasized repeatedly in this Appendix, we have not engaged in extensive data mining. Our objective is simply to suggest that that it is hard to reconcile observed data with the standard hypotheses. Of course, as we argue in the text, the observed money supply may depend on many other variables than income and the interest rate, and controlling for those variables, one should obtain a better fit.

Since the costs of adjusting money balances are small, it might be argued that there is little reason that individuals are not on their money demand curve. Still, one can view money balances as a residual, and if individuals cannot adjust other elements of their spending, then money balances will be off the demand curve in the event of an income (or interest rate) shock. We have estimated the demand function for money, assuming flexible lags, and the Keynesian monetary equation is still rejected.

79  The analysis becomes only slightly more complicated if inflationary expectations depend on the level of output in equilibrium.

80  If inflationary expectations (ie) are a function of the gap between actual and potential output, with potential output fixed for the moment, then ie = H(Y). Writing the IS curve as $Y = Z(R) = Z(r - i^e) = Z(r - H(Y))$, or $Y = Z^{\wedge}(r)$

81  Aggregate demand is a function of the real interest rate, and the IS curve only determines the nominal interest rate (the opportunity cost of holding money). But if expectations about prices or price changes are fixed, a change in nominal interest rates translates directly into a change in real interest rates. A more general case is discussed later.

Figure 7.3 and an associated regression undermine the credibility of the determination of the (nominal or real) interest rate through a Keyesian LM framework.

82  A11d: $\alpha = 59.5758$, 95%CI $= [51.0058, 68.1457]$; $\Upsilon = 20.4850$, 95%CI $= [11.0189, 29.9511]$; $R^2 = 0.0745$. A11e: $\alpha = 0.0075$, 95%CI $= [0.0065, 0.0086]$; $\Upsilon = 0.0029$, 95%CI $= [0.0018, 0.0041]$, $R^2 = 0.1008$. In these regressions, the "effective federal funds rate" is used as a proxy for the nominal interest rate.

83  Moreover, the coefficient on the nominal interest rate is of the *wrong* sign, that is an increase in the nominal interest rate is associated with a higher Y, for a given real interest rate. In fact, this is not as surprising as it seems. Since the nominal interest rate is the real interest rate plus the rate of inflation, an increase in the nominal interest rate *given a real interest rate* is equivalent to an increase in inflation. We would expect an increase in inflation to be associated with a higher level of real (and nominal) output. The association between the nominal interest rate and real output thus being picked up is the standard Phillips curve. But we are not picking up the hoped for relationship between the interest rate as determined by the government and the level of economic activity.

84  A similar analysis, though, applies if we look beneath the surface, say to the relationship between investment or consumption and (real) interest rates – the channel through which monetary policy is supposed to have much of its effect. Most studies (unmassaged) suggest that income and substitution effects are broadly offsetting.

## Bibliography

Akerlof, George A., Blanchard, Olivier, Romer, David, & Stiglitz, Joseph E. (eds.). (2014). *What Have We Learned? Macroeconomic Policy after the Crisis.* Cambridge, MA and London: MIT Press.

Akerlof, George A., & Shiller, Robert J. (2015). *Phishing for Phools: The Economics of Manipulation and Deception.* Princeton, NJ: Princeton University Press.

Andrews, D. (2003). "Tests for Parameter Instability and Structural Change with Unknown Change Point: A Corrigendum," *Econometrica*, 71(1): 395–397.

Berle, A. A., & Means, G. C. (1932). *The Modern Corporation and Private Property.* New York, NY: Harcourt, Brace and World, 2nd ed. 1967.

Blanchard, Olivier, Romer, J. D., Spence, M., & Stiglitz, Joseph E. (eds.). (2012). *In the Wake of the Crisis.* Cambridge, MA: MIT Press.

Buffet, Warren. (2003, November 10). "America's Growing Trade Deficit Is Selling the Nation out from Under Us. Here's a Way to Fix the Problem: And We Need to Do It Now," *Fortune.*

Calvo, Guillermo A. (1998). "Capital Flows and Capital-Market Crises: The Simple Economics of Sudden Stops," *Journal of Applied Economics*, 1(1): 35–54.

Chapman, B., Higgins, T., & Stiglitz, Joseph E. (eds.). (2014). *Income Contingent Loans: Theory, Practice and Prospects.* Houndmills, UK and New York: Palgrave Macmillan.

Dasgupta, Partha, & Stiglitz, Joseph E. (1977, December). "Tariffs vs. Quotas as Revenue Raising Devices Under Uncertainty," *American Economic Review*, 67(5): 975–998.

DelliGatti, D., Gallegati, M., Greenwald, B., Russo, A., & Stiglitz, Joseph E. (2012). "Mobility Constraints, Productivity Trends, and Extended Crises," *Journal of Economic Behavior & Organization*, 83(3): 375–393.

DelliGatti, D., Gallegati, M., Greenwald, B., Russo, A., & Stiglitz, Joseph E. (2016). "Sectoral Imbalances and Long Run Crises," in *The Global Macro Economy and Finance*, F. Allen, M. Aoki, J.-P. Fitoussi, N. Kiyotaki, R. Gordon, and J. E. Stiglitz (eds.), IEA Conference Volume No. 150-III, Houndmills, UK and New York: Palgrave, pp. 61–97. Originally presented at World Congress of IEA, Jordan, June 2014.

Galbraith, James K. (2012). *Inequality and Instability: A Study of the World Economy Just before the Great Crisis.* New York: Oxford University Press.

Giovannoni, Olivier G. (2014, March 3). "What Do We Know about the Labor Share and the Profit Share? – Part III: Measures and Structural Factors," Bard College.

Giovannoni, Olivier G. (2015, January 3). "Inequality: Challenge of the Century?," Presentation to the ASSA meetings, Boston.

Greenwald, Bruce, & Stiglitz, Joseph E. (1986). "Externalities in Economies with Imperfect Information and Incomplete Markets," with B. Greenwald, *Quarterly Journal of Economics*, 101(2): 229–264.

## 180 *Joseph Stiglitz*

Greenwald, Bruce, & Stiglitz, Joseph E. (1989, May). "Toward a Theory of Rigidities," *American Economic Review*, 79(2): 364–369.

Greenwald, Bruce, & Stiglitz, Joseph E. (1990). "Asymmetric Information and the New Theory of the Firm: Financial Constraints and Risk Behavior," *The American Economic Review*, 80(2): 160–165.

Greenwald, Bruce, & Stiglitz, Joseph E. (1991, October). "Toward a Reformulation of Monetary Theory: Competitive Banking," *Economic and Social Review*, 23(1): 1–34. Also NBER Working Paper 4117.

Greenwald, Bruce, & Stiglitz, Joseph E. (1993a). "Financial Market Imperfections and Business Cycles," *The Quarterly Journal of Economics*, 108(1): 77–114.

Greenwald, Bruce, & Stiglitz, Joseph E. (1993b). "Monetary Policy and the Theory of the Risk-Averse Bank," Working Papers in Applied Economic Theory 93–04, Federal Reserve Bank of San Francisco.

Greenwald, Bruce, & Stiglitz, Joseph E. (2003). *Towards a New Paradigm in Monetary Economics*. Cambridge: Cambridge University Press.

Greenwald, Bruce, Stiglitz, Joseph E., & Weiss, Andrew. (1984, May). "Informational Imperfections in the Capital Market and Macroeconomic Fluctuations," *American Economic Review*, American Economic Association, 74(2): 194–199.

Guzman, Martin, & Stiglitz, Joseph E. (2013, December). "Monetary Policy and Capital Controls: Coordination in a World with Spillovers," Presented at the RIDGE Workshop at Central Bank of Uruguay.

Guzman, Martin, & Stiglitz, Joseph E. (2015). "Pseudo-Wealth and Consumption Fluctuations," Discussion paper, Columbia University.

Guzman, Martin, & Stiglitz, Joseph E. (2016). "A Theory of Pseudo-Wealth," in *Contemporary Issues in Macroeconomics: Lessons from the Crisis and Beyond*, Joseph E. Stiglitz and Martin Guzman (eds.), IEA Conference Volume, No.155-II, Houndmills, UK and New York: Palgrave Macmillan. (Paper presented at a special session of the International Economic Association World Congress, Dead Sea, Jordan, June 2014, sponsored by the OECD.)

Hahn, F. (1966). "Equilibrium Dynamics with Heterogeneous Capital Goods," *The Quarterly Journal of Economics*, Oxford University Press, 80(4): 633–646.

Kay, John. (2015). *Other People's Money: The Real Business of Finance*. PublicAffairs.

Kreamer, Jonathan. (2015). "Credit and Liquidity in the Macroeconomy," PhD Dissertation, University of Maryland, College Park.

Neary, Peter, & Stiglitz, Joseph E. (1983). "Towards a Reconstruction of Keynesian Economics: Expectations and Constrained Equilibria," *Quarterly Journal of Economics (Supplement)*, 98: 199–228.

Ohlin, B. (1937). "Some Notes on the Stockholm Theory of Savings and Investment II," *The Economic Journal*, 47: 221–240.

Robertson, D. H. (1934). "Industrial Fluctuation and the Natural Rate of Interest," *The Economic Journal*, 44: 650–656.

Shell, Karl, & Stiglitz, Joseph E. (1967, November). "Allocation of Investment in a Dynamic Economy," *Quarterly Journal of Economics*, 81: 592–609.

Stiglitz, Joseph E. (1985). "Credit Markets and the Control of Capital,"*Journal of Money, Banking, and Credit*, 17(2): 133–152.

Stiglitz, Joseph E. (1988). "On the Relevance or Irrelevance of Public Financial Policy," in *The Economics of Public Debt*, Proceedings of the 1986 International Economics Association Meeting, London: Macmillan Press, pp. 4–76.

Stiglitz, Joseph E. (1994). *Whither Socialism?* Cambridge, MA: MIT Press. (Expanded from a paper presented at the Wicksell Lectures, May 1990).

Stiglitz, Joseph E. (1998a). "More Instruments and Broader Goals: Moving Toward the Post-Washington Consensus," 1998 WIDER Annual Lecture, Helsinki, January; subsequently published in *Development Issues in the 21st Century*, G. Kochendorfer Lucius and B. Pleskovic (eds.), Berlin: German Foundation for International Development, pp. 11–39; and Chapter 1 in *The Rebel Within*, Ha-Joon Chang (ed.), London: Wimbledon Publishing Company, 2001, pp. 17–56.

Stiglitz, Joseph E. (1998b). "Central Banking in a Democratic Society," *De Economist* (Netherlands), 146(2): 199–226. (Originally presented as 1997 Tinbergen Lecture, Amsterdam, October).

Stiglitz, Joseph E. (2002a). "Information and the Change in the Paradigm in Economics," abbreviated version of Nobel lecture, *American Economic Review*, 92(3): 460–501.

Stiglitz, Joseph E. (2002b). *Globalization and Its Discontents*, New York: W. W. Norton & Company.

Stiglitz, Joseph E. (2003). *The Roaring Nineties: A New History of the World's Most Prosperous Decade.* W. W. Norton & Company.

Stiglitz, Joseph E. (2010). *Freefall: America, Free Markets, and the Sinking of the World Economy.* W. W. Norton & Company.

Stiglitz, Joseph E. (2012). *The Price of Inequality: How Today's Divided Society Endangers Our Future.* W. W. Norton & Company.

Stiglitz, Joseph E. (2014). "The Lessons of the North Atlantic Crisis for Economic Theory and Policy," in *What Have We Learned? Macroeconomic Policy after the Crisis*, George Akerlof, Olivier Blanchard, David Romer, and Joseph E. Stiglitz (eds.), Cambridge, MA and London: MIT Press, pp. 335–347.

Stiglitz, Joseph E. (2015a, April). "Fed Policy, Inequality, and Equality of Opportunity," paper presented to the Ninth Biennial Federal Reserve System Community Development Research Conference, April 2015, and to be published in proceedings; available online at http://rooseveltinstitute.org/fed-policy-inequality-and-equality-opportunity/.

Stiglitz, Joseph E. (2015b, May). "New Theoretical Perspectives on the Distribution of Income and Wealth Among Individuals: Part IV," NBER Working Papers 21192.

Stiglitz, Joseph E. (2015c). "Monetary Policy in a Multipolar World," in *Taming Capital Flows: Capital Account Management in an Era of Globalization*, Joseph E. Stiglitz and Refet S. Gurkaynak (eds.), IEA Conference Volume No. 154, UK and New York: Palgrave Macmillan.

## 182  Joseph Stiglitz

Stiglitz, Joseph E. (2015d). "New Theoretical Perspectives on the Distribution of Income and Wealth Among Individuals: Part I," NBER Working Papers 21189, May.

Stiglitz, Joseph E. (2016a). *The Euro: How a Common Currency Threatens the Future of Europe*. W. W. Norton & Company.

Stiglitz, Joseph E. (2016b). "The Measurement of Wealth: Recessions, Sustainability and Inequality," in *Contemporary Issues in Macroeconomics: Lessons from The Crisis and Beyond*, Joseph E. Stiglitz and Martin Guzman (eds.), IEA Conference Volume, No.155-II, Houndmills, UK and New York: Palgrave Macmillan. (also NBER Working Paper 21327, July 2015. Paper presented at a special session of the International Economic Association World Congress, Dead Sea, Jordan, June 2014 sponsored by the OECD.)

Stiglitz, Joseph E. (2016c). "New Theoretical Perspectives on the Distribution of Income and Wealth among Individuals," in *Inequality and Growth: Patterns and Policy, Volume I: Concepts and Analysis*, Kaushik Basu and Joseph E. Stiglitz (eds.), IEA Conference Volume No. 156-I, Houndmills, UK and New York: Palgrave Macmillan.

Stiglitz, Joseph E. (2016d). *Towards a General Theory of Deep Downturns*, IEA Conference Volume, 155-VI, Houndmills, UK and New York: Palgrave Macmillan, 2016; previously NBER Working Paper 21444, August 2015 and Presidential Address to the 17th World Congress of the International Economic Congress, Dead Sea, Jordan, June, 2014.

Stiglitz, Joseph E. (2016e). "The State, the Market, and Development," to be published in *Mapping Development Economics: The Past, Present and Future*, Tony Addison and Finn Tarp (eds.) and WIDER Working Paper 2016/1, January 2016, originally presented at UNU-WIDER 30th Anniversary Conference held September 2015 in Helsinki, Finland, available online at www.wider.unu.edu/sites/default/files/wp2016-1.pdf.

Stiglitz, Joseph E., & Weiss, Andrew. (1981, June). "Credit Rationing in Markets with Imperfect Information," *American Economic Review*, American Economic Association, 71(3): 393–410.

Stiglitz, Joseph E., & Weiss, Andrew. (1986). "Credit Rationing and Collateral," in *Recent Developments in Corporate Finance*, Jeremy Edwards et al. (eds.), New York: Cambridge University Press, pp. 101–135.

Stiglitz, Joseph E., & Yun, Jungyoll. (2013, May). "Optimal Provision of Loans and Insurance against Unemployment from a Lifetime Perspective," National Bureau of Economic Research Working Paper 19064.

Stiglitz, Joseph E., & Yun, Jungyoll. (2014). "Income Contingent Loans for the Unemployed: A Prelude to a General Theory of the Efficient Provision of Social Insurance," in *Income Contingent Loans: Theory, Practice and Prospects*, Joseph E. Stiglitz, Bruce Chapman, and Timothy Higgins (eds.), Houndmills, UK and New York: Palgrave Macmillan, pp. 180–204.

Stiglitz, Joseph E., & Yun, Jungyoll. (2016). "Income-Contingent Loan as an Unemployment Benefit," Columbia University working paper.

Tobin, J. (1970). "Money and Income: Post Hoc Ergo Propter Hoc?," *The Quarterly Journal of Economics*, 84(2): 301–317.

Turner, Adair. (2015). *Between Debt and the Devil: Money, Credit, and Fixing Global Finance*, Princeton, NJ: Princeton University Press.

Weitzman, Martin. (1974). "Prices vs. Quantities," *Review of Economic Studies*, 41(4): 477–491.

Yellen, Janet. (2014, October 17). "Perspectives on Inequality and Opportunity from the Survey of Consumer Finances," Remarks by Janet L. Yellen Chair Board of Governors of the Federal Reserve System at the Conference on Economic Opportunity and Inequality Federal Reserve Bank of Boston, Boston, MA.

# 8 Money and market failures

## A theoretical perspective

*Anjan Mukherji\**

In a recent paper, I had looked at the question of market failures (Mukherji 2016). While trying to indicate the ways that one may tackle these failures, the role of the government or rather the extent of the activities that the government or its agencies would have to carry out were mentioned. In all of these discussions, there was no mention of money or any financial assets. The purpose of this note is to fill this gap. There is also a feeling among many[1] that money markets or markets for financial assets are quite different from the markets for say

---

\* The main purpose of this paper is to record my indebtedness to my friend and colleague for many years, Deepak Nayyar. Deepak has been an outstanding example of a person who sets lofty standards in whatever he did; he is a distinguished scholar and, what is rare among academic persons, a very able administrator as well. His movement from either the lofty chambers in the North Block or even the splendour of the Viceregal Lodge of Delhi University, back to the dingy offices in CESP and settling down without any apparent discomfort, amazed me. He has been always very helpful and exceedingly generous towards his friends and colleagues and his kindness towards even mere acquaintances is legendary. When the editors approached me for a contribution, I felt honoured to be asked to contribute to this venture. My only worry has been whether I would be able to produce something worthy for the occasion. I thank the Editors, specially Ananya Ghosh Dastidar, for their patience; I am also indebted to Vivek Suneja for a careful reading of the manuscript and for helpful suggestions. I also record my indebtedness to Lord Meghnad Desai and Amal Sanyal for their encouraging comments on an earlier version. A still earlier version was presented as a part of my lecture at the International Centre for Theoretical Sciences (ICTS) programme on "Modern Finance and Microeconomics: A Multidisciplinary Approach" (Code: ICTS/Prog-memf/2015/12) during December 2015 and benefitted from comments received from participants. The support is gratefully acknowledged.

## Money and market failures 185

potatoes or cars or labour. We hope to shed some light on this aspect as well.

At the outset, we should alert the reader that by the phrase 'market failure' we shall mean a broader than usual class of situations. Usually the term 'market failure' is used to imply a situation where the competitive equilibrium is inefficient, but as in our earlier contribution, we will use the term to include situations where the competitive equilibrium may not even exist and when even if there is a competitive equilibrium, it is unstable and cannot be approached. In other words, whenever the market ceases to function as we would like it to, we shall describe it to be a case of market failure.[2]

In Mukherji (2016), we considered a standard general equilibrium model with an activity analysis model of production with a fixed and finite number of factors and basic activities. The relationship between an equilibrium and optimum was established and the First Fundamental Theorem of Welfare Economics (Arrow 1950) was deduced from first principles, using the definition of efficient states and that of a competitive equilibrium; basically the standard argument used for the smooth $2 \times 2 \times 2$ case, was extended to derive the proof. This method has the advantage that we can pinpoint what can possibly go wrong and lead to a market failure. The principal condition that may affect the connection between equilibrium and efficiency is the fact that on the one hand, at the equilibrium, consumers and producers may react to identical prices which leads to the MRS (Marginal Rates of Substitutions) across individuals being equal to one another and indeed equal to the MC (Marginal Cost), while on the other hand efficiency may require MRS across individuals to differ from one another and in particular, differ from the MRT (the Marginal Rate of Transformation, the absolute value of the slope of the production possibility schedule). The last being the same as the MC: Once prices are introduced, conditions for equilibrium and efficiency fall apart. Thus what we were doing in that paper was trying to extend the argument to situations where slopes like MRT are not well defined. It was shown there that this could be done, and analogous conditions could be derived, in which the equality of MRS across individuals continued to play a central role since the utility functions were taken to be differentiable, so that MRS was well defined.

The three situations analysed in Mukherji (2016), were externalities, asymmetric information and manipulation (or reneging from the competitive trades). In each case, individuals and decision makers, in general, found it more attractive to use prices different from the market prices or found that opportunity costs were not perfectly captured by the market prices; further it could be that MRS across individuals were not identical at an efficient state. Consequently, market failure resulted. Our point of focus here is somewhat different; we consider the problems associated with the introduction of money into the standard general equilibrium model. And then see what this means for our discussion of market failures. This discussion is particularly of interest given the history of the financial crashes that we have witnessed around the world. To quote the foremost authority, Kenneth Arrow (2013) said, writing about the 2008 financial crash, "the failure of the markets for various kinds of derivative securities to perform properly is an essential element of the current financial crisis" (p. 5). What we wish to examine is whether there is something which makes the market of financial securities prone to failure and if so, attempt to identify why this maybe so. A first step in this direction would be to examine the consequence of introducing money into the standard model and examine whether there is any particular reason to expect the market to falter.

We begin by looking at the standard case to keep our treatment self-contained. Thereafter, we consider the problems associated with the introduction of the demand for money. The final section contains the implications of our exercise.

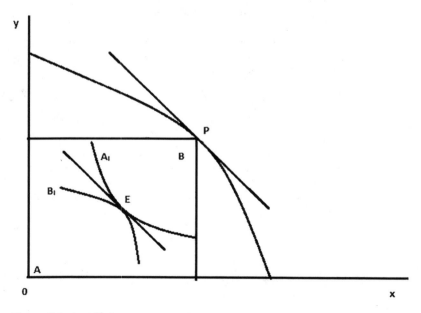

*Figure 8.1* An efficient state

## Preliminaries

Consider a situation where two goods are produced by means of two scarce factors which are owned by two individuals A and B (e.g. Bator 1957) and assume that the production occurs under very standard assumptions. We try to pin down the conditions for efficiency in this set up. Figure 8.1 will be useful in pinning down these conditions.

To consider an efficient state, production must occur at a point such as P on the production possibility locus; since the production below the frontier can be improved upon, producing more of both the goods and within the restrictions placed by the availability of resources. Thus the box depicts amount of goods available for redistribution between A, B. For efficiency keeping A at the level $A_1$, we try to locate the maximum that B can achieve given the production at P. This consideration leads us to the distribution depicted by the point E, an efficient distribution. Note that first of all the slope of the indifference curves at E must be the same and further the common slope at E = slope at P. These three conditions viz., production on the frontier, indifference curves have the same slope and finally the common slope should match the slope of the production possibility locus characterise efficiency.

We have already indicated why efficiency involves production on the frontier. Next, if the distribution to individuals places them at points where the indifference curves cross, then there are better redistribution points available for both. The final condition which requires that the common slope of the indifference curves match the slope of the production possibility locus may be seen thus: Suppose this is not so. To fix matters, suppose the common slopes of the indifference curves is –2 while the slope of the production possibility locus is –1. What does this mean? It means that first of all that at the margin, a reduction of production of good x, releases enough factors to produce one unit of y; whereas both individuals consider 1 unit of x to be equivalent to 2 units of good y. Let us reduce the production of y by 2 units; we can then produce 2 more units of good x; we can remove 2 units of good y that was given to A for instance, and give A, 2 units of x; this would make A better off, since he required only one unit of x to be compensated; thus A is better off while nothing has been done to B and hence the earlier situation could not have been efficient.

The reason why a competitive equilibrium induces this state may now be easily seen. At a competitive equilibrium, first of all, there must be full employment so that production occurs on the frontier; secondly, price ratio equals the marginal cost, so that the slope of the production possibility locus happens to be the ratio of prices, which in

## 188  *Anjan Mukherji*

turn is precisely equal to the slope of each indifference curve slope, by virtue of utility being maximised. Hence MRS must equal one another. In this entire discussion, notice the crucial assumption that everyone, producers and individuals, face the same set of prices. It is this which is crucial for the competitive equilibrium to induce an efficient state. We have shown in Mukherji (2016) how these conditions can be inferred under more general situations.

Market failure occurs when something goes wrong with this line of argument and the connection between the competitive equilibrium and the optimum breaks down, and when the competitive equilibrium, if it exists, is not optimal. Thus it would be possible to generate a feasible state, different from the equilibrium, where no one was worse off and someone was actually better off. This discrepancy between the two needs to be examined a bit more closely since we wish to see how or why the discrepancy arises. In other words, whereas we had examined why the two states may be identical, we now wish to see how or why these two states may differ. Notice first of all that the competitive equilibrium is about individuals maximising utility at the given prices and the firms maximising profits at the same prices. In the description of an optimal state, the prices do not figure.

For an equilibrium, say $E$ failing to be optimal means that we must be able to redistribute resources to obtain a state $Y$, such that no one is worse off at $Y$, compared to $E$ while some one is better off at $Y$. At the equilibrium $E$, by definition there is a price system say $p$ at which utility is maximised given resources and firms maximise profits at the same price configuration. Now consider the configuration $Y$ and consider the allocation to each individual $h$ at that state, say $y_Y^h$; let us write the allocation at $E$ to each individual as $y_E^h$; no individual is worse off at $Y$ compared to at $E$, by definition. We shall also write the outputs (of goods and demand for factors, writing demand for factors as negative supply, the usual sign convention) of firm $j$ as $z^j$ and then index it by the state we are considering; thus at $E$, demand equals supply at equilibrium entails, $\sum_h y_E^h = \sum_j z_E^j$ and feasibility ensures that there is $z_Y^j$ such that $\sum_h y_Y^h \leq \sum_j z_Y^j$. Once again by definition, since at price $p$, $y_E^h$ is utility maximising given resources, it follows that the bundles $y_Y^h$ cannot be cheaper than $y_E^h$ at prices $p$ for each $h$, since $y_E^h$ is not only utility maximising, it must also be the cheapest way of attaining that level of utility. Thus we have that $p.y_E^h \leq p.y_Y^h \forall h$ with the inequality strict for that individual who is better off at $Y$ and so we have $p.\sum_h y_E^h < p.\sum_h y_Y^h$. The strict inequality is crucial.

*Money and market failures* 189

Using next, the feasibility conditions and the equilibrium conditions, it follows that we must have $p.\sum_j z_E^j < p.\sum_j z_Y^j$ and hence for some $j$, we must have $p.z_E^j < p.z_Y^j$ but that raises a problem: Since the $z_E^j$ must also be profit maximising at $p$ which implies that this inequality cannot hold, since the product $p. z$ implies the profits associated with the activity $z$, given the sign convention, we adopted. Thus no such state $Y$ can exist given an equilibrium $E$: This is the proof of the claim that the equilibrium induces an optimal state.

Where can this argument break down? Notice that if individuals while maximising utility, instead of evaluating bundles' worth, use prices which are different from the market price or if the firms while maximising profits evaluate costs by using prices which are different from market prices or if individuals differ in their assessment of worth and so do firms, then clearly, the neat argument not only breaks down but shatters into many pieces and we have market failure. The worst case scenario is where the equilibrium may disappear altogether (an extreme form of what is reported in Akerlof, 1970). An intermediate case, which is a lot more plausible is when firms decide to renege on their commitment to produce the competitive output (Mukherji 2014) or when individuals renege on supplying the factors necessary.

We try to examine, next, what happens when we introduce money into the standard general equilibrium model.

## Demand for money

A proper consideration of money or other financial assets complicates matters on one count: It requires the introduction of time into the framework within which people make decisions; thus decision makers have to necessarily plan for the future. This extension is required to admit the role of money as a 'store of value'. Without time or multiple periods over which decisions are being planned, money has the role of medium of exchange or transaction and that is easily accommodated into our earlier framework by the ruse of treating a good as the numeraire; the only problem is that the numeraire, or the unit of account, has also direct effect on individual's utility. If that is not there, then people will not hold money, unless it is mandated to use money while making transactions. So, in this set-up, there is no saving with all income being spent. And there is no latching on to money. In fact, the acceptability of money is open to question.

First we need to remind ourselves that money is usually thought of not only as a medium of exchange but also as a store of value. So far as the former aspect is concerned, matters are simple. The numeraire that we may introduce into the general equilibrium model, is also something that satisfies this property. Since it too acts as a medium of exchange. For example, if good $n$ is the numeraire good, then we can think of $n-1$ markets; and in the $i$-th for example, good $i$ is exchanged against good $n$.[3] Theoretically this was not very satisfactory since it assumed that there was a direct utility from possessing units of the good $n$ over and above its usefulness in transacting business; but this of course was a nominal problem, since the presence of $n$ in the utility function of individuals could be due to the usefulness in buying other commodities. The problem lay elsewhere; it is to the notion of the store of value aspect that I would like to turn to next.

With many periods over which we examine decision making, we can make things more interesting and closer to what one may consider reality to be. With decision making over multiple periods, actually, financial assets like stocks and bonds also find a natural environment but then since these assets usually yield interest, which in fact may be certain, like fixed deposits with banks for example, the question of holding on to money resurfaces once again and we have addressed this elsewhere. But that is not the point of major concern here. For the moment let us keep such financial assets aside and look at the only question of introduction of money into the kind of general equilibrium model that we have considered so far.

The phrase 'store of value', conjures up the image of holding onto some things for some time at least as a guard against what the future may spring upon us. Thus it is essential to bring in time into our consideration. However as soon as this is done, we need to be able to handle uncertainty satisfactorily, since time introduces the notion of a future, about which we cannot have full or even partial knowledge. And money was basically thought of as a hedge against this uncertain future. In standard general equilibrium constructs, the way such matters were handled has been thought to be unsatisfactory.

Formally speaking, the standards were set by the contribution of Arrow (1953, 1963–64) and Debreu (1959), who thought of each good to have not only a place but time attached to it. Thus a loaf of bread available at New Delhi on 25 April 2015 was a different good from the loaf of bread available in Kolkata on 25 April 2015 and indeed was different from a loaf of bread available at New Delhi on 25 April 2014. Thus analytically of course this extension to millions of markets poses no real problems though it does tax our imagination considerably. If we look around, and decide that today we wish to buy a loaf of bread available in New Delhi next year, I do not know whether

Money and market failures  191

it would be possible to do so; although there is a very good chance that one may get committed to some asylum or the other for trying to do so. Alternatively some con artist may transact and when the next year appears, you have nothing to show for what you had paid. In spite of the intellectual elegance, the Arrow and Debreu contributions needed the introduction of a complete set of futures markets, which was clearly not plausible. A more plausible approach and one which is much closer to what we actually engage in is to consider the notion of a Hicksian week, or formally, the notion of a *temporary equilibrium*.

### Temporary equilibrium

Let us think of two periods, today and tomorrow. We know what happens today and there are expectations that each decision maker has about what lies ahead. Each decision maker takes decisions on sales and purchases on today's markets, based on what the person expects to happen tomorrow; if, based on these expectations, today's markets clear at some prices, then we have a temporary equilibrium. Tomorrow is another beginning of another two period problem; or maybe, tomorrow is just a sequence of tomorrows, and today, based on what we expect to happen tomorrow, we make decisions. Hicks in Value and Capital (1939) made the suggestion that we consider a decision period unit as a week during which production decisions are planned, based on anticipated demand and thus arose the notion of the Hicksian week. The idea of a Temporary equilibrium came about precisely from such a notion. A formal definition, and properties thereof may be found in Grandmont (1982), but we shall look at an application of such an construct to a simple model. These models of decision making were made well known by Malinvaud (1977) and Benassy (1982) and we look into such matters next.

### An application: The three-good Benassy-Malinvaud model

We shall use the three-good Benassy-Malinvaud model to analyze the effect of introducing money into the discourse. We shall not use the full model; rather we shall use a specification of the consumption side of things and then that too only the consumption from the household sector. As we hope to show that would be adequate for our purpose. We consider households who take decisions over two periods, today, indexed by 1 and tomorrow, indexed by 2; all variables will be so indexed so that the index will make clear whether we refer to a today variable or whether it relates to tomorrow. The only goods

## 192 *Anjan Mukherji*

which households are interested in are consumption goods $c_i$, $i = 1,2$ so that the utility function of household $h$ is given by $U^h(c_1, c_2)$ and is assumed to be of the standard type (strictly quasi-concave and differentiable with strictly positive partial derivatives). The household $h$ has an income $w_1^h$, today and expects an income $w_2^h$ tomorrow; we are actually abstracting from the labour market wherein the household would have sought employment in each period and would have been either partially or fully employed. The initial endowment of household $h$ is a sum of money $m_0^h$; money has to be used to buy commodities in each period and can be stored from today to tomorrow and this activity is costless. The consumption good cannot be so stored. For such households, to determine consumption today, given the state of expected prices and income in the next period, the following maximisation problem needs to be solved:

$$\text{Maximise } U^h\left(c_1, c_2\right) \text{ subject to } p_1 c_1 + m_1^h \leq m_0^h + w_1^h$$
$$\text{and } p_2 c_2 \leq w_2^h + m_1^h$$

Some explanations are in order. First of all, to solve the above, we need to state that all the variables indexed by 2 must necessarily be uncertain since they pertain to tomorrow and as such are expected variables. This is the crucial point. Next, please note that in period 2, it must be the case that the demand for consumption by household $h$, must satisfy:

$$c_2^h = \frac{w_2^h + m_1^h}{p_2^h}$$

this is so since it is the last period and all income must be spent, given that we have assumed that utility is monotonic. Also note that the expected price is indexed by $h$ since different people are expected to have different expectations. Consequently the utility maximisation problem reduces to:

$$\text{Maximise } U^h(c_1, \frac{w_2^h + m_1^h}{p_2^h}) \text{ subject to } p_1 c_1 + m_1^h \leq m_0^h + w_1^h$$

Under the standard conditions that we have invoked, the following first-order conditions are necessary and sufficient (see Mukherji 1989):

$$\frac{\partial U^h}{\partial c_1} = \lambda_h p_1 \text{ and } \frac{\partial U^h}{\partial c_2} \frac{1}{p_2^h} = \lambda_h$$

*Money and market failures*  193

so that we have, at any possible demand configuration,

$$\frac{\dfrac{\partial U^b}{\partial c_1}}{\dfrac{\partial U^b}{\partial c_2}} = p_1 \, / \, p_2^b$$

Notice that the right hand side will vary across persons, generally, since $p_2^b$ denotes expected prices and will vary from person to person. Thus at equilibria, if they exist, MRS across individuals will no longer be identical. Clearly then, we have reached an impasse since we do not expect anything else to intrude into the efficiency considerations, we would expect that efficiency would require MRS to be equal across individuals. And equilibria will be expected to be inefficient. Notice the reason for this is straightforward to see, since there is no market for $c_1$, $c_2$ trading and there is the only possibility of trading $c_1$ against $m_1$ and then hopefully in the next period $c_2$ with $m_1$. Thus with money, or indeed any other financial asset, when expected prices enter into consideration, we are to face this problem of possible inefficiency. This is generic to the problem and cannot be wished away.

One will realise why some have invoked the assumption of perfect foresight, that is, agents today are able to forecast the equilibrium price tomorrow. In that case, notice that the problems indicated previously disappear since $p_2^b = p_2$, the equilibrium price for all individuals. Notice too that this means that we have dispensed with uncertainty playing a significant role. Which is why it does appear that markets over time will contain an element of inefficiency.

## Conclusions

So what do we conclude from our discussion? Whenever there is uncertainty, the assessment of the possible outcomes is bound to vary from decision maker to decision maker, consequently the formulation of the problem that each decision maker will solve is bound to vary. In general equilibrium constructs, in the simplest possible case, we saw that the assessment of the future prices is unlikely to match and consequently, the driving force behind the First Fundamental Theorem of Welfare Economics, for example, that people have identical MRS is likely to break down. In this situation, it appears that markets are much more likely to fail.

What happens when we do introduce the markets where one can trade $c_1$ for $c_2$, the so-called futures market? In our simple set-up, notice

194 *Anjan Mukherji*

that first of all the reason for holding money disappears. And we are back into a situation where the store of value property of money is absent. However, the efficiency of equilibrium seems to be restored? With price in current markets being common across individuals, the problem raised earlier may disappear but the chances of agents honouring tomorrow contracts made today may run into problems of the type that we have raised earlier. In fact, with courts unable to enforce contracts, if agents renege on their commitment, market failure is possible as we have argued earlier in Mukherji (2014). As we had said in the introduction, in the standard set-up without money, we had located some reasons for markets to fail. The same reasons exist when one introduces money or other financial instruments. In fact with money and other financial assets, assessment of future prices causes another reason for individual decision makers, both firms and consumers to adjust to market prices differently.[4] In fact with no money or financial assets, the presence of externality leads to a breakdown of the markets; further, it is well known that the effort to decentralise the optimum, by searching for a uniform set of prices, breaks down. One set of prices may get profit-maximising behaviour to be exhibited, but not utility maximising behavior; while the other set of prices get consumers to maximise utility but these do not elicit the profit maximising supplies (see, for instance Mukherji 2002, p. 105). It is this dichotomy which gets amplified.

We would like to mention the connection that the aforementioned has with the occurrence of a financial crisis. Episodes characterised as a financial crisis have periodically plagued the real world from time to time. These are generally thought of as examples of market failures too, as we indicated at the outset using a quote from Arrow (2013) referring to the 2008 financial crisis. If this is acceptable, then what we have put forward earlier may provide the foundation of an explanation of why such crises appear from time to time in almost a cyclical fashion. Financial crises are generally thought of as a sharp decline in asset prices accompanied by the failure of many financial and non-financial firms. Of course the problem is to identify why this sharp decline occurs and why firms fail. There is an influential view that it is primarily due to asymmetric information, see for instance Mishkin (2015).[5] The following were among the main factors identified for the occurrence of financial crashes in the developed world (Mishkin 2015):

- increases in interest rates
- increases in lender uncertainty
- effect of asset markets on balance sheets

Money and market failures 195

- problems in the banking sector; and in emerging economies, an additional cause maybe
- fiscal imbalances of the government.

The increases in lender uncertainty is the path through which asymmetric information plays a major role and which indirectly also creates problems in the banking sector. But that is precisely how market failures take place.[6] There is also the view of Milton Friedman and followers that it is the government which is the culprit and it is government monetary policy which triggers off financial crises, and, but for the government intervention, everything would have worked well. Clearly though, market failure due to differences in expectations giving rise to unequal MRS, is not the effect of monetary policies.

Finally, to sum up, in the presence of money or financial assets and therefore uncertainty, markets may fail because of the usual reasons: Externalities, asymmetric information and reneging on contracts; there is however an additional reason, as we have pointed out, why markets may fail. And this is due to agents assessing the future differently. The complication which arises from expectations is therefore not something which can be explained away: It is no longer a question of imposing correct taxes, or that of ensuring some guarantee of quality, but ensuring what decision makers feel about the future. Fixing that, of course, is a very tall order.

## Notes

1 See, for example, textbooks like Houthakker and Williamson (1976).
2 See for instance Ledyard (1987) for a similar interpretation of the term 'market failure'.
3 It is this aspect which led critics such as Joan Robinson to refer to the Walrasian general equilibrium model to be a prisoner-of-war economy; in POW camps cigarettes were used as the numeraire or the unit of account. Every good or service had a price in terms of cigarettes. The analogy was used in a derogatory fashion, since it did not amount to depicting a real economy. Be that as it may, the model is capable of explaining some things which critics do not care to realise.
4 In this connection, in multi-period models, imagine an asset, say a house, which is bought today with a loan from say a bank, since its price is way beyond the person's income. Clearly the loan has to be paid off in future periods. So long as the agent is able to meet the EMIs in each period, there is no problem. But consider a situation where the agent is unable to meet the payments because of any one of many reasons, and the bank seizes the house and tries to sell the house off. Now if the house is able to fetch the price necessary to provide the bank a reasonable return, the system continues. But if the bank is unable to do so because the price of the house was

## 196 *Anjan Mukherji*

inflated to begin with, or for some other reason, the entire system crashes. The sub-prime crash of the US was the result of one such situation.

5 In fact, an earlier study, Mishkin and White (2003), analysed 15 stock market crashes in the US over the last century and concluded that it is financial instability which should be the key matter of concern for monetary policy framers and not stock market crashes. I am indebted to Priyadarsini Nair for a reference to the net version of this paper.

6 It is not clear though why the fiscal imbalances of only emerging markets create problems; it may be because these imbalances occur because of different reasons, that is, reasons different from the ones causing imbalances in the developed world.

## Bibliography

Akerlof, G. A., (1970), The Market for "Lemons": Quality Uncertainty and the Market Mechanism, *Quarterly Journal of Economics*, 488–500.

Arrow, K. J., (2013), Economic Theory and Financial Crisis, *Procedia Social and Behavioral Sciences*, 77, 5–9.

Arrow, K. J., (1963–64), The Role of Securities in the Optimal Allocation Risk Bearing, *Review of Economic Studies*, 31, 91–96 (first in French, in *Econometrie*, Colloques Internationaux du Centre National la Recheche Scientifique, Vol XI, 941–973, 1953).

Arrow, K. J., (1950), An Extension of the Basic Theorems of Classical Welfare Economics, In *Proceedings of the Second Berkeley Symposium in Mathematical Statistics and Probability*, ed., J. Neyman, University of California, Berkeley, 507–532.

Bator, F. M., (1957), The Simple Analytics of Welfare Maximization, *American Economic Review*, 47, 22–59.

Benassy, J.-P., (1982), *The Economics of Market Disequilibrium*, Academic Press, New York.

Debreu, G., (1959), *The Theory of Value: An Axiomatic Analysis of Economic Equilibrium*, Wiley, New York.

Grandmont, J. M., (1982), Temporary Equilibrium Theory, In *Handbook of Mathematical Economics*, Volume 2, ed., K. J. Arrow and M. D. Intrilligator, North Holland, Amsterdam, 879–922.

Hicks, J. R., (1939), *Value and Capital*, Clarendon Press, Oxford, UK.

Houthakker, H. S., and P. J. Williamson, (1996), *The Economics of Financial Markets*, Oxford, New York.

Ledyard, J. O., (1987), Market Failure, In *The New Palgrave Dictionary of Economics*, ed., J. Eatwell, M. Milgate and P. Newman, Macmillan, New York and London.

Malinvaud, E., (1977), *Theory of Unemployment Reconsidered*, Basil Blackwell, Oxford.

Mishkin, F. S., (2015), *The Economics of Money, Banking and Financial Markets*, Global Edition, Pearson, New York.

Mishkin, F. S., and E. N. White, (2003), U.S. Stock Market Crashes and Their Aftermath: Implications for Monetary Policy, In *Asset Price Bubbles: The*

*Implications for Monetary, Regulatory and International Policies*, ed., W. B. Hunter, G. G. Kaufman and M. Pormerleano, MIT Press, Cambridge, MA.

Mukherji, A., (2016), Market Failures: Almost Always?, In *Themes in Economic Analysis*, ed., S. Guha, R. Kundu and S. Subramanian, Routledge, New Delhi.

Mukherji, A., (2014), Is Competitive Behaviour a Best Response? In *Emerging Issues in Economic Development: A Contemporary Theoretical Perspective*, ed., S. Marjit and M. Rajeev, Oxford University Press, Delhi.

Mukherji, A., (2002), *An Introduction to General Equilibrium Analysis: Walrasian and Non-Walrasian Equilibria*, Oxford University Press, Delhi.

Mukherji, A., (1989), Quasi-Concave Optimization: Sufficient Conditions for a Maximum, *Economic Letters*, 30, 341–343.

# 9 Persuasion and coercion
## A transaction costs perspective on income distribution

*Vivek Suneja*

As is well known, transaction cost economics, also referred to as new institutional economics, explores the nature of costs involved in conducting economic transactions and the nature of institutional arrangements that may help in economising on such costs. In this chapter, we argue that transaction cost theories have not adequately addressed the question of income distribution. Transaction asset specificity and team production (that give rise to economic rent) play a central role in the theory of the firm. However, existing theory has little to say on the degree and on the nature of bargaining-related transaction costs that are likely to be involved in the division of team output or economic rent. This chapter explores how cultural norms and bargaining power can influence the efficiency of transacting as well as the pattern of income distribution under team production. Our discussion also suggests a new explanation for the phenomenon of efficiency wages.

## Transaction cost theory: Rationale and limitations

Coase, in his seminal paper on the nature of the firm, asked how the institution of the firm differs from the institution of the market, and why some transactions are carried out within firms while others are carried out in the market (Coase 1937). His answer was that a firm may be supposed to exist when the allocation of economic resources becomes dependent upon the direction of an entrepreneur–coordinator rather than occurring in response to market determined prices. The firm arises because there is a cost of using the price mechanism. According to Coase, the costs involved in the use of the price mechanism include costs relating to search, price discovery and the negotiation and concluding of separate contracts for each transaction. There has subsequently been considerable research on identifying market making costs (see, e.g. Carter, Casson and Suneja 1998).

The marketing costs can be reduced by forming a firm where authority is accorded to an entrepreneur to direct the activity of other factors of production within certain limits. However, as the heterogeneity, spatial distribution and the number of transactions organised within a firm increases, the ability of the entrepreneur to allocate factors to their best use diminishes. Firms and markets are two alternative ways of 'organising' or coordinating economic activity, and transactions will be allocated to firms or markets depending upon which of these institutions can achieve better coordination with lower transaction costs.

Several researchers have built upon the key insight provided by Coase. Williamson in his significant contributions to this field over the last four decades has worked on how transactions can vary from each other, and how appropriate institutional arrangements can help in reducing transaction costs (e.g. Williamson 1975, 1985, 1996, 2013).

Williamson characterises transactions in terms of three main dimensions: Transaction asset specificity, uncertainty and frequency of recurrent transactions. He demonstrates that if economic agents are assumed to be boundedly rational and opportunistic, then transactions characterised by high asset specificity, high uncertainty and high frequency of recurrence will be more efficiently organised through the firm than through the market.

The Williamson argument can be summarised as follows. When assets possessed by the (potential) transactors are specific to the transaction such that the assets are more productive in their joint use than in any alternative transaction, then there is an economic logic for deploying these assets together. (Transaction asset specificity may be physical, site or human in nature.) However, the presence of transaction specific assets often transforms a large numbers trading situation into a small numbers or bilateral trading situation. The trading opportunities with other transactors are now less attractive because they do not possess the co-specialised assets that can help reduce production costs. This transformation of trading possibilities is likely to give rise to bargaining costs between the owners of the assets. Furthermore, asset specificity also creates the possibility of moral hazard, because once the agents who possess the co-specialised assets decide to transact with each other, they are effectively 'locked' into the relationship. The threat to discipline a defaulter by switching to other transactors is no longer effective. If transactors foresee this possibility, they may decide not to transact and then the production efficiency gains that can arise from bringing the co-specialised assets together shall not be realised.

Williamson states that asset specificity by itself does not necessitate a switch from the market to the firm as the most efficient way to conduct such transactions. The (potential) transactors could in principle agree upon a long term legally binding contract that would take into account all possible future contingencies. However, if there exists a relatively high degree of uncertainty (stemming from the external environment or generated by asymmetric information) then, given that transactors are boundedly rational and opportunistic, the costs of writing and enforcing such a comprehensive, complete contract are likely to be prohibitively high. The transactors could agree on an open-ended, incomplete contract and renegotiate terms as events unfolded (thereby economising on bounded rationality) but the assumption of opportunism along with presence of imperfect or asymmetric information may rule out such a possibility. Williamson argues that under such conditions, it would be more efficient to organise the transaction within a firm rather than through the market. Common ownership diminishes the incentive to sub-optimise. The firm has greater access to information, and can use fiat to settle disputes which may be cheaper than using adjudication.

The use of the governance structure of the firm to facilitate transactions is however not costless. Since the employee (who in the market setting was an autonomous trader) is no longer motivated by profit maximisation considerations and is no longer disciplined by market competition, he may have an incentive to shirk in the performance of his job. While the firm may deploy monitoring mechanisms to try and control shirking, this will entail costs, especially if the information needed to measure employee productivity is imperfect or imperfectly available to management.

Ouchi investigates the role of trust and social norms in dealing with evaluation and control issues. He distinguishes between three organisational control mechanisms: Markets, bureaucracies and clans (Ouchi 1979). While bureaucracies rely on the laying down of rules and on supervision, clans rely on engineering cultural norms that induce agents to be self-monitoring. Similarly, Casson examines the role that trust and culture can play in reducing transaction costs (Casson 1991). It is important to note that trust in these models does not simply represent a calculated faith in the expected actions of the other that is based on purely materialistic grounds. The transactors suffer an *emotional* penalty if they renege on an explicit or an implicit agreement or expectation (or equivalently benefit from an emotional reward when they refrain from doing so). Transaction costs are reduced through a *cultural* mechanism. Support for this hypothesis has been found in several studies. For example, Suneja finds that firms effectively use trust building strategies to reduce opportunism-related costs when input

*Persuasion and coercion* 201

monitoring and output monitoring are costly (Suneja 1997a, 1997b). Suneja concludes that a key role of the institution of the firm is the creation of trust which enhances the efficiency of transacting.

A key contribution to the transaction cost literature and the theory of the firm comes from Alchian and Demsetz (1972). They argue that it is 'team production' that accounts for the institution of the firm. Team production is defined as the case when team output (when the inputs are used jointly) is greater than the sum of outputs when the inputs are used separately. This can happen because of technological indivisibilities, the existence of fixed factor proportion technology (Leontief production function) or the existence of synergies/complementarities between inputs used in the production process. Team production makes it difficult to determine individual productivity from looking at the output that has been (jointly) produced. The team players may consequently be tempted to freeride and reduce their individual contributions to the team production process. Alchian and Demsetz argue that the institution of the firm arises to address this problem. To prevent freeriding by any of the team members, a central party is entrusted with the task of monitoring the inputs/behaviours of the players. To ensure that the central party does not shirk in his task of monitoring the inputs of team players, the central agent is made to receive residual income (profit) – it is hence in his interest to not shirk in his monitoring task. The firm thus arises as an institutional arrangement with the aim of minimising transaction costs relating to monitoring under conditions of team production.

There are two weaknesses in the Alchian and Demsetz theory of the firm that are of interest to us. First, as Alchian and Demsetz observe, the ability of the central agent to discern a player's contribution to the team production process by monitoring his observable inputs may be imperfect and costly. It may hence be difficult to prevent employees from shirking (freeriding).

Second, Alchian and Demsetz do not adequately address the issue of how the team output is to be distributed between the team players. There is consequently little discussion of the nature of or the degree of transaction costs that may be involved in the process of the division of team output.

Williamson's theory of the firm suffers from a similar omission. Transaction asset specificity is key to the Williamson analysis of transaction costs. The joint use of transaction-specific assets in production increases productivity relative to use of non-specific assets. Williamson does not however explicitly address the question of how the ensuing economic rent will be distributed between the owners of the specific

202   *Vivek Suneja*

assets. The process of division of economic rent may entail significant transaction costs. The investigation of this matter might raise questions similar to that which are likely to arise when investigating the nature of transaction costs associated with the division of output under team production. We now take up this important and neglected issue.

## Distribution under team production: Bargaining power and cultural norms

Let there be two individuals A and B.

Assume A owns a particular production input X and B owns a production input Y (the inputs may be physical or human in nature).

Assume that when A uses input X in the production process on his own, it generates an output of 0. Similarly assume that when B uses input Y in the production process on his own, it generates an output of 0.

Assume that inputs X and Y are complementary in nature (synergies exist in their joint use). Assume that when inputs X and Y are jointly used in the production process, this yields an output of 100. So we have a case of team production here: The team output (when the inputs are used jointly) is greater than the sum of outputs when the inputs are used separately.

As a simplifying assumption, let us further suppose that inputs X and Y are identical. The output produced when inputs are used jointly is greater than when the inputs are used separately because of the presence of indivisibility in production.

Let us assume that A is poor while B is wealthy, and this fact is known to both A and B.

Would A and B agree to team produce by pooling their inputs? They can be expected to do so as long as they can agree on a division of the surplus of 100 that is acceptable to both of them. The division of the team surplus will depend on the outcome of bargaining between A and B. Assuming that the bargaining process consumes economic resources (time spent on bargaining has a positive opportunity cost), A and B will jointly produce if the transaction cost entailed in bargaining is less than the surplus of 100, and furthermore if the bargaining outcome is acceptable to both A and B.

Given our above assumptions, can we expect that team production will proceed smoothly with low bargaining costs? Would B use the asymmetric bargaining power (engendered by the unequal distribution of wealth) to seek a bargaining outcome where he appropriates more than half of the surplus? Would such an outcome be acceptable to A?

Several scenarios are possible (by adding varying assumptions) of which the following are of interest to us:

1 Suppose A is desperate to earn an income. Then he may immediately accept any offer B may make to him (in excess of an income of zero) without engaging in any bargaining. Bargaining costs would then be zero. In case A's degree of desperation is lower, he might be willing to risk spending some time in bargaining in the hope of seeking a more favourable outcome. However, given the expected asymmetry in the time discount rate between A and B owing to the differences in their wealth (the expected asymmetry in the capacity for sustaining a protracted period of bargaining) we would expect a relatively early settlement and relatively low bargaining costs.

2 Suppose A cares not just about his expected income but also about 'fairness'. Suppose A subscribes to the fairness norm of 'equal contribution, equal reward'. If his attachment to such a norm is sufficiently strong (he derives sufficient utility from adherence to such an emotional/cultural norm) he may even be prepared to starve rather than accept a grossly 'unfair' distribution of team output.[1] Suppose B does not subscribe to such a norm of fairness but instead derives utility from adhering to a different norm of fairness which posits that it is fair to seek the maximum share of the pie that one's bargaining power can command. In this situation, we can expect to see a relatively high degree of bargaining costs. In the extreme case, where A and B derive a great degree of 'non-pecuniary' utility from their commitment to their respective (and different) cultural norms of 'fair' play, the bargaining costs may be raised to a level that we have bargaining failure and team production fails to materialise

3 Suppose A and B both subscribe to (derive utility from) the norm of 'equal contribution equal reward'. Then B may not aggressively seek a greater than equal share of the pie despite his greater bargaining power. If B derives a sufficiently high degree of utility from adherence to such a fairness norm, bargaining costs can be expected to be low and team production can be expected to proceed smoothly.

## Implications

Our discussion suggests that the bargaining power of the players and the nature and strength of beliefs of the players with regard to distribution norms/bargaining norms can influence the efficiency of bargaining

## 204  Vivek Suneja

(degree of bargaining costs) as well as influence the pattern of the division of output/economic rent under team production.[2]

As mentioned earlier, new institutional economics or transaction cost theories assume that economic institutions in a free market economy tend to evolve in such a way that transactional efficiency is enhanced. If we accept this premise, we can then ask how institutional mechanisms may evolve that attempt to minimise bargaining-related transaction costs under team production. Since both the bargaining power of the team players as well as the bargaining norms can impact upon bargaining costs, institutional mechanisms may evolve that attempt to influence these two variables in the desired direction.

Consider the issue of bargaining norms. Norms are generally considered by mainstream economists as cultural variables that lie outside the purview of economic theory. Our analysis however suggests that cultural norms may have a significant impact on bargaining related transaction costs and on the pattern of the division of team output. Consequently, institutional mechanisms may evolve that influence the nature of norms such that transactional efficiency is enhanced. Within firms, efforts may be made to create norms that permit agreements to be reached regarding division of team output with low bargaining costs. A key task of the entrepreneur may be the creation and sustenance of such a corporate culture. Instituting such a culture may involve 'persuasion' – convincing team players to subscribe to desired bargaining norms. Such 'persuasion' is likely to involve expenditure of economic resources (the opportunity cost of time involved, costs relating to communication, negotiation, associated symbolic or ritual activity etc.). As long as the economic expenditure involved in such cultural activity is less than the expected reward in the form of reduction in bargaining costs, such 'persuasion' activity would be economically desirable.

Culture need not be restricted to intra-firm norm formation. Industry-wide norms or professional or regional or national culture can help in reducing transaction costs. Widely shared cultural norms can in effect serve as a public good that potential transactors can benefit from. In view of the public good nature of such cultural norms, the state may need to invest in norm creation of the desired kind.

Cultural norms can be expected to interact with bargaining power to influence both the efficiency of bargaining and the pattern of division of output. If, say, all players subscribe to the 'equal contributions equal rewards' norm, we are likely to have low bargaining costs and an equitable distribution of output, ceteris paribus. On the other hand, if consensus is engineered on the norm of 'reward should be based on bargaining power', and if bargaining power is unequally distributed between the transactors, we might have low bargaining costs and an unequal distribution of output. As an example, a 'feudal' or 'servile' culture may be sought to be created by the feudal or capitalist class so as to reduce (implicit or explicit) bargaining costs while ensuring an unequal division of income. In such a case, the cultural activity of influencing norms (referred to earlier as 'persuasion') reinforces the 'coercion' role played by the unequal distribution of bargaining power in facilitating reduction in transaction costs and bringing about an unequal division of income. A society or economy can hence potentially enhance transactional efficiency by bringing about a highly unequal distribution of bargaining power while persuading the participants that such a situation is legitimate or inevitable. Here is a possible case of conflict between the goals of transactional efficiency and equity. Transaction efficiency is brought about by maintaining inequity in the distribution of wealth or inequity in the access to resources or capital (including human capital), thereby skewing the distribution of bargaining power.

This result is of course not inevitable. As discussed previously, if transactors derive utility from subscribing to an equity norm, then we can have an equitable division of output and low bargaining costs, even when bargaining power may not be equally distributed.

## Relation to theories of income distribution

We now briefly examine how our perspective on distribution of team output relates to some of the prominent theories of income distribution.

As is well known, the standard Neo-classical model of income distribution does not take into account team production. The production function in the standard general equilibrium model permits calculation of marginal productivity of the individual factors of production. With factor and product markets assumed to be perfectly competitive, and given the other standard assumptions of general equilibrium theory, it can be shown that the factors of production receive a reward that is determined by their marginal productivity, and that the equilibrium is Pareto-efficient. Bargaining is unnecessary and transactions between the factors of production take place 'efficiently' with zero bargaining-related transaction costs. The question of norms with respect to bargaining or fairness in income distribution does not arise. No factor is regarded to have a higher bargaining power than any other. The positions of labour and capital with respect to income distribution are symmetric – all factors of production are regarded to be on the same footing.

## 206   Vivek Suneja

As discussed previously, new institutional economics or transaction cost economics relaxes some of the unrealistic assumptions of the standard Neo-classical general equilibrium model. Information available to transactors is no longer assumed to be perfect. Coase demonstrates how market-making costs may make the firm a more efficient organiser of transactions than the market. Williamson builds on the Coase insight and demonstrates how the presence of transaction specific assets can raise bargaining- and monitoring-related costs in the presence of uncertainty and information asymmetry when the transactors are assumed to be boundedly rational and opportunistic. Williamson hypothesises that the co-specialised assets will then be brought under common ownership but this may give rise to shirking costs. Others such as Ouchi and Casson build a theory of trust and corporate culture to suggest how monitoring costs can be reduced if employees suffer an emotional penalty if they 'cheat' on the firm. However, none of these theories explicitly address the question of how the distribution of economic rent takes place. Given that significant bargaining costs may be associated with the process of determining the distribution of economic rent, these theories remain incomplete because they fail to adequately address a key source of transaction costs. The team-based theory of the firm proposed by Alchian and Demsetz suffers from the same lacuna: It does not address how the division of team output or economic rent takes place. It hence fails to take into account the bargaining costs that may be involved in the process of the determination of division of team output.

This chapter focuses on the issue of transaction costs associated with the process of income determination under team production. Under team production – which can be caused by technological indivisibilities, fixed factor proportion technology (Leontief production function) or other kinds of complementarities/synergies between production inputs – reliable measures of individual factor productivity are no longer available. Standard Neo-classical theory of income distribution based on measurable marginal products of individual inputs cannot be applied to explain how the team output will be distributed. As we have discussed previously, the degree of bargaining costs (the efficiency of transacting) as well as the pattern of output division is likely to depend both upon the bargaining power of the players as well as on the nature of the cultural norms that the players subscribe to.

Let us take a brief look at Marxian theories of distribution. Marx's theory of distribution is significantly different from the Neo-classical theory of distribution. In Marx's theory of labour value, the differential access to capital and to ownership of means of production, and

Persuasion and coercion   207

the existence of the reserve army of unemployed labour, enables capital to appropriate 'surplus value' from labour. Labour and capital are regarded to be in a fundamentally asymmetric position with regard to their role in the production and market exchange process. This asymmetry leads to the unequal distribution of income.

Marxian theory, similar to our team production analysis, does not apply marginal productivity theory to explain factor incomes. The bargaining power of the players is regarded to be a key determinant of the pattern of division of output. Marxian theory also emphasises the role of norms and 'ideology' in explaining the dynamics of the production and exchange process.

Finally, we wish to examine how our analysis of distribution under team production relates to 'efficiency wage' theories. Efficiency wage theories seek to explain why firms may pay higher than market clearing wages when not induced to do so by collective bargaining pressures or minimum wage legislation. Efficiency wage theories argue that payment of wages that are higher than market clearing lead to higher labour productivity through various mechanisms such as through reduced shirking by employees (e.g. Shapiro and Stiglitz 1984), lower worker turnover (e.g. Stiglitz 1974) and better self-selection opportunities for high quality workers (e.g. Weiss 1980). There are also efficiency wage theories which explain the payment of higher than market clearing wages by taking into account the influence of norms on behaviour (e.g. Akerlof and Yellen 1990).[3]

How can our analysis of income division under team production explain the existence of wages in excess of market clearing levels? Consider the case of team production in a particular firm where labour and capital both subscribe to a fairness norm that links rewards to contributions. As argued previously, subscription to such a norm might lead to a reduction in bargaining costs. Now suppose that while no change occurs in this firm's financial situation (its revenue, cost, value added remain unchanged), the labour market moves from a situation of full employment to less than full employment. In the absence of labour and capital subscribing to the 'rewards linked to contributions' norm, capital would be tempted to renegotiate the division of team output. The emergence of unemployment has raised capital's bargaining power. Capital can potentially replace the firm's incumbent workers with the unemployed available outside at a lower wage if the incumbents refuse to accept a lower wage. However, since both labour and capital have been assumed to subscribe to the 'rewards linked to contributions' norm, then since no (inter-temporal) change has occurred in factor contributions and no change has occurred in the firm's income, we

208  *Vivek Suneja*

would not expect to see any renegotiation with respect to the shares of labour and capital in team output. Wages will not fall despite the fact that we now have unemployment rather than full employment in the labour market – wages shall demonstrate the 'wage stickiness' that is often observed in practice.

What would we expect if instead of both labour and capital subscribing to the 'rewards linked to contributions' norm, only labour subscribes to such a norm? Our explanation of sticky wages (based on team production and bargaining norms) might still hold good under certain circumstances. If labour derives sufficient utility from its adherence to the 'rewards linked to contributions' norm (labour is strongly and demonstrably committed to this cultural norm), then capital may find it in its self-interest to accommodate this fact in its bargaining strategy, since otherwise the fruitless bargaining effort may reduce the pie available for distribution. If this is the case, we would expect that as long as the firm's income remains unaltered, capital will not insist on renegotiating the division of income despite the change in the situation in the labour market from one of full employment to less than full employment.

In view of the preceding discussion, we can argue that higher than market clearing wages may not be paid solely out of fairness or norm related considerations. Payment of a higher than market clearing wage may lead to greater efficiency in the distribution of team output. The 'efficiency' wage may lead to greater efficiency in bargaining: It may pay for itself by bringing about a saving in bargaining costs.

## Conclusions

This chapter argues that transaction cost theories have not so far adequately addressed the question of income distribution. They have largely ignored consideration of bargaining costs that are likely to arise during the income division process. This is a significant omission in view of the important role played by transaction asset specificity and team production in the theory of the firm. In this chapter, we have examined issues relating to income distribution under conditions of team production. In particular, we have discussed the role of cultural norms and of bargaining power in determining both the efficiency of transacting and the distribution of team output. We relate our findings to some of the prominent theories of income distribution. Finally, we suggest a new explanation for the phenomenon of efficiency wages under conditions of team production.

## Notes

1 'The passion for equality seeps into every corner of the human heart, expands and fills the whole. It is no use telling them that by this blind surrender to an exclusive passion they are compromising their dearest interests; they are deaf' (Tocqueville 1969, p. 505).
2 There is a large literature on bargaining theory. For an overview and an excellent discussion, see Elster (1989a), Chapter 3: Bargaining. For an overview and discussion of the literature on bargaining norms, see Chapter 6: Bargaining and Social Norms (Elster 1989a).
3 These theories examine the influence of various norms (including those relating to fairness) in their explanation of efficiency wages. Our analysis differs from such theories in that we examine the role of bargaining and distribution norms in the explicit context of team production. Furthermore, our analysis examines how bargaining/distribution norms and bargaining power may impact upon the *efficiency* of bargaining under conditions of team production *by lowering bargaining-related transaction costs*.

## Bibliography

Akerlof, G. A., & Yellen, J. L. (1990). The fair wage-effort hypothesis and unemployment. *The Quarterly Journal of Economics*, 255–283.
Alchian, A. A., & Demsetz, H. (1972). Production, information costs, and economic organization. *The American Economic Review*, 62(5), 777–795.
Arrow, K. J., & Debreu, G. (1954). Existence of an equilibrium for a competitive economy. *Econometrica: Journal of the Econometric Society*, 265–290.
Austen, S. (2003). *Culture and the labour market*. Edward Elgar Publishing.
Carter, M., Casson, M., & Suneja, V. (eds.) (1998). *The economics of marketing*. Edward Elgar Publishing.
Casson, M. (1991). *The economics of business culture*. Clarendon.
Coase, R. H. (1937). The nature of the firm. *Economica*, 4(16), 386–405.
Elster, J. (1989a). *The cement of society: A survey of social order*. Cambridge: Cambridge University Press.
Elster, J. (1989b). Wage bargaining and social norms. *Acta Sociologica*, 32(2), 113–136.
Høgsnes, G. (1989). Wage bargaining and norms of fairness – a theoretical framework for analysing the Norwegian wage formation. *Acta Sociologica*, 32(4), 339–357.
Kahneman, D., Knetsch, J. L., & Thaler, R. H. (1986a). Fairness and the assumptions of economics. *Journal of Business*, S285–S300.
Kahneman, D., Knetsch, J. L., & Thaler, R. H. (1986b). Fairness as a constraint on profit seeking: Entitlements in the market. *The American Economic Review*, 728–741.
Marx, K. (1867). *Capital: A critique of political economy*. Vol. 1. London and New York: Penguin.
Ouchi, W. G. (1979). *A conceptual framework for the design of organizational control mechanisms*. New York: Springer, 63–82.

## 210 Vivek Suneja

Shapiro, C., & Stiglitz, J. E. (1984). Equilibrium unemployment as a worker discipline device. *The American Economic Review*, 74(3), 433–444.

Stiglitz, J. E. (1974). Alternative theories of wage determination and unemployment in LDC's: The labor turnover model. *The Quarterly Journal of Economics*, 194–227.

Suneja, V. (1997a). Monitoring and trust in firms: An investigation of sales force motivation strategies. Doctoral dissertation, University of Reading, Doctoral Supervisor: Mark Casson.

Suneja, V. (1997b). Output monitoring, input monitoring and trust building: A conceptual model and empirical investigation of sales force motivation strategies in multinational firms. Proceedings of the Annual Conference of the Academy of International Business, Leeds, UK.

Tocqueville, A. de (1969). *Democracy in America*. New York: Anchor Books.

Weiss, A. (1980). Job queues and layoffs in labor markets with flexible wages. *The Journal of Political Economy*, 526–538.

Williamson, O. E. (1975). *Markets and hierarchies*. New York: Free Press, 26–30.

Williamson, O. E. (1985). *The economic institutions of capitalism*. Simon and Schuster.

Williamson, O. E. (1996). *The mechanisms of governance*. Oxford: Oxford University Press.

Williamson, O. E. (2013). *The Transaction Cost Economics Project*. Edward Elgar.

Yellen, J. L. (1984). Efficiency wage models of unemployment. American Economic Review, Papers and Proceedings of the Ninety-Sixth Annual Meeting of the American Economic Association, 200–205.

# 10 Dual economy models with fixed terms-of-trade

*Amitava Bose*

Supply and demand frequently fail to match in a market economy. When that happens, there will be pressure on the market price and the level of output to change. Neo-classical economics assumes 'price flexibility', the precise implication of which is that price adjustment will succeed in clearing the market. However, many a time, price flexibility in this sense may fail and in that case the burden of adjustment falls on the level of production. This chapter explores the role of production in market clearing using the model of a dual economy consisting of a backward agricultural sector and a progressive manufacturing sector.

Dual economy models add up to a family that is large. Moreover, there are important differences within the family, some being Ricardian and others Keynesian. Ricardian models assume that expenditure is *always* equal to income, the equality looking rather like an internal budget constraint. An example of the operation of a budget constraint in this context is the requirement that investment be financed by the investor's own saving. This is of course at sharp variance with the Keynesian class of models that regards saving and investment (hence also income and expenditure) as outcomes of *independent* decision making; equality between the two is seen as a market clearing adjustment for the credit market in Keynesian models.

In the dual economy models covered in this chapter, the economy consists of two sectors, 'Agri' (agriculture) and 'Non-agri' (manufacturing and services lumped together), each producing a different final product. The two sectors are linked through flow of resources and exchange of final product. Here again two approaches can be distinguished. In most dual economy models, the relative price of the agricultural good (inter-sectoral terms of trade) is the equilibrating variable (either by itself or in conjunction with the level of non-agricultural production). However, in this chapter, the focus is on an alternative approach in which the relative price is *given* – it does not respond to

## 212 *Amitava Bose*

current excess demands – and instead it is the level of non-agricultural production that is the *sole* equilibrating variable.

An important underlying assumption here is that the level of non-agricultural output is *demand-determined*. The role of the agricultural sector is to produce demand for the non-agricultural sector. That is the theme of this chapter.

The following notation is used throughout. The index used for the agricultural sector (called 'Agri') is x and that for the non-agricultural sector (called 'Non-agri') is y. On the supply side, the marketable surplus of agricultural goods (called 'food') is denoted by X. The output of non-agricultural goods is denoted by Y.

On the demand side, the aggregate demand for Non-agri or y-goods is denoted by AD. The Non-agri or y-sector's demand is $D_y$ for y-goods and $D_x$ for Agri or x-goods. The demand for y-goods from the Agri or x-sector is denoted by F. The respective rates of growth of output are $g_y$ and $g_x$. The relative price of x-goods in terms of y-goods is denoted by p.

### The Ricardian approach

The two 'budget constraints' in this system are

(1) $D_y + D_x = Y$
(2) $F = pX$

The definition of aggregate demand for y is

(3) $AD = D_y + F$

Together these equations imply

(4) $AD - Y = pX - D_x$

We will focus on the market for x-goods. In that context, (4) is useful in clarifying how adjustments in Y help to clear the market for x-goods. Moreover (4) implies that if demands are budget constrained then the following equilibrium condition clears both markets simultaneously:

(5) $D_x = pX$

Next, we consider the demand function for food or the x-good. Given that the relative price p is fixed, assume that $D_x$ depends only on Y. Thus $D_x = D(Y)$. In particular, consider

(6) $D(Y) = mY, 0 < m < 1$

Then

(7) $Y = pX/m$

## Causation

The character of the model depends on which variables are flexible, that is, which ones adjust to bring about the equality in (5), and which variables are fixed, that is, are autonomous. Here it is assumed that pX is given and Y is the equilibrating variable. Then it follows from (7) that Y is determined by pX. The interpretation of (7) as a 'foreign trade multiplier' for the y-sector is straight-forward.[1]

## External demand multiplier and adjustments in non-agricultural output

Here we will discuss how an exogenous expansion of the Agri or x-sector stimulates 'external demand' for the y-sector, leading to a multiplier effect and how, output of the Non-agri or y-good adjusts to clear the market for Agri or x-goods.

Starting from an equilibrium suppose that pX goes up. That creates an excess supply of agricultural goods or x-goods at the initial level of Y. However, the budget constraint (2) implies that the increased pX stimulates F, the 'external demand' for y. That boosts AD as per (3).

Now in these models, the basic short-run adjustment is that Y adjusts to AD. The increase in AD stimulates Y and that in turn creates additional demand for the x-good, thereby reducing excess supply.

## Balanced and unbalanced growth

As long as p is fixed, with given m, (7) implies that if X has a rate of growth $g_x$ then Y must also grow at the same rate: $g_x = g_y$. Therefore, market clearing adjustment in Y at fixed p implies 'balanced growth'.

This balanced growth result, however, is rather special. The demand function in (6) implies that the income elasticity of demand for agricultural goods ('food') is unity. That is an unrealistic supposition. If the growth process is such that additional incomes accrue mostly to better paid workers, then this income elasticity is very likely to be less than unity.

## 214  *Amitava Bose*

Hence, we replace (6) by the following demand function:

(8)  $D_x = mY^\sigma, 0 < \sigma < 1$

Agri or x-sector equilibrium then entails

(9)  $mY^\sigma = pX$

Log-differentiating both sides w.r.t. time,

(10)  $\sigma g_y = g_x$

Since $\sigma < 1$ this implies that $g_y > g_x$

Thus when growth is biased in favour of upper and middle income groups, the Non-agri or y-sector (that can also be described as the 'modern sector') persistently maintains a higher rate of growth than the Agri or x-sector (also the 'traditional sector'). This is necessary for market clearing.

### Contemporary relevance: Growth of the services sector

The conclusion that growth has to be unbalanced to ensure market clearing is of considerable contemporary relevance for India. The two noteworthy characteristics of recent Indian growth are its impressively high level together with its unimpressively low 'inclusiveness'. The growth process has also been accompanied by structural changes that do not conform to the sequence predicted by development theorists. India appears to have entered the phase of services-led growth earlier than scheduled. The share of the services sector in non-agricultural output has been increasing at the expense of the manufacturing sector. This has been causing significant changes in the composition of employment resulting from the fact that the skilled-to-unskilled labour ratio is much higher in services (such as IT and banking) than it is in manufacturing (and ancillaries). It is therefore the case that growth has been accompanied by a redistribution of income in favour of better paid skilled workers in preference to poorly paid unskilled labour. As a consequence, the fraction of additional incomes that are re-spent on food has been coming down, given the fact that the marginal propensity to consume food is higher for lower income groups.

This reasoning justifies adopting the assumption that food demand is less-than-unit-elastic when growth is services-oriented. Growth keeps redistributing income and that keeps changing the composition of demand. If relative prices are constant, then, to maintain supply-demand equality, such continuing shifts in the composition of demand – away from food and other primary products – must be matched by equivalent changes in the composition of outputs. Such changes in output composition require appropriate disequalisation of growth rates across sectors. Uneven output growth is a corollary of changes in the composition of demand.

### Role of agriculture vis a vis services as the 'leading' sector

It has been assumed that Y is flexible and X is given. It follows from (7) and/or (9) that Y is determined by X, and $g_y$ is determined by $g_x$. The modern Non-agri or y-sector may be the faster growing sector but that does not mean it is the *leading sector*. On the contrary the modern sector (services-'led') is totally subservient to the traditional Agri or x-sector.

- *The role of* Y *is to create sufficient demand for the given* X.

Thus, in this model, though the growth rate of the modern sector persistently outstrips that of the backward sector, it is the latter that determines the former. In the framework adopted here the only way the modern sector can increase its growth rate, *given* the agricultural growth rate, is by making its growth income-wise more top-heavy. That will reduce the income elasticity of demand for food ($\sigma$) thereby raising $g_y$ for unchanged $g_x$.

### The realisation problem

The budget constraint (2) implies that suppliers of Agri goods ('farmers') decide on their expenditure on Non-agri goods y depending on *potential* income pX – regardless of whether this will in fact be *realised* in terms of sales revenue.[2] However, consider the less optimistic scenario where farmers' demand for y depends on realised revenue from sales of X. Suppose pX goes up. Initially the realised income will still be the previous value of $D_x$, say $mY(0)\sigma$, and there is no increase in the demand for y. Thus the working of the multiplier (on pX) is far from automatic – it depends on the extent to which the increase in agricultural production is accompanied by an essentially autonomous increase in the Agri or x-sector's demand for y (i.e. export demand for y).[3]

## 216    *Amitava Bose*

To see this explicitly, replace (2) by

(2)$'$ $F = D_x$

Then (3) gets replaced by

(3)$'$ $AD = D_y + D_x$

There is then no effect of a change in pX on AD. In fact, given the budget constraint (1) it follows that $AD = Y$. The level of Y is indeterminate from the demand side and has to be determined from supply constraints.

## The Keynesian approach

The point of departure for Keynesian macroeconomics is rejection of Say's Law. Following Keynes one can assume that some components of demand in the Non-agri or y-sector such as investment demand are autonomous (i.e. not income-constrained). There is a well-developed financial sector and that effects a separation of investment from the saving of the investor. The demand for the Non-agri or y-good can be written as the sum of the following components:

(1) Investment demand (I); (2) Consumption demand (bY); (3) External demand (F):[4]

(11) $AD = I + bY + F$

The level of production of the y-good is demand-determined; i.e. Y adjusts to AD. So

(12) $Y = AD$

From (2), farmers' demand for the y-good is assumed to be constrained by income: $F = pX$. Therefore

(13) $Y = (I + pX)/(1-b)$

This shows that improvements in agricultural production stimulate non-agricultural production in much the same way that increases in autonomous investment expenditure do.

Next, define saving S residually as follows:

(14) $Y = S + bY + D_x$

The following property is important: While (13) implies that $[S + D_x = I + pX]$, it does not follow that $D_x = pX$ (food market is cleared) – unless it is *additionally* the case that

(15) $I = S(Y)$ [where $D_x = D(Y)$ has been used]

This is unlike the Ricardian case in which (15) would be an identity. Clearly there is now an inconsistency between (13) and (15) – there is only one variable (viz., Y) to play around with; see Figure 10.1 – which, for simplicity, has been drawn assuming $D(Y) = mY$. While (13) asserts that pX has a multiplier impact on Y, (15) implies that Y is independent of pX. Thus we have to drop one of the market clearing conditions.

If Y is determined by AD (i.e. there is Y-equilibrium) then $I > S$ implies $pX < D(Y)$, an excess demand for food. If $I < S$ in Y-equilibrium (as in Figure 10.1) then $pX > D(Y)$, indicating an excess supply of food. In the former case, farmers would end up with some extra financial saving if they run down food stocks to meet the increased demand while sticking to an expenditure of pX on the Non-agri good (instead of increasing that to $D(Y)$). In the latter case they would have to either borrow to maintain demand at pX or cut down their demand from pX to $D(Y)$. Farmers now face a 'realisation problem'. Whether F is sensitive to pX depends on the extent to which farmers' expenditure is linked to current sales of food and this has an important bearing on determination of Y.[5]

### Growth consequences

There are two possible solutions for Y as is clear from Figure 10.1. These two solutions will be denoted as $Y_d$ and $Y_x$. Let $Y_d$ solve (13), that is, when Y is determined by AD. Let $Y_x$ solve (3): $D(Y^x) = pX$; then Y is determined by pX.

*Case I:* $Y = Y_d$

From (13), $(1-b)Y = I + pX$, it follows that

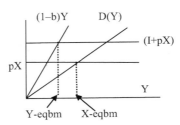

*Figure 10.1* The two equilibria in the Keynesian case

## 218   *Amitava Bose*

(16) $g_y = \lambda g_I + (1-\lambda)g_x$, $0 \leq \lambda \leq 1$ where $\lambda \equiv I/(I + pX)$

Assume that $g_I$ and $g_x$ are given constants. Then differentiation with respect to time yields[6]

(17) $\dot{g}_y = \lambda(1 - \lambda)(g_I - g_x)^2 > 0$ for $0 < \lambda < 1$. Therefore

(18) $g_y \to \max(g_I, g_x)$ as $t \to \infty$

Thus

> *I(a):* For $g_I > g_x$, it follows that $g_y > g_x$ for all t and not only is there persistently uneven growth but, since $\lambda \to 1$ as $t \to \infty$, there is *divergently uneven* growth over time.

However,

> *I(b):* For $g_I \leq g_x$, it follows that $g_y \to g_x$ from below and there is balanced growth in the long-run (the disparity is temporary).

*Case II:* $Y = Y_x$

In this case with $D(Y) = Y^\sigma$,

(19) $mY^\sigma = pX$, $0 < \sigma \leq 1$

Therefore, $\sigma g_y = g_x$ and it follows that

$[g_y - g_x] = [(1 - \sigma)g_x/\sigma]$ is constant and non-negative.

*Comparing $Y_d$ and $Y_x$:* From definitions it follows that

(20) $Y_d = [I + m(Y_x)^\sigma]/(1-b) \equiv A + a(Y_x)^\sigma$

Therefore

(21) $Y_x - Y_d = [(1-b)Y_x - I - m(Y_x)^\sigma]/(1-b)$ is increasing in $Y_x$; it is negative for small values and positive for large values of $Y_x$. Let $Y_z$ solve

(22) $Y_z = [I + m(Y_z)^\sigma]/(1-b)$

Then $Y_x < Y_z \Rightarrow Y_x < Y_d; Y_x > Y_z \Rightarrow Y_x > Y_d$ and $Y_x = Y_z \Rightarrow Y_x = Y_d$

Consider the respective influences of I and X on $Y_z$ and $Y_x$. From (19), $Y_x$ is independent of I, and from (22), $Y_z$ is increasing in I. If I is small and X is large – as would be the case in the initial stages of development – then $Y_x > Y_z$ is likely resulting in $Y_x > Y_d$. In such a case there would be too little demand for X from the Non-agri or y-sector: The agricultural surplus would fail to find a market. On the other hand, if I is large and X is small there would be an excess demand for Agri or x-goods; growth is likely to lead to 'food inflation'.

### Resolving the inconsistency: The credit market

In the Keynesian case, one encounters the problem that both markets cannot clear at the same time. It follows from (13) that $S - I = pX - D_x$. There are then two possible repercussions of $pX \neq D_x$. The first is a change in p – this has been ruled out here. But there is another possibility. An excess supply of food would mean an excess supply of saving (by sellers of food) over investment. If this persists then it points to a financial market failure. To get over this one can introduce an interest rate mechanism and invoke an investment function $I = I(r)$. Then the model becomes

(23) $\quad I(r) + pX = (1-b)Y$
(24) $\quad D(Y) = pX$

Now there is no necessary inconsistency between the two market clearing conditions. The latter equation is a subsystem that determines Y: $Y = Y_x$. Inserting this value in (23) would yield the equilibrium value of r.

## Conclusions

In this chapter, a dual economy framework was adopted and two alternate approaches, a Ricardian and a Keynesian one were used to analyse the consequences of economic growth in context of a developing economy with fixed inter-sectoral terms of trade. Apart from fixed relative prices, the model also assumed that output of the modern sector was demand determined and was the sole equilibrating variable.

Using the Ricardian approach, it was shown under reasonable assumptions that unbalanced growth, necessary for market clearing in the model, had considerable contemporary relevance for India. The Keynesian model, *inter alia*, characterised the conditions under

## 220  *Amitava Bose*

which growth could lead to food inflation and showed the relevance of the interest rate mechanism and credit markets in the equilibrating process.

## Notes

1  See Bhaduri and Skarstein (2003).
2  pX could correspond to some trend value.
3  Relevant in this context is the Kalecki-Robinson dictum: 'Capitalists get what they spend' implying that spending is independent of income. Here pX is essentially non-wage income in agriculture. See Kalecki (1971).
4  'External demand' is demand for y from the x-sector. 'Internal demand' means the demand for y from the y-sector itself. It is assumed that there is no investment demand for y from farmers.
5  That in turn would seem to depend on whether the excess of pX over mY is regarded as temporary or not.
6  Noting that $\lambda = \lambda(1-\lambda)(g_I - g_x)$

## Bibliography

Bhaduri, A. and R. Skarstein (2003): Effective demand and the terms of trade in a dual economy: a Kaldorian perspective, *Cambridge Journal of Economics*, 27(4): 583–595.

Kalecki, M. (1971): *Selected Essays on the Dynamics of the Capitalist Economy 1933–1970*, Cambridge: Cambridge University Press.

# 11 Comprehending the 'in-formal'

## Formal-informal conundrum in labour under capitalism

*Saumyajit Bhattacharya* *

The concept 'informal economy' first arose in the early 1970s in the work of the anthropologist Keith Hart (1973) in his famous paper on informal income opportunities and urban unemployment in Ghana and its concurrent generalised use in the ILO framework (ILO 1972). The setting and the contexts of these are crucial to understand the popularity that the concept assumed in the next few decades.

Development economics was dominated by the influential work of Arthur Lewis (1954), who visualised capitalist accumulation in the developing economies in a paradigm where an expanding modern capitalist sector drew its labour supply from a subsistence sector, which formed an unlimited reservoir of 'surplus labour', almost waiting to be productively withdrawn to the urban accumulation process. The essential paradigm was one of duality. The capitalist sector where production decisions were guided by marginal calculus, where the marginal gains to productivity of employing each additional labour must be more than or equal to the prevailing wage, stood in contradistinction to the subsistence sector where the motive of capital accumulation was absent and thus work did not follow such marginal calculus of instrumental rationality. Work got shared amongst the multitude of 'surplus population', that is in each subsistence enterprise or family farm, everybody contributed, but nobody worked to their productive limit. Labour thus remained underemployed in the subsistence sector and the 'surplus labour' so constituted in macroeconomic terms was an expression of hidden unemployment or what was called 'disguised unemployment'. There was so much labour potential if only all individuals worked to their full capacities and this reservoir of surplus labour could be withdrawn to the industries

---

* The author expresses sincere thanks to Sumangala Damodaran and Naveen Kanalu for valuable discussions and comments.

222  *Saumyajit Bhattacharya*

waiting to be set up and expanded and thus absorbed readily into the capitalist accumulation process.

However, the subsistence sector was not in a cocoon of a pre-capitalist culture, where motives of individual gain and betterment got subsumed to duty and tradition. The logic of capitalism had already made its announcement in the desires of this surplus reservoir – the surplus population could be lured by the potential of earning higher individual income in the urban capitalist sector. As long as the capitalist sector could offer a wage rate significantly higher than the average rural income, workers would continuously be migrating to the capitalist sector at that constant wage differential constituting a cheap unlimited labour supply until the reservoir would be exhausted at some distant future. Till then profits could be reinvested in capitalist industry and accumulation could continue unabated without any tendency of a rise in wages choking out profits. The duality was therefore one of an economic structure – not a duality in psychology or culture.

The developmental realities of the postcolonial economies did not easily correspond to this appealing economic logic. The promise of unlimited migration and unlimited absorption of the surplus population was turning into a nightmare. The nascent industrial experiences of the developing countries were witnessing the formation of a huge underbelly of urban class who were not being absorbed in the industrialisation process. They were populating the urban slums, flooding the streets, perceived as adding to crime in cities. If they were not being absorbed in industry and leading such precarious lives in cities, why were they pouring in still? Logically the migration should have halted. In this context came a major contribution from Harris and Todaro (1970). That the surplus population migrates in lure of an industrial job, because of its higher wage level, and they hang around waiting until the one day that they will get absorbed. As some get absorbed, the expectations rise for the others waiting behind – they see their chances of getting an industrial job in the next lot. The more such employment is created, the more the expectation, the more the migration and the more the hanging around and waiting – and the more the urban unemployment.

This is where the 'informal sector' story fits in. What do they do when they hang around? They find all kind of rudimentary opportunities – menial service jobs, street occupations, part-time employment, often finding multiple insecure sources of income. The informal sector, so constituted, allows them to subsist and persist in the urban areas. It is a sector which gives temporary refuge to aspirants of industrial jobs. The participants in informal sector are not organically there – they are temporarily there in waiting. It is a sector for refuge; a sector in waiting to be ultimately abolished by vigorous accumulation of the capitalist sector, whether such a dream gets fulfilled or remains ever illusory.[1]

Ironically, Keith Hart's pioneering coinage of the term 'informal sector' and its motivations differ quite starkly from the popular interpretation that it soon assumed. He, in fact, questioned Todaro's vision in seeing the informal migrants or the urban 'hanger-arounds' as merely waiting to get employed in the formal sector to secure a formal wage. For him "the magnetic force of the town may be derived from the multiplicity of income opportunities rather than merely from wage levels", including that "the migrant could look to the prospect of accumulation, with or without a job, in the informal economy of the urban slums" (Hart 1973, p. 88).

## Alternative discourses of informality – an evaluation

In the discourse on informality that evolved, however, quite different standpoints can be delineated. Whereas duality seems to be a fundamental premise, the inherent notions of this dual structure have different articulations of the separation.

1   The extended Lewisian framework is one of economic structural dualism, where the formal and informal sectors operate on different principles of economic organisation. Further, the capitalist accumulation and growth process is essentially in the formal sector and the informal sector has little to do with it except for being a repository of labour supply and a refuge. A clear separation of the formal and informal and a one-way link (of labour supply) from the informal to the formal was a structural feature of this framework. However, as mentioned earlier, the duality does not extend to the culture of individuals. Individuals in the informal sector were 'rational' (in the economic sense) and responded to 'economic incentives', thus allowing the sector to be a latent reserve pool of labour waiting to be absorbed.

2   A contrasting version exists, where the inhabitants of the informal domain are entirely excluded from the capitalist growth process, even as a reserve labour pool. A variant of this is to pose capitalist accumulation as essentially a sphere of 'big processes' and 'modern technology' often coterminous with monopoly capitalism. By implication the informal sector is technologically backward, with low productivity, carrying the remnants of pre-capitalist/artisanal production relations and processes, having no (or at best weak)

## 224 Saumyajit Bhattacharya

organic links with the modern sector and is waiting for the inevitable destruction with the march of modernity. Thus the inhabitants of such an excluded informal sector are victims of postcolonial modernity and development. In spite of their marginalisation and dispossession by the processes of primitive accumulation, capitalist development cannot incorporate this relative surplus population, even as a 'reserve army of labour', and bypasses them completely (Sachs 1991; Sanyal 2014). A version of this line of thinking sees this as a challenge for the postcolonial states, where, in the context of their total economic exclusion from the accumulation process, they nevertheless need to be politically included for the construction of a complex hegemony (Sanyal 2014) and the compulsions of electoral democracy, through fiscal transfers and other livelihood policies, thus reversing some of the effects of the primitive accumulation (Chatterjee 2008; Sanyal 2014). In spite of this reversal, however, the excluded still remains capitalism's 'others', to be managed by nuanced 'governmentality',[2] both national and global, so that they do not grow into a dangerous class.

3  Another parallel and a relatively new discourse is one where the informal is treated as the 'precariat' (Standing 2009, 2011). Once again, there is a sense of exclusion in this discourse. Its origin lies in a strand of social exclusion discourse, where the excluded were seen to be outside the productive processes – in crime, delinquency and the shadow (parallel) economy or in various disabilities. Though members of the precariat need not occupy this shadowy terrain, they are "dangerously" poised, "flanked by an army of unemployed and a detached group of socially ill misfits living of the dregs of the society" (Standing 2011, p. 8). They themselves are in precarious conditions and thus making the social process of accumulation precarious. They constitute the "global reserve army" yet they are too precarious to qualify as 'labour' and are in fact a new "dangerous class in the making". Though, the precariat is "globalisation's child" and it plays a crucial role therein as the "reserve army" but its conceptualisation as the "dangerous class", not as the norm and *not as labour*, makes it essentially an aberration – a catastrophe in capitalism rather than its normal functioning (Standing 2011, pp. 5 and 7).

4  Quite another view is that the informal economy lacks Weberian rationality. Particularly, the modern state apparatus with its legal paraphernalia and bureaucracy and public organisation/regulation of economic life is largely absent from this sphere.[3] The processes that go on in the informal economy are unlike formal capitalist

*Comprehending the 'in-formal'* 225

processes – non-contractual (absence of written contract), unregulated and unorganised (a lack of organisation and structure). This may not imply an absence of organisation/regulation and structure per se but these organisations and structures are guided by 'social regulation' that is alien to modern organisation principles of the state and developed capitalism (Harriss-White 2010). The emphasis here is not so much on size, productivity or technology but rather the social organisation principle and the nature of regulation. The modern writ of the state is absent here.

5   A variant of this sees much of the informal economy as petty commodity production (PCP) in contradistinction to capitalist 'labour'. Further, it is the labourist conceptualisation of work that is causal for the state to neglect and marginalise the particularities of the 'petty producers/petty economy' and allow the 'social regulation' of this sector to prevail (Harriss-White 2010). Thus this sector is allowed to be exploited by capital in multifarious forms and its inherent accumulation potential is stifled or neglected by indifferent state machinery obsessed with formal structures and paraphernalia. This neglect of the state arises essentially out of a misconception, a misplaced priority or a mindset obsessed with Weberian rationality – it is not a strategic choice of the accumulation paradigm (it is at best a tactic of administration) – to make itself absent and allow the sector to be self-regulated and not muddle with it. It is a failure of the state to regulate in its capacity and intent.

6   A contesting and contradictory variant of this is that the informal sector is a repository of a potential for capitalist accumulation. But it is the bureaucratic regulatory apparatus of the state that stifles its energies and hinders its potential (De Soto 1989, 2000). The state is not absent here, but it is present in the negative sense with its harsh regulations and an entire neglect of any structure of incentives for realising its native accumulation potential. The sector has its masses waiting to be capitalists and embrace capitalism; it is only the vested interest of state and big capital that snuffs out that potential.[4]

These different articulations of informality listed are not always consistent or coherent, and can be mutually contesting, yet they share a common trait. That is, there is an inherent duality between the formal and the informal, whether they are economically structural, technological or socially organisational. Further, howsoever the link between the formal and informal may be conceived, the mainspring of capitalist

## 226 *Saumyajit Bhattacharya*

accumulation process does not lie there. The informal economy thus may be bypassed, exploited, managed or stunted by capitalist accumulation and the accompanying manoeuvres by the state, yet the energies and obsessions of that accumulation paradigm do not lie there.

Before we evaluate this discourse further let us have a look at the ground reality of informality and its place in capitalist globalisation. I limit this discussion essentially to some synoptic features of informality in India because here we find perhaps one of the most extensive and fertile grounds of generation of 'informality'. The National Commission for Enterprises in the Unorganised Sector (NCEUS) (NCEUS 2007, 2009) estimated the total number of informal workers spread across both the formal as well as informal sectors in 2004–05 to be about 167 million, that is about 84 percent of the non-agricultural workforce.[5] Further not only is informal sector employment growing faster than formal sector employment, formal jobs are declining in absolute terms and the growth of formal sector jobs are entirely because of informal job growth in the formal economy. The NCEUS recorded that informal workers constitute about 45 percent of the non-agricultural formal sector workforce and by all evidence of the above mentioned trends this share must have grown since then. We are therefore witnessing a phenomenon of pervasive informalisation in the entire economy. The sheer size and dynamism of this phenomenon is enough to suggest that this is no dual or marginal story and in my opinion informalisation and informal labour lie at the heart of capitalist accumulation process in India.

A significant part of the informal economy in the contemporary world is intrinsically linked to the formal economy in more than one way. Activities in the informal economy are directly linked to and often constitute an essential part of the processes of production, exchange and accumulation both at the national and, increasingly, at global levels.

What is at the core in the interaction and dynamics between the formal-informal is a range of flexibilities that can be ascribed to the informal economy or processes. This flexibility in turn proves to be a crucial element in depressing costs, both in the short and the long run, and is particularly used by large capital to its advantage. Different forms and arrangements of this process can be observed in current global production and distribution networks. Observing the operation of the global commodity chains, one finds that some of the crucial stages of production and supply are in fact located in the developing world in sectors and processes that are 'informal'. This allows large multinational capital a process of flexible subcontracting and the ability to shift supply networks and production processes from one country or sector to another with ease. The fact that crucial suppliers of products, processes and components are small firms in the informal economy gives a strong leverage to large capital in its bargaining position. But this in itself is not the crucial point about the role of informality since this would then be no different from a story of oligopolistic firms dealing with competitive suppliers spread across countries. The informality that characterises these small enterprises can in turn be utilised in the process of accumulation that will be difficult to carry out in case of small firms in a formal sector context. The lack of regulatory environment, the flexibility or absence of labour contracts, the ability to stretch hours of operation at ease are some of the crucial means by which these informal enterprises themselves operate, survive and chart out their competitive advantage. The major brunt of this flexibility falls on labour employed in these enterprises or on even smaller organisational forms – the self-employed and the homebased workers which in turn supply to them. It is this flexibility and managing to keep transaction and labour costs to the minimum, which is at the core of the dynamics of these small enterprises that allows them to survive and provides them the competitive edge. It is this advantage that is ultimately and crucially made use of by large capital in its search of global profits and accumulation.

A different process of creating informality is also visible in the era of globalisation. This is informalisation that has resulted from 'rationalisation' and restructuring processes in the formal sector. This has two broad manifestations. One, where the formal sector firm itself carries out informal employment and processes and the other where downsizing of labour in the formal sector or recessionary tendencies, particularly for domestic industries in certain sectors, associated in various cases of structural adjustment have forced people to the informal economy for their livelihood and survival.

There are two distinct processes in which informalisation of employment takes place in formal sector firms. One is to employ labour without any permanent wage or employment contract or provide any employment benefit. The other is to contract operations that were earlier performed by employees of the firm to smaller or 'specialised' enterprises. A particular form of this is to contract out operations to labour contractors or suppliers, where, even if particular employees are regularly working in the principal firm, they are not de-facto considered the employees of the principle firm and are therefore denied any rights, which they would have otherwise had. The suppliers of such workers are often informal sector enterprises, where no such granting of rights or obligation for the employees they provide is practiced. However, the suppliers of workers in many cases are large service sector firms, even multinationals, where informal employment practices are rampant and neither they nor the principal employers take any responsibility for such workers.

Thus informalisation is not a story of a dualistic economy, where the marginalised sections shunned by the capitalist growth process find residual avenues to survive through a host of activities. The informal workforce is inextricably a part of the very capitalist growth process.

This is neither to deny the presence of any marginalised or excluded sector nor the denial of informal work not connected to the central accumulation drives, but to stress that to conceptualise the informal sector or the occupants therein essentially as disjointed from or untouched by the capitalist accumulation process does the greatest disservice to any coherent conceptualisation of the current global capitalist regimes and even those of the past.

A relevant point to mention here is a whole range of occupations, not directly integrated to the circuits of capital, such as paid domestic work and other petty services, nevertheless perform vital roles in maintaining the domain of reproductive work and consumption, on which the entire domain of productive work and its level of productivity and wage formations depend. Thus unpaid or low paid reproductive or petty work 'subsidises' corporate firms such that they can pay a lower level of wages than they could have otherwise, because the cost of living of the 'productive' worker remains contained (Malos 1975; Antonopoulos and Hirway 2010). Thus to see even such occupations in terms of a disjointed need economy (Sanyal 2014), unrelated to capital accumulation, misses out one of the fundamental features of the regime.

In light of this discussion, how do we evaluate the conceptualisation of informalisation synoptically presented in points (1) to (6)? Any conceptualism of structural dualism, where the informal economy is seen as a mere reservoir of labour or with rudimentary processes and technology misses the point completely. Not only are there multidirectional complex causalities running between the 'formal' and the 'informal' economy, the informal economy itself is a part of a core strategy of capitalist accumulation and is as much (in fact more of) a crucial dimension as the formal processes and sectors.

Neither can we generalise anything about technological backwardness, as many sophisticated technical tasks are being handed to informal arrangements and networks by large capital. Similarly, the conceptualisation of much of the informal economy as PCP misses

*Comprehending the 'in-formal'* 229

the most crucial point of the inherent dynamics that through these informal processes and work arrangements surplus value is extracted by capital by both mechanisms that Marx called 'absolute' and 'relative' surplus value extraction (Marx 1984). Informality, devoid of any regulatory norms, provides the most flexible arrangements of stretching the workday as well as extracting intensive work. In conjunction its presence in high value added sectors also represent easy productivity gains, which are not shared with labour, increasing the 'degree of exploitation' (i.e. the rate of surplus value) (Marx 1984).

If we now consider informality as the absence of state regulation (or more aptly as being socially regulated), the question is not whether state regulation is absent, which it obviously is. The issue is can this absence be seen as neglect or 'marginalisation'. My contention is that this is not neglect or a product of marginalisation at all but a deliberate choice by the state. The crucial role that informality plays in the general accumulation process cannot be 'marginalised' or left to 'social regulation' by chance. The state allows such 'social regulation' by deliberately absenting itself so that such informality can be generated and regenerated in the process of expanded reproduction of capital, so that capital gets the most flexible field of domination and exploitation that it desires in such an accumulation milieu.

Similarly, viewing the inhabitants of the informal economy through a lens of exclusion also does great disservice to an adequate conceptualisation of the reality. Conceptualising them as the excluded 'others' of the capitalist economy, only to be managed by state and 'governmentality' for political hegemony or compulsion, entirely misses out the central role they play in the accumulation regime. Likewise, defining the 'precariat' distinct from labour as a new emerging dangerous class beclouds our understanding of the accumulation process. Whereas, indeed the majority in the informal economy lead a precarious life and are indeed excluded from the fruits of accumulation, these discourses, in spite of capturing these sensitivities, obfuscate more than they reveal of the accumulation process, particularly in their specific discourse trajectories. The 'precariat' and the 'socially excluded' are seen not at the centre stage of accumulation but as those who are there because the system cannot carry them. Whereas the exclusion discourse covers many different strands and clearly there are sections that are excluded in capitalist growth processes, such a term semantically does lot of disservice to the actual nature of accumulation. A part of the social exclusion discourse arose from the European context, where sections of population were seen not integrated culturally or involved in illegal activities/crime (Levitas 2005). This is not the space to have detailed

## 230 *Saumyajit Bhattacharya*

evaluation of such a discourse, the point here is that whereas the social exclusion discourse has its own place, its extension to the informality discourse is rather inappropriate and 'social exclusion' is perhaps most unsuitable a term for understanding the subjects of informality. Its own grounds notwithstanding, the use of the social exclusion discourse in this context obfuscates the fact that these informal structures, processes and those in it are very much at the heart of the social process of accumulation. It is these social structures that are used; it is those who are thought to be the excluded who foremost contribute to the capitalist value exploitation process. Capital does not exclude them, nor does it or the state keep the regeneration of such conditions to chance. It is only that the fruits of the accumulation process are excluded from them. It is quintessential exploitation of labour, akin to keeping wages at subsistence level or below it and the construction of mechanisms to see such pathetic subsistence reproduced. The absence of the state from regulation is a deliberate choice. Otherwise, the reproduction of such pathetic conditions of subsistence and vulnerability will be impossible in the framework of a regulatory apparatus of a modern 'democratic' state. It is not irrelevant here to remind ourselves that the first hundred years of industrial capitalism in England also saw such 'apathy' from the state about much of its labouring population. Perhaps London's East End in the mid-nineteenth century is a stark example of informal economic organization which can rival in scale any of today's slum areas of the Global South. Henry Mayhew's investigations for the Morning Chronicle in the 1850s, published as London Labour and the London Poor (1861–62) or W. F. Whyte's American study Street Corner Society (1943) reminds us that such 'informality' is not any preserve of the 'failure of development' story (Mayhew 2008; Whyte 1993).

## Informality as a negative semantic – the norm of formality

In the face of such pervasive and vigorous informalisation how are these dualistic conceptualisations maintained where informalisation is seen as the 'other' of the capitalist growth process? I argue that this lies in the normative semantics of formality/informality and the political ideology that it generates.

Thus the conceptualisation of informality is a negative semantic itself. In-formal that which is not formal implying that capitalist accumulation or 'modern economic growth' is a process of formality – a formality of contracts, processes and organisations. Similarly, the

## Comprehending the 'in-formal' 231

term used for the informal sector in India is 'unorganised sector'. The NCEUS has even used the term 'unorganised labour' for informal labour (NCEUS 2007, 2009). Once again the negative semantic is at work. Modern growth, whether in public or private sector, is conceptualised as an organised process. This is not unorganised labour as in not unionised, for the existence of labour unions in the 'unorganised' sector does not make either the sector or that labour 'organised' according to official depiction in India. It is unorganised because the very entity in its existence is supposed to lack Weberian rationality and organisation – something that is haphazard, unstructured or ad hoc.

At a more abstract level, the conceptualisation of capitalist growth inherently views the market processes and institutions as autonomous and in neutrality from various social entities such as race, caste and gender. Networks and ties that are social and not 'purely' economic are not features of such an imagined production/exchange process. Thus both the organisations and their hierarchies are seen to operate as abstract processes devoid of social sensitivities – these processes are general and generalisable devoid of any organic local markers; the local may only be an add on to a general structure. The informal or the unorganised lack that 'neutrality'; they are embedded in concrete social networks of kinship, traditions and localisms. Even though any consideration of concrete history of labour is contradictory to such a conceptualisation that is devoid of social embeddedness (Granovetter 1985), such an ideology, particularly transmitted through formal economics textbooks and models, has tremendous sway. It is pertinent to remind ourselves that the most 'formalised' practice of labour process in capitalism, the Fordist labour process, did not originate in such labour market 'neutrality'. Henry Ford chose to man his Michigan auto plant with new migrant labour, who would easily accept the regimentation of the Fordist labour process. Even a higher wage rate and a regularised workday could not entice the existing labour force to accept the 'rationalisation' of the labour process (Tonkiss 2006).

However, the formation of the norm of formality goes much deeper than this abstraction of market neutrality. It is so intrinsic to the conceptualisation of capitalist labour process that even when these 'structures of formality' face relentless attacks under Neo-liberal regimes, the 'informal' still remains, in terms of its identity, outside the arena of 'normal' labour in capitalism. The process of this norm formation happens in diverse and opposed political quarters.

In the discourses of the apologists of Neo-liberalism, informality arises due to imperfections or rigidities in the labour market. Thus even though labour rights are relentlessly attacked and the labour

## 232 Saumyajit Bhattacharya

regime made more and more flexible and casual, the presence of large mass of 'informal' labour is explained because of existing labour rights of formal labour and rigidities that trade union politics and labour regulations create, making it impossible to absorb the informal mass in the formal sector or forcing capital to contract out to escape from rigid regulation and politics.[6] Of course, the argument is flawed in its basic logic. If the only way the informal can be made a part of the formal is by abolishing the basic tenets of 'formal' labour (that is, the various rights and provisions of employment security) – if labour can be hired and fired at will – then what remains of that formality is where the informal are supposed to be integrated. Thus while attempting to informalise labour in general and while attacking the tenets of formality, informal labour is still treated as the other – something which exists not because of strategies of capital but because of hindrances to capital.

Such a norm formation of formality is not an exclusive preserve of Neo-liberal ideologues. In fact, on the other side of the fence, even mainstream trade unions are themselves quite resistant to see the problem of the 'informal' as a core issue in labour politics today. The trade unions of the North for a long time has had a paternalistic attitude to the issue, advising their cousins in the South to incorporate these workers/issues in their political coverage as an add-on approach reminiscent of the WID (women in development) approach to the women's question in developmental paradigm (Rathgeber 1989). The problem was seen as peculiar to the developing countries, where the lack of democratic modernisation and continuation of pre-capitalist practices were held responsible for prevalence of such structures. That this is a core strategy of capital, including multinational capital, particularly in the phase of globalisation and is not only limited to a third world experience, was not central to the discourse for a long time. As a result, it remained an add-on approach. Even though increasing number of pronouncements were made on informal labour/informal economy, it did not get systemic attention.

The mainstream trade unions of the South also follow a somewhat similar trajectory. Whereas they have to confront the problem of growing 'informality' in day-to-day practice and they no longer can be oblivious to the informalisation of the 'formal sector' (i.e. the casualisation and rampant flexibilisation of what used to be a 'formal' labour space), and many trade unions do indeed try organising informal labour in small enterprises, these are often seen not as core issues of labour politics. They remain as additional issues or when within a structure of a formal enterprise/corporation, the issue becomes one of regularisation; of how to incorporate rather than how to see this as an organic structure in itself. In practice of course, often it is difficult to delineate between such incorporation strategies and organic strategies, but in their programmatic preoccupations much of organised labour remains straddled with structures where informality is external to or is a deviation from the norm.

Often, it is this apathy to prioritise the discourses and politics of informal labour in mainstream trade union politics which provides fodder to the alternative radical discourses discussed earlier, such as those by the protagonists of 'precariat' and PCP in contradistinction to labour. However, in their critique they give up much more than is necessary. They create an alternative dualism where formal labour, state and capital are often placed in the same box, all standing in opposition to the hapless informal subjects derided, neglected and marginalised by the formal structural entities – be it state, capital or labour. Surprisingly and perhaps entirely without intent, such a discourse finds a strange parallel with the Neo-liberal critique of formal labour that formal labour and its ideology stand as the ultimate barrier to the salvation of the 'masses waiting to be incorporated' in the capitalist accumulation process.[7]

## Deconstruction of the norm of formality – a historical grounding

It is therefore pertinent to deconstruct this norm formation of formal labour, both in history and theory. The constitution of the norm of labour as formality is often presented as a historical character of labour in capitalism. What are the tenets of this 'formality'? A long-term employment, with well-defined contracts with various securities including retirement benefits, security against arbitrary dismissals and the right to collective bargaining with a conditional right to strike – all these and many more form the core of the formality.

But looking back one observes that such rights of labour have not only been largely absent in most of the period of capitalism, they have also been largely absent in geographies mapping the capitalist spread. This body of rights as a fully practiced norm happened only after the Second World War even in the advanced capitalist countries and ran its full course only up to the end of the so called golden age. The periphery of capitalist expansion anyway saw these rights in a much more incomplete and contingent way.

The most important legal theoretical premise in the application of the law of contract in the realm of capital-labour relation is to assume

## 234 *Saumyajit Bhattacharya*

a formal symmetry between the two parties – that they are both bound by contractual obligations (and nothing beyond it) till the contract lasts and after that they can both terminate the contract freely without any further obligation. This seemingly equal contractual situation hides the basic asymmetry between the two parties that the capitalist as the owner of means of production and the labourer devoid of it, are fundamentally in absolutely unequal positions to enter the 'equal contract'. Not only does this inequality arise from the inequality of their starting position, which was recognised quite early on very succinctly by Adam Smith (1976), but fundamentally it also arises from the ending position of the contract that entails the legal premise of right to property over the produced commodity that forms the very basis of value exploitation by the capitalist. As Marx (1984) eloquently exposed: The capitalist as an owner of the means of production has the exclusive and total claim to the product and the surplus value, whereas labour, the producer of surplus value, does not have any claim to it. That is the law of contract in its undiluted form, and it entails the fundamental prerogative of the employer and posits a legal symmetry on asymmetries both at starting and ending positions of the contract.

Even this camouflaging legal symmetry did not arise since the genesis of industrial capitalism. In Britain, well into a hundred years of industrial revolution that governed the capital – labour relation was not a labour contract as discussed previously but the centuries-old law of master and servant according to which rules of status allowed a master to control his servant through obligations of obedience, loyalty and fidelity. Breach of obligations by the worker (but not the master) allowed a liberal use of penal sanctions that were enforceable before magistrates (Kerr 2004). These rules spread in different forms through much of the British Empire in the nineteenth and early twentieth centuries. In Britain, these rules of status were abolished in 1875 and employment was brought into the framework of the general law of contract by which an employer obtained the right to control the labour of his employee in much the same way as the rules of status allowed him to do so before 1875. The law of contract that substituted for these rules also allowed the employer the exclusive right to dispose of the worker for reasons of his choosing, subject to the giving of adequate notice. In other words, the employer's prerogative was supreme in the relationship between the employer and the employee. The framework of the law of contract, while replacing the rules of status, carried with it explicit traces of the fundamentally unequal relationship, both overtly and covertly. It was only through intense struggles of labour that the overt elements of inequality in the premises of the law of contract were

*Comprehending the 'in-formal'* 235

gradually moderated through the next three-quarters of a century. But, in spite of various collective gains made by labour in the first half of the twentieth century, workers received only a week's notice before termination of employment and hardly any severance payments or state protection against dismissal before the Second World War.

The legal framework of 'formal labour' has emerged historically only after the Second World War, particularly in the context of the shadow of the cathartic era of depression and war, and the subsequent rise of social democracy and the construction of the welfare states in Europe. It was also undoubtedly a result of the undercurrents in the realm of international politics to take the wind out of the sail of socialist forces, particularly in the face of rising strength of the labour movement, or the general consensus not to go back to the unemployment situation of the depression period and the instability of the war years and also strong technological reasons in the large-scale Fordist industrialisation, where capital demanded more stable labour (Bhattacharya 2007).

The legal framework of formal labour that emerged thus primarily questioned the exercise of employer prerogative and therefore had built into it the provisions that made unfair dismissal legally and statutorily not possible and also making the state the upholder of these protective provisions (Anderman 2004). In legal theoretic terms, it recognises the inherently unequal/asymmetrical nature of the employer/employee relationship and is predicated on the idea that while the contract should enable production to take place smoothly, it should do so without giving the more powerful party in the contract, the employer, the ability to use his power (Bhattacharya 2007).

This phase of fundamental ascendance of labour rights, encompassed in the structure of 'formal labour', however had quite a short span of vigour. It lasted between the end of the Second World War and the beginning of the 1970s, often referred to as the 'golden age of capitalism'. The advent of Neo-liberal ideology and practices since the mid-1970s brought a harsh challenge to such an embodiment of labour rights and soon created conditions of its speedy reversals.

Thus, reviewing the experience of capitalist labour one sees that the norm of 'formal labour' was established at a rather late and contingent stage of capitalism and experienced in its fullness for quite a limited span of time. Further, such an enablement was rather limited in the experience of capitalist expanse beyond the advanced capitalist countries both in the extent and coverage of these rights. The Neo-liberal reversal of the labour rights of 'formal labour' in the very countries where they originated and got established and particularly the ease and

236  *Saumyajit Bhattacharya*

speed of this reversal make us question how much this was a norm, anyway, of labour in capitalism. How can an experience so short and so limited in extent be considered a norm? Not only the ideology and practice of 'employer's prerogative' – the expression of the basic asymmetry in capital-labour relations has surfaced with force but also much more of its 'originary' tendencies such as overt dominance and rampant flexibility have been the core of Neo-liberal labour reforms everywhere. Further, the rampant casualisation, flexibilisation and vulnerability that we observe in sites of global value chain production today, mostly in the developing economies (but not only there) is not any aberration of or deviation from the capitalist labour process but rather its full expression. Globalisation, as a manifestation of the limitless expanse of capital and its limitless fragmentary potential, while inscribing the meta-narrative of exploitation and accumulation in a grand totality not witnessed hitherto, has used uneven geographies to its core in expressing its organic originary tendencies, unhindered by contingencies. It is crucial to realise that these 'originary' tendencies are not originary just in the sense of tendencies in its nascent stage, but they are indeed organic – the expression of its latent intent – something which announces itself from the very beginning and remains latent, always waiting to find full expression whenever conjunctures are suitable. Viewed this way, it is the paradigm of 'informal labour' rather than 'formal labour', which forms the norm in the immanent and organic tendencies of capitalism.

## The norm of formality as the essence of class struggle

It is however pertinent to ask what precisely has been the experience, achievements and politics involved in 'formal' labour and is there anything of essence in treating it as the norm?

First and foremost, formality can be conceptualised as a process of advancement of labour rights beyond the law of contract. We have discussed how the evolution of the law of contract being applied to labour with the abolition of the master-servant act was itself a product of labour struggles and came almost hundred years after the advent of capitalist industrialisation. Even after this, in no way was this a symmetric situation; the premise of the law of contract in formal symmetry hides the basic asymmetry of capital-labour relation. Therefore the constitution of countervailing rights of labour in both collective action and employment securities is a product of the recognition of this basic asymmetry, which came as a result of intense struggles of labour and the contingent post–Second World War situation, both political

*Comprehending the 'in-formal'* 237

and economic, in the advanced capitalist countries. These rights by recognising the basic asymmetry of the relation attempt to redress the balance through provision of labour rights. Irrespective of whether these rights depoliticised labour or helped incorporate labour politics within the ambit of contestations internal to capitalism, they mark out an undeniable advance for labour within the immanent tendencies of capitalism.

Let us examine them in some detail. The provision of long-term employment and laws against arbitrary dismissal essentially deny capital its most important instrument – the freedom to hire and fire – to treat labour as merely a contractual entity which is contractually prepaid before the realisation and appropriation of the surplus and therefore in organic terms denied having any claim over the surplus or to the continuity of the circuits of capital. It is an ultimate expression of the negative freedom of labour that Marx eloquently analysed – of its being free from any claim to the means of production or to the product or surplus that labour power produces. To deny or constrict that to a considerable extent, as these rights did, is unquestionably an advance in contestation and denial of one of capitalism's central tenets of functioning.

The formal can also be understood in a spatial-temporal dimension. Formal labour not only has a sense of a regulated and determined workspace and a strict definition of hours of work (with overtime benefits if they were exceeded) but also the separation of the home and the workplace and the binaries constructed therein have deep significance in the politics of labour. Even though this binary separation is a prime marker of estrangement of labour – the work process being alienated from the life of labour and separated out, it also formed dialectically the most important basis for the expression of its positive freedom that the labourer's social life is not tied to the workplace or work regimentation and obligations. This separation is the first step in contesting bondage. It did not originate naturally with the arrival of capitalist relations, as a rudimentary survey of history will indicate, but was a product of its advance through contestations. This freedom of course was perhaps the most incomplete and particularly situated in a gendered terrain of the male breadwinner. The separation of male labour from the home was also the basis of gradually relegating women only to housework, and the constitution of the double burden of work, when women re-entered formal workspaces.

Parallel to this process was the struggle to reduce the workday. This constituted one of the most crucial contestations against capital: The struggle of labour to reduce the extraction of absolute surplus value

## 238 Saumyajit Bhattacharya

and its concomitant manoeuvre by capital to instead take recourse to the extraction of relative surplus value. Yet to analyse the dynamics of capitalism as a linear shift from extraction of absolute to relative surplus value will be travesty of history. Capital never ceases to seek opportunities for extracting absolute surplus value because, in class terms, that is the most unambiguous expression of power over labour – of tying the worker in temporal magnitude – to reduce the free time available to labour and to further extend the surplus labour time above necessary labour time. Only possibilities of trade-offs with higher relative surplus value (productivity gains) or fashioning the labourer as a consumer and the need to make consumption time available (the increasing commoditisation of life and leisure) could bring in a shift from absolute to relative surplus value extraction. Fordist strategies which proactively reduced the absolute workday and simultaneously increased the wage floor with its concomitant intensified monitoring and rigidification of the intensity of work and work schedules represent such a shift. The production-consumption 'fits' that stereotypical Fordist regimes represented was the other side of the same coin (Tonkiss 2006). In a different contingent situation in spatial terms, the geographies of low-wage sweatshop labour, with its time flexibilities, can be easily adopted if absolute surplus value can become a crucial form of extraction of surplus value, particularly where the worker's consumption in the geography of production sites becomes less relevant in a paradigm of global commodity chains, where the consumption of the final product is designed for a distant 'global' locale, away from the local geographies of the fragmentary chain of producers.

In the quest to retain the formal in spatial-temporal terms labour thus fights for its relative freedom in a time sense, it does so as well in a spatial sense. Designated workspace with securities of safety and hygiene is not only an issue of comfort and life hazard, it creates the profound sense of claim of the worker to the production site and production process, a claim which capital in its organic tendencies always tend to deny. This not only creates a sense of belonging to the workspace, which, however false, constitutes a sense of recognition and self-worth of labour, but it also creates one of the most crucial basis of organisation, camaraderie and collective action against capital.

## Conclusions

Informal labour practices constitute some of the most blatant reversals of the gains that 'formal' labour made in spatial-temporal domains. Footloose and flexible labour not only lacks employment security, it

*Comprehending the 'in-formal'* 239

also lacks a sense of attachment and recognition and it lacks a crucial spatial engagement that can form the basis for counterclaims and collective action at the workspace. A deconstruction of the concrete strategies of 'informalisation' often boils down to the negation of spatial-temporal gains of labour. For example, working without a fixed workspace, a mobile salesman with a laptop and cell phone not only is exploited in terms of stretched time, but also any possibility of association and collective action is reduced without a space for meeting and belonging and perceiving the workplace as one's own. Similarly, homebased work by disturbing the workplace/home binary not only stretches work and is an obvious example of the extraction of absolute surplus value, but the very sense of being labour with its rights vis-à-vis capital is denied when spatially the work is situated at home. In fact, the spatial-temporal displacement here creates a sense of homebased work as non-work or not quite work or additional work, even though it often stretches much longer than any norm of workday if time-use calculations are considered. The selection of primarily women as homebased workers solidifies this spatial-temporal dimension of exploitation in the very gendered nature of this work and goes to its ultimate in rendering an intense labour exploitation process to a category of 'not quite work' and its concomitant debasement of the self-worth of the worker.

Once they are taken as issues in the politics of labour – then one can see capital, unless contingent, has a tendency to always try to negate and negotiate formality and create 'informal' tendencies and labour's oppositional politics lie in creating 'formal' tendencies. It is for this reason that capital in its general obfuscatory manoeuvres projects the informal as the 'other', so that its own machinations are not revealed, even when it strives to pull down the apparatus of formality. And it is this which is laudable in labour's opposition to informality and informalisation.

Thus how do we deal with the norm of formality? If we retain the norm beyond instrumentality, it can only be done with a political agenda. That is not to treat informality as the other but rather the organic that is always present as a tendency in strategies of capital, which labour fights for contesting and negotiating subjugation and exploitation. So it is in this sense that the formal can be treated as the desired norm of labour – as both an objective and the vindication of the struggle against capital. And it is in this sense that discourses deriding 'formal labour' miss the point and serve the agenda of capital in the ultimate analysis, whatever their colour and predilections.

## 240 Saumyajit Bhattacharya

## Notes

1 Harris and Todaro's focus was on the motives of the continuous surplus migration and policies to arrest it; they did not essentially compose an informal sector story. However, the overall discourse soon took that shape, particularly in pedagogic practices of Development Economics, integrating the informal sector dynamics to the outgrowth of a failed Lewisian story; Ray (1998) is a very good example.
2 This original Foucauldian concept has been extended by both Chatterjee (2004, 2008) and Sanyal (2014, pp. 170–176) in Post-colonial contexts. For the original concept introduced by Foucault, see Foucault (1991)
3 Keith Hart's comprehension of the informal sector is more in this sense.
4 Hart's original contribution at length discussed petty accumulation as a motive and lure for many of those in the informal sector. But contrary to De Soto's assertion and hope in vigorous possibilities of capitalist accumulation in this sector, Hart sees such possibilities largely stifled, just creating an eternal illusory hope of salvation.
5 Almost the entire agricultural sector except for plantations and corporate farming falls under informal sector in India. In 2004–05 this was estimated to be 97.6 percent of the total agricultural sector workforce.
6 Basu, Fields and Debgupta (2004); Besley and Burgess (2004); Fallon and Lucas (1991). For a critique, see Bhattacharya (2008).
7 For a detailed critique, see Bhattacharya (2014).

## Bibliography

Anderman, S. (2004): 'Termination of Employment – Whose Property Rights?' in Barnard, C., Deakin, S. and G. Morris (eds) *The Future of Labour Law*, Hart Publishing, Oxford and Portland Oregon.

Antonopoulos, R. and I. Hirway (2010): *Unpaid Work and the Economy: Gender, Time Use and Poverty in Developing Countries*, Palgrave Macmillan.

Basu, K., G. S. Fields and S. Debgupta (2004): *Retrenchment, Labor Laws and Government Policy: An Analysis with Special Reference to India*, Paper written for World Bank, Washington, DC. [http://siteresources.worldbank.org/INTDECSHRSMA/Resources/india.pdf]

Besley, T. and R. Burgess (2004): 'Can Labour Regulation Hinder Economic Performance? Evidence from India', *Quarterly Journal of Economics*, Vol. 119, No. 1, pp. 91–134.

Bhattacharya, S. (2007): 'Vicissitudes of the Relationship between State, Labour and Capital: An Appraisal of the Neo-Liberal Labour Market Reforms in India and Beyond', *Labour, Capital and Society*, Vol. 40, Nos. 1 and 2.

Bhattacharya, S. (2008): 'The Changing Discourse of Neoliberal Labour Reforms: From Labour Suffering Temporarily for Transition to Labour Creating the Obstacles to Transition', *Indian Journal of Labour Economics*, Vol. 51, No. 4.

Bhattacharya, S. (2014): 'Is Labour Still a Relevant Category for Praxis? Critical Reflections on Some Contemporary Discourses on Work and Labour in Capitalism', *Development and Change*, Vol. 45, No. 5, pp. 941–962.

## Comprehending the 'in-formal' 241

Breman, J. (2002): *The Labouring Poor in India: Patterns of Exploitation, Subordination, and Exclusion*, Oxford University Press, Oxford.

Chatterjee, P. (2004): *The Politics of the Governed: Reflections on Popular Politics in Most of the World*, Columbia University Press, New York.

Chatterjee, P. (2008): 'Democracy and Economic Transformation in India', *Economic and Political Weekly*, Vol. 43, No. 16, pp. 53–62.

De Soto, H. (1989): *The Other Path: The Invisible Revolution in the Third World*, Harper & Row, New York.

De Soto, H. (2000): *The Mystery of Capital: Why Capitalism Triumphs in the West and Fails Everywhere Else*, Bantam Press, London.

Fallon, P. and R. Lucas (1991): 'The Impact of Changes in Job Security Regulations in India and Zimbabwe', *World Bank Economic Review*, Vol. 5, No. 3.

Fields, G. (1984): 'Employment, Income Distribution and Economic Growth in Seven Small Open Economies', *Economic Journal*, Royal Economic Society, Vol. 94, No. 373.

Foucault, M. (1991): 'Governmentality' in Burchell, G., Gordon, C. and G. Miller (eds) *The Foucault Effect: Studies in Governmentality*, The University of Chicago Press, Chicago.

Galli, R. and D. Kucera (2004): 'Labour Standards and Informal Employment in Latin America', *World Development*, Vol. 32, No. 5.

Granovetter, M. (1985): 'Economic Action and Social Structure: The Problem of Embeddedness', *American Journal of Sociology*, Vol. 91, No. 3.

Harris, J. R. and M. P. Todaro (1970): 'Migration, Unemployment and Development: A Two-Sector Analysis', *American Economic Review*, Vol. 60, No. 1.

Harriss-White, B. (2010): 'Globalization, the Financial Crisis and Petty Production in India's Socially Regulated Informal Economy', *Global Labour Journal*, Vol. 1, No. 1.

Hart, K. (1973): 'Informal Income Opportunities and Urban Employment in Ghana', *The Journal of Modern African Studies*, Vol. 11, No. 1, pp. 61–89.

ILO (1972): *Employment, Incomes and Equality: A Strategy for Increasing Productive Employment in Kenya*, International Labour Organisation, Geneva.

Kerr, I. (2004): 'Labour Control and Labour Legislation in Colonial India: A Tale of Two Mid-Nineteenth Century Acts', *South Asia: Journal of South Asian Studies*, Vol. 37, No. 1, April.

Levitas, R. (2005): *The Inclusive Society? Social Exclusion and New Labour*, Palgrave.

Lewis, W. A. (1954): 'Economic Development with Unlimited Supplies of Labour', *Manchester School of Economic and Social Studies*, Vol. 22.

Malos, E. (ed.) (1975): *The Politics of Housework*, The New Clarion Press, New York.

Marx, K. (1984): *Capital Volume I*, Progress Publishers, Moscow.

Mayhew, H. (2008): *London Labour and the London Poor*, Wordsworth Classics of World Literature, Wordsworth Editions Limited, Hertfordshire.

NCEUS (2007): *Report on Conditions of Work and Promotion of Livelihoods in the Unorganised Sector*, National Commission for Enterprises in the Unorganised Sector, Government of India, New Delhi.

## 242  Saumyajit Bhattacharya

NCEUS (2009): *The Challenge of Employment in India: An Informal Economy Perspective*, National Commission for Enterprises in the Unorganised Sector, Government of India, New Delhi.

Rathgeber, E. M. (1989): *WID, WAD, GAD: Trends in Research and Practice*, International Development Research Centre, Ottawa.

Ray, D. (1998): *Development Economics*, Princeton University Press, Princeton, NJ.

Sachs, I. (1991): 'Growth and Poverty: Some Lessons from Brazil' in Dreze, J. and A. Sen (eds) *The Political Economy of Hunger*, Oxford Clarendon Press.

Sanyal, K. (2014): *Rethinking Capitalist Development: Primitive Accumulation, Governmentality and Post-Colonial Capitalism*, Routledge, New Delhi [Paperback edition].

Smith, A. (1976): *The Wealth of Nations*, Oxford Clarendon Press, UK.

Standing, G. (2009): *Work after Globalisation: Building Occupational Citizenship*, Edward Elgar, UK and USA.

Standing, G. (2011): *The Precariat: The New Dangerous Class*, Bloomsbury Academic, London, NY.

Tonkiss, F. (2006): *Contemporary Economic Sociology: Globalisation, Production, Inequality*, Routledge, UK.

Whyte, W. F. (1993): *Street Corner Society: The Social Structure of an Italian Slum*, University of Chicago Press, Chicago.

# 12 Multiple efficient rules and inefficient outcomes

*Satish K. Jain*[*]

A liability rule, a rule for apportioning liability between the victim and the injurer, is efficient if it has the property of invariably inducing both the victim and the injurer to behave in ways which result in the minimization of total social costs of interaction.[1] Most of the rules used by the courts have turned out to be efficient. These include, among others, the rules of negligence, negligence with the defense of contributory negligence, comparative negligence, and the strict liability with the defense of contributory negligence.

If the court always uses the same liability rule for deciding on the liability shares of the two parties, and the rule used by the court is an efficient rule, then one can be sure that every outcome would be efficient. This chapter is concerned with the question of efficiency of outcomes when the court uses more than one liability rule. If every liability rule used by the court is efficient and there is no uncertainty as to which liability rule will be applied in which cases, then again one can be sure that every outcome would be efficient. But can one be sure of the efficiency of outcomes when in any particular instance it is not known in advance as to which of the liability rules will be used by the court, even given that all liability rules used by the court are efficient? In this chapter, it is shown that when there is uncertainty regarding as to which liability rule will be used by the court in which instances, then in general there is no guarantee that the outcomes would be efficient, even if all the liability rules used by the court are efficient.

Let $f_1$ and $f_2$ be two efficient liability rules. Suppose the court sometimes employs $f_1$ for apportioning liability between the parties,

---

[*] I wish to thank Kaushal Kishore for proofreading the final draft of the chapter and pointing out a typographical error.

244  *Satish K. Jain*

and at other times employs $f_2$ for the purpose. Let $f_1$ be such that when neither party takes any care it makes the victim liable for less than half of the harm; and let $f_2$ be such that when neither party takes any care it makes the victim liable for more than half of the harm. If there is uncertainty regarding whether $f_1$ will be used or $f_2$ will be used in any particular instance, then according to the theorem established in this chapter, in some cases, outcomes will not be efficient.

The policy implication that emerges from the analysis of this chapter is that the use of a single efficient liability rule is in general preferable to the use of multiple efficient liability rules. If only one efficient liability rule is used one can be certain that the outcomes will be efficient. Under special circumstances, it is possible that outcomes would be efficient even with the use of multiple efficient liability rules. For instance, if there is no uncertainty regarding the domains of application of the rules, that is to say, for each case it is known with certainty as to which rule will be applicable, then, even with the use of multiple efficient rules, there will be no inefficiency. However it is clear that, unless there are important non-efficiency considerations, purely on efficiency grounds the use of a single liability rule in general is preferable over the use of multiple efficient liability rules.

The analysis of this chapter also has an important implication of methodological import. If in a jurisdiction it turns out that in a particular period every case was decided by applying an efficient liability rule, from this alone one cannot infer that the outcomes during the period were efficient. To infer the efficiency of outcomes, one needs to know whether throughout the relevant period only one efficient liability rule was used or more than one, and, in case more than one efficient liability rule was used, whether any of the conditions which make the use of multiple efficient liability rules unproblematic was satisfied.

The chapter is divided into five sections, including this introductory section. The second section contains the definitions and assumptions, and spells out the framework of analysis. The third section states and proves the theorem that if two efficient liability rules are such that one of them assigns less than half of the loss to the victim and the other more than half of the loss when neither party takes any care, then, if there is uncertainty regarding which of the two rules will be used in which cases, inefficiency is possible in some cases. The penultimate section illustrates the theorem with an example. The concluding section contains some remarks regarding further investigations into the problem.

## Definitions and assumptions

We consider accidents resulting from interaction of two parties, assumed to be strangers to each other, in which, to begin with, the entire loss falls on one party to be called the victim (plaintiff). The other party would be referred to as the injurer (defendant). At times, the victim would be referred to as individual or party 1 and the injurer individual or party 2. We denote by $c \geq 0$ the cost of care taken by the victim and by $d \geq 0$ the cost of care taken by the injurer. Costs of care would be assumed to be strictly increasing functions of indices of care, that is, care levels; consequently, costs of care themselves can be taken to be indices of care. Let

$C = \{c \mid c$ is the cost of some feasible level of care which can be taken by the victim$\}$

and

$D = \{d \mid d$ is the cost of some feasible level of care which can be taken by the injurer$\}$.

We will identify $c = 0$ with victim taking no care; and $d = 0$ with injurer taking no care.

We assume:

$$0 \in C \wedge 0 \in D. \tag{A1}$$

Assumption (A1) merely says that, for each party, taking no care is always a feasible option.

Let $\pi$ denote the probability of occurrence of accident and $H \geq 0$ the loss in case of occurrence of accident. Both $\pi$ and $H$ will be assumed to be functions of $c$ and $d$; $\pi = \pi(c, d)$, $H = H(c, d)$. Let $L = \pi H$. $L$ is thus expected loss due to accident.

We assume:

$$(\forall c, c' \in C)(\forall d, d' \in D)\big[[c > c' \rightarrow L(c,d) \leq L(c',d)] \\ \wedge [d > d' \rightarrow L(c,d) \leq L(c, d')]\big]. \tag{A2}$$

That is to say: A larger expenditure on care by either party, given the expenditure on care by the other party, does not result in greater expected accident loss.

Total social costs (*TSC*) are defined to be the sum of cost of care by the victim, cost of care by the injurer, and expected loss due to accident;

246 *Satish K. Jain*

$TSC = c + d + L(c, d)$. Let $M = \{(c', d') \in C \times D \mid c' + d' + L(c', d')$ is minimum of $\{c + d + L(c, d) \mid c \in C \wedge d \in D\}\}$. Thus $M$ is the set of all costs of care configurations $(c', d')$ which are total social cost minimizing. It will be assumed that:

$$C, D \text{ and } L \text{ are such that } M \text{ is nonempty.} \qquad (A3)$$

In order to characterize a party's level of care as negligent or otherwise, a reference point (the due care level) for the party needs to be specified. Let $c^*$ and $d^*$, where $(c^*, d^*) \in M$, denote the due care levels of the victim and the injurer respectively. We define nonnegligence functions $p$ and $q$ as follows:

$p : C \mapsto [0,1]$ such that:[2]

$$
\begin{aligned}
p(c) &= \frac{c}{c^*} \quad \text{if } c < c^*; \\
&= 1 \quad \text{if } c \geq c^*
\end{aligned}
$$

$q : D \mapsto [0,1]$ such that:

$$
\begin{aligned}
q(d) &= \frac{d}{d^*} \quad \text{if } d < d^*; \\
&= 1 \quad \text{if } d \geq d^*.
\end{aligned}
$$

$p$ and $q$ would be interpreted as proportions of nonnegligence of the victim and the injurer respectively. The victim would be called negligent if $p < 1$ and nonnegligent if $p = 1$. Similarly, the injurer would be called negligent if $q < 1$ and nonnegligent if $q = 1$.

In case there is a legally binding due care level for the plaintiff, it would be taken to be identical with $c^*$ figuring in the definition of function $p$; and in case there is a legally binding due care level for the defendant, it would be taken to be identical with $d^*$ figuring in the definition of function $q$. Thus implicitly it is being assumed that the legally binding due care levels are always set appropriately from the point of view of minimizing total social costs.

A liability rule is a function $f$ from $[0,1]^2$ to $[0,1]^2$, $f: [0,1]^2 \mapsto [0,1]^2$, such that: $f(p,q) = (x, 1-x)$. Thus a liability rule is a rule which specifies the proportions in which the two parties are to bear the loss in case of occurrence of accident as a function of proportions of nonnegligence of the two parties.

The context in which a liability rule can be applied is completely specified if in addition to $C, D, \pi$ and $H$ we also specify the configuration of due care levels $(c^*, d^*) \in M$. The set of all applications satisfying (A1)–(A3) would be denoted by $\mathcal{A}$.

## Multiple efficient rules and inefficient outcomes    247

Let $EC_1(c, d)$ and $EC_2(c, d)$ denote expected costs of the victim and the injurer respectively. We have: $EC_1(c, d) = c + xL(c, d)$ and $EC_2(c, d) = d + (1 - x)L(c, d)$.

Both parties are assumed to prefer smaller expected costs to larger expected costs and be indifferent between alternatives with equal expected costs.

A rule is defined to be efficient for a given application belonging to $\mathcal{A}$ iff $\left(\forall\left(\overline{c},\overline{d}\right) \in C \times D\right)\left[\left(\overline{c},\overline{d}\right)\right.$ is a Nash equilibrium $\rightarrow\left(\overline{c},\overline{d}\right) \in M]$ and $\left(\exists\left(\overline{c},\overline{d}\right) \in C \times D\right)\left[\left(\overline{c},\overline{d}\right)\right.$ is a Nash equilibrium]. In other words, a rule is efficient for a given application iff (1) every $\left(\overline{c},\overline{d}\right) \in C \times D$ which is a Nash equilibrium is total social cost minimizing, and (2) there exists at least one $\left(\overline{c},\overline{d}\right) \in C \times D$ which is a Nash equilibrium. A rule is defined to be efficient iff it is efficient for every application belonging to $\mathcal{A}$.

Efficient liability rules are characterized by the negligence liability condition, that is, a liability rule is efficient for every application belonging to $\mathcal{A}$ iff satisfies the condition of negligence liability. Negligence liability requires that if one of the two parties is negligent and the other nonnegligent then the negligent party must bear the entire loss, that is, $\left[\left(\forall p \in [0,1)\right)\left[x(p,1) = 1\right] \wedge \left(\forall q \in [0,1)\right)\left[x(1,q) = 0\right]\right]$.

The negligence rule and the negligence with the defense of contributory negligence are among the most important of liability rules. Under the negligence rule the injurer is liable for the entire loss iff he is negligent; and he is not at all liable iff he is nonnegligent. Under the negligence with the defense of contributory negligence, the injurer is liable for the entire loss iff he is negligent and the victim is nonnegligent; and he is not at all liable otherwise. More formally, $f$ is the negligence rule iff $\left(\forall p \in [0,1]\right)\left(\forall q \in [0,1)\right)\left[f(p,q) = (0,1)\right] \wedge \left(\forall p \in [0,1]\right)\left[f(p,1) = (1,0)\right]$; and $f$ is the negligence with the defense of contributory negligence rule iff $\left(\forall p \in [0,1)\right)\left(\forall q \in [0,1]\right)\left[f(p,q) = (1,0)\right] \wedge \left(\forall q \in [0,1)\right)\left[f(1,q) = (0,1)\right]$ $\wedge f(1,1) = (1,0)$. As both the rules of the negligence and the negligence with the defense of contributory negligence satisfy the negligence liability condition, they are efficient for all applications belonging to $\mathcal{A}$.

## Efficiency implications of using more than one liability rule

**Theorem 1.** Suppose the court sometimes uses efficient liability rule $f_1$ and at other times efficient liability rule $f_2$. Suppose there is uncertainty as to which of these two liability rules will be used for which cases. Then inefficiency is possible if $f_1(0,0) = \left(x_1^0, 1 - x_1^0\right), f_2(0,0) = \left(x_2^0, 1 - x_2^0\right)$, $x_1^0 < \dfrac{1}{2}, x_2^0 > \dfrac{1}{2}$.

## 248 Satish K. Jain

*Proof.* Let $f_1(0,0) = \left(x_1^0, 1 - x_1^0\right), f_2(0,0) = \left(x_2^0, 1 - x_2^0\right), x_1^0 < \frac{1}{2}, x_2^0 > \frac{1}{2}.$
Choose a positive number $\in$ such that:

$$0 < \in < min\left\{\frac{1 - 2x_1^0}{2x_1^0}, \frac{2x_2^0 - 1}{2\left(1 - x_2^0\right)}\right\} \quad if \ x_1^0 > 0 \wedge x_2^0 < 1$$

$$0 < \in < \frac{2x_2^0 - 1}{2\left(1 - x_2^0\right)} \quad if \ x_1^0 = 0 \wedge x_2^0 < 1$$

$$0 < \in < \frac{1 - 2x_1^0}{2x_1^0} \quad if \ x_1^0 > 0 \wedge x_2^0 = 1$$

$$0 < \in \quad if \ x_1^0 = 0 \wedge x_2^0 = 1$$

Choose $\alpha, \beta \in [0, 1]$ such that:

$$0 \le (1 - \alpha) < \frac{1 - 2(1 + \in)x_1^0}{2(1 + \in)\left(x_2^0 - x_1^0\right)} \text{ and } 0 \le \beta < \frac{1 - 2(1 + \in)\left(1 - x_2^0\right)}{2(1 + \in)\left(x_2^0 - x_1^0\right)}.^3$$

Now, let the victim expect $f_1$ with probability $\alpha$ and $f_2$ with probability $1 - \alpha$; and let the injurer expect $f_1$ with probability $\beta$ and $f_2$ with probability $1 - \beta$.

Consider the following application belonging to $\mathcal{A}$.

$C = D = \{0,1\}$; and $L(c, d)$, $(c, d) \in C \times D$, is as given in the following array:

|  |  | $d$ | |
|---|---|---|---|
|  |  | 0 | 1 |
| | 0 | $2 + 2\epsilon$ | $1 + \epsilon$ |
| $c$ | | | |
| | 1 | $1 + \epsilon$ | 0 |

TSC are uniquely minimized at $(1,1)$.

Let the configuration of due cares $(c^*, d^*)$ be $(1,1)$.

The victim's expected costs $EC_1(c, d)$ for different configurations $(c, d) \in C \times D$ are as given in the following array:

|  |  | $d$ | |
|---|---|---|---|
|  |  | 0 | 1 |
| | 0 | $(\alpha x_1^0 + (1 - \alpha)x_2^0)2(1 + \epsilon)$ | $1 + \epsilon$ |
| $c$ | | | |
| | 1 | 1 | 1 |

The injurer's expected costs $EC_2(c, d)$ for different configurations $(c, d) \in C \times D$ are as given in the following array:

| | | $d$ | |
|---|---|---|---|
| | | 0 | 1 |
| | 0 | $(\beta(1 - x_1^0) + (1 - \beta)(1 - x_2^0))2(1 + \epsilon)$ | 1 |
| $c$ | | | |
| | 1 | $1 + \epsilon$ | 1 |

We have:

$$EC_1(1,0) - EC_1(0,0)$$
$$= 1 - \left(\alpha x_1^0 + (1 - \alpha)x_2^0\right)2(1 + \epsilon)$$
$$= \left(1 - 2(1 + \epsilon)x_1^0\right) - 2(1 + \epsilon)(1 - \alpha)\left(x_2^0 - x_1^0\right)$$
$$= 2(1 + \epsilon)\left(x_2^0 - x_1^0\right)\left[\frac{1 - 2(1 + \epsilon)x_1^0}{2(1 + \epsilon)\left(x_2^0 - x_1^0\right)} - (1 - \alpha)\right]$$
$$> 0, \tag{1}$$

as

$$(1 - \alpha) < \frac{1 - 2(1 + \epsilon)x_1^0}{2(1 + \epsilon)\left(x_2^0 - x_1^0\right)}.$$

$$EC_2(0,1) - EC_2(0,0)$$
$$= 1 - \left(\beta\left(1 - x_1^0\right) + (1 - \beta)\left(1 - x_2^0\right)\right)2(1 + \epsilon)$$
$$= 1 - \left(\beta\left(x_2^0 - x_1^0\right) + \left(1 - x_2^0\right)\right)2(1 + \epsilon)$$
$$= \left[1 - \left(1 - x_2^0\right)2(1 + \epsilon)\right] - \beta\left(x_2^0 - x_1^0\right)2(1 + \epsilon)$$
$$= 2(1 + \epsilon)\left(x_2^0 - x_1^0\right)\left[\frac{1 - 2(1 + \epsilon)\left(1 - x_2^0\right)}{2(1 + \epsilon)\left(x_2^0 - x_1^0\right)} - \beta\right]$$
$$> 0, \tag{2}$$

as

$$\beta < \frac{1 - 2(1 + \epsilon)\left(1 - x_2^0\right)}{2(1 + \epsilon)\left(x_2^0 - x_1^0\right)}.$$

250  *Satish K. Jain*

(1) and (2) imply that (0,0), which is not TSC-minimizing, is a Nash equilibrium. Thus efficiency does not obtain under this application.

We have shown that whenever two efficient rules are such that one of them assigns the victim less than half of the loss and the other one more than half of the loss in case of both parties taking zero care then there exists an application for which the outcome will be inefficient for certain values of subjective probabilities with which the two parties expect the use of the rules by the court. Therefore the theorem stands established.

**Corollary 1.** Suppose the court sometimes uses the negligence rule and at other times the negligence with the defense of contributory negligence rule. Suppose there is uncertainty as to which of these two rules will be used for which cases. Then inefficiency is possible.

*Proof:* Both the rules of negligence and the negligence with the defense of contributory negligence are efficient. Under the negligence rule $x(0,0) = 0$ and under the negligence with the defense of contributory negligence rule $x(0,0) = 1$. Thus the conditions of the Theorem are satisfied and consequently it follows that inefficiency is possible.

**Remark 1.** The possibility of inefficiency with the use of more than one efficient rule when there is uncertainty regarding which rule will be used for which cases was first pointed out in Jain (2016). There it was shown that if the court sometimes uses the negligence rule and at other times the incremental negligence rule, and if there is uncertainty regarding as to which of these rules will be used for which cases, then inefficiency is possible, even though both the negligence rule and the incremental negligence rule are efficient. This result, however, cannot be derived as a corollary from the Theorem of this chapter because the incremental liability rule does not belong to the class of the standard liability rules. The incremental liability rule belongs to the class of the incremental liability rules. While a liability rule apportions the loss between the two parties on the basis of the nonnegligence proportions of the two parties; an incremental liability rule determines on the basis of the nonnegligence proportions of the two parties (1) which of the two parties would be the non-residual liability holder, and (2) the proportion of the incremental loss, which can be ascribed to the negligence of the non-residual liability holder, to be borne by the non-residual liability holder. Under the incremental negligence rule, the injurer is liable for the entire incremental loss which can be ascribed to his negligence iff he is negligent; and not at all liable iff he is nonnegligent.

**Remark 2.** It is immediate that if the court employs more than two efficient liability rules and there is uncertainty as to which of the rules

### Multiple efficient rules and inefficient outcomes 251

will be used for which cases, then inefficiency is possible if we have for one of the rules $x(0,0) < \dfrac{1}{2}$ and for another of the rules $x(0,0) > \dfrac{1}{2}$.

## An illustrative example

**Example 1.** Suppose the court sometimes uses the negligence rule and at other times the negligence with the defense of contributory negligence rule. Suppose there is uncertainty as to which of these two rules will be used for which cases.

Consider the following application belonging to $\mathcal{A}$.

$C = D = \{0, 1\}$; and $L(c, d)$, $(c, d) \in C \times D$, is as given in the following array:

|       |     | $d$ |     |
|-------|-----|-----|-----|
|       |     | 0   | 1   |
|       | 0   | 3   | 1.5 |
| $c$   |     |     |     |
|       | 1   | 1.5 | 0   |

TSC are uniquely minimized at $(1,1)$.

Let the configuration of due cares $(c^*, d^*)$ be $(1,1)$.

Let the victim expect the negligence rule with probability $\dfrac{3}{4}$ and the negligence with the defense of contributory negligence rule with probability $\dfrac{1}{4}$; and let the injurer expect the negligence rule with probability $\dfrac{1}{4}$ and the negligence with the defense of contributory negligence rule with probability $\dfrac{3}{4}$.

The expected costs of the victim $EC_1(c, d)$ for different configurations $(c, d) \in C \times D$ are as given in the following array:

|       |     | $d$           |     |
|-------|-----|---------------|-----|
|       |     | 0             | 1   |
|       | 0   | $\frac{3}{4}$ | 1.5 |
| $c$   |     |               |     |
|       | 1   | 1             | 1   |

The expected costs of the injurer $EC_2(c, d)$ for different configurations $(c, d) \in C \times D$ are as given in the following array:

|       |     | $d$           |     |
|-------|-----|---------------|-----|
|       |     | 0             | 1   |
|       | 0   | $\frac{3}{4}$ | 1   |
| $c$   |     |               |     |
|       | 1   | 1.5           | 1   |

252　*Satish K. Jain*

We have:

$$EC_1(1,0) - EC_1(0,0) = 1 - \frac{3}{4} = \frac{1}{4} > 0, \text{ and}$$

$$EC_2(0,1) - EC_2(0,0) = 1 - \frac{3}{4} = \frac{1}{4} > 0.$$

Therefore $(0,0)$ is a Nash equilibrium. As $(0, 0) \notin M$, it follows that efficiency does not obtain.

## Conclusions

This chapter has derived a sufficient condition on the structure of liability rules under which there will be inefficiency for some application and for some choice of subjective probabilities with which the various rules are expected by the two parties. Put another way, a necessary condition has been formulated for efficiency to be obtained for all applications and for all possible choices of subjective probabilities with which the various rules can be expected by the two parties. What is required for a complete solution to the problem is the formulation of a necessary and sufficient condition under which efficiency will obtain for all applications and for all possible choices of subjective probabilities with which the various rules can be expected by the two parties. Knowledge of such a necessary and sufficient condition would enable one to know which sets of efficient liability rules can be used together by the courts without any possibility of inefficiency on account of uncertainty regarding which rule will be used for which cases.

## Notes

1 On the efficiency of liability rules, see Brown (1973); Landes and Posner (1987); Shavell (1987); Jain and Singh (2002); and Jain (2015), among others.
2 Let $a$ and $b$ be real numbers such that $a < b$. We use the standard notation to denote: $\{x \mid a \leq x \leq b\}$ by $[a, b]$, $\{x \mid a \leq x < b\}$ by $[a, b)$, $\{x \mid a < x \leq b\}$ by $(a, b]$, and $\{x \mid a < x < b\}$ by $(a, b)$.
3 $x_1^0 > 0 \rightarrow \epsilon < \dfrac{1 - 2x_1^0}{2x_1^0}$

$\rightarrow 2x_1^0(1+\epsilon) < 1$

$\rightarrow \dfrac{1 - 2(1+\epsilon)x_1^0}{2(1+\epsilon)\left(x_2^0 - x_1^0\right)} > 0.$

## Multiple efficient rules and inefficient outcomes    253

$$x_1^0 = 0 \to \frac{1-2(1+\epsilon)x_1^0}{2(1+\epsilon)(x_2^0 - x_1^0)} = \frac{1}{2(1+\epsilon)x_2^0} > 0$$

Therefore there exists an $\alpha \in [0,1]$ such that $0 \leq (1-\alpha) < \dfrac{1-2(1+\epsilon)x_1^0}{2(1+\epsilon)(x_2^0 - x_1^0)}$.

$$x_2^0 < 1 \to \epsilon < \frac{2x_2^0 - 1}{2(1-x_2^0)}$$

$$\to 2(1-x_2^0)\epsilon < 2x_2^0 - 1$$

$$\to 2(1-x_2^0)\epsilon < 2(x_2^0 - 1) + 1$$

$$\to 2(1-x_2^0)(1+\varepsilon) < 1$$

$$\to \frac{1-2(1+\epsilon)(1-x_2^0)}{2(1+\epsilon)(x_2^0 - x_1^0)} > 0.$$

$$x_2^0 = 1 \to \frac{1-2(1+\epsilon)(1-x_2^0)}{2(1+\epsilon)(x_2^0 - x_1^0)} = \frac{1}{2(1+\epsilon)(1-x_1^0)} > 0$$

Therefore there exists a $\beta \in [0,1]$ such that $0 \leq \beta < \dfrac{1-2(1+\epsilon)(1-x_2^0)}{2(1+\epsilon)(x_2^0 - x_1^0)}$.

## Bibliography

Brown, John Prather (1973), 'Toward an Economic Theory of Liability', *Journal of Legal Studies 2*, pp. 323–350.

Jain, Satish K. (2015), *Economic Analysis of Liability Rules*, New Delhi: Springer.

Jain, Satish K. (2016), 'Uncertainty Regarding Interpretation of the "Negligence Rule" and Its Implications for the Efficiency of Outcomes', *Asian Journal of Law and Economics 7*, pp. 147–168.

Jain, Satish K. and Singh, Ram (2002), 'Efficient Liability Rules: Complete Characterization', *Journal of Economics (Zeitschrift für Nationalökonomie) 75*, pp. 105–124.

Landes, William M. and Posner, Richard A. (1987), *The Economic Structure of Tort Law*, Cambridge, MA: Harvard University Press.

Shavell, Steven (1987), *Economic Analysis of Accident Law*, Cambridge, MA: Harvard University Press.

# 13 Auctions with an inferior outside option

*Krishnendu Ghosh Dastidar*[*]

This chapter analyzes auctions of a single indivisible item in a setting in which consumers have identical utility functions for two goods but different income levels. Incomes are private information and consumers' preferences display income effects. We assume that all bidders' outside options are inferior, since their incomes are low. In this setting we show that bidding ones' value for the indivisible object is a symmetric equilibrium in first-price, second-price and all-pay auctions. We also show that the expected revenue is the highest with all-pay auctions and lowest with second-price auctions.

Consider a two-good world where one good is perfectly divisible and the other good is indivisible. The divisible good is available in a store at a fixed price of 1 and one unit of the indivisible good is sold in an auction. There are buyers with commonly known preferences over these two goods. Buyers' incomes are their private information. They maximize utility under their budget constraint; that is, they decide how much to bid at the auction for the indivisible item and spend rest of the income not used at this auction to purchase the divisible good.

---

[*] I am deeply honoured to be able to contribute to this volume of essays dedicated to Prof. Deppak Nayyar, who is among the best minds in our country. Prof. Nayyar is a superb teacher with remarkable ability to express any argument succinctly and an academician with exemplary integrity and commitment to his profession. More importantly, he is a wonderful human being. For this chapter, I would like to thank Masaki Aoyagi, Subrata Guha and Anjan Mukherji for constructive suggestions. An earlier version of the chapter was written when I was a Visiting Foreign Scholar at the Institute of Social and Economic Research, Osaka University in 2013–14. ISER provided me with excellent research facilities and stimulating intellectual ambience and I am grateful for that. The usual disclaimer applies.

## Auctions with an inferior outside option    255

In this setting we define a buyer's *value* for the indivisible object to be *the maximum price he is willing to pay and able to pay* for it. Also, each individual's *outside option* is the utility of consuming only the divisible good by devoting his entire income to the purchase of this good at the given fixed price. We define the outside option for the individual to be *inferior* if it is *lower* than the utility of consuming *only* the indivisible object.[1] This happens when his income is low enough. In such a case, it can be shown that the value for the indivisible object will be his entire income. Consequently, when the individual's *outside option is inferior*, then in an auction where the indivisible object is up for sale, the individual will have the incentive to bid his entire income. In this chapter we show that under some restrictions, bidding one's value (which is equal to one's income) of the indivisible object is a symmetric equilibrium in first-price, second-price and all-pay auctions. The fact that bidding ones' value can be an equilibrium even in all-pay auctions is surprising and counterintuitive. We also show that the expected revenue is the highest with all-pay auctions and lowest with second price auctions. We provide specific numerical examples for illustrative purposes.

The canonical model of auctions with private values assumes that preferences are quasilinear, valuations are private information and incomes are high enough.[2] It may be noted that when incomes are high enough the outside options are superior. In contrast, we deal with the case where the outside options are inferior for everybody (i.e. incomes are low). We consider a more general class of utility functions that allow for income effects.[3] We assume that all individuals have the same utility function but have different incomes. An example of this would be a specific sociocultural milieu where people tend to have similar tastes but differ in their incomes. This assumption reflects the fact that they have the same cultural, social and historical background so that their tastes and values are sufficiently close to justify the assumption of identical preferences. On the other hand, the members of a given society have different skills and productivities and this is reflected in the differences in their incomes. However, incomes of all individuals in this society are low enough and this implies their outside options are inferior. This will be possibly true in certain poor socioeconomic categories (especially in emerging economies like India). Anecdotal evidences suggest that due to some cultural reasons people from such communities often crave for certain items like gold (or precious stones) and they are willing to pay large sums to acquire such goods. This implies that for such a class of relatively poor people who belong to this sociocultural milieu, the utility of acquiring only

## 256   *Krishnendu Ghosh Dastidar*

the indivisible item (say a gold ornament) is much higher than the utility of consuming only the divisible good (say food) by devoting his entire income to the purchase of this good.

For example, demand for gold in India has been very resilient even in the most trying circumstances. The World Gold Council noted "Indian consumers have been steadfast in their desire for gold, even in the face of very challenging circumstances – most notably, extreme adverse squeeze on rural incomes" (see Ramarathinam, 2016).

In our model, the *value* of the object is the maximum price that an agent is *willing to pay and able to pay*. It may be noted that this is different from one particular strand in the literature. We draw attention to the very interesting and influential paper by Che and Gale (1998) where preferences are quasilinear and valuation (which is independent of income) is the maximum price that an agent is willing to pay (but not necessarily able to pay). In short, the *definition of value* used in our chapter is *different* from the one used in Che and Gale (1998).

Saitoh and Serizawa (2008) and Sakai (2008) analyze second-price auctions on general preference domains (that include non-quasilinear preferences) and show such auctions satisfy efficiency and strategy-proofness. We approach the problem differently and consider a case where preferences are common knowledge, but budgets are private information. Proposition 1, where we show that choosing a bid equal to the value of the indivisible item is a weakly dominant strategy, is similar to the results derived in Saitoh and Serizawa (2008) and Sakai (2008).

Dastidar (2015) has a similar approach, but that paper deals with bidders whose outside options are superior (all incomes are high enough). In contrast, we concentrate on bidders whose outside options are inferior. We analyze first-price, second-price and all-pay auctions in such a scenario.

The rest of the chapter is organized as follows. In the second section we provide the model and the main assumptions of our exercise. In the third we discuss these assumptions and also prove a few preliminary results with illustrative examples. The fourth section provides the main results of our exercise. In the final section we give some concluding remarks. Lastly, the appendix provides explanations/definitions of some of the terms used in this chapter.

## The model

We closely follow Dastidar (2015) and consider a two-good world where an individual $i$ has utility function $U(x, y)$ where $x \in [0, \infty)$ and $y \in \{0, 1\}$. This means that any non-negative amount of good $x$ can be consumed but in case of good $y$ there are only two choices. Either one unit of good $y$ can be consumed or it cannot be consumed. Individual $i$'s income is $m_i$. We provide the first set of assumptions.

**Assumption A1.** Utility is additively separable. That is, $U(x, y) = u(x) + h(y)$ where $x \in [0,\infty)$ and $y \in \{0,1\}$, $u(0) = 0$, $h(0) = 0$ and $h(1) = \gamma > 0$. This clearly means that $U(0, 0) = 0$, $U(0, 1) = \gamma$, $U(x, 0) = u(x)$ and $U(x, 1) = u(x) + \gamma$.

**Assumption A2.** $u(x)$ is strictly increasing in $x$. It is continuous in $x$ for all $x \in [0,\infty)$ and differentiable w.r.t. $x$ for all $x \in (0,\infty)$.

**Assumption A3.** $\lim_{x\to\infty} u(x) > \gamma$.

Let price of $x$, $P_x = 1$ and price of $y$ be $p$. Note that since $u(x)$ is continuous and strictly increasing in $x$ and since $\lim_{x\to\infty} u(x) > \gamma$ there exists a unique $k > 0$ s.t. $u(k) = y$.

Hence

$$u(m_i) \leq \gamma \text{ iff } m_i \leq k$$

**Remark.** Note that the individual's *outside option* is the utility of consuming only the divisible good by devoting his entire income to the purchase of this good at the given fixed price. Hence the outside option of an individual with income $m_i$ is $u(m_i)$. The utility of consuming *only* the indivisible object is $\gamma$. The outside option will be inferior if $u(m_i) \leq \gamma$. This means that the outside option is inferior if the individual's income is below $k$.

The individual's utility maximization problem is as follows:

$$\max_{x \in [0,\infty),\, y \in \{0,1\}} u(x) + h(y) \qquad \text{s.t. } x + py \leq m_i.$$

There are two possible cases. (1) $m_i \leq k$ (inferior outside option) and (2) $m_i > k$ (superior outside option)

We now derive the value for good $y$ (the maximum price that the consumer is *willing and able* to pay for $y$) for each of these two cases.

### Valuation for good $y$

*Case 1* (inferior outside option) $m_i \leq k \Leftrightarrow \gamma \geq (m_i)$.

It may be noted that if $p \leq m_i$ and the individual purchases $y$ he can spend $m_i - p$ on $x$ and get $u(m_i - p) + \gamma$.[4] If he does not purchase $y$ and spends his entire income on $x$ he gets $u(m_i)$. Here note that for all $p \in [0, m_i]$

$$u(m_i - p) + \gamma \geq \gamma \geq u(m_i)$$

## 258 *Krishnendu Ghosh Dastidar*

Therefore the individual will buy good $y$ (that is choose $y = 1$) iff $m_i - p \geq 0 \Leftrightarrow p \leq m_i$. Hence, for this case, the maximum price he is willing and able to pay for good $y$ (his value for $y$) is $v_i = m_i$.

*Case 2* (superior outside option) $m_i > k \Leftrightarrow \gamma < u(m_i)$

From our assumptions it follows that for each $m_i$ there exists a unique $c(m_i)$ s.t. $u\big(c(m_i)\big) + \gamma = u(m_i)$. Clearly $c(.)$ is strictly increasing in $m_i$. Now

$$
\begin{aligned}
u(m_i - p) + \gamma &\geq u\big(c(m_i)\big) + \gamma = u(m_i) \\
\text{iff } m_i - p &\geq c(m_i).
\end{aligned}
$$

Therefore, the individual will buy good $y$ (that is choose $y = 1$) iff $m_i - p \geq c(m_i) \Leftrightarrow p \leq m_i - c(m_i)$. That is, the maximum price he is willing and able to pay for good $y$ (his value for $y$) is $v_i = m_i - c(m_i)$.

Therefore we get that values are functions of income.

$$
v(m_i) = \begin{cases} m_i \text{ if } m_i \leq k \\ m_i - c(m_i) \text{ if } m_i > k \end{cases}
$$

where $c(m_i)$ is such that $u\big(c(m_i)\big) + \gamma = u(m_i)$.

**Comment.** Note that $u(m_i) \leq \gamma$ iff $m_i \leq k$. Intuitively speaking, when an agent's income is lower than $k$, the agent's outside option is inferior as the utility of consuming only the divisible good, $u(m_i)$, by devoting the entire income to the purchase of $x$ is so low that he would be better off using the entire income to buy the indivisible object $y$. Consequently, when the outside option is inferior, the value, $v(m_i)$, for $y$ is equal to the agent's income, $m_i$. On the other hand, when the agent's income is high (i.e. $m_i > k$), his outside option is superior. In this case, the utility of consuming only the divisible good, by devoting the entire income to the purchase of $x$ is so high that, even if he could, an agent would not spend his entire income on $y$. As a result, the value for $y$ will be lower than the income.

**Basic Story.** Our basic story is as follows. There are $n$ individuals in a society. All have the same preference ordering (i.e. the same utility function) but different incomes. Individual $i$'s income is private information.[5]

Bidder $i$ knows that $M_i = m_i$ but does not know $M_j$ ($j \neq i$). Suppose good $x$ is available at a store at price 1, while one unit of good $y$ can be obtained in an auction. We consider three types of auctions viz. first-price, second-price and all-pay auctions. Price of good $y$ will be determined in the Bayesian Nash equilibrium of the auction. This

## Auctions with an inferior outside option    259

essentially means that the consumer is no longer a price-taker since his bid affects the equilibrium price of $y$. If an individual bids zero in the auction and does not obtain good $y$ then he spends his entire income on good $x$ and earns utility $u(m_i)$. This is his outside option. Consequently, in any equilibrium, the expected payoff to the individual will be at least $u(m_i)$. In no circumstances can a bidder with income $m_i$ pay more than $m_i$ for any good. If a bidder $i$ were to bid more than $m_i$ (in the auction for good $y$) and default, then a penalty would be imposed. If he defaults he cannot obtain good $y$ (even if his bid is the highest). In case the penalty amount exceeds his income, he has to forfeit his income. That is, in case of default, his total payment would be equal to the minimum of {penalty, $m_i$}.

We now provide our next assumption.

**Assumption A4.** The random variables $M_1 \ldots M_n$ are identically and independently distributed. Each random variable $M_i \in [0, \beta]$, where $\beta > 0$, has the same distribution function $F(.)$ and density $f(.)$. That is, each bidder $i$ believes that competitors' incomes are given by $M_j \in [0, \beta]$ with distribution function $F(.)$ and density function $f(.)$.

In any auction the set of actions available for any bidder is $[0, \infty)$. Individual $i$'s problem is to choose a strategy $b_i(m_i) : [0, \beta] \to [0, \infty)$ so as to maximize the expected value of $u(x) + h(y)$.

**Remark.** *First note that since a penalty would be imposed in case of default, for any bidder with income $m_i$, choosing $b_i = 0$ weakly dominates any bid $b_i > m_i$ in any auction.*

Before giving our main results, we need to provide some preliminaries on order statistics and some additional assumptions.

**Order Statistics: Some notations.** We would be interested in $M_{(1)}$ (highest order statistic) and $M_{(2)}$ (second highest order statistic). The corresponding distribution functions and density functions are $F_1(.)$, $F_2(.)$ and $f_1(.), f_2(.)$. Note that

$$F_1(h) = F^n(h) \text{ and } F_2(h) = F^n(h) + n\left[F^{n-1}(h) - F^n(h)\right]$$

$$f_1(h) = nF^{n-1}(h)f(h) \text{ and } f_2(h) = n(n-1)F^{n-2}(h)\left[1 - F(h)\right]f(h)$$

Another useful random variable is $Z = \max\{M_j\}_{j \neq i}$. To any individual this is the maximum of the others' incomes. The distribution and density function of $Z$ is $G(.)$ and $g(.)$ respectively. Clearly

$$G(z) = F^{n-1}(z)$$

$$g(z) = (n-1)F^{n-2}(z)f(z)$$

260  *Krishnendu Ghosh Dastidar*

We will now provide our last set of assumptions.

**Assumption A5.** $G(t) - G(s) \geq G(t-s)$ for all $t \geq s$, $t \in [0, \beta]$ and $s \in [0, \beta]$.

**Assumption A6.** $G(t)\left[\gamma - u(\beta)\right] \geq u(t)$ for all $t \in [0, \beta]$.

Under assumptions A1–A6 we will analyze three types of auctions viz. (1) first-price auction (2) second-price auction and (3) all-pay auctions. But before that we provide some preliminary results and discussion on our assumptions.

## Discussion of assumptions and preliminary results

We assumed (in A1) that $U(x, y) = u(x) + h(y)$ where $x \in [0,\infty)$ and $y \in \{0,1\}$, $u(0) = 0$, $h(0) = 0$ and $h(1) = \gamma > 0$. Note that the assumption of additive separability of utility is consistent with (1) risk neutrality, (2) risk aversion and (3) risk loving.[6]

For example, if $U(x, y) = x + 3y$ the bidders are risk neutral. If $U(x, y) = \ln(1 + x) + 3y$ then bidders are risk averse and if $U(x, y) = x^2 + 3y$ then bidders are risk lovers. The other assumptions (A2 and A3) about the utility function are standard.

We now show that convexity of $G(.)$ is a sufficient condition for assumption A5 to hold.

**Lemma 1.** *If $G(.)$ is convex then* $G(t) - G(s) \geq G(t-s)$ *for all* $t \geq s$, $t \in [0, \beta]$ *and* $s \in [0, \beta]$.

**Proof.** Note that $G(.): [0, \beta] \to [0, 1]$. We have $G(0) = 0$, $G(\beta) = 1$ and $G(t)$ is increasing in $t$. This means that lemma 1 is trivially true for the following two cases: (1) $t = s$ and (2) $t > s = 0$.

Now suppose $t > s > 0$. Since $G(.)$ is convex we have

$$\frac{G(t) - G(t-s)}{s} \geq \frac{G(t-s) - G(0)}{t-s}$$

$$\Rightarrow G(t) - G(t-s) \geq \frac{s}{t-s} G(t-s) \tag{1}$$

Again, since $G(.)$ is convex we have

$$\frac{G(t) - G(s)}{t-s} \geq \frac{G(s) - G(0)}{s}$$

$$\Rightarrow G(s) \leq \frac{s}{t-s}\left[G(t) - G(s)\right] \tag{2}$$

*Auctions with an inferior outside option* 261

Now using (1) and (2) we have

$$G(t) - G(t-s) - G(s)$$
$$\geq \frac{s}{t-s} G(t-s) - \frac{s}{t-s}[G(t) - G(s)]$$
$$= \frac{s}{t-s}\left[-\{G(t) - G(t-s) - G(s)\}\right]$$
$$\Rightarrow G(t) - G(t-s) - G(s) \geq -\frac{s}{t-s}[G(t) - G(t-s) - G(s)] \qquad (3)$$

Note that since $t > s > 0$ we have $\dfrac{s}{t-s} > 0$.

Now, if possible let $G(t) - G(t-s) - G(s) < 0$ for some $t > s > 0$. Then, from (3) we get that $-\dfrac{s}{t-s}[G(t) - G(t-s) - G(s)] < 0$. Since $\dfrac{s}{t-s} > 0$ this means we must have $G(t) - G(t-s) - G(s) > 0$. But this is a contradiction. Hence, we must have $G(t) - G(t-s) - G(s) \geq 0$ for all $t > s > 0$. ∎

**Comment.** Note that convexity of $G(.)$ is a *sufficient* condition (but not a necessary condition) for assumption A5 to hold. For example, take a two-bidder case. Let $F(t) = \dfrac{t^2}{12}(7 - 2t)$ and $\beta = 2$. Since $n = 2$, we have $G(t) = F(t)$ and $G(.)$ is clearly not convex. Here,

$$G(t) - G(s) - G(t-s) = \frac{t^2}{12}(7 - 2t) - \frac{s^2}{12}(7 - 2s) - \frac{(t-s)^2}{12}(7 - 2(t-s))$$
$$= \frac{1}{6}s(7 - 3t)(t-s)$$
$$\geq 0 \text{ for all } t \geq s \text{ and } t \in [0,2] \text{ and } s \in [0,2].$$

Note that $u(m)$ is the outside option for the bidder with income $m$. The utility of consuming *only* the indivisible object is $\gamma$. We can interpret $(\gamma - u(m))$ to be the *prize* for winning the indivisible good $y$ at a price $m$. Now $\gamma - u(\beta) \leq \gamma - u(m)$ for all $m \in [0, \beta]$. Assumption A6 states that $G(t)[\gamma - u(\beta)] - u(t) \geq 0$ for all $t \in [0, \beta]$. Note that this assumption will hold if the prize for winning the indivisible item, $\gamma - u(m)$, is high enough for all $m \in [0, \beta]$.

Below we provide examples of distribution functions and utility functions that satisfy all our assumptions. For all our examples we assume $n = 2$.

## 262  Krishnendu Ghosh Dastidar

1  Let $\beta = 1$, $F(.)$ is uniform over [0, 1] and $U(x, y) = \ln(1 + x) + 10y$. Note that here $\gamma = 10$, $u(\beta) = \ln 2 = 0.69315$ and $G(t) = t$. Routine computations show that

$$G(t)\big[\gamma - u(\beta)\big] - u(t) = t(10 - \ln 2) - \ln(1 + t)$$
$$= 9.3069t - \ln(1 + t)$$
$$\geq 0 \text{ for all } t \in [0,1].$$

2  Let $\beta = 2$ and $F(t) = \dfrac{t^2}{12}(7 - 2t)$ for $t \in [0, 2]$. Let $U(x, y) = x^2 + 14y$. Here $\gamma = 14$, $u(\beta) = 4$ and $G(t) = \dfrac{t^2}{12}(7 - 2t)$. Note that

$$G(t)\big[\gamma - u(\beta)\big] - u(t) = \frac{t^2}{12}(7 - 2t)(14 - 4) - t^2$$
$$= \frac{1}{6}t^2(29 - 10t)$$
$$\geq 0 \text{ for all } t \in [0,2].$$

## Equilibrium in auctions

**Inferior outside option.** Here we consider the case where bidders have an inferior outside option. We take $k$ as a critical benchmark of the level of incomes. If $\beta < k$ (i.e. all incomes are below $k$) then the outside option any bidder with income $m$ is $u(m) < \gamma$. *In this paper we exclusively deal with the case where $\beta < k$.* This means that the outside option is inferior for everybody. Since $\beta < k$ we have $m_i < k$ and $v(m_i) = m_i$ for all $i$. We first analyze the case of second-price auction. In this case the result is identical to the standard result in auction theory.

**Proposition 1.** *In a second-price auction for any $m_i \in [0, \beta]$, it is a weakly dominant strategy for bidder i to bid his own value. That is, the following is a symmetric Bayesian Nash equilibrium of the second price auction: $b^{II}(m_i) = v(m_i) = m_i$.*

**Proof.** Let the maximum of the bids of bidders 2, 3 ... $n$ be $z$. Let bidder 1's income be $m_1$ which is also his valuation. Let bidder 1's bid be $b_1$.

First suppose $m_1 > z$. If $b_1 = m_1$ then bidder 1 wins the auction, pays an amount $z$ and the payoff to bidder 1 is $u(m_1 - z) + \gamma$. If $z < b_1 < m_1$ then bidder 1 still wins the auction and the payoff would be the same.

# Auctions with an inferior outside option 263

If $b_1 < z$ then bidder 1 loses the auction and spends the entire income on good $x$ and the payoff will be $u(m_1)$. Since $m_1 < k$, we have the following (see the assumptions and the discussion in the second and third sections above):

$$u(m_1 - z) + \gamma > \gamma > u(m_1)$$

Hence, when $m_1 > z$ it's a weakly dominant strategy to quote a bid $b_1 = m_1$.

Now suppose $m_1 < z$. If $b_1 = m_1$ then then bidder 1 loses the auction and spends the entire income on good $x$ and the payoff will be $u(m_1)$. Any bid $b_1 < m_1$ will fetch the same payoff. If $m_1 < b_1 < z$ then also bidder 1 loses the auction and gets the same payoff. If $b_1 > z$ then bidder 1 is the highest bidder but he has to pay $z > m_1$ to obtain the object. Since he cannot pay more than his income, he has to default and cannot obtain the object. Moreover, he has to pay a penalty for defaulting. This means his payoff would be strictly lower than $u(m_1)$. Hence, when $m_1 < z$ it's a weakly dominant strategy to quote a bid $b_1 = m_1$.

**Comment.** While the proof is very standard, it may be noted that our framework is different from the canonical model. Proposition 1 shows that the original result of Vickrey (1961) on second-price auctions is very robust to changes in model specifications.[7]

We now analyze symmetric equilibria in first-price and all-pay auctions. We noted earlier, for any bidder with income $m_i$, choosing $b_i = 0$ weakly dominates any bid $b_i > m_i$. *This means that in any equilibrium* $b_i \leq m_i$. Proposition 2 deals with the cases of both first-price auction and all-pay auction.

**Proposition 2.** *Choosing a bid equal to income, i.e. $b^1(m_i) = m_i$, is a symmetric Bayesian Nash equilibrium in a first-price auction as well as in an all-pay auction.*

**Proof.** We first consider a *first-price auction*. Let bidders 2, 3 ... $n$ bid $m_2, m_3 \ldots m_n$. Bidder 1's income is $m_1$ and he chooses a bid equal to $b_1$. If he wins the auction his payoff is $u(m_1 - b_1) + \gamma$. If he loses then he spends his entire income on good $x$ and his payoff is $u(m_1)$. The probability that he wins is the probability that the maximum of $\{m_2, m_3 \ldots m_n\}$ is less than $b_1$. Then bidder 1's expected payoff is as follows (see the subsection under the second section above for the notations on order statistics):

$$\pi_1(b_1, m_1) = G(b_1)[u(m_1 - b_1) + \gamma] + (1 - G(b_1))u(m_1)$$
$$= G(b_1)[\gamma + u(m_1 - b_1) - u(m_1)] + u(m_1) \qquad (4)$$

## 264 *Krishnendu Ghosh Dastidar*

From (4) we get

$$\pi_1(0, m_1) = u(m_1) \text{ and}$$

$$\pi_1(m_1, m_1) = G(m_1) [\gamma - u(m_1)] + u(m_1) \tag{5}$$

When $m_1 = 0$ then clearly the optimal bid is zero. Now suppose $m_1 \in (0, \beta]$. Note that assumption A6 implies that $\gamma - u(m_1) > 0$. Also, $G(m_1) > 0$ for all $m_1 \in (0, \beta]$. This means (using (5 above) $\pi_1(m_1, m_1) > \pi_1(0, m_1)$ for all $m_1 \in (0, \beta]$. Now note that

$$\begin{aligned}
\pi_1(m_1, m_1) - \pi_1(b_1, m_1) &= [G(m_1) - G(b_1)][\gamma - u(m_1)] - G(b_1)u(m_1 - b_1) \\
&\geq G(m_1 - b_1)[\gamma - u(m_1)] - G(b_1)u(m_1 - b_1) (\text{using assumption A.5}) \\
&\geq G(m_1 - b_1)[\gamma - u(m_1)] - u(m_1 - b_1)(\text{since } G(b_1) \leq 1) \\
&\geq 0 (\text{using assumption A6}).
\end{aligned}$$

Therefore the best bid is $b_1 = m_1$. That is, $b^I(m_1) = m_1$ is a symmetric Bayesian Nash equilibrium in a first-price auction.

We now consider an *all-pay auction*. Let bidders 2, 3 . . . $n$ bid $m_2, m_3$ . . . $m_n$. Bidder 1's income is $m_1$ and he chooses a bid equal to $b_1$. If he wins the auction his payoff is $u(m_1 - b_1) + \gamma$. If he loses then he spends $m_1 - b_1$ on good $x$ and his payoff is $u(m_1 - b_1)$. The probability that he wins is the probability that the maximum of $\{m_2, m_3 \ldots m_n\}$ is less than $b_1$. Then bidder 1's expected payoff is as follows:

$$\begin{aligned}
\pi_1(b_1, m_1) &= G(b_1)[u(m_1 - b_1) + \gamma] + (1 - G(b_1))u(m_1 - b_1) \\
&= G(b_1)\gamma + u(m_1 - b_1).
\end{aligned} \tag{6}$$

From (6) we get

$$\pi_1(0, m_1) = u(m_1) \text{ and}$$

$$\pi_1(m_1, m_1) = G(m_1)\gamma \tag{7}$$

When $m_1 = 0$ then clearly the optimal bid is zero. Now suppose $m_1 \in (0, \beta]$. Note that assumption A6 implies that $G(m_1)\gamma > u(m_1)$. This means (using 7 above) $\pi_1(m_1, m_1) > \pi_1(0, m_1)$ for all $m_1 \in (0, \beta]$. Now note that

$$\begin{aligned}
\pi_1(m_1, m_1) - \pi_1(b_1, m_1) &= [G(m_1) - G(b_1)]\gamma - u(m_1 - b_1) \\
&\geq G(m_1 - b_1)\gamma - u(m_1 - b_1)(\text{using assumption A5}) \\
&> 0 (\text{using assumption A6}).
\end{aligned}$$

Therefore the best bid is $b_1 = m_1$. That is, $b^{AP}(m_1) = m_1$ is a symmetric Bayesian Nash equilibrium in an all-pay auction.∎

**Comment.** The result that bidders bid all their income on the item for sale both in a first-price and in an all-pay auction is surprising. A possible intuition behind these results could be as follows. The outside option for any bidder with income $m$ is $u(m)$. Note that $u(m) < \gamma$, where $\gamma$ is the utility of consuming only the indivisible good. Earlier we noted that $(\gamma - u(m))$ to be the *prize* for winning the good $y$ at a price $m$. Now consider a bidder whose $u(m)$ is very low and the *prize* for winning the good $y$ is very high. This means that the incentive to obtain the indivisible object at any cost is very high. Consequently, the bidder will quote the maximum possible amount to get the object. Even if the probability of winning is low, since the outside option is very poor and the utility gain from obtaining the indivisible item is sufficiently large, this bidder will bid as much as he can in both first-price and all-pay auctions. In Dastidar (2015) the agents' outside options are superior (incomes are high enough) and in equilibrium the bids in first-price and all-pay auctions are below the bidder's values.[8] This clearly shows that the equilibrium behaviour crucially depends on the outside options.

The expected revenues in this case for first-price, second-price and all-pay auctions are as follows: $R^I = \int_0^\beta bf_1(b)db$, $R^{II} = \int_0^\beta bf_2(b)db$ and $R^{AP} = n\int_0^\beta bf(b)db$. We now provide the revenue-ranking result.

**Proposition 3.** $R^{AP} > R^I > R^{II}$.

**Proof.** The expected revenues in this case are as follows.

$$\text{First-price: } R^I = \int_0^\beta bf_1(b)db = \int_0^\beta bdF_1(b)$$

$$\text{Second-price: } R^{II} = \int_0^\beta bf_2(b)db = \int_0^\beta bdF_2(b)$$

$$\text{All-pay: } R^{AP} = n\int_0^\beta bf(b)db$$

266  *Krishnendu Ghosh Dastidar*

First note that $F_1(h) = F^n(h)$ and $F_2(h) = F^n(h) + nF^{n-1}(h)(1 - F(h))$. Since $F_1(h) < F_2(h)$ for all $h \in (\alpha, \beta)$ we have $R^I > R^{II}$.

Also note that

$$
\begin{aligned}
R^I &= \int_0^\beta h f_1(h) dh = n \int_0^\beta h F^{n-1}(h) f(h) dh \\
&< n \int_0^\beta h f(h) dh \left( \text{since } F^{n-1}(h) < 1 \text{ for all } h \in [0, \beta) \right) \\
&= R^{AP}.
\end{aligned}
$$

Hence we have $R^{AP} > R^I > R^{II}$.∎

**Comment.** In a nutshell, when bidders' outside options are inferior (incomes are low enough), revenue equivalence fails to hold. Expected revenue in a first-price auction is strictly higher than that in a second-price auction. An all-pay auction fetches the highest expected revenue. We now discuss some similarities between our results and some related results in the literature.

In Dastidar (2015) the bidders' outside options are superior (incomes are high enough). There expected revenue in a first-price auction is equal to that in a second-price auction. But there also the all-pay auction fetches the highest expected revenue. In Che and Gale (1996) all bidders have a known common value $v$ for the object (i.e. identical preferences) but they differ in their incomes. This is similar to our model except the following: (1) Che and Gale (1996) assume quasilinear preferences while we don't. (2) In Che and Gale (1996) the valuation is common knowledge while income is private information. In our framework, the values are equal to incomes and they are private information. Che and Gale (1996) show that, in a first-price auction, buyers whose incomes are below a critical level bid their incomes while buyers above the critical level bid below their incomes. *In their model for all-pay auctions, bids are always below the incomes.* They also show that the first-price auction may have strictly higher expected revenue than the second-price auction and the all-pay auction may have strictly higher expected revenue than the first-price auction.

In Che and Gale (1998), where types are two-dimensional (valuation $v_i$ and wealth $w_i$ are both private information), it is possible to have a symmetric equilibrium in a first-price auction where bids are equal to incomes and the expected revenue in first price auctions will be strictly higher than the expected revenue in second price auctions.

*Auctions with an inferior outside option* 267

We have shown that bidders bid their values (equal to incomes in our framework) in a symmetric equilibrium in all three auctions. This, together with the fact that $R^{AP} > R^I > R^{II}$ (proposition 3) is somewhat close in spirit to Che and Gale (1996, 1998). *This is despite the differences in the models and in the definitions of valuations.*[9]

## Conclusions

Auctions where bidders' outside options are inferior have not been adequately analyzed in the standard literature. In this chapter an attempt is made to fill this gap within an extremely simple framework. In contrast to the benchmark model, we considered a more general class of utility functions. This paper analyzed auctions of a single indivisible item in a setting in which consumers have the same utility function for two goods – the item for sale at auction and a divisible good that can be bought at a given market price – but different incomes (which are private information). In our framework, value of the indivisible object is defined to be the maximum price that a bidder is *willing* to pay and *able* to pay. We demonstrated that when bidders' outside options are inferior, the value of the indivisible object is equal to the income. We showed that while Vickrey's (1961) result on second price auction is very robust, bidding ones' own value is an equilibrium even in first-price and all-pay auctions. An all-pay auction fetches the highest expected revenue. We propose the following for possible future research.

1   In our model we have not dealt with the effects of introduction of a reserve price and computation of optimal reserve price. This is left for future research.

2   Dastidar (2015) deals with the case where all bidders have superior outside options (all incomes are above $k$). We have not analyzed the case where some bidders' outside options are inferior and the other bidders' outside options are superior (i.e. when some incomes are below $k$ and other incomes are above $k$). Derivation of equilibrium in all the three auctions, effects of reserve price and revenue-ranking results in such a scenario should be an interesting research problem.

# Appendix

We now provide an explanation of some of the terms used in this chapter. There is a seller who has a single indivisible object. The seller does not know how much any buyer would be willing to pay for it. If the seller were to know each buyer's value for the object, he could just approach the buyer who values it most. This strategy is infeasible when he does not know their values. The reason the seller holds an auction is because his information about the possible buyers is imperfect; the auction is intended to produce the best sale price in part by identifying the best bidder. A *standard auction* is where the object is sold to the highest bidder.

**The terms.** The *value* (or reservation price) for a bidder $i$, denoted by $v_i$, is the maximum amount of money he would be willing to pay for the object. In game (auction) theory jargon, $v_i$ is the type of bidder $i$.

The symmetric, independent, private value (SIPV) model of auctions make the following assumptions.

1  *Private values*: The private information of a bidder is his own value for the object, and it does not depend on what the other bidders know.
2  *Independent types*: $v_1$; $v_2....v_n$ are independently distributed.
   Bidder $i$ believes that $v_1$; $v_2..v_{i-1}$; $v_{i+1}..v_n$ are random variables to which he can attribute a joint probability distribution. Each bidder believes that the other types are distributed independently of his own.
3  *Symmetry*: Each random variable $v_i$ has the same distribution.
4  *Risk neutrality:* The bidders are risk neutral.

Some standard auctions are as follows:

1  *First-price auction (FPA)*: The bidders simultaneously submit sealed bids. The highest bidder wins and pays a price equal to his bid.

2 *Second-price auction (SPA)*: The bidders simultaneously submit sealed bids. The highest bidder wins and pays a price equal to the second highest bid.

3 *All-pay auctions (APA)*: The bidders simultaneously submit sealed bids. The highest bidder wins. Each bidder must pay an amount equal to his bid, regardless of whether he wins or not.

4 *English auction (EA)*: Bids are oral. The auctioneer (the seller) starts the bidding process at some price. The bidders proclaim successively higher bids until no bidder is willing to bid higher. The bidder who submitted the final bid wins and pays a price equal to his bid. For private value auctions, EA is outcome equivalent to SPA.

5 *Dutch auctions (DA)*: The seller starts with a very high price. Then the price declines continuously on a "wheel" until one bidder yells "stop". That bidder wins and pays the price at which the wheel stopped. The DA is outcome equivalent to the FPA.

It may be noted that in each of these auction examples, if there is tie at the top (i.e. if there are $k$ highest bidders), we assume that each such bidder wins with probability $1/k$.

A *procurement auction* is one where the auctioneer is a *buyer* instead of being a seller. The bidders are the sellers. Each bidder possesses one unit of an identical object which is being offered for sale. In a standard procurement auction the *lowest bidder* wins. Here, in an FPA the lowest bidder wins and sells the object to the auctioneer (who is the buyer) at that price. Similarly, in an SPA, the lowest bidder wins and sells the object to the auctioneer at the second lowest price and so on. It may be noted that procurement auctions are just standard auctions in reverse.

Auction theory's most celebrated theorem, *The Revenue Equivalence Theorem*, basically states that for SIPV auctions with risk neutral bidders the expected price (which is the same as the expected revenue) at which the good is sold is same across all the four standard auctions. For the most general formulation of this theorem, see Klemperer (2004).

# 270 *Krishnendu Ghosh Dastidar*

## Notes

1  The outside option for the individual will be superior if it is higher than the utility of consuming only the indivisible object.
2  See Krishna (2010) for all the major results around the canonical model.
3  It may be noted that a quasilinear utility function, where demand depends only on price – at least for large enough levels of income – and there are no income effects to worry about, is more appropriate for modeling a situation where the demand for a good isn't very sensitive to income. For example, demand for paper or pencils is not likely to change with changes in income. Most likely, any increase in income would go into consumption of other goods. (see page 165 of Varian 1992).
4  If $p > m_i$ then the individual cannot purchase $y$ and he has to spend the entire income on good $x$ and get $u(m_i)$.
5  As per standard convention we use capital letters for random variables and small letters for realized values of random variables.
6  In our framework an individual would be risk neutral iff $\dfrac{\partial^2}{\partial x^2} U(x,y) = u''(x) = 0$ and risk averse iff $\dfrac{\partial^2}{\partial x^2} U(x,y) = u''(x) < 0$. For an explanation about why this is so see Kreps (1990, chapter 3).
7  Dastidar (2015) has a similar result.
8  As noted before, when incomes are high enough (i.e. $m_i > k$) then the values are less than $m_i$.
9  In the Che-Gale approach, the valuation of an indivisible item is the maximum price that the individual is willing to pay (but not necessarily able to pay). That is, it is possible for the valuation to exceed wealth (i.e. $v_i > w_i$) in the Che-Gale framework. In our model, the valuation is defined to be the maximum price that an individual is willing to pay and able to pay. In our case, for low enough incomes we always have $v_i = w_i$.

## Bibliography

Che, Y.-K., and I. Gale (1996) Financial constraints in auctions: Effects and antidotes in *Advances in Applied Microeconomics*, vol. 6, Ed. M. Baye, JAI Press Inc.

Che, Y.-K., and I. Gale (1998) Standard Auctions with Financially Constrained Bidders *Review of Economic Studies* 65 pp. 1–22.

Dastidar, K.G. (2015) Basic Auction Theory Revisited *International Journal of Economic Theory (special issue in honour of Makoto Yano)* 11 pp. 89–106.

Klemperer, P. (2004) *Auctions: Theory and Practice* Princeton University Press Princeton, New Jersey, USA.

Kreps, D. (1990) *A Course in Microeconomic Theory* Princeton University Press, Princeton, NJ, USA.

Krishna, V. (2010) *Auction Theory* (2nd Edition) Academic Press, San Diego, CA, USA.

Ramarathinam, A. (2016) The Barbarious Relic in the Time of Drought *Mint*, 21 April, 2016.

Saitoh, H., and S. Serizawa (2008) Vickrey Allocation Rule with Income Effect *Economic Theory* 35 pp. 391–401.

Sakai, T. (2008) Second Price Auctions on General Preference Domains: Two Characterisations *Economic Theory* 37 pp. 347–356.

Varian, H.R. (1992) *Microeconomic Analysis* (3rd Edition) W.W. Norton and Company, New York, USA.

Vickrey, W. (1961) Counterspeculation, Auctions, and Competitive Sealed Tenders *Journal of Finance* 16 pp. 8–37.

# Part IV

# Lessons from development experiences

# Emerging economies

# 14 Beyond *Catch Up*

## Some speculations about the next twenty-five emerging economies

*Sudipto Mundle*[*]

Deepak Nayyar's recent book *Catch Up* (Nayyar 2013) is a fascinating narrative of change, divergence and convergence between different regions of the world since the 16th century, and especially during the last 200 years. An economist's narrative, but written in a Braudel-like *long duree* perspective (Braudel 1973), the book belongs to the grand empirical tradition of Clark (1940); Kuznets (1966); and Chenery (1969). In the closing chapters of the book Nayyar has identified a group of fourteen countries that appear most significant for the process of 'catch up'. Then in the very last chapter he has identified another ten developing countries which could be following in the footsteps of the next fourteen, and also two 'least developed countries', Bangladesh and Tanzania. Included in this list of twenty-six countries is Taiwan, which is no longer recognised by the United Nations, and its partner institutions like the World Bank, as an independent country and therefore dropped from their published data sets. That leaves twenty-five developing countries, the Next Twenty-five, which Nayyar has identified as having the most potential for 'catching up' with the developed countries.

This chapter speculates about the prospects of these twenty-five countries by about the middle of the 21st century, that is over the next thirty-five years or so.[1] The first part of the chapter presents some elements of a theory of economic history that can frame the assessment of these prospects. The second presents the assessment based on the framework developed in the first part and the third concludes.

---

[*] Deepak Nayyar has had a long, distinguished career ranging from being Vice Chancellor of Delhi University and Chief Economic Adviser of the Indian government to publishing a remarkable book as an amateur photographer. However, his most enduring contribution is as a scholar, a leading heterodox economist whose reputation stretches well beyond India.

276  *Sudipto Mundle*

## Elements of a theory of economic history

### Forecasting and speculating about the future

The term 'speculation' is deliberately chosen rather than prediction or forecast to describe the assessments presented in this chapter. That is because a prediction or forecast is a probabilistic statement about the future, and the probabilities decline quite sharply for assessments that go beyond a year or two. So to describe the possible scenarios described here as forecasts would be pretentious.

In his book *A Theory of Economic History*, in which Hicks described as following in the footsteps of Marx rather than Toynbee, Hicks adopted a probabilistic or 'statistical' approach as he calls it (Hicks 1969). He explained that it may be possible to generalise analytically about some of the principal drivers of change in a group of societies or countries which may have some key features in common. Such a generalised model may reasonably account for the broad direction of change of the group as a whole. However, such a model would typically not be able to explain changes that may occur in a particular country. That is because those particular changes may have been driven by elements specific to that country which are not a part of the general model.

Clearly, if theories of economic history can only be applied in this probabilistic sense in interpreting the past, for which the facts are already known, it is that much more challenging to apply them for forecasting the future. Nayyar prudently limited himself to some general observations about emerging trends that may be important in determining the future. If we wish to imprudently push the envelope further, and attempt to assess the future prospects of individual countries in the Next Twenty-five group, then it is best to describe such assessments as speculations rather than forecasts.

While recognising that the goal here is to speculate rather than forecast, it is nevertheless important to ensure that as far as possible these speculations are based on facts rather than fantasy. And for that it is best to follow the procedural discipline of forecasting based on Bayesian probabilities (Silver 2012).

### Initial conditions, path dependence and determinants of change

As Nayyar observes in *Catch Up*, nothing is pre-ordained about the development path of a country. At any given point of time, the legacy of a society's entire past history is reflected in its present conditions.

These present conditions are the initial conditions that lay down the boundaries of the possible, feasible paths for the future. Particularly important among these initial conditions are the endowments of resources, technical knowledge and institutions – the rules or conventions according to which a society is organised and conducts its affairs.

Which of the many feasible paths a country actually takes at each point of time, for each point can indeed be a turning point, will depend on the interaction among different elements of the initial conditions, in particular resource endowments, technical knowledge and institutions. To the dynamics of these interactions must be added unanticipated shocks, either positive or negative, that can suddenly shift the trajectory of a country, rather like a monsoon flood that can suddenly change the course of a river. We must also add to this the cumulative impact of incremental change. As chaos theory has taught us, the cumulative impact of small, imperceptible change can in fact lead to sudden, dramatic change or 'discontinuities' beyond a tipping point. Of these two sources of dramatic shift in a country's development path, future shocks will be unanticipated by definition. As for the cumulative impact of incremental change, to the extent that such incremental change is already present in the initial conditions, an alert observer needs to look out for possible signals of such change in the middle of all the noise.

### The agrarian barrier to industrial growth

Setting aside the unanticipated sources of dramatic change, a theory of economic history needs to focus on the interactions between the three components of initial conditions identified earlier: Resource endowments, technical knowledge and institutions. It needs to indicate the broad path of development along which these interactions might drive a country. In a paper published over thirty years ago, I had used a model of economic history developed along these lines to illustrate how the history of industrialisation in different countries and regions of the world was crucially related to enabling changes in the agrarian barrier to industrial growth, the backward and forward linkages between agriculture and industry. The changes were in turn related to interactions between resources, technology and institutions in agriculture (Mundle 1985).

Agrarian systems were classified into three broad types, based on the relationship between two classes of people in agrarian societies, surplus producers and surplus appropriators:[2] Type A, in which surplus producers organise production but the productivity gains are captured

278   *Sudipto Mundle*

by a class of surplus appropriators; Type B, in which surplus appropriators organise production and also capture the productivity gains; and Type C, where surplus producers organise production and also capture the productivity gains.[3] These are ideal types. The real world would consist of combinations of these ideal types.

In other words, I had classified agrarian systems in terms of how well the prevailing institutions aligned technical capability and command over resources, for example, labour and capital in capitalist agriculture, with the incentive to innovate and raise productivity. Abstracting from other drivers of industrialisation, such as long-distance trade, Type A agrarian systems would trap countries in a vicious circle of stagnant agriculture and arrested industrialisation, for example, India before independence or the Second Serfdom in Russia and large parts of eastern Europe till the late 19th century. Type B agrarian systems would generate virtuous circles of capital-intensive technological innovation and rising productivity in agriculture and industrialisation, for example, England, Scotland and large parts of western Europe, because the surplus appropriators had strong incentives to invest much of the surplus in productivity enhancing investments. Type C agrarian systems would generate virtuous circles of labour-intensive technological innovations and rising productivity in agriculture along with industrialisation, for example, Japan post the Meiji Restoration.

### Inclusive versus extractive institutions

Some of these elements have reappeared in a recent institutional theory of economic history that has become quite influential (Acemoglu and Robinson 2012). Acemoglu and Robinson recognise the role of interactions between technology, resource endowments and institutions, but identify institutions as the key drivers of change. They distinguish between inclusive and extractive institutions, and between economic and political institutions. Inclusive economic institutions ensure property rights, a level playing field among agents and a wide sharing of the fruits of growth, thereby providing the incentive for innovation, investment, skill development and a rapid rise to prosperity. Conversely, extractive institutions enable a small elite to extract all the fruits of growth at the cost of insecurity and deprivation of the majority, thereby suppressing or dampening the incentives for innovation, investment and skill formation. Such institutions are therefore associated with stagnation or slow growth.

Extractive political institutions, where a small elite monopolises political power, reinforce extractive economic institutions, which in turn reinforce the elite's monopoly of political power, thereby perpetuating a vicious cycle of stagnation. Conversely, inclusive political institutions promote the emergence of inclusive economic institutions, thereby generating a virtuous circle of rising prosperity. So, of the many possible paths that are feasible for a given set of initial conditions, it is the prevailing nature of institutions that will determine which path a nation will follow.

Acemoglu and Robinson emphasise that theirs is not a deterministic theory of economic history. No nation's path is pre-ordained. They argue that world history has been generally characterised by the vicious circle of extractive institutions and stagnation as the norm. But when specific conjunctures and circumstances enabled a nation to break out of this negative symbiotic relationship, the nation could shift to a path of growth and prosperity driven by the virtuous circle of inclusive institutions. In this context the authors emphasise the key role of critical junctures in shifting nations from one path to another and also the accumulation of incremental changes, which they describe as institutional drift. By critical junctures, they mean transformative shocks to society, such as the 'black death' that greatly de-populated Europe, the political revolution that ended absolute monarchy in England, the rise of the Atlantic trade, etc. They point out that it is at such critical junctures that institutional drift can lead to divergent paths, as for instance between France and England.

Critical junctures and institutional drift are indeed powerful drivers of economic history. But these drivers do not necessarily have to go together. As was mentioned earlier, chaos theory tells us that the cumulative impact of incremental change, institutional drift, can on its own lead to dramatic change beyond a tipping point even without critical junctures. There is another, deeper, sense in which the Acemoglu-Robinson institutional theory of economic history needs an amendment in order to enhance its predictive power. The classification of all institutional arrangements into inclusive and extractive is possibly too broad to sufficiently discriminate between different paths of development.

By way of illustration, agrarian systems of Type A in my classification described previously would clearly be classified as stagnation inducing extractive institutions in the Acemoglu-Robinson theory, and my agrarian systems of Type C would be classified as growth promoting inclusive institutions in their theory. But what about the agrarian systems described as Type B, where a privileged class that controls production and appropriates the surplus also has the capacity, resources and incentives to invest in productivity-enhancing innovations and

## 280 *Sudipto Mundle*

growth in agriculture? Such systems can also promote industrialisation through the backward and forward linkages between the two sectors.

Do we have here a counter-example to their theory, where an extractive institutional set up generates a virtuous circle of growth, or should we describe systems such as capitalist farming as being inclusive? If we choose the latter, then we can no longer differentiate between, say, the large scale, capital intensive, capitalist farms in large parts of the USA, Europe, Australia, Argentina, etc. and the small, labour-intensive, owner-cultivated peasant farms that are typical in Japan and much of Asia. Yet, we know that the long-term dynamics of these different institutional systems, and their implications for industrial growth may be quite different.

Authoritarian systems of socialism present another awkward category. Such systems are unambiguously classified as extractive by Acemoglu and Robinson, but they invoke an auxiliary concept of centralisation to account for growth in such societies. If extractive institutions come along with a high degree of political centralisation, they argue, the political power elite can reinvest large volumes of the extracted savings to keep growth going for some time even in the absence of any inclusive sharing of the fruits of growth. Here, we see the tight link between extractive institutions and stagnation in their theory getting stretched to accommodate historical experience that is not compatible with the core theory.

Besides, what is the time horizon for the accommodation of such special cases? The fact that the Soviet Union did eventually collapse does not detract from the fact that this authoritarian system of extractive institutions grew dramatically over a period of seventy years. China, another authoritarian, socialist nation is still rising quite rapidly and now rivalling the USA. Acemoglu and Robinson predict that China's rise will not be sustained because of its extractive institutions. Chinese growth has indeed slowed in recent years. But it is still one of the fastest growing economies in the world, and is projected to surpass the size of the USA within a couple of decades, a projection that has not been seriously questioned. The Chinese case is discussed in further detail later.

The point of this discussion is to suggest that an institutional theory of economic history needs to be adequately nuanced. In particular, we need to recognise that certain types of extractive institutions may also be conducive to growth, and that in some nations extractive and inclusive institutions may co-exist. Acemoglu and Robinson recognise that extractive political institutions may co-exist with inclusive economic institutions in transitional periods, but maintain that under stable conditions the two sets of institutions will be aligned to each other.

*Beyond* Catch Up    281

However, the experience of rapid growth under authoritarian regimes in socialist countries and in East Asia in the latter half of the 20th century suggests that the co-existence of inclusive economic institutions and extractive political institutions may be sustained for decades. They cannot be explained away as merely transitional economic phenomena.

The discussion so far has equated development with growth. This is a very narrow definition of development compared to the concept of development as freedom proposed by Sen (1999). Incorporating his concept of the many varieties of freedom into Acemoglu and Robinson's institutional theory of economic history greatly enhances the predictive power of the theory. Sen points out that the connection between freedom of individual agency and social development is "influenced by economic opportunities, political liberties, social powers, and the enabling conditions of good health, basic education, and the encouragement and cultivation of initiatives", adding that "The institutional arrangements for these opportunities are also influenced by the exercise of people's freedoms, through the liberty to participate in social choice and in the making of public decisions that impel the progress of these opportunities".[4]

That is a very comprehensive description of the constitutive elements of inclusive economic and political institutions. Sen also adds that freedom of individual agency in one dimension contributes to strengthening free agency of other kinds, the sum of freedoms is greater than the parts, which echoes the synergy between inclusive economic and political institutions in Acemoglu and Robinson. However, there is no suggestion that freedom of individual agency can only exist if it exists simultaneously in all dimensions. In Sen's framework, it is conceivable that a society allows economic opportunities, provides basic education, good health care, etc. but not political freedom or the freedom to participate in social choice and the making of public decisions. In other words, the co-existence of inclusive economic institutions along with extractive political institutions is possible. I have cited several examples previously of such combinations producing high growth over fairly long periods of time.

Based on the foregoing discussion of actual historical experience, it is helpful to modify the Acemoglu and Robinson classification, allowing for four rather than two broadly defined types of economic and political institutions:

Inclusive–progressive
Inclusive–populist
Exclusive–progressive
Exclusive–extractive

## 282 *Sudipto Mundle*

*Inclusive–progressive* institutions, both economic and political, are those that are inclusive and at the same time committed to development. The *Inclusive–populist* institutions are those which are inclusive, but with the state deploying its resources for populist measures rather than development. Such institutions may be required for the survival of weak political elites in fractionalised polities. The opposite of inclusive institutions are exclusive institutions, both economic and political, that are narrowly elitist, possibly even authoritarian. If political economic conditions drive elites in such societies to be growth promoting, such institutional conjunctures can be described as *Exclusive–progressive*. On the other hand, when elites in exclusive institutions siphon off resources, and incentives are not aligned to promote growth, these institutions may be described as *Exclusive–extractive*. Clearly, the ideal composition would be to have both economic and political institutions that are inclusive and progressive. The worst possible combination would be to have political and economic institutions that are both exclusive and extractive.

The institutional theory of economic history, modified as to accommodate important experiences in the history of global development, provides us a framework with considerable predictive power for assessing the prospects of the Next Twenty-five, listed in Table 14.1 below.

### The next twenty-five emerging economies

As a prelude to such assessment, it is important to recognise that size matters. There are a number of fundamental global challenges as well as opportunities facing all countries, including the twenty-five of interest to us. How a country responds to these challenges and opportunities depends on its internal conditions, technological capabilities and institutions. It also depends on a country's size. Large countries may exercise market power, and draw strength from their command over resources. These opportunities would not be available to small open economies. Some illustrations follow.

Globalisation is a major challenge and also an opportunity. Its impact on a country can be benevolent or malevolent, depending on how the country responds to it. The response will depend, among other factors, on the country's resource endowments, which is a function of its size. For example, a large country with a large, low-cost, manufacturing labour force can capture global markets, further strengthen its competitiveness and emerge as a global manufacturing hub. This is not an option for a small country.

*Table 14.1* Selected indicators of the next twenty-five emerging economies

| Country name | GDP per capita (current US$), 2014 | Population, total, 2014 (in million) | GDP at market prices (current US$ billion), 2014 | Annual average GDP growth 2007 to 2014 | Land area ('000 sq. km), 2015 | Population density (people per sq. km of land area), 2014 | Life expectancy at birth, total (years) | World population share, 2014 (percent) |
|---|---|---|---|---|---|---|---|---|
| (0) | (1) | (2) | (3) | (4) | (5) | (6) | (7) | (8) |
| World | 10,739 | 7,259.69 | 77,960.61 | 1.66 | 129,736 | 55.96 | 71.5 | 100.00 |
| **Very large countries** | | | | | | | | |
| China | 7,590 | 1,364.27 | 10,354.83 | 7.66 | 9,388 | 145.3 | 75.8 | 18.79 |
| India | 1,582 | 1,295.29 | 2,048.52 | 6.03 | 2,973 | 435.7 | 68.0 | 17.84 |
| **Very small countries*** | | | | | | | | |
| Tunisia | 4,421 | 11.00 | 48.61 | 2.30 | 155 | 70.8 | 74.1 | 0.15 |
| Honduras | 2,435 | 7.96 | 19.39 | 2.40 | 112 | 71.2 | 73.1 | 0.11 |
| **Asia** | | | | | | | | |
| Korea, Rep. | 27,970 | 50.42 | 1,410.38 | 2.76 | 97 | 517.3 | 82.2 | 0.69 |
| Malaysia | 11,307 | 29.90 | 338.10 | 3.99 | 329 | 91.0 | 74.7 | 0.41 |
| Turkey | 10,515 | 75.93 | 798.43 | 2.78 | 770 | 98.7 | 75.2 | 1.05 |
| Thailand | 5,977 | 67.73 | 404.82 | 2.50 | 511 | 132.6 | 74.4 | 0.93 |
| Iran, Islamic Rep. | 5,443 | 78.14 | 425.33 | 1.10 | 1,629 | 48.0 | 75.4 | 1.08 |
| Indonesia | 3,492 | 254.45 | 888.54 | 4.94 | 1,812 | 140.5 | 68.9 | 3.51 |
| Philippines | 2,873 | 99.14 | 284.78 | 4.52 | 298 | 332.5 | 68.3 | 1.37 |
| Vietnam | 2,052 | 90.73 | 186.20 | 5.03 | 310 | 292.6 | 75.6 | 1.25 |
| Bangladesh | 1,087 | 159.08 | 172.89 | 5.19 | 130 | 1,222.1 | 71.6 | 2.19 |

*(Continued)*

*Table 14.1* (Continued)

| Country name | GDP per capita (current US$), 2014 | Population, total, 2014 (in million) | GDP at market prices (current US$ billion), 2014 | Annual average GDP growth 2007 to 2014 | Land area ('000 sq. km), 2015 | Population density (people per sq. km of land area), 2014 | Life expectancy at birth, total (years) | World population share, 2014 (percent) |
|---|---|---|---|---|---|---|---|---|
| **Africa** | | | | | | | | |
| South Africa | 6,484 | 54.00 | 350.14 | 1.72 | 1,213 | 44.5 | 57.2 | 0.74 |
| Egypt, Arab Rep. | 3,366 | 89.58 | 301.50 | 3.14 | 995 | 90.0 | 71.1 | 1.23 |
| Nigeria | 3,203 | 177.48 | 568.51 | 5.21 | 911 | 194.9 | 52.8 | 2.44 |
| Kenya | 1,358 | 44.86 | 60.94 | 4.17 | 569 | 78.8 | 61.6 | 0.62 |
| Tanzania | 955 | 51.82 | 48.06 | 5.55 | 886 | 58.5 | 64.9 | 0.71 |
| **Latin America** | | | | | | | | |
| Chile | 14,528 | 17.76 | 258.06 | 3.15 | 744 | 23.9 | 81.5 | 0.24 |
| Venezuela, RB** | 12,772 | 30.69 | 381.29 | 0.90 | 882 | 34.8 | 74.2 | 0.42 |
| Argentina | 12,510 | 42.98 | 537.66 | 3.08 | 2,737 | 15.7 | 76.2 | 0.59 |
| Brazil | 11,727 | 206.08 | 2,416.64 | 2.65 | 8,358 | 24.7 | 74.4 | 2.84 |
| Mexico | 10,326 | 125.39 | 1,294.69 | 1.64 | 1,944 | 64.5 | 76.7 | 1.73 |
| Colombia | 7,904 | 47.79 | 377.74 | 3.64 | 1,110 | 43.1 | 74.0 | 0.66 |
| Ecuador | 6,346 | 15.90 | 100.92 | 3.99 | 248 | 64.0 | 75.9 | 0.22 |

Source: World Development Indicators (weblink: http://data.worldbank.org/indicator), retrieved on 02–06–2016

* Countries with less than 15 million population (0.2 percent of global population)

** Data are for 2012; except population, land area and life expectancy at birth data, which are for 2014.

Global warming and the energy crisis is another example. There are few sceptics who still question the link between global warming and the growing consumption of fossil fuels. At the same time, with costs declining in alternative technologies, the world may be at the cusp of a switch to an altogether different energy paradigm based on renewables. It is a critical juncture. Whether or not a country grasps this great market opportunity will depend, among other things, on its command over resources, and that is a function of its size.

Much the same can be said about the water crisis. With the needs of many countries running ahead of the availability of fresh water, it is a major global challenge today. At the same time, desalination technologies exist for converting abundant saline water from the oceans into potable fresh water. Costs are still very high but declining. Among those countries that have the technological capability and incentives to turn this challenge into a major market opportunity, only those would succeed that have the necessary scale and command over resources.

A fourth and final example of paradigmatic change is the emergence of microchip-based technologies that have revolutionised products, production techniques and communications across the world. There are vast new opportunities unfolding as a consequence of this great disruptive change. The size of countries, their internal markets and their command over resources, including labour, capital and knowledge, will be key determinants of the winners and losers in this Schumpeterian gale of creative destruction.

Since size matters, the set of twenty-five countries have been classified into three broad groups in the following discussion. First, there are the two very large countries with populations exceeding a billion each: China and India. At the other end, using a cut-off of fifteen million population size, approximately one-fifth of one percentage point of the global population, we have two very small countries, Honduras and Tunisia. In assessing the prospects of the remaining twenty-one countries, the discussion is focused on comparing the countries in Asia with those in Africa and Latin America. It addresses the question of why the 'catch up' process seems to be working quite powerfully in Asia, particularly East Asia, but not in the other two regions.

### China and India: Two very large countries

China and India are often bracketed together mainly because of their large size. No other country has a population size even remotely close to the 1.3 billion people in each of these two countries. The per capita income in both countries is quite low, much more so in India than in

## 286  Sudipto Mundle

China. Yet both are among the largest economies in the world when their low per capita income is multiplied by their large populations. This large economic size gives them command over vast domestic resources, a great deal of market power and consequent geo-political influence. These similarities notwithstanding, it is really the differences between them that are more relevant in speculating about their future paths.

It is fascinating that the pendulum of economic power, which swung away from these two giant countries at the beginning of the second millennium, is again swinging back in their direction after a thousand years. Around the year 1000, China and India accounted for about half of global GDP, and also about half of the global population (Nayyar 2013). That situation began to change from the 15th century, gradually at first and then at a rapid pace during the 19th and 20th centuries. Even as recently as in 1820, the two countries still accounted for about half of global GDP, and about 57 percent of world population. But by 1950, their combined share declined to only 9 percent of global GDP, while they still accounted for about a third of global population. Since then, their relative decline has been arrested and both countries are again on the ascendant, especially China. Both are now among the largest economies in the world. In PPP (purchasing power parity) terms China is already the largest and India the third largest.

The Second World War also marked the end of the period of global colonialism. Several newly independent countries, including China and India, embarked on a new era of development from the 1950s onwards. At the time both per capita income and overall economic size were about the same in the two countries. They were not much different even at the beginning of the 1980s. But following the launch of its liberalisation reforms, starting in 1979, China has left India far behind. This is despite the fact that India also launched its liberalisation programme in 1991. It is astonishing that in a little over thirty years, China's per capita income (US$7,500 in 2014) has risen to five times that of India (US$1,582 in 2014), and the Chinese economy is also five times the size of India.[5] What accounts for the vastly different performance in the two countries? An answer to that question is quite critical for an assessment of their future prospects.

One reason, possibly the primary reason, is that the two countries have very different institutional structures. In our terminology China's political institutions are exclusive, allowing no political freedom for the vast majority of its citizens, but they are progressive. The state is deeply committed to development. And its economic institutions are inclusive. Particularly in the years following the socialist revolution,

*Beyond* Catch Up    287

the Chinese state has deployed vast resources in enabling widely dispersed social freedoms, in particular improvement of education and health services, along with different rounds of egalitarian land reforms and infrastructure development.

India's political institutions are inclusive. It is remarkable, perhaps even unique among developing countries, that a robust system of parliamentary democracy has flourished for over sixty years, with a free and vocal press, the toleration of dissent as a right, and so forth. The state is also committed to development. In our terminology, India's political institutions are inclusive and progressive. It's economic institutions, on the other hand, are exclusive.[6] Unlike China, India did not experience a cathartic, but equalising, socialist revolution. As a result the inclusive political institution of democracy came to rest on a deeply unequal and extractive socio-economic system, the caste system, reified over millennia. The challenge to this entrenched system is relatively recent. It started with anti-caste movements in the southern states in the early 20th century, and then spread to the north more recently. This entrenched exclusion is still reflected, as many authors have noted, in India's abysmal neglect of human development, especially basic education and basic health care. That has greatly compromised both human development as well as growth in India.[7] Moreover, India could not introduce egalitarian land reforms except in a few states.

A consequence of China's inclusive economic system and human development, especially mass education, was the availability of a huge educated workforce. This workforce could be readily harnessed and trained as skilled industrial workers as China's relentless growth over three decades transformed it into the manufacturing hub of the world by the end of the 20th century. In contrast, despite fairly high growth for over two decades, India has faced the paradox of a large surplus labour and low-labour productivity alongside the severe scarcity of a skilled workforce.

A second reason for the difference in growth performance between China and India is the difference in quality of governance and service delivery. The Chinese command and control system, though exclusive and authoritarian, is effective in both reforming and implementing policies. In contrast, as Vijay Joshi points out in his recent book, policy making and implementation in India is hobbled by three major constraints: 'Collective action gridlock', deficits in state competence and accountability and crony capitalism.[8]

Looking to the future, will China continue to soar to the top, as predicted by Arvind Subramanian (2011), or will both China and India regress towards mean global growth as predicted by Pritchett

288  *Sudipto Mundle*

and Summers (2013)? They have argued that three decades of high growth experienced by China and India is very unusual and that both countries are likely to slow down. Both countries have indeed slowed down significantly compared to the growth rates they recorded during the first decade of the 21st century (Mundle 2015a). Is this a secular trend, a one-time adjustment or a temporary phenomenon?

China's long period of high growth was led by exports and high public investment. It is now attempting a shift to growth led by domestic consumption along with public investment. This adjustment may partly account for the recent slowdown. The investment pillar of this new growth strategy seems quite robust (Mundle 2016a). However, even the reduced 'new normal' growth target of 6.5 percent will require sustained productivity growth. As Mody (2015) suggests, that will in turn require substantial institutional reform away from what is still a state-led economy, weighed down by zombie firms and zombie banks, towards a more market-oriented system. The new consumption pillar of growth will also require an incomes policy that substantially ratchets up the purchasing power of the working class, particularly unorganised sector workers. Such reforms would become a critical juncture if they were to happen. An even more far-reaching critical juncture could arise when China's inclusive economic institutions, and in particular its growing and increasingly affluent middle class (Silverstein et al. 2012), collide against the restrictions of an authoritarian regime that lacks political legitimacy. Bardhan and many others regard this as the greatest challenge for China's future growth.

In India, the situation is quite the reverse. The political institutions are relatively inclusive. But the economic institutions are exclusive and highly unequal, excluding large segments of the population from decent basic education and health care, among other deprivations. The prospects of high growth in the future will depend on whether or not the economic institutions get better aligned with India's inclusive political institutions.[9] Whether such a critical juncture will occur is difficult to foresee. However, there are some signals of a possible institutional drift towards more inclusive economic institutions.

Political power in India has become much more decentralised in recent years, as several regional parties with charismatic leaders have emerged as major players in India's federal political system. Such decentralisation has been nudged forward with greater fiscal empowerment of state governments by successive Finance Commissions, especially the 14th Finance Commission. Moreover, these regional political parties are beginning to compete on the basis of performance alongside traditional identity politics. Growth and social development as well as

## Beyond Catch Up

public spending on infrastructure, education and health are beginning to emerge as important factors in political competition.

### Honduras and Tunisia: Two very small countries

Honduras and Tunisia are the two smallest countries in the Group of Twenty-five. For the large countries, interaction with globalisation is a two-way process. They influence the process of globalisation, just as globalisation influences them. For the small countries, the causality runs entirely one way. Outcomes in these countries are largely determined by the tides of global political and economic developments that reach their shores.

In some ways Honduras and Tunisia are very similar. Both have small populations of less than fifteen million. Both are growing at very modest rates of just over 2 percent, and both have fairly high life expectancy of over seventy-three and seventy-four years, respectively (Table 14.1). Their economic structures are also very similar, with services accounting for around 60 percent of GDP, and agriculture for around 10 percent only, with mining, manufacturing, utilities and construction accounting for the balance (Table 14.2). However, per capita income in Tunisia at $4,421 in 2014 was almost double that of $2,435 in Honduras. This difference in standards of living is attributable to their different histories and their present location in the global geo-political economic system.

Honduras was 'discovered' and colonised by Spain at the beginning of the 16th century like much of Latin America. It remained a part of the Spanish colonial system of surplus extraction till the early 19th century, when it declared independence with the ebbing of Spanish power, first as part of a Central American federation, then on its own. Like the rest of the region, it was increasingly drawn into the US sphere of influence, formalised in its occupation by US marines in 1900. It has remained a part of the US backyard since then, with bases in the country for the US war on drugs. Occasionally, there have been tensions with neighbours. But it is a member of the Organisation of American States, and in 2006 joined the US-led North American Free Trade Agreement. One of the poorest countries in the region, it exports bananas, coffee and other agricultural products, sea food, beef and some gold and other minerals. However, the major businesses are largely owned by US companies such as United Fruit Company and Standard Fruit Company, and the economy is heavily dependent on foreign aid. Honduras is literally a classic case of what is sometimes described as a 'banana republic', characterised by exclusive economic and political institutions.

*Table 14.2* Structure of production in the next twenty-five emerging economies, 2014

| Country name | Agriculture, hunting, forestry, fishing (ISIC A-B) (percent of GDP) | Mining, manufacturing, utilities (ISIC C-E) (percent of GDP) | of which: Manufacturing (ISIC D) (percent of GDP) | Construction (ISIC F) (percent of GDP) | Services (ISIC G-P) (percent of GDP) | Exports of goods and services (percent of GDP) | Imports of goods and services (percent of GDP) | Net exports of goods and services (percent of GDP) |
|---|---|---|---|---|---|---|---|---|
| (0) | (1) | (2) | (2.a) | (3) | (4) | (5) | (6) | (7) = (5)–(6) |
| World | | | | | | 29.7 | 29.49 | 0.22 |
| **Very large countries** | | | | | | | | |
| China | 9.39 | 35.58 | 28.08 | 6.99 | 47.30 | 22.6 | 18.92 | 3.70 |
| India | 15.66 | 20.24 | 15.82 | 7.40 | 48.79 | 23.2 | 25.51 | -2.33 |
| **Very small countries*** | | | | | | | | |
| Tunisia | 9.01 | 23.48 | 15.47 | 4.57 | 59.36 | 44.6 | 55.38 | -10.75 |
| Honduras | 12.69 | 18.99 | 17.03 | 5.27 | 60.73 | 46.9 | 65.74 | -18.87 |
| **Asia** | | | | | | | | |
| Korea, Rep. | 2.14 | 30.36 | 27.62 | 4.51 | 54.19 | 50.6 | 45.31 | 5.34 |
| Malaysia | 9.06 | 36.16 | 23.95 | 4.37 | 49.29 | 73.8 | 64.61 | 9.24 |
| Turkey | 7.13 | 19.56 | 15.83 | 4.56 | 57.72 | 27.7 | 32.18 | -4.45 |
| Thailand | 10.48 | 34.29 | 27.72 | 2.55 | 52.67 | 69.2 | 62.59 | 6.60 |
| Iran, Islamic Rep. | 7.54 | 33.46 | 11.68 | 8.89 | 51.82 | 24.2 | 18.89 | 5.27 |
| Indonesia | 13.38 | 31.99 | 21.02 | 9.88 | 42.25 | 23.7 | 24.48 | -0.75 |
| Philippines | 11.32 | 24.79 | 20.52 | 6.44 | 57.51 | 28.7 | 32.39 | -3.73 |
| Vietnam | 18.12 | 33.17 | 17.46 | 5.33 | 43.38 | 86.4 | 83.13 | 3.28 |
| Bangladesh | 15.35 | 19.55 | 16.61 | 6.76 | 53.64 | 19.0 | 25.52 | -6.53 |

| | (1) | (2) | (2.a) | (3) | (4) | (5) | (6) | |
|---|---|---|---|---|---|---|---|---|
| **Africa** | | | | | | | | |
| South Africa | 2.23 | 22.77 | 11.91 | 3.66 | 61.02 | 31.3 | 33.11 | −1.86 |
| Egypt, Arab Rep. | 13.85 | 33.76 | 15.72 | 4.45 | 43.58 | 14.4 | 22.98 | −8.54 |
| Nigeria | 19.99 | 21.11 | 9.64 | 3.54 | 54.15 | 18.4 | 12.54 | 5.90 |
| Kenya | 27.33 | 12.63 | 10.03 | 4.85 | 47.96 | 16.4 | 33.88 | −17.48 |
| Tanzania | 28.91 | 10.50 | 5.60 | 12.46 | 41.04 | 19.5 | 29.89 | −10.41 |
| **Latin America** | | | | | | | | |
| Chile | 3.05 | 24.84 | 11.29 | 7.26 | 56.21 | 33.8 | 32.29 | 1.48 |
| Venezuela, RB** | 4.98 | 38.18 | 12.57 | 8.00 | 43.87 | 24.8 | 29.51 | −4.75 |
| Argentina | 6.91 | 19.22 | 12.26 | 5.06 | 53.07 | 14.8 | 14.49 | 0.29 |
| Brazil | 4.75 | 14.80 | 9.33 | 5.21 | 60.71 | 11.2 | 33.46 | −1.07 |
| Mexico | 3.13 | 28.55 | 16.74 | 7.14 | 55.94 | 32.4 | 13.92 | −2.73 |
| Colombia | 5.76 | 23.69 | 11.24 | 9.38 | 51.66 | 16.0 | 21.44 | −5.40 |
| Ecuador | 8.72 | 26.23 | 13.83 | 11.13 | 49.47 | 28.6 | 30.11 | −1.54 |

Source: Column (1), (2), (2.a), (3), (4) are from UN STAT database

(weblink: http://unstats.un.org/unsd/snaama/dnllist.asp) and Col. (5) & (6) from World Development Indicators (weblink: http://data.worldbank.org/indicator), retrieved on 02–06–2016

* Countries with less than fifteen million population.
** Export and Import data in Venezuela, RB are for 2013.

292  *Sudipto Mundle*

Tunisia's antecedents are very different. Originally settled by the Phoenicians in the 12th century BCE, it had an ancient civilisation and its city state of Carthage once dominated the entire western Mediterranean region. Present-day Tunisia was integrated into the Ottoman Empire in the 16th century, then occupied by France in the 19th century. It remained a French protectorate till 1956, when it became an independent republic. However, the first free and fair election in fifty years was held only in 2011. Before that Tunisia was ruled by two strong men. Bourguiba ruled till 1987, then Ben Ali till 2011, allegedly through repeated re-election in rigged elections.

While their monopoly of power and corruption provoked angry opposition, the continuity and stability also enabled Tunisia to develop a diversified economy, with strong trade links to countries in Europe. Rain fed agriculture supports 50 percent of the work force but contributes only 10 percent of GDP. Services, especially tourism, oil and gas, mining of phosphates and other minerals and light manufactures account for the rest. Oil, minerals, chemicals, textiles, olive oil and other agricultural produce are the major exports; France, Italy, Spain, Germany and Libya are the major trading partners. The 2011 elections were a turning point, with a moderate Islamic party coming to power, heading a centre-left ruling coalition; Sunni Muslims account for the bulk of the population. Rising Islamic fundamentalism remains a major threat, with sometimes tourists being targeted to damage the economy. But while Islam is recognised as the national religion, the ruling coalition and the new constitution adopted in 2014 are secular and progressive.

To summarise, Tunisia's institutions have long antecedents and are by and large inclusive and progressive, though facing serious risks from religious fundamentalists. If that threat can be managed, Tunisia could cross a threshold of, say, US$10,000 at current prices and approach the present living standards of Turkey or Malaysia by the middle of this century. In contrast Honduras, which is still locked into an exclusive and extractive institutional nexus, may reach a threshold of say US$5,000 at current prices, more or less comparable to the average standard of living in Thailand today.

### Comparing Asia, Africa and Latin America

Figure 14.1 presents a scatter diagram plotting the recent average growth rates of the 'Next Twenty-five' group of countries against their per capita incomes. There is a distinct inverse relationship between per capita income and growth, as shown by the fitted regression line. It is

*Beyond* Catch Up 293

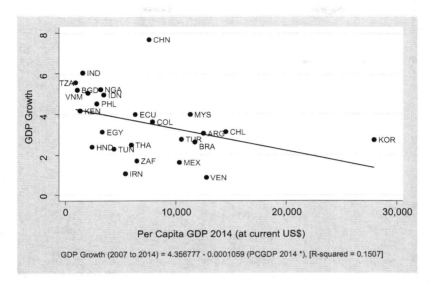

*Figure 14.1* GDP growth 2007 to 2014 and per capita GDP 2014

Source: World Development Indicators (weblink: http://data.worldbank.org/indicator), retrieved on 02-06-2016

Note: * Implies statistical significance at 10 percent level.

Country Code: ARG-Argentina, BGD-Bangladesh, BRA-Brazil, CHL-Chile, CHN-China, COL-Colombia, ECU-Ecuador, EGY-Egypt, Arab Rep., HND-Honduras, IND-India, IDN-Indonesia, IRN-Iran, Islamic Rep., KEN-Kenya, KOR-Korea, Rep., MYS-Malaysia, MEX-Mexico, NGA-Nigeria, PHL-Philippines, ZAF-South Africa, TZA-Tanzania, THA-Thailand, TUN-Tunisia, TUR-Turkey, VEN-Venezuela RB, VNM-Vietnam

tempting to interpret this as an illustration of the Pritchett-Summers hypothesis of regression to mean. However, that would be misleading since none of the countries in the group barring South Korea have reached advanced country (OECD) levels of per capita income. What the figure shows, along with Table 14.1, is a bunching of most Asian and African countries, including those with relatively high growth rates of around 4 percent to 5 percent, at low per capita income levels of between $2,000 and $6,000. In contrast the Latin American countries are bunched at a higher per capita income range of around $10,000 to $15,000 along with lower rates of growth. In other words, we have high growth in several low per capita income countries of Asia and Africa and low growth in the middle income countries of Latin America – the middle income trap.

## 294  *Sudipto Mundle*

### Asia

The end of the colonial era around the middle of the 20th century was a critical juncture in most Asian countries. New institutional arrangements emerged in these newly independent countries ruled by new national governments. Like China and India discussed earlier, most Asian countries moved to a path of high economic growth. The exceptions to this pattern are South Korea, Turkey, Thailand and Iran (Table 14.1). South Korea is now an advanced country, a member of the OECD group. After three decades of very high growth, the Pritchett-Summers process of regression to mean has kicked in. Turkey, with per capita income of over $10,000 and aspiring to join the European Union, has been impacted for decades by conflicts in the Middle East. The same applies to Iran, which was under US-led sanctions for many years. Both countries are yet to emerge from this abnormal period of economic growth. The case of Thailand is interesting and is discussed further later.

Setting aside the outliers, the hallmark of the Asian development path of the late 20th century, particularly in East and Southeast Asia, was high growth combined with inclusion, as highlighted in the World Bank's widely cited report on the East Asian Miracle (World Bank 1993). Country-specific variations apart, the core institutional model was the same as that seen earlier in the case of China, namely, inclusive economic institutions combined with exclusive but progressive, growth-oriented, political institutions. These political institutions were either authoritarian dictatorships, as in East Asian countries like South Korea and Taiwan or communist countries like Vietnam and China, where political power was monopolised by a monolithic communist party.

In this institutional model the fruits of growth were widely shared through strong emphasis on human development, basic education and health care, along with infrastructure. Sometimes these human development programmes were combined with egalitarian land reforms or programmes of income transfer to poor households. As explained in the context of China, the focus on basic education and health were not only ends in themselves but also laid the foundation for a skilled but low-cost industrial workforce that became the competitive backbone of east Asia's rapid export-led growth once the forces of market competition and open trade regimes were allowed to work. On the question of market forces, the authoritarian regimes essentially followed a pragmatic approach. While the market mechanism was increasingly relied on, the regimes did not hesitate to pursue a 'picking winners'

Beyond Catch Up    295

type industrial policy and other support mechanisms if they helped to push manufacturing growth. Among the two socialist Asian countries, market-oriented reforms were initiated in China from 1979, and in Vietnam the *Doi Moi* liberalisation programme started ten years later in 1989.

The main challenge in this institutional model, as we saw in the case of China, is the mismatch between inclusive economic institutions and extractive political institutions. In some cases, as in South Korea, the authoritarian regime itself initiated the transition to more inclusive political institutions as rising incomes and the emergence of an articulate, self-conscious, middle-class generated political demands for such reform. Malaysia, where per capita income has crossed $11,000 and growth remains high, will most likely reach advanced country standards by the middle of the century and will need to follow South Korea in making its political institutions more inclusive. In other cases, like Vietnam, political power has remained the exclusive domain of the Communist Party (Fforde and De Vylder 1996). Thailand is a case where demands for political liberalisation, arising in the wake of rising incomes and the emergence of the middle class, have been suppressed by successive military dictatorships. This has disrupted the growth model and a secular slowdown of growth has followed (Phongpaichit and Baker 1997).

Looking to the future, those countries which successfully introduce inclusive political institutions better aligned with their inclusive economic institutions are likely to sustain or raise their rates of growth. By the middle of the 21st century, they will have doubled or even tripled their per capita incomes. In those countries which fail to make this alignment between inclusive economic and political institutions, growth will decelerate, eventually leading to rising tensions and political strife.

### Africa

The Asian paradigm outlined previously is a useful benchmark for assessing the prospects of countries from Africa and Latin America in the Next Twenty-five group. For the countries in Africa, the basic institutional model is one of exclusive-extractive economic institutions, usually combined with similarly exclusive-extractive political institutions. There are of course country-specific variations around this basic model. In countries where the variations are towards more inclusion, their future prospects are also more optimistic. In countries

## 296 Sudipto Mundle

where the variations are more deeply extractive, future prospects will remain gloomy. Some remarks relating to specific countries follow.

Nigeria is the largest, most populous economy in Africa, with a GDP of around \$570 billion and a population of over 177 million persons. Its average growth of over 5 percent per year is entirely due to Nigeria's large reserves of oil, which accounts for virtually all its export incomes and also the revenues of the government. However, oil is also the biggest curse for its people, who remain desperately poor with 75 percent of them surviving on subsistence agriculture. It is telling that the expectancy of life in Nigeria, at less than fifty-three years, is the lowest among all the countries in the Group of Twenty-five. Nigeria's political and economic institutions are deeply extractive, with a narrow self-serving elite focused on extracting all the profits flowing from oil. As a consequence, it is almost a failed state, collapsing under the onslaught of rebels in the Niger delta and the ruthless Boko Haram Islamic fundamentalists. The latter started out in the North, but now seem to be spreading throughout the country. Nigeria's prospects for the future are quite bleak.

South Africa, the second largest economy in Africa, is generally seen as the most promising among all the countries of Africa. Under Dutch and later British colonial rule since the 17th century, South Africa remained an agricultural economy till the discovery of diamonds and gold at the beginning of the 19th century. It then soon became one of the world's largest producers of these precious products. During the 20th century the country diversified into manufacturing, then services, which now accounts for over 60 percent of GDP. Both before and after the discovery of precious minerals, the white immigrant ruling elite practiced a ruthless 'apartheid' system of racial segregation to exploit the indigenous population.

Politically and formally apartheid was finally abolished with a peaceful transition to democracy, as Nelson Mandela became President in 1994. Despite this transition to a more inclusive political system, South Africa has regressed under Mandela's successors, and the old exclusive-extractive economic institutions have survived. The white minority population still controls much of South Africa's mines and industries, while indigenous black workers make up 75 percent of the workforce. They are badly paid and working conditions remain very poor. Not surprisingly, though per capita income in South Africa is the highest among the African countries at about \$6,500, life expectancy is the second lowest after Nigeria at 57.2 years. The future prospects of the country depend largely on whether or not it experiences a critical juncture that replaces the present extractive economic institutions by those that are more inclusive.

Egypt is the third largest economy in Africa, and the second highest in per capita income. It embarked on a state-led, self-reliant path of industrialisation in the early 1950s. Though a third of the workforce is still dependent on agriculture, Egypt has a well-diversified industrial base of mining, manufacturing and construction that accounts for about 40 percent of its GDP, with another 44 percent coming from services (Table 14.2). Market-oriented reforms were introduced in 1990s, when the weaknesses of the earlier model surfaced. But Egypt continues to grow at a modest pace of around 3 percent.

This is presumably because Egypt's institutions are authoritarian and exclusive, varying from progressive to extractive at different points of time. Egypt has remained under authoritarian military rule for over sixty years, despite the brief flowering of the pro-democracy movement in Tahrir Square in 2011. Its resources and attention are diverted towards combating the rise of Islamic fundamentalism and the continuing tensions of the Middle East. Absent any major political development that shifts the country to a more inclusive, non-authoritarian system, Egypt can be expected to continue along its modest growth path.

The two neighbouring countries of Tanzania and Kenya in East Africa are both largely agrarian, with much of the population surviving on subsistence agriculture and animal husbandry. Some mining and light industries in agro-processing and consumer goods have also developed. The two were under German and British colonial control in different periods since the 19th century, though Kenya had been originally colonised by Portugal in the 16th century. Both became independent in the 1960s. However, while Tanzania enjoyed two decades of stable rule under Julius Nyerere, who also established inclusive economic institutions, Kenya struggled under turbulent, and often corrupt, civilian rule. As a consequence, its institutions are neither strong nor inclusive. Future prospects depend on how effectively the two countries can promote capitalist development based on inclusive institutions (Sender and Smith 1986). Both countries are growing at 4 to 5 percent per year at present. However, given its stronger institutional legacy, Tanzania has the better prospect of doubling or tripling its per capita income by the middle of the 21st century.

### Latin America

In Latin America also, as in Africa, the specific conditions of individual countries can be described as variations around a core model of extractive economic institutions, often reinforced by extractive

## 298 Sudipto Mundle

political institutions, that is common to all the countries. This institutional model also explains why these countries found it difficult to keep growing beyond middle-income levels to catch up with the levels of income in the advanced countries.

The Latin American countries were colonised during the 16th century, mostly by Spain. The exception was Brazil, the largest country (accounting for half the South American continent), which was colonised by Portugal. Extractive economic institutions, reinforced by similar political institutions, were employed to extract vast surpluses in gold and other precious metals, agriculture and livestock over the next 300 years (Gunder Frank 1970; Furtado 1976; Acemoglu and Robinson 2012). This colonial system of surplus extraction ended with the Napoleonic wars and the decline of the Iberian powers early in the 19th century. Following political independence, power shifted to elected rulers who sometimes replaced self-appointed local monarchs. However, the elected rulers were frequently overthrown by authoritarian military dictatorships on grounds of corruption or misrule. Sometimes they themselves became quite authoritarian, for example, Peron in Argentina.

In the economic sphere there followed a whole century of development as these countries became integrated into the new globalised economic system that evolved following the industrial revolution in Britain. In the new international division of labour, the Latin American countries became exporters of raw materials in exchange for manufactures from the metropolitan hubs of world capitalism, first Britain and later the USA, which also controlled the global financial and transportation systems (Furtado 1976).

Different Latin American countries were integrated in different ways into the global system. Some became specialised as suppliers of meat and other temperate climate agricultural products, others specialised in the supply of tropical agricultural products, yet other countries specialised in the supply of mineral products (Furtado 1976). Each country therefore became heavily dependent on the vagaries of international trade in its commodity of specialisation. These variations notwithstanding, the economic institutions in all the countries came to be characterised by a two-tier structure of extraction. Internally surplus is extracted by a narrow elite: The owners of the latifundia (huge landholdings of thousands of hectares), the mine owners or the urban bourgeoisie in the port cities who control the trade. However, these economies are closely controlled by foreign capital, mostly US corporations that extract a large share of the surplus externally. Sometimes the same multinational corporation owns the land, plantations or mines and also controls trade.

*Beyond* Catch Up   299

Despite the establishment of this centre-periphery structure of surplus extraction, the half century or so since the late 19th century was also the period of rising Latin American prosperity. Incomes rose steadily in the periphery, with correlated advancement in education, health and other social indicators. The middle-income status of these countries evident today is largely attributable to this long period of stable growth (Furtado 1976). The system was broken by the two world wars, and more importantly the great depression of 1929, when the global demand for the particular products in which these countries had narrowly specialised collapsed. With their global links disrupted, the countries of Latin America moved towards a path of import substitution–based industrialisation, often led by the state. However, inadequacy of the home market undermined those efforts, bringing down their pace of growth.

The failure of import substitution strategies to revive growth underlined the importance of inclusive economic institutions and shared prosperity for a home market–based model of growth. However, the abortive attempts at import substitution did succeed in creating a diversified industrial base in several of these countries. During the past half century or so, these Latin American countries have been attempting to reintegrate with the global economy, drawing on the strength of this diversified industrial base in addition to their traditional comparative advantage in primary products. This has been challenging since the global economy has become a moving target, itself getting restructured. Also, high wages in these middle income Latin American countries have made them uncompetitive vis-à-vis their Asian competitors in many industries and services. Apart from these general remarks about the Latin American experience, a few observations about some specific countries are in order to give a more nuanced picture of that experience.

The case of Brazil is especially interesting because it is not only the largest but also the most representative of the Latin American pattern of growth. Initially integrated into the centre-periphery structure based on exports of coffee from its southern estates, Brazil led the switch to an import substitution–based growth strategy when export led growth collapsed in the early 20th century. The new strategy was driven by the state, which had set up a modern steel industry during World War II, and followed up with a major infrastructure development program in the 1950s. The establishment of Petrobras, following the discovery of oil, gave a spurt to this industrially diversified growth effort. However, in the absence of inclusive economic institutions, the effort soon ran out of steam. This was mainly due to inadequacy of

## 300 *Sudipto Mundle*

domestic demand, a consequence of poor wages and low purchasing power of the working class in a labour surplus economy according to Furtado (1976). Brazil came to be seen as the classic case of a failed model of growth based on the consumption of the rich.

Following a succession of military coups since the mid-sixties, civilian rule was re-established in Brazil with the election of Cardoso in 1985. Despite his attempts at fiscal prudence and market-oriented reforms, Brazil soon ran into a major debt crisis, requiring a massive IMF rescue package of $30 billion in 2002. Brazil's approach shifted radically towards inclusive growth with the election of Lula de Silva, Brazil's first working-class president. Lula pursued a strategy of fiscal prudence combined with pro-poor policies, a large increase in minimum wages and the famous Bolsa Familia conditional cash transfer program that lifted a fifth of Brazil's population out of poverty. Though he was highly popular, constitutional limits required Lula to hand over power after two terms to his trusted chief of staff Dilma Rouseff. She was impeached for a corruption scam in Petrobas in early 2016 and had to resign. Now Lula himself is being charged. While resigning, Rouseff stated that her removal was in fact a *coup d'etat*.

Argentina is interesting because, unlike Brazil and much of Latin America, it is (along with Uruguay) a case of growth under conditions of labour scarcity. Like Australia and New Zealand, it was integrated into the 19th-century global economy as the supplier of temperate agricultural products, grain and meat. It had vast, open grazing lands in the Pampas, but little labour. Hence, production and exports were heavily dependent on high wage immigrants from Europe. Though some industries have developed in agro-processing and consumer goods, Argentina remains one of the world's main exporters of meat and grain. It is the classic example of the Latin American *Latifundia* agrarian system. The estate owners and the trading bourgeoisie constitute the narrow elite which has continued to dominate Argentina, mostly through a succession of ruthless dictatorships, whether civilian or military. The country is yet to make a transition to more inclusive economic and political institutions.

While all countries in Latin America are strongly influenced by US economic and political interests, the Mexican case is particularly interesting because of its close proximity to the USA. It demonstrates both the disadvantages as well as advantages of that proximity.

The home of the ancient Mayan and Aztec civilizations, Mexico once included the US states of California, Texas, Nevada, Utah and large parts of Arizona, New Mexico, Wyoming and Colorado. Following the collapse of the Spanish empire, these territories were ceded

*Beyond* Catch Up    301

to the USA either in war or through treaties, for example, the Treaty of Guadalope Hidalgo (1848). There have been contentious issues between the USA and Mexico, as also other Latin American countries, over the control of oil. While foreign capital is now barred from this sector, US corporates remain a dominant force in other sectors of the Mexican economy and can influence policy to serve their interests. Mexico is also, unfortunately, a source and transit route for drugs flowing into the USA, and has suffered for decades on that account.

On the positive side, Mexico has also benefitted from the large inflow of US capital and technology, and free access to its vast market as a member of NAFTA since 1994. There is large-scale migration of labour from Mexico, a labour surplus country, to the USA. Also, when fiscal profligacy has led Mexico to debt crises, as for instance after the collapse of oil prices in 1986 and again in 1995, the USA provided massive assistance, either bilaterally or through multilaterals like the IMF, World Bank and Inter-American Development Bank.

Venezuela is an interesting case as a small country with massive deposits of a valuable resource. It has one of the world's largest known deposits of oil. However, it also reveals the fragility of a country dependent on the export of a single commodity. Mostly ruled by military strongmen or corrupt civilians following the end of colonial rule, Venezuela experienced a critical juncture with the election of Hugo Chavez in 1998. A popular leftist leader, Chavez attempted to pull Venezuela out of US domination and initiated inclusive policies as Lula had done in Brazil. However, his efforts were fiscally profligate, mainly predicated on revenues from oil, and could not be sustained following the collapse of oil prices. Now his authoritarian successor Maduro has destroyed the inclusive economic and political institutions Chavez had nurtured, thereby plunging Venezuela into a chaotic abyss.

Finally, there is Chile, which is perhaps the only Latin American country that has enjoyed the benefits of relatively inclusive economic institutions. Chile's record was sullied by the military coup and murder of Allende in 1973, followed by fifteen years of brutal dictatorship under Pinochet. However, Chile has actually had a long democratic tradition going back to the end of colonial rule in 1833. Chile was integrated into the global economy based on the supply of copper, and it was the struggle over control of this raw material that brought down the Allende government (Furtado 1976). Nevertheless, successive elected governments had nudged Chile towards diversified industrialisation from the early 20th century, with a consequent dampened effect of copper export shocks. These governments also invested in

302　*Sudipto Mundle*

education and health, rather like the states in East Asia. As a consequence Chile has the highest per capita income among all the middle-income countries of Latin America at around $15,000, and the highest life expectancy at over eighty-one years (Table 14.1). Among the group of Next Twenty-five, Chile has a per capita income and life expectancy that is second only to South Korea, which is already a developed country. There is a high probability that by the middle of the 21st century, Chile too will have become a developed country.

## Conclusions

This chapter has tried to speculate about the future prospects of the Group of Twenty-five countries that Nayyar had identified in *Catch Up* as having the potential to achieve developed country living standards. The speculation has been based on a theory of economic history which attributes causal primacy to economic and political institutions. The chapter has also addressed the question of why the catch up process clearly visible in many countries of Asia is not much in evidence in Africa and Latin America. It turns out that sustained high growth in Asia is being driven by the existence of inclusive economic institutions. By the same token, the absence of 'catch up' in most countries of Africa and Latin America is attributable to the prevalence of exclusive-extractive economic institutions, usually combined with similar political institutions. The chapter suggests that inclusive economic institutions can co-exist with exclusive political institutions during the period of catch up. However, in the long run, the latter will have to be reformed as rising prosperity and the emergence of a middle class raises the demand for inclusive political institutions.

## Notes

1 The list is adopted from Nayyar (2013) without further scrutiny of why certain countries were included in the list and not some others. It includes, for instance, South Korea, which is already a developed country. On the other hand it excludes all former CIS countries, some of which could reach developed country status by the middle of this century.
2 'Surplus' was defined as the residual of production over and above the share going as consumption necessary for subsistence of the actual producers, for example, slaves in a slave society, serfs in feudal societies or wage labourers in a capitalist system of production. These producers would by definition also be the producers of the surplus. The slave owners, feudal lords or capitalist employers would be the surplus appropriators.
3 For an alternative typology, see Senghaas (1985).
4 Sen (1999) page 5.

## Beyond Catch Up    303

5 Those who make much of India's growth rate slightly exceeding that of China during the past two years should remember that a 1 percent growth in China adds as much volume of additional output in absolute terms as 5 percent growth in India.
6 Comparisons that suggest inequality in China is higher and rising faster than in India can be quite misleading (Mundle 2015b). After factoring in differences in levels of education and health and asset distribution, including egalitarian land reforms in China, Bardhan (2015) concludes that inequality is higher in India compared to China. See also Acharya and Mehrotra (2017).
7 For a comparative assessment of human development in China and India, see Sen (1999) and Bardhan (2011) among others. On the elitist bias of India's education policy, see Mundle (2016b). For recent discussions of the adverse impact of poor human development in India on manufacturing growth and employment, see Institute of Human Development (2016); Acharya (2016); and Ninan (2015).
8 For detailed discussions of each of these three constraints, see Bardhan (2011, 2015) and Ninan (2015).
9 For a recent paper contrasting the experiences of selected countries in East Asia and South Asia from a similar perspective, see Acharya and Mehrotra (2017).

## Bibliography

Acemoglu, D. and J.A. Robinson (2012), *Why Nations Fail*, Crown Publishers, USA.

Acharya, S. (2016), Why India Won't Grow at 8% Plus, *Business Standard*, 8 June, 2016.

Acharya, S. and S. Mehrotra (2017), Planning for Human Development: Lessons from the Asian Experience, *Indian Journal of Human Development (forthcoming)*.

Bardhan, P. (2011), *Awakening Giants, Feet of Clay: Assessing the Economic Rise of China and India*, Princeton University Press, NJ.

Bardhan, P. (2015), *Globalisation, Democracy and Corruption*, Front Page, London and Kolkata.

Braudel, F. (1973), *Capitalism and Material Life 1400–1800*, Harper and Row, New York.

Chenery, H.B. (1969), *The Process of Industrialisation*, Economic Development Report no. 146., Project for Quantitative Research in Economic Development, Center for International Affairs, Harvard University, Cambridge, MA.

Clark, C. (1940), *The Conditions of Economic Progress*, Macmillan, London.

Fforde, A. and S. de Vylder (1996), *From Plan to Market: The Economic Transition of Vietnam*, Westview Press, Boulder.

Furtado, C. (1976), *Economic Development of Latin America*, 2nd Edition, Cambridge University Press, Cambridge, UK.

Gunder Frank, A. (1970), *Capitalism and Underdevelopment in Latin America*, Penguin Books, Hammondsworth, UK.

## 304  *Sudipto Mundle*

Hicks, J. (1969), *A Theory of Economic History*, Oxford University Press, London.

Institute of Human Development (2016), *India Employment Report: India's Employment Challenge and the Imperatives of Manufacturing Led Growth*, Oxford University Press, New Delhi.

Joshi, V. (2016), *India's Long Road: The Search for Prosperity*, Penguin Books, London.

Kuznets, S. (1966), *Modern Economic Growth: Rate, Structure and Spread*, Yale University Press, New Haven.

Mody, A. (2015), When Crisis Comes Home, *Indian Express*, 27 August, 2015.

Mundle, S. (1985), The Agrarian Barrier to Industrial Growth, *Journal of Development Studies*, vol. 22 No. 1, pp. 49–80.

Mundle, S. (2015a), The Tortoise and the Hare, *Mint*, 18 September, 2015.

Mundle, S. (2015b), Inequality and Growth, *Mint*, 23 October, 2015.

Mundle, S. (2016a), Reflections on a Short Passage Through China, *Mint*, 15 July, 2016.

Mundle, S. (2016b), Employment, Education and the State, Radha Kamal memorial lecture delivered at the 58th Annual Conference of the Indian Society of Labour Economics, Guwahati, 24 November, 2016.

Nayyar, D. (2013), *Catch Up*, Oxford University Press, Oxford.

Ninan, T.N. (2015), *The Turn of the Tortoise: The Challenges and Promises of India's Future*, Penguin Books, London.

Phongpaichit, P. and C. Baker (1997), *Thailand: Economy and Politics*, Oxford University Press, Oxford.

Pritchett, L. and L. Summers (2013), *Asiaphoria Meets Regression to Mean*, National Bureau of Economic Research Working Paper no. 20573.

Sen, A. (1999), *Development as Freedom*, Oxford University Press, Oxford.

Sender, J. and S. Smith (1986), *The Development of Capitalism in Africa*, Methuen and Co., London.

Senghaas, D. (1985), *The European Experience: A Historical Critique of Development Theory*, Berg Pub Ltd.

Silver, N. (2012), *The Signal and the Noise: The Art and Science of Prediction*, Penguin Books, London.

Silverstein, M.J., A. Singhi, C. Liao and D. Michael (2012), *The $10 Trillion Prize: Captivating the Newly Affluent in China and India*, Harvard Business Review Press, Boston.

Subramanian, A. (2011), *Eclipse: Living in the Shadow of China's Economic Dominance*, Peter G. Peterson Institute, Washington.

Tolnai, G. (1960), *The Growth of Big Industry and Domestic Market in the Third World*, Akademiai Kiado, Budapest.

World Bank (1993), *The East Asian Miracle: Economic Growth and Public Policy*, Oxford University Press, Oxford.

# 15 Latin America's development record and challenges in historical perspective

*José Antonio Ocampo*[*]

Deepak Nayyar's *Catch Up* (2013) is an outstanding account of the participation of developing countries in the world economy, focusing on the post–Second World War period, but going back to the historical precedents, and notably to the "Great Divergence" of these countries from the developing world, that took place in the nineteenth and first half of the twentieth centuries. This chapter follows that tradition and concentrates on Latin America.

This region has many peculiarities within the broader economic history of the developing world. First of all, it is the part that was most deeply transformed by colonization (together with the Caribbean), and also the first to become politically independent on a broad scale as a result of the Napoleonic wars, particularly Napoleon's invasion of the Iberian Peninsula in 1808. This was possibly one of the factors for a second difference with other developing regions. As Nayyar recognizes in his book (Nayyar, 2013, chapter 2), Latin America was a partial exception to the "Great Divergence", and indeed a relative success story during the "first globalization"[1] and the interwar period of the twentieth century, when the region became (together with Central and Eastern Europe and parts of the Middle East) a sort of "middle class of the world". Third, it is the most unequal region of the world. I should add that it is a region highly dependent on commodities, a feature that it shares, however, with several other developing regions.

---

[*] This chapter is prepared for my friend Deepak Nayyar's festschrift. It borrows from a statement delivered on the occasion of the 50th anniversary of the Latin American and Caribbean Institute for Economic and Social Planning, ILPES (Ocampo, 2013), and my joint economic history of Latin America written with Luis Bértola (Bértola and Ocampo, 2012). The literature on the topics analyzed here is massive. Therefore, I am highly selective in the references included.

# 306 *José Antonio Ocampo*

This chapter analyzes the long-term evolution of Latin America in the global context with broad strokes. The first section analyzes the process of convergence and divergence over the past two centuries. The second takes a look at the associated social and institutional dimensions. On the basis of the historical record, the last outlines some critical issues for the future development of the region.

## Latin America's development record

The two centuries covered by this analysis can be divided into four different periods:[2] (1) the post-independence decades (1820 to 1870); (2) the commodity export-led growth period that coincided with the first globalisation (1870 to 1929); (3) the period of State-led industrialisation[3] (or "development from within", in the terminology of the United Nations Economic Commission for Latin America and the Caribbean [ECLAC]), which was bound by two major crises, one of a global character (the Great Depression of the 1930s), and another of a regional character (the debt crisis and the associated "lost decade" of the 1980s); and (4) the period of market reform, which began in the 1980s (in some countries, notably Chile, in the 1970s) and has coincided with the second globalisation. Since Latin America is a diverse region – though less so in this regard than Asia – these phases did not start or end at the same time in every country.

### *Broad trends*

Performance can be looked at from two different perspectives: the relative position of the region in the global economy, and the speed of growth during different historical periods. The first look (Table 15.1) indicates that there has been a long-term divergence of Latin America vis-à-vis developed countries in terms of GDP per capita (about 27 percentage points between 1820 and 2014), but that it was concentrated in the post-independence period (20 percentage points between 1820 and 1870) and during the "lost decade" of the 1980s (8 percentage points between 1980 and 1990). In some periods, Latin America has grown faster than the developed countries, particularly during the period of commodity export-led growth, but those positive phases have only compensated temporarily and, in a partial way, the adverse long-term trend. This was generally reinforced by periods of retrogression in Latin America and by other developments such as the post–Second World war "golden age" (1950 to 1973) in Western Europe that led to a widening gap vis-à-vis the developed world.

*Table 15.1* Relative position of Latin America in the world economy

|  | 1820 | 1870 | 1913 | 1929 | 1950 | 1973 | 1980 | 1990 | 2008 | 2014 |
|---|---|---|---|---|---|---|---|---|---|---|
| Per capita GDP vs. |  |  |  |  |  |  |  |  |  |  |
| Developed countries | 55.5% | 35.8% | 36.7% | 39.6% | 36.2% | 31.9% | 34.2% | 26.0% | 27.0% | 29.0% |
| Other developing regions | 118.4% | 128.3% | 179.1% | 224.7% | 223.5% | 215.6% | 229.5% | 186.9% | 145.3% | 128.2% |
| World average | 101.8% | 87.8% | 100.1% | 116.0% | 115.8% | 109.0% | 120.6% | 98.4% | 93.5% | 96.5% |
| Share in world GDP | 1.9% | 2.6% | 4.2% | 5.2% | 7.2% | 8.2% | 9.5% | 8.0% | 7.8% | 8.0% |

Source: Bértola and Ocampo (2012). Original data, except for Latin America, from Angus Maddison. 2014 estimates according to United Nations growth data for the period 2008–2014

## 308  José Antonio Ocampo

During the first phase (1820 to 1870), although the region lost ground relative to the developed world, it gained vis-à-vis most of the countries that make up what is considered today to be the developing world (Table 15.1).[4] The strong relative position within that group was significantly reinforced during the phase of commodity export-led growth, when the region achieved a prominent place (with GDP per capita more than twice the average of other developing regions), which it maintained during the era of State-led industrialisation. The market reform period is, therefore, the only one during which the region lost ground relative to the rest of the developing world and, in particular, to Asia.

As a result of these combined trends, Latin America's per capita GDP fell relative to the world average during the post-independence period, but gained during the commodity export-led growth phase and held its position during State-led industrialisation, with a level slightly above the world average. It fell in relative terms during the market reform era, largely due to the retrogression that took place during the lost decade.

What these trends show is that the narrower per capita GDP gap that separated Latin America from the developed world at the time of the industrial revolution is an unclear indicator of the capacity of countries to join the structural transformation that it implied. The technological capacities and institutional features were much more important, and Latin America lagged behind, particularly in the former. However, the region was successful in joining the wave of economic growth during the first globalisation and establishing a leading position within the developing world, which was maintained during the period of State-led industrialisation. The most recent development period is, therefore, the only one in which the region has experienced a relative decline. The strong loss experienced during the debt crisis of the 1980s is the major explanation of that lag, but the most important trend, the decline vis-à-vis Asia, has other determinants, notably, as we will see, in terms of the trends in industrialisation.

Looking at growth rates tells a slightly different story. It indicates in particular that Latin America made its greatest strides in economic development during the period of State-led industrialisation. This is reflected in Figure 15.1, which shows economic growth in moving averages for the decades ending in the year indicated in the graph. The annual growth rates of over 5 and 6 percent posted toward the end of State-led industrialisation had been achieved only briefly during the previous development phase, particularly during the decade before the First World War and in the 1920s. Conversely, growth rates following the economic reforms, which were implemented precisely to hasten

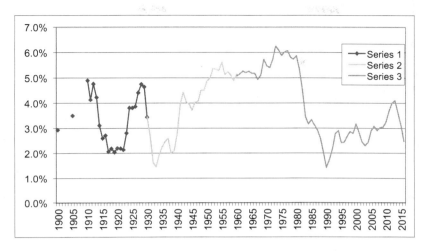

*Figure 15.1* Latin America: Moving average of decade-long growth rates

Source: Series 1 and 2 from Bértola and Ocampo (2012). Series 3 from ECLAC.

Notes: Series 1 includes Argentina, Brazil, Chile, Colombia, Cuba, Ecuador, Mexico, Peru, Uruguay, and Venezuela (the first two data points exclude Cuba and Ecuador); Series 2 includes all countries, except Bolivia, Panama, Paraguay, and the Dominican Republic; Series 3 includes all countries

economic growth, have been much lower, fluctuating generally around 3 percent per year, but temporarily reaching 4 percent in 2003–13.

A comparison between per capita and overall GDP growth shows one important feature: Per capita growth was lowered during State-led industrialisation by explosive population growth. This fact should be interpreted in a positive way, as it reflected Latin America's capacity to absorb one of the fastest population growth rates in world history, and the very rapid urbanization that accompanied it. This is also reflected in the fact that Latin America's share in world GDP, which had increased since the post-independence period, and very rapidly during the period of commodity export-led growth (when it doubled, from 2.6 percent in 1870 to 5.2 percent in 1929), continued to increase at a steady pace during State-led industrialisation, peaking at 9.5 percent in 1980. In contrast, the region has benefited in recent decades, in terms of per capita GDP, by the fall in population growth and associated "demographic dividend" (the fall in dependency rates), but this has not compensated the slower GDP growth that has characterized the market reform period.

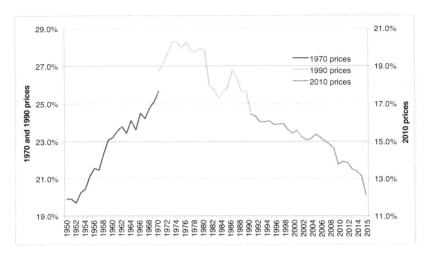

*Figure 15.2* Latin America: Share of manufacturing in GDP, 1950–2015
Source: ECLAC

It should be added that the region's population growth has exceeded that of the world over the whole two centuries, converging to the latter only recently. Population dynamics has been associated more with high fertility than with international migration, but has been supported by immigration in particular countries in some periods (Argentina and Uruguay, in particular, but also Brazil, Chile, Cuba, and Venezuela).

Overall, since the second and fourth stages discussed coincided with globalisation processes, Latin America was evidently a winner during the first globalisation but was unable to take advantage of the second. The region's export performance has been good in recent decades, as well as its capacity to attract capital; therefore, the major reason for this can be traced to the de-industrialisation that has taken place since the 1980s (Figure 15.2), which has been premature, in the sense that it has taken place at an early stage of development (Palma, 2011). This contrasts with the continuous industrialisation of one of the most successful developing country regions, notably East Asia. This confirms the findings from extensive research that shows a strong association of development success with industrialisation (see, e.g., Rodrik, 2014).

## Emerging patterns

Development was uneven within the region, particularly during the commodity-export-led growth period (1870 to 1929). By the First World War, the countries of the Southern Cone (Argentina, Chile, and Uruguay) and Cuba had increased their edge over the rest of the region. From that point on, there was a tendency toward convergence in regional development levels, partly because the leaders began to lag and partly because other countries became more successful. The latter case was true especially for the two largest countries (Brazil and Mexico), but also of a few medium-sized countries (Venezuela and Colombia) and small ones (Costa Rica, Ecuador, and Panama, in particular). Nevertheless, there were a few countries (Nicaragua and Bolivia, in particular) that were left behind. This process of regional convergence came to a halt during the lost decade of the 1980s, giving way to a growing divergence once again.[5]

The economic growth of individual countries shows another strong pattern: the tendency of Latin American countries to grow rapidly for extended periods of time during which they narrow the income gap separating them from the developed countries, but these growth spurts then also give way to lengthy periods during which this gap widens again. This process can be described as a one of "truncated convergence". Cuba is perhaps the first and most prominent example of this pattern: after having been one the world's export success stories of the nineteenth and early twentieth centuries, its per capita income flattened out almost completely from around 1915 onwards. Much the same thing occurred in the Southern Cone, which surged ahead until the First World War but then slowed down significantly. This was particularly the case in Argentina, which was one of the world's greatest development success stories during the first globalisation. Following in its footsteps was Venezuela, which was Latin America's star performer from the 1920s to the 1960s, thanks to its oil boom and its ability to spread its benefits; but this period was followed by a strong relative decline since the mid-1970s. Brazil and Mexico, the prime success stories of the period of State-led industrialisation, followed this same path since the lost decade. In the absence of "growth miracles", but also of major crises, Colombia seems to have found the key to maintaining a slower but steady development path. To a lesser extent, this is also the story of the two most successful small economies: Costa Rica and Panama.

Interruptions in growth patterns have been associated historically to major crises, most of them of external origin and in this sense a

## 312  José Antonio Ocampo

reflection of the region's external vulnerability. The impact of the debt crisis of the 1980s has already been noted and is particularly remarkable in this regard, as it generated a region-wide slowdown of economic growth, which was particularly strong in the two largest economies. The overriding vulnerability factor throughout the region's economic history has been dependency on commodities, whose prices have been highly volatile and especially so during the First World War, the Great Depression, and since the mid-1970s. This situation has been compounded by the volatility associated with the countries' pro-cyclical access to external financing, which has been at the root of some of the region's most extreme business cycles: the boom of the second half of the 1920s, which was followed by the deep downturn and the defaults of almost all Latin American countries in the 1930s; the capital inflows surge of the second half of the 1970s, which gave way to the debt crisis and lost decade of the 1980s; the surge of 1991–97, which was cut short when external financing dried up after the 1997 East Asian crisis and the 1998 Russian default, whose effects lasted for half a decade; and the boom which preceded the North Atlantic financial crisis of 2008–09,[6] which was cut short by the crisis but soon renewed with even greater intensity, but has been followed by a contraction of external financing in recent years – which, however, has so far been less intense than the previous "sudden stops" of external financing of the 1930s, 1980s, and 1998–2003.

### Some implications

One of the effects of the region's external vulnerability has been its sharply volatile economic growth during the phase of market reforms. This is clear when we compare the unstable growth rates for the period 1990–2015 with those for 1950–80 (Table 15.2). In a sense, this was a return to the volatile growth that had been typical up to the Second World War, and that was only interrupted in the three decades and a half of rapid State-led industrialisation. The recent market reform

*Table 15.2* GDP growth in Latin America: Dynamics and volatility

|  | Average growth | Standard deviation | Coefficient of variation |
| --- | --- | --- | --- |
| 1950–80 | 5.5% | 1.7% | 31.3% |
| 1990–2015 | 3.1% | 2.2% | 73.5% |

Source: Author's estimates based on ECLAC data

period has, therefore, seen not only slower but also more unstable economic growth. The greater volatility reflects not only external shocks associated with terms of trade and external financing but also the dominance of pro-cyclical macroeconomic policies (i.e. expansionary fiscal, monetary, and exchange rate policies during booms, contractionary policies during crises). Only recently have a few countries reverted to counter-cyclical fiscal policies, as, for instance, the counter-cyclical fiscal rules of Chile since 2000 and the counter-cyclical monetary policies of a few central banks during the North Atlantic financial crisis and during the succeeding recovery period. One of the outcomes of this is that although progress has been made toward achieving price stability and avoiding financial crises, less has been achieved in another major area of macroeconomic stability (one which is in fact often overlooked when the term is used): in terms of *real* macroeconomic stability (i.e. avoiding sharp business cycles).

What this discussion indicates is that the "Black Legend"[7] about State-led industrialisation that has been spread in the orthodox interpretations of Latin American development is not founded in a careful review of historical facts. This stage of development was not only one of prolonged, rapid, and stable growth, but also, as we will see in the next section, of social progress. It was even, at least since the 1960s (and before, in the case of the smaller economies), a stage of export growth and diversification, when the classic model of "development from within" gave way to a "mixed model" that characterized the last stages of State-led industrialisation, which combined import substitution with export promotion and regional integration. It would be an illusion, however, to think that the region could return today to a development pattern typical of this period, whose origins were linked to the collapse of the first globalisation more than anything else.

Part of the "Black Legend" is also the view that State-led industrialisation was a period in which Latin America lacked macroeconomic discipline. This is also largely wrong. Until the early 1970s, a tendency toward high inflation was absent except in the Southern Cone and Brazil, and most countries did not exhibit a lack of fiscal discipline until the second half of that decade, when large flows of external financing began to pour into the region. Thus, broad-based runaway inflation was only a feature of the 1980s, and in this sense more an effect than a cause of the debt crisis (Bértola and Ocampo 2012, chapters 4 and 5).

The State-led model obviously had flaws, the main one being its inability to build a solid technological base. This flaw was deeply entrenched, as it was rooted in the lag in industrial development that

# 314   *José Antonio Ocampo*

occurred during the first globalisation, cumulative lags in education (see next section), and the even greater backwardness of the region in terms of the construction of a scientific-technological base of its own. But this problem was compounded by the premature de-industrialisation that has taken place during the market reform period, and which has been associated with the slowing of the upward trend in productivity levels (a widely recognized trend) which most of the Latin American economies had experienced until the mid-1970s (see, e.g., IDB, 2010).

The adverse trends typical since the 1980s were temporarily interrupted by strong regional performance in 2003–08 and, to a lesser extent, 2008–13. The basic underlying factor was the new commodity prices boom – the "super-cycle" of commodity prices, as it has been widely called – that characterized these years, largely fed by Chinese demand, which also generated a regional export boom toward the Asian giant. Part of the additional export revenues were used to generate a strong reduction in external debt ratios in 2003–08. This allowed some countries to adopt counter-cyclical policies when faced with the North Atlantic financial crisis, and a growing number of countries to access international capital markets. The collapse of commodity prices in 2014–15 put an end to this period and it remains to be seen whether this would be compounded, as in the past, by capital flight and the increasing difficulties in accessing external finance – though, as indicated, this effect has been relatively weak so far. In any case, the commodity price collapse led first to a strong slowdown in South America and to a recession in 2015–16, which eliminated the view that faster growth in 2003–13 had finally vindicated the positive effects of market reforms.

## Social and institutional development

Social progress was slower in coming to Latin America as compared to growth. The deplorable state of education in the early twentieth century, even in countries at the forefront of the region's development drive, attests to this.

### *Broad trends*

Human development indicators began to improve slowly vis-à-vis those of industrial countries in the early twentieth century, but the most important advances were registered throughout most of the region during the era of State-led industrialisation (Figure 15.3).

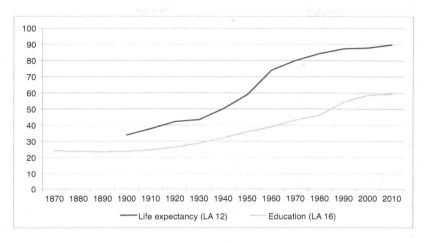

*Figure 15.3* Latin America: Human development indices vs. developed countries
Source: Table 1.9, p. 34, Bértola and Ocampo (2012)

Progress in these indicators tended to slow down during the last two decades of the century. Although some advances continued to be made in education, the gap with developed countries continued to be large, and was compounded with significant quality problems.

The few available studies on poverty reduction prior to 1980 indicate that in the twentieth century the greatest progress was also made during the period of State-led industrialisation, and particularly during the 1970s (Prados de la Escosura, 2007; Londoño and Székely, 2000). Starting in 1980, this favorable trend came to an end and indeed was followed, not by a "lost decade" but by an entire "lost quarter-century" in terms of poverty reduction, as the 1980 poverty levels were only surpassed in the early part of expansion witnessed in the 2003–13 period. This recent expansion gave way to a sharp reduction in poverty, the fastest since the 1970s, which was coupled with an improvement in income distribution in many countries and a rising middle class.[8]

The historical trends in inequality in different countries of the region are complex and highly variable, and do not follow a unique pattern. The colonial legacy of highly segmented economic and social structures continues, of course, to weigh upon the region's societies, but the impact of that legacy has been influenced by other factors that have had varying effects on different countries. The factors that had the most widespread adverse effects on distribution were the first globalisation,

## 316   *José Antonio Ocampo*

the 1980s debt crisis, and the economic liberalisation of the late twentieth century. For countries that had large labor surpluses (essentially all of them except for those of the Southern Cone), the pressure that they generated during much of the twentieth century also had negative effects on income distribution. The situation was further compounded by the adverse impact of a long list of military dictatorships.

Positive forces have also been at work, however. In the final analysis, the greatest steps forward in terms of the promotion of social equality were clearly the abolition of slavery in the nineteenth century, which was a long time in coming in some countries (Brazil and Cuba), and the lengthier process of erosion of the various forms of rural servitude which were quite prevalent even in the early twentieth century in most Latin American countries and continued to exert an influence for far longer. The urbanization process did a great deal to open up new opportunities for people who had been subject to the strict social segmentation characteristic of the region's rural areas. Advances in education, which were also a long time in coming, helped to create a more level playing field and were arguably one of the main driving forces behind the improvement in income distribution experienced in the early twenty-first century – although there was unevenness in the quality of education made available to different social groups. The massive influx of European migrants to the Southern Cone also had positive long-term distributional effects, basically because they brought with them skills, knowledge, and, especially, institutions (including trade unions) that helped to spread the benefits of development. Other countries in the region have also made institutional changes that generated greater equity, such as those brought about by the social democratic revolution in Costa Rica in the mid-twentieth century and by the socialist revolution in Cuba.

### Emerging patterns

These varying forces affecting income distribution came together in dissimilar ways in different countries, and there is not enough information to determine exactly what their net effect was, but we can discern two major cycles. The first started with a deterioration in income distribution that lasted until the start of the twentieth century or even later in economies that had extensive labor surpluses. This was followed by an improvement in distribution, which occurred earlier (starting in the 1920s) in the Southern Cone thanks to the institutional forces mentioned previously, and later on (in the 1960s or 1970s) in other countries (Colombia, Costa Rica, Mexico, and Venezuela); however, there were

*Latin America's development record* 317

some countries, such as Brazil, where such improvement failed to take place at all. The second cycle opened with another deterioration in distribution that once again began in the Southern Cone during the military dictatorships of the 1970s, but then spread across the region in the late twentieth century, reflecting the adverse distributive effects of economic adjustment during the debt crisis and the adverse distributive effects (at least initially) of market reforms. Then most Latin American countries witnessed an improvement in distribution in the first decade of the twenty-first century, a trend that has put Latin America in the spotlight as it contrasts with adverse distributive trends worldwide. The specific reasons for this improvement are still subject to debate but certainly include a reduction in wage-skill premiums, which reflect the increase in educational levels. From a long-term perspective, and although it is impossible to corroborate this assertion with hard data, Latin America's high degree of inequality in income distribution is probably worse today than it was before the region experienced its first burst of economic growth in the closing decades of the nineteenth century.

Individual countries have taken quite different paths in terms of their institutional development, understood here as the organization of the State and, more generally, society, to supply social and public goods. This is true even of countries that share a common border and that have followed similar development paths in other aspects, with the only explanatory factor being the varying political histories of different countries. One common denominator (with the partial exception of no more than a handful of countries) is that economic liberalism was not synchronized with political liberalism, which did not truly take hold until the last two decades of the twentieth century (and, even so, has recently suffered a number of setbacks). Another common denominator has been a tendency to embrace rentism in the form of a reliance either on the earnings derived from natural resources or on the gains to be derived from maintaining a "rent seeking" relationship with the State.

As for the relationship existing between the State and the market, the greatest progress in terms of the development of State-run activities was made again during the stage of State-led industrialisation. However, in many cases, the associated institutions had begun to take shape during the preceding stage of commodity-export development – in the development of state railroads and the first stages of putting in place a mass supply of social services, for example. During the industrialisation phase, the countries of the region (with the exception of Cuba and a few other nations during their short-lived experiments with socialism) developed a mixed economic model similar to that prevalent in Western Europe and were, accordingly, far less Statist than most of the developing countries

# 318 *José Antonio Ocampo*

of Asia and Africa – a fact that is often overlooked in the literature. This was also true of development planning, which generally took the form of "indicative planning", to use a French concept.

## Some implications

Economic liberalisation led to a major redefinition of the roles of the State and the market beginning in the 1970s in a few countries and in the mid-1980s in most of the rest. Nonetheless, this redefinition did allow public-sector banks and firms to survive in a majority of the countries – notably in the latter case in oil and mineral resources. More importantly, perhaps, it was associated with a significant increase in public social expenditure in all of them from 1990 onwards. In the course of this process, some State bodies (notably finance ministries and central banks) grew stronger, but others (planning agencies and those responsible for productive development policies for the industrial and agricultural sectors) were weakened or disappeared altogether. Oddly enough, the upturn in social spending was not coupled with a similar trend in investment in infrastructure during the past few decades. This has generated a sizeable backlog in infrastructure (see, e.g., CAF, 2014). In addition, the mix of de-industrialisation and inadequate attention to science and technology has generated a large lag vis-à-vis major competitors or reference groups, notably compared to East Asia and developed economies whose production structures rely on natural resources (ECLAC, 2012).

Disappointment with the results of market reforms prompted the region's policymakers to take a more positive view of the role of the State at the turn of the century. This triggered the emergence of various left-wing political movements, but this shift was also evident in countries placed at the center or even at the right of the political spectrum. As a result, Latin America began to figure at the forefront of a process of renewed State building that has come to encompass a broader range of countries around the world. Nonetheless, it is a process that has differed across countries and has clearly been flawed in some instances. One of the most glaring shortcomings has been a failure to devote more attention to productive development policies.

## Rethinking Latin America's development agenda

Given the combination of historical legacies and foreseeable international scenarios, there is a strong need to rethink Latin America's development strategies. The relevant international scenarios include

*Latin America's development record*   319

the "new normal" of slow world economic growth, even stronger slowdown of international trade and the end of the super-cycle of commodity prices. It also includes the likely impact of the slowdown in Chinese economic growth on the former processes, and the renewed uncertainties surrounding the availability of external finance to developing countries. The advances that have already been made in some areas such as macroeconomic stability, poverty reduction, and income distribution need to be consolidated and expanded upon.

*Economic policies*

In the macroeconomic sphere, the inroads already made in terms of lowering inflation, improving fiscal sustainability, and reducing debt ratios must be consolidated. But it is also clear that a great deal more remains to be done in order to reduce Latin American economies' long-standing external vulnerability and associated growth volatility. This implies, above all, building capacities and support for counter-cyclical macroeconomic policies. Some countries' responses to the 2008–09 North Atlantic financial crisis were a step forward in this regard, but the new adverse scenario of 2014–16 have unfortunately implied a return to the pro-cyclical macroeconomic policies that have prevailed in the past. This requires international support, notably actions to reduce the strong pro-cyclical patterns of capital flows toward developing economies; but it also calls for reversing the tendency to spend or even over-spend windfall revenues, as reflected in the patterns of domestic demand during the recent commodity boom (see, in this regard, IMF, 2013).

The challenges to be faced in promoting the development of the production sector are even more formidable. This area has been a problematic one for many Latin American countries during the market reform phase, especially in terms of productivity performance. The region's economic history and the more successful productive development efforts mounted by East Asian countries both indicate that high growth rates cannot be achieved simply by ensuring sound macroeconomic policies and specializing according to static comparative advantages. Proactive production sector strategies are also needed. This topic was intentionally left off the governments' agendas during the market reform phase, and no determined effort has been made to reverse this situation since then. There is need for a strategy that not only includes re-industrialisation but also development of modern services and exploitation of the opportunities for technological upgrading of the natural resources sector (see, on the latter, Pérez, 2010). At

320  *José Antonio Ocampo*

the core of this strategy should be a quantitative leap in the design of proactive technology policies, which is an area that was also largely ignored during the phase of State-led industrialisation. This effort should go hand in hand with the consolidation of the advances made in education and the elimination of the shortcomings in the education system, especially in terms of quality. It should also be accompanied by significant efforts to reduce the lags in infrastructure development, particularly road infrastructure.

Given the projections of sluggish growth in international trade, it is essential not only to boost competitiveness and improve the quality of the export basket, but also to strike a balance between the domestic and external markets. There are three options in this regard, which can be mixed in diverse ways according to national conditions. The first is to use the opportunities offered by the domestic market and, particularly, by the market generated by a rising middle class. However, a strategy focused exclusively on the domestic market will only work for Brazil and, to a much lesser extent, for some middle-sized countries. A second strategy, exploiting the opportunities to an "expanded domestic market" created by a genuine revitalization of integration processes, is a more broadly-based opportunity. However, this requires overcoming the political constraints that have been weakening and, in some cases, actually sabotaging regional integration processes. The third strategy focuses on diversifying exports in two different ways: By improving the technological content (or knowledge-intensiveness) of the export basket, and by working to expand the region's exports to fast-growing Asian economies, particularly China. These two strategic courses of action are complementary, since one of the main challenges is that of diversifying the region's exports to the Asian giant.

## Social policies

In terms of social policy, the main challenge continues to be to pay off the debt to society represented by the striking inequalities inherited from the past. The challenge here is not only to continue to improve the human development indicators and to reduce poverty, but to focus the attention on inequality as such. It should be borne in mind that, in addition to being the region with the most glaring inequalities in the world, Latin America's human development is also skewed to an enormous degree by those same high levels of inequality. This is reflected in the segmentation in the provision of education, health, and social protection, among others. It also includes the high levels of labor market informality that reflect different job opportunities but also unequal access to social protection, to the extent that the latter is tied to contributory systems to which informal workers lack access.

The work to be done in this area includes three major elements. The first is access to secondary and higher education and improving the quality of education made available to lower-income groups. The second is the development of universal social protection systems. One of the priorities in this connection is to design systems that eliminate segmentations in service delivery, notably in health services, as well as the design of systems that mix contributory and noncontributory pillars to give equal access to informal workers. The third involves a greater fiscal redistribution effort, which can be channeled through both the tax system and public spending. In this respect, it is important to realize that, although differences do exist in pretax income distribution and public expenditure, one of the chief differences in terms of income distribution vis-à-vis the OECD countries is precisely the very limited redistribution achieved via taxation.

## Conclusions

The lessons of history indicate that, in any event, social advances will not be long-lasting unless they are coupled with necessary changes in production. The key link is the creation of high-quality jobs, with quality being defined in terms of skills, job stability, and social protection coverage. This is an area in which a great deal remains to be done in view of the substantial deterioration of job quality that occurred in almost all the countries of the region between the outbreak of the debt crisis and the early years of the twenty-first century, as reflected in particular in rising labor market informality. This deterioration has been partially reversed during the 2003–13 growth period, but much remains to be done. Action in this area should be closely tied in with the effort to improve the production structure and, in order for that to happen, high-quality job creation must be one of the central objectives of a production-based development policy.

## Notes

1 Following recent historiography, I will use the term "first globalization" to refer to the period of global integration unleashed in the second half of the nineteenth century, and particularly in the last three decades, by the maritime and railroad transport revolutions, the spread of the telegraph and the very open trade polices of England and a few other countries (the Netherlands). In turn, I will use the "second globalization" to refer to the most recent process of global integration since the 1960s.

## 322 José Antonio Ocampo

2 See Bértola and Ocampo (2012) and the complementary book by Bulmer-Thomas (2014).
3 Following Cárdenas et al. (2000) and Bértola and Ocampo (2012), I prefer this term to "import substitution industrialization" because the latter captures only one – and not necessarily the most important – element of this period of development.
4 Throughout this chapter, the concept of developing countries encompasses the so-called emerging economies.
5 See the details of these different periods of divergence and convergence of different countries' levels of development in Bértola and Ocampo (2012). It should be underscored, however, that regional divergence has been more limited than that of Asia since the 1960s.
6 I use this term rather than the most common one of "global financial crisis" to underscore that, although the crisis had global effects, it was concentrated in the U.S. and Western Europe.
7 This term has been used mainly to refer to the demographic effects of the European conquest of the Americas.
8 On the evolution of poverty vis-à-vis 1980, see the successive publications of ECLAC's *Social Panorama of Latin America*. On the trends in income distribution and the rise of the middle class, see, among many studies, López-Calva and Lustig (2010) and World Bank (2013).

## Bibliography

Bértola, Luis and José Antonio Ocampo (2012), *The Economic Development of Latin America since Independence*, Oxford: Oxford University Press.
Bulmer-Thomas, Victor (2014), *The Economic History of Latin America since Independence* (3rd ed.), Cambridge: Cambridge University Press.
CAF (Development Bank of Latín America) (2014), *Infraestructura en el desarrollo de América Latina*, Caracas: CAF.
Cárdenas, Enrique, José Antonio Ocampo and Rosemary Thorp (eds.) (2000), *Industrialization and the State in Latin America: The Postwar Years*, Volume 3 of *An Economic History of Twentieth-Century Latin America*, Houndmills, Oxford: Palgrave, in association with St. Antony's College.
ECLAC (Economic Commission for Latin America and the Caribbean) (2012), *Cambio estructural para la equidad: Una visión integrada del desarrollo*, Santiago: ECLAC.
IDB (Inter-American Development Bank) (2010), *The Age of Productivity: Transforming Economies from the Bottom Up*, Washington, DC: Inter-American Development Bank.
IMF (International Monetary) (2013), *World Economic and Financial Surveys, Regional Economic Outlook, Western Hemisphere: Time to Rebuild Policy Space*, Washington, DC: IMF, May.
Londoño, Juan Luis and Miguel Székely (2000), "Persistent Poverty and Excess Inequality: Latin America, 1970–1995", *Journal of Applied Economics*, 3(1), 93–134.

López-Calva, Luis Felipe and Nora Lustig (eds.) (2010), *Declining Inequality in Latin America: A Decade of Progress*, New York; Washington, DC: Brookings Institution Press and UNDP.

Nayyar, Deepak (2013), *Catch Up: Developing Countries in the World Economy*, New York: Oxford University Press.

Ocampo, José Antonio (2013), *The History and Challenges of Latin American Development*, Statement delivered on the occasion of the 50th anniversary of the Latin American and Caribbean Institute for Economic and Social Planning (ILPES), Santiago: Economic Commission for Latin America and the Caribbean.

Palma, José Gabriel (2011), "Why Has Productivity Growth Stagnated in Latin America since the Neo-Liberal Reforms?", in José Antonio Ocampo and Jaime Ros (eds.), *The Oxford Handbook of Latin American Economics*, Oxford: Oxford University Press, chapter 23.

Pérez, Carlota (2010), "Dinamismo tecnológico e inclusión social en América Latina: Una estrategia de desarrollo productivo basada en los recursos naturales", *Revista de la CEPAL*, 100(April), 123–45.

Prados de la Escosura, Leandro (2007), "Inequality and Poverty in Latin America: A Long-Run Exploration", in Timothy J. Hatton, Kevin H. O'Rourke and Alan M. Taylor (eds.), *The New Comparative Economic History: Essays in Honor of Jeffrey G. Williamson*, Cambridge: MIT Press, chapter 12.

Rodrik, Dani (2014), "The Past, Present and Future of Economic Growth", in Franklin Allen and others, *Toward a Better Global Economy*, Oxford: Oxford University Press, chapter 2.

World Bank (2013), *Economic Mobility and the Rise of the Latin American Middle Class*, Washington, DC: World Bank.

# 16 The global financial crisis and policy challenges in EMEs

*Ananya Ghosh Dastidar* *

This chapter attempts to delineate some of the key challenges for macroeconomic policy in emerging market economies (EMEs)[1] in the wake of the global financial crisis. In particular it questions the relevance of the 'Asian model'[2] of export-led growth in the aftermath of the crisis and emphasizes the importance of fostering growth in domestic markets. It contends that, going forward, a key challenge for EMEs would be to create adequate policy space for accommodating the increasingly complex interactions between asset prices, exchange rates and capital flows and their feedbacks for the real economy. This calls for a creative yet pragmatic approach to policy making that strikes the right balance between free market forces and the regulatory role of the state especially in managing capital flows and maintaining financial stability.

The chapter is structured as follows. The impact of the crisis provides the basic context for understanding emerging challenges for policy; hence the first section briefly touches on the channels of transmission of the crisis to the EMEs and their patterns of post-crisis recovery. This is followed by a discussion on key issues related to certain systemic fragilities in EMEs that were essentially bred by the processes of globalisation and market orientation. Against this backdrop, the third section identifies priorities for policy and the final section concludes.

---

\* The author is grateful to Rajeev Malhotra and Vivek Suneja for their extremely helpful comments and suggestions on an earlier draft of this chapter and would also like to thank Shantanu Roy and other participants at the Economics Seminar Series at the Department of Policy Studies, TERI University for useful comments. The usual disclaimer applies.

## Impact of the crisis and post-crisis recovery

The following discussion essentially highlights that global integration of their economies played a crucial role in transmitting the impact of the crisis to EMEs as well as in shaping their subsequent economic trajectories, with policy being an important catalyst in the entire process.

There is a large literature on this which identifies international trade and cross-border capital flows, two fundamental facets of global integration, as key channels of transmission of the effects of the crisis.[3] In the immediate aftermath of the crisis there was a significant dip in economic growth in late 2008–09 in most developing countries (see e.g. Akyuz, 2012, 2013; Blanchard et al., 2010), owing to the sharp contraction in export demand from USA and EU. Capital flows, the other important facet of globalisation, also shaped the impact of the crisis, with 'sudden stops' (especially in late 2008–09, when growth rates in advanced economies became negative) leading to sharp currency depreciation in the developing world. The slowdown of export demand affected investment and job creation in the export sector (and via linkage effects, the rest of the economy), whereas currency depreciation[4] led to balance sheet losses for firms exposed to foreign currency debt, with negative implications for asset creation by firms and for the investment climate in general. Alongside, drying up of remittance inflows was another critical factor adding to the growth slowdown, especially in parts of the developing world where migrants' remittances provide significant support for household consumption and investment of families that are dependent on them.

The initial downturn, however, was followed by strong growth recovery by 2010, accompanied by revival of trade and capital flows, strengthening currencies and build-up of foreign exchange reserves. Countercyclical policy responses, especially expansionary fiscal policies, adopted simultaneously across developed and emerging nations (especially large countries like India, China and Brazil) were seen as a major driver of this phenomenon (Nayyar, 2011; Rakshit, 2012). While fiscal expansion revived domestic demand, increase in capital inflows provided much needed balance of payments (BOP) support for financing current account deficits fueled by domestic demand led expansion. On the downside, the revival of capital inflows led to strengthening of emerging market currencies with negative implications for exports (Akyuz, 2014). Ironically this occurred at a time when developed countries aggressively pursued easy money policies, persistently holding interest rates at the zero lower bound and maintaining weak currencies to foster export growth.

## 326 *Ananya Ghosh Dastidar*

Yet, growth recovery in emerging markets proved relatively short-lived and pre-crisis growth rates remained elusive. In fact the persistent sluggishness in global demand, despite sustained pursuit of unconventional monetary policies in the industrialised world has been variously described as the downward phase of a 'debt super cycle' (Rogoff, 2016) as well as 'secular stagnation' (Summers, 2016). By 2012, the onset of a gradual slowdown in growth rates became evident, even in large economies like India and China that had spearheaded the earlier recovery, led in particular by a slowdown in private investments (Dastidar, 2014). With early signs of growth recovery, fiscal consolidation was back on the policy agenda along with monetary policy focus on inflation targeting, in line with economic orthodoxy. This was arguably an important factor behind the subsequent slowdown (Rakshit, 2012). After all, withdrawal of the policy stimulus in emerging economies came at a time when, despite early signs of recovery in the OECD, global demand remained sluggish and accompanied by weak and volatile commodity prices.

At the current conjuncture, the financial crisis appears to be finally over and recovery seems well under way, with rise in job creation and fall in unemployment rates in the USA, signs of firming commodity prices, revival of exports and growth rates picking up in commodity exporting as well as importing countries. However, what remains a matter of deep concern is that private investments continue to remain sluggish in emerging markets.

So is it going to be back to 'business as usual' with countries relying on export-led or export-induced growth[5] as in the pre-crisis phase? Or are there specific lessons to be drawn for EMEs from the post-crisis experience, for robust recovery in growth and employment creation in the medium run? The following discussion draws attention specifically to a few key features inherent in the economic systems of EMEs which were themselves fostered by the process of globalisation and which fundamentally shape the context for policy challenges lying ahead.

## Key issues and challenges

The global crisis exposed anew certain fragilities inherent in the economic systems of emerging nations. These were shaped by the economic reforms adopted across developing countries since the 1980s decade, which broadly involved dismantling state-led, inward looking development strategies and adoption of market-oriented reforms involving trade liberalisation, flexible exchange rates, easing of restrictions on capital flows and deregulation of the financial sector.[6] While

*The global financial crisis* 327

market oriented policies fostered growth and led to poverty reduction *inter alia*, they also, (1) enhanced inequalities in income and wealth, (2) led to excessive dependence on external markets, perhaps even at the cost of domestic markets and (3) created vulnerability in the financial sector via complex inter-linkages between asset prices, leverage, interest rates, exchange rates and international capital flows.

As we discuss later, each of these trends created certain systemic vulnerabilities that were instrumental in shaping the impact of the crisis and whose implications must be clearly grasped while designing policies for sustained recovery in growth and employment.

### Widening inequalities

It is now well recognized that globalisation was accompanied by an increase in inequalities in income and wealth in emerging economies.[7] Several factors inherent in the very process of globalisation contributed to this trend (Nayyar, 2006, 2013). For instance, contrary to the implications of standard trade theory, the pattern of North-South trade actually enhanced the skilled-unskilled wage gap in emerging economies in Asia as well as Latin America.[8] In emerging economies, skilled workers who were absorbed in manufacturing and services sectors engaged in production mainly for exports, benefitted directly from globalisation, leading to the emergence of a prosperous middle class. While large masses of unskilled workers, lacking access to education and opportunities for skill formation, often languished in low productivity agriculture and informal sectors and benefitted indirectly from the trickle down effects of high growth. Advances in technology and the breaking up of the global value chain reinforced this tendency by increasing the share of capital and high-skilled workers and reducing the share of low-skilled workers in value added in emerging economies (Timmer et al., 2014). Apart from international trade, there is also evidence to indicate that the process of financial globalisation, involving capital account liberalisation and financial development, also contributed to widening inequality especially between the top and middle income groups in emerging economies (Das and Mohapatra, 2003).

An important implication of increase in inequality is that this phenomenon imposes constraints on the size of the domestic market. The overall savings rate tends to increase with rising inequality between wage- and profit-incomes, as propensities to consume out of wage incomes are typically higher than those out of profits and income from capital (see, e.g. Carvalho and Rezai, 2016). In this way increase in inequality can undermine the strength of domestic markets. Yet, the

## 328  Ananya Ghosh Dastidar

sheer importance of a large and growing domestic market cannot be overemphasized as it can be a critical factor behind successful industrialisation[9] and for sustaining investment-led growth, especially under conditions of sluggish external demand.

Sustained increase in aggregate demand is crucial for the success of any strategy of investment-led growth. While increases in investments fuel growth in income and consumption in the short run, they also add to capacity creation in the medium run. Hence any negative demand shock (e.g. fall in domestic or export demand) that reduces capacity utilization and causes actual output to fall below potential tends to lower investments further (owing to fall in capacity utilization), leading to even lower demand via multiplier effects in the short run. In this way, by laying out too much capacity, an investment boom can actually create recessionary conditions in the presence of adverse demand shocks.[10] Therefore, widening inequalities can potentially undermine strategies of investment-led growth by creating a problem of inadequate aggregate demand.

In the case of countries relying on external markets, widening inequality in trade partners can constrain growth in the size of export markets; this may be especially problematic in a scenario where a large number of countries are competing in the same market. Hence the phenomenon of sharply increasing inequalities across developed countries (Atkinson and Piketty, 2012; Dabla-Norris et al., 2015) may well be a deep cause for concern for the future of emerging economies' growth strategies based on export markets.

### Dependence on external markets

An important characteristic of the economic systems largely prevalent in emerging nations is dependence on external markets and wide acceptance of export-led growth, following the East Asian model. East Asian economies have been largely regarded as success stories shaped by globalisation. Strategic state intervention led to successful industrialisation strategies based on exports at a time when external markets presented ample scope for growth. The growth strategy of these economies is regarded as a model for other emerging nations as it demonstrates both how external markets can be exploited to foster industrialisation and employment creation and the importance of FDI inflows in this process.

While export-led growth can be a successful strategy followed by small countries with limited domestic markets, from the point of view of the global economy, success of such a strategy is conditional

*The global financial crisis* 329

upon expansion and spillover of domestic demand especially of large economies into external markets. Prior to the crisis, the spectacular exports growth in emerging markets (especially from 2003 to 2007), was closely linked to mounting current account deficits in large industrial economies like the USA (Krugman, 2008). However, reliance on such a strategy naturally exposes economies to the risks associated with fluctuations in global demand conditions. In fact, the jeopardies of dependence on external markets came to the fore during the financial crisis, when the sharp fall in global demand had a disproportionate impact on trade volumes owing to the phenomenon of global value chains and large volumes of intra-industry trade that characterizes production and exports of manufactures in emerging economies (Eichengreen, 2009). Subsequently, the revival of commodity prices and exports, especially following the adoption of domestic investment-led growth in large countries like China, forcefully demonstrated the necessity of demand expansion for success of export strategies at a global level (Akyuz, 2013).

The fragility inherent in an economic system with excessive reliance on export-led growth is apparent especially under conditions of sluggish world demand. In this case nominal exchange rate movements become crucial for export success, especially when there are a large number of counties competing for a share of a limited global market. This can lead to a beggar-thy-neighbor spiral of competitive exchange rate depreciation where no country emerges as a 'winner' and problems are transmitted from one to the other in a musical chair sequence.

These problems were recently underscored by the exchange rate policies of developed countries in the post crisis era, which demonstrated limited consideration for global spillover effects; rather, these countries' own export performance and its linkages with their domestic economies appeared to be the primary concerns shaping such policy decisions. Post-crisis recovery in the world economy has been characterized by emerging market currencies facing real appreciation and developed country currencies facing real depreciation (Rajan, 2016). As such, recovery in the industrial world has come on the back of weak currencies supported by interest rates held at the zero lower bound (and even negative rates). Such strategies display a determination to compete for a share of a sluggish global market, rather than a willingness to undertake domestic expansion to boost global demand.

The tendency of industrial countries to also rely on external rather than domestic demand to fuel growth and its implied limits on the potential for export-led growth, should be an important consideration underlying the adoption of such strategies for EMEs, going ahead.

## 330 *Ananya Ghosh Dastidar*

### Enhanced financial risks

Financial globalisation, comprising financial deregulation and liberalisation of international capital flows was an important facet of market oriented policy reforms in EMEs. This process went hand in hand with trade liberalisation and exchange rate flexibility.[11] While it gave domestic agents greater freedom to take advantage of arbitrage opportunities, it enhanced exchange rate volatility, forged closer interlinkages between domestic and international asset markets in emerging economies and escalated leverage and systemic risks especially via real and financial sector feedback effects.

Asset price booms (both stock prices as well as real assets like land and housing) had become a common phenomenon in EMEs in the pre-crisis period (Akyuz, 2012, 2013, 2014; Nagaraj, 2013). While financial deregulation and financial sector reforms in EMEs paved the way for development of asset markets, surge in foreign capital inflows contributed to creation of asset price bubbles and excessive leverage that could undermine financial stability. Alongside, high rates of economic growth and emergence of prosperous middle and upper-middle classes (mainly skilled workers and professionals who benefitted the most from globalisation) spurred the demand for assets.

A related phenomenon was the growth in leverage among financial entities, firms as well as households. On the supply side, the rising value of collaterals enhanced willingness to lend, whereas on the demand side, growing incomes and its increasing concentration spurred demand for assets and loans to finance them. Simultaneously there was significant systemic exposure to foreign currency loans that enhanced exchange rate risks. This was facilitated by the easing of restrictions on cross-border capital flows that allowed for interest rate arbitrage, given the low rates of interest in developed countries like the USA and Japan and relatively higher rates in emerging economies pursuing inflation targeting (Krugman, 2008).

The systemic vulnerabilities fostered by these developments came to the fore with the onset of the crisis (see Acharya, 2016). As different phases of monetary policy in the USA unfolded[12] in response to the crisis and with post-crisis economic recovery, emerging markets witnessed considerable volatility in capital flows and exchange rates that affected asset markets and balance sheets, especially of leveraged entities in EMEs. While sharp exchange rate depreciations escalated values of liabilities denominated in foreign currency, the collapse in asset prices led to tumbling collateral values, leading to balance sheet losses and inducing debt defaults.[13] These developments had spillover

## The global financial crisis 331

effects for the real as well as financial spheres; balance sheet losses contributed to slowdown in investment demand by reducing operational profits and leading to shelving of investment projects, whereas collapse in collateral values induced debt defaults, affecting the asset side of the balance sheet of lending agencies, especially banks. Since financial sector entities like banks forge a key link between savings and investments, any disruption in this sector can have lasting negative repercussions on investments, growth and employment creation (Reinhart and Rogoff, 2009).

Thus the problem of excessive leverage that lay at the heart of the sub-prime crisis continued unabated in emerging markets, sowing the seeds of a possible future slowdown, or even a crisis, when asset prices crash or capital flows retreat in response to developments elsewhere (e.g. eventual rise in interest rates in the USA). The combination of asset price collapses and exchange rate depreciation could magnify balance sheet losses, enhance debt defaults and significantly worsen balance sheets of financial entities. The resultant financial instability could have negative real sector feedback effects, triggering a downturn in investments both from the supply side (e.g. mounting defaults affect banks' capacity to lend) as well as demand side (e.g. through mounting balance sheet losses).

This discussion highlights several issues that require urgent policy attention in EMEs for reviving and sustaining growth and maintaining macroeconomic stability.

## Policy priorities

Attaining pre-crisis rates of growth, reviving private investments and managing financial and macroeconomic stability are among the top concerns of policymakers in emerging markets.

### *Strengthening domestic demand*

Given the importance of aggregate demand expansion both for the success of export-led growth as well as for investment-led growth, managing aggregate demand holds the key for growth recovery in the EMEs. The main challenge here would be to achieve a stable and broad-based structure of the domestic market. That is, alongside demand generation, equal importance must be placed on making domestic demand more broad based. This can be achieved mainly by increasing the share of wages, which can occur only with large scale employment generation through industrialisation (Nayyar, 2014).

## 332 *Ananya Ghosh Dastidar*

It is also important to stabilize incomes at the bottom end of the distribution. This is necessary in order to reduce severe downward dips in demand in the face of negative shocks when consumption at the lower tail of the income distribution tends to collapse, in the absence of adequate means for self-insurance among the relatively poor and vulnerable. Consumption smoothing at the lower end of the income distribution can be especially important in countries where domestically produced goods have a large weight in the consumption basket of the poor, creating significant linkage effects for domestic producers.

In this context, widening inequalities in emerging economies, as well as developed market economies, become a matter of deep concern. As argued previously, increasing the concentration of income tends to undermine domestic demand and the size of the domestic market. This calls for measures aimed at reducing inequalities in income and, more importantly, from a long-run point of view, in access to education and health facilities that are critical for human capital formation. Here, the importance of public provision of health and education cannot be overemphasized.

While such programmes would bear fruit in the medium to long term, in the short run, fiscal stimuli can boost autonomous demand required to induce increase in consumption levels in EMEs leading to increases in capacity utilization and investment demand. Typically public expenditure tends to crowd in private investments in EMEs, but focusing only on the creation of capacity may not be sufficient if there are problems related to inadequate aggregate demand.

Fiscal expansion focused on an increase in government expenditures tends to have implications for public debt, but instead of abandoning fiscal policy as a tool, this calls for creative, out-of-the-box thinking in designing fiscal tools (Feldstein, 2016; Summers, 2016). After all, fiscal policy would not generate financial risk as in case of unconventional monetary policies[14] and, rather than increase in spending, the focus could be more on revenue-based measures. These could involve, for example, improvements in institutional and incentive-based measures for enhancing tax compliance, investment tax credits financed by increase in corporate taxes and so on.

### Capital flow management

Another issue relates to the implications of relatively free capital mobility and financial development in EMEs. On the one hand this enhances currency volatility primarily owing to volatility in short-term flows, on the other hand, currency movements induced by capital flows can

The global financial crisis 333

undermine export performance. In the post-crisis period, episodes of 'sudden stop' have been interspersed with those of 'capital surge' affecting exchange rates, with consequences for exports as well as balance sheets (both in the real and financial sectors) exposed to foreign assets and liabilities.

In the post-crisis period, prolonged episodes of near zero and even negative rates of interest in the industrialised countries led to surge in capital inflows in EMEs in search of returns. While these inflows helped finance current account deficits, they also effectively postponed structural reforms aiming at reduction in the size of the deficits. Currency appreciation induced by the capital surge had adverse implications for export competitiveness. This created pressure on emerging market central banks to carry out foreign exchange intervention to maintain competitive exchange rates and led to accumulation of foreign exchange reserves. In part this was useful as it provided a safeguard against possible currency volatility (induced, for instance, by volatility in capital flows). However, to the extent that capital inflows could only be partially sterilized (e.g. owing to the debt implications of open market operations), they led to an increase in money supply and contributed to inflation and consequent real exchange rate appreciation, further affecting export performance in emerging markets.

Therefore, managing foreign capital flows is an important area that requires policy attention. It has become clear that neither a blanket ban, nor full capital account convertibility are feasible options at the current conjuncture. In this context, regulating inflows logically makes the most sense as that would obviate the need for restrictions on outflows. In particular, the policy stand has to be fairly nuanced as different types of flows may need different regulations depending on their role, quality, duration etc. Such measures would have important implications for the central banks' role in carrying out interventions, sterilization measures and policies for controlling inflation.

### Managing real and financial sector feedbacks

Finally, a critical policy issue relates to macroeconomic management, for which the core problem is achieving stability in interest rates, exchange rates and inflation in an era of volatile capital flows and financially integrated global markets. The core concerns of policymakers in this context is the design and implementation of appropriate policies to prevent excessive leverage and to manage the feedbacks between the real and financial sectors that take place via changes in interest rates, asset prices and exchange rates, against a backdrop of international capital mobility and changing balance sheet effects of real and financial sector entities. This involves managing the 'financial trilemma' (Schoenmaker, 2013) involving internationally open financial markets, national sovereignty over financial policy and financial stability. This calls for an extensive use of macro prudential tools along with monetary policy tools to manage real and financial sector inter-linkages mediated via asset markets. It also underscores the need for management of capital flows, especially with a view to control asset price and exchange rate volatility.

A slew of macro prudential measures has been adopted across EMEs mainly aimed at controlling lending behavior of banks and concentrating on the housing market. These include, for example, calibrating loan market variables such as loan-to-value (LTV) and debt-to-income (DTI) ratios, adjusting risk weights in banks' lending portfolios, in tune with movement in asset prices (Borio, 2014; Haldane, 2014) etc. The basic idea being that policy-induced counter-cyclical movement in these variables would prevent excessive leverage on the upward phase of an asset price boom and even act as an endogenous mechanism preventing (or slowing down) the creation of a bubble. These could be useful tools therefore for managing feedbacks from the financial to the real sector. Moreover, such policies also involve periodic changes in regulations governing foreign exchange hedging options available to firms in line with external market conditions. Evidence suggests that these measures were used successfully in emerging economies as diverse as India, Brazil and South Korea (Chakrabarty, 2014; da Silva, 2016; Kim, 2014) to prevent negative spillovers, from the housing sector into the financial sector, from blowing out of proportion as in case of the US sub-prime crisis.

However, several issues need attention regarding design and implementation of macro-prudential measures – for one, it is not always easy to separate a normal boom (accompanying the upward phase of a business cycle) from a potential bubble while one is 'in' the boom (i.e. while asset prices are rising). Second, given the complexity of financial markets and associated financial entities, it is not clear how such regulation would be implemented for banks as well as non-bank entities operating in the 'shadow banking sector'. This is problematic especially in emerging economies where the institutional structure of financial supervision is still in an evolving phase, with the countries being at various stages of financial deregulation and financial development. Third, there is ample scope for revisiting the inter-relations (including feedback effects) and coordination of macro-prudential policies with conventional monetary policy, financial sector regulations and

The global financial crisis  335

management of foreign capital flows. A clearer understanding of these issues would contribute to improved coordination between macroprudential and conventional monetary policies (Shin, 2016).

Addressing the policy priorities in EMEs in the wake of the crisis ultimately calls for reviving and redesigning the role of the state especially for reining in volatilities unleashed by market forces in a globalized world.

## Conclusions

In the current scenario, when a large number of emerging countries are pursuing policies of export-led growth, on the supply side there is a great deal of competition, making exchange rate management absolutely critical for sustained growth in exports. On the demand side, export markets remain volatile with unconventional monetary policies still in place in industrialised countries like the USA, Japan and the EU. In this scenario, for emerging economies the importance of policies fostering growth in domestic markets and putting in place mechanisms for mitigating external shocks, especially related to exchange rates, becomes paramount. At the same time, managing capital flows with a view to maintaining real and financial sector stability becomes important for achieving macroeconomic stability.

In the event of yet another crisis in the future (even if it is not of the proportions of the global financial crisis), it is wise to remember that the world economy is in a far more vulnerable position in terms of crafting a policy response, with governments carrying high debt burdens and central banks coping with change in asset quality and much expanded balance sheets. In this context, EMEs must concentrate on fostering growth in stable and broad-based domestic markets, concentrating especially on reducing income inequality, as this can be a crucial component in policies meant to weather future global shocks.

## Notes

1  The term 'EMEs' is used to broadly refer to countries in the developing world comprising both developing as well as emerging market economies.
2  The Asian experience, though diverse, can be seen as being broadly based on success of manufactures and services exports, in contrast to the case of Latin American and especially African countries where primary exports remain dominant.
3  See Dastidar (2015a) for a comprehensive survey of the literature on the impact of the crisis on EMEs.
4  However, currency depreciation also had a positive impact on emerging market exports (Blanchard et al., 2010).

## 336    Ananya Ghosh Dastidar

5  Export-led growth refers specifically to the East Asian model and refers to a conscious strategy of growth adopted by the state with export promotion at its heart. In contrast Dastidar (2015b) defines export induced growth as growth in aggregate output caused by an increase in exports where such increase in exports is not directly policy induced. Dastidar (2015b) argues that countries like India experienced export-induced growth in the pre-crisis period.

6  The process of globalisation picked up momentum during the 1990s and 2000s decades in terms of geographical spread and deepening of market oriented reforms in the developing world, with the extent and sequencing of reform measures showing significant differences across nations. See Stiglitz et al. (2006) for a rich discussion on the diversity of development experiences and macroeconomic implications of economic reforms.

7  For evidence on trends in inequality over the decade of the 1990s and 2000s, see Dabla-Norris et al. (2015).

8  As per the tenets of standard trade theory (Heckscher-Ohlin theory of international trade), such trade should have reduced the gap between skilled and unskilled workers in the South via specialization in the production and exports of unskilled labor-intensive commodities. However, the reverse was observed in practice (see Wood, 1995, for an analysis of initial trends in the skilled-unskilled wage gap in the South).

9  Murphy et al. (1989) demonstrate the importance of the domestic market for industrialisation especially when entering world trade is costly and, in this context, they argue that income distribution must be sufficiently broad based so as to generate demand for a broad range of manufactures.

10  Rakshit (2016) demonstrates the importance of boosting aggregate demand for reviving investment-led growth in case of India which experienced an investment boom in the pre-crisis period and is currently facing a prolonged slowdown in private investments.

11  In the wake of the Asian crisis and collapse of fixed exchange rate regimes in Latin American countries like Mexico and Argentina, most developing nations had opted for managed floats (Reinhart and Rogoff, 2009).

12  US monetary policy introduced quantitative easing (QE) from 2009, in a phased manner (via QE1, QE2 and QE3) till the end of 2013. The last phase of QE was tapered off between 2013 and 2014 in a gradual rollback of the bond buying program. Thereafter, with clear signs of recovery in the US economy, there was a small hike in the federal funds rate (which still remained below 0.5 percent) at the end of 2015; and now with strengthening of US recovery, markets are expecting further rise in US interest rates as well as imminent exit from unconventional monetary policies.

13  Rakshit (2016) links the mounting nonperforming assets on the balance sheets of lenders in India's financial sector with poor performance by firms, especially in India's infrastructure sector, during the growth slowdown. These firms were highly leveraged with exposure to foreign debt, as the policy incentive structure had effectively encouraged such borrowings given the low rates of interest in international markets in the pre-crisis period.

14  Low interest rates on safe assets under unconventional monetary policy regime enhances agents' incentives to opt for investing in projects with higher returns and high risk, thereby increasing risk exposure of the financial system as whole.

## Bibliography

Acharya, V. (2016): "A Comparative Analysis of Financial Sector Health in the United States, Europe, and Asia", in O. Blanchard, R. Rajan, K. Rogoff and L. Summers (eds), *Progress and Confusion: The State of Macroeconomic Policy*, International Monetary Fund, MIT Press: Massachusetts.

Akyuz, Y. (2012): *The Financial Crisis and the Global South: A Development Perspective*, Pluto Press: London.

Akyuz, Y. (2013): "Waving or Drowning: Developing Countries after the Financial Crisis", *Economic and Political Weekly* 48, pp. 38–48.

Akyuz, Y. (2014): *Liberalization, Financial Instability and Economic Development*, Anthem Press: New Delhi.

Atkinson, A.B. and T. Piketty (eds) (2012): *Top Incomes: A Global Perspective*, Oxford University Press: Oxford.

Blanchard, O., M. Das and H. Faruqee (2010): "The Initial Impact of the Crisis on Emerging Market Countries", Brookings Paper on Economic Activity (Spring), pp. 263–323 (with comments by K.J. Forbes and L. Tesar).

Borio, C. (2014): "Macroprudential Policy and the Financial Cycle: Some Stylized Facts and Policy Suggestions", in G. Akerlof, O. Blanchard, D. Romer and J. Stiglitz (eds), *What Have We Learned? Macroeconomic Policy after the Crisis*, International Monetary Fund, MIT Press: Massachusetts.

Carvalho, L. and A. Rezai (2016): "Personal Income Inequality and Aggregate Demand", *Cambridge Journal of Economics* 40, pp. 491–505.

Chakrabarty, K. (2014): "Framework for the Conduct of Macroprudential Policy in India: Experiences and Perspectives", *Financial Stability Review* 18, Banque de France, pp. 131–144.

Dabla-Norris, E., K. Kochhar, N. Suphaphiphat, F. Ricka and E. Tsounta (2015): "Causes and Consequences of Income Inequality: A Global Perspective", IMF Staff Discussion Note: SDN/15/13, June.

Das, M. and S. Mohapatra (2003): "Income Inequality: The Aftermath of Stock Market Liberalization in Emerging Markets", *Journal of Empirical Finance* 10, pp. 217–48.

Da Silva, L.A.P. (2016): "Some Lessons of the Global Financial Crisis from an EME and a Brazilian Perspective", in O. Blanchard, R. Rajan, K. Rogoff and L. Summers (eds), *Progress and Confusion: The State of Macroeconomic Policy*, International Monetary Fund, MIT Press: Massachusetts.

Dastidar, A.G. (2014): "The Global Recession and Developing Economies in Asia: Evidence from China and India", in G.G. Das (ed), *Current Issues in International Trade: Methodologies and Development Implications for the World Economy*, Nova Publishers: USA, pp. 3–26.

Dastidar, A.G. (2015a): "The Global Recession and Emerging Economies", *Journal of Business Thought* 1, pp. 3–13.

Dastidar, A.G. (2015b): "India's Experience with Export-Led Growth", in J. Ghosh (ed), *India and the International Economy*, ICSSR Research Survey and Explorations in Economics, Vol. 2, Oxford University Press: New Delhi.

## 338 Ananya Ghosh Dastidar

Eichengreen, B. (2009): "Comments in 'Collapse in World Trade: A Symposium of Views'", *The International Economy*, Spring.

Feldstein, M. (2016): "The Future of Fiscal Policy", in O. Blanchard, R. Rajan, K. Rogoff and L. Summers (eds), *Progress and Confusion: The State of Macroeconomic Policy*, International Monetary Fund, MIT Press: Massachusetts.

Haldane, A. (2014): "Macroprudential Policy in Prospect", in G. Akerlof, O. Blanchard, D. Romer and J. Stiglitz (eds), *What Have We Learned? Macroeconomic Policy after the Crisis*, International Monetary Fund, MIT Press: Massachusetts.

Kim, C. (2014): "Korea's Experiences with Macroprudential Policy", in G. Akerlof, O. Blanchard, D. Romer and J. Stiglitz (eds), *What Have We Learned? Macroeconomic Policy after the Crisis*, International Monetary Fund, MIT Press: Massachusetts.

Kose, A. and E. Prasad (December 2010): "Emerging Markets Come of Age", *Finance & Development* 47(4).

Krugman, P. (2008): *The Return of Depression Economics and the Crisis of 2008*, Penguin Books: London.

Murphy, K.M., A. Shleifer and R. Vishny (1989): "Income Distribution, Market Size and Industrialization", *Quarterly Journal of Economics* 104, pp. 537–64.

Nagaraj, R. (2013): "India's Dream Run, 2003–2008: Understanding the Boom and Its Aftermath", *Economic and Political Weekly* 48, pp. 39–51.

Nayyar, D. (2006): "Globalization, History and Development: A Tale of Two Centuries", *Cambridge Journal of Economics* 30, pp. 137–59.

Nayyar, D. (2011): "The Financial Crisis, the Great Recession and the Developing World", *Global Policy* 2, pp. 20–32.

Nayyar, D. (2013): *Catch Up: Developing Countries in the World Economy*, Oxford University Press: New Delhi.

Nayyar, D. (2014): "Why Employment Matters: Reviving Growth and Reducing Inequality", *International Labour Review* 153(3), pp. 351–64.

Rajan, R. (2016): "Going Bust for Growth", in O. Blanchard, R. Rajan, K. Rogoff and L. Summers (eds), *Progress and Confusion: The State of Macroeconomic Policy*, International Monetary Fund, MIT Press: Massachusetts.

Rakshit, M. (2012): "Keynes and the Contemporary Economic Crisis", *Money & Finance*, ICRA Bulletin, September, pp. 43–87.

Rakshit, M. (2016): "India's Post-Crisis Macroeconomic Slowdown: Some Perspectives", *Money & Finance*, ICRA Bulletin, April, pp. 49–84.

Reinhart, C.M. and K.S. Rogoff (2009): *This Time Is Different*, Princeton University Press: Princeton and Oxford.

Rogoff, K. (2016): "Debt Supercycle, Not Secular Stagnation", in O. Blanchard, R. Rajan, K. Rogoff and L. Summers (eds), *Progress and Confusion: The State of Macroeconomic Policy*, International Monetary Fund, MIT Press: Massachusetts.

Schoenmaker, D. (2013): *Governance of International Banking: The Financial Trilemma*, Oxford University Press: London.

## The global financial crisis  339

Shin, H.S. (2016): "Macroprudential Tools, Their Limits, and Their Connection with Monetary Policy", in O. Blanchard, R. Rajan, K. Rogoff and L. Summers (eds), *Progress and Confusion: The State of Macroeconomic Policy*, International Monetary Fund, MIT Press: Massachusetts.

Stiglitz, J., J.A. Ocampo, S. Spiegel, R. Ffrench Davis and D. Nayyar (2006): *Stability with Growth: Macroeconomics, Liberalization and Development*, Oxford University Press: Oxford.

Summers, L. (2016): "The Age of Secular Stagnation: What It Is and What to Do about It", *Foreign Affairs* 2, February.

Timmer, M.P., A.A. Erumban, B. Los, R. Stehrer and G.J. de Vries (2014): "Slicing Up Global Value Chains", *The Journal of Economic Perspectives* 28, pp. 99–118.

Wood, A. (1995): "How Trade Hurt Unskilled Workers", *Journal of Economic Perspectives* 9, pp. 57–80.

# 17 Land deals in Africa
## Host country effects in the presence of skill formation*

*Gouranga G. Das*

> *"Just like heaven. Ever'body wants a little piece of land."*
> John Steinbeck, *Of Mice and Men*, Chapter 4,
> paragraph 64, p. 74

Development policies centering on trade, macroeconomics, and development are major foci of Deepak Nayyar's valuable contributions in economics. Nayyar (2013) offers analysis on the Global South and their catch-up phenomena, documenting the role of global engagement as well as state-led development for growth and structural change of the developing economies. One of his concerns is that moving out of agriculture is not the way for development for stagnating poor economies as it displaces peasant production. Moreover, Nayyar (2012) discussed at length on the differences across developing and developed economies regarding human development and institutions for macroeconomic outcomes. In particular, based on the idea of expansion of 'capabilities and opportunities', he highlighted the importance of institutions, education, and human development for adopting modern technologies in agriculture and, hence, inferred strong 'positive causation from human development to macroeconomics at low levels of income and low levels of human development' (Nayyar 2012, p. 18) for less developed nations.

In this chapter, taking that flavor of works we analyze the issue of land rush in the African context, quite different from the Indian case. In the transition from agriculture to modern industry, as part of the development process, accumulation of physical capital, human

---

\* Acknowledgments are due to UNU-World Institute of Development Economics Research (WIDER), Helsinki, Finland, for helpful feedback. Special thanks go to Augustin Fosu and Paul Collier for valuable discussions. The usual disclaimer applies.

capital, has been given central importance in the economic development literature while the role of land being underemphasized. However, land acquisition for nonagricultural uses is not uncommon in history. As the economy industrializes, land is acquired for developing roads, transport infrastructure, urbanization, building dams, and also for building industries generating employment. Land tenure and land reform programs giving property rights and ownerships to the farmers are pathways to economic development. A study by Antonelli et al. (2015) shows negative socio-economic impact of land use changes (livelihoods, self-sufficiency in food, and access to resources) in countries such as Indonesia, Cambodia, Benin, and Burkina Faso. In fact, in the context of EU land deals they found significant evidences of very low levels of human development indices (HDI), and poor development in countries such as Sierra Leone, Guinea, and Mozambique.

However, if conversion of land leads to eviction and displacement of people from their livelihoods and rights, it subsequently results in resistance.[1] This has been the case of India where with her escalating growth (7.5 percent for 2015) the demand for transfer of land for industry, urbanization, and other projects raised hue and cry, led to conflicts, and ultimately led to the adoption of a new Act for adequate compensation (Singh 2016; Dinda 2016). What makes land deals in Africa distinct is trans-border acquisition causing spatial shift of 'immobile' land services.

Transnational large-scale land acquisition is a recent phenomenon, triggered by three-pronged nature of the 2008–2009 crises: First, world food market experienced acute shortages with higher food prices driven by export bans, drought in some breadbaskets such as Russia, Australia, and Ukraine, and adverse supply conditions; second, the fuel crisis, rise in oil prices, and climate change propped up food-agrofuel competition; and, third, bioethanol policies induced conversion of land from food production to biofuel crops causing land-use changes, further aggravating the price spiraling. As emerging countries experiencing high demand (like China, South Korea, India) and those without self-sufficiency in grains (like mostly Gulf states) were looking for solutions to get away with steep prices in world markets afflicted with severe resource crunch, private and state investors, and global agribusiness companies engaged in securing land for food safety and energy supply. These new spate of activities – called 'land deal or grab' – evolved to circumvent the adverse consequences. As international actors tap into lands beyond their borders, in the wake of systemic food-feed-fuel crises, without proper design such deals reducing land for agriculture or, displacement of tillers, could be threat to food security.

342  *Gouranga G. Das*

Driven by distrust on world market's capability to export, the grabbers grow food and export/cash crops on land in host (mostly poor) nations and import back their *'own'* food, and/or agrofuel, which would have otherwise been provided either domestically or from world market via imports – *a kind of offshore outsourcing to import food and biocrop (unlike intermediates, materials, or services) produced relatively cheaply abroad in the target.* There are differences in terms of contract negotiations and often, it does not involve direct land acquisitions, rather food *supplies via contract farming* or investment in irrigation or rural infrastructure – the latter being welcomed to some extent, because that could generate beneficial effects to spill over to other segments (Daniel and Mittal 2009, 2010; Kugelman and Levenstein 2009).

Data on the magnitude of land rush differ widely across different sources and, hence, the conundrum exists due to contradictions, lack of consensus on definitions, and methodological differences (Edelman 2013). About 20 million hectares of farmland (i.e. worth $20–$30 billion of land value with conservative estimates) in least-developed countries (LDCs) were under consideration for such deal (International Food Policy Research Institute [IFPRI], as quoted in *The Economist* May 23rd, 2009). Further, according to the report, the food importers like Saudi Arabia, Kuwait, China, and South Korea 'have opted to grow food on land they own or control abroad rather than import it through international trade (p. 63, ibid.)'.[2] According to Oxfam (2011), the magnitude is 227 million hectares of land. Edelman (2013) and Anseeuw et al. (2013) mention that the Land Matrix (2014) provides greater transparency and reliability. Land Matrix partnership's Global observatory (2014) based on the Land Matrix online public database offers worldwide pictures of 1,305 deals (195 intended covering 16 million hectares, 1,029 concluded for 38.3 million hectares, and 81 failed contracts for 7.3 million hectares) from negotiation to the stage of operational use.[3] They estimate that between 2000 and 2010, globally about 83 million hectares of purchased or leased land have been under such 'deal' (Anseeuw et al. 2012a). According to the latest report of Land Matrix (October 2014), between June 2013 and September 2014, concluded deals increased by 27 percent and the intended size under each sub-deal increased. The principal investor countries are OECD nations (52 percent, 718 deals with the United States, the UK, and Netherlands being the first 3 of top 10 investors) and also the emerging growth engines such as China, India, South Korea, Singapore, Hong Kong, and Malaysia, and lower middle income countries (21 percent, 292 deals). Upper middle-income oil-exporting countries (15 percent, 200 deals) Saudi Arabia, Kuwait, or Qatar are aggressively involved in farmland acquisition in mainly developing and transition countries.

*Land deals in Africa* 343

The *target regions* are these: Sub-Saharan African (SSA) economies (e.g. breadbasket Sudan, Mozambique, Congo, Sierra Leone), as well as other countries like Cambodia, Indonesia, the Philippines, Vietnam, Brazil, Laos, etc. It is a global phenomenon where Africa and Asia account for 80 percent of the global grabbed area, although the Land Matrix database (2013) had revised global estimates downwards to 42.3 million ha with 20.2 million ha located in Africa.

Despite the large number of deals, only a small fraction is currently being utilized for pure agricultural purposes while food production and shifting to non-food crops or biofuel production remain the main drivers (*mixed deals*) (Land Matrix October 2014). Target crops had biases biofuel feedstock for oilseed cultivation (oil palm and jatropha) of 60.4 percent of the total area, while timber and pulpwood products accounted for 15 percent; sugar crops, 13.2 percent; and food crops (roots, cereals, tubers, and vegetables) constitute 6.7 percent of the area in SSA (Schoneveld 2014). Water availability is critical for land deals as yields on land depend on a stable and secure supply of water. Using data from multiple sources, Rulli, Saviori, and D'Odorico (2013) developed a quantitative hydrological model to assess the alarming rates of water grabbing for crop and livestock production (green water or rainwater, and blue or irrigation water) associated with land deals, and showed that 'the per capita volume of grabbed water often exceeds the water requirements for a balanced diet and would be sufficient to improve food security and abate malnourishment in the grabbed countries' (ibid., p. 892). Also, it reports that 'global land grabbing ($469.4 \times 10^5$ ha) is associated with a maximum rate of water grabbing of about $454 \times 10^9 m^3$ per year. Overall, about 60 percent of the total grabbed water is appropriated, through land grabbing, by the United States, United Arab Emirates, India, United Kingdom, China, and Israel' (ibid., p. 893).

Schoneveld (2014) bridges the gaps in empirical evidence on geographical and sectoral patterns for 563 selected farmland projects for 2005–2013 in SSA and mentions that opacity of the deals and information makes reconciliation of different sources of data covering different time periods and sectors hard to judge (Table 17.1).[4]

According to Edelman, Oya, and Borras Jr. (2013), as 'sweeping conclusions' are drawn that require more rigorous grounding of claims about impacts, for scrutiny of failed projects and for (re)examination of the social differentiation, the agency of the contending social classes, and forms of grassroots resistance, the debate centers around 'contested definitional, conceptual, methodological and political issues' (ibid., p. 1517). This implies the necessity of understanding the interactions between key elements inhibiting (or favoring) the prospective

*Table 17.1* Top-10 investor and target countries for pure and mixed deals

| | | 'Pure' agrofuel deal | | | 'Mixed' deals with agrofuel | | |
|---|---|---|---|---|---|---|---|
| | Investor country | Investor region | Size under contract (ha) | Investor country | Investor region | Size under contract (ha) |
| 1 | Netherlands | Europe | 904,700 | United Kingdom | Europe | 796,905 |
| 2 | United Kingdom | Europe | 726,419 | Singapore | Asia | 656,294 |
| 3 | Malaysia | Asia | 479,178 | India | Asia | 584,332 |
| 4 | Canada | Americas | 276,437 | Malaysia | Asia | 430,194 |
| 5 | France | Europe | 230,000 | Hong Kong | Asia | 421,310 |
| 6 | Republic of Korea | Asia | 206,661 | Saudi Arabia | Asia | 250,000 |
| 7 | Italy | Europe | 176,849 | South Africa | Africa | 206,103 |
| 8 | China | Asia | 172,789 | Portugal | Europe | 161,000 |
| 9 | Romania | Europe | 130,000 | Zimbabwe | Africa | 150,000 |
| 10 | Spain | Europe | 65,273 | Switzerland | Europe | 126,800 |

| | 'Pure' agrofuel deal | | | 'Mixed' deals with agrofuel | | |
|---|---|---|---|---|---|---|
| | Target country | Target region | Size under contract (ha) | Target country | Target region | Size under contract (ha) |
| 1 | Brazil | Americas | 896,307 | Indonesia | Asia | 1,066,150 |
| 2 | Madagascar | Africa | 569,558 | Sierra Leone | Africa | 817,726 |
| 3 | Indonesia | Asia | 400,000 | Ethiopia | Africa | 444,800 |
| 4 | Senegal | Africa | 207,500 | Ghana | Africa | 421,808 |
| 5 | Burkina Faso | Africa | 200,000 | Papua New Guinea | Oceania | 390,286 |
| 6 | Ethiopia | Africa | 175,400 | Mozambique | Africa | 232,093 |
| 7 | Kenya | Africa | 160,000 | Liberia | Africa | 220,000 |
| 8 | Papua New Guinea | Oceania | 135,178 | Zambia | Africa | 206,103 |
| 9 | Lao People's Democratic Republic | Asia | 134,361 | Timor-Leste | Asia | 100,000 |
| 10 | Mozambique | Africa | 125,335 | Ukraine | Europe | 80,000 |

Source: www.landmatrix.org, data as of 2 June 2014. Adaptation from Nolte, Ostermeier, and Schultze (2014), Tables 1 and 2.

# 346  *Gouranga G. Das*

outcomes of such deals in a framework structured to capture the quintessential mechanism for making the deals beneficial for agriculture-led development. Das (2013), the first of its kind, modeled in a general equilibrium framework to show the 'immiserizing effects' of such deal when there are food price inflation and opacity of such investment in land deal encapsulated via payment of land-premium. However, possible remedies of getting over the 'pauperizing' effects are discussed in von Braun and Meinzen-Dick (2009), Deininger et al. (2011), and Collier and Venables (2012a, 2012b). For sustainable development and well-being, food security must be ensured for growing population and hence, shrinking the space of agricultural production is not way out. In fact, in the Indian context, Dinda (2016) has mentioned that for sustainable development one form of non-cash compensation could be offering jobs and skill formation.

Developing the debate and rationale in a global context, this chapter adds value by offering an analytical framework showing the following: How could the design and arrangements of these deals be made favorable for improving the investment climate via facilitating socio-economic-institutional infrastructure (say, job creation, skill-formation via education-led human capital, enforcement mechanisms, and accountability via governance and rule of law)? Government's role as facilitator is of paramount importance for turning the hollow deals into profitable investment opportunities. This is important for inclusive growth and development. The next section briefly presents the debate. The final section of this chapter offers an analytical model, and is then followed by the conclusion.

## Nature of the problem, lacunae, and a framework

### The debate

The nature and magnitude of vast tracts of land acquisitions by private investors spawned debate about the positive and negative impacts on local communities. The debates about the rationale for such activities are contested claims about impacts – positive or negative – on targeted developing economies. Benefits are perceived in terms of expected development outcome underlying the *primary motive* of farmland investment, that is, to resolve food supply problem and avoiding the protectionist impulse for overcoming shortage of staple crops or developing alternative green technology, training, and infrastructure. For the *host countries* suffering from incidence of chronic poverty, food-shortage, hunger, and malnutrition, the *incentives* are manifold: The foreign investment in farming enables them to get better agricultural inputs like seeds and fertilizers, investment in superior agricultural technology like green revolution, modernization via foreign capital, human resource development via extension services, direct financial benefits via land fees, to name a few – all these contributing to improve farm productivity per worker and growth in crop yields per unit of farmland. On the other hand, the potential threats are (1) the displacement of local people or smaller farmers from livelihood, (2) the relative risk of land-use competition between different crops due to incipient biofuel sector and escalation of global demand for renewable energy causing conversion of major crops, and (3) the absence of mechanisms for regulating land conversion due to weakness in regulatory power, enforcement mechanisms, and the weak bargaining power of the farmers.

The study by IFPRI (April 2009) mentions that the proliferation of land acquisitions are targeted by the countries with higher capital endowment and water scarcity (say Gulf States) and high population with food insecurity (emerging engines like India or China) towards the host countries depending on their geographical proximity, but mostly, on the basis of their low labor cost, abundance of land and water, and favorable climate for crops. Arezki, Deininger, and Selod (November 2011) presented a study by IMF determining the factors behind such activities by employing a gravity model with indicators of agro-ecological suitability and land rights security along with bilateral investments. Their findings confirm that '*weak land governance and tenure security*' attract foreign investors although quality of business climate does not matter much.

Impacts of such projects are too hard to gauge whether host countries benefit in terms of food security, or the diversification of bioenergy sources, and *soft and hard infrastructure*. There are also growing concerns over the impact on the rural poor's livelihood. Under the arrangement, as the host economy suffers from a poor investment climate, low yield per acre, dearth of sophisticated agricultural R&D or other mechanized equipment (better seeds, tractors, fertilizers, irrigation facilities), and inadequate infrastructure, there is abysmally low underinvestment in agriculture. Therefore, an inflow of investment in land could have potential positive effects such as increased productivity to overcome these techno-infrastructural deficiencies, employment generation, overcoming capital-shortage for effective utilization of land, undertaking farmland production by improving productivity of land and labor, promoting health and education for skill, and, thereby, improving well-being (Deininger et al. 2011).[5]

According to Cotula (2009, 2011), the value of direct financial transfer (land fee or rent) that the investors pay for governmental land

348  *Gouranga G. Das*

allocations are very low nominal rates (less than USD 2/ha/year to USD 5/ha/year) or not charged at all (e.g. case of Sudan, Senegal, Madagascar). This is due to low rents resulting from underdeveloped formal land market, weak negotiating and regulatory position of the host government, and uncertainty about land values. Also, as international development organizations such as World Bank or FAO reports that the land fees are an insignificant part of negotiations as the host is more interested in investor commitments to prospective economic benefits such as diversifying the economic base, capital formation, stimulating the local economy and local livelihoods, training and job creation, and infrastructure development than direct compensation via land fees (Cotula 2011). Often, various tax incentives or duty exemptions are granted for enticing investment in strategic sectors like agriculture or modernizing primary economic base. As financial transfers assume insignificance for the host, macroeconomic benefits such as job creation in agriculture via supply chains, investments to stimulate the economy, sectoral development via capital inflow, skill formation, and training were key areas of perceived benefits expected from foreign investors' commitments, ushering in new agricultural biotechnology for productivity-enhancement, quality improvement of agricultural products, and employment prospects via skill formation (Zoomers 2010).

Emerging evidences from case studies suggest that the benefits might not occur and there might be *negative impacts* or potential threats for the local population, especially concerning access to land and water resources, and might lead to internal conflict (Osabuohien 2014). Social and environmental impact assessment of such displacement is required as the rural poor suffer from losses of minimum subsistence under customary tenure (Cotula 2011; Cotula et al. 2009). This might cause a change in livelihood due to shift of occupations, and hence might cause a change in the rural community, a loss of social capital, and a lack of accessibility to local resources (Daniel and Mittal 2009; Antonelli et al. 2015). In that case, a code of conduct is necessary for compensation of the displaced in land deal. As Anseeuw et al. (2012b) mentions, there are further adverse impacts: Revenue loss due to tax exemptions, and petty lease fees, loss of access to common property such as grasslands and forests, lack of legal recognition of customary resource ownership causing inadequate compensation, vulnerability of women due to discrimination in their land rights and poverty, insecure and low-paid jobs creation, etc. Schoneveld (2014) shows that biodiversity and ecosystem losses due to land use conversions is a threat as host 'governments are ill-equipped or disinclined to regulate land

*Land deals in Africa* 349

conversion' for new opportunities for rent-seeking or for attracting foreign capital. Land reform effort in the developing countries has been thwarted by land grab deals by investors and hence formal land tenure scheme is weak and undeveloped in the host nations.[6] Sources of these negative impacts are attributed to 'key failures of governance' resulting in 'power asymmetries' – unequal bargaining power of the farmers vis-à-vis the state, and government's weak mechanism and regulatory ability vis-à-vis the international investors – that push the local people with customary land rights and minimal negotiation power out of the deal (Anseeuw et al. 2012b; Borras and Franco 2012).

This causes a lack of access to land for food production, threatening poor rural communities as a wealthy investor gains control over food supply. In order to reduce the threats and facilitate beneficial opportunities for all parties, governments should have a role to play for enforcement and accountability of the investors so as to ensure investors' commitments for job creation, skill formation and training for employment, infrastructure development, and reducing income loss and food insecurity, etc.

### Constraints and conditions for beneficial investment

From the preceding discussion on negative impacts, we see that the malicious impacts of resource rents, the reduced accountability of government, and the misuse of power for rent-seeking activities are constraints (European Report on Development 2009, ERD henceforth). The World Bank Report (Deininger et al. 2011) reiterates this apprehension that although investments could lead to higher productivity in longer run, the lack of transparency and secretive or veiled tactics between the buyers and sellers (lack of governance) could be detrimental to this optimism. The report *does not* unequivocally lend support to the much hyped 'benefits' of running such deal, but warns against the mismanagement due to weak governance and corrupt underhand dealing. Moreover, by presenting a mixed picture across 14 countries in Africa, Latin America, Europe, and Asia, the report points out the failure on the part of most of the host governments to ensure rights to land and livelihood for the benefit of the local people, thus undermining the potential benefits via improved productivity. Normally, resource-rich countries get higher doses of FDI. However, the other host of factors like physical infrastructure, human capital, efficient legal system, political stability, corruption, and governance matter much for attracting FDI in the extractive industries. According to the ERD (2009), although the foreign investments in land is gaining prominence with the hope

350    *Gouranga G. Das*

that exchanging abundant resources (land and water with rising value) with scarce ones such as capital, infrastructure, skills, and technological progress will deliver benefits, but the ill-conceived deals could be counter-productive depending on the 'key' factor of serving local interest in land and natural resources. Soete and Habiyaremye (2010) discussed the *'paradox of plenty'* in terms of exploitation of tremendous endowment while crowding out the accumulation of social, human, and knowledge capital.[7] From the reports so far available, it is evident that the lack of appropriate institutional framework leads to the emergence of an unholy nexus between policy makers, governments, and the stakeholders (foreign as well as domestic private investors) so as to expropriate the landowners (smallholders and those with customary rights) via exploiting the advantages of existing 'weakest form of governance'. Weak governance, corruption, and malfunctioning state machinery make the host countries vulnerable. These countries typically suffer from low human development reflecting inadequate human capital, inability to mobilize domestic resources, weak infrastructure, and exposure to risk of conflict breakout. This, in turn, could make FDI and other factors ineffective to help transitioning from fragility to resilience. Although national law exists in some countries, often it leads to an inappropriate code of conduct via bribery, malpractices such as underhand dealings (i.e. 'veil of secretive tactics').

In order to overcome the inhibiting factors and achieve resilience, as mentioned by the ERD (2009), several *preconditions*, inter alia, are the following: Building social cohesion and state (building to ensure social compact between state and citizens), adhering to a long-term view, facilitating expansion of social and human capital, forming optimal governance structure, escalating the process of broader development objectives, and stabilizing the government with legitimacy. For such investments to have beneficial and sustained effect on host economies' pursuit of development, Quoting Deininger et al. (2011):

> Currently none of the African countries of interest to investors achieves even a quarter of its potential productivity. Rather than just focus only on an expansion of uncultivated land, it is important that investors and governments support improvements in technology, infrastructure, and institutions that can improve productivity on existing farmland.

For proper design and implementation of such deals, Von Braun and Meinzen-Dick (2009) suggests a *'dual-approach'*: First, by establishing a transparent code of conduct for the host and the foreign investors,

_Land deals in Africa_ 351

and, second, by designing appropriate policies by the host government to tap the opportunities and controlling the adverse effects so as to improve _investment climate_. If FDI in agriculture leads to positive spillovers via educational attainment and skill acquisition and domestic policy facilitates it, then the result could have beneficial impacts. Human capital development and skilled formation is important for seizing the benefits of good governance and enhancing productivity. In other words, if government or public institutions need transparencies, strengthening efficient 'legal' services by the specialized training of a skilled workforce (i.e. those who have already achieved tertiary or higher level of education or have expertise to undertake training to become legal professionals) is a way to prohibit expropriation or extortionary practices that might shroud the land deals.

As weak institutions, lack of government mechanism for enforcement, and accountability of investor commitments lead to power asymmetries and curb the bargaining power of the small farmers, the targeted countries need to strengthen governance, institution, and transparency for strengthening their negotiation capacity and implementation of code of conduct (dual approach). For a panel of 157 nations during 2000–2011, Bujko et al. (2014) presented evidence on how weak institutions and enforcement systems harboring corrupt practices led to large land deals at the expense of local people. This is critical as expected development outcomes need job creation, employment generation, technical viability, defining property rights, and better institutions (Deininger and Byerlee 2012). In fact, Collier and Venables (2012a, 2012b) has discussed the hindrances of shortages of capital, skill, and governance capacity in Africa, and emphasized the importance of these factors for productivity-enhancing investment in agronomic knowledge and better investment climate thanks to pioneer investors with superior skill. In the same vein, Antonelli et al. (2015) call for research on adoption of responsible land acquisitions to encourage transparency as the target countries suffering from low HDI are vulnerable to social and environmental unsustainable livelihood. Davis, D'Odorcio, and Rulli (2015a, 2015b) linked this vulnerability to the malnourishment, deforestation, and income loss of local communities. Importantly, they find that without an influx of technology and human development Africa, having most of the large-scale deals (53 percent of global agricultural land grabbed and 65 percent of food crop deals) would suffer from food and climate insecurity as well as less employment opportunities.

In this chapter, we offer a model to show how the government could overcome the negative impact of an ill-conceived land deal for reaping

## 352 Gouranga G. Das

expected positive development outcome via channelizing resources into productive investment.[8]

## Analytical framework for land deal

### Core model

Training and skill for inclusive development is important for sharing the benefits. Under chronic food shortage, and potential famine the poor host country is more than willing to offer a reasonably higher premium in alternative forms. Also, because of enforceability and compliance problems with investment commitments, these deals are 'risky' in terms of social instability, food insecurity, and land mismanagement. Although Kleemann and Thiele (2015) recognized the paucity of skilled and qualified labors in target regions and the lack of positive spillovers via better infrastructural facilities (e.g. machinery, seeds, fertilizers), unlike ours, they have considered welfare implications of displacements of small farmers from land. However, it supports our conjecture that governments should be facilitators for productive investments, technology transfer, and employment generation for improving welfare. In the Indian context, Das and Saha (2015) deploy a two-sector growth model with Hicks-Neutral technical progress to show the adverse welfare effects on farmers, and also on the industrialists with rehabilitation and remuneration (R&R) transfers to the displaced. In a different vein, here a stylized, perfectly competitive model, based on Jones (1965, 1971), is developed by reinstating and augmenting Das's (2013) model with skill formation and transparency aspect. This kind of 'land grab' is an *asymmetric replica* of outsourcing in food sector *without* encompassing value chain slicing. There are models based on Heckscher-Ohlin and its derivatives to explore such aspects (Jones 2000; Marjit and Acharyya 2003; Das 2009; Weiss 2008; Beladi, Marjit, and Oladi 2006; Feenstra and Hanson 2003).

Four sectors in the economy are the following: Low-skilled manufacturing (M), agricultural export sector (A), intermediates export sector using skilled labor (Z), and non-tradable *subsistence* sector (X).[9] M and Z are low skill manufactures and skilled sectors respectively. X is an indigenous sector (e.g. handicraft, or grazing cattle, medicinal plants, or wood products). Host countries, like Africa, have abundant land (T), out of which, say $T_o$, is *outsourced* for farm production, crop exports, and the rest of it ($T_d$) is kept for locals attracting low return. Also, it is endowed with an unskilled population (U), but skilled workers (S) and capital (K) are scarce. Skilled labor is specific to Z. K is only

*Land deals in Africa* 353

mobile across M and Z. $T_o$ and $T_d$ are specific *nonhomogeneous* land for sectors A and X respectively. Thus, returns to $T_o$ ($r_o$) and that to $T_d$ ($r_d$) differ. Mobility of unskilled labor ensures a uniform low wage ($w_u$) across M, A, and X. On the contrary, the immobility of specific land types causes the return to vary across A and X. But K, being mobile across M and Z, attracts uniform returns ($r_k$), whereas skilled labor, specific to Z, attracts wage ($w_s$) higher than $w_u$.

$$M = M(L_u, K)$$
$$A = A(L_u, T_o)$$
$$X = X(L_u, T_d)$$
$$Z = Z(L_s, K)$$

The following notations are used in the model:

$P_j$: Exogenous prices for $j^{th}$ good, $\forall j \in \{M, A, X, Z\}$
M: Import-competing (importable) low-skill manufacturing sector
A: Agricultural staple crops sector subject to outsourced production and exports
X: Non-traded agriculture and related sector
Z: High-skill sector (exportable)
$w_u$: Unskilled labor's wage
$w_s$: Skilled wage. Assume that originally, $w_s > w_u$[10]
$r_k$: Return to capital[11]
$T_o$: Land outsourced (i.e. subject to land deal)
$T_d$: Land preserved via customary rights for locals and used in non-traded agricultural sector or, fallow land with inferior quality used for peripheral activities like cattle-raising, grazing, primary products, forestry, etc. $T_o + T_d = T$
$r_o$: Return to $T_o$
$r_d$: Return to $T_d$.
$r_p$: Premium paid per unit of land leased, creating a wedge between $r_d$ and $r_o$
$a_i^j = i^{th}$ input required to produce 1 unit of $j^{th}$ final good, i = U, S, K, $T_o$, $T_d$
$\theta_{lj} = w_l a_l^j / P_j$ is the distributive share of $l^{th}$ labor-types in the production of $j \in \{M, A, X, Z\}$, $\forall l \in \{S, U\}$
$\theta_{kj} = r_k a_k^j / P_j$ is the distributive share of capital-owner for $j \in \{Z, M\}$
$\theta_{tj} = r_t a_t^j / P_j$ is the distributive share of $t^{th}$ specific landowner for $j \in \{A, X\}$, $\forall t \in \{T_o, T_d\}$

354 *Gouranga G. Das*

$\lambda_{ij} = \dfrac{a_i^j Y_j}{f_i}$ = jth commodity's input share in ith factor's endowment, where Y is generic output and $f$ is generic endowment; $\sigma_j, \forall_j \in \{M, A, X, Z\}$ is elasticity of substitution

$\bar{K}, \bar{S}, \bar{U}$, and $\bar{T}_d$: factor endowments of respective primary inputs[12]
"^" = proportional changes for a variable, *say* V, such that generically $\hat{V} = \dfrac{dV}{V}$

Competitive equilibrium with zero pure profit condition implies:

$$a_u^M w_u + a_k^M r_k = P_M \tag{1}$$

$$a_u^A w_u + a_{To}^A r_o = P_A \tag{2}$$

$$a_u^X w_u + a_{Td}^X r_d = P_X \tag{3}$$

$$a_s^Z w_s + a_k^Z r_k = P_Z \tag{4}$$

Prices for M, A, and Z are world prices because of small open economy and, for X, it is numeraire. Now, we add a skill formation sector and a composite legal sector (for appropriate code of conduct and governance).[13]

G: Government's expenditure (resources) facilitating human capital/skill, legal-institutional services such as quality governance, rule of law, etc.[14]
L: Sector providing legal-institutional services, kind of *social capital*
S: Skilled workers[15]

Efficient and quality legal services (L) are attributed to skilled lawyers, judicial system, and transparent government; thus, appropriate level of 'G' facilitates shaping of 'L' with the help of legal skilled professionals who come from the reserve of 'S' in the economy. As 'G' improves with a functioning government, 'L' is high, implying better governance. As 'S' develops more, it contributes to better quality or services of 'L'. Hence:

$$L = L(G, S) \text{ where } \partial L/\partial S = L_S \geq 0, \partial L/\partial G = L_G \geq 0.$$

Better quality of such services enables more trust, transparency, cooperation, and thus leads to productivity growth (Das 2009). In fact, *given* L, if 'G' is high for enacting the rule of law and governance is

*Land deals in Africa*   355

adequate, then 'S', being released, could be utilized in Z (hi-tech or innovative sectors). Also, that can boost production of both skill-user sectors, viz., L and Z.

In fact, rationale for invoking such mechanism could easily be grounded in the context of *E-government* in achieving the MDGs. In particular, we quote UN (2010)[16] that:

> E-Government is the use of ICT for strengthening governance and public institutions. It can help make public service delivery more agile and less costly. Similarly, e-government can be useful in the implementation of regulatory reforms by making processes more transparent and by streamlining activities.
>
> (p. 74)

To model it, we introduce the following technological coefficients:

$a_G^S, a_G^L$ : Per unit requirement of 'G' for production of 'S' and 'L' respectively, that is for providing regulatory framework or strengthening governance.[17]

Typically, $a_G^L$ represents a technological coefficient proxying mechanism design for governance control such that higher value of it implies a better code of conduct ensuring better property rights. In other words, *assuming* $a_G^L.L = \overline{G} \Rightarrow$ *with such technical progress,* $\hat{L} = -\hat{a}_G^L = g_L > 0$. The intuition here is that, akin to technical change, as government's governance mechanism improves (via better resources, endowment of skilled lawyers, or proficiency in institutions), then legal service improves in quality, which results in a higher level of output. For the educated professionals or skill sector, assuming government programs for educational attainment of the unskilled and training the semiskilled contribute to better human capital-induced skill, we write:

$$S = S(G, U) \ where \ \frac{\partial S}{\partial G} = S_G \geq 0, \frac{\partial S}{\partial U} = S_U \geq 0 \frac{\partial}{\partial G}\left(\frac{\partial S}{\partial U}\right)$$
$$= S_{GU} \geq 0.$$

Mutual development of 'S' and 'L' *via* 'G' creates conducive institutional environment for better designing of land rights instruments. We assume that L-sector uses relatively more 'G' as compared to the 'S-sector'. Thus, L- and S-sectors are linked via mobile input 'G' – 'G' contributes doubly, via skill acquisition as well as through better governance framework. Production functions above are assumed to exhibit

# 356   Gouranga G. Das

linear homogeneity and diminishing returns. The following technical coefficients are introduced:

$a_u^S$ : Per unit requirement of unskilled worker going into skill formation sector

$a_S^L$ : Per unit requirement of skilled workers for governance via legal professionals

Thus, for a *price system* we add, on top of Eqs. (1)–(4), two more P = AC relationships:

for skill sector, $a_u^S.w_u + a_G^S.r_G^* = w_S$  (4a)

and, for governance sector, $a_S^L.w_S + a_G^L.r_G^* = w_L$  (4b)

where $w_L$: Return to legal services or payment for such service providers for protecting land rights and taking care of extortions, corrupt practices.[18]

$r_G^*$: Return to government investment in educational and social infrastructure. This could also be construed as the price of public education for skilling the unskilled, and also for supplying such human capital for the legal sector for transparency. As this is often out of altruism or philanthropy by the government, it is exogenously fixed by the authorities.[19]

Full employment ensures the following:

$$a_u^M.M + a_u^A.A + a_u^X.X + a_u^S.S = \overline{U}$$  (5)

$$a_s^Z.Z + a_s^L.L = S$$  (6)

$$a_k^M M + a_k^Z Z = \overline{K}$$  (7)

$$a_{To}^A A = T_o$$  (8)

$$a_{Td}^X X = \overline{T}_d$$  (9)

Although the endowment of unskilled workers is fixed (at a given point of time in the economy), we assume that skill formation sector increases 'S' over time via training of the fixed pool of the unskilled; thus, there is flow of skill. Additionally, for constrained government resources:

$$a_G^L.L + a_G^S.S = \overline{G}$$  (9a)

$$r_o = r_d + r_p \text{ where } r_p > 0.[20]$$  (10)

Now, we have in total 12 equations (1, 2, 3, 4, 7, 8, 9) plus (4a), (4b), (9a), (5), and (6) to determine 12 variables: $w_s$, $w_u$, $r_K$, $r_d$, $w_L$; M, A, X, Z, S, L, $T_O$. We solve for $w_s$, $w_u$, $r_k$, $r_d$, and M, A, X, and Z. Given *exogenous* $r_p$ and $P_j$ ($\forall j$), we solve for $w_u$ and $r_d$ from (2) and (3). Using (10), we get $r_o$ as unique and this leaves room for policy makers to use as an instrument for manipulation to suit purpose in hand. We see that $r_o$ and $r_p$ move in unison with each other. Substituting $w_u$ in (1), we get $r_k$. Finally, from (4), we obtain $w_s$ by eliminating $r_k$. For outputs, equation (8) and (6) determine A and Z respectively. As $\overline{K}$ is given exogenously, plugging Z in (7), we derive M. Then, plugging M and A in (5), we get X. Equation (8) determines $T_o$ as a function of level of A, factor returns, and technological coefficients. Considering unit value isoquant and unit cost minimization, the technological coefficients, $a_i^j$ are determined by:

$$a_i^j = a_i^j(w_l, r_k, r_t), \forall l = s, u; t = T_o, T_d; j = M, A, X, Z \qquad (11)$$

X is the non-traded numeraire sector. All other sectors are traded where the *small* host country is a *price-taker* in the world market. As an illustration, suppose we incorporate L-services in the sector 'X' facing the threat of land grab via 'deal' under secretive tactics or improper 'code of conduct' (see ERD 2009; Von Braun and Meinzen-Dick 2009; Deininger et al. 2011) in the sense that 'L' protects their rights to land and enables them to produce output (as an input into production process) such that: $X = X(L_u, T_d, L)$ and $a_L^X.X = L$ where $a_L^X$ is the technological coefficient. It is obvious that, if 'L' increases, then the output of 'X' increases via ensuring a better code of conduct; in turn, it causes $T_d$ to be used more so as to limit land grab activities, resulting in a fall in $T_o$. At the same time, unskilled workers released from 'A' sector can be trained via 'S' sector to become skilled; as 'S' increases it leads to development of human capital and good quality L-services.

### Equations of change

For enumerating proportional changes for the equation system (1) to (4), (4a), and (4b), employing envelope theorem (Jones 1965), we derive the factor-return shares – $\theta_{lj}$, $\theta_{kj}$, $\theta_{tj}$ – to obtain:

$$\theta_u^M \hat{w}_u + \theta_k^M \hat{r}_k = \hat{P}_M \qquad (12)$$

$$\theta_u^A \hat{w}_u + \theta_{To}^A \hat{r}_o = \hat{P}_A \qquad (13)$$

$$\theta_u^X \hat{w}_u + \theta_{Td}^X \hat{r}_d = \hat{P}_X \qquad (14)$$

358   *Gouranga G. Das*

$$\theta_s^Z \hat{w}_u + \theta_k^Z \hat{r}_k = \hat{P}_Z \tag{15}$$

$$\theta_u^S . \hat{w}_u + \theta_G^S . \hat{r}_G^* = \hat{w}_s \tag{15a}$$

$$\theta_G^L . \hat{r}_G^* + \theta_S^L . \hat{w}_s = \hat{w}_L \tag{15b}$$

where cost-shares, $\theta_G^S + \theta_u^S = 1, \theta_G^L + \theta_S^L = 1$ and endowment shares, $\lambda_G^S + \lambda_G^L = 1, \lambda_u^S + \lambda_u^X + \lambda_u^A + \lambda_u^M = 1$.

Following Jones (1965), using (4a) and (4b), from unit-value isoquant:

$$\hat{a}_G^L = -\theta_S^L \sigma_L (\hat{r}_G^* - \hat{w}_S) \text{ and } \hat{a}_S^L = \theta_G^L \sigma_L (\hat{r}_G^* - \hat{w}_S) \tag{4c}$$

$$\hat{a}_u^S = \theta_G^S \sigma_S (\hat{r}_G^* - \hat{w}_u) \text{ and } \hat{a}_G^S = -\theta_u^S \sigma_S (\hat{r}_G^* - \hat{w}_u) \tag{4d}$$

Also, from (10), $\hat{r}_o = \hat{r}_p + \hat{r}_d$ with $\hat{r}_p \geq 0$. \tag{16}

Using (16) in (13 and 13b) we can determine the changes due to premium alterations:

$$\hat{A} - \hat{X} = \hat{a}_{Td}^X - \hat{a}_{To}^A = (\hat{w}_u - \hat{r}_o) \left[ \theta_u^X \sigma_X - \theta_u^A \sigma_A \right] + \hat{r}_p \theta_u^X \sigma_X \tag{17}$$

From (5), $\lambda_u^M \hat{M} + \lambda_u^A \hat{A} + \lambda_u^X \hat{X} + \lambda_u^S \hat{S} = \hat{U} - [\lambda_u^M \hat{a}_u^M + \lambda_u^A \hat{a}_u^A + \lambda_u^X \hat{a}_u^X + \lambda_u^S \hat{a}_u^S]$ \tag{5.1}

From (6), $\lambda_S^Z \hat{Z} + \lambda_S^L \hat{L} = \hat{S} - [\lambda_S^Z \hat{a}_S^Z + \lambda_S^L \hat{a}_S^L]$ \tag{6.1}

From (9a), analogously, $\lambda_G^L \hat{L} + \lambda_G^S \hat{S} = \hat{G} - [\lambda_G^L \hat{a}_G^L + \lambda_G^S \hat{a}_G^S]$ \tag{9a.1}

From (6), $\hat{Z} = -\hat{a}_s^Z = [-\theta_k^Z \sigma_z (\hat{r}_k - \hat{w}_s)] < 0$ \tag{6a}

Using (6a) and (4c) in (6.1), with $\widehat{r_G^*} = 0$, we simplify to get:

$$\lambda_S^L \hat{L} = \hat{S} + \lambda_S^Z \sigma_Z \theta_K^Z (\hat{w}_S - \hat{r}_K) + \lambda_S^L \sigma_L \theta_G^L \hat{w}_S - \lambda_S^Z \hat{Z} \tag{9b}$$

On further simplification,

$$\hat{L} = \hat{S} \Big/ \lambda_S^L + \frac{\lambda_S^Z}{\lambda_S^L} \sigma_Z \theta_K^Z (\hat{w}_S - \hat{r}_K) + \sigma_L \theta_G^L \hat{w}_S - \frac{\lambda_S^Z}{\lambda_S^L} \hat{Z} \tag{9b.1}$$

Collecting terms from earlier:

$$\hat{L} = [\hat{S} \Big/ \lambda_S^L + \sigma_L \theta_G^L \hat{w}_S] - \frac{\lambda_S^Z}{\lambda_S^L} [\hat{Z} - \sigma_Z \theta_K^Z (\hat{w}_S - \hat{r}_K)]$$

Right running head: *Land deals in Africa* 359

As before, from (9a.1), (4c), and (4d) we write:

$$\lambda_G^L \hat{L} = \hat{G} - \lambda_G^S . \hat{S} - \lambda_G^L \theta_S^L \sigma_L \hat{w}_S - \lambda_G^S \theta_u^S \sigma_S \hat{w}_u \text{ (assuming } \hat{r}_G^* = 0).$$

$$\Rightarrow \hat{L} = \frac{\hat{G}}{\lambda_G^L} - \frac{\lambda_G^S}{\lambda_G^L} \hat{S} - \theta_S^L \sigma_L \hat{w}_S - \frac{\lambda_G^S}{\lambda_G^L} \theta_u^S \sigma_S \hat{w}_u \qquad (9c)$$

This equation shows that

with $\hat{w}_S = \hat{w}_u = 0, \hat{G} > 0$, we get $\hat{L} = \dfrac{\hat{G}}{\lambda_G^L} - \dfrac{\lambda_G^S}{\lambda_G^L} . \hat{S} > 0,$ iff $\hat{G} > \hat{S} \geq 0.$

With $\hat{w}_S = \hat{r}_K = 0, \hat{L} = \dfrac{1}{\lambda_S^L}[\hat{S} - \lambda_S^Z . \hat{Z}] \Rightarrow \hat{L} > 0,$ iff $\hat{S} > \lambda_S^Z . \hat{Z}$

$\hat{S} > 0,$ iff $\hat{G} > \lambda_G^L . \hat{L}$ while $\lambda_S^L \neq 0$ (from 9c)

This implies that if an increase in government expenditure/resources in providing services exceeds its share spent on increasing provision of better institution via strong governance/rule of law, then the rest of G is used for financing spending on human capital/education so that skill is augmented. Thus, both social and human capitals are conjointly increased via public policy support (G). Both, in turn, contribute to improvement in quality of legal-institutional framework. Intuitively, if $S > 0$ and $\hat{Z} = 0$, given $\hat{w}_S \geq 0, \hat{w}_S \geq \hat{r}_K, \hat{L} > 0$. That is, with an increase in skills or human capital, legal professional services go up to contribute better quality governance and if production of Z falls, the more skilled workforce gets absorbed into L-sector with the net impact depending on the term $(\hat{S} - \lambda_S^Z \hat{Z})$. This is clear because if the wages of skilled workers go up in the S-sector, then more exodus of unskilled workers leads to further skill formation, fall in the return to capital in M- and Z-sectors; if increase in Z is not much compared to increase in S, it will cause skilled migration to L-sector from Z and lead to increase in L-output. Also, if 'L' is at quite optimal level, then a share of skilled workers in L might decline with more 'S' leading to increase in Z-production (i.e. via $\lambda_S^Z \hat{Z} = \hat{S} + \lambda_S^Z \sigma_Z \theta_K^Z (\hat{w}_S - \hat{r}_K) + \lambda_S^L \sigma_L \theta_G^L \hat{w}_S - \lambda_S^L \hat{L}).$

Similarly, from (5.1),

$$\hat{S} = -\left[\frac{\lambda_u^M}{\lambda_u^S}\hat{M} + \frac{\lambda_u^A}{\lambda_u^S}\hat{A} + \frac{\lambda_u^X}{\lambda_u^S}\hat{X}\right] + \frac{\lambda_u^M}{\lambda_u^S}\theta_k^M \sigma_M (\hat{w}_u - \hat{r}_k)$$

$$+ \frac{\lambda_u^A}{\lambda_u^S}\theta_{T_o}^A \sigma_A (\hat{w}_u - \hat{r}_o) + \frac{\lambda_u^X}{\lambda_u^S}\theta_{Td}^X \sigma_X (\hat{w}_u - \hat{r}_d) + \theta_G^S \sigma_S (\hat{w}_u - \hat{r}_G^*) \qquad (18)$$

## 360 Gouranga G. Das

With $\hat{M} = \hat{A} = \hat{X} = 0$ and $\hat{r}_k = 0 = \hat{r}_0 = \hat{r}_d = \hat{r}_G^*$, then from (18), write:

$$\hat{S} = \frac{\hat{w}_u}{\lambda_u^S}[\lambda_u^M \theta_k^M \sigma_M + \lambda_u^A \theta_{T0}^A \sigma_A + \lambda_u^X \theta_{Td}^X \sigma_X + \lambda_u^S \theta_G^S \sigma_S] > 0$$

Consider the following comparative statics analysis (ceteris paribus) for sectors 'L' and 'S' only. This enables us to trace the policy impacts (of government's exogenous shocks) on enacting 'code of conduct' (via 'L') and attainment of human capital (via 'S').

*Proposition 1:* Improvement in governance for a better code of conduct will increase output.

*Proof:* Improvement in governance mechanism to ensure a better 'code of conduct' is modeled via the technological coefficient (see above) $a_G^L$ such that, *ceteris paribus*, nonuniform technical progress, occurring only in legal sector, represents increasing efficiency of the host country government's designing of stronger governance. Thus,

$$\hat{a}_G^L = -g_L, g_L > 0 \,, \hat{a}_S^L = 0 \text{ whereas } \hat{a}_h^m = 0, \forall h$$
$$\text{and } \forall m = S, M, A, X, Z.$$

Using Eqs. (4b), (15b), and envelope condition (at *given* factor prices), we derive:

$$\theta_S^L \hat{a}_S^L + \theta_G^L \hat{a}_G^L = \hat{w}_L \tag{19}$$

$$\Rightarrow -g_L \theta_G^L = \hat{w}_L \Rightarrow 0 > \hat{w}_L. \tag{19.1}$$

Also, at given factor prices in L-sector, using envelope condition and (19), we have $\hat{w}_S = 0 = \hat{r}_G^* \Rightarrow$ from (15a), $\hat{w}_u = 0$ and hence, from Eqs. (12)–(15), $\hat{r}_k = \hat{r}_0 = \hat{r}_d = 0$.

With technical change, a final price change due to factor price changes is *less* as technical progress compensates via cost-reduction and factor-saving.

From (9a.1):

$$\lambda_G^L \hat{L} = \hat{G} - [\lambda_G^L(-g_L) + \lambda_G^S.0] - \lambda_G^S \hat{S} \Rightarrow \hat{L} = \frac{\hat{G}}{\lambda_G^L} + \lambda_G^L g_L - \lambda_G^S \hat{S}$$

$$\Rightarrow \text{ with } \hat{S} = 0, \hat{L} = \frac{\hat{G}}{\lambda_G^L} + \lambda_G^L g_L > 0$$

Improvement in efficiency in governance mechanism (presumably changes in technology translate into quality changes and alter input coefficients) leads to a reduction in government coefficients in 'L', and makes its provision cheaper, that is, easily accessible by the local people in the host. Thus, better governance improves rule of law, makes land rights conditions better, and makes social capital affordable so as to facilitate better functioning.

Using (9c) with (19.1), with $\hat{w}_u = 0$ we invoke:

$$\hat{L} = [\frac{\hat{G}}{\lambda_G^L} + \sigma_L g_L \theta_G^L] - \frac{\lambda_G^S}{\lambda_G^L}\hat{S} \Rightarrow \text{ while } g_L > 0, \hat{L} > 0 \text{ iff } [\frac{\hat{G}}{\lambda_G^L} + \sigma_L g_L \theta_G^L] > \frac{\lambda_G^S}{\lambda_G^L}\hat{S}$$

$$\Rightarrow \text{ iff } \hat{G} + \lambda_G^L \sigma_L g_L \theta_G^L > \lambda_G^S \hat{S}$$

Consider the changes in input coefficients to changes in input prices as well as technical change, and, thus, we get conditions for impacts on output and prices of technological changes as:-

With $\hat{r}_G^* = 0$, using (15a) and (15b) respectively

$$\theta_u^S.\hat{w}_u = \hat{w}_s = \frac{\hat{w}_L + g_L \theta_G^L}{\theta_S^L} \Rightarrow \hat{w}_u = \frac{\hat{w}_s}{\theta_u^S} = \frac{\hat{w}_L + g_L \theta_G^L}{\theta_u^S \theta_S^L} \qquad (15a.1)$$

$$\theta_S^L.\hat{w}_s = \hat{w}_L + g_L \theta_G^L \Rightarrow \hat{w}_s = \frac{\hat{w}_L + g_L \theta_G^L}{\theta_S^L} \qquad (15b.1)$$

As $\theta_u^S < 1$, $\frac{1}{\theta_u^S} > 1 \Rightarrow \hat{w}_u > \hat{w}_S$.

*Corollary:* If the X-sector is facing the threat of eviction and land grab takes recourse to services or inputs from L-sector (that is legal protection establishes code of conduct to prevent violation of land rights), then with the improved efficiency of governance mechanism and better quality and easy access, X-sector gains and incidence of land grab might fall.

As before, L = L(S, G) and S = S(U, G), keeping G fixed for this sector.

For linking legal services to land acquisitions, for example, to protect property rights via strong governance and legal land rights, we postulate that $a_L^X.X = L$ where $a_L^X$ is the per unit requirement of legal input for X-sector facing the threat of eviction or land grab. Thus, $\hat{X} = \hat{L} - \hat{a}_L^X$. With $\hat{a}_L^X = -g_X, g_X > 0$, this signifies that legal sector protecting land rights become efficient so that technological coefficient

## 362 Gouranga G. Das

improves indicating improvement in governance or code of conduct, then we get $\hat{X} = \hat{L} + g_X > 0$

To illustrate the role of better quality 'L' in protecting land rights of the small land-holders (manifested in rising output of traditional agriculture, X-sector), let us suppose S = S(U), that is by some training or schooling mechanism, the unskilled labor's quality is improved to translate into a skilled personnel. Then, (4b) remains unaltered while from price equation (4a), we get $a_u^S.w_u = w_S \Rightarrow \theta_u^S \hat{w}_u = \hat{w}_S$ and $\hat{S} = -\hat{a}_u^S = g_u$ (rise in technical efficiency in skill upgrading) > 0.

Under this specific example, (9a) modifies to: $a_G^L.L = \overline{G} \Rightarrow \hat{L} = -\hat{a}_G^L = g_L > 0$. This yields:

$$\hat{X} = \hat{L} + g_X = g_L + g_X > 0. \tag{15a.2}$$

Also, from (4c), we write:

$$\hat{L} = -\hat{a}_G^L = +\theta_S^L \sigma_L \hat{w}_S > 0, \text{ while } \hat{r}_G^* = 0 \Rightarrow \hat{X} = \theta_S^L \sigma_L \hat{w}_S + g_X. \tag{15a.3}$$

Intuitively, as more skilled labor force augments professional competencies, better quality 'code of conduct' comes into shape resulting in increase in the output of the small-holder agriculture sector. As X expands, more unskilled workers migrate from 'A', the sector subject to land acquisition, to 'X' and to 'S', causing a squeeze in the production of 'A'. This could lead to expansion in the 'Z'-sector using specific skilled labor. Thus, motives for landgrab subside while the innovative manufacturing sector benefits along with small-holder agriculture. Welfare improves and immiserizing effect, encountered in the basic core model (Das 2013), is withered away. From (15a) and (15b), in this specific illustration, we invoke:

$$\theta_S^L.\hat{w}_s = \hat{w}_L = \theta_S^L.[\theta_u^S.\hat{w}_u](\textit{fixed } \hat{r}_G^* = 0).$$

Hence, from (15a.3) $\hat{X} = \sigma_L \hat{w}_L + g_X$ and $\hat{w}_L > \hat{w}_u > 0$.

Returns to skilled, governance sector professionals, and unskilled increase and as $\hat{w}_L > 0$, $\hat{X} > 0$.

Therefore, if returns or payment to legal professionals rise via better quality services, governance mechanism, and skills, then production in domestic subsistence or small-holder traditional sector expands attributable to host government's developing better socio-institutional

Land deals in Africa    363

capital (along with human capital). With S = S (U, G), from either (9b.1) or (9a.1), $\hat{L} > 0$ and hence, $\hat{X} > 0$.

Considering the P = AC equation in X-sector we can modify Eq. (3) and, hence, Eq. (14) to:

$$a_u^X w_u + a_{Td}^X r_d + a_L^X w_L = P_X \tag{3a}$$

$$\Rightarrow \theta_u^X \hat{w}_u + \theta_{Td}^X \hat{r}_d + \theta_L^X \hat{w}_L = \hat{P}_X \tag{14a}$$

Using envelope condition, we write:

$$\theta_u^X \hat{a}_u^X + \theta_{Td}^X \hat{a}_{T_d}^X + \theta_L^X \hat{a}_L^X = 0, \text{ where } \theta_u^X + \theta_{Td}^X + \theta_L^X = 1 \tag{14a.1}$$

$$\Rightarrow \hat{a}_L^X = \left(\theta_u^X + \theta_{Td}^X\right)\hat{a}_L^X - \left(\theta_u^X \hat{a}_u^X + \theta_{Td}^X \hat{a}_{T_d}^X\right)$$

$$\Rightarrow \hat{a}_L^X = \theta_{Td}^X \left(\hat{a}_L^X - \hat{a}_{T_d}^X\right) + \theta_u^X \left(\hat{a}_L^X - \hat{a}_u^X\right)$$

From this relationship, it is evident that technical expertise or efficiency in governance/legal sector is the cost-share weighted average of its differences from the primary factor-augmenting technical change in land and unskilled workers; thus, we could say that if $\hat{a}_L^X > \hat{a}_u^X$ and $\hat{a}_L^X > \hat{a}_{T_d}^X$, then surely $\hat{a}_L^X > 0$. Exploiting previously developed relationships in terms of isoquant and its properties (alike Eqs. 17a, b, c, d), we can also derive that:

$$\hat{a}_L^X = -\theta_{Td}^X \sigma_{LTd}(\hat{w}_L - \hat{r}_d) - \theta_u^X \sigma_{LU}(\hat{w}_L - \hat{w}_u)$$
$$\Rightarrow \hat{a}_L^X = -[\theta_{Td}^X \sigma_{LTd}(\hat{w}_L - \hat{r}_d) + \theta_u^X \sigma_{LU}(\hat{w}_L - \hat{w}_u)] \tag{15a.4}$$
$$\Rightarrow \hat{X} = [\theta_{Td}^X \sigma_{LTd}(\hat{w}_L - \hat{r}_d) + \theta_u^X \sigma_{LU}(\hat{w}_L - \hat{w}_u)] > 0,$$
when $\hat{w}_L > \hat{w}_u$ and $\hat{w}_L > \hat{r}_d$.

*Proposition 2:* Uniform technical progress in the sector (L) proxying better quality of governance mechanism will lead to increase in output and reduction in wage inequality.

*Rationale:* Here $\hat{a}_S^L = \hat{a}_G^L = -g_L(g_L > 0)$. Then, we derive:

$$\theta_S^L \hat{a}_S^L + \theta_G^L \hat{a}_G^L + \theta_S^L \hat{w}_s + \theta_G^L \hat{r}_G^* = \hat{w}_L \text{ and, with } \hat{r}_G^* = 0,$$
$$\theta_S^L \hat{w}_s = \hat{w}_L + g_L \tag{20}$$

364   *Gouranga G. Das*

Considering system of equations (12)–(15) plus (20) and (15a.1), we find:

$$\hat{w}_S = \frac{\hat{w}_L + g_L}{\theta_S^L} \text{ and } \theta_S^L[\theta_u^S.\hat{w}_u] = \hat{w}_L + g_L \Rightarrow \hat{w}_u = \frac{\hat{w}_L + g_L}{\theta_S^L \theta_u^S} > 0.$$ Fol-

lowing a previous proposition, we can infer that $\hat{w}_S - \hat{w}_u = -\frac{g_L + \hat{w}_L}{\theta_S^L}\left(\frac{\theta_G^S}{\theta_u^S}\right)$

$\Rightarrow [\hat{w}_S - \hat{w}_u] < 0.$ Therefore, inequality declines as quality of governance, attributable to quality-augmentation of the skilled workers (upgrading technical expertise of skill going into legal profession, $\hat{a}_S^L > 0$) escalates as well as improved government transparency ($\hat{a}_G^L > 0$), improves translating into higher level of social capital formation ($\hat{L} > 0$). Intuition is that as returns to skill increases ($\hat{w}_s > 0$) and that of returns to quality-governance also inflates ($\hat{w}_L > 0$), more unskilled workers are trained to become skilled and upgrading takes place in S- and L-sectors. Thus, from fixed pool of untrained workers the unskilled moves to S and subsequently, to L-sector, resulting in rise in unskilled wage for the sectors M, A, and X; with more unskilled becoming skilled, the rise in skilled workers via the skill formation sector leads to fall in wage. It implies that the increase in skilled wage (following ensuing shocks and changes) is less pronounced than that in the unskilled case, but the skill-unskilled wage gap still remains with narrowing of the differentials.

Using Eq. (15): $\theta_S^Z[\frac{\hat{w}_L + g_L}{\theta_S^L}] + \theta_K^Z \hat{r}_K = 0 \Rightarrow \hat{r}_K = -\frac{\theta_S^Z}{\theta_K^Z \theta_S^L}(\hat{w}_L + g_L) < 0.$

Therefore, $[\hat{w}_s - \hat{r}_K] > 0 \Rightarrow$ from (9b), $\hat{L} > 0.$

*Proposition 3:* Improvement in human capital-induced skill formation, via public investment in education, training, and schooling (i.e. augmenting technical expertise and efficiency of skilled and unskilled represented by increase in technological coefficients in G-input), leads to an expansion of skill formation and innovative sector and helps averting land outsourcing.

*Proof:* Here $\hat{a}_G^S = \hat{a}_u^S = -g_S (g_S > 0).$

Then, we derive that:

$$\theta_G^S \hat{a}_G^S + \theta_u^S \hat{a}_u^S + \theta_u^S \hat{w}_u + \theta_G^S \hat{r}_G^* = \hat{w}_S$$
$$\Rightarrow -g_S + \theta_u^S \hat{w}_u = \hat{w}_S \Rightarrow \theta_u^S \hat{w}_u = \hat{w}_S + g_S \tag{21}$$

And $\theta_S^L \hat{w}_S = \hat{w}_L$ (22)

If $\hat{w}_L = 0$, from (22), $\hat{w}_S = 0$ and from (21), $\hat{w}_u = \dfrac{g_S}{\theta_u^S} > \hat{w}_S = 0$

If $\hat{w}_L > 0$, from (22), $\hat{w}_S = \dfrac{\hat{w}_L}{\theta_S^L} > 0 \Rightarrow \hat{w}_S > \hat{w}_L (as, \dfrac{1}{\theta_S^L} > 1)$, and from dividing (22) by (21), on simplification:

$$\frac{\hat{w}_s}{\hat{w}_u} = \frac{\hat{w}_L \theta_u^S}{\hat{w}_L + \theta_S^L g_S} \Rightarrow \hat{w}_S < \hat{w}_u.$$

As $\hat{w}_L(>0)$ increases, this causes migration of unskilled to skilled and legal sector. Also, as technical progress in unskilled indicates a quality improvement leading to skill formation, in the absence of productivity improvements of the skilled workers, marginal productivity of unskilled workers increases causing its wage to rise and, hence, wage gap declines.

From (9a.1), $\lambda_G^S.\hat{S} = \hat{G} + \lambda_G^S g_S - \lambda_G^L \hat{L} \Rightarrow \hat{S} = g_S - \dfrac{\lambda_G^L}{\lambda_G^S} \hat{L} \; (if \; \hat{G} = 0)$.

Also, $\hat{S} > 0$, if $g_S > \dfrac{\lambda_G^L}{\lambda_G^S} \hat{L} \Rightarrow$ if $\lambda_G^S g_S > \lambda_G^L \hat{L}$; that is, increase in public expenditure on education/skill formation augments skilled workforce into the innovative manufacturing sector (Z). This has significance for the land deal issue because for a host country with *already existing* better governance and judicial system for protecting local's rights, the pernicious or bad 'syndrome' is absent and hence, she needs to invest less on building good socio-institutional capital (i.e. in L-sector's output) and thus, she can put more effort in building educational infrastructure to have educated workforce, who might contribute to the development of further technical expertise via innovation.

## Conclusions

Terminological differences aside, 'outsourcing' (*á la*The Economist 2009) farm production to relatively land-abundant nations across borders, for producing staple crops, and exporting them back to mitigate the adverse effects of food insecurity is kind of off-shoring, and

366 *Gouranga G. Das*

is quite distinct from materials or service outsourcing. According to ERD (2009, p. 68),

> assessing the contribution of FDI to food security is not an easy task . . . is a daunting task to address the concerns of the various stakeholders (private sector of investor and host countries as well as the governments). . . . In order to safeguard the concerns of the various parties, it may be useful to develop a framework to highlight the particular aspects of investments, which need to be evaluated so that the negative impacts can be minimized in the future and they can be rendered more sustainable.

Based on this type of conjectures, this chapter constructs a model for eliciting useful conclusion. The model offers insights that (1) government should seek enforceable investor commitments and ensure accountability via promoting quality institutions; (2) investment in education and skill is crucial for employment of the displaced rural people, and better negotiation power; and (3) building up technological efforts (via investment in new technology) and skill formation, infrastructure developments will have favorable effects.

In fact, Deininger et al. (2011) cautions against the optimism of achieving higher productivity if 'veil of secret tactics between the dealmakers' prevails as it undermines the much avowed objective of improving hosts' labor productivity. Fazekas and Burns (2012) supports our conjecture that skill and knowledge 'is directly relevant to governance as a critical input to the process, a resource for political decision-making, and an instrument for policy implementation', thus, human capital formation drives policy change via institution (ibid., p. 10). This is in conformity with our conjectures that public investment in education leads to employment generation, increases capacity to negotiate by balancing power, enables stronger property rights, and facilitates a better institutional, economic, and social environment so that the negative impacts of unequal power are curbed.

## Notes

1 Acquisition and eviction experience associated with land deals is found in history, for example, the enclosure movement in Britain or land conversion in the United States, and even in developing nations like China, East Asia, South-East Asia for public or private purposes. This issue is so important that even Nobel laureate poet Tagore from Bengal wrote 'Two

## Land deals in Africa 367

Acres of Land (Do Bigha Jameen)' and subsequently in 'The Robbery of Soil' in 1922 by L. K. Elmhirst to warn against malpractices of corrupt aggression on land resulting in social divisions. In this chapter, we deal with land acquisition in developing countries of Africa.

2 The Economist (May 7th 2011) reports that it has swelled to 80 million hectares equal to the farmland of Britain, France, Germany, and Italy. Extensive listing of media reports on overseas land investments is available on IFPRI's website at www.ifpri.org/ pubs/bp/bp013Table01.pdf. IFPRI's blog at http://ifpriblog.org/2009/04/24/landgrab.aspx.

3 The 2014 database is much more detailed and significantly upgraded from the 2012 beta version with dynamic interface. See http://www.landmatrix.org/en/ and http://landmatrix.org/en/announcements/tagged/analytical%20report/

4 The list of media reports on land deals are presented in a table spanning five pages in their policy brief. Since 2009 various reports and data sets have come out and debates draw largely upon those datasets with contested methodologies and differences in coverage, time periods, and regional coverage, making the research suffer from misconceptions on the subject. For example, Anseeuw et al. (2012b) and Kugelman (2013) present figures as large as 203 and 230 million ha. See www.landmatrix.org/en/about/, https://exposingtheinvisible.org/resources/land-matrix and Nolte et al. (2014).

5 Foreign direct investment in land could bring benefits, see *New Agriculturist* at www.new-ag.info/en/developments/devItem.php?a=782

6 In fact, recent evidences show that in Laos land grabs have pushed subsistence farmers into poverty, hunger and higher mortality, and conflicts, and promoted a lack of access to education and health (See United Nations, IRIN News at www.irinnews.org/report/100116/laos-land-grabs-drive-subsistence-farmers-into-de accessed on 01/12/2014).

7 See UNCTAD (2008).

8 In this chapter, we do not model 'power-relations' or bargaining power' or 'ill-design'; rather, it is perceived as consequences of 'lack of governance' or 'corruption' or 'cronyism' in a host lagging in adequate literacy to comprehend such deals. We show how productive investment in human capital could achieve better design and implementation of investment in land by facilitating conducive governance structure and institution; it implies that if the foreign investors invest in education and literacy for the local communities, deliver requisite training, then the benefits could be shared between the stakeholders with improvement in institution building, efficacy, and balance of power. This will replace weak institutions with corrupt elites as educated local people will have more bargaining power than the uneducated.

9 Although cash crop production like rubber, sugar, and banana are quite common historically (like the banana republic), the new trend induced primarily by food shortage (due to trade bans and slump in production in major grain producers) is a way to shift to cereal or staples. Sector 'A' is a kind of 'booming staple crops sector' where the boom happens due to land-shifting via land deals signed by the actors. Subsistence sector does grazing cattle, raises medicinal plants, or herbs, which are predominantly non-tradeable.

368   *Gouranga G. Das*

10  Even in developing economies, skilled labor attracts considerably higher wages than their unskilled counterpart, although levels are *lower than* the rich nations. Income gap is persistent in these nations with incidence of poverty.

11  K is domestic capital or conceived as composite capital made of foreign and domestic types. Given the primary focus, we *do not distinguish* capital by origin. However, the model could be extended to incorporate foreign capital with higher premium and could study the impact of differences in relative premium between land outsourced and foreign capital on income and output. In this model, *implicit presumption* is defined by the following: Being naturally capital scarce, and foreign capital inflow is already internalized in the economy via composite K whereas, being *naturally* land-abundant, the impact of foreign acquisition of immobile land is not absorbed at all.

12  In these countries, 'Emigration' is more common due to home economy's conditions. It causes brain drain or skill shortages, hindering the development prospect and inhibiting technical progress.

13  A much more complex formalization could split skills in categories (e.g. distinguishing between specific skills for legal and innovation). However, this is beyond the scope of this chapter.

14  We do not model political economy aspects such as elections or the overthrow of corrupt governments.

15  Intra-skill classification is not distinguished. Every skill professional is assumed to be malleable to perform designated works.

16  The United Nations (November 2010). Millennium Development Goal 8, the Global Partnership for Development at a Critical Juncture. MDG Gap Task Force Report 2010.

17  As will be illustrated later, improvement in 'L' could be modeled akin to technological change in this sector in the sense that *better mechanism design* to overcome weak rule of law and building stronger governance resembles improvement in technical efficiency of government machinery via training, human capital, and better technological facilities like GPS, GIS, ICT, etc.

18  $W_L$ could be a lawyer's official salary without being bribed. Thus, $W_L$ is quasi-fixed in the sense that the user of services of L-output has no control over it, i.e. the sector using such services 'pays' (in the form of tax or service fees) this amount as fixed by the government or judicial systems.

19  This assumption is logical as the government often provides education with prices (irrespective of levels) fixed by it at a point of time.

20  Agricultural investment in such economies is highly risky, especially in continents like Africa. Not only that, there is risk of riots and protests by civil societies in these countries (e.g. in Haiti, Congo, and Bangladesh there were eruptions of riots instigated by food shortage) causing disruptions of smooth operations. Also, Kugelman and Levenstein (2009) documents such evidence in terms of lavish tax incentives and hefty security arrangements for investors in the case of Pakistan (see P. 3). Madagascar's case of overthrowing the government following South Korea's Daewoo logistics bid to acquire large chunk of farmland in 2008 is noteworthy. Without addressing weak governance or mismanagement or any secretive deal, the

*Land deals in Africa*  369

host government indulges in malpractices and covers up by paying incentives, thus creating hindrances for 'sharing the benefits' with the people and transparent code of conduct. However, risk analysis in production decision is assumed away.

## Bibliography

Anseeuw, Ward, M. Boche, T. Breu, M. Giger, J. Lay, P. Messerli, and K. Nolte (2012a). *Transnational Land Deals for Agriculture in the Global South.* Analytical Report based on the Land Matrix Database. CDE/CIRAD/GIGA, Bern/Montpellier/Hamburg.

Anseeuw, Ward, Jann Lay, Peter Messerli, Markus Giger, and Michael Taylor (2013). Creating a Public Tool to Assess and Promote Transparency in Global Land Deals: The Experience of the Land Matrix. *The Journal of Peasant Studies*, 40 (3), 521–530. DOI: 10.1080/03066150.2013. 803071

Anseeuw, Ward, Liz A. Wily, Lorenzo Cotula, and Michael Taylor (January 2012b). *Land Rights and the Rush for Land: Findings of the Global Commercial Pressures on Land Research Project.* International Land Coalition, Rome.

Antonelli, M., Giuseppina Siciliano, M. Emma Turvani, and Maria Cristina Rulli (2015). Global Investments in Agricultural Land and the Role of the EU: Drivers, Scope, and Potential Impacts. *Land Use Policy*, 47, 98–111.

Arezki, Rabah, Klaus Deininger, and Harris Selod (November 2011). What Drives the Global Land Rush? IMF Working Paper, WP/11/251. IMF Institute, Washington, DC.

Beladi, H., S. Marjit, and R. Oladi (2006). Uniform Technical Progress: Can It be Harmful? *Pacific Economic Review*, 11 (1), 33–38.

Borras, Saturnino M., Jr. and Jennifer C. Franco (2012). Global Land Grabbing and Trajectories of Agrarian Change: A Preliminary Analysis. *Journal of Agrarian Change*, 12 (1), S, 34–59.

Bujko, Matthias, Christian Fischer, Tim Krieger, and Daniel Meierrieks (2014). *How Institutions Shape Land Deals: The Role of Corruption*, Discussion Paper Series, Wilfried-Guth-Stiftungsprofessur für Ordnungs- und Wettbewerbspolitik, Universität Freiburg, No. 2014–02.

Collier, P. and A. J. Venables (2012a). Land Deals in Africa: Pioneers and Speculators. *Journal of Globalization and Development*, 3 (1), 1–22.

Collier, P. and A. J. Venables (2012b). Greening Africa? Technologies, Endowments and the Latecomer Effect. CSAE Working Paper WPS/2012–06. Oxford University, 1–25.

Cotula, L. (2011). *Land Deals in Africa: What Is in the Contracts?* International Institute for Environment and Development (IIED), London.

Cotula, L. (2013). *The Great African Land Grab? Agricultural Investments and the Global Food System.* IAI/RAS/WPC, London/New York.

370 *Gouranga G. Das*

Cotula, L., S. Vermeulen, R. Leonard, and J. Keeley (May 2009). *Land Grab or Development Opportunity? Agricultural Investment and International Land Deals in Africa*. IIED/FAO/IFAD, London/Rome.

Daniel, Shepard and Anuradha Mittal (2009). *The Great Land Grab: Rush for World's Farmland Threatens Food Security for the Poor*. The Oakland Institute, Oakland, USA.

Daniel, Shepard and Anuradha Mittal (2010). *Misinvestment in Agriculture*. The Oakland Institute, Oakland, CA, USA.

Das, Gouranga G. (December 2009). A Hybrid Production Structure in Trade: Theory and Implications. *International Review of Economics*, 56 (4), 359–375, Springer-Verlag.

Das, Gouranga G. (February 2013). "Moving" Land across Borders: Spatial Shifts in Land Demand and Immiserizing Effects. *Journal of Economic Policy Reform*, 16 (1), 46–67. DOI: 10.1080/17487870.2012.761459

Das, Satya and Anuradha Saha (2015). Land Acquisition and Industrial Growth. *Indian Growth and Development Review*, 8 (2), 163–183.

Davis, Kyle F., Paolo D'Odorcio, and M. C. Rulli (2015a). Land Grabbing: A Preliminary Quantification of Economic Impacts on Rural Livelihoods. *Population and Environment*, 1–14. DOI: 10.1007/s11111-014-0215-2

Davis, Kyle F., Paolo D'Odorcio, and M. C. Rulli (2015b). The Global Land Rush and Climate Change. *Earth's Future*, 3. DOI: 10.1002/2014EF000281

Deininger, Klaus and Derek Byerlee (2012). The Rise of Large Farms in Land Abundant Countries: Do They Have a Future? *World Development*, 40 (4), 701–714.

Deininger, Klaus, Derek Byerlee, J. Lindsay, A. Norton, H. Seold, and M. Stickler (Eds.) (2011). *Rising Global Interest in Farmland: Can It Yield Sustainable and Equitable Benefits?* World Bank Publications, Washington, DC.

Dinda, Soumyananda (2016). Land Acquisition and Compensation Policy for Development Activity. *Journal of Land and Rural Studies*, 4 (1), 111–118.

*The Economist* (2009). *Buying Farmland Abroad: Outsourcing's Third Wave*. May 23rd 2009, 55–57.

*The Economist* (2011). *The Surge in Land Deals: When Others Are Grabbing Your Land*. May 7th 2011, 57–58.

Edelman, Marc (2013). Messy Hectares: Questions about the Epistemology of Land Grabbing Data. *The Journal of Peasant Studies*, 40 (3), 485–501.

Edelman, Marc, Carlos Oya, and Saturnino M. Borras (2013). Global Land Grabs: Historical Processes, Theoretical and Methodological Implications and Current Trajectories. *Third World Quarterly*, 34 (9), 1517–1531.

European Report on Development (ERD) (2009). *European University Institute and Robert Schuman Centre for Advanced Studies*. European Commission.

Fan, Shenggen (October 1, 2010). *Five Steps to Prevent a Repeat of the 2007–08 Food Crisis*. International Food Policy Research Institute (IFPRI).

Fazekas, M. and T. Burns (2012). Exploring the Complex Interaction between Governance and Knowledge in Education. OECD Education Working Papers, No. 67, OECD Publishing. http://dx.doi.org/10.1787/5k9flcx 21340-en

Feenstra, R. C. and G. Hanson (2003). Global Production Sharing and Rising Wage Inequality: A Survey of Trade and Wages. In: Choi, E. K. and Harrigan, R. J. (Eds.), *Handbook of International Trade*. Blackwell, Cornwall.

Jones, R. W. (1965). The Structure of Simple General Equilibrium Models. *Journal of Political Economy*, 73, 557–572.

Jones, R. W. (1971). A Three-factor Model in Theory, Trade, and History. In: Bhagwati, J. N. and Kindleberger, C. P. (Eds.), *Trade, Balance of Payments and Growth: Papers in International Economics in Honor of Charles P. Kindleberger*, Vol. 1, pp. 3–21. North Holland, Amsterdam.

Jones, R. W. (2000). *Globalization and the Theory of Input Trade*. MIT Press, Cambridge, MA, USA.

Jones, R. W. and S. Marjit (2009). Competitive Trade Models and Real World Features. *Economic Theory*, 41, 163–174.

Kleemann, Linda and Rainer Thiele (May 2015). Rural Welfare Implications of Large-Scale Land Acquisitions in Africa: A Theoretical Framework. *Economic Modelling*, 51, 269–279.

Kugelman, Michael (2013). Introduction. In: Kugelman, M. and Levenstein, S. L. (Eds.), *The Global Farms Race: Land Grabs, Agricultural Investment, and the Scramble for Food Security*. Island Press, Washington, DC, USA.

Kugelman, Michael and Susan L. Levenstein (Eds.) (2009). *Land Grab? The Race for the World's Farmland*. Woodrow Wilson International Center for Scholars, Washington, DC.

Land Matrix (October 2014). Land Matrix Newsletter. www.landmatrix. org/media/filer_public/b2/48/b24869d1-ff17-4cb2-8bc3-5c55ef6a3e0c/ lm_newsletter_3-4.pdf

Land Matrix Global Observatory (2014). Land Matrix Dataset. International Land Coalition (ILC), Centre de Coopération Internationale en Recherche Agronomique pour le Développement (CIRAD), Centre for Development and Environment (CDE), German Institute of Global and Area Studies (GIGA) and Deutsche Gesellschaft für Internationale Zusammenarbeit (GIZ). Accessed on 08/01/2015 http://www.landmatrix.org/en/.

Marjit, S. and R. Acharyya (2003). International Trade, Wage Inequality and the Developing Economy: A General Equilibrium Approach. Physica-Verlag. Germany.

Messerli, P., M. Giger, M. Dwyer, T. Breu, and S. Eckert (2014). The Geography of Large-Scale Land Acquisitions: Analysing Socio-Ecological Patterns of Target Contexts in the Global South. *Applied Geography*, 53, 449–459.

372 *Gouranga G. Das*

Meyer, John W. (1977). The Effects of Education as an Institution. *American Journal of Sociology*, 83 (1), 55–77.

Nayyar, Deepak (2012). Macroeconomics and Human Development. *Journal of Human Development and Capabilities*, 13 (1), February 2012, 7–30.

Nayyar, Deepak (2013). *Catch Up: Developing Countries in the World Economy*. Oxford University Press, Oxford and New York

Newman, C., F. Tarp, and K. van der Broeck (2015). Property Rights and Productivity: The Case of Joint Land Titling in Vietnam. *Land Economics*, 91 (1), 91–105.

Nolte, Kerstin, Martin Ostermeier, and Kim Schultze (2014). *Food or Fuel – The Role of Agrofuels in the Rush for Land: GIGA Focus*. German Institute of Global and Area Studies. No. 5. ISSN 2196–3940. urn:nbn:de:0168-ssoar-396661

OECD (2010). *Perspectives on Global Development 2010: Shifting Wealth*. OECD Development Centre, Paris.

Osabuohien, Evans (2014). Handbook of Research on In-Country Determinants and Implications of Foreign Land Acquisitions. *IGI Global*, 2015, 1–430. Web. 11 January 2015. DOI: 10.4018/978-1-4666-7405-9

Oxfam (2011). Land and Power: The growing scandal surrounding the new wave of investments in land. 151 Oxfam Briefing Paper. UK (https://www.oxfam.org/en/pressroom/pressreleases/2011-09-22/oxfam-warns-modern-day-land-rush-forcing-thousands-greater)

Rulli, M. C., Antonio Saviori, and Paolo D'Odorico (January 15, 2013). Global Land and Water Grabbing. *PNAS (Proceedings of the National Academy of Sciences)*, 110 (3), 892–897. DOI: 10.1073/pnas.1213163110

Sanyal, K. K. and R. W. Jones (1982). The Theory of Trade in Middle Products. *American Economic Review*, March, 16–31.

Schoneveld, G. C. (2014). The Geographic and Sectoral Patterns of Large-Scale Farmland Investments in Sub-Saharan Africa. *Food Policy*, 48, 34–50.

Singh, S. (2016). Land Acquisition in India: An Examination of the 2013 Act and Options. *Journal of Land and Rural Studies*, 4 (1), 66–78.

Smaller, Carin and Howard Mann (May 2009). *A Thirst for Distant Lands: Foreign Investment in Agricultural Land and Water*. International Institute for Sustainable Development, Canada.

Soete, Luc and Alexis Habiyaremye (2010). The Global Financial Crisis and Africa's "Immiserizing Wealth". United Nations University-MERIT Research Brief No. 1, pp. 1–7

United Nations (2010). Millennium Development Goal 8, the Global Partnership for Development at a Critical Juncture. MDG Gap Task Force Report 2010. New York: United Nations.

UNCTAD (2008). Development and Globalization: Facts and Figures. New York and Geneva: United Nations Conference on Trade and Development (UNCTAD). (http://unctad.org/en/Docs/gdscsir20071_en.pdf)

Von Braun, Joachim and Ruth Meinzen-Dick (2009). "Land Grabbing" by Foreign Investors in Developing Countries: Risks and Opportunities. IFPRI Policy Brief No. 3, pp. 1–9. IFPRI, Washington DC.

Weiss, Matthias (2008). Skill-Biased Technological Change: Is There Hope for the Unskilled? *Economics Letters*, 100, 439–441.

Zoomers, A. (2010). Globalization and the Foriegnisation of Space: Seven Processes Driving the Current Global Land Grab. *Journal of Peasant Studies*, 37 (2), 429–447.

# Indian economy

# 18 Major policy debates in the Indian economy
## Some reflections

## Y. V. Reddy*

The Indian economic history has been characterized by a number of policy debates. It is very pertinent to quote from Nayyar (2006), who commented:

> The second half of the 20th century witnessed remarkable swings of the pendulum in perceptions about economic development in independent India. In the early 1950s, India was a path setter, if not a role model. And the optimism extended beyond those who had a dream about India. For some, its mixed economy was an answer to the challenge posed by communism in China. For others, its strategy represented a non-capitalist path to development. For yet others, who recognised the problems of industrial

---

* Professor Deepak Nayyar joined the Indian Administrative Service and left it with no loss of time to devote himself to academics. I started my career as a research scholar in Economics, and moved on quickly to join the Indian Administrative Service. We were destined to work together in the Ministry of Finance, Government of India, where he was Chief Economic Adviser, while I was Joint Secretary, in charge of Balance of Payments. That was in the early 1990s, when the balance of payments crisis hit us. I worked closely with him, and was impressed by his determination, devotion to duty, penchant for detail and command over the subject. This period reaffirmed his willingness to be a practitioner of policy-making, but his departure demonstrated his greater commitment to academics. He proved to be an able and popular educationist when he became the Vice Chancellor of Delhi University. He is also recognized as an eminent teacher of Economics to multiple generations of students in elite institutions in India and abroad. I am a witness to the esteem that he commands – be it in South-South Centre, Geneva, or New School for Social Research, New York. I am honoured by the invitation to contribute to this volume, and am delighted to do so. In this effort, I must acknowledge the benefit of advice and assistance of Professor Partha Ray, another admirer of Professor Deepak Nayyar.

376 *Y. V. Reddy*

capitalism, India was on the road to their ideal of a social democracy and a welfare state. Just 25 years later, in the mid-1970s, perceptions were almost the polar opposite. India became an exemplar of everything gone wrong. For some, the slow growth and the persistent poverty in the economy represented failure. For others, the inefficient industrialisation was a disaster. For yet others, the political democracy was unaffordable if not unviable. Another 25 years later, in the early 2000s, there was a dramatic change in perceptions once again. The same India came to be seen as a star performer, if not a role model. For some, rapid economic growth turned the lumbering elephant into a running tiger. For others, the impressive economic performance combined with strong institutions which have matured over time in a political democracy mean that India may be the next Asian giant competing with, if not displacing, China. For yet others, India's economy is the latest poster child to demonstrate the virtues of markets and openness.

(p. 1451)

In this festschrift for Professor Nayyar, this chapter proposes to track some of those policy debates from the perspective of a practitioner. Needless to add, the treatment is highly personal and selective and does not claim any exhaustiveness! Furthermore, for expository convenience, the slicing of the time period is done purely in decadal terms – whereas history may not have jumps and breaks only at the time points demarcating the decades.

## 1950s: Mahalanobis versus Vakil-Brahmananda model

Nation building started at a time and in an economy that was savaged by the world war in particular and the colonial rule in general. The Indian economy – especially those of West Bengal, North-East and Punjab – was grappling with the cruel reality of partition. Admittedly, the nations had statesmen who, despite their strong personalities and ideological differences, provided strong leadership to the process of integration of princely states and nation building. To confront the challenges facing the nation, two distinct policy paths were envisaged, namely, the Bombay Plan and the National Plan. The latter prevailed with the establishment of Planning Commission, despite some discomfort in the cabinet.

Ravaged by the World War II, it was a period of reconstruction of the global economy. Bretton Woods institutions were born and, with a number of countries becoming independent from erstwhile

## Policy debates in the Indian economy 377

colonial powers, the sun started setting in the then infamous British Empire. With the emergence of the North Atlantic Treaty Organization (NATO), the birth of East Germany in 1949, and the Warsaw Pact of 1955, the Cold War was firmly in place. While the global polity had an alternative to the NATO powers, global economy too had found an alternate to the standard Anglo-Saxon model of capitalist development – people dreamt big in terms of an active state intervention to kick-start an otherwise stagnant economy with massive public investment. We were, no doubt, influenced by this global trend in deciding on our preferred development path.

In terms of Indian economic policy debate during this period, perhaps the thematic difference between Nehru-Mahalanobis strategy and Vakil-Brahmananda approach is worth mentioning. While Mahalanobis strategy was influenced by post-revolution Russian industrialisation experience and emphasized the capital goods sector, the foundation of the Vakil-Brahmananda model was the idea that growth could occur via transfer of surplus labour from the agricultural sector to capital goods sector even with an unchanged average consumption of wage goods. Was this debate about a choice between what matters more for growth – a capital goods constraint or a wage goods constraint? Without going into a discussion on the relative foundation of these two competing paradigms, it may not be an exaggeration to say that, in terms of implementation in the policy space, the Vakil-Bramhnanda strategy was a non-starter. From the vantage point of the present time, it is also interesting to note that Nehruvian vision of large-scale industrialisation since the Second Plan was not exactly in consonance of Gandhian ideas of economic reconstruction in terms of a self-sufficient village economy.

In retrospect, has this period missed any key policy issue? Has the intellectual debate regarding pursuing particular forms of investment strategy overlooked any significant concerns? Looking back, it appears that the economic debate of the period seems to have missed the importance of education and health. While the name of Milton Friedman does not get exactly associated with such humane issues, it may be pertinent to quote from him what he wrote in his memorandum submitted to the Government of India when he was working for some months as a consultant to the Ministry of Finance at the invitation of the Indian Government:

> The present writer is convinced that the fundamental problem for India is the improvement of the physical and technical quality of her people, the awakening of sense of hope, the weakening of rigid

378   Y. V. *Reddy*

social and economic arrangements, the introduction of flexibility of institutions and mobility of people, the opening up of the social and economic ladder to people of all kinds and classes. And what gives an outsider like the present writer a feeling of optimism and hope about the future of India, makes one feel that India is on the move and will continue to move, is that so much is being done and such a good beginning has been made on this fundamental problem of creating the human and social basis for a dynamic and progressive economy.

(Friedman, 1955)[1]

Interestingly, in terms of growth outcome, the 1950s (and in fact, the Nehru years of 1950–1964) turned out to be a great performer. The period 1951–1964 in fact experienced high GDP growth of 4 percent (compared to China's growth of 2.9 percent during the same period) and a per capita growth of 1.9 percent. Thus, the Indian economy started well in terms of growth in these early years.

## 1960s: The devaluation of 1966

In some sense, the 1960s witnessed the building up of various tensions across the globe as a prelude to the more difficult decade of the 1970s. This is perhaps best reflected in the transformation of US Presidency from Kennedy (in 1961) to Nixon (in 1969). In Russia, the ouster of Khrushchev in October 1964 who was replaced by Brezhnev as the First Secretary of the Central Committee of the Communist Party of Soviet Union – a position he held till 1982. While Communist-led guerrillas started their struggle in Vietnam as early as 1958, with an active intervention from US President Lyndon Johnson, by 1965 the US-Vietnam War gained its full momentum. On the economic front, there were confusing signals in President Kennedy's tax cut programmes that could have boosted the US economy, but by the time Lyndon Johnson came to power inflation began to raise its ugly head in the US.

For India too, the 1960s were difficult years. After Nehru's death in 1964, Lal Bahadur Shastri's stint as the Prime Minister was cut short by his death in 1966. Subsequently, amidst much internal conflict within the then ruling Congress Party – primarily between old guards and younger leaders – Mrs. Indira Gandhi became Prime Minister. There were two wars – the Sino-India war of 1961 and the second war with Pakistan in 1965. There were two successive droughts in 1965 and 1966. While growth suffered in the second half of this decade, inflation, fueled by food prices and associated supply shocks, started spiraling up.

## Policy debates in the Indian economy    379

A major policy debate of this period was perhaps the devaluation of the rupee in June 1966, whereby the rupee-dollar exchange rate was adjusted from 4.76 to 7.50. It was reported that "Shastri felt that devaluation was acceptable if it was necessary to ensure sufficient imports of cereals; but that T TKrishnamachari . . . was resolutely opposed to it" (Joshi and Little, 1994; p. 75). The reaction to the devaluation among the economists too had been diverse. While Jagdish Bhagwati, T. N. Srinivasan or K. N. Raj (later) supported it, economists like V. M. Dandekar, or P. S. Lokanathan opposed it. The spread of opinions led a commentator to conclude:

> Thus, the response of the academic economists and the Press was evenly spread among the critics and the supporters; the industrial and business groups largely approved; and these facts somewhat mitigated the fierce political storm that the June 1966 devaluation raised in the country, cutting across nearly all the political parties on the Right and on the Left.
>
> (Sundaram, 1972; p. 1933)

The other important economic debate that generated quite a bit of commotion towards end of this decade is the nationalization of fourteen commercial banks in 1969. In fact, the Ordinance promulgating bank nationalization was challenged in the court of law on the ground that the ordinance had violated Fundamental Rights (Ghosh, 2015). In terms of political tensions of the period, bank nationalization can be seen as an outcome in the context of Mrs. Gandhi's leaning towards left. While the young Turks in the party (like Chandra Sekhar or Mohan Dharia) stood by Mrs. Gandhi in support of bank nationalization, senior leaders in the Congress Syndicate (such as Kamaraj or S. K. Patil) opposed it. Economists' community too was divided in their support of bank nationalization. While K. N. Raj was the major exponent of bank nationalization, P. R. Brahmananda spoke out against it (Raj, 1974; Brahmananda, 2000).

In the midst of this heated debate of the role of government in economic activity has the intellectual discourse of this period neglected the issue of the impact of two wars on the economy? While the debate about the assumption of a closed economy as well as strategy of import substituting industrialisation is well known, the impact of wars in India and the global geo-political changes (such as Cuban Missile crisis of 1962) seemed to have been ignored. In retrospect it appears that importance of neighbours, even in a closed economy, remained a neglected issue in this period.

## 380   Y. V. Reddy

### 1970s: Equity and efficiency?

In the beginning of the 1970s, the world economy witnessed the ugly face of inflation in the US – largely viewed as a failure of the easy monetary policy regime of US Fed Chairman Arthur Burns (Hetzel, 1998). By 1974, the first oil shock hit the global economy when a number of oil producing nations decided to punish the western countries in response to their support for Israel in the Yom Kippur war against Egypt causing the crude oil price to rise from $3 per barrel to $12.

Mrs. Gandhi won handsomely in the general election of 1971 and the results of the state elections of 1972 further cemented her victory. However, the political glory of Indo-Pakistan war and liberation of Bangladesh in the beginning of the decade was marred by the gloomy days of emergency. In economic terms, the 1970s was perhaps a lost decade – with the droughts of 1972 and 1973, the average decadal growth turned out to be around 3 percent (the lowest decadal growth since 1950s) with two years of negative growth (1972–1973 and 1979–1980). Indicators of unrest like riots, students' movements and workdays lost also reveal the extent of political uncertainty in the country (Rudolph and Rudolph, 1987).

The 1970s was tumultuous with the average inflation rate touching 9.0 percent. The maximum inflation in 1974–1975 at 25.2 percent was mainly attributed to the failure of *kharif* crops in 1972–1973, as well as the hike in crude oil prices in 1973. In response to the strong anti-inflationary measures taken by the authorities, the minimum inflation rate for the decade at (–)1.1 percent was recorded in the following year, that is 1975–1976. The year 1979–1980, however, witnessed a strong resurgence of inflationary tendencies due mainly to poor agricultural output and the second hike in international oil prices (Reddy, 1999).

How do we characterize the period from the vantage point of 2016? Instead of taking the traditional positions of left versus right ideologies, Nayyar (1998) described the period of 1967–1980 as one of co-option and mediation and went on to say:

> There was a recognition of two realities. For one, the rich peasantry had emerged as a new force demanding its due share in benefits derived from economic policies and seeking an upward mobility in the political process. For another, the poor, who had not seen any improvement in their living conditions, did exercise their right to vote in a political democracy. . . . . . In the sphere of economics, the response was twofold. First, there was a strong, new, emphasis on agriculture. . . . Second, poverty alleviation programmes began

Policy debates in the Indian economy   381

life in independent India, albeit on a modest scale. . . . The slogan of *garibi hatao*, even if it was mere words, captured the popular imagination. But the rhetoric went further to the nationalisation of banks and the abolition of privy purses. It was these steps which gave Indira Gandhi, who dominated politics in this period through the democratic, populist and authoritarian phases of her rule, a stranglehold on the political process.

(p. 3125)

Has the economic discourse of this period treated emergency as a distinct but unrelated political happening? While legitimately there are accounts of the political impact, the study of its economic impact is somewhat limited. Of course, one hears some folklore of certain temporary efficiency gains (like the running of the trains on time), but what led to the inability of such perceived gains to get translated into electoral outcomes? An editorial in *Economic and Political Weekly* (Vol. 13, No. 46, Nov. 18, 1978, pp. 1870–1871) looked into the "Gains' of Emergency" in the light of the Reserve Bank's study of the finances of large public limited companies in the private sector for 1976–1977 (RBI Bulletin, July 1978) and commented:

> Against the build-up of fixed assets by the companies, largely with the help of government policies and through government financial support, it is interesting to see the private sector's performance in respect of employment generation. The average employment in the private manufacturing sector during the four quarters of 1975–76 was 40.53 lakhs, but in 1976–77 it declined to 40.48 lakhs. 1976–77 was also the year when under cover of the Emergency, employers had gone on lock-out sprees and man-days lost due to lock- outs had shot up sharply from a little over 4 million in, 1975 to 9.95 million in 1976. The industrial working class was thus the victim of a decline in its share in the value of production, of a fall in employment in the private industrial sector, and of an industrial relations offensive by employees.

## 1980s: The IMF loan

Globally the 1980s was a turbulent decade and started with the second oil price shock coinciding with the Iraq-Iran War. But, it is important to remind us that, during this decade, Ronald Reagan served as the President of the US from 1981 to 1989 and, on the other side of the Atlantic, Margaret Thatcher served as the prime minister of England

## 382   *Y. V. Reddy*

from 1979 to 1990. The duo Reagan-Thatcher dominated the turn-around of the global economic philosophy away from socialism and increasingly towards free markets. Towards the end of the decade, the world witnessed thawing of the thirty-year-long Cold War. It was epitomized in the fall of the Berlin Wall on 9 November, 1989 and the reunification of the East and West Germany on 3 October 1990.

In India, after a short spell of the Janata Party government during 1977–1979, the Congress (I) swept back to power in January 1980 and Mrs. Indira Gandhi became the Prime Minister. A number of commentators have pointed out that her second regime was a much-changed one from her earlier one during 1966–1977 (Jalan, 2012). Illustratively, it has been noted, "Evidence shows that the post-Emergency Indira Gandhi was a different Indira Gandhi: She downplayed redistributive concerns and prioritised economic growth; sought an alliance with big business; adopted an anti-labour stance; put brakes on the growth of public sector industries" (Kohli, 2006). After Mrs. Gandhi's tragic assassination in 1984, Rajiv Gandhi came to power. There is an influential view that it was during Rajiv Gandhi's regime (1985–1989) that initial attempts of liberalisation started taking place.

What was the key economic debate of this period? While the later years of the decade might have been seen as the initial signs of liberalisation and the associated debate, the IMF loan in the early 1980s was marred with controversy. In 1981–1982, India borrowed SDR 3.9 billion (as against the approval of SDR 5 billion) from the IMF under an Extended Fund Facility, the largest arrangement in IMF history at that time. What was the political reaction to the IMF loan? It is pertinent to turn to the then Finance Minister Pranab Mukherjee in that context:

> At that time, the government had negotiated with the IMF a loan in the form of Extended Funding Facility to the tune of 5 billion SDRs. This IMF loan had raised enormous heat and dust in the media. . . . . . . . As usual, I was at the receiving end of fierce criticism from all quarters, especially the Left parties. They raised a hue and cry, alleging that the economic sovereignty of the country had been compromised and that subsidies would have to be discontinued. P Rammurthy, a prominent CPI(M) leader, . . . warned me: "You are on very slippery ground." I assured him: "I would tread carefully." . . . . . . The final installment of the SDR amounting to $1.1 billion was not required. I wrote to the IMF that we didn't need the money and instead paid back the entire loan in due course. This was perhaps the first time in the history of the IMF

## Policy debates in the Indian economy 383

that a borrowing country didn't take the full amount of the loan. My Budget speech of 1984 reflected this proud moment.

(Mukherjee, 2008)

What was the crux of the left critique against the IMF loan of 1981? A deep insight of the critique can be accessed in a summary of a seminar organized by the All-India Peace and Solidarity Organization on Planning and Self-Reliance in 1981 in the pages of the *Economic and Political Weekly* (BM, 1981). It was noted:

> The two-day seminar, chaired by P N Haksar and R C Dutt, retired ICS, was attended by a galaxy of Left-oriented intellectuals. . . . Three distinct strands of thinking were revealed as the discussions at the seminar proceeded. P N Haksar and others like him were nostalgic about the 'golden' Nehru era when, it was suggested, India had made great strides towards self-reliance. . . . . Then there were young academics who demarcated themselves from the other participants in the seminar by their forthright position that the entire content and direction of the development process in India after gaining political independence had been so oriented that it could not promote and had not promoted equity or self- reliance. . . . . . Most remarkable, however, was the stand of what may be characterised as senior academics with high reputations of scholarship as well as high positions in the academic Establishment with its complex linkages with the power Establishment. . . . . While their lines of argument had a rich variety, they were at great pains to find alibis for the IMF deal and plead for understanding for the difficulties and dilemmas facing the established system. There was, they argued, great risk in shaking the system too much since alternatives to it were either not available or were not desirable. This is a familiar line of argument which turns those who are ideologically supposed to stand for radical changes in society as the final desirable goal into votaries of the *status quo* in the short and medium term, favouring working relationships with the established power structure.

(BM, 1981)

The approval process of the loan within the IMF was also not free from controversy. A number of countries like the US and Australia were against the loan. There was worry that the loan could be used as medium-term financing for India's capital investments. Finally, the loan was approved, with only the US abstaining (Boughton, 2001).

## 384   Y. V. *Reddy*

Has there been sufficient debate within the country regarding the reasons behind the situation in which India had chosen to go to the IMF? In retrospect it does not seem so. Was going to the IMF the only alternative? Why did India refuse to take the final instalment? Was it due to improvement of India's balance of payments or was there any difference about adherence to IMF conditionality on the part of India? Were the seeds for balance of payments crisis of 1991 sown in 1980s? Several such questions remain unanswered.

### 1990s: Growth and poverty?

The fall of the Berlin Wall in 1989, the subsequent dissolution of Soviet Union in December 1991, and emergence of the Chinese economy as a major economic power (as a result of the economic reform programmes that started in 1979) are perhaps some of the major global happenings of the 1990s.The ethos of the period, however, went beyond the binary choice of liberalisation versus sticking to a dirigisme regime. A major happening of this period was perhaps the East Asian crisis of 1997, wherein countries like Malaysia, Thailand, Korea, Philippines, and Indonesia were seriously affected by the contagion effect of capital flight and the associated attack on their currencies. Many of these countries were considered to be macroeconomically sound and, thus, the attack on the currencies of these countries could not be brushed aside as being driven only by sentiments. This, in fact, called for a new sense of fundamentals, which may need to be enlarged to include the state of financial system (Reddy, 1998a).

At the domestic level the decade started with the crisis of 1991 when the foreign exchange reserves of India came to as low as covering only three weeks of essential import. From the hindsight one can discern two sources of external shocks in 1991. First, the second Iraq war and the consequent impact on oil prices led to a substantial increase in oil imports bill – the impact was exacerbated by a decline in Middle East–based workers' remittances. Second, Indian trading partners like Russia also experienced slow growth. There is evidence to show that economy was under stress due to unsustainable twin deficits, namely, on current account and fiscal. At the same time, there was great deal of political instability in the latter part of Rajiv Gandhi's years, and significantly in the post–Rajiv Gandhi years, with two Prime Ministers within a span of one and half years (V. P. Singh – December 2, 1989 to November 10, 1990 – and Chandra Sekhar – November 10, 1990 to June 21, 1991). Interestingly, in such a situation of crisis, the initiation of reforms by the minority government under the Prime Minister Narasimha Rao (1991–1996) attracted less of a controversy than what

*Policy debates in the Indian economy* 385

happened in 1981. India approached the IMF and during 1991–1993 borrowed a total of SDR 2.2 billion under two standby arrangements, and in 1991 it borrowed SDR 1.4 billion under the Compensatory Financing Facility.

The liberalisation process in India was multipronged and non-linear; it embraced both macroeconomic as well as structural polices. The ambit of the reform process was diverse and included spheres like fiscal consolidation, monetary policy, financial sector reform, industrial and trade policy, agricultural policy, infrastructure development, as well as social sector improvement. A full treatment of these polices as well as their assessment is beyond the scope of the present chapter, and interestingly there was great deal of convergence among the broad issues of macroeconomic policies. But, in the spirit of highlighting the major policy debate of the period, this section will delve into the issue of growth-poverty nexus.

The fact that reforms had led to higher growth in 1990s has been fairly well established. However, growth and macroeconomic stability are not ends by themselves – for a country like India the issue of poverty eradication has been an essential ingredient of public policy. What has been a source of debate is whether this increase in growth has been poverty reducing as well. A major controversy in this regard has been the non-comparability of poverty numbers in pre- and post-1990s period. As per the data revealed by the 55th Round of NSSO sample (for 1999–2000) there had been a considerable poverty decline between 1993–1994 (50th round) and 1999–2000 whereby the all-India headcount ratio declined from 36 percent to 26 percent. However, the 55th Round is not directly comparable to the 50th Round, due to changes in questionnaire design on account of mixed recall period (30 days versus 7 days).[2] Nevertheless, as Angus Deaton and Jean Dreze have shown in a painstaking exercise, even after adjusting the data, the direction of movement of head-count ratio of poverty does not change though its extent of reduction over the period 1993–1994 through 1999–2000 becomes subdued (Deaton and Dreze, 2002). It is indeed encouraging to know that the growth has not occurred in India at the cost of poverty alleviation – perhaps a combination of forces of higher growth together with government intervention towards poverty eradication seemed to have worked well.

## 2000s: Opening up the external capital account

The decade witnessed a challenge to US supremacy in global economy from China. It was also a period of what has been described as 'Great Moderation', to be followed by the global financial crisis or North

## 386 Y. V. Reddy

Atlantic Crisis. There was excess price volatility in global commodity markets, especially of food and fuel.

The end of the 1990s and the early part of the twenty-first century has been marred with a number of crises in the emerging economies, the East Asian crisis of 1997, the Russian debt crisis of 1998, and Argentinean debt crisis of 1998–2002. While each crisis could have distinct features – there has been some commonality in their genesis. One of the lessons learnt from all these crises is the criticality of compulsions of impossible trinity, whereby no nation can defend the three objectives of independent monetary policy, fixed exchange rate, and a free capital account simultaneously. Furthermore, global experience has shown us that instead of operating at the vortexes of the triangle a country can chose a combination of different policy combination. However, coinciding with the bouts of global financial flows since 2000, countries all over the world have been under pressure to liberalize their capital account – such pressures emanated both from the global financial market players as well as various global international institutions (at least till the genesis of the global financial crisis in 2007–2009).

In India, two committees, both headed by Mr. Tarapore, delved into the conditions under which Indian capital account can be liberalized. Conditions of fiscal prudence, low inflation, and banking stability (low NPA) have been emphasized in particular. In general, public policy in India recognized the following: "(1) appropriate management of capital account is critical for both growth and stability; (2) the cautious approach to capital account has given us leeway; (3) there are preferences in regard to different types of capital flows; (4) some fiscal costs are consciously incurred as necessary on account of sterilization; (5) monetary and exchange rate management are very complex in the context of well-known trilemma; and (6) in the current complex global environment, India cannot be immune to global development but we should maintain domestic drivers to growth" (Reddy, 1998b; p. 4).

In the true Indian tradition of plurality, such a view on calibrated capital account liberalisation faced considerable criticism – directly or indirectly. A mere mention of Tobin tax on unwarranted capital inflows by the present author drew substantial hostility from select market participants in January 2005. Some official reports (such as the *Report of the High Powered Expert Committee on Making Mumbai an International Financial Centre*, 2007, Ministry of Finance) also held a contrarian position.

A significant section of economists argued that accelerated capital account convertibility would enhance the growth of economy and that

## Policy debates in the Indian economy  387

the 'control mentality' and 'conservatism' was holding back country's progress. However, the global financial crisis of 2008 altered the course of debate, and it centred around the policy responses to the crisis.

## Conclusions

In retrospect, one gets an impression that policy debates in India have tended to underestimate importance of experiences of other developing countries and impact of global economy on the Indian economy. One also gets an impression that strategies with long-term implications were given less attention in the mainstream policy debates. It is difficult to assess the influence of thinking of political leadership on the range of issues or alternatives. I wondered why the economic ideology advanced by Swatantra Party, led by C. Rajagopalachari, which predates President Reagan and Prime Minister Thatcher, did not find a pride of place in debates on economic policy in India.

## Notes

1  Friedman, Milton (1955): "A Memorandum to the Government of India", available at http://indiapolicy.org/debate/Notes/friedman.htm
2  Deaton and Dreze (2002; p. 3730) noted, "The experimental questionnaire used a seven-day recall period for food, pan, and tobacco, as well as a 365-day recall period for less frequently purchased goods such as durables, clothing, footwear, educational and institutional medical expenditures. Prior to 1999–2000, the traditional '30-day recall' questionnaire and the experimental questionnaire were administered to different (and independent) samples of households. These alternative questionnaires produced two independent series of expenditure estimates, with a fairly stable 'ratio' of the lower estimates based on the traditional questionnaire to the higher estimates based on the experimental questionnaire. In 1999–2000, the 30-day recall and seven-day recall periods for food, pan and tobacco were used for the same households, in two adjacent columns on the same pages of a single questionnaire".

## Bibliography

B. M. (1981): "The Left and the IMF Loan", *Economic and Political Weekly*, 16 (51), December 19.

Boughton, James M. (2001): *Silent Revolution: The International Monetary Fund 1979–1989*, Washington, DC: IMF.

Brahmananda, P. R. (2000): "Bank Nationalisation: Story of Ad Hocism and Arbitrariness", *Hindu Business Line*, July 26.

Deaton, Angus and Jean Dreze (2002): "Poverty and Inequality in India a Re-Examination", *Economic and Political Weekly*, September 7.

## 388 Y. V. Reddy

Ghosh, D. N. (2015): *No Regrets*, New Delhi: Rupa.

Hetzel, Robert L. (1998): "Arthur Burns and Inflation", *Federal Reserve Bank of Richmond Economic Quarterly*, 84 (1), Winter 1998.

Jalan, Bimal (2012): "Indira Gandhi", in Kaushik Basu and Annemie Maertiens (eds.): *The New Oxford Companion to Economics in India*, Delhi: Oxford University Press, Vol. 1, pp. 282–284.

Joshi, Vijay and I. M. D. Little (1994): *India: Macroeconomics and Politics: 1964–1991*, Delhi: Oxford University Press.

Kohli, Atul (2006): "Politics of Economic Growth in India, 1980–2005 (Part I: The 1980s)", *Economic and Political Weekly*, April 1.

Mukherjee, Pranab (2008): "How We Repaid the IMF Loan", Op-Ed in Business Standard, February 29, 2008, available at www.business-standard.com/article/opinion/pranab-mukherjee-how-we-repaid-the-imf-loan-108022901035_1.html

Nayyar, Deepak (1998): "Economic Development and Political Democracy – Interaction of Economics and Politics in Independent India", *Economic and Political Weekly*, 33 (49).

Nayyar, Deepak (2006): "Economic Growth in Independent India", *Economic and Political Weekly*, 41 (15), April 15.

Raj, K. N. (1974): "Monetary Management and Nationalisation of Banking in India", in Ashok Mitra (ed.) *Economic Theory and Planning: Essays in Honour of A K Das Gupta*, Calcutta: Oxford University Press, pp. 302–329.

Reddy, Y. V. (1998a): "Asian Crisis: Asking Right Questions", Speech at the India International Centre, New Delhi, May 1, 1998, available at https://rbidocs.rbi.org.in/rdocs/Speeches/PDFs/2489.pdf

Reddy, Y. V. (1998b): "Management of the Capital Account in India – Some Perspectives", Inaugural address at the Annual Conference of the Indian Econometric Society, Hyderabad, January 3, 2008.

Reddy, Y. V. (1999): "Inflation in India: Status and Issues", Speech Delivered at the Centre for Economic and Social Studies, Hyderabad, August 17, 1999, available at www.rbi.org.in

Rudolph, L. I. and Rudolph, S. H. (1987): *In Pursuit of Lakshmi: The Political Economy of the Indian State*, University of Chicago Press.

Sundaram, K. (1972): "Political Response to the 1966 Devaluation: III: The Press, Business Groups and Economists", *Economic and Political Weekly*, 7 (38), September 16, pp. 1929–1933.

# 19 Reversing premature deindustrialisation for job creation

## Lessons for *Make-in-India* from industrialised and East Asian countries

*Nagesh Kumar*[*]

For a country undergoing a youth bulge in its demographic transition such as India, with nearly 65 percent of its population in the working age group, creation of adequate and productive jobs for nearly 12 million people who join the workforce every year is one of the most pressing development policy challenges. Nayyar (2014) has highlighted the importance of job creation for sustaining growth itself and for reducing inequalities. However, the employment elasticity of growth has been falling constantly since the turn of the century. The issue of job creation is linked with the nature of technological change, the structural transformation that a country experiences as well as productivity trends. It would appear that India has had a dramatic structural transformation in terms of a declining share of agriculture in the GDP, but it has bypassed industry in general and manufacturing in particular. While the services sector has contributed to India's dynamism over the past decade, it could not pull people out of low productivity activities

[*] This chapter has evolved through several presentations made by the author over the past couple of years including at the IGIDR Silver Jubilee Conference in Mumbai in October 2013; the Sixth Annual Day Lecture at the Symbiosis School of Economics in Pune in March 2014; the IHD Conference on Desirable Future for India, held in New Delhi in March 2014; the ISID Foundation Day Lecture delivered in New Delhi on 1 May 2014; ICRIER's Annual G-20 Conference held in New Delhi in August 2014; and most recently at the NITI Aayog/RIS/UN Consultation on SDGs held in New Delhi on 2 August 2016 and has benefited from discussions. Swayamsiddha Panda provided valuable research assistance. However, the views expressed are personal and should not be attributed to any of the cited institutions or to the United Nations or its member states.

390   *Nagesh Kumar*

in agriculture leaving it to sustain nearly half of India's workforce. Far from industrialising, we find evidence that India has witnessed a premature deindustrialisation with rising dependence on imports in final consumption, corroborating earlier observations, using different methodology and data sources.

History corroborates that few countries if at all have attained prosperity without industrialisation (Kaldor 1967). In that context, the launch of the *Make-in-India* campaign by the Prime Minister of India in 2015 that seeks to exploit the potential of manufacturing for India's development is timely. The *Make-in-India* campaign is also consistent with the objectives of the Agenda 2030 on Sustainable Development adopted at the United Nations Summit in September 2015 comprising 17 Sustainable Development Goals that recognizes the transformative potential of industry and seeks to enhance the share of the sector in employment and GDP (SDG-9.2). Industrialisation through manufacturing is also critical for SDG-8 on accelerating growth and productive jobs creation.

It is in this context that this chapter reviews the compulsions for building a manufacturing sector in India. It then reviews the challenges faced in that process and makes a compelling case for public intervention for fostering industrial development. It also reviews the experiences of industrialised and East Asian countries to draw lessons for India for building productive capacities through extensive public interventions in their process of industrialisation. It concludes with some lessons for policy.

## Structural transformation, vertical linkages and job creation

Employment growth not keeping pace with growth rates of GDP in India has been an acknowledged fact resulting in declining employment elasticity of growth process particularly since the turn of the century (Figure 19.1). The employment elasticity of growth could decline as a result of labour-saving technological innovations or capital-intensive or automated modes of production. However, a more important determinant of employment creation is the nature and speed of structural transformation that an economy is going through. Indian economy has indeed gone through a substantial structural transformation with the share of agriculture in GDP coming down dramatically from over 50 percent to under 15 percent over the post-Independence period. This has been accompanied by share of services nearly doubling from 30 percent to nearly 60 percent. However, the industry has been bypassed

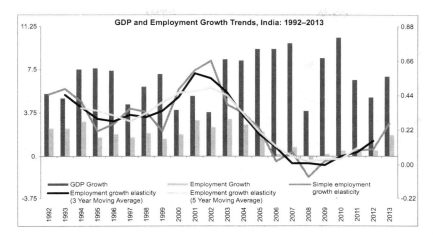

*Figure 19.1* GDP and employment growth and elasticity in India, 1992–2013
Source: Based on UNESCAP Statistical Database. Available from www.unescap.org/stat/data/statdb/DataExplorer.aspx

by the structural transformation with the share of manufacturing and other industries stagnating and even declined after peaking around 1995 (Figure 19.2). The services-oriented structural transformation has given to India robust economic growth rates but could not provide adequate jobs commensurate with its nearly 60 percent share in the GDP absorbing only about a quarter of the workforce (Aggarwal and Kumar 2015). This lopsided structural transformation has led to agriculture supporting nearly half of the workforce with about 15 percent share of the GDP, reflecting their low productivity. Neglect of industry especially manufacturing has cost the country in terms of creation of productive jobs for nearly 12 million workers that join the workforce every year especially because the manufacturing sector has the highest backward and forward linkages of any productive sector (see Figure 19.3). Hence, its potential of creating direct and indirect jobs remained underexploited. It is its potential to create jobs and contribute to sustainable prosperity that industrialisation has been included in the SDGs. The SDG target 9.2 seeks to raise share of industry in the GDP, doubling for LDCs. India has one of the lowest share of manufacturing sector in the GDP among key Asian countries (Figure 19.4). Compared to the East Asian average of around 30 percent, the share of manufacturing in India is under 15 percent. It has declined slightly over the years after peaking in the mid-1990s. Therefore, the SDG target

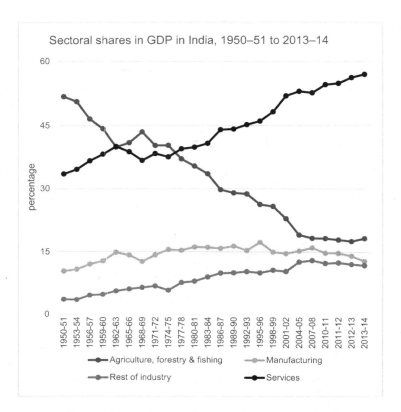

*Figure 19.2* Shares of agriculture, industry and services in GDP, 1951–2014

Source: Based on National Accounts Statistics, Ministry of Statistical Planning and Implementation, India

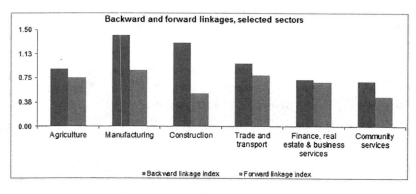

*Figure 19.3* Backward and forward linkages generated by productive sectors in India based on input-output tables

Source: Based on Bose and Kumar (2016)

*Reversing premature deindustrialisation* 393

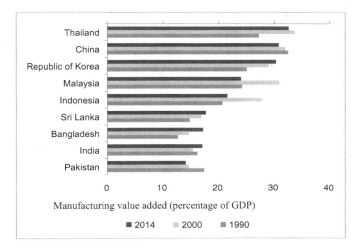

*Figure 19.4* Share of manufacturing in GDP of select Asian countries
Source: Based on the World Development Indicators database, World Bank

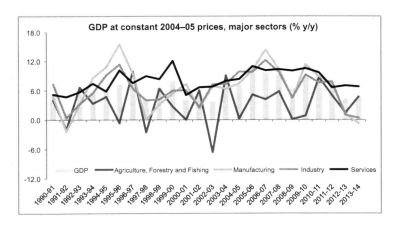

*Figure 19.5* Growth rates of GDP and major productive sectors, 1990–2014
Source: Author's computations based on CEIC database originally drawn from National Accounts Statistics, CSO, India

for doubling of industry's share in GDP for LDCs is very relevant for India. The deceleration of manufacturing growth started around 2007 (Figure 19.5).[1] The deceleration of manufacturing growth has been largely responsible for India's inability to reach the 9.5 percent rate of growth of GDP achieved during 2003–08 period.

394 *Nagesh Kumar*

## Premature deindustrialisation and 'hollowing-out' of Indian manufacturing: The role of liberalisation and currency appreciation

Has India been deindustrialising prematurely? To examine this question, we analyzed the trends in share of imports in final consumption in India across broad sectors using Input-Output Tables for 2001–11 period obtained from the World Input Output Database (WIOD) created at the Groningen University (see Timmer et al. 2015). The analysis summarized in Table 19.1 shows a sharp rise in the share of imports in final consumption over the 2001–11 period, particularly in Electrical and Optical Equipment (from 20 percent to 52.2 percent), Machinery, n.e.c. (from 5.9 percent to 15.1 percent), Transport Equipment (from 0.5 percent to 4.7 percent) and Other Non-Metallic Minerals (8.3 to 37.1 percent). The rising share of imports in final consumption or import dependence would tend to corroborate deindustrialisation taking place in India at least in select sectors with the declining dependence on local manufacturing.

This finding of deindustrialisation in India is consistent with a number of studies that have found that the process of deindustrialisation happening in developing countries (see Dasgupta and Singh 2006; Felipe, Mehta and Rhee 2014; Amirapu and Subramanian 2015; Rodrik 2015). These studies have generally attempted to capture the extent of deindustrialisation in terms of the declining share of manufacturing employment in total or manufacturing value added in GDP, however, they have reached a similar conclusion as here using the import dependency of final consumption. In particular, Amirapu and Subramanian (2015) report strong evidence of deindustrialisation in India.

That the share of manufacturing begins to decline after a certain level of per capita income is reached as services begin to attain a greater prominence, as happened in most of the industrialised countries, has been a stylized fact. However, deindustrialisation happening in developing countries is an issue that warrants attention. Rodrik (2015) in particular found deindustrialisation to be happening prematurely in most African, Latin American and Asian countries and only manufacturer exporters in Asia escaped this phenomenon. Rodrik also finds the turning point to be at around US$5,500 (in 1990 prices) per capita levels.

### Factors explaining premature deindustrialisation

In India's case, the deindustrialisation has begun much more prematurely compared to other countries and it is important to examine the possible factors responsible for it. Infrastructure deficits, land

*Table 19.1* Share of imports used in final consumption expenditure in major industry groups, 2001–11

| | 2001 | 2002 | 2003 | 2004 | 2005 | 2006 | 2007 | 2008 | 2009 | 2010 | 2011 |
|---|---|---|---|---|---|---|---|---|---|---|---|
| Mining and quarrying | 7.1 | 8.4 | 9.0 | 10.9 | 12.3 | 13.5 | 14.4 | 14.7 | 16.7 | 20.3 | 17.5 |
| Food, beverages and tobacco | 0.5 | 0.4 | 0.3 | 0.5 | 0.7 | 0.9 | 0.9 | 0.8 | 1.0 | 0.9 | 0.7 |
| Textiles and textile products | 5.4 | 2.2 | 2.3 | 1.8 | 2.0 | 2.3 | 2.7 | 2.6 | 1.8 | 2.0 | 2.4 |
| Leather, leather and footwear | 4.3 | 3.3 | 3.3 | 3.5 | 3.8 | 5.1 | 4.7 | 4.6 | 3.2 | 3.9 | 4.5 |
| Wood and products of wood and cork | 11.1 | 4.5 | 6.4 | 15.4 | 20.9 | 12.6 | 11.1 | 15.1 | 16.0 | 22.5 | 19.5 |
| Pulp, paper, paper, printing and publishing | 8.7 | 8.6 | 6.3 | 7.3 | 8.5 | 10.7 | 9.9 | 4.3 | 3.3 | 3.9 | 3.8 |
| Coke, refined petroleum and nuclear fuel | 7.3 | 8.7 | 8.9 | 8.8 | 9.1 | 8.5 | 8.6 | 8.0 | 3.0 | 2.8 | 3.2 |
| Chemicals and chemical products | 10.4 | 12.2 | 12.0 | 12.6 | 12.1 | 15.4 | 16.7 | 11.7 | 18.4 | 15.3 | 15.4 |
| Rubber and plastics | 7.2 | 7.0 | 8.1 | 9.7 | 10.8 | 11.5 | 11.9 | 10.7 | 9.7 | 10.8 | 11.2 |
| Other non-metallic mineral | 8.3 | 3.8 | 3.6 | 8.7 | 19.6 | 9.7 | 10.2 | 35.1 | 29.7 | 34.1 | 37.1 |
| Basic metals and fabricated metal | 4.3 | 2.0 | 3.1 | 5.5 | 7.6 | 6.5 | 6.4 | 7.1 | 8.1 | 10.1 | 9.4 |
| Machinery, n.e.c. | 5.9 | 4.1 | 6.6 | 8.2 | 9.4 | 8.9 | 9.4 | 11.5 | 12.7 | 14.8 | 15.1 |
| Electrical and optical equipment | 20.0 | 15.2 | 18.0 | 32.6 | 21.4 | 49.5 | 39.8 | 23.8 | 58.1 | 49.1 | 52.2 |
| Transport equipment | 0.5 | 0.5 | 1.1 | 1.2 | 2.3 | 2.7 | 4.7 | 8.0 | 4.9 | 4.1 | 4.7 |
| Manufacturing, n.e.c.; recycling | 86.0 | 43.4 | 49.1 | 71.3 | 84.2 | 81.2 | 80.6 | 82.7 | 80.5 | 84.6 | 84.0 |
| Electricity, gas and water supply | 0.1 | 0.0 | 0.1 | 0.1 | 0.1 | 0.5 | 0.5 | 0.5 | 0.4 | 0.3 | 0.3 |
| Construction | 0.1 | 0.1 | 0.1 | 0.1 | 0.2 | 0.3 | 0.3 | 0.3 | 0.3 | 0.3 | 0.3 |
| **Total manufacturing** | 8.1 | 4.9 | 4.9 | 6.9 | 8.1 | 7.9 | 7.9 | 8.5 | 9.4 | 11.1 | 10.4 |

Source: Author's computations from Input-Output Tables of India available in the World Input-Output Database. Available from www.wiod.org/new_site/database/niots.htm

acquisition challenges and high cost of capital due to monetary tightening may be responsible for the deceleration of growth of manufacturing in India over the past decade. Amirapu and Subramanian (2015) blame it on an inappropriate specialization of skill-intensive industries in which India did not possess comparative advantage. However, by now, many countries have successfully gained comparative advantage in newer industries through strategic interventions by the development state. These include the Republic of Korea developing a competitive steel industry and other modern industries or Brazil building a competitive aerospace industry. India herself is known for building a comparative advantage in generics pharmaceutical industry and emerging as a global leader. The comparative advantage can thus be acquired.

A more important role in the deindustrialisation in India seems to have been played by import liberalisation and exchange rate movements. India has undertaken reforms to liberalize the trade regime since 1991. Although tariffs have been brought down gradually ever since 1991, liberalisation began to bite particularly since 2000 when the quantitative restrictions on imports and performance requirements such as local content requirements were withdrawn. The Information Technology Agreement (ITA) 1996 of WTO as a signatory of which India eliminated custom duties on imports of final IT products also adversely affected the domestic manufacturing of electronic hardware. ITA (and some bilateral FTAs with the East Asian countries) led to the removal of tariffs on the imported finished goods, but the inputs and raw materials for local manufacture continued to remain subject to duties and taxes, thus eroding their competitiveness. This is consistent with Rodrik (2015) who argues that while technological progress can explain deindustrialisation in the advanced countries, trade and globalisation have played a bigger role in the deindustrialisation of developing countries. Santos-Paulino and Thirlwall (2004), in an empirical study using a panel of 22 developing countries from across the continents, have found trade liberalisation leading to import growth at a much higher rate than export growth that has worsened the balance of payments situation, and have made a case for a careful sequencing of the liberalisation of exports and imports.

In India's case, another and perhaps more important factor seems to be real appreciation in the exchange rate of Indian rupee particularly since 2007 (Figure 19.6), which has prompted outsourcing of manufacture by Indian companies in order to save costs. The outsourcing has been practiced widely by a number of Indian companies

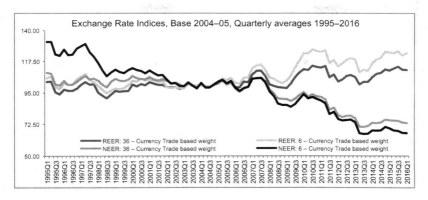

*Figure 19.6* Movements in nominal and real effective exchange rate of Indian rupee
Source: RBI (2016) *Database on Indian Economy*, RBI

owning well-known brand names to get their products manufactured in other countries, mainly China, and continue selling them under their brand names. Outsourcing of production was practiced even for a number of home electrical and electronic appliances that tend to be price sensitive like electric fans, toasters, mixer-grinders, juicers, wall clocks, TVs, refrigerators, air conditioners etc. This also explains a sharp rise in import dependence in final consumption in Electrical and Optical Equipment from 20 to 52 percent in just a decade as observed in Table 19.1. Rising import dependence of consumption in India especially through the outsourcing of production abroad is akin to the phenomenon observed in Japan that has been described as the 'hollowing out' of Japanese manufacturing (Horaguchi 2004). While in Japan, such hollowing out was caused by labour scarcities, in India, at the other end of labour abundance, outsourcing of production was leading to a widespread loss of jobs and potential jobs that could have been created to produce home appliances, the manufacturing of which tends to be labour intensive.

Indian rupee has tended to appreciate despite widening trade deficits due to increasing short-term capital inflows coming to Indian capital markets to make quick returns. In 2007/8, just before the onset of the global financial crisis, the Indian economy received FII inflows of US$28 billion (Kumar 2014).

# 398 *Nagesh Kumar*

## Rebuilding a competitive and sustainable manufacturing sector in India: Lessons from industrialised and East Asian newly industrialising countries

The foregoing discussion has underlined the fact that Indian economy has not been able to harness the potential of manufacturing for its development and has in fact been deindustrialising prematurely. In the context of the compulsions to create productive jobs, India has to reverse the process of deindustrialisation and exploit the opportunities for establishing manufacturing plants within the country. In that context, the recent *Make-in-India* campaign launched by the NDA Government in 2015 is timely and relevant. Services acted as the engine of growth over the past 15 years, manufacturing needs to drive economic growth over the next 15 years to help achieve SDG targets regarding growth, jobs and industrialisation. As Kaldor (1967) has argued persuasively, growth of manufacturing will not only drive economic growth but will also enhance productivity of the economy overall with increasing returns to scale, which could be dynamic in nature. Industrialisation has been an engine of economic transformation all across the world. As Kaldor argued, with the exception of Australia, New Zealand and Canada, no country has grown rich without relying on manufacturing. Similar assertions on criticality of manufacturing have been made by Stiglitz, Lin and Patel (2013) and Salazar-Xirinachs, Nübler and Kozul-Wright (2014).

### *Import-substitution versus export-promotion*

Traditionally, import substituting (IS) industrialisation and export-oriented (EO) industrialisation are considered as two alternative routes to build manufacturing industries. India pursued an IS route in the period up to 1990. Even though it is generally believed that the East Asian countries pursued an EO route to industrialisation (World Bank 1993), they have actually pursued a strategy having elements of both IS and EO simultaneously to harness the economies of scale required to be competitive in international markets.

In any case, in the context of slowdown of the global economy as at present, an EO-based strategy can be challenging given an environment of excess capacities throughout the Asian and the Pacific regions, the growing threat of protectionism in the industrialised countries and the temptation of dumping by those with deep pockets. In such circumstances, it might also be critical to look at new opportunities for

*Reversing premature deindustrialisation*  399

strategic import substitution. As observed earlier, India has high levels of import dependence in a number of sectors such as electrical, electronics and optical equipment, non-electrical machinery and defence equipment, among others that provide opportunities for strategic import substitution. Annual imports of electronics themselves are of the order of US$40 billion and are growing rapidly with projections of US$400 billion of imports by 2025. Similarly India is importing around $30 billion of non-electrical machinery, $15 billion of transport equipment, $30 billion of chemicals and artificial resins, project imports of around $10 billion and around $15–20 billion of defence equipment. An effort needs to be made to start the domestic manufacture of these products. An ESCAP study analyzing opportunities for building productive capacities in South Asia using product space maps also found opportunities for strategic import substitution in India (Freire 2012). As in the East Asian countries, the focus of manufacturing industries should be on exploiting the economies of scale for competitiveness so that they could survive in domestic and international markets. The biggest opportunity for India for make-*in*-India is making-*for*-India, leveraging its large domestic market. It goes without saying that the competitive manufacturing plants exploiting scale economies would also be able to tap opportunities that may arise in the international markets.

### Rationale for public intervention for industrial development

In the foregoing analysis, a compelling case has been made for switching over to a manufacturing-led growth, especially to harness its higher potential of direct and indirect job creation. However, building the competitive manufacturing capacities does not happen in a vacuum and often requires considerable hand-holding and interventions by the government playing the role of a development state. Collectively these interventions are called industrial policy, a term which has become fashionable again across the world including in the industrialised world after falling out of favour for a while (*The Economist* 2010; Stiglitz et al. 2013; Salazar-Xirinachs, Nübler and Kozul-Wright 2014). Wade (2014) highlights how industrial policy has been revived in the US, otherwise a strong proponent of trade liberalisation in multilateral trade negotiations.

The case for state interventions has continued to be made in the theoretical literature at regular intervals. The argument for infant industry protection had been around for very long time since List (1909) and was used to justify high tariff barriers imposed in the US in its period

## 400 *Nagesh Kumar*

of industrialisation, as documented by Chang (2002). Infant industry protection later on was used to justify the incorporation of chapter on trade and development in the General Agreement on Tariffs and Trade in the 1960s. The literature on the Developmental State has documented extensive state intervention for industrialisation employed in the East Asian countries (Johnson 1982). Strategic Trade Theory has also justified state intervention that can be welfare enhancing, shifting profits from international to domestic firms under certain conditions (Brander and Spencer 1985). More recently the New Structural Economics has justified state intervention for building industrial capabilities (Lin 2012).

The need for state intervention arises from the inability of markets to give the correct investment signals in enabling the technological capacity of new industries when there are high and uncertain learning costs and high levels of pecuniary externalities (see Kumar and Gallagher 2007 for a review). For many reasons, including weak capital markets, restrictive intellectual property laws, lack of information, poor coordination, imperfect competition and the need for scale economies, underinvestment in technologically dynamic sectors can occur (Arrow 1962; Nelson and Winter 1982; Lall 2005). Historically, to address these market failures, governments have encouraged joint ventures and technological transfer agreements with foreign firms to foster technological capabilities of domestic firms. Firms may under-invest in the training of their workers because of fears of high labour turnover (Rodrik 2004). Besides investing heavily in skill development, higher education and funding and subsidizing research and development (R&D) activity, they have encouraged knowledge spillovers through vertical inter-firm linkages. Intellectual property rights have been loosened to facilitate the absorption of spillovers of R&D activity of foreign firms. Technological and industrial upgrading has been fostered through government procurement, export subsidies, subsidized capital and tariff protection. History is rich in lessons of strategic interventions employed by industrialised as well as newly industrialising countries in the process of their industrialisation, as documented extensively in the literature (Amsden 2001; Lall 2005; Wade 2003; Chang 2002; Kumar and Gallagher 2007, among many others). The strategic interventions that may be relevant in India's case are as follows.

### Privileged access to domestic market

For manufacturing plants to have higher productivity and competitiveness, it is important that they are able to exploit scale economies. To enable domestic firms a privileged or preferential access to their

## Reversing premature deindustrialisation 401

national markets to enable them to reap economies of scale, governments have employed a variety of interventions. These include high tariffs and non-tariff barriers to protect local manufacturing from imports. Although industrialised countries today are champions of trade liberalisation in multilateral trade negotiations, it is interesting to see how tariffs have been used as a tool of development policy by most of the developed countries in the early phases of their development. European countries, the US and Japan have employed high tariffs extensively to protect their infant industries in the early phases of their development and liberalized their trade regimes only when their industries gained competitiveness. Thus,

> Britain was protectionist when it was trying to catch up with Holland. Germany was protectionist when trying to catch up with Britain. The United States was protectionist when trying to catch up with Britain and Germany, right up to the end of the World War II. Japan was protectionist for most of the twentieth century up to the 1970s, Korea and Taiwan to the 1990s.
>
> (Wade 2003)

Protectionism in the developed countries has not been limited to only the pre-War period. Most of the developed countries adopted the Multi Fibre Agreement (MFA) that enabled them to impose quantitative restrictions on imports of textiles and clothing. The MFA quotas have finally been phased out, under the WTO's Agreement on Textiles and Clothing (ATC), by 31 December 2004. However, industrialised countries continue to employ high peak tariffs on select labour-intensive products such as textiles and clothing, leather goods, among others. The incidence of contingent protection for example anti-dumping duties, on these products is also very high.

The East Asian countries have emulated the industrialised countries in their own process of industrialisation. Chang (2002) highlights the role that protection has played in emergence of Hyundai, POSCO among other enterprises in the Republic of Korea as world's leading enterprises in their respective industries. Malaysia has protected Proton with high tariffs on imported cars ranging up to 300 percent and had resisted the liberalisation of tariffs under ASEAN Free Trade Agreement. Nearly full access to the domestic market enabled Proton to grow to competitive scales and even export its vehicles to 26 countries. Similarly NTBs have been employed extensively and have included different unique and stringent standards (as Japan setting its electric current at an unconventional 100 volts), registration requirements on

402 *Nagesh Kumar*

pharmaceuticals imports in China, among other barriers. WTO's SPS and TBT Agreements allow countries to impose standards and other requirements to protect human health and the environment, which have been used extensively to deter foreign competition to protect the fledgling domestic industry.

Therefore, a privileged access to the domestic market for local producers through tariff and non-tariff barriers could enable them to reap scale economies. India has maintained a wide space between bound and applied tariffs for most industrial products. However, given the liberalisation commitments within the framework of bilateral and regional FTAs, NTBs provide more viable options for building manufacturing capacities and allowing them to grow to a certain scale before being exposed to competition.

In order to prevent rent-seeking behaviour of domestic enterprises–provided protection, the East Asian countries normally fostered domestic competition while protecting them from external competition, for instance, between Toyota and Honda, or between Sony and Panasonic, between LG and Samsung, or Hyundai and Daewoo. Also the protection can be for a limited period and phased out gradually as the domestic capacities become well entrenched.

### Government procurement for supporting domestic production

A number of developed countries have used government procurement as a policy tool to foster the deepening and diversification of domestic industrial structure. The US Government adopted the Buy American Act in 1933 that mandates preference for the purchase of domestically produced goods over foreign goods in US Government procurement. The provisions of the Act have also been used as local content requirements (LCRs). For instance, in order to qualify as a domestic product to claim a 25 percent price preference under the Buy American Act, a Hungarian manufacturer of buses had to buy US-made engines, transmissions, axels and tyres (Krugman and Obstfeld 2000: 205). EU also has provisions for minimum local requirement and preference for European firms in government procurement (Corrales-Leal and Sugathan 2003). A number of countries, including developed countries like Switzerland, impose offset requirements in government procurements especially of defence equipment where the exporters have to undertake obligations to import or outsource a certain proportion of the value of exports from the importing country. India has recently started to use some local content or offset requirements in its defence procurements. However, a recent ruling by the WTO dispute panel against India's

## Reversing premature deindustrialisation 403

domestic content requirements under its solar energy mission shows that some of the multilateral trade rules need to be reviewed to recover policy space eroded in the Uruguay Round under TRIMs agreement.

### Performance requirements on foreign enterprises and proactive FDI promotion

The WTO Agreement on TRIMs (Trade Related Investment Measures) has taken away the ability of governments to impose some types of performance requirements on foreign investors. Among the specific types of performance requirements (PRs), local content requirements have been employed by most of the developed countries at one time or other for deepening their industrial structure (Kumar 2005). In particular, governments have employed LCRs in the auto industry to promote the backward integration and localization of value added activities. For instance, when Ford Motor Company took over a minority stake in the UK in 1960, 'a string of conditions on exports, earnings retentions, employment and import policies were imposed' (UNCTAD 2003: 266). Countries like Australia, Canada, France, Japan, among others, have made extensive use of PRs. Australia (and New Zealand) imposed 50 percent domestic ownership requirements in natural resource projects, and also employed offset policies under which larger government contracts required new domestic activity of 30 percent of their import content. Canada enacted a Foreign Investment Review Act (FIRA) in the early 1970s, through which an extensive set of PRs (called undertakings) were imposed to ensure the reaping of 'significant benefit' by Canada from the operations of FDI (UNCTAD 2003). Japan also imposed PRs at the time of approvals depending upon the contribution to technology development, exports or import substitution, competition to Japanese industry, 50 percent foreign ownership and required the president of the joint venture to be a Japanese (UNCTAD 2003). Thailand has emerged as the third largest exporter of automobiles in Asia and the Pacific by using performance requirements on Toyota and Honda by initially imposing LCRs to deepen production linkages and, once integrated production bases developed, to impose export performance requirements to virtually turn these facilities into globally sourcing hubs for certain models (Kumar 2005). India's emergence, for instance, as a competitive exporter of auto parts in recent times owes to a particular strategic intervention by the government in the form of an erstwhile performance requirement that required foreign-owned companies to balance imports by foreign exchange earnings (Kumar 2005). While

## 404 Nagesh Kumar

some performance requirements such as LCRs have been outlawed by WTO's TRIMs Agreement, others like export performance requirements can still be imposed by host governments. Again there is a case for a review of TRIMs Agreement for retrieving the policy space by developing countries in the context of their SDG commitments (Correa and Kumar 2003). Quantitative studies have found a trade-off between the quantity and quality of FDI in terms of effect of performance requirements. While performance requirements may affect the quantity or magnitude of FDI adversely, the quality of those that come in terms of their depth and vertical integration, export-orientation and R&D activity improves (Kumar 1998, 2000, 2002).

Proactive targeting which involves inviting MNEs to undertake certain investment proposals on the basis of agreed parameters could also be a useful tool for attracting the right kind of investments, as demonstrated by the case of the Maruti-Suzuki joint venture in India.

### Investment and export incentives

Under the WTO Agreement on Subsidies and Countervailing Measures (SCM), many possible subsidization measures such as export subsidies and investment incentives have been phased out except for low income countries with a per capita income up to US$1,000. However, investment incentives and subsidies have historically been widely practiced in developed countries to give to their enterprises a competitive advantage. Examples include large sums of subsidies doled out to investors by governments in developed countries to industrial enterprises such as US$484 million given to Ford in Portugal in 1991 for creating 1,900 jobs or $300 million to Mercedez-Benz in Alabama in 1996 for creating 1,500 jobs (Kumar and Gallagher 2007). The billions of dollars or euros given as subsidies to Boeing and Airbus by the US Government and the EU countries are well known. The European governments have been giving the so-called launch aid to Airbus while Boeing gets huge subsidies from the US Government for R&D projects. The aircraft subsidies dispute has been one of the biggest feuds at the WTO dispute settlement. Another dispute running at the WTO dispute settlement concerned the policy of the US Government to pass on the anti-dumping duties collected from the foreign exporters to the US enterprises under the Byrd Amendment, which has since been deemed illegal by the WTO. WTO has also deemed illegal the subsidies given to exporters under the Foreign Sales Corporation Act totalling US$4 billion annually on the basis of a complaint brought by the EU.[2] Developed country governments also assist their exporters through export

# Reversing premature deindustrialisation 405

credits extended to importing countries tied to imports from them. Reportedly the developed country export credit agencies had outstanding guarantees of US$500 billion in 2000 to their firms in developing countries and had issued US$58 billion worth of new export credits for goods and services exported by their firms. The European Community Structural Funds consist of over 540 programmes, including areas such as agriculture, R&D, industry, among others, besides several regional funds such as European Regional Development Fund, European Social Fund, the European Agriculture Guidance and Guarantee Fund. The EU has allocated a total of euro 347 billion placed at the disposal of the Structural Funds for the period of 2007–13, making them the largest share of total EC budget.

The East Asian countries have supported their industrialisation through various kinds of subsidies. Republic of Korea has directed subsidized credit to the chaebols or their national champions in their formative years. The Chinese Government has been offering a variety of subsidies and incentives including subsidized infrastructure in the special economic zones. Malaysia offers a range of incentives to manufacturing enterprises under its pioneer industry programme. India's Biocon Ltd has been lured by the pioneer industry incentives to locate a billion dollar insulin plant in Malaysia. In the early post-Independence period, India had also established term-lending institutions to support industrialisation by providing long-term capital viz. the Industrial Development Bank of India (IDBI), the Industrial Finance Corporation of India (IFCI) and the Industrial Credit and Investment Corporation of India (ICICI). However, over time, as capital markets developed, two of them have moved on to become full-scale retail banks (ICICI Bank and IDBI) and IFCI has turned its attention to infrastructure financing (Nayyar 2015; Kumar 2016b). However, the government has recognized the importance of providing directed credit to industry and has started MUDRA and Stand-Up programmes to SMEs and the start-ups recently.

*Infrastructure support*

A number of countries have supported their industrialisation by providing infrastructure support by investing in development of social and physical infrastructure such as development of transport corridors passing through lagging or backward regions. Others have been more proactive and have invested more directly by building industrial infrastructure such as special economic zones, technology parks and industrial estates, which are often offered to prospective entrepreneurs

406  *Nagesh Kumar*

at subsidized or nominal prices. China has fostered its industrialisation by establishing special economic zones (SEZs) in coastal areas and by investing in physical infrastructure development all across the country. In addition, provincial and local governments in China also offer a variety of support to potential entrepreneurs including subsidized land and utilities to attract investments. By lowering the initial set-up costs, such industrial infrastructure can incentivize and facilitate rapid industrialisation.

### Supporting technological development and R&D activity for sustainable products

In order to retain and further sharpen the technological edge of their corporate enterprises, governments of industrialised countries have been supporting the technological activities of national enterprises through a wide variety of government-industry complexes and direct and indirect subsidies and tax breaks. In the US, the federal government accounted for $125.7 billion, or 30 percent, of US total R&D in 2011, a substantial part of this funding was to support directly or indirectly the activities of US firms.[3] The governments in France, Germany, the UK and the US, for instance, accounted for 48.8, 37, 34 and 47 percent respectively of total gross R&D expenditure in their countries with a substantial proportion of the funding directly going to business enterprises (see Kumar and Siddharthan 1997 for more details). In the EU, the national programmes for supporting corporate R&D are complemented by the European Union's Framework Programmes for subsidizing corporate R&D to the tune of 50 percent. The Eighth Framework Programme (FP8) (2014–20) has a budget of Euro 80 billion.

Among the East Asian countries, in Republic of Korea the government was spending 0.42 percent of the GDP in directly or indirectly supporting business R&D, the highest in OECD countries.[4] With respect to learning in private firms, East Asian tigers – like the developed countries before them – also spent a great deal of effort providing education and training to their people. This was done by spending a significant amount of funds on education (including providing scholarships to obtain PhDs in developed countries), clustering schools in export-processing zones, requiring that foreign firms hire nationals and train them on the job and subsidizing training programs in domestic firms (Kim and Nelson 2000; Amsden 2001).

Strengthening the enterprise-level innovative activity assumes a greater criticality in the context of sustainability considerations for the

*Reversing premature deindustrialisation* 407

future manufacturing activity in terms of intensity of products in terms of energy, natural resources and emissions. Given the international commitments undertaken by India under the Paris Agreement, carbon intensity of the production will have to decline progressively. Growing environmental consciousness among consumers within the country and in export markets will increasingly put a premium on greener products. Only through investment in innovative activity focused on sustainability can the enterprises stay in competition. Heavy subsidization of enterprise level R&D activity by governments in industrialised and newly industrialising countries directly and indirectly puts them at an advantage vis-à-vis others.

The Indian Government has been providing tax incentives to enterprises to encourage corporate R&D activity. However, it has been argued that a more direct subsidization may yield greater benefits in select strategic sectors in terms of sharpening the competitive edge of Indian enterprises (Kumar and Aggarwal 2005). Under WTO's Agreement on Subsidies and Countervailing Measures, the subsidization of up to 50 percent of precompetitive R&D expenditure is non-actionable.

An important strength of Indian enterprises, now recognized worldwide, has been their frugal engineering capability emanating from their experience in serving a market where the volumes lay at bottom of the income pyramid. This frugal engineering capacity has led to development of some of the cheapest products and processes anywhere in the world, ranging from generic pharmaceuticals and vaccines, automobiles, home appliances, medical diagnostic equipment, among others. This capacity can be harnessed to develop greener and more affordable products that can become a source of competitive advantage in the era of sustainability. The R&D incentives and subsidies could be directed to harness this frugal engineering capacity of Indian enterprises.

### TRIPs and intellectual property protection policy

There is extensive evidence suggesting that the developed countries of today have used lax intellectual property rights to absorb spillovers of innovative activity in other countries during the process of their industrialisation. They started demanding stringent IPR standards from others after emerging as the source countries of innovations to provide monopoly rights to their enterprises to exploit the inventions. The US is a typical case in this regard. The US has been seeking to strengthen IPR protection through bilateral negotiations and through unilateral sanctions under the Super 301 Priority Watch Lists before using multilateral trade negotiations in the Uruguay Round to harmonize the IPR

408    *Nagesh Kumar*

protection under the TRIPs Agreement. However, history suggests that the US has followed a discriminatory IPR regime in its period of industrialisation. Between 1790 and 1836, as a net importer of technology, the US restricted the issue of patents to its own citizens and residents. Even in 1836, the patents' fees for foreigners were fixed at 10 times the rate for US citizens (CIPR 2002).

The East Asian countries such as Japan have similarly used extensively weak IPR regimes to facilitate the absorption of foreign inventions and did not recognize product patents until the mid-1970s. Republic of Korea did not have product patents till the mid-1980s to facilitate absorption of innovations of others (Kumar 2003). India herself has benefited from soft IPRs in building a globally competitive generic pharmaceutical industry that serves as a major sourcing base for affordable medicines and vaccines for developing countries. Although some of the policy space has been eroded under the TRIPs Agreement, yet there are still a number of flexibilities available and can be used for instance, the criteria for patentability and compulsory licensing provisions on account of public health considerations. Furthermore, in order to foster the frugal engineering activity in the context of sustainable and affordable products as discussed above, India may adopt a petty patents regime or utility models that provide a short duration protection to incremental innovations (Kumar 2003). In Japan, petty patents have been used effectively to foster innovative activity of SMEs among other enterprises.

### Competitive exchange rates

East Asian countries have widely used managed exchange rates as a tool for fostering industrialisation. Japan has extensively used the depreciated exchange rate of yen to boost competitiveness of its exports before the Plaza Accord of 1985. Even in recent times, exchange rate management has been an important component of stimulus policy adopted by the Japanese government. The US sought to depress the exchange rate of dollar through policy coordination among major economies at the Plaza Accord in 1985. The Chinese Government has kept a tight leash on the exchange rate of yuan during 1979–94 during which a dual exchange rate was maintained, followed by a hard peg during 1995–2005. It has allowed the exchange rate of yuan to move within a narrow band since 2005, as international pressure mounted with growing trade surpluses.

As observed earlier, appreciation of the rupee in real terms over the past decade has adversely affected local manufacturing in India,

# Reversing premature deindustrialisation 409

encouraging offshore outsourcing of production. What would serve the cause of local manufacturing is a competitive and slightly depreciating real exchange rate. It is an important challenge for Indian policy makers especially in view of the pressure on the exchange rate to appreciate from the short-term capital inflows attracted by the dynamism and robust macro-fundamentals of India's economy. From that point of view some kind of capital controls in the form of taxes on short-term capital inflows would be fruitful not only in moderating the volatility and upward pressure on exchange rate of the rupee while also generating some revenue.

## RTAs and preferential access to markets

Non-discrimination enshrined in the most-favoured nation (MFN) clause is a bedrock of multilateralism trade regime within the GATT framework. But rules provided an exception from MFN for regional economic integration (REI) (Art. XXIV of GATT) to take care of the exceptional situation of critical interdependence between economies. However, in the 1990s, the exception was exploited by developed economies to form a number of groupings, a trend led by the formation of a Single European Market and of the North American Free Trade Agreement (NAFTA), EFTA and European Economic Space, APEC, among others. Major implication of the formation of large trade blocs of 1990s was that a large proportion of world trade began to take place outside MFN, on a preferential basis. This was because of high share of advanced economies in world trade (73 percent in 1990, 65 percent in 2000 and 51 percent in 2012) and a very large proportion of their trade taking place within the region (63 percent of EU's $5.8 trillion in trade was intra-regional; 49 percent of NAFTA's $2.37 trillion in trade was intra-regional). There was a domino reaction world-wide with MERCOSUR being formed in Southern America, SADC and SACU in Africa, among others. Besides trade diversion, participation in FTAs also influences magnitude and quality of FDI inflows (Kumar 2002). Recently, there has been another fresh trend of the formation of mega FTAs of a transcontinental type, led again by advanced economies that will have major implications for the world trade further eroding the remit of MFN. This trend started with launch in 2011 of the Trans-Pacific Partnership (TPP) negotiations bringing together the US and Japan, Australia and New Zealand, among other countries.[5] It was followed up with the launch in July 2013 of the EU-US Transatlantic Trade and Investment Partnership (TTIP) negotiations. The implications of TPP and TTIP, in case

410 *Nagesh Kumar*

they come into force, would be that virtually entire mutual trade of advanced economies – intraregional as well as interregional – would be conducted on preferential basis with existing regional blocs (EU and NAFTA) and their new emerging interregional trade blocs. Thus they will further erode MFN (Kumar 2016a).

With the bulk of trade of their major trade partners going off the MFN, developing countries like India need to look at the policy options. In any case, the advanced economies have been facing an uncertain and subdued economic outlook in a post-global financial crisis phase and the growth rate of world trade has come down dramatically. India has concluded preferential trade agreements with Sri Lanka, SAARC, Singapore, Thailand, ASEAN, Japan and the Republic of Korea. India is also part of Regional Comprehensive Economic Partnership of East Asia (RCEP) negotiations that are currently ongoing to evolve a comprehensive trade agreement between ASEAN and its six dialogue partners. RCEP, when concluded, is poised to become an important regional grouping that shall provide to its members, including India, a preferential access to a large and dynamic region in Asia and the Pacific. However, India's experience with FTA/RTAs so far suggests that Indian enterprises have not been able to exploit the market access that they gain through these agreements, but enterprises from the partner countries were able to get a toehold in the Indian market. The preferential market access obtained by the government through these negotiations is of no use unless exploited by the Indian enterprises to enhance their exports.

## Conclusions

The foregoing discussion has shown that there is a compelling case for strategic interventions for reversing the premature deindustrialisation that the Indian economy has faced, particularly to meet the challenge of job creation. In this context there are useful lessons from experiences of present-day developed countries which have extensively employed infant industry protection, industrial policy and performance requirements, soft intellectual property protection regimes, investment incentives and R&D subsidies, government procurement and regional economic integration, among other policies in their process of industrialisation. Many of these policies have also been effectively and successfully emulated by the newly industrialising economies in East Asia to build internationally competitive modern industries despite the lack of the apparent comparative advantage.

## Reversing premature deindustrialisation 411

The elements of industrial policy that may be relevant for the contemporary Indian situation could include infrastructure support and help with land acquisition, facilitation of approvals through single window clearances and ease-of-doing business, infant industry protection and pioneer industry programmes, preferences in public procurement, direction of subsidized credit and skill development, among others. Some of these are being addressed within the framework of the *Make-in-India*, Stand-Up India and MUDRA schemes. Maintaining a competitive exchange rate is perhaps most critical in an open economy environment of low tariff barriers for the development of manufacturing as demonstrated by the experiences of the East Asian countries. Domestic competition should be fostered in order to prevent the rent-seeking behaviour of domestic enterprises–provided protection from external competition. In any case the protection from external competition should be for a limited period and phased out gradually as the domestic capacities get entrenched.

In the world of trade alliances, facilitating strategic access to markets through preferential trade agreements can be an important determinant of development of industry. In that respect, India's participation in the ongoing RCEP negotiations has the prospect of giving to India preferential access to a very large market bringing together Japan, China and ASEAN among other countries and an opportunity to participate in the regional value chains.

Innovation is an important driver of modern manufacturing and competitiveness. Here government support through direct subsidies and through petty patents to enterprises may help to harness Indian strengths in frugal engineering and software design for developing new, more efficient and resource-saving products and processes for domestic and international markets.

Another important tool for developing competitive manufacturing capabilities is to leverage the large domestic market for attracting FDI in manufacturing. The exporters of manufactured goods to India could be pushed to set up manufacturing plants in India through a facilitating regime to serve not only the domestic market but also for global and regional sourcing to take advantage of abundant skilled and low-cost labour and scale economies. Performance requirements and proactive targeting could be a useful tool for attracting the right kind of investments. As some of the performance requirements have been outlawed under WTO's TRIMs Agreement, India along with like-minded countries could seek a review of TRIMs Agreement to retrieve the policy space.

## 412 Nagesh Kumar

### Notes

1 Nayyar (1978) had observed stagnation in India's industrial growth during the mid-1960s and mid-1970s too.
2 See for details World Trade Organization website: www.wto.org/english/tratop_e/dispu_e/cases_e/ds108_e.htm
3 See for more details National Science Foundation website: www.nsf.gov/statistics/seind14/index.cfm/chapter-4/c4s1.htm
4 See for more details OECD website: www.oecd.org/sti/scoreboard-2015-interactive-charts.htm
5 However, recently the Trump Administration has pulled the US out from the TPP negotiations although other countries have decided to move ahead without the US.

### Bibliography

Aggarwal, A. and Nagesh Kumar (2015), 'Structural Change, Industrialization, and Poverty Reduction: The Case of India', in W. Naude, A. Szirmai and N. Horaguchi eds. *Structural Change and Industrial Development in the BRICS*, Oxford: Oxford University Press: 199–243.

Amirapu, Amrit and Arvind Subramanian (2015), *Manufacturing or Services? An Indian Illustration of a Development Dilemma*, WP 409, Washington, DC: Centre for Global Development.

Amsden, Alice (2001), *The Rise of the Rest: Challenges to the West from Late Industrializing Countries*, Oxford: Oxford University Press.

Arrow, Kenneth J. (1962), 'The Economic Implications of Learning by Doing', *Review of Economic Studies* 29(3), June 1962: 155–173.

Bairoch, Paul (1993), *Economics & World History: Myths and Paradoxes*, Chicago: The University of Chicago Press.

Baumol, J. and Oates (1988), *The Theory of Environmental Policy*, Cambridge: Cambridge University Press.

Birdsell, N., D. Rodrik and A. Subramanian (2005), 'How to Help Poor Countries', *Foreign Affairs*, July/August 2005.

Bose, Sukanya and Abhishek Kumar (2016), *Growth of Finance, Real Estate and Business Services: Explorations in an Inter-Sectoral Framework*, WP 162, New Delhi: National Institute of Public Finance and Policy.

Brander, J.A. and B.J. Spencer (1985), 'Export Subsidies and International Market Share Rivalry', *Journal of International Economics* 18: 83–100.

Burton, J. (1983), *Picking Losers . . .? The Political Economy of Industrial Policy*, London: Institute for Economic Affairs.

Chang, Ha-Joon (2002), *Kicking Away the Ladder: Development Strategy in Historical Perspective*, London: Anthem.

CIPR (2002), *Integrating Intellectual Property Rights and Development Policy*, London: Commission on Intellectual Property Rights. Available from www.iprcommision.org.

Corrales-Leal, Werner and Mahesh Sugathan (2003), *Spaces for Development Policy: Revisiting Special and Differential Treatment*, Geneva: ICTSD.

## Reversing premature deindustrialisation 413

Correa, Carlos M. and Nagesh Kumar (2003), *Protecting Foreign Investment: Implications of a WTO Regime and Policy Options*, London: Zed Press.

Dasgupta, Sukti and Ajit Singh (2006), *Manufacturing, Services and Premature Deindustrialization in Developing Countries, RP# 2006/49*, Helsinki: UNU/WIDER.

*Economist* (2010), 'Picking Winners, Saving Losers: Industrial Policy Is Back in Fashion', *Have Governments Learned from Past Failures?*, 5 August. Available from www.economist.com/node/16741043.

Felipe, J., A. Mehta and C. Rhee (2014), *Manufacturing Matters . . . but It's Jobs That Count*, Economics Working Paper 420, Manila: Asian Development Bank.

Freire, Clovis (2012), *Strategies for Structural Transformation of Economies in South and South-West Asia*, SSWA Development Papers #1204, New Delhi: ESCAP-SSWA. Available from http://sswa.unescap.org.

Gallagher, Kevin P., ed. (2005), *Putting Development First: The Importance of Policy Space in the WTO and IFIs*, London: Zed Books.

Hirschman, Albert (1958), *The Strategy of Economic Development*, New Haven: Yale University Press.

Hobday, Michael (1995), *Innovation in East Asia: The Challenge to Japan*, England and USA: Edward Elgar Publishing Limited.

Horaguchi, Haruo (2004), *Hollowing-Out of Japanese Industries and Creation of Knowledge-Intensive Clusters*, Faculty for Business Administration, Hosei University.

Imbs, Jean and R. Waczraig (2003), 'Stages of Diversification', *American Economic Review* 93(1), March: 63–86.

Johnson, Chalmers (1982), *MITI and the Japanese Miracle*, Stanford, CA: Stanford University Press.

Kaldor, N. (1967), *Strategic Factors in Economic Development*, Ithaca, NY: New York State School of Industrial and Labour Relations, Cornell University.

Kim, Linsu and Richard Nelson (2000), *Technology, Learning, and Innovation: Experiences of Newly Industrializing Economies*, Cambridge: Cambridge University Press.

Krugman, Paul and M. Obstfeld (2000), *International Economics*, (Fourth Edition), McGraw Hill.

Kumar, Nagesh (1998), 'Multinational Enterprises, Regional Economic Integration, and Export-Platform Production in the Host Countries: An Empirical Analysis for the US and Japanese Corporations', *Weltwirtschaftliches Archiv* 134(3): 450–483.

Kumar, Nagesh (2000), 'Explaining the Geography and Depth of International Production: The Case of US and Japanese Multinational Enterprises', *Weltwirtschaftliches Archiv* 136(3): 442–476.

Kumar, Nagesh (2002), *Globalization and Quality of Foreign Direct Investment*, New Delhi: Oxford University Press.

Kumar, Nagesh (2003), 'Intellectual Property Rights, Technology and Economic Development: Experiences of Asian Countries', *Economic and Political Weekly* 38(3): 209–226.

Kumar, Nagesh (2005), 'Performance Requirements as Tools of Development Policy: Lessons from Experiences of Developed and Developing Countries for the WTO Agenda on Trade and Investment', in Kevin Gallagher ed. *Putting Development First*, London: Zed Press (also an RIS DP 52#/2003 available from www.ris.org.in).

Kumar, Nagesh (2011), 'Intellectual Property Rights, Technology and Economic Development: Experiences of Asian Countries', in Christopher May ed. *The Political Economy of Intellectual Property Rights*, Vol. 3, Cheltenham: Edward Elgar: 209–226.

Kumar, Nagesh (2014), 'Reforms and Global Economic Integration of the Indian Economy: Emerging Patterns, Challenges and Future Directions', in A. Goyal ed. *The Oxford Handbook of the Indian Economy in the 21st Century*, New Delhi: Oxford University Press: 209–246.

Kumar, Nagesh (2016a), 'G-20, Multilateralism and Emerging Mega-Trade Blocs: Options for India and Asian Developing Countries', in R. Kathuria and N.K. Nagpal eds. *Global Economic Cooperation*, Springer: 233–240.

Kumar, Nagesh (2016b), *National Development Banks and Sustainable Infrastructure in South Asia, GEGI WP 003*, Global Economic Governance Initiative, Boston University.

Kumar, Nagesh and A. Aggarwal (2005), 'Liberalization, Outward Orientation and In-House R&D Activity of Multinational and Local Firms: A Quantitative Exploration for Indian Manufacturing', *Research Policy* 34: 441–460.

Kumar, Nagesh and Kevin P. Gallagher (2007), *Relevance of 'Policy Space' for Development: Implications for Multilateral Trade Negotiations*, Geneva: ICTSD. Available from www.researchgate.net/publication/247236671_Preserving_Policy_Space_at_the_WTO.

Kumar, Nagesh and K.J. Joseph (2007), *International Competitiveness & Knowledge-Based Industries in India*, New Delhi: Oxford University Press.

Kumar, Nagesh and N.S. Siddharthan (1997), *Technology, Market Structure and Internationalization: Issues and Policies for Developing Countries*, London and New York: Routledge.

Lall, Sanjaya (2005), 'Rethinking Industrial Strategy: The Role of the State in the Face of Globalization', in Kevin P. Gallagher ed. *Putting Development First: The Importance of Policy Space in the WTO and IFIs*, London: Zed Books.

Lin, Justin Yifu (2012), *New Structural Economics: A Framework for Rethinking Development*, Washington, DC: The World Bank.

List, Friedrich (1909), *The National System of Political Economy*, London: Longmans, Green & Co.

Moran, Theodore H. (1998), *Foreign Direct Investment and Development*, Washington, DC: Institute for International Economics.

Nayyar, Deepak (1978), 'Industrial Development in India: Some Reflections on Growth and Stagnation', *Economic and Political Weekly* 13(31–33), August: 1265–1278.

## Reversing premature deindustrialisation 415

Nayyar, Deepak (2014), 'Why Employment Matters: Reviving Growth and Reducing Inequality', *International Labour Review* 153(3): 351–364.

Nayyar, Deepak (2015) 'Birth, Life and Death of Development Finance Institutions in India', *Economic and Political Weekly* 50(33), 15 August: 51–60.

Nelson, Richard and S.J. Winter (1982), *An Evolutionary Theory of Economic Change*, Cambridge: Harvard University Press.

Rodrik, Dani (2004), *Industrial Policy for the 21st Century*, Vienna: United Nations Industrial Development Organization.

Rodrik, Dani (2015), *Premature Deindustrialization, WP #20935*, National Bureau of Economic Research.

Salazar-Xirinachs, J.M., I. Nübler and R. Kozul-Wright, eds. (2014), *Transforming Economies: Making Industrial Policy Work for Growth, Jobs and Development*, Geneva: International Labour Office.

Santos-Paulino, A. and A.P. Thirlwall (2004), 'The Impact of Trade Liberalization on Exports, Imports and the Balance of Payments of Developing Countries', *The Economic Journal* 114: F50–F72.

Stiglitz, J.E., Justin Y. Lin and E. Patel (2013), *The Industrial Policy Revolution II: IEA Conference Volume No 151–11*, Houndsmill: Palgrave Macmillan.

Timmer, M.P., E. Dietzenbacher, B. Los, R. Stehrer and G.J. de Vries (2015), 'An Illustrated User Guide to the World Input – Output Database: The Case of Global Automotive Production', *Review of International Economics* 23: 575–605.

UNCTAD (2003), *Foreign Direct Investment and Performance Requirements: New Evidence from Selected Countries*, New York: United Nations.

Wade, Robert (2003), *Governing the Market*, (Second Edition), Princeton, NJ: Princeton University Press.

Wade, Robert (2014), 'The Paradox of US Industrial Policy: The Development State in Disguise', in J.M. Salazar-Xirinachs, I. Nübler and R. Kozul-Wright eds. *Transforming Economies: Making Industrial Policy Work for Growth, Jobs and Development*, Geneva: International Labour Office: 379–396.

World Bank (1993), *The East Asian Miracle: Economic Growth and Public Policy*, A World Bank Policy Research Report, Oxford University Press, New York.

# 20 Globalisation and the slowdown of the Indian economy

## A demand-side view

*Mritiunjoy Mohanty**

The Government of India (GOI) has argued that the 'great recession' in the aftermath of the 2008 financial crisis alongside supply-side bottlenecks within the economy are the main culprits behind the current investment slowdown. This chapter argues that the nature and pattern of integration and its impact on demand growth are equally if not more implicated. The chapter is divided into six sections: the first synoptically explores the slowdown from the demand and supply sides; the second looks at the resulting current account dynamics; the third analyses patterns of trade integration into the global economy; the fourth discusses the role of manufacturing trade in the slowdown; the fifth discusses the impact of manufacturing trade on private corporate investment and growth; finally the sixth section concludes.

## Growth slowdown – the demand and supply sides

As is now well established, and Table 20.1 makes clear, the first decade of the 21st century saw a sharp increase in average rates of growth of the Indian economy as compared with any other prior period (see for example Mohanty and Reddy 2010).

---

* It is a great honour to contribute to the festschrift for my teacher, thesis supervisor and friend Professor Deepak Nayyar. Many a lesson have I learned from him both inside and outside of class. In academic terms, however, perhaps the most abiding has been on how to frame a research question – as sharply and clearly as possible – and what to expect from an answer – to leave enough space in the analysis to incorporate the unexpected. This contribution is to honour one of Deepak's abiding research interests – globalisation and the macro-dynamics of growth and development, for example, Nayyar (1978, 1996, 2003, 2006, 2010, 2011, 2013).

   This is a shorter and substantially revised version of Mohanty (2015b). I am grateful to Sushil Khanna for discussions around an earlier draft of this chapter. Comments from Ananya Ghosh Dastidar are also gratefully acknowledged. Neither of course is responsible for errors that remain.

## Globalisation and the slowdown of the Indian economy   417

This increase in rates of growth was associated with significant increases in investment and savings ratios alongside a deepening of integration with the global economy (see e.g. Mohanty 2013: pp. 204–9[1]). As Table 20.1 makes clear this phase was interrupted by the global financial crisis of 2008. Even though the economy rebounded quickly, the recovery could not be sustained as investment growth collapsed leading to a slowdown of the economy. And as GOI (2016b) notes there has been a significant slowdown in employment growth as well and a related increase in unemployment.

During the high-growth phase demand, growth was investment driven – defined as investment's contribution to demand growth being greater than consumption's (i.e. $\Delta$investment > $\Delta$consumption) (see Mohanty and Reddy 2010: pp. 51, 57; Mohanty 2015b: p. 3). During the slowdown, the brunt of the output adjustment has been borne by gross and fixed investment. As a result demand growth has become consumption driven (i.e. $\Delta$consumption > $\Delta$investment). Increase in Investment demand accounted for only 14 percent of demand growth during the slowdown – a decline of more than 75 percent in comparison with the high growth phase (see Mohanty 2015b: pp. 3–4). Investment growth – both in the high-growth phase (see Khanna 2015: pp. 53–4), as well as in the slowdown (see RBI 2014: p. 17), has been driven by private-corporate investment. As both RBI (2014: p. 2) and GOI (2015) note, the slowdown in investment is largely the result of the contraction of private corporate fixed investment.

*Table 20.1* GDP and expenditure aggregates – growth rates (percent p.a.[a] and at constant 2004/5 prices)

|  | *2003/4[c]–7/8* | *2008/9* | *2009/10– 10/11* | *2011/12– 13/14* |
|---|---|---|---|---|
|  | *High-growth* | *Crisis[b]* | *Rebound* | *Slowdown* |
| GDP at market prices | 8.8 | 3.9 | 9.4 | 5.5 |
| Consumption | 7.2 | 7.7 | 8.3 | 6.2 |
| Gross investment | 18.5 | –1.6 | 13.7 | 2.1 |
| Gross fixed-investment | 16.2 | –51.4 | 9.3 | 4.3 |
| Exports | 17.8 | 14.6 | 7.5 | 9.7 |
| Imports | 20.1 | 22.7 | 6.7 | 8.4 |

Source: Author calculations on the basis of data from Reserve Bank of India's Handbook of Statistics on the Indian Economy (15th September 2014)

Notes:
a p.a. refers to per annum;
b 'Crisis' refers to global financial crisis of 2008;
c India's fiscal year begins on 1st April of a given year and ends on 31st March of the next year.

418 *Mritiunjoy Mohanty*

*Table 20.2* Supply-side contributions to GDP growth (percent)

|  | 2003/4–7/8 | 2009/10–10/11 | 2011/12–13/14 |
| --- | --- | --- | --- |
| Agriculture, forestry and fishing | 10.4 | 8.2 | 10.0 |
| Mining & quarrying | 1.5 | 1.7 | –0.5 |
| Manufacturing | 17.5 | 18.3 | 7.6 |
| EGWS[a] | 1.8 | 1.3 | 2.0 |
| Construction | 10.6 | 5.6 | 6.3 |
| THTC[b] | 31.1 | 34.1 | 21.1 |
| FIRE&B services[c] | 18.7 | 19.2 | 40.6 |
| Community, social & personal | 8.4 | 11.8 | 12.8 |

Source: Same as Table 20.1

Notes:
a EGWS: Electricity, gas and water supply;
b THTC: Trade, hotels, transport and communication;
c FIRE&B Services – Finance, real estate and business services.

As Table 20.2 establishes, the manufacturing sector was one of the leading contributors to GDP growth during the high-growth phase and the rebound. During the slowdown, manufacturing becomes one of the smallest contributors (along with construction) to GDP growth after mining and quarrying. It is worth noting however that the deceleration in manufacturing growth had started before the slowdown. Manufacturing therefore has undergone a protracted slowdown and a contraction in output (see Mohanty 2015b: pp. 6–9).

Therefore two important drivers of demand and supply growth – gross and fixed-investment and manufacturing – have decelerated very sharply and we have to understand their deceleration to understand the slowdown. But before that we need to introduce another element germane to our discussion.

## The current account balance and the investment-savings balance

We had noted earlier that the economy rebounded very quickly after the 2008 financial crisis. However, as Table 20.3 makes clear, there was one crucial difference. The high growth phase was characterised by low current account deficits. The rebound, on the other hand, saw a sharp increase in current account deficits, averaging almost 3 percent. Not only was it the case that the current account deficit increased

## Globalisation and the slowdown of the Indian economy  419

*Table 20.3* Macroeconomic balances (percent at current prices-old series)

|  | 2003/4–7/8 | 2008/9 | 2009/10–10/11 | 2011/12–12/13 | 2013/14 |
|---|---|---|---|---|---|
| Investment[b]/GDP | 33.4 | 35.5 | 36.4 | 35.2 | 30.4[a] |
| Savings[c]/GDP | 33.3 | 32.0 | 33.7 | 30.7 | 28.7[a] |
| CAB[d]/GDP | –0.3 | –2.3 | –2.8 | –4.5 | –1.7 |

Source: Same as Table 20.1 except where indicated

Notes:
a Author's estimates on the basis of 2011/12 base year data from GOI (2015) and CSO (2015);
b Refers to gross investment;
c Refers to gross savings;
d CAB – Current account balance.

during the rebound, it continued to *widen* over the slowdown as well. The average for 2011/12–2012/13 was 4.5 percent (see Table 20.3) before a sharp correction in 2013/14 to less than 2 percent.

The flip side of the current account balance is of course the investment-saving balance. During the rebound, demand-growth continued to be investment driven, fixed-investment growth was significantly slower than in the high growth phase (see Mohanty 2015b: pp. 3–4). The Government of India maintains that the increased demand for gold and silver, most of which had to be imported, meant high gross investment ratios as well as an increase in the current account deficit via the trade deficit.

However, as Table 20.3 also tells us, savings ratios declined quite sharply and indeed declined more than investment ratios, thereby contributing to widening of the current account deficit to almost 5 percent in 2012/13. Therefore an increase in the demand for gold and silver and an increase in the oil import bill due to increase in oil prices cannot be the only reasons for the worsening of the current account deficit. In 2013/14 the current account deficit narrowed very sharply to 1.7 percent (as compared with almost 5 percent the previous year) but came at the cost of a very sharp decline in the investment ratio. Put differently, had savings ratios not declined in the manner they did, it would have required a much smaller drop in investment ratios to close the significant and sustained current account deficit that opens up after the 2008 financial crisis.

All of this created for interesting investment-saving dynamics. During the high-growth phase Δinvestment (i.e. increase in investment)

420  *Mritiunjoy Mohanty*

and Δsaving (i.e. increase in savings) were roughly in balance, with the former slightly higher (51 percent) than the latter (49 percent)[2]. However Δsaving (49 percent) was clearly greater than Δfixed-investment (42 percent). Roughly the same pattern holds during the rebound. During the slowdown however both Δinvestment (28 percent) and Δfixed-investment (28 percent) are clearly greater than Δsaving (18 percent).We will have occasion to address later the implications of these dynamics for growth stability.

Returning to the issue of the current account deficit, the slowdown phase was therefore characterised by three trends – a sharp deceleration and eventual contraction in fixed-investment growth; a significant deceleration and eventual contraction in manufacturing growth; and an appreciable and sustained widening of current account deficit, which more than doubles. For the GOI, the global economic slowdown, the institutional failures in allocation of natural resources, the increase in the demand for gold and silver and the increase in oil prices explain all three trends. In our understanding however the nature and pattern of Indian economy's integration into the global economy had some role to play in explaining all three trends as well.

## Patterns of trade integration and the slowdown

We now turn to analyse one element of this pattern of integration – trade in goods and services – and its impact on growth dynamics.

As Table 20.4a clearly indicates, the speed of integration clearly accelerates in the first decade of the 21st century. In the last decade of the 20th century – the first post-reform decade – integration in terms of total trade in goods and services increased relatively slowly. It increased from 19 percent (two-year average for 1992/93–1993/94) to a little more than 27 percent (two-year average for 2001/2–2002/3). In the next decade however this ratio doubles – going from a little more than 27 percent to almost 54 percent (two-year average for 2012/13–2013/14).

The bulk of the increase happens in the high-growth phase during which total trade increases by more than 60 percent – from a little more than 27 percent to 45 percent (two-year average for 2006/7–2007/8). During this period, continuing a trend from the first post-reform decade, the increase in the total trade ratio is driven by both goods and services trade – goods trade ratio increases from almost 21 to 33 percent and services trade from 7 to 12 percent.

# Globalisation and the slowdown of the Indian economy 421

*Table 20.4a* Average trade ratios (percent of GDP)

|  | 1992/93–1993/94 | 2001/2–2002/3 | 2006/7–2007/8 | 2009/10–2010/11 | 2012/13–2013/14 |
|---|---|---|---|---|---|
| Goods exports | 7.4 | 9.5 | 13.2 | 13.9 | 16.4 |
| Services exports | 1.8 | 3.7 | 7.5 | 7.1 | 8.0 |
| Goods imports | 8.2 | 11.1 | 19.9 | 21.3 | 25.1 |
| Services imports | 1.5 | 3.0 | 4.4 | 4.5 | 4.3 |
| Goods trade[a] | 15.6 | 20.6 | 33.2 | 35.2 | 41.6 |
| Services trade[b] | 3.4 | 6.8 | 11.9 | 11.7 | 12.2 |
| Total trade[c] | 18.9 | 27.3 | 45.1 | 46.9 | 53.8 |
| Total trade less crude oil and g-s[d] imports | 16.8 | 23.4 | 37.4 | 38.3 | 42.6 |
| Total trade less crude oil and g-s imports and POL[e] exports | 16.6 | 22.9 | 35.2 | 36.1 | 39.3 |

Source: Same as Table 20.1

Notes:
a Goods trade is defined as total of goods exports and imports;
b Services trade is defined as total of services exports and imports;
c Total trade is defined as goods trade + services trade;
d 'g-s' refers to gold and silver;
e 'POL' refers to petroleum, oil and lubricants (refinery products).

Post the 2008 financial crisis however the pace of integration slows down substantially. During the rebound, total trade increased by less than 2 percent with all of it coming from goods trade. Services trade actually sees a small decline in its share. Over the growth slowdown, the pace of integration actually quickens again and total trade increases by 7 percent, to reach almost 54 percent. The bulk of the increase in integration comes from goods trade – the share of goods trade increases by almost 6.5 percent as opposed to services trade by 0.5 percent.

It is important to recognise that the trade integration result stands even when we strip out oil and gold-silver imports – total trade less oil and gold and silver imports increases by almost 60 percent during the high growth phase – rising from 23.4 (two-year average for 2001/2–2002/3) to 37.4 percent (two-year average for 2006/7–2007/8). Similarly, during the slowdown, total trade less oil and gold and silver imports increases by more than 4 percent to 43 percent (two-year average for 2012/13–2013/14).

## 422   Mritiunjoy Mohanty

*Table 20.4b* Average oil and non-oil goods trade ratios (percent of GDP)

|  | 1992/93–1993/94 | 2001/2–2002/3 | 2006/7–2007/8 | 2009/10–2010/11 | 2012/13–2013/14 |
|---|---|---|---|---|---|
| Goods exports | 7.4 | 9.5 | 13.2 | 13.9 | 16.4 |
| Non-POL exports | 7.2 | 9.0 | 11.1 | 11.6 | 13.1 |
| Goods imports | 8.2 | 11.1 | 19.9 | 21.3 | 25.1 |
| Non-crude-oil imports | 8.4 | 8.2 | 10.3 | 13.7 | 15.1 |
| Non-crude-oil/non-g-s imports | 6.1 | 7.1 | 12.2 | 12.7 | 14.0 |

Source: Same as Table 20.1

Therefore the following conclusions may be drawn about the pattern of integration: *First*, during the first decade of the 21st century – the second post-reform decade – the pace of trade integration with the global economy increases appreciably; *second*, the bulk of the integration happens during the high-growth phase and is driven by *both* goods and services trade; *third*, integration continues to deepen during the slowdown but is driven almost *entirely* by goods trade; *finally* and importantly all of these conclusions hold even when we remove oil and gold-silver imports from total trade.

Given the importance of goods trade in driving integration particularly during the slowdown, Table 20.4b allows us to explore goods trade in somewhat greater detail. The following conclusions emerge: First, in the first post-reform decade (1992/93–2002/3) – goods trade integration is driven by both exports and imports, with an export ratio increasing by 2 percent and import ratio by 3 percent; second, goods trade remains in deficit, but the bulk of the increase in import intensity (2 percent out of 3 percent) is due to increase in oil and gold-silver imports; third, therefore in the *first post-reform decade* non-oil/non-gold-silver import integration is relatively slow and *trade integration is driven by exports.*

In the high-growth phase (2003/4–2007/8) – which saw a sharp increase of 12.6 percentage points in the goods trade ratio (33.2 percent–20.6 percent in Table 20.4a) – the exports ratio increased by almost 4 percentage points (13.2 percent–9.5 percent in Table 20.4a) while imports ratio increased by almost 9 percentage points. The increase in import intensity remains true even we strip out oil and gold-silver imports – non-oil/non-gold-silver imports share increases by 5 percentage points.

*Globalisation and the slowdown of the Indian economy* 423

*Therefore, in the high-growth phase, trade integration is also driven by non-oil/non-gold-silver imports,* even as exports share sees an appreciable increase.

On the basis of Table 20.4a we know that during the slowdown import ratio increased by 3.8 percentage points (25.1 percent–21.3 percent), of which 1.3 percentage points is accounted for by non-crude oil/non-gold-silver imports whereas goods export ratio increases by 2.5 percentage points. If we consider averages for the first two years of the slowdown (2011/12–2012/13) the goods import ratio rises by 4.8 percent, of which 1.9 percent is accounted for by non-oil/non-gold-silver imports. The goods export ratio over this period rises by 2.3 percent. Therefore despite a *slowing economy, non-oil/non-gold-silver imports accounted for a substantial proportion of the increase in imports* – a 40 percent of the increase in goods imports ratio.

On the basis of Table 20.4b we can say that clearly crude oil imports – and to some extent gold-silver imports – distort the extent of import integration. Oil imports which accounted for 3 percent of GDP (11.1 percent–8.2 percent) for the period 2001/2–2002/3 (little more than 25 percent of total imports) increased to 10 percent of GDP for the period 2012/13–2013/14 (40 percent of total imports). Gold and silver imports fluctuate between 1 and 2 percent of GDP over this period. Therefore the Government of India's position that the deterioration in the current account is on account of rising oil import bill and gold-silver imports is certainly not incorrect. But as we have seen it is not the whole story.

Finally, on the basis of Table 20.4a, we can say that petroleum and refinery product exports have seen an increasing importance in the country's export profile – rising from 0.5 percent of GDP (23.4 percent–22.9 percent) and a little more than 5 percent of total exports (average for 2001/2 to 2002/3) to 3.3 percent of GDP and more than 20 percent of total exports (average for the period 2012/13 to 2013/14). Clearly then, in the last decade, crude oil and related products have had an important role to play in the evolution of India's foreign trade in goods. But their growing importance perhaps hides more than it reveals.

We noted earlier that trade integration with the global economy was driven by goods trade in the high-growth phase and particularly so during the slowdown. In turn goods trade during both phases has been driven by rising import intensity despite substantially improved export performance. Finally, oil imports notwithstanding, *non-oil/non-gold-silver imports have been important drivers of import integration.*

424  *Mritiunjoy Mohanty*

*Table 20.5* Average trade and current account balances (as percent of GDP)

|  | 1992/3– 2002/3 | 2003/4– 2007/8 | 2009/10– 2010/11 | 2011/12– 2013/14 |
|---|---|---|---|---|
| Goods trade deficit | –2.8 | –5.4 | –8.1 | –9.5 |
| Non-oil goods balance | 0.7 | –1.4 | –3.4 | –3.6 |
| Non-oil/non-gold goods surplus | 1.5 | 1.4 | 1.1 | 2.2 |
| Services trade surplus | 0.4 | 2.6 | 2.6 | 3.6 |
| Pvt. transfers surplus | 2.5 | 3.2 | 3.5 | 3.4 |
| Current Account Deficit | –0.7 | –0.3 | –2.8 | –3.5 |

Source: Same as Table 20.1

The importance of oil imports in driving India's goods trade deficit is clear from Table 20.5. The deficit on account of oil imports rises from 4 percent of GDP [–5.4 percent–(1.4 percent)] during the high-growth period to 6 percent [–9.5 percent–(3.6 percent)] in slowdown. However equally importantly, the non-oil/non-gold goods trade has consistently been in surplus in both the first and second post-reform decades. Clearly then gold and silver imports did have some role to play in the worsening of India's current account deficit during the rebound and the slowdown, in line with the GOI's position in this regard. However a more disaggregated analysis of the patterns of integration allows a more nuanced understanding of the role of manufacturing trade in the slowdown.

## Manufacturing trade and the slowdown

As we have noted elsewhere (Mohanty 2013: pp. 221–2), in terms of global integration, the three major sectors are very differently situated. The average agricultural trade ratio for the period 2008/9–2010/11 was 11.9 percent; over the same period, manufacturing's trade ratio was 142 percent; for services it was 19.8 percent. Even if we consider the narrower sub-sector 'financial and business services', its trade ratio was 57.8 percent – significantly below manufacturing.[3] Therefore manufacturing – which at 2004/5 constant prices accounts for 15–16.3 percent of India's GDP (over the period 2002/3–2013/4) – is the economy's most globally integrated sector. In addition, the manufacturing sector accounts for almost 80 percent of India's exports (Mohanty 2013: Table 8.6, p. 203). For manufacturing, both the pace and nature of integration changed significantly in the first decade of the 21st century – the high-growth phase.

*Globalisation and the slowdown of the Indian economy* 425

*Table 20.6* Manufacturing sector trade ratios (percent of manufacturing GDP)

| | 1992/93–2002/3 | 2003/4–2008/9 | 2009/10[a] | 2010/11–2012/13 | 2013/14 |
|---|---|---|---|---|---|
| Manufacturing (X+M)[b] | 82.0 | 134.9 | 142.5 | 172.3 | 201.7 |
| Manufacturing (X+M) less POL exports | 80.6 | 124.0 | 128.1 | 150.8 | 173.5 |
| Manufacturing (X–M) | 10.2 | 8.5 | 4.9 | 13.5 | 26.8 |
| Manufacturing (X–M) less POL[c] exports | 8.9 | –2.3 | –9.5 | –7.9 | –1.3 |

Source: Same as Table 20.1

Notes:
a For India the trade effects of 2008 global financial crisis become visible in the fiscal year 2009/10. Therefore in both Tables 20.6 and 20.7 the fiscal year 2008/9 has been included in the high-growth period;
b X refers to exports and M to imports;
c POL refers to 'petroleum, oil and lubricants'.

As Table 20.6 details, manufacturing's average trade ratio (as a proportion of manufacturing GDP) for the period 1992/3–2002/3 – the first post-reform decade – was 82 percent. Manufacturing export and import ratios were at 46 percent and 36 percent, respectively. The non-POL manufacturing export ratio was 45 percent. In the *first post-reform period*, therefore, both manufacturing export ratio *as well as* non-POL manufacturing export ratio were greater than the manufacturing import ratio and the sector generated an overall *as well as* non-POL trade surplus.

During the high-growth period – 2003/4–2008/9 – the average trade ratio rose to 135 percent, an increase of 65 percent as compared with the earlier period. Manufacturing's exports ratio rose to 72 percent, non-POL exports to 61 percent and imports to 63 percent. There are some noteworthy aspects about this phase: First, import integration is much sharper than export integration; second, during the high-growth phase, manufacturing imports were the driver of the manufacturing sector's integration into the global economy; third, the non-POL export ratio is lower than the import ratio; finally, therefore, during the *high-growth phase, non-POL manufacturing trade is in deficit*, whereas overall manufacturing trade continues to be in surplus as opposed to the first post-reform decade where *both* were in surplus (see also Chaudhuri 2013, with regard to the manufacturing trade deficit).

## 426 Mritiunjoy Mohanty

Over the slowdown, trade integration of the manufacturing sector increased further to 172 percent: The export ratio rising to 93 percent, the non-POL export ratio to 71.5 percent and import ratio to 79 percent. Over this period the increase in the export ratio (29 percent) was only slightly greater than in the import ratio (25 percent), but the latter continued to increase much faster than non-POL export ratio (17 percent). Therefore during the *slowdown, the deficit in non-POL manufacturing trade widened even further as compared with the high-growth phase*, as Table 20.4b clearly indicates. Overall, manufacturing trade however continued to remain in surplus.

Therefore it is reasonable to argue that not only has manufacturing sector's integration increased sharply but that it has also been asymmetric – import integration increasing much faster than exports, particularly, as Table 20.6 makes clear, when we have excluded petroleum product exports. Put differently, rising POL exports mask an increasing deficit in non-POL manufacturing trade, which opens up during the high growth period (2 percent of manufacturing GDP), widens substantially during the slowdown (8 percent of manufacturing GDP). As we will see in a moment, this has deleterious consequences for investment growth.

### Growth, private corporate investment and manufacturing trade

Before we move on to analyse the consequences of manufacturing trade, it is important to note one particular aspect of private corporate investment in manufacturing. We have already noted that in both the high-growth and slowdown phases, investment growth was driven by private, corporate investments. And for the accumulation of the private corporate sector, the manufacturing sector is of particular importance. As Mazumdar (2008: p. 70) notes, "the manufacturing sector absorbs the major part of private corporate investment and . . . private corporate sector dominates the investment in registered manufacturing" (see also Khanna 2015: pp. 55–6).

In addition, manufacturing accounts for a substantial proportion of investment in the economy. Manufacturing accounted for between 33 and 37 percent of gross capital formation between 2004/5 and 2007/8 and averaged 34 percent for that period. In 2009/10, 2010/11 and 2011/12 it accounted for 31.2, 32.7 and 25.7 percent of gross investment respectively (see Chandrasekhar and Ghosh 2013). All this to say that what happens in manufacturing has important implications for private corporate investment behaviour as well as overall investment in the economy.

## Globalisation and the slowdown of the Indian economy 427

Why was private corporate investment growth so robust over this period? Whereas there are a large number of factors including financial market liberalisation, there are two factors that are central from our standpoint: First were investment subsidies inherent in the under-pricing of assets and natural resources (see Mohanty 2012); and the second was access to international markets for goods and services and capital, one aspect of which was manufacturing trade.

Putting together data from Tables 20.4a, 20.6 and 20.7, the following conclusions emerge: During the first post-reform decade (1992/3–2002/3), integration was driven by exports of goods and services though the pace of integration was relatively slow. Manufacturing exports grew faster than manufacturing imports (see Table 20.7) and both overall and non-POL manufacturing trades generated surpluses.

During the high-growth phase that followed, however, the pace of integration accelerated dramatically particularly for imports. The average rate of growth of non-oil/non-gold-silver imports increased by more than 60 percent whereas that of exports increased at a much slower pace of 25 percent (on the basis of Table 20.7). As we have already noted, during this period, the manufacturing sector generated a small non-POL deficit as opposed to a surplus in the previous period. Even though integration is driven by imports, continued expansion of manufacturing exports saw the commodity composition change towards higher value added commodities (see Mohanty 2013: Tables 8.5 and 8.6, pp. 201–3).[4]

*Table 20.7* Export and import growth rates (percent p.a. in current rupees)

|  | 1992/93–2002/3 | 2003/4–2008/9 | 2009/10[a] | 2010/11–2012/13 | 2013/14 |
|---|---|---|---|---|---|
| Imports | 18.4 | 29.3 | –0.8 | 25.5 | 1.7 |
| Exports | 17.6 | 22.1 | 0.6 | 25.0 | 15.9 |
| Oil and gold-silver imports | 22.0 | 30.8 | 5.2 | 30.4 | 0.0 |
| Non-oil-non-gold-silver imports | 17.3 | 28.4 | –4.5 | 22.2 | 3.1 |
| Manufacturing exports | 18.3 | 22.4 | –1.5 | 25.2 | 16.3 |
| Non-oil manufacturing exports | 18.0 | 19.8 | –3.5 | 22.4 | 16.8 |
| Manufacturing imports | 17.1 | 30.3 | –6.3 | 22.4 | 2.6 |
| Capital-goods-imports | 19.5 | 31.3 | –5.4 | 18.6 | –0.1 |

Source: Same as Table 20.1

Note:
a Please see notes to Table 20.6 with regard to fiscal year 2009/10.

428  *Mritiunjoy Mohanty*

We know that, in this phase, demand-growth was investment-driven (particularly fixed-investment) and that the manufacturing sector was an important driver of supply-side growth. Investment-driven growth meant, as we have seen, an increase of 8 percent in the fixed-investment share (at constant prices) over a short five-year period. As Table 20.7 makes clear, in this phase, manufacturing imports and capital goods imports grow faster than overall imports. In addition capital goods imports grows faster than oil and gold-silver imports!

Clearly then growth in domestic capacity (manufacturing sector growth) and imports moved together. Access to imported inputs both in the intermediate and capital goods ensured that the investment boom was sustained without domestic capacity or capability appearing as a constraint. This observation however has to be contextualised. As Chandra (2012: p. 102) has argued, the impact of trade liberalisation of early 1990s was disproportionately borne by the capital goods sector which according to a large number of estimates (including of the World Bank) was efficient (see Chandra 2012: pp. 98–102). Therefore, had the capital goods sector not been damaged by macro-policy, the import requirements and technological spillovers of the investment-driven high-growth phase would have been very different. Returning to the issue at hand, we also know that the period produced a non-POL manufacturing trade deficit. And as Chaudhuri (2013: pp. 46–9) notes, the failure to produce new capital goods was an important reason for this deficit and that the Neo-liberal policy regime was directly implicated in the failure (see also Chandra 2012: p. 102).

Be that as it may, the coming together of increases in the investment ratio, manufacturing ratio, export ratio (alongside a diversification towards higher value-added exports) created a virtuous cycle of what Kaldor (1970, 1972) has termed "cumulative causation" – where demand-growth, working itself through manufacturing exports and Verdoorn's law, triggers productivity growth which in turn leads to more demand-growth (see also Setterfield 2011: pp. 413–14). The fact that the leakage – non-POL manufacturing trade deficit – was relatively small, sustained it as a demand-driven process with important productivity spillovers given that overall demand growth was investment-driven.

During the slowdown this virtuous cycle of cumulative causation *reversed* itself. The non-POL manufacturing trade balance moved significantly into deficit territory – 8 percent of manufacturing GDP for the period 2010/11–2012/13 (Table 20.6). The worsening of the manufacturing non-POL trade balance was accompanied by decline

## Globalisation and the slowdown of the Indian economy 429

in gross investment ratio – from 39 percent during the rebound to 37 percent for the period 2012/13–2013/14 – and stagnation in the fixed investment ratio as investment growth – both gross and fixed – slowed down sharply (see Table 20.1). As we have seen already, manufacturing growth slowed down significantly, turning into a laggard sector from being a driver of supply-side growth (see Table 20.2). And as Table 20.7 makes clear, even though import growth slows down, as do fixed-investment and GDP growth, both manufacturing and capital goods imports growth remain reasonably robust. Indeed manufacturing imports and non-POL export growth are not very dissimilar.

Manufacturing import growth not only led to a non-POL trade deficit but also by displacing domestic production particularly in the capital goods sector, adversely affected profitability expectations, helping the slowdown in investment feed on itself – the virtuous cycle of cumulative causation had turned into a vicious cycle. Manufacturing imports and rising import propensities, including of capital goods, by displacing domestic capacity, contributed to the downward spiral in private corporate investment by further damaging expected profitability already adversely affected by the withdrawal, due to political economy reasons, of implicit investment subsidies inherent in the under-pricing of land and other natural resources[5] (see Mohanty 2012).

The RBI accepts that imports displaced domestic capacity. It noted (2012: p. 19) that "*Capital goods production also contracted sharply*, though this was partly on account of *substitution by imported capital goods*. Hence, investment decelerated faster than other components of domestic demand" [emphasis added]. And even though our data ends in 2013/14, all evidence suggests that the slowdown in overall investment and private corporate investment persists (see RBI 2016: p. 15; GOI 2016a, Vol.1: p. 13). This despite the fact that the private corporate sector has seen a robust growth in savings (see GOI 2016a, Vol.1: p. 13). In addition the GOI admits that capacity utilisation in manufacturing is low and that all evidence points "towards the existence of significant excess capacities in sectors like capital goods and consumer durables" (see GOI 2016a, Vol.1: p. 15). That the weakness in capital goods and durable goods is persistent can be gauged from the fact that the maximum sectoral IIP (Index of Industrial Production) values were reached way back in March 2011 for capital goods and October 2012 for consumer durables.

At first brush this narrative of output adjustment would seem to be a good candidate for a balance of payments constrained growth process working itself through Verdoonian productivity spillovers, and the interaction of export and investment growth and thereby endogenising

## 430 Mritiunjoy Mohanty

the Harrodian natural growth rate as well as ensuring that it is equal to the actual growth rate (see Thirlwall 2011: pp. 22–3; Setterfield 2011: pp. 411–24).

Be that as it may, we feel that the balance of payments constrained growth model is an inappropriate lens with which to view India's recent growth dynamics largely because it misses out on the central role played by investment (particularly private corporate investment) and capacity utilisation in this process that I have outlined previously (see also Razmi 2016: p. 1592). In our view a Kaleckian model with a Bhaduri and Marglin (1990) or Kurz (1990) type investment function and where capacity utilisation is an adjusting variable in both the short and medium/long term may be more apposite, the debate around the 'normal' rate of capacity utilisation notwithstanding (on the debate see Skott 2008; Lavoie 2010; and Hein et al. 2012). I for one do not believe in the uniqueness of the 'normal' rate of capacity utilisation at least in part because, as Taylor notes (2004: p. 198), "structuralist models don't blend happily with natural rates." This is not to deny the importance of Harrodian instability. Rather to argue that it is possible to contain it and yet have a demand-constrained growth process that has, both in the short and medium/long term, Kaleckian attributes of paradox of costs (see Lavoie 2010; Dutt 2010; and Hein et al. 2012).

From a stability standpoint, as we have already noted in the second section perviously, with $\Delta$saving being greater than $\Delta$fixed-investment during the high growth phase, the process exhibited Keynesian stability[6] at least with regard to fixed-investment. During the slowdown however the process was clearly Keynesian unstable with both $\Delta$investment and $\Delta$fixed-investment being greater than $\Delta$saving. Stability issues apart, India's growth is arguably demand constrained given that the economy seems to have reached a low level equilibrium characterised by low levels of investment growth, significant excess capacity and high levels of unemployment and underemployment.

## Conclusions

Without doubt then the global financial crisis and the 'great recession' that followed had a significant impact on India's growth trajectory. This is particularly true of the relative slowing down in services exports during the slowdown as a result of which trade integration gets dominated by goods trade. And certainly the increase in oil prices and the continuing increase in the import of gold and silver had an impact on current account balances. Therefore the international

# Globalisation and the slowdown of the Indian economy 431

conjuncture and behavioural aspects outside the government's control have acted as catalysts. But we also argue that the oil trade – crude oil imports and petroleum and refinery product exports – overstates the extent of integration and mask important structural tendencies such as persistent deficits on non-oil manufacturing trade. Equally importantly neither (increase in oil prices and gold-silver imports) explain the sharp deceleration in fixed-investment growth and the contraction in manufacturing output that characterise the slowdown. In our analysis, the centrality of private corporate investment and the manufacturing sector to the high-growth phase and the slowdown is explained, in part, by the patterns of integration and its impact on growth dynamics.

We have argued that, during the high-growth phase, the pattern of integration into the global economy created a virtuous cycle of cumulative causation where manufacturing trade, private corporate investment and manufacturing growth fed off each other. During the slowdown, this process reversed itself, creating a vicious cycle of cumulative causation where a deceleration in private corporate investment through the expected profitability channel was reinforced by manufacturing imports displacing domestic capacity. Given the centrality of private corporate investment to investment and thereby the growth process, we have argued that using a Kaleckian lens (as opposed to a balance of payments constrained growth model view), where investment is driven by expected profitability and capacity utilisation, is an adjusting variable in both the short and long term is more appropriate.

We have also suggested that for all the advances in the Indian economy's technological capabilities, import integration during this phase of investment-led growth exacerbated an old structural problem – inability to produce new capital goods – by destroying hard-earned capability in this sector. And as Nayyar (2013: p. 146) has noted,

> However, technological developments in firms at a micro-level is also shaped by technological capabilities in the economy at a macro-level. National technological capabilities are the outcome of a complex interaction between incentives, capabilities and institutions. . . . It becomes possible for late industrializers to complete the transition once they develop technological capabilities both at the micro-level in firms and at the macro-level in the economy.

As India's economy passes through this current phase of turbulence it would be more than useful to keep this learning squarely in focus.

## 432  *Mritiunjoy Mohanty*

## Notes

1  The English version of Mohanty (2013) is available as Mohanty (2015a). The appropriate page reference for Mohanty (2013: pp. 204–9) is Mohanty (2015a: pp. 6–16).
2  That is to say that ($\Delta$investment/$\Delta$GDP) is 51 percent and ($\Delta$saving/$\Delta$GDP) is 49 percent.
3  As a result of revision of GDP data since the publication of Mohanty (2013), there will be some change in these ratios. The broad magnitudes however and therefore the conclusions do not get altered. For Mohanty (2013: pp. 221–2) see Mohanty (2015a: pp. 23–4); for Mohanty (2013: Table 8.6, p. 203), see Mohanty (2015a: Table 6, p. 11).
4  See also Mohanty (2015a): Tables 5 and 6, pp. 10–11.
5  Rajan (2013) agrees that correction of the under-pricing was one of the causes of the growth slowdown but attributes causes with which I am not in agreement. See Mohanty (2013: pp. 230–1; 2015a: pp. 28–9) for my understanding.
6  This might reflect Harrodian stability as well given that, as Hein et al. (2011: p. 589) note, the two are difficult to disentangle in practice. However this is not to deny, as they go on to note (p. 592), that one can "have Keynesian stability and Harrodian instability simultaneously." Therefore the need to separately contend with Harrodian instability.

## Bibliography

Bhaduri, Amit and Stephen Marglin, (1990), 'Unemployment and the Real Wage: The Economic Basis for Contesting Political Ideologies', *Cambridge Journal of Economics*, Vol. 14(4): 375–93.

Chandra, Nirmal K., (2012), 'Appraising Industrial Policies of India and China from Two Perspectives – Nationalist and Internationalist' in Amiya Bagchi and Anthony D'Costa (eds.) *Economic and Social Transformation of China and India*, Delhi: Oxford University Press.

Chandrasekhar, C.P. and Jayati Ghosh, (2013), 'Unleashing the Animal Spirits', *Business Line*, 23rd December.

Chaudhuri, Sudip, (2013), 'Manufacturing Trade Deficit and Industrial Policy in India', *Economic and Political Weekly*, Vol. 48(8): 41–50.

CSO, (2015), Press Note on Advance Estimates of National Income 2014–15, Central Statistics Office, Ministry of Statistics & Programme Implementation, Government of India, New Delhi, 9th February.

Dutt, Amitava K., (2010), 'Reconciling the Growth of Aggregate Demand and Aggregate Supply' in Mark Setterfield (ed.) *Handbook of Alternative Theories of Economic Growth*, Cheltenham: Edward Elgar, pp. 220–40.

GOI, (2012), Economic Survey 2011–12, Ministry of Finance, Government of India, New Delhi.

GOI, (2015), Economic Survey 2014–15, Vols. 1&2, Ministry of Finance, Government of India, New Delhi.

GOI, (2016a), Economic Survey 2015–16, Vols. 1&2, Ministry of Finance, Government of India, New Delhi.

## Globalisation and the slowdown of the Indian economy   433

GOI, (2016b), Report on Fifth Annual Employment-Unemployment Survey 2015–16, Vol. 1, Ministry of Labour and Employment, Government of India, Chandigarh.

Hein, Eckhardt, Marc Lavoie and Till van Treeck, (2011), 'Some Instability Puzzles in Kaleckian Models of Growth and Distribution: A Critical Survey', *Cambridge Journal of Economics*, Vol. 35: 587–612.

Hein, Eckhardt, Marc Lavoie and Till van Treeck, (2012), 'Harrodian Instability and the "Normal Rate" of Capacity Utilisation in Kaleckian Models of Growth and Distribution – a Survey', *Metroeconomica*, Vol. 63(1): 139–69.

Kaldor, Nicholas, (1970), 'The Case for Regional Policies', *Scottish Journal of Political Economy*, Vol. 17(3): 337–48.

Kaldor, Nicholas, (1972), 'The Irrelevance of Equilibrium Economics', *Economic Journal*, Vol. 82(328): 1237–55.

Khanna, Sushil, (2015), 'The Transformation of India's Public Sector: The Political Economy of Growth and Change', *Economic and Political Weekly*, Vol. 50(5): 47–60.

Kurz, Heinz D., (1990), 'Technical Change, Growth and Distribution: A Steady State Approach to Unsteady Growth', in Heinz D. Kurz (ed.) *Capital, Distribution and Effective Demand: Studies in the Classical Approach to Economic Theory*, Cambridge, UK: Polity Press.

Lavoie, Marc, (2010), 'Surveying Short-Run and Long-Run Stability Issues with the Kaleckian Model of Growth' in Mark Setterfield (ed.) *Handbook of Alternative Theories of Economic Growth*, Cheltenham: Edward Elgar, pp. 132–56.

Mazumdar, Surajit, (2008), 'Investment and Growth in India under Liberalisation: Asymmetries and Instabilities', *Economic and Political Weekly*, Vol. 43(49): 68–77.

Mohanty, Mritiunjoy, (2012), 'The Growth Model Has Come Undone', *The Hindu*, 11th July.

Mohanty, Mritiunjoy, (2013), 'Mondialisation et croissance de l'économie indienne' in Serge Granger, Karine Bates, Mathieu Boisvert and Christophe Jaffrelot (eds.) *L'Inde et ses Avatars: Pluralités d'une puissance*, Montreal: Presses de l'Université de Montréal, pp. 189–231. (English version available as Mohanty (2015a)).

Mohanty, Mritiunjoy, (2015a), 'India: Globalisation and Growth', Working Paper Series WPS No. 762, IIM Calcutta, May.

Mohanty, Mritiunjoy, (2015b), 'Globalisation and the Slowdown of the Indian Economy: Another View', Notes d'analyse du PRIAS Policy Note No.4, Pôle de recherche sur L'Inde et l'Asie du Sud (PRIAS), Centre d'Études et de Recherche Internationales (CERIUM), Université de Montréal. September.

Mohanty, Mritiunjoy and V.N. Reddy, (2010), 'Some Explorations into India's Post-Independence Growth Process, 1950/1–2002/3: The Demand Side', *Economic and Political Weekly*, Vol. 45(41): 47–58.

Nayyar, Deepak, (1978), 'Transnational Corporations and Manufactured Exports from Poor Countries', *Economic Journal*, Vol. 88: 59–84.

Nayyar, Deepak, (1996), 'Free Trade: Why, When and for Whom?', *Banca Nazionale del Lavoro Quarterly Review*, Vol. 49: 333–50.

## 434  Mritiunjoy Mohanty

Nayyar, Deepak, (2003), 'Globalization and Development Strategies', in John Toye (ed.) *Trade and Development: Directions for the 21st Century*, Cheltenham: Edward Elgar.

Nayyar, Deepak, (2006), 'Globalization, History and Development: A Tale of Two Centuries', *Cambridge Journal of Economics*, Vol. 30: 137–59.

Nayyar, Deepak, (2010), 'China, India, Brazil and South Africa in the World Economy: Engines of Growth?' in Amelia Santos-Paulino and Guanghua Wan (eds.) *Southern Engines of Global Growth*, Oxford: Oxford University Press.

Nayyar, Deepak, (2011), 'The Financial Crisis, the Great Recession and the Developing World', *Global Policy*, Vol. 2: 20–32.

Nayyar, Deepak, (2013), *Catch Up: Developing Countries in the World Economy*, Oxford: Oxford University Press.

Rajan, Raghuram, (2013), 'Why India Slowed', *Project Syndicate*, 30th April.

Razmi, Arslan, (2016), 'Correctly Analysing the Balance-of-Payments Constraint on Growth', *Cambridge Journal of Economics*, Vol. 40: 1581–08.

RBI, (2012), Reserve Bank of India's Annual Report 2011–12 Reserve Bank of India, Mumbai.

RBI, (2014), Reserve Bank of India's Annual Report 2013–14, Reserve Bank of India, Mumbai.

RBI, (2016), Reserve Bank of India's Annual Report 2015–16, Reserve Bank of India, Mumbai.

Setterfield, Mark, (2011), 'The Remarkable Durability of Thirlwall's Law', *PSL Quarterly Review*, Vol. 64(259): 393–427.

Skott, Peter, (2008), 'Theoretical and Empirical Shortcomings of the Kaleckian Investment Function', Working Paper 2008–11, University of Massachusetts, Amherst.

Taylor, Lance, (2004), *Reconstructing Macroeconomics: Structuralist Proposals and Critiques of the Mainstream*, Cambridge, USA: Harvard University Press.

Thirlwall, Anthony P., (2011), 'Balance of Payments Constrained Growth Models: History and Overview', School of Economics Discussion Papers, University of Kent.

# 21 Is land a bottleneck for economic development in India?

*Ram Singh*

India needs to industrialize rapidly to sustain economic growth. To achieve that objective, the country will have to expand its infrastructure networks. The availability of suitable land is critical for industrial as well as infrastructure projects. The country is already witnessing a demand for land in a proportion much larger than what has been the case so far. Moreover, urbanization is also going to be an integral part of the process of development. There are several estimates that suggest India is urbanizing rapidly. By 2050, India's urban and semi-urban areas are going to account for 55 percent of the population, amounting to about 900 million people. Urbanization will further intensify the pressure for transfer of agricultural land to nonagricultural use. Indeed, the success of economic policy will depend on whether adequate land is being made available for industrial and urban development projects.

Of course, we need to ensure that the available land is used efficiently. Optimum land use can be achieved through implementation of suitable 'master plans', surface-area ratios and other zonal regulations. Various studies show that existing planning and governance processes for urban areas leave much to be desired. The state of the land use policies for urban areas is even worse. The land already available is not being used efficiently. Moreover, there is wide gap between the additional land needed for urban housing and other development projects, on the one hand, and the land that is actually available, on the other hand. Indeed, a considerable amount of work is required to ensure optimum use and supply of land for urban projects.

The focus of this chapter is on the issue of transfer of agricultural land for industrial, housing and the other urban developmental projects. The transfer of land from agriculture to other desirable objectives can be arranged through various processes. For instance, land transfer can be facilitated through voluntary transactions between the existing land owners and the potential project developers. Alternatively, the process of land transfer could allow for compulsory acquisition of land, as is the case with standard use of the eminent domain. It could also be a complex mix of these two processes.

We examine the existing rules that govern transfer of agriculture land to the industrial, housing and the other urban projects through voluntary transactions. We show that the existing institutional and regulatory structure precludes a large number of potentially profitable transactions over transfer of land from current usage to the use for industrial and urban development. As a result, there has been a natural tendency among the companies and developers to approach the state government to get the required land. Further, we examine the tax structure applicable to the land transaction, including the *stamp duty* and *property tax*. We show that not only these taxes fail to achieve the intended objectives, they create an artificial demand for land by encouraging speculative investment in land. The result is that land becomes excessively costly, which, in turn, reduces the profitability of the industrial and the other urban projects.

The use of eminent domain to transfer of agricultural land for non-agricultural use is going to be governed by the Right to Fair Compensation and Transparency in Land Acquisition, Rehabilitation and Resettlement Act, 2013. We examine the provisions of the Act and show that the new law seriously restricts the scope of misuse of eminent domain for land acquisition for companies. Unlike in the past when the state governments were able to use eminent domain to acquire land for urban development as well as for various business activities, land acquisition for companies faces serious scrutiny under the new Act.

In the second section, we examine the existing regulatory framework governing agriculture land, its usage and transactions in agricultural land. We analyze the effects of the regulatory framework on transfer of agriculture land to the other sectors of the economy. This is followed by an analysis of the various taxes applicable to land transactions, the ownership of land and the implications of those taxes on the functioning of market in agriculture land. In the fourth section, the provisions of the Right to Fair Compensation and Transparency in Land Acquisition, Rehabilitation and Resettlement Act, 2013 is examined. The objective of the section is to analyze the scope of the use of eminent domain for land transfer under the new law. It is followed by the concluding section that highlights some suggestions for the future course of policy action to improve the functioning of land markets in India.

## Existing land use regulations: An impediment to efficient land use

The existing institutional and regulatory frameworks governing land and its usage are highly restrictive. First of all, there are restrictions on the purchase of agricultural land itself. Agricultural land is a state subject, that is, the subject belongs to the 'State List'. Some states allow only the agricultural land owners and their progeny to buy agricultural land. Several other states allow 'non-farmers' to own agricultural land. Nonetheless, all states allow 'non-farmer' to buy agricultural land for nonagricultural purposes.

However, the transfer of agricultural land for other purposes is highly regulated. For using agricultural land for other purposes requires a Change in Land-Use (CLU) clearance from the state government, in addition to several other clearances from the local authorities. Besides, there are ceiling regulations which limit the size of the agricultural land that can be owned. The land ceiling regulations mean that it is impossible to buy agricultural land at a scale generally needed for setting up big industries. Moreover, one cannot avoid land ceiling regulations on agricultural land by converting the land as nonagricultural, because to get CLU clearance for agricultural land, one must own the land beforehand. The institutional and regulatory frameworks governing land and its uses, therefore, leave little scope for the transfer of land to intended purposes. These regulations make the already dormant market of agricultural land more difficult to work efficiently. They generate a tendency among the industrialists, companies and developers to have no other way but to approach the state government to acquire the land for the nonagricultural use.

Even when the land needed for the project is well within the ceiling limit, the regulatory holdup is a serious matter. The regulations are a major source of rent-seeking for the officials concerned. For the small, medium-sized industries and real estate projects, the formal and 'informal' cost of getting regulatory clearances has been estimated to be comparable to the cost of land itself. The net result is that these regulations avert a large number of potential profitable land transactions, and exert a downward pressure on the price of the land that could be potentially transacted. Thereby, fewer projects are feasible than would be the case in the absence of the said rules. It seems wrong, therefore, to attribute the dormancy of the market in agriculture land to market frictions, high transaction costs and the hold-up. Certainly these are some of relevant constraints. However, the constraining land use regulations seem to be the more critical reason for lack of transactions in agriculture land.

438   *Ram Singh*

Thus, the only option left to the industrialists, companies and developers is to approach the state government to acquire the land for their big projects. The use of eminent domain becomes a preferred option for project developers. It means that the clearances that were to be taken are not needed anymore, as these are automatically given at the time of the land acquisition and land transfer to the project developers. It is much faster and easier for the project developers to bribe the state for the use of eminent domain. Indeed, in the past, this option has been better for the private companies as the effective price of land is much cheaper then what they would have paid in voluntary transactions. Singh (2012) shows that under land acquisition the compensation received by the farmers is only a fraction of the real market value of their land. The travesty of the regulatory structure for agricultural land is that it is aimed at safeguarding the interests of farmers and the agriculture. In reality, it ends up doing just the opposite, and becomes a major source for the local authorities and the state to exploit both the potential buyers of the land, as well as the farmers.

## Taxes on land transactions

Under the Registration Act of India, 1908, any sale of an immovable object/property valued more than Rs.100 can only be made through a registered instrument. When a property is registered, the parties involved in the transaction are liable to pay certain taxes and fees. If these taxes are very high they can have two adverse implications. First, they can incentivize the transaction parties to underreport the value of their transactions, resulting in a significant loss of revenue to the exchequer. Second, they can cripple the growth of urban land markets as well, and therefore can hamper an efficient use of the land. There are several instances where both of these phenomena are at work in the land markets in India.

To start with, consider the Stamp Duty levied under the Registration Act of India, 1908. It is an ad valorem tax, that is, its value increases with the value of the transacted instrument, which makes it a progressive tax in nature and effect. Depending on the nature of the instrument, the power to levy stamp duty can lie with either the state concerned or the union or both. Stamp duty of property is in the state domain. It is one of the major sources of the revenue for the state. There are several problems with the prevalent stamp duty regimes in India. It is generally very high compared to the international standards and thus induces tax evasion, principally through underpricing of transactions.

*Land a bottleneck for development?* 439

Depending on the state concerned, it varies from less than 5 percent to 8 percent of the 'market value' of the property.

The market value is assessed on the basis of the 'circle rates' (minimum land rates, revised from time to time by the local government) or a sale-deed of a similar property. For the purpose of the stamp duty, the market value cannot be less than the circle rate of the area. However, problem is that the circle rates are still well below the true market value of the land. To overcome these limitations, some states have increased the rate in recent times. For example, the Delhi Government has amended the Indian Stamp Act thrice within last 15 years. The circle rates have been revised twice since 2007, the last being in December 2012, in view of the sharp increase in the value of land during the past decade or so. It has divided Delhi into eight categories/colonies according to the ambiance of the area, and the availability of the space and has set circle rates accordingly. Similarly, the Bombay Stamp Act (1958) presents a detailed set of guidelines in determination of the market value of the property, the CCRA (Chief Controlling Revenue Authority) is liable to send a copy of annual statements of the average rates of land situated in the state (divided into tehsil, municipal corporation and local body area) to the sub-registrar office for the area under his prerogative after which it is liable to get scrutinized and corrected by the Registering Office.

Even in Delhi and Mumbai, the circle rates have failed to keep pace with the market value of the land. Therefore, the circle rate-based determination of the stamp duty has not served the intent of the government to collect the stamp duty on the market value of the transactions. Moreover, the declared values of the transacted properties are generally equal to or slightly above the circle rates, but significantly less than the true market value. As a result, land transactions have emerged as a significant source of black money.

In fact, the stamp duty has led to generation of additional corruption. The Indian Stamp Act provides for verification of the market value of property for the objective of calculating stamp duty payable. For the purpose of verification, the authorities can consider the circle rates as well as the sale-deeds of similar properties. Since properties and their market values can vary on many counts, this clause gives huge discretionary power to the authorities to extract bribe from the transacting parties. Therefore, the extant regime has turned into a major source of corruption and disputes.

The provisions of the Capital Gains tax on land transactions make things worse. Under the Income Tax Act, 1961, whenever somebody buys a property, the seller of the property gets endowed with the capital

440   *Ram Singh*

which is taxable. The capital gains tax is around 20 percent and is one of the major liabilities for the seller which strengthens the incentives for the seller to greatly under-report the true value of the transaction.

Land in urban areas are subject to Property Tax as well. The Property Tax is independent of the amount of transaction and the stamp duty payable of the land rather, it is calculated with the Unit Area Method, which determines the value of land in a similar way as circle rates. Also it is a prime source of revenue for the local municipal authorities. It is seen that there is scope to falsify the officially stated documents because they are usually very difficult or costly to verify; this gives property owners a way to manipulate and misreport their true property tax.

None of the existing regulations and taxes serve the intent of the government to assess the true value of land. Indeed, due to manipulation and misapplication of the relevant taxes and regulations, the real-estate sector has become the breeding ground for black income. A typical developer-sponsored housing project requires 50 to 60 regulatory approvals, including the infamous CLU clearance. The property developer needs to pay huge bribes to get these clearances. Wide-ranging anecdotal evidence suggests that bribes and 'informal fees' are said to increase the cost of housing projects by at least 25 to 30 percent. Obviously, the land developers and builders pass the costs of bribes and kickbacks on to the final buyers. However, they would need to generate black money to pay the bribes. They do so by under-stating their income and overstating the expenses. Due to unreasonably high prices, even the layman has incentives to generate black income to afford a house, wherever possible. Finally, to save on the stamp duty and other taxes, the buyers and sellers in the property market leave 20–30 percent of the transactions unreported, further adding to the pool of black money. While it is difficult to put the exact number on the amount of black income generated by the real-estate sector, it will not be unreasonable to argue that this sector is, perhaps, the single largest contributor to the pools of black money and income in the country. Furthermore, the underreporting has a direct relation to the widely discussed inadequate compensation of the acquired land by the government which then mostly results in litigation and thus adds to the overall costs.

To curb the problem of underreporting many new proposals have been made. There is a proposal of revising the circle rates twice a year so that they reflect the true value of the land and make the stamp duty payable on those fixed circle rates. Though this proposal puts a huge burden on the administration to keep on revising circle rates

*Land a bottleneck for development?* 441

periodically with the fluctuations in the prices of land, but its fixed nature makes underreporting inevitable, both for the buyers and the sellers. Another one is the "use of e-governance in valuation of properties and use of manpower for collecting more disaggregated information about true market value of the properties" (Mukherjee, 2013). Taking 'Punitive Action' on the parties that are found guilty is also suggested to prevent the parties from misconduct in future.

At the same time, the existing tax regime encourages speculative investment in agricultural land, resulting in increasing the cost of land for other purposes. To see how, note that under Section 10 of the Indian Income Tax Act, 1961, agricultural income is exempted from income tax. The exempted income includes rent or revenue derived from use of agricultural land, including from the building situated on such land. Further, agricultural land is exempted from capital gains tax, if land is situated beyond municipality limits or gains are reinvested in agricultural land. Naturally, people have reasons to invest in agricultural land to park their black money and also to convert it into white money. Such investments increase the price of land, making it unnecessarily costly for other purposes.

## Land acquisition: Past, present and future

To help put things in perspective: Until about two decades ago, the compulsory acquisition of land under eminent domain mainly used to be for provisions of roads, railways, school, dams, mega-plants etc. The acquisition for such activities was infrequent and therefore was rarely questioned. However, the last one and half decades or so experienced a phenomenal rise in the number of compulsory acquisitions. Due to increased urbanization, land has been acquired for urban development and other infrastructure projects.

However, it was the acquisition for private companies that was the major cause behind the numerous protests against land acquisitions. Many state governments went overboard to acquire land for companies. In numerous instances, agriculture land was acquired, citing public purpose, but subsequently transferred to private companies. Moreover, they started to use the emergency clause to acquire land for all sorts of activities of companies, including ones that even remotely cannot serve any public purpose. The states were able to do all this by exploiting ambiguities in the archaic Land Acquisition (LA) Act, 1894. The judicial apathy on a crucial issue has also facilitated a ruthless trampling of farmers' rights. Courts rarely questioned the legitimacy of the acquisition per se.

## 442 *Ram Singh*

In such a scenario, the private interests, rather than public purpose, came to dictate the decision making of the state governments. This phenomenon became especially pronounced during the XI Five-Year Plan. The plan had made the 'special economic zones' and other 'public-private partnerships' the mainstay for improving provisions of public goods. Purportedly, the partnerships were formed to tap private funds for infrastructure and public services like education, health etc. However, in the guise of these partnerships, excess land was acquired to be used by the companies for real-estate and other commercial purposes. Post-acquisition, companies made huge fortunes by leasing out the 'developed' land.

What made things worse was the fact that the compensation to the acquisition-affected owners was invariably less than the market value of the land. Actually, the very basis and process of determining compensation under the Act was seriously flawed. Section 23 of the Act entitled the owners to market value of property plus a solatium of 30 percent. However, compensation was required to be determined on the basis of the floor price fixed by the state, or the average of registered sale-deeds of similar land. As discussed previously, the circle rates as well as the sale-deeds were below the true market value of the land. The result was that the owners were under-compensated, making them resort to litigation to seek better compensation. A study of judgments of Punjab and Haryana High Court by the author shows that the average compensation provided by the courts has been significantly higher than the government-awarded compensation. It is in that context that the Right to Fair Compensation and Transparency in Land Acquisition, Rehabilitation and Resettlement Bill was passed by the Parliament.[1]

The major change in the law pertains to the increase in the compensation for acquisition affected owners[2] and the serious checks on the misuse of eminent domain law for land acquisition for companies. Moreover, the new law provides for Resettlement and Rehabilitation (R&R) benefits for people affected by large projects. The scope of forceful land acquisition for companies has been seriously restricted. Land acquisition for private companies has been restricted to a set of 'public purpose' activities. The term 'public purpose' has been better defined to make meaningful distinction between land acquisition for public purpose and private purposes.[3] Moreover, the new law does not permit use of urgency clauses except when there is genuine emergency or natural calamity. The acquisition for developers of private industrial, housing and other projects has been restricted to 20 percent of the required land – that too after the project developer has received prior

## Land a bottleneck for development? 443

permission of 80 percent of the owners. The law provides for compensation up to two times the assessed market value in urban areas, and up to four times in the rural areas. The market value will be assessed on the basis of stamp-duty rates or sale-deeds.

It is no surprise that the new law has come in for sharp criticisms from the private sector, especially the developers and industrialists. Some fear is that, under the new law, due to higher compensation the land price will skyrocket; as a result, housing, urban development and industrial projects will suffer. Gloom and doom has been predicted for private projects in particular, and the economy at large. The fact is that the provisions of the Bill will not apply to most of the private projects. As long as land is purchased directly from the owners, the developers of small- and medium-size projects will not have to provide annuity payments, jobs and the other R&R benefits to project affected people. For such projects, the decision on whether there should be R&R of project affected people is left to the discretion of the states. There is a consensus that the condition of R&R should not apply to projects over less than 50 acres in urban areas and 100 acres in rural areas. Within these limits if the project developers find it difficult to buy the required land, it can only be on account of the poor land records and the other issues discussed earlier, because of which the transaction cost of land deals can be very high. The need is to rectify these infirmities rather than continue with the past misuses.

However, the Act seems to discriminate between projects of the central government and others. Its provisions – such as social impact assessment (SIA), increased compensation to the land owner and the R&R benefits for the project affected people – will apply to all projects of the private and the state government. The same conditions will not apply to as many as 13 categories of projects of the central government. The list of exempted projects includes those in mining, coal and railways.

Besides, the law is open to strategic manipulations and litigation. Under it, as is the case under the extant law, government officials are required to assess compensation on the basis of sale-deeds. There is a tendency among officials to play it safe and award compensation using relatively low value sale-deeds. In contrast, courts tend to use higher value sale-deeds. Consequently, the average of court-awarded compensation is several times higher, as is confirmed by study of Punjab and Haryana High Court judgments. Obviously, acquisition-affected parties have reasons to approach courts to get their due. The incentive to litigate will be even stronger under the new law since the compensation

## 444   *Ram Singh*

rate will be two to four times the assessed market rate under the new law; gains from litigation will be multifold.

To see why, note that the previous law provided for compensation including solatium, equal to 1.3 times the 'market value' of the property. In contrast, the new law has increased compensation up to four times for the rural areas, and two times the market value for urban areas. Now, consider an agriculture land measuring just 100 square meters. Suppose, a LAC (the government official responsible for making compensation award at the time of acquisition) uses a circle rate of say Rs.1000 per-sq-meter for determining compensation, and the court uses a sale-deed rate of say Rs.1,400. Under the old law, since the multiplier was 1.3, the total compensation would have gone up by Rs.42,000. By comparison, under the new law, since the multiplier is four, the compensation will increase by Rs.1,60,000! That is, gains from litigation will be much greater under the new law – given the proclivity of the LACs and courts to use a different basis. The gains and therefore the incentive to litigate increases further, as the land size and/or the difference between sale-deeds and circle rates goes up.[4]

The new law does not address the fundamental causes behind litigation over compensation. The excessive litigation under the old law was due to the fact that the land acquisition collectors (LACs) and courts used a different basis for determining compensation – generally, LACs used low-value circle rates, but courts used relatively high-value sale-deeds. All that the new law does is replace the ADJ court with a 'Land Acquisition Rehabilitation and Resettlement Authority' (LARRA) to adjudicate compensation related disputes. This replacement cannot reduce litigation. However, the cost of disputes and litigation will ultimately be borne by the states.

To sum up, the Right to Fair Compensation and Transparency in Land Acquisition, Rehabilitation and Resettlement Act 2013 is better than the previous law. However, it has some serious flaws too. The Act offers enough opportunities to the resourceful and politically connected to make money simply by concocting sale-deeds. Besides, it induces strategic litigation over compensation.

## Conclusions

We have shown that at present several institutional and regulatory hurdles thwart the transfer of agriculture land for other desirable purposes. Some of these regulations make the large-scale purchases

*Land a bottleneck for development?* 445

of land, say for setting up of a big industry, totally impossible. Even when the land required for the project is within the permissible limits in terms of the size of landholding, the costs of regulatory clearances is a significant component of the project costs. As a result, these 'regulatory' costs preclude a large number of potentially profitable transactions. Moreover, they put heavy downward pressure on the price of transactions that still remain feasible, so the sellers get a raw deal. At the same time, the buyers are no better off, as the significant fraction of the surplus is siphoned off in the form of bribes and the other costs of greasing the system.

### A way forward

Things can be made much better by setting right the institutional and regulatory infirmities. The land use regulations need to be transparent and consistent. The existing regulations are discretionary and therefore a source of rent-seeking. Transparent zoning regulations will be a better alternative. Different zones should be set up for different activities. In addition, in the zoned areas, the basic infrastructure such as roads, water, sanitation and the power lines should be provided by the state. Having done that there should be no more regulations imposed on the land, its use, sales and purchases, as long as the land use is among the permitted ones. As long as the land is used for the purposes permitted by these regulations, there should be no further interference with voluntary land transactions.

Moreover, transactions cost of land transfers can be reduced greatly by making the ownerships and land-type records publicly available and verifiable. These measures as such will go a long way in facilitating voluntary transactions by clearing uncertainty over ownership. Indeed, the poor land records lead to avoidable disputes. Moreover, the land and the related assets cannot be used as collaterals for raising loans from the banks. Consequently, farmers' access to bank credit has been limited. Indeed, the poor land records have held back not only the development of an efficient land market, but also the overall development of the economy. Collective bargaining between the owners and the developers can also reduce the transaction cost of land deals. It should be pointed out that these measures can be initiated only by the state government concerned; since the land, its usage and the contracts over land are all in the state-list.

On a positive note, the new land acquisition law (LARR, 2013) will nudge the states to undertake much needed reforms related to the ownership, transfer and use of the land. Under the new land acquisition law, the states will have to deal with the issue of land acquisition for private projects. It is true that the terms of the Act do not directly apply to small- and medium-size projects, as long as land is purchased directly from the owners – these terms are to be decided by the states. There is consensus that the condition of R&R should not apply to projects involving less than 50 acres in urban areas and 100 acres in rural areas. However, even within these limits, whether the project developers will actually be able to buy the required land will depend on the transaction costs – which depend on whether land titles are clear or not, and whether records are updated or not. Similarly, the success of big projects will turn on the negotiation process and the terms governing lease agreements over land. Therefore, there is incentive for the states to undertake the previously suggested reforms. The states failing to do so will pay a high price.

At the same time, the LARR, which otherwise is laudable, can be improved further. For instance, it will be a good idea to differentiate among the various types of the public-private partnerships (PPPs). These partnerships have been used by the center as well as the states to mobilize private funds for public goods and services – the land is provided by the government concerned. Many of the national and state highways, ports, airports and urban development projects have been funded through this mechanism. The new law subjects all PPPs for infrastructural development by the states and the urban local bodies to the requirement of prior consent, regardless of the issue of ownership over land. If a state government or municipality would need land for a road or flyover funded through PPP, it will require consent of at least 70 percent of land owners. At the same time, as per the law, the center can carry on with this practice with PPPs. For instance, for the highways PPPs the center will continue to acquire land using the National Highways Act, 1956, which provides for extremely low compensation and no meaningful R&R benefits. This discrimination is unwarranted and goes against the spirit of federalism.

PPPs, if used carefully, can be an effective instrument for funding of urban development projects. Indeed, there is no valid reason to treat land acquisition for PPPs differently from the acquisition for publicly funded projects, as long as the land is used for a genuine public good, its ownership remains with the government and there is no real-estate component to the project. The provisions of the new law restricting scope for PPPs need to be amended.

## Notes

1 For analysis of the new land acquisition laws, see Chakravorty (2011); Desai (2011); Ghatak and Ghosh (2011); Guha (2007); Sarkar (2007); Sarkar (2011); Sarma (2011); Singh (2012); and Singh (2013).
2 The law also provides additional benefits including 20 percent of the developed land if acquisition for urban development projects, land for irrigation projects, fishing rights, resettlement and rehabilitation benefits in the event of displacement or loss of livelihood.
3 The term was vaguely defined under the previous Land Acquisition Act, 1894, which made no real distinction between land acquisition for genuine public purpose and companies.
4 For more on this issue, see Singh (2013).

## Bibliography

Bhaduri, Amit and Medha Patkar (2009): "Industrialisation for the People, by the People, of the People", *Economic and Political Weekly*, 44(1), 10–13.

Chakravorty, Sanjoy (2011): "A Lot of Scepticism and Some Hope", *Economic and Political Weekly*, 46(41), 29–31.

Desai, Mihir (2011): "Land Acquisition Law and Proposed Changes", *Economic and Political Weekly*, 46(26, 27), 95–100.

Gaurav, Sarthak and Srijit Mishra (2011): "Size-Class and Returns to Cultivation in India: A Cold Case Reopened", *Indira Gandhi Institute of Development Research Working Paper*, October, WP-2011-027

Ghatak, Maitreesh and Parikshit Ghosh (2011): "The Land Acquisition Bill: A Critique and a Proposal", *Economic and Political Weekly*, 46(41), 65–72.

Guha, Abhijit (2007): "Peasant Resistance in West Bengal a Decade before Singur and Nandigram", *Economic and Political Weekly*, September 15, 3706–3711.

Land Acquisition, Rehabilitation and Resettlement Bill, 77–2011 (LARR) (2011): Available at: http://164.100.24.219/BillsTexts/LSBillTexts/asintroduced/land%20acquisition%2077%20of%202011.pdf.

Malloy, Robin P. (2008): *Private Property, Community Development, and Eminent Domain*. (Edited), Ashgate Publishing Ltd, Hampshire, UK.

Morris, Sebastian and Ajay Pandey (2007): "Towards Reform of Land Acquisition Framework in India", *Economic and Political Weekly*, June 2, 2083–2090.

Mukherjee, V. (2013). "Determinants of Stamp Duty Revenue in Indian States", *South Asian Journal of Macroeconomics and Public Finance*, 2(1), 33–58.

Nielsen, Kenneth Bo (2011): "Land, Law and Resistance", *Economic and Political Weekly*, 46(41), 38–40.

Ramanathan, Usha (2011): "Land Acquisition, Eminent Domain and the 2011 Bill", *Economic and Political Weekly*, 46(44), 10–14.

Sarkar, Abhirup (2007): "Development and Displacement: Land Acquisition in West Bengal", *Economic and Political Weekly*, 42(16), 1435–1442.

## 448 *Ram Singh*

Sarkar, Swagato (2011): "The Impossibility of Just Land Acquisition", *Economic and Political Weekly*, 46(41), 35–38.

Sarma, E. A. S. (2011): "Sops for the Poor and a Bonus for Industry", *Economic and Political Weekly*, 46(41), 32–34.

Singh, Jaivir (2006): "Separation of Powers and the Erosion of the Right to Property in India", *Constitutional Political Economy*, 17(4), 303–324.

Singh, Ram (2012): "Inefficiency and Abuse of Compulsory Land Acquisition: An Enquiry into the Way Forward", *Economic and Political Weekly*, 47(19), 46–53.

Singh, Ram (2013): "The New Land Law: Are the States Up to the Challenge?" in *The Ideas for India Portal*, (available at www.ideasforindia.in/article.aspx?article_id=208).

# Index

Page numbers in *italics* indicates figures; and those in **bold** indicate tables.

Abbas, Tahir 91–93
ABP arguments: climate 65, 69–70; criticisms 67–73; culture 66, 71–73; ethnic diversity 66, 70–71; geography 64–65, 67–69; institutions 67, 73; natural resource 65, 70
Acemoglu, Daron 65, 278–281
acquisition of land, in India 441–444
ad-valorem tax 438
Afghanistan 93
Africa 295–297; environment degradation in 82; exclusive-extractive economic institutions 295–296; landlockedness 65; Muslims in 88–89; per capita endowments 70; population density 70
Agenda 2030 on Sustainable Development 390
agrarian barrier to industrial growth 277–278
agrarian systems: classification 277–278; surplus appropriators 278; surplus producers 277–278
Agreement on Subsidies and Countervailing Measures (SCM) 404
Agreement on Textiles and Clothing (ATC) 401
agricultural income 441
agricultural land 435; CLU clearance 437; regulatory frameworks

437–438; as state subject 437; taxes on transactions 438–441; usage for other purposes 437
agriculture: declining share in Indian GDP 389, 390, 391, *392*; FDI in 351
agrofuel 342
Airbus 404
Alchian, A. A. 201, 206
All-India Peace and Solidarity Organization on Planning and Self-Reliance in 1981 383
Al-Shabaab 83
*American Economic Review* 62
Amirapu, Amrit 394, 396
analytical framework, for land deals 352–365; core model 352–357; equations of change 357–365
Anseeuw, Ward 342, 348
Antonelli, M. 341, 351
apartheid system of racial segregation 296
Arezki, Rabah 347
Argentina: dictatorships 300; during first globalisation 311; *Latifundia* agrarian system 300; as supplier of agricultural products, grain and meat 300
Argentinean debt crisis of 1998–2002 386
Aristotle: human functioning 53; Nicomachean Ethics 53; *Politics* 69

# 450 *Index*

Armstrong, Karen 55
ASEAN Free Trade Agreement 401
Asia 294–295; export-led growth
  294; institutional model 294–295;
  market mechanism 294–295;
  Muslims in 86–88
Asian financial crisis (1997) 67
atomized society 51
auctions: all-pay 269; assumptions
  and preliminary results 260–262;
  canonical model of 255; credit
  155–157; Dutch 269; English 269;
  equilibrium in 262–267; first-
  price 268; with inferior outside
  option 254–267; model 256–260;
  procurement 269; Revenue
  Equivalence Theorem, The 269;
  second-price 256, 269; SIPV 268;
  standard 268–269
authoritarian systems of socialism 280

bad neighbourhoods 65, 68–69
Balliol College, University of
  Oxford 4
Bangladesh: India and 68, 69;
  liberation of 380
banks/banking 152–159; capital
  157–158; capitalism and 155;
  in modern economy 152, 153;
  as moneylenders 155; supply of
  money 152; traditional view
  of 152
bargaining power 155; and cultural
  norms 202–205; implications
  203–205
Bayesian probabilities 276
Begg, Moazzam 92–93
Benin: Muslims in 88
Berlin Wall, fall of 382, 384
Bhaduri, Amit 12
Bhagwati, Jagdish 379
Bill & Melinda Gates Foundation 151
Biocon Ltd 404
Boeing 404
Boko Haram 83, 91, 295
Bolsa Familia conditional cash
  transfer program 300
Bombay Plan 376
Bombay Stamp Act (1958) 439
Borras, Saturnino M. 343

Bosnian Muslims 93
Brahmananda, P. R. 379
Brazil 299–300, 311; Bolsa Familia
  conditional cash transfer program
  300; debt crisis 300; as failed
  model of growth 300; import
  substitution-based growth
  strategy 299; military coups 300;
  Petrobras 299
Bretton Woods institutions 376
Brexit 25
bribes 440
British Empire 377
Brooks, Harvey 50
Burns, Arthur 380
Buy American Act in 1933 402
Byrd Amendment 404

Canada 69; FIRA 403
capital account liberalization in
  India 386–387
capital gains tax 439–440
capitalism 41; banks and 155;
  consciousness for sustainable
  development 50–56; economic
  crisis 41–47; environmental crisis
  47–50; relationship between
  humans, nature and commodities
  in 51
carbon dioxide 47; *see also*
  greenhouse gas emissions
cash crops 342
*Catch Up: Developing Countries in
  the World Economy* (Nayyar) 35,
  275, 276, 305
CCRA *see* Chief Controlling
  Revenue Authority (CCRA)
central banks 130; credit supply
  regulation 153; in modern
  economy 152
Chakravarty, Sukhamoy 4
Chang, Ha-Joon 400, 401
Change in Land-Use (CLU)
  clearance 437
chaos theory 277
Chavez, Hugo 301
Chayanovian theory of the 'peasant
  economy' 61
Che, Y.-K. 256, 266–267
Chenery, H. B. 275

## Index 451

Chief Controlling Revenue Authority (CCRA) 439
Chile 306; "Black Legend" 313; counter-cyclical fiscal policies 313; democratic tradition 301; dictatorship 301; diversified industrialisation 301; life expectancy 302; per capita income 302
China 26, 285–289; as authoritarian socialist nation 280; domestic consumption 288; economic institutions 286–287; educated workforce 287; extractive institutions 280; future prospects 287–288; global GDP and 286; India outsourcing manufacturing to 397; large economic size 286; Muslim communities in 87; per capita income 285–286; political institutions 286; population size 285, 286; public investment 288; purchasing power parity (PPP) 286; Second World War 286; special economic zones (SEZ) 406; subsidies and incentives 405; support to entrepreneurs 406
Chinese economy 385
circle rates 439; revising 440–441
civil wars 78
Clark, C. 275
Clash of Civilizations, The (Huntington) 66
climate, ABP arguments 65; criticisms 69–70; diseases 65, 69; economic development and 65
climate change 47–48
CLU see Change in Land-Use (CLU) clearance
Coase, R. H. 198, 199, 206
cold climate 69
Cold War 377, 382
Collier, P. 346, 351
Colombia 311
colonialism, and horizontal inequalities 80–81
commercial banks, nationalization of (1969) 379

commodities: accumulation of 51; atomized society and 51; market-based production system and 51; relationship between humans, nature and 51–53
Compensatory Financing Facility 385
complexity: making sense of 24
Conference of Parties (COP-21) 48; see also Paris Agreement
conflict: inequalities causing 79–80; international interventions in 78; within nations 78; vertical inequality and 78
Congo: per capita endowments 70
Congress Party 378
constant velocity 165–166
Corden, Max 4
Costa Rica: social democratic revolution in 316
Cote d'Ivoire 82
Cotula, Lorenzo 347–348
credit: auctions 155–157; correlation between money and 134–135; demand for 138–139; domestic control over creation of 153–155; importance of 132–135; supply of 135–138; targeted regulation of 153; theory and macroeconomic stability 127–161; uses of 139–140
credit card companies 156
cross-border networks and social mobilisation 100–101
Crusades 93
Cuba 311; per capita income 311; socialist revolution in 316
cultural discrimination, against Muslims 85–86
cultural norms, bargaining power and 202–205
culture, ABP arguments 66; criticisms 71–73

Dandekar, V. M. 379
Das, Gouranga G. 346
Das, Satya 352
Dastidar, K. G. 256, 265, 266, 267
Deaton, Angus 385
Debreu, Arrow 161
deflation 152

## 452 Index

deindustrialisation in developing countries 394
deindustrialisation in India: exchange rate movements 396–397, 397; factors affecting 394, 396–397; import liberalization 396; ITA and 396; outsourcing 396–397; share of imports in final consumption 394, 395
Deininger, Klaus 346, 347, 350, 366
Delhi School of Economics 4
demand: for credit 138–139; for gold in India 256; for money 165–167
democratisation of governance 104
Demsetz, H. 201, 206
Denmark: Muslims in 86
Dependency theory 61–62
de Tocqueville, A. 79
devaluation of the rupee in 1966 379
developed economies: groupings 409; MFA 401; offset requirements in government procurements 402; protectionism in 401
developing countries: agricultural sector in 61; capitalist accumulation in 221; deindustrialisation in 394; economic problems 61; Great Divergence 305; land reform effort 349; markets in 44; Structural Adjustment Programs (SAP) 63
development: economic 24–25; of human capabilities 53–54; as multi-dimensional phenomenon 24; paths to 24; political 25; variables influencing 24
development economics 61; Third World Debt Crisis of 1982 63; work of Arthur Lewis 221
development path 276–277
Dinda, Soumyananda 346
diseases 65, 69
distortionary effects, of monetary policy 142–143; creating jobless recovery 144–145; inter-sectoral misallocations 144; mispricing of risk 143–144

distributive effects, of monetary policy 142, 145–146
D'Odorico, Paolo 343, 351
domestic market, privileged access to 400–402
domestic production: government procurement and 402–403
Dreze, Jean 385
droughts: of 1965 and 1966 378; of 1972 and 1973 380
dual economy models 211–219; Keynesian approach 216–19; overview 211–212; Ricardian approach 212–216

Earth: threat to life on 47–48
East Asia 26; ethnic homogeneities 71; industrialisation through subsidies 405; intellectual property protection policy 407–408; manufacturing industries 399; miracle economies 64; subsidies in 405; technological development and R&D 406–407
East Asian crisis of 1997 386
East Germany 377; reunification with West Germany 382
Eatwell, John 46
*Economic and Political Weekly* 381
economic crisis 25, 41–47; fragility and instability 45–47; growing financial sphere 42–43; market deregulation and 43–45; Multinational Corporation 42; structural changes and 42–43; systemic risk and measurement problem 45
economic instability 45–47
economic policy and human rights 98–117; cross-border networks and social mobilisation 100–101; democratisation of governance 104; economic heterodoxy 105–117; globalisation and internalisation 100–104; indicators 107–110, 109; inequalities 101–104; normative framework 106–107
economics 4; assumptions and 30; behavioural assumptions and 30; discipline of 30; Nayyar's contribution to the discipline of 15–18

*Index* 453

economic theory: and public policy 29–33

*Economist, The* 342

Edelman, Marc 342, 343

efficient liability rules 243–252; definitions and assumptions 245–247; illustrative example 251–252; implications of using more than one 247–251; Nash equilibrium 247; negligence liability condition 247

Egypt 297; authoritarian and exclusive institutions 297; industrialisation 297; Islamic fundamentalism 297; per capita income 297; Yom Kippur war 380

Einstein, Albert 24

electronic financial system 150–161; banking system 152–159; current account deficit management 159–161; economic theory and macro-stability 161; transactions system 151–152

electronics: imports of 399

elements of economic history theory 276–282; development path 276–282; present/initial conditions 276–277; speculation 276

emerging economies 35–36; *see also* emerging market economies (EME); twenty-five emerging economies

emerging market economies (EME) 324–335; capital flow management 332–333; external markets dependence 328–329; financial risks 330–331; inequalities 327–328; issues and challenges 326–331; managing real and financial sector feedbacks 333–335; policy priorities 331–335; strengthening domestic demand 331–332; *see also* twenty-five emerging economies

employment elasticity of Indian GDP 389, 390, *391*

employment growth, and Indian GDP 390, *391*

environmental crisis 27, 47–50; global warming and climate change 47–48; green technologies and market failures 48–50; Paris Agreement 48

Equality Commission Review 85

ethical behaviour 54

Ethiopia 68

ethnic diversity, ABP arguments 66; criticisms 70–71; distrust and 66; poor economic performance 66; violent conflicts and 66

Etounga-Manguelle, Daniel 66

Europe: Muslims in 84–86

European Agriculture Guidance and Guarantee Fund 405

European Community Structural Funds 405

European Regional Development Fund 405

European Report on Development (ERD) 349–350

European Social Fund 405

exchange rate: China 408; India 408–409; Japan 408; US 408

exchange rates 408–409

exclusive-extractive institutions 282

exclusive-progressive institutions 282

export: manufacturing 424–430, **425, 427**; subsidies and incentives 404–405; trade integration and 421–424, **422**

export-promotion *vs.* import-substitution 398–399

Extended Fund Facility 382

external balance 114–115

extractive *vs.* inclusive institutions 278–282

farming, foreign investment in 346–347

farmland, in least-developed countries (LDC) 342

Fei, John 62

financial fragility 45–7; structural changes and 42–43

FIRA *see* Foreign Investment Review Act (FIRA)

First World War: Southern Cone countries 311

floor price 342

food importers 342

food security, land deals and 346

food supplies via contract farming 342

foreign exchange reserves of India 384

## 454  *Index*

foreign investment, in land: constraints and conditions 349–352; ERD on 349–350; farming 346–347; World Bank Report on 349

Foreign Investment Review Act (FIRA) 403

Foreign Sales Corporation Act 404

formality: class struggle 236–238; deconstruction of the norm 233–236

fragility *see* financial fragility

France: Muslims in 84, 85

*Frankenstein* (Shelley) 72

Friedman, Milton 130, 377–378

Furtado, C. 300

Gale, I. 256, 266–267

Gandhi, Indira 378, 379; assassination in 1984 382; general election of 1971 380; second regime (1980-1984) 382; state elections of 1972 380

Gandhi, Rajiv 382

Gandhian ideas of economic reconstruction 377

Ganguli, Pankaj 4

GDP growth rate of India: employment elasticity 389, 390, *391*; employment growth and 390, *391*; major productive sectors and *393*; services 390, 391, *392*; share of agriculture in 389, 390, *392*; share of manufacturing and other industries 390–391, *392*

General Agreement on Tariffs and Trade (GATT) 6

geography, ABP arguments 64–65; bad neighbourhoods 65, 68–69; criticisms 67–69; landlockedness 65, 67–68

Germany: culture 72; economic development 72; Muslims in 86

Ghana: economic divergence between South Korea and 66

Glass-Steagall Act of 1933 45

globalisation 25; evolving dimensions of 26–28; horizontal inequalities drivers and 82–83; human rights and 100–104; Nayyar on 12–13, 17–18

global warming 47; climate change and 47–48

gold demad in India 256

"Goldilocks" economy 152

Gourevitch, J.-P. 84

governance, democratisation of 104

government procurement: offset requirements in 402–403; for supporting domestic production 402–403

Great Depression 130, 312

Great Moderation 385

Great Recession 128

greenhouse gas emissions 47

green technologies 48; market failures and 48–50

Greenwald, Bruce 132, 135, 140

group identities 80

growth slowdown: current account balance 418–420; demand and supply sides 416–418; investment-savings balance 418–420; manufacturing trade and 424–426; trade integration and 420–424

Gulick, Sidney 72

Habiyaremye, Alexis 350

Hajj pilgrimage 91

Haq, Mahbub Ul 53

Hart, Keith 221, 223

heterodox economic policy 28, 110–114

Hicks, J. 276

Hicks, John 4

Hindu-Muslim violence 68

Hirschman, Albert 62

HIV/AIDs among Muslim 88

Honduras 289, 292; as a banana republic 289; economic structure 289; growth rate 289; NAFTA 289; per capita income 289; population 289; Spanish colonial system 289; standard of living 292; US and 289

horizontal inequalities 28; colonialism and 80–81; conflict and 83–93; contemporary conflicts 83; drivers of 80–83; environment degradation and 82; geographic advantages and disadvantages 81–82; globalisation and 82–83; government policy and 82; migration flow and 81, 82; oil market and 83; *see also* Muslims

*Index*  455

human capabilities: concept of 53; development of 53–54
human functioning: Aristotle on 53, 54; sustainable development and 53, 54
human rights 28
human rights, economic policy and 98–117; cross-border networks and social mobilisation 100–101; democratisation of governance 104; economic heterodoxy 105–117; globalisation and internalisation 100–104; heterodox economic policy 110–114; indicators 107–110, *109*; inequalities 101–104; macroeconomic policy 114–117; normative framework 106–107; overview 98–99
humans: atomized society and 51; market-based production system and 51; relationship between commodities, nature and 51–53
Hussain, Shah 52

Iberian Peninsula: Napoleon's invasion of 305
Igbo, in Nigeria 81
IMF *see* International Monetary Fund (IMF)
import: manufacturing 424–429, **427**; trade integration and 421–424, **422**
imported labour 81
import-substitution *vs.* export-promotion 398–399
inclusive-populist institutions 282
inclusive-progressive institutions 282
inclusive *vs.* extractive institutions 278–282
income distribution: efficiency wage theories 207; Marxian theory 206–207; Neo-classical theory 205, 206; relation to theories of 205–208; rewards linked to contributions norm 207–208; team production 202–205; *see also* bargaining power; transaction cost
Income Tax Act, 1961 439–440; Section 10 of 441
incremental liability rule 250

India: bad neighbourhood effect 68, 69; Bangladesh and 68, 69; caste system 287; economic institutions 287, 288; extractive socio-economic system 287; Finance Commissions 288; future prospects 287–288; global GDP and 286; Hindu-Muslim violence 68; job creation in 389–410; large economic size 286; military conflicts between Pakistan and 68; parliamentary democracy 287; per capita income 285–286; political institutions 287, 288; political power in 288; population 285, 286, 389; purchasing power parity (PPP) 286; Second World War 286; technological development and R&D 407
Indian Administrative Service (IAS) 4
Indian economy 36–38; crisis of 1991 384; inflation rate in 1970s 380; land in 435–446; liberalization process 385; nationalization of commercial banks (1969) 375–387; nation building 375; Nayyar on 375–376; 1980s 382–385; 1950s 376–378; 1990s 384–385; 1970s 380–381; 1960s 378–379; performance requirements 403–404; policy debates 375–387; political instability 384; services sector 389–390; slowdown of 416–430; structural transformation 390–393; term-lending institutions 405; 2000s 386–387
Indian Stamp Act 439
India's Exports and Export Policies in the 1960s (Nayyar) 10
individual risks 45
Indonesia: Muslim communities in 87
Industrial Credit and Investment Corporation of India (ICICI) 405
industrial development, state intervention for 399–400
Industrial Development Bank of India (IDBI) 405
Industrial Finance Corporation of India (IFCI) 405

## 456 *Index*

industrial growth, agrarian barrier to 277–278
industrial revolution 47
inequalities 26, 28; conflict and 79–80; human rights and 101–104; implications of consistent and persistent 90–93; Latin America 315–316; vertical 28, 78, 79, 80, 94, 400; *see also* horizontal inequalities
inferior outside option, auctions with 254–267; assumptions and preliminary results 260–262; equilibrium in 262–267; model 256–260
informal economy 221
informality: alternative discourses 223–230; as negative semantic 230–233
informal sector: participants in 222–223; for refuge 223; rudimentary opportunities in 222
Information Technology Agreement (ITA) 396
infrastructure support 405–406
initial conditions 276–277; incremental change 277; interaction among elements of 277
Indo-Pakistan war of 1965 378
Indo-Pakistan war of 1971 380
institutional theory of economic history 278–282
institutions 277
institutions, ABP arguments 67; Asian financial crisis (1997) 67; criticisms 73
intellectual property protection policy 407–408
Inter-Governmental Panel for Climatic Change (IPCC) 47
internal balance 114
internalisation, human rights and 100–104
international banking 42, **43**
International Food Policy Research Institute (IFPRI) 342
International Monetary Fund (IMF) 63, 67; Extended Fund Facility 382; loan to India 381–384
international trade 43, **43**
investment incentives 404–405

IPCC *see* Inter-Governmental Panel for Climatic Change (IPCC)
Iran: US-led sanctions 294
Iraq 93
Iraq-Iran War 381
Iraq war 384
Islam 91; conflict between the West and 91; divisions within 90; regressive interpretation of 93
Israel: Yom Kippur war 380

Janata Party government (1977–1979) 382
Japan: culture 72; depreciated exchange rate of yen 408; intellectual property protection 408; minority problems 71
job creation, in India 389–410; *see also* manufacturing
Joshi, Vijay 287

Kaldor, Nicholas 398, 428
Kenya 297; Al-Shabaab 83
Keynesian approach 216–219; growth consequences 217–219; resolving inconsistency 219
Keynesian demand for money 166–167
Keynesian equilibrium 167–171
Keynesian internal balance 114
Kikuyu, in Kenya 81
Kleemann, Linda 352
Korea: culture of 72; regional divisions 71
Krishnamachari, T. T. 379
Kuznets, S. 275

LAC *see* land acquisition collectors (LAC)
land, in India 435–446; acquisition 441–444; circle rates 439; demand 435; eviction and displacement of people 341; optimum use 435; overview 435–436; regulatory frameworks 437–438; taxes on transactions of 438–441; urbanization 435
land acquisition
Land Acquisition (LA) Act, 1894 341; Section 23 of 342
land acquisition collectors (LAC) 444

## Index 457

Land Acquisition Rehabilitation and Resettlement Authority (LARRA) 444, 445–446

land deals in Africa 340–365; acquisition for non-agricultural uses 341; agricultural purposes 343; analytical framework for 352–365; benefits/positive impact 346–348; constraints and conditions for investment 349–352; debate 346–349; drivers of 343; dual-approach 350–351; eviction and displacement of people 341; farmland in LDCs for 342; immiserizing effects of 346; impact and outcomes 343, 346–349; investor countries 342, **344–345**; Land Matrix on 342–343; negative impacts 348–349; preconditions 350; socio-economic impact 341; sustainable development and 346; target regions for 343, **344–345**; tenure and reform programs 341; water availability for 343; weak institutions and enforcement systems 351

land deals in EU 341

landlockedness 65, 67–68

Land Matrix 342–343

land rush 342

LARRA *see* Land Acquisition Rehabilitation and Resettlement Authority (LARRA)

Latin America 297–302; abolition of slavery 316; colonization 298; colonization and 305; counter-cyclical fiscal policies 313, 314; debt crisis of the 1980s 308, 312; de-industrialisation 310, 314; dependency on commodities 312; development agenda 318–321; development record 306–314; economic growth 308–309, *309*; economic policies 319–320; educational advancement 316; European migrants to 316; export performance 310; external vulnerability 312; globalisation and 310; human development indicators 314–315, *315*; import substitution-based industrialisation 299; income distribution 315–317; inequalities 315–316; international division of labour 298; international trade and 298; interruptions in growth patterns 311–312; liberalization and 318; market reforms 312–313, 318; middle-income status 299; Napoleonic wars and 305; Nayyar on 305; overview 305–306; per capita GDP 308, 309; population growth 309, 310; poverty reduction 315; regional convergence 311; relative position in world economy 306–308, *307*; share in world GDP 309; social and institutional development 314–318; social expenditure 318; social policies 320–321; State-led industrialisation 308, 309, 313–314; surplus extraction 298, 299; truncated convergence 311; urbanization process 316; *see also* specific Latin American countries

liability rules *see* efficient liability rules

liberalization of Indian economy 385; capital account 386–387

Lichbach, M. I. 79

life: threat to 47–48

Lin, Justin Y. 398

liquidity trap 140; *see also* monetary policy

local content requirements (LCR) 403–404; in government procurements 402–403

Lokanathan, P. S. 379

London bombings 93

macroeconomic imbalances 115

macroeconomic policies 114–117; broadening goals of 116–117; EMDCs and 117; flexibility in 114, 115–116; orthodox tradition and 114; stability with growth 116

*madhabs* 91

Mahalanobis strategy 377

*Make-in-India* campaign 390, 398

458 *Index*

making-*for*-India 399
Malaysia: Biocon Ltd 405; incentives to manufacturing enterprises 405; Muslim communities in 86–87; per capita income 295; Proton 401
Malhotra, Rajeev 113
Mandela, Nelson 296
manufacturing 389–411; competitive exchange rates 408–409; deceleration of growth 393, *393*; deindustrialisation and 394–398; government procurement 402–403; gross capital formation 426; import-substitution *vs.* export-promotion 398–399; infrastructure support 405–406; intellectual property protection policy 407–408; investment and export incentives 404–405; outsourcing 396–397; performance requirements on foreign enterprises 403–404; private corporate investment 426–430; privileged access to domestic market 400–402; proactive FDI promotion 403–404; rebuilding competitive and sustainable 398–410; RTAs and preferential access to markets 409–410; share in Asian countries 391, *393*; slowdown and 424–426; state intervention 399–400; structural transformations and 390–393; technological development and R&D 406–407; trade ratio 424–426, *425*
Maoist guerillas in India 68
market capitalism 26
market failure: green technologies and 48–50
market failures, money and 184–193
markets: deregulation decisions 43, 44–45; in developing countries 44; local administration and 44; Nayyar on 43–44; preferential access to 409–410; in rural areas 44; state institutions and power structures configuring 44; Third world countries 43
Maruti-Suzuki joint venture 404
Mazumdar, Surajit 426
Meinzen-Dick, Ruth 346, 350–351

MERCOSUR 409
methane 47; *see also* greenhouse gas emissions
Mexico 300–301, 311; Mayan and Aztec civilizations 300; migration of labour from 301; NAFTA 301; oil and 301; US and 300–301
MFA *see* Multi Fibre Agreement (MFA)
MFN *see* most-favoured nation (MFN)
migration flows 28
Mody, A. 288
monetary policy: creating jobless recovery 144–145; distortionary effects 142–143; distributive effects 142, 145–146; inter-sectoral misallocations 144; limitations on effectiveness of 140–142; liquidity trap 140; mispricing of risk 143–144; ZLB 131, 140; *see also* banks/banking; credit; money
money 127–130; correlation between credit and 134–135; demand for 165–167; Keynesian equilibrium 167–171; market failures and 184–193; quantity theory of 163–165; *see also* credit; monetary policy
moneylenders 155
most-favoured nation (MFN) 409, 410
MUDRA 405
Mukherjee, Pranab 382–383
Multi Fibre Agreement (MFA) 401
Multinational Corporation 42
Muslims 28; in Asia 86–8; Bosnian 93; Christian attacks on 93; conflicts/differences within 90–91; consistent and persistent inequalities implications 90–93; cultural discrimination 85–86; in Europe 84–86; global connections among 91–93, *92*; Hajj pilgrimage 91; HIV/AIDs 88; *Ummah* 91; in West Africa 88–89
Muslims countries: imbalance in political power 89; less well off as compared to non-Muslim countries 89; majority 89, *90*; Security Council and 89

# Index 459

Napoleon's invasion of Iberian Peninsula 305
Nash equilibrium 247
nationalization of commercial banks (1969) 379
National Plan 376
natural resource, ABP arguments 65; abundance generating perverse politics 65; criticisms 70
nature: atomized society and 51; relationship between humans, commodities and 51–53
Nayyar, Deepak 3–18; academic career/engagement 5–6, 10; academic writings 9; analysis on the Global South 340; as an IAS officer 4, 6; as chief economic adviser to the government of India 6; contribution to discipline of economics 15–18; on determining future 276; educational background 4; field of study 9–10; on globalisation 12–13, 17–18; heterodox approach to economics 16; on Indian economy 375–376; 'India's Exports and Export Policies in the 1960s' 10; on international migration 11; on international trade 10–11; introduction 3; on macroeconomic constraints 18; on macroeconomics of development 11–12, 18; marriage 9; on period of 1967-1980 380–381; professional milestones 4–9; research interests 9; work 9–15; on world economy 13–14
Nayyar, Rohini 9
NDA Government 398
negligence liability 247
Neo-classical economics 29, 61; mono-economics characteristic of 62; price incentives 62; universal applicability of 63–64
Neo-liberalism 155
Nepal: Maoists civil war 68
Netherlands: Muslims in 84–85, 86
Nicomachean Ethics (Aristotle) 53
Nigeria 91; Boko Haram Islamic fundamentalists 83, 296; GDP 296; Igbo 81; oil reserves 296; subsistence agriculture 296
nitrous oxide 47; see also greenhouse gas emissions
non-petroleum, oil and lubricants (POL) trade 425–426, 427–429
North American Free Trade Agreement (NAFTA) 409
North Atlantic Crisis 385–386
North Atlantic Treaty Organization (NATO) 377
NTBs 401–402
Nyerere, Julius 297

offset requirements, in government procurement 402–403
one-size-fits-all approach 63
outside option 254, 255; see also auctions; inferior outside option, auctions with
outsourcing 396–396
Oxfam 342
Oya, Carlos 343

paradox of plenty 350
Paris Agreement 48; countries committed to 48; weakness 48
partition 376
Patel, E. 398
per capita endowments 70
per capita income: African countries 70, 293; Asian countries 293; Chile 302; China 285–286; Cuba 311; Egypt 297; Ethiopia 68; Honduras 289; India 285–286; Latin American countries 293, 306, 307, 308, 309; low income countries 404; Malaysia 295; Muslim populated regions 88; South Africa 70, 296; Tanzania 297; Tunisia 289; Turkey 294; twenty-five emerging economies 283–284, 292–293, 293; Uzbekistan 68
performance requirements (PR) 403–404
Philippines: Muslim communities in 87–88
Planning Commission 376
Plaza Accord of 1985 408

460  *Index*

policy debates, in Indian economy 375–387; anti-inflationary measures 380; capital account liberalization 386–387; devaluation of the rupee in 1966 379; growth and poverty 384–385; IMF loan 381–384, 385; nationalization of commercial banks 379
policymaking: creative and pragmatic approach to 26–27
political centralisation 280
political inequalities, Muslims 86
*Politics* (Aristotle) 69
Polynesian origin 71
poor farmers 44
post-colonial developing economies 62
postcolonial economies: developmental realities of 222
poverty alleviation, in India 385
PPP *see* public private partnerships (PPP)
preferential access to markets 409–410
pre-mature deindustrialisation, in India *see* deindustrialisation in India
price incentives 62
princely states, integration of 376
Pritchett, L. 287–288, 293, 294
private corporate investment 426–430
privileged access to domestic market 400–402
proactive FDI promotion 403–404
Property Tax 440
protectionism: in developed economies 401; in East Asian countries 401–402
Proton 401
public intervention for industrial development 399–400
public policy: economic theory and 29–33
public private partnerships (PPP) 446
Punjab: poor peasants of 52

quantity theory of money 163–165
quantum physics 29

racism 66
Raj, K. N. 4, 379

Ranis, Gustav 62
Rao, Narasimha 384–385
rationality: Neo-classical theory 54; self and 54–55
Ray, N. C. 4
RBI 429
RCEP *see* Regional Comprehensive Economic Partnership of East Asia (RCEP)
Reagan, Ronald 381, 382
real-estate sector: black income 440; bribes 440; regulatory approvals and 440
Regional Comprehensive Economic Partnership of East Asia (RCEP) 410
regional economic integration (REI) 409
regional trade agreements (RTA) 409–410
Registration Act of India, 1908 438
rehabilitation and resettlement (R&R) 343
REI *see* regional economic integration (REI)
relational selfhood 54
research and development (R&D) 400, 406–407
resource endowments 277
retail banks 45; Glass-Steagall Act of 1933 45; imprudent investment activities 45
Revenue Equivalence Theorem, The 269
Ricardian approach 211–216; adjustments in non-agricultural output 213; agriculture vis a vis services 215; balanced and unbalanced growth 213–214; causation 213; external demand multiplier 213; realisation problem 215–216; services sector growth 214–215
Right to Fair Compensation and Transparency in Land Acquisition, Rehabilitation and Resettlement Act 2013 444
risk measurement 45
risks: individual 45; systemic 45
Robinson, James A. 278–281

Rodrik, Dani 74n3, 394, 396
Roma people 93
Rouseff, Dilma 300
Rulli, M. C. 343, 351
rupee: appreciation 396, 397, 397, 408–409; devaluation 379; exchange rate 379, 396, 397
Russell, John 72
Russian debt crisis of 1998 386
Rwanda: ethnic cleansing 71; homogeneity 71

Saha, Anuradha 352
Saitoh, H. 256
Sakai, T. 256
sale: of an immovable object/property 438
Saviori, Antonio 343
Scandinavian countries 70
Schoneveld, G. C. 343, 348–349
scientific discoveries 50
Second World War 42; end of global colonialism 286
self and rationality 54–55
self-awareness 54
self-sufficient village economy 377
Selod, Harris 347
Sen, Amartya 4, 53, 54, 281
Serizawa, S. 256
services sector growth: in India 389–390, 392, 398; Ricardian approach 214–215
17 Sustainable Development Goals 390
Shastri, Lal Bahadur 378, 379
Shelley, Mary 72
Shia 91
SIA see social impact assessment (SIA)
Singapore 69
Single European Market 409
Sino-India war of 1961 378
SIPV see symmetric, independent, private value (SIPV) model
Skidelsky, Robert 44–45
slowdown see growth slowdown
social capital 81
social impact assessment (SIA) 443
social mobilisation, cross-border networks and 100–101
Soete, Luc 350
soil: disposal of toxic materials into 48

solar energy mission 403
Solow, Robert 4
South Africa 296; apartheid system of racial segregation 296; colonial rule 296; diamonds and gold 296; life expectancy 296; per capita endowments 70; per capita income 296; transition to democracy 296
South Asia: bad neighbourhood effects 68, 69; diverse cultures and religious beliefs 52
Southern Cone countries 311
South Korea 62–63; as advanced country 294; authoritarian regime 295; culture 66; economic divergence between Ghana and 66
Soviet Union 26; dissolution of 385
Spain: Muslims in 86
speculation about future 276
Spence, Michael 45
Sri Lanka: Tamil-Sinhalese ethnic war in 68
Srinivasan, T. N. 379
St. Stephen's College, Delhi 4
stamp duty: circle rates 439; on land/property transactions 436, 438–441
Standard Fruit Company 289
standard liability rules 250
Stand-Up programmes 405
start-ups 405
state intervention for industrial development 399–400
Stiglitz, Joseph E. 132, 135, 140, 398
Streeten, Paul 4
Structural Adjustment Programs (SAP) 63
structural transformation of Indian economy 390–393
St Xavier's School, Jaipur 4
Subramanian, Arvind 394, 396
Sub-Saharan Africa 27–28; bad neighbourhood effects 69; SAPs failure in 67
subsidies: in East Asia 405; investment and export 404–405; in US 404–405
subsistence sector 221–222

462 *Index*

Sufi poetry 52
Sufism 91
Summers, L. 287–288, 293, 294
Sunnis 91
Super 301 Priority Watch Lists 407
supply: of credit 135–138
surplus appropriators, in agrarian systems 278
surplus labour 221–222; migration of 222
surplus producers, agrarian systems 277–278
sustainable development 27, 50–56; alternative perspective 54–55; development of human capabilities 53–54; human functioning 53, 54; land deals and 346; normative basis of 55–56; relationship between humans, commodities and nature 51–53
Sustainable Development Goals of United Nations 390
Switzerland 402; ethnic diversity 71
Syed, Najam Hussain 53
symmetric, independent, private value (SIPV) model 268
systemic risk 45

Tagore, Rabindranath 52
Taiwan 62–3; Chinese in 71
Tamil-Sinhalese ethnic war in Sri Lanka 68
Tanzania 71, 297
taxes on land transactions 438–441
technical knowledge 277
technological development 406–407
temperature increase 47
Thailand 294; as automobile exporter 403; Muslim communities in 87–88; political liberalisation demand 295
Thatcher, Margaret 381–382
theory of economic history: application 276; elements of 276–282; institutional 278–282
*Theory of Economic History, A* (Hicks) 276
Thiele, Rainer 352
Third World Debt Crisis of 1982 63

threat to life on Earth 47–48
total social costs (TSC) 245–246
toxic materials: disposal into soil 48
TPP *see* Trans-Pacific Partnership (TPP)
trade, and slowdown: integration pattern of 420–424; manufacturing 424–426, *425*
transaction cost: cultural norms 202–205; overview 198; theory 198–202; *see also* bargaining power; income distribution
Transatlantic Trade and Investment Partnership (TTIP) 409–410
transnational large-scale land acquisition: bioethanol policies 341; financial crisis of 2008-2009 and 341; food market and 341; fuel crisis and 341
Trans-Pacific Partnership (TPP) 409–410
Treaty of Guadalope Hidalgo 301
TRIPs Agreement 407–408; *see also* intellectual property protection policy
tropical climate 69
tropical diseases 69
TSC *see* total social costs (TSC)
TTIP *see* Transatlantic Trade and Investment Partnership (TTIP)
Tunisia 292; diversified economy 292; economic structure 289; French occupation 292; growth rate 289; institutions 292; Islamic fundamentalism 292; Ottoman Empire 292; per capita income 289; Phoenicians 292; population 289; religion 292; standard of living 292
Turkey: European Union and 294; per capita income 294
Tutsis 71, 80–81
twenty-five emerging economies 282–302; Africa 295–297; Asia 294–295; classification 285; energy crisis and 285; globalisation and 282; global warming and 285; growth rates against per capita incomes 292–3,

## Index  463

293; Latin America 297–302; microchip-based technologies and 285; selected indicators of 283–284; two small countries 289, 292; two very large countries 285–289; water crisis and 285

UK: Muslims in 84, 86
*Ummah* 91
Unit Area Method 440
United Fruit 289
United Nations: Agenda 2030 on Sustainable Development 390; 17 Sustainable Development Goals 390
United Nations Economic Commission for Latin America and the Caribbean (ECLAC) 306
urban areas lans: Property Tax 440; Unit Area Method 440
US: Buy American Act in 1933 402; IMF loan to India and 383; inflation (1970s) in 380; investment and export incentives in 404–405; Mexico and 300–301; technological development and R&D 406
uses of credit 139–140
Uzbekistan 68

Vakil-Brahmananda model 377
Vedanta Treatise 52
Venables, A. J. 346, 351
Venezuela: inclusive policies 301; military rule 301; oil boom 311; oil deposits 301; relative decline since the mid-1970s 311
vertical inequalities 28, 78, 79, 80, 94, 400
Vietnam: Communist Party 295; *Doi Moi* liberalisation programme 295
Von Braun, Joachim 346, 350–351

Warsaw Pact of 1955 377
Washington Consensus 115
weak land governance and tenure security 347
Webb, Beatrice 72
Weitzman, Marty 161
West Africa: Muslims in 88–89
West Germany: reunification with East Germany 382
Williamson, O. E. 199–200, 201–202, 206
work of Deepak Nayyar 9–15
World Bank 63, 67
world economy: in 1980s 381–382; in 1950s 376–377; in 1990s 384; in 1970s 380; in 1960s 378; oil shock (1974) 380; 2000s 385–386
World Gold Council 256
World War II 376
WTO: Agreement on Subsidies and Countervailing Measures (SCM) 404; Agreement on Textiles and Clothing (ATC) 401; Agreement on Trade Related Investment Measures (TRIMs) 403–404; Byrd Amendment 404; Foreign Sales Corporation Act 404; on India's domestic content requirements 402–403; Information Technology Agreement (ITA) 396; TRIPs Agreement 407–408

X-rays: discovery of 50

Yom Kippur war 380

zero lower bound (ZLB) 131, 140; *see also* monetary policy
zero net emissions 48